ARMAGNAC
Vieille réserve
1820
1820
Vieux Cognac
of France
Pear Brandy
Bottled for JURGENSEN'S of CALIFORNIA
SPECIAL OLD RESERVE
BOND & LILLARD
NET CONTENTS ONE PINT
BOTTLED IN BOND UNDER U.S. GOVERNMENT SUPERVISION
REBEL YELL
6
Years Old
ONE QUART
REBEL YELL
Southern Sour Mash
Straight Bourbon Whiskey from old Kentucky
Exclusively for
TH' DEEP SOUTH

DRINK

The Ultimate Cocktail Book

Drink

13-Digit ISBN: 978-1-60433-831-7
10-Digit ISBN: 1-60433-831-8

This book may be ordered by mail from the publisher. Please include $7.99 for postage and handling.
Please support your local bookseller first!

Books published by Cider Mill Press Book Publishers are available at special discounts for bulk purchases in the United States by corporations, institutions, and other organizations. For more information, please contact the publisher.

Cider Mill Press Book Publishers

"Where good books are ready for press"

501 Nelson Place
Nashville, Tennessee 37214

cidermillpress.com

Typography: Adobe Garamond, Brandon Grotesque, Lastra, Sackers English Script

Image Credits: see page 821

Printed in China

23 24 25 26 27 DSC 9 8 7 6 5

DRINK

The Ultimate Cocktail Book

KURT MAITLAND

CIDER MILL PRESS
BOOK PUBLISHERS

A NOTE ON THE PHOTOGRAPHS

Throughout this book, images correspond to recipes as follows: if there is only 1 image, it depicts the recipe at the top of the page; if there are 2 images, they depict the first two recipes on the page, top first, bottom second; if there are 3 images, starting top left and moving clockwise, they depict the first three recipes on the page; if there are 4 images, starting top left and moving clockwise, they depict the first four recipes on the page.

CONTENTS

FOREWORD

CLAY RISEN

Here's what happens the first time you meet Kurt Maitland. Assuming spirits are on the menu, conversationally speaking, you might be hit with a disquisition, worthy of a Cambridge oral examination, on the finer points of Speyside single malt production in the 1980s. Or you might find yourself on the receiving end of a comparative analysis examining rum production in Cuba versus Jamaica. He might throw in a firsthand report from the most recent Berlin Bar Convention, including a rhetorical sidebar about his visit to an obsessive German whisk(e)y collector (as I've learned from Kurt, besides the Japanese, no one hoards whisk(e)y like the Germans). He will almost certainly tell you about his latest trip to the Scottish island of Islay, home to peat-monster distilleries like Ardbeg and Lagavulin—and if you listen long enough, he might well persuade you to join him on his next adventure. In short, one does not listen to Kurt Maitland; one *experiences* him.

I first met Kurt at the Brandy Library, circa August 2015. The Brandy Library, despite its name, is New York's premier whisk(e)y bar (in a nice twist, it also has one of the city's best brandy collections). We were there for a semi-private tasting; some distillery was rolling out its latest expression, and a few reporters, like me, and insiders, like Kurt, were invited to get an early taste. I had heard of Kurt already—his reputation as a walking encyclopedia of whisk(e)y preceded him among Manhattan's spirits cognoscenti. We made our introductions, and by the time the second hand on my watch had completed a single sweep, we were deep into a debate about the finer points of various independent bottlers of single malt scotch. When I stumbled out of the bar an hour later, slightly tipsy from the tasting and fully hammered on our conversation, I'm pretty sure I had agreed to buy a plane ticket to Sapporo the following month, so we could check out the Yoichi distillery on Hokkaido.

I am, to a myopic degree, a whisk(e)y person, so it was only much later when I realized that Kurt is not just a whisk(e)y geek—that he is somehow as knowledgeable about rum or vodka or tequila as he is about bourbon and rye. And not just as straight spirits; as this book attests, his fluency in the mixological arts knows no bounds.

Usually, I do not like people like this—know-it-alls who just want to show off their giant brains. But then, that's not Kurt. For all his knowledge and insight, he is never one to lord his intelligence over someone else. He is, above everything, a conversationalist, a guide, a joyful kid in the land of potent potables who simply wants to share his experiences and insights, likes and dislikes, with anyone willing to give him the time.

Kurt is among the most generous people I know. I have been to parties at his apartment, a cozy abode overflowing with bottles, like a roadside chapel of booze, where he spent hours pouring from his rarest of rare bottlings while pulling LPs from his equally enormous record collection. He is not a hoarder; the collections, like his immense knowledge, exist primarily so he can share them with his friends, and soon-to-be friends.

Likewise, this book is nothing if not that—generous. It is, as it should be immediately obvious, a near-complete compendium of cocktails, with more recipes than an average home bartender could make in a lifetime. It is also a primer in the principles of cocktail mixing, going behind the recipes to explain the origins of Martinis, Bloody Marys, Old Fashioneds, and other "mother sauce" cocktails. There are many great cocktail books, but this is the only cocktail book you'll ever need.

And that's true not just because it is comprehensive. You'll never need another because you'll never find another that is at once so authoritative and yet so personal, so intelligent yet so intimate, so wide-ranging and yet so clear and specific. It is, in other words, unmistakably the product of a writer at once all-knowing and self-effacing, someone whose greatest joy in life comes from sharing what he knows with friends and strangers alike. I feel lucky to know Kurt Maitland, and I hope you feel just as lucky after reading this book.

—Clay Risen

Clay Risen, the deputy op-ed editor at *The New York Times*, is the author of *Single Malt: A Guide to the Whiskies of Scotland* and the spirits bestseller *American Whiskey, Bourbon & Rye: A Guide to the Nation's Favorite Spirit.* He has written about spirits for numerous publications, including *The New York Times, Fortune, The Atlantic,* and *Bloomberg Businessweek*, and he has also authored several books about 20th century American history.

INTRODUCTION

WHO AM I AND WHY AM I HERE?

Since you have opened this book it is safe to assume that you have some interest in the subject at hand, which is drinks, specifically cocktails. If not, I still hold out hope that these pages contain something of interest to all readers. If you are here for the main event, I'm pleased to make your acquaintance. I'll be your guide for this tour around the world of drinks. There's lots of ground to cover in this expansive landscape of libations, from tools of the trade, spotlights on bars and bartenders, histories of classic cocktails, garnish guides, and, of course, drink recipes (including a healthy amount of nonalcoholic drinks, which, I'm happy to say, are more of the infusion variety than mocktails). You can focus on your favorite spirit, read the whole thing from cover to cover, jump around, or use the index to help you navigate the book.

So, now that we've had a bit of a preamble, let's talk about me for a bit. Not that this book is about me in the slightest (well, maybe a little bit), but it's only fair that you know a bit about your guide and how I got here.

While I have a Scottish surname and a German first name, my background is West Indian. My parents are from the Caribbean (Trinidad and Grenada, to be specific). The drinks that I grew up around were rum punches, shandies, basic cocktails, and, of course, beer. I wasn't drinking any of them, mind you. They were just the alcoholic drinks I recall at my folks' parties and family gatherings.

Truth be told, I didn't drink much pre-college. I got the occasional little sip from whatever Dad was drinking, in response to my questions about what a Screwdriver or Rum and Coke tasted like. Looking back, I'm not sorry I didn't indulge. I probably saved myself from the "I don't drink such and such," "mistakes were made when I was young" drama that prevents adults from enjoying certain spirits. Southern Comfort, I'm looking at you. Not to pick on Southern Comfort in any way, but my own informal research indicates that SoCo is involved in a disproportionate amount of the events that put people off "brown" liquor for life.

In college, beer was around as it always is, but I have to say it didn't hold much appeal for me. Everyone was drinking bad beer. I think I got more pleasure my freshman year sitting back and watching it all play out (from failed keg stands to praying to the porcelain god and other drunken hijinks) than I would have ever had drinking. A lot of what I drank in those days was influenced by my friend, Leslie Chiu. She grew up in Hong Kong, while my middle school and high school years were spent in Allentown, Pennsylvania. She was hipper and cooler than me, and nothing about that has changed in the intervening years. Through her, I had my first tastes of basic drinks like Vodka Gimlets and Gin & Tonics. We also spent a decent amount of time drinking Jameson's Irish Whiskey. (Leslie has formally requested that I mention that we both have since grown up and moved on to expensive single malts as our primary whiskies of choice. No disrespect for "Jamie" intended.)

After college, I became friends with Richard Thomas. You may know of him as the editor of The Whiskey Reviewer website (where I am deputy editor and you can find the majority of my writing on spirits to this day). But when we first met he was my then-roommate's boss. She brought me to his house for a summer party, and Richard and I have been friends ever since. He is from Lexington, Kentucky, and knows more about bourbon than I ever will. Bourbon was our first bond, with whisk(e)y in all its varieties, talking politics, and watching boxing deepening the friendship in the years that followed. (The fight that always comes to mind is when we sat in a bar on Capitol Hill in DC and watched 45-year-old George Foreman knock out Michael Moorer to regain the heavyweight title.)

By now you may have noticed that cocktails haven't made much of an appearance in my early alcohol-related recollections, and rumor has it this a cocktail book. You are still in the right place and they do appear in this tale, but, in all honesty, the '80s, and much of the '90s, were quite the wasteland in terms of cocktails, with some very notable exceptions. Between the late '80s and the late '90s, cocktail legend Dale DeGroff made his reputation behind the bar at the Rainbow Room. But, contrary to popular belief, not everyone lives in, or visits, New York City. For the "average" person, one who wasn't a member of a club, didn't spend much time in hotel bars, or wasn't an experienced drinker, a cocktail was mainly of the Jack & Coke, Bloody Mary, Whiskey Ginger, and Long Island Iced Tea variety. There was also the guilty pleasure of the Margarita slurry that came out of the machine perched at the back end of the bar, but the less said about that the better. These cocktails did the trick, i.e., got you drunk. But from the standpoint of flavor, and from the perspective of the cocktail renaissance we're living through today, they were the cheap beer at college I couldn't be bothered to nurse a hangover with. Even if you had a hankering for one of these cocktails you might have heard of, let's say a Daiquiri, you'd often have the joy of witnessing the spectacle of a bartender fumbling around for a tattered copy of basic cocktail assembly notes that were stashed behind the register or some other part of the bar. They probably had to move the Tom Collins mix out of the way to find them. (There is nothing wrong with a Tom Collins cocktail. Just avoid the mix; turn to page 130, and make it yourself.)

If you like cocktails, be glad those days are over.

My own delving into cocktails really began when I moved to New York City in the early 2000s. While my enjoyment of bourbon continued (lots of Maker's Mark neat was consumed at the Kettle of Fish in the West Village), cocktails slowly started creeping into my life. They would be offered at parties and events I attended.

The first of two big cocktail revelations for me was receiving DeGroff's book *The Craft of the Cocktail* as a Christmas gift. I got the book during a stretch of joblessness in the mid-2000s. Perhaps there was the idea that I would try my hand at bartending to earn some extra cash, or at the least get out of the house. I stuck to simple recipes like the Bee's Knees (see page 180) or the Godfather (a version of this classic appears in the Flask Cocktails chapter, see page 685). They were drinks that were easy to make and a pleasure to drink. By messing around at home, I learned what should be obvious: cocktails made with fresh ingredients taste better. This invaluable lesson changed how I thought about cocktails and what I would look for in the wilds of New York.

My second formative exposure to well-made cocktails was Louis 649. I first came across the bar wandering around the East Village, either after a party or an unsuccessful date. At the time, they hosted a lot of live jazz and I was drawn in, hearing it bopping out of the open windows that night. It was right across from La Plaza Cultural de Armando Perez, a park that was home to a few of Manhattan's puny population of willow trees (nicknamed Cher, Krusty, and Wally, which, like my cherished Louis 649, are no longer part of the landscape). The bar had a European feel. Dark woods and tiles, with creamy walls and exposed brick accented with the occasional painting. As I recall, I sat at the end of the bar furthest from the band and took it all in. It was designed to be similar in look and feel to a New Orleans bar. Let's clarify, a classic New Orleans bar. The ones that don't have neon everywhere and '80s cover bands on tap every night. It was dimly lit, with nooks and crannies for people on dates or small gatherings of friends that wanted privacy, and stools at the white-tile bar for those whose who wanted to be close to the action. The bar's name came from Louis Armstrong and its address (649 East Ninth Street). Against the exposed-brick back of the bar stood a small but quality collection of spirits that the bartenders ably mixed into memorable cocktails. I made friends with the owner Zach Sharaga (you will hear from Zach later in this book) and had the pleasure of watching him ply his craft on a nightly basis. Here was proof that fresh ingredients and an inventive mind could do wonders with spirits. From that first night I was hooked and became a regular patron until it closed due to the damage Hurricane Sandy inflicted on the bar. Birthday gatherings, New Year's parties, if someone special was in town, more often than not, I was at Louis 649. I loved that bar so much that when I split up with a girlfriend whom I had introduced to the bar, I negotiated Louis as part of the breakup. I couldn't lose my bar and her at the same time. That would have been unthinkable.

Digging around in my files (it's gotten to the point in my spirit writing life that I do have files, like I'm an actual researcher or something), I found notes from what was my first formal cocktail class. "Notes" may be a stretch. It's a one-page handout with my handwriting all over the back. It's dated 3/22/11, the class was called "Cocktail 101—How to Mix Cocktails at Home," and it took place at, you guessed it, Louis 649 (see pages 18-19).

Zach gave me some important tips during this class. As you can see we worked through just a few basic cocktails—Martini, Pimm's Cup, Daiquiri, Manhattan, and the bartender's favorite, the Negroni. Zach started off with a review of the basic bar tools and hints about how to deal with ice and glassware. I remember how much he stressed the importance of ice. He was a believer in starting with big pieces of ice. Better to break up a big piece than to rely on the slivers coming out of the dispenser on your refrigerator door.

Think of this book as a bigger, better version of that handout I marked up years ago. That single page was a starter for me and, hopefully, this will be the same for you; or, if you consider yourself a cocktail aficionado, there are ample recipes contained within to surprise and delight your spirited sensibilities. You'll find bartenders from around the world telling you how they like to make cocktails, what influences their creations, and their favorite drinks and spirits. I've provided histories of spirits and some of the classic cocktails, as well as tips on garnishes and how to make simple syrups and shrubs. And then there are the more than 1,100 recipes—old standbys, variants, and newfangled concoctions—for you to explore and tinker with. I fully expect you to modify every recipe that you try so that it works for your tastes and your palate.

Cocktails took their first steps during the years of Prohibition. They were the child of necessity, born of laws preventing the "good stuff" from being available and the need to make rotgut substitutes palatable. Now you can get craft gins and small-batch spirits everywhere you look, and cocktails are no longer charged with making the bad palatable. Instead, they make the good better and the excellent sublime. It's basically alchemy you can practice in a standard kitchen.

So, to be clear, what you have in your hands is a "spirit" cookbook, where I've compiled cocktails from many sources so you don't have to. If you are making a cocktail for yourself or punch for a party, there should be something that you can use to enhance the experience. If I can do that much, I'll feel like I've done my job.

Now before you run off to start mixing, let me give you a bit of the methodology I used when compiling the recipes. You can safely skip this part, but it might help to clear up why cer-

Chill Glassware
·Prep Garnishes

Shake ~~EAt~~ Any ~~[illegible]~~ Citrus ~~citrus~~-based Drink

Louis 649

Tuesday Night Tasting – 3/22/11
Cocktails 101 – How to Mix Cocktails at Home

Tools you'll need:
One Large Steel Shaker
One Pint-Size Mixing Glass
One Bar Spoon
(Oxo) One Hawthorn Strainer (Need)
One Julep Strainer (Need)
Jigger(s)
Y-peeler (Need)
Microplane (Need)
Lemon/Lime Hand Juicer

Booze Basics, Et cetera:
Gin
Rye Whiskey
Rum → Santa Clarasa / Flor de Cana
Pimm's No. 1 (Need)
Sweet Vermouth
Dry Vermouth
Campari
Angostura Bitters
Fresh Lemons and Limes
White Granulated Sugar

Tips:

Simple Syrup – Mix two parts sugar to one part boiling water. Shake to dissolve and let cool. Refrigerate for up to one week.

Glassware – Try to keep as many as you'll be using in your freezer. Don't forget the Arm & Hammer or your glasses and ice, which absorb odors, will make your cocktails taste like frozen Wiener Schnitzel.

COCKTAILS

Gin Vermouth – ↑ *Martini* ~ *Pimm's Cup* (↓ Pimm's Lemon) ~ *Daiquiri* ~ *Manhattan* ~ *Negroni* (↑ Campari)

Martini—
5/1 — Gin/Vermouth
2.5 Gin / .5 Vermouth

—Collins Glass
—Double Old Fashioned Glass

Pimm's Cup
2.0 oz Pimms / .5 Lemon juice
.5 Lime juice
3/4 simple syrup / Club soda
(enough to top off glass
Garnish with cucumber

Daiquiri
2.0 oz Rum / 1 oz lime / 3/4 Sugar (simple syrup)
garnish with a wheel of lime (Shaken)

Rye	Sweet Vermouth	Bitters
2 oz	1 oz	2 dashes

Manhattan

Negroni
Gin 1oz
Sweet Vermouth 1oz
Campari 1oz

Cheaper ingredients first

More Ice is better

Ingredients then ice —

tain spirits make limited appearances. All books contain the author's biases, and this one is no exception. So let's get those out of the way.

I've avoided what I consider to be "better performed by professionals" drinks. These aren't necessarily difficult creations but involve some slightly hazardous step that is better suited to a controlled environment. There are plenty of drink options that you can enjoy without the risk of burning down your house.

You also won't find much in the way of typical "shots" here. Mainly because I feel that many shots aren't cocktails and I would like to think you don't need my help in prepping a shot. The "shots" that I have included are more like mini-cocktails that you might begin or end a party with (i.e., the Lemon Drop, page 109). This bias comes from my experiences in the whisk(e)y world. This is a bit off topic, but I feel that Irish whiskey as a category is never given its due because it's often seen as a part of the beer-and-a-shot combo that's so common in bars. I'd like every spirit to be respected and maybe avoiding "shots" will help. (Don't mind the soapbox I am standing on, thank you.)

I don't like flavored whiskies—this goes back to the importance of natural ingredients. If you want a cinnamon flavor for your whisk(e)y, I would prefer that you get some cinnamon sticks and use them to make an infusion. It's the same reason the following recipes call for fresh lemon and lime juice, versus using the concentrated versions. It's about the taste and I'm doing this for your own good. With that in mind, I did my best to limit recipes that rely on artificial flavoring.

I'm not trying to get you drunk—you don't need my help for that and for me that is not what this book is about. What I really want is for you to make drinks that you can enjoy and share with friends and family because the drink should be the cherry on top of an event. (Apparently, my soapbox is getting more use than I originally planned.)

There are more infusions in this book than mocktails—part of that is because the infusions appealed to me more as I was working on the book and I thought they would be a great way to balance out all of the cocktails. The other reason was that a real-life encounter influenced this editorial decision. While working on *Drink*, I had a friend from out of town coming over and she wanted to bring a friend with her who didn't

drink. I had another friend over who was going to make cocktails and I didn't want him doing both, as he was a guest. I needed something that tasted good and showed my teetotaling guest that I was looking out for her (making me an even better host, of course). Having some soda or seltzer around wasn't really going to cut it in my mind. As I mentioned above, I was already working on the book and I had infusions on my mind. I have to say, it worked like a charm. I made the Blueberry and Orange Water (see page 732) and the Orange and Mango Water (see page 731). Not only were they easy to make, the people drinking alcohol liked them as a way to take a break from drinking firewater. Infusions are one of the things I learned during this process that I'm happiest to share. The other thing is that the infusions can be modified to make a drink because you can take the same recipes and use vodka, gin, or moonshine to make an infusion. It's win-win for all involved.

Finally, I tried to stick to the basics (which I know seems ridiculous in a book sporting over 1,100 cocktails, but hear me out). I made the editorial decision that wine, vodka, whisk(e)y, tequila, rum, and gin recipes would form the core of this book. They are the most common spirits you come across and have access to, and should cover a lot of what you'll want to make. Believe me when I say that plenty of other spirits make an appearance, but the aforementioned spirits make up the majority of the recipes. You'll also notice that beer hasn't been mentioned other than in my sardonically tinged nostalgic romps. It's there, but I'll admit that as a category it is getting lapped by the other drink options. Perhaps that will be my second book or something.

Hopefully, my rambling hasn't scared you off and by now you are ready to start mixing, shaking, and stirring up your own cocktails. I will reappear on occasion, but I'm not the star of the show. The recipes are, and they are ready and waiting. The final ingredients are your time and attention.

Kurt Maitland

A BRIEF HISTORY OF COCKTAILS

I know, you want to start drinking. I'm not stopping you. Go on. But once you've made that first drink, perhaps you'll want to sit back and learn a bit about how cocktails came to be.

The stories associated with the creation of cocktails—many of which still refer to their origin as being the "Nectar of the Gods"—are part of mixology's magic. Most spirits were first used as healthful tonics, and the herbs, roots, and flowers indeed offered healing (and still do). Over time, though, the beverages pivoted from medicinal remedies to spirited ways to celebrate the joys of life.

At their best, cocktails combine stories about their ingredients and their pedigree. Consider the Jazz Age, when frothy cocktails as we know them premiered—bathtubs filled with gin and bubbly champagne fueling swoon-worthy parties and speakeasies where the festivities roared on in secrecy, which only added to the cocktail mystique. Or a total lack of craft and concern for quality. During Prohibition, when the objective was to get drunk and speakeasies were far more concerned with quantity sold, cocktails came together to mask the tastes of the spirits that were being made as quickly as possible by bootleggers. One noteworthy exception to this was Captain Bill McCoy. A "Rum Runner" who made his own product, his dedication to providing the best for his customers earned his product the name "the real McCoy." So there's some trivia for you.

While a properly made Martini has been of the utmost import since Ian Fleming introduced 007 in 1953, and other basic cocktails have been part of the cultural landscape for much of the 20th century, we are currently living through an unprecedented cocktail renaissance that has walked hand-in-hand with the locavore revival. In 2012, The James Beard Foundation introduced the Outstanding Bar Program category "in recognition of the artisanal creations using seasonal, homegrown herbs, produce and ingredients." Craft cocktails are now seen as unique to a place, country, people, season, holiday, or event; they invoke a memory and the joy of entertaining. Drinks are ritual, a celebratory tradition marking events from sports, such as the Kentucky Derby, to cultural or religious celebrations, including Mardi Gras and Christmas. Cocktails make the party. And its "altar," the bar, takes priority at nearly every event.

Our connection to a particular cocktail can remain steadfast; James Bond's passion for his Martini is legendary, and, similarly, we may never stray from our favorite drink. We believe the character and style of what we drink mirrors our quintessence; "my drink" makes a statement. "Bourbon with ginger and a twist, please," conjures one type. "A Cosmopolitan straight up," followed by a wink, suggests another.

Cocktails also lay claim to their own form, metrics, and language: there are jiggers, ponys, shots; they are straight up and on the rocks, neat

and dirty, shaken or stirred. There's a chaser, a split, top-shelf, and tiki.

And we see how cocktail culture has influenced our everyday conversations: there's a "straight shooter," the saying "down the hatch," or "washing it down" and "highball" (which was a railway term for "signal to proceed," signaled by lifting a ball). We know the person dispensing drinks from behind a bar is called a bartender. Did you know that a clumsy bartender is called a "shoemaker" while a quick and capable one is a "mechanic"?

Cocktails are also potent, and not just as drinks. They have power and influence. They continue to be social arbiters. Think about it: they not only possess their own times of day—Cocktail Hour or Happy Hour, a Nightcap, and the Morning After—there's also a special place or intimate hideaway for our communion with cocktails. In fact, we devote entire rooms to this intimate relationship: there's the cocktail lounge, bar, bar car on the train, tiki bar, and more.

The mystery continues further when considering the moniker "cocktail." The first published reference to a cocktail appeared in the *Farmer's Cabinet* in 1803. No one really knows where it originated, but stories abound, though with cocktail folklore and legend, inevitably shared over a few drinks, things can get a bit muddled. Who doesn't love to hear a good story about how a classic or traditional cocktail came to be, or how artful mixologists continue to raise the, ahem, "bar" for evermore exotic cocktail creations along with their imaginative, fanciful names?

Here are a few popular ideas about how the "cocktail" could have come to be named:

- It is a reference to a rooster's tail (or cock-tail) being used as a Colonial drink garnish.
- Bartenders stirred drinks with a rooster's feather.
- In New Orleans around 1800, a cocktail was derived from the French *coquetier*—an egg cup—connected to a drink, naturally.
- Or, *coquetier* came from mixed drinks in the Bordeaux region and was introduced by French officers during the American Revolution.
- After the Aztec goddess, Xochitl (an indigenous word for "flower"). Xochitl was also the name of a Mexican princess who served drinks to American soldiers.
- Cock-ale was a mixture of spirits and bitters fed to fighting cocks, and spectators would toast the cock with the most feathers left in his tail at the end of the fight.

TOOLS OF THE TRADE, GARNISHES, AND ICE

No matter their origins, cocktails are here to stay. As mixologists prove time and time again, the creation of cocktails is an art. And if you want to practice this art at home, you'll need some tools. The pros can do a lot with a little, but there are some basic objects and supplies you will need to play this game. The same way that a chef needs better knives than a civilian, when making cocktails, one needs more than a spoon.

For our purposes, tools go beyond strainers and jiggers and include the glassware and basic spirits. Below we list the must-haves for a basic bar setup. Keep in mind that you don't have to break the bank to start your home bar, but between the spirits, the glassware, and the bar tools, a little money will need to be spent.

On the tool front, you can find basic bar and glassware sets on specialty sites like Cocktail Kingdom, as well as at other online retailers; as with anything, the options will fit lots of budgets. If you are tight on funds, don't be deterred by used items. Soap and water come pretty cheap, and you might find some real bargains on vintage gear to boot. Same goes for antique shops and yard sales. Hell, your parents might have some of the tools you need stashed away in a closet or basement. Nothing wrong with a little scavenging for a good cause.

Here is a rundown on the basics:

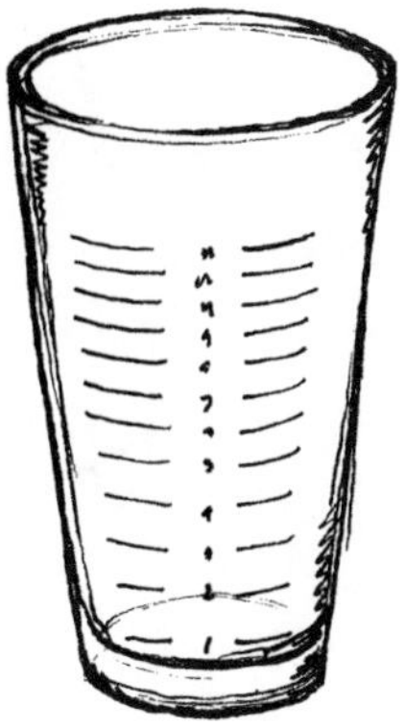

MIXING GLASS

Typically a standard pint glass, a mixing glass is nothing more than a tall glass in which to stir a drink. A mixing glass is not specialized equipment—in a pinch, you can use any glass large enough to hold the necessary ingredients along with a few ice cubes.

COCKTAIL GLASS

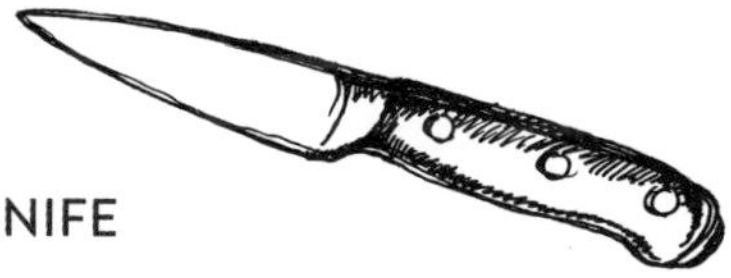

PARING KNIFE

JIGGER

A jigger is just a fancy name for the most common measuring tool in a mixologist's arsenal. Shaped like a shot glass (and with approximately the same capacity), a jigger allows you to quickly and easily measure either "parts" or ounces.

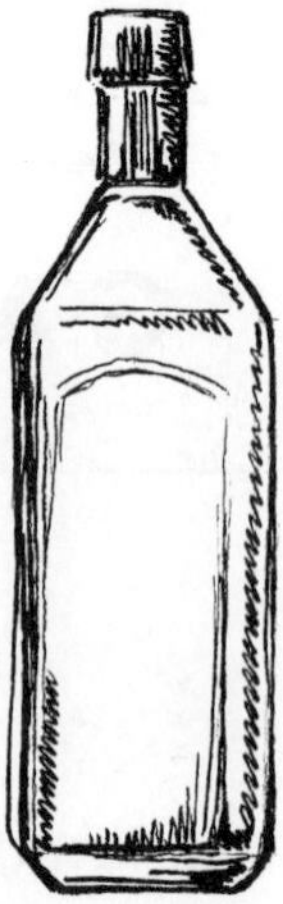

BOTTLE FOR HOMEMADE BITTERS & INFUSIONS

HIGHBALL GLASS

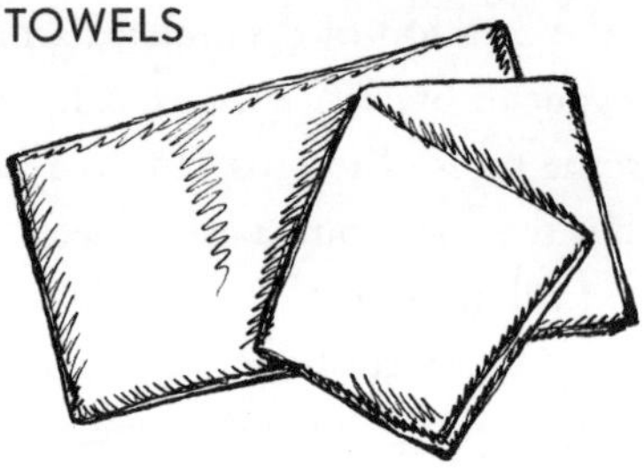

BAR TOWELS

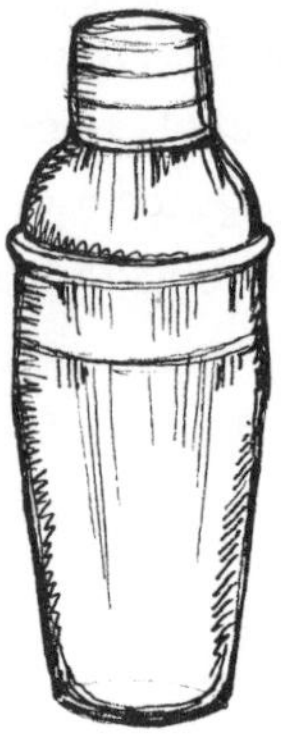

COCKTAIL SHAKER

A cocktail shaker is a container about the size of a pint glass, usually made from metal, with a screw top. The shaker provides a simple way to mix a cocktail, both combining the necessary ingredients and chilling them with ice. A basic cocktail shaker is relatively inexpensive, and you are better off purchasing this specific tool than trying to jury-rig a shaker for yourself.

CHAMPAGNE FLUTE

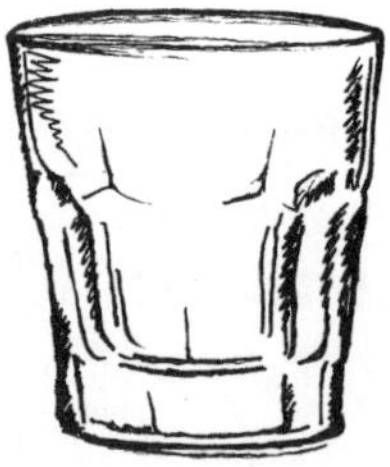

ROCKS GLASS

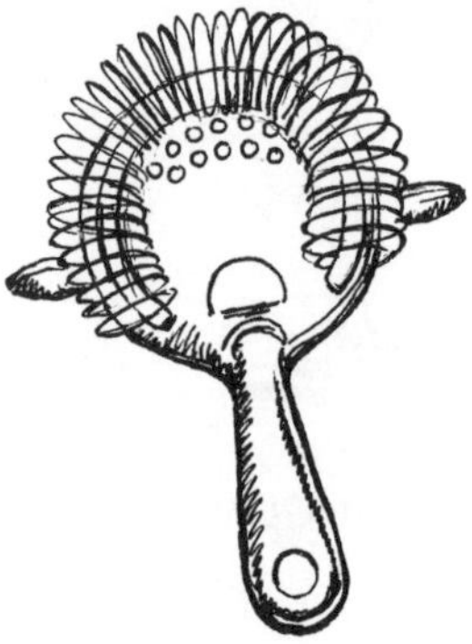

STRAINER

Used in tandem with either a mixing glass or cocktail shaker, the strainer simply strains the cocktail after it has been mixed. This keeps the ice cubes (in the case of a mixing glass) or broken ice chips (in the case of a cocktail shaker) out of your drink. Because ice waters down a drink when it melts, the strainer is an important tool for keeping your cocktail pure.

MUDDLER

Similar to a pestle, this simple tool is used to mash (muddle) ingredients such as fruits or herbs. Muddling fruits releases the juice within, adding a fresh quality to a drink, while muddling certain herbs helps activate their flavors. A simple muddler can often be found on the top end of a cocktail shaker, though fancier, specialized muddlers are available for minimal cost.

SHOT GLASS

COUPE

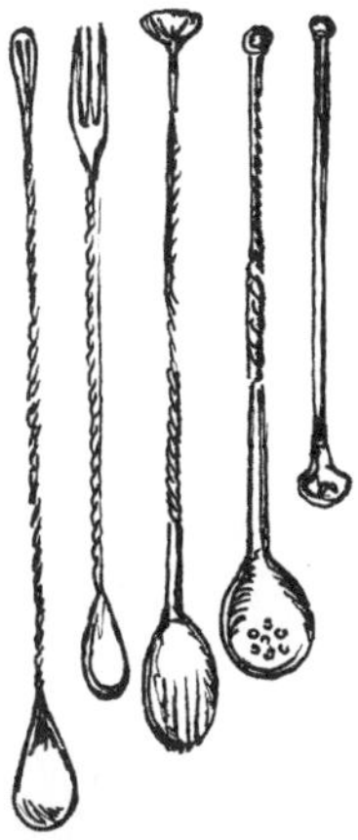

COCKTAIL STIRRER

There are plenty of fancy cocktail stirrers, but most take the form of a small spoon with a long handle. Used in conjunction with a mixing glass, the purpose of the cocktail stirrer is exactly as it sounds: to quickly and easily stir any cocktail. If you don't have a designated cocktail stirrer, you can use any spoon—you just may find it more difficult to navigate the ice cubes.

If you have rocks, highball, and all-purpose cocktail glasses on hand, you'll be able to manage most drinks. But here are some insights about the differences in some of the more common glassware:

Highball and Collins glasses are tall and skinny and basically interchangeable, though Collins glasses are taller.

The coupe glass has replaced the traditional V-shaped cocktail glass and is good for drinks served "up."

Nick & Nora glasses are bell-shaped, falling somewhere between the coupe and a wine glass, and still mostly used by professionals; any drink being served in one of these can just as easily be poured into a coupe.

Rocks glasses are meant for neat drinks and spirits on the rocks and are between 8 and 10 ounces; double rocks glasses are typically only a couple ounces larger and used for cocktails served over ice.

SELECTING YOUR SPIRITS

As for spirits, this is a trickier proposition. I'm of a mind that you shouldn't go cut-rate on your spirits. Simply put, working with subpar ingredients is counterproductive. After all, this is something that you and your family and friends will consume and hopefully enjoy. The best you can get should be your go-to option.

With that in mind, here are some personal rules about basic home bar spirit selection:

1. If you are on a budget, vodka is more forgiving than cheap gin, whisk(e)y, or tequila. Therefore, better to skimp on the vodka than the others.

2. Always remember that inexpensive is different from cheap. For example, George Dickel Rye and Old Overholt are inexpensive ryes that lots of bars use to create an Old Fashioned. Can you get better ryes to work with? Yes. But you don't have to.

3. Avoid flavored spirits (except in the case of vodka, where it can come in handy). You will get better flavors and better cocktails if you do it yourself when possible.

4. Keep an eye on what's up with your local spirits scene. You might find some great gins or other spirits that don't break the bank and offer great value or flavors that can make your cocktails more unique.

GARNISHES

Creative, boundary-pushing, dare I say avant-garde mixologists add the damnedest things to cocktails these days, from ginger-serrano syrup to activated charcoal (more for coloring than flavoring). While I don't expect you to have an industrial-strength centrifugal juicer or a sous vide cooker, these basic methods and tricks of the trade will improve your home bartending game.

BASIC GARNISHES

CITRUS FRUITS

Originally from Asia, cultures the world over have long extolled the healthy properties of citrus fruits. Pliny the Elder noted the ability of citrus fruits to act as an antidote to poison when taken in wine; in Europe, royalty grew citrus because of its nutritional benefits; and let's not forget those "Limeys," the members of the British navy who sucked limes to fight off scurvy.

The earliest acknowledged reference to citrus peel as cocktail garnish appeared in the first drink book published in the U. S.: Jerry Thomas's 1862 *The Bar-tender's Guide*. Not long after, in 1892, William Schmidt mentioned the

use of citrus and fruits in his book, *The Flowing Bowl*: "lemons, oranges, the delicious pineapple, choice grapes, and strawberries, raspberries, and cherries." Limes came later.

Citrus as garnish has more or less been codified over the years so that we think a lemon twist simply must be used with a Sidecar or Sazerac or Martini—and that there is no substitute for a lime with a cool and refreshing Gin & Tonic. And while it's true that today the most popular citrus garnishes are lemon, lime, and orange, with grapefruit "squeezing" in not far behind, it's also true that there is an astounding array of citrus varieties readily accessible to today's inventive and creative mixologists. Think of yuzu or tangelo or pummelo as potential garnishes just as the earliest bartenders experimented with the "exotic" lemon, lime, or orange.

Citrus is a member of the *Rutaceae* family of flowering plants—their leaves are aromatic and the flowers feature a heady fragrance designed to attract pollinators and creative cocktail enthusiasts. Use all of a citrus plant's parts in creating garnishes and finishing touches. The flowers and the blossoms are edible.

Rubbing parts of the glass with the citrus rind probably came about for two reasons: first is taste—as the essences of the citrus oils are expressed during the rubbing. And second, the citrus was so exotic and rare at the time of the nascent cocktail culture that bartenders and saloon owners wanted to use every last drop. It was a sign of conspicuous consumption to use citrus and they weren't about to waste any of it.

Probably more than any other category of garnish, citrus requires a set of tools to get garnishes with the proper precision:

Zester and peeler (and micro zester): cocktail garnish enthusiasts consider the functional zester and peeler a must-have because it offers two functions: it provides the ability to cut the citrus peel easily and adds a more intense flavor element by separating the zest from the pith.

Channel knife: a classic bar tool, the must-have channel knife creates swanky visual garnishes.

Bar knife (with pronged tip): doing double duty, this knife slices and cuts the garnish; the tip makes it easy to stab cherries (and olives and peppers, and more).

Y-shaped garnish peeler: a professional tool for the urbane cocktail aficionado, the Y stands for "yes" as far as being the workhorse of the bar—and kitchen; it readily peels citrus—and vegetables—for those pretty, decorative garnishes.

Rimmer with citrus well: a lovely addition to the bar, the rimmer makes it easy to add salt or sugar to glass rims while the citrus well holds wedges or zests to add to the drink. Pretty and useful.

Citrus juice squeezer: a handheld, ice cream scoop-looking hinged implement with one scoop resting on top of the other, the squeezer is designed to extract every last drop from citrus, while a built-in strainer prevents seeds from making their way into your cocktail.

Citrus reamer: the classic, rather medieval-looking reamer captures or extracts maximum citrus juice as the tool's pointed tip and flared edges can readily snuggle into a citrus fruit's corners to capture all the tart and tangy pulp and juice.

CRAFTING CITRUS GARNISHES

Zest: it's just as easy and fun to say and repeat this happy onomatopoeia as it is to create zest. Make certain to remove the colored skin of the fruit from the bitter white pith, using a certain amount of learned pressure.

Using a citrus zester: utilize a comfortable amount of pressure to drag the sharp-edged side of the tool down the fruit to produce long, thin, curly strips of zest.

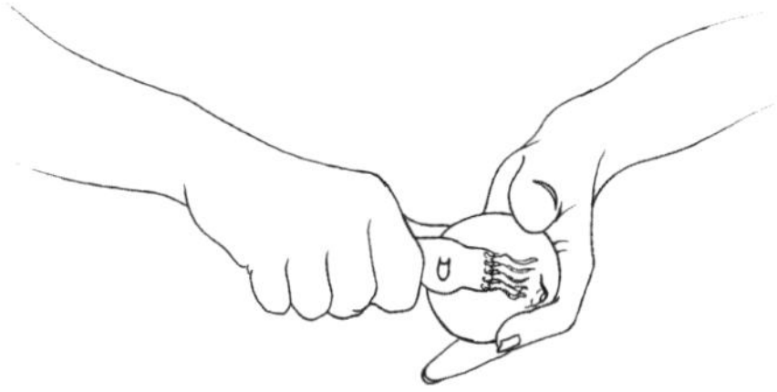

Using a microplane: over a cutting board or plate, hold the microplane in one hand, and use a downward motion and moderate pressure to drag the citrus against the blades of the microplane. Turn the fruit as you go, removing just the colored portion of the skin. The zest will gather in the groove underneath the microplane.

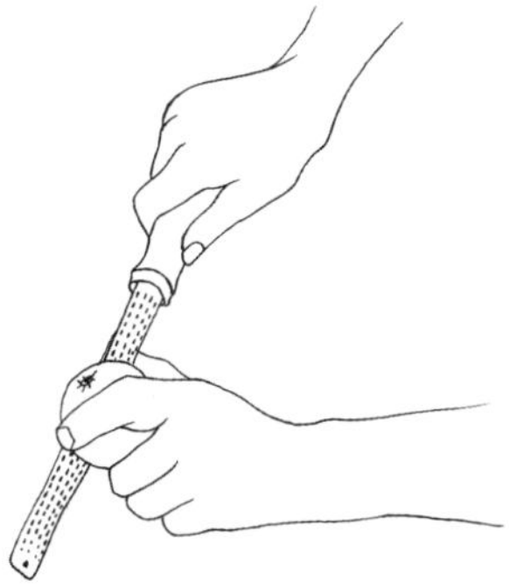

Using a vegetable peeler: the vegetable peeler easily enables peeling of citrus zest from top to bottom or around the fruit, so you can rim the glass and twist it over the cocktail to express the essential oils before floating in the drink. You can also use the peel to flavor a simple syrup.

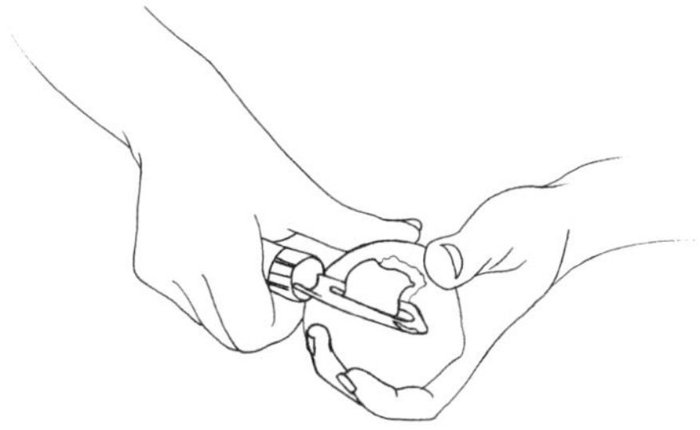

Wedge: this ubiquitous and easy-to-make garnish does require a bit of technique. First, slice ¼" off each end of a citrus fruit. Next, cut the fruit in half, lengthwise, and set one of the halves cut side down on your cutting board. Finally, slice it at an angle, lengthwise, and you should have a perfect little wedge. You want to design moderate-sized wedges that allow the drinker to readily squeeze the wedge. Slice a cut in the midsection of the wedge to perch the garnish on the glass rim. You can set out your garnished glasses pre-party or cuddle the wedges in decorative bowls—preferably glass bowls—in order to dramatize their colorful skins.

Wheels: cut a citrus wheel by slicing the fruit in half crosswise. Make another parallel cut about ⅛" to ¼" in from the edge of the first cut. A wheel is presented on the rim of a glass, so you need to make another cut from the center of the wheel out to the edge so it can perch on the rim of the glass.

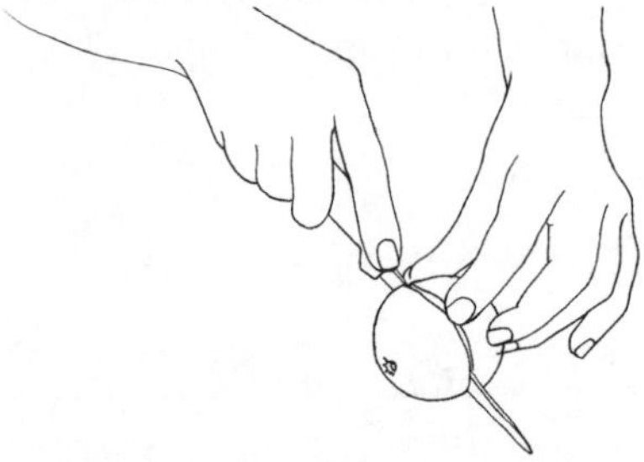

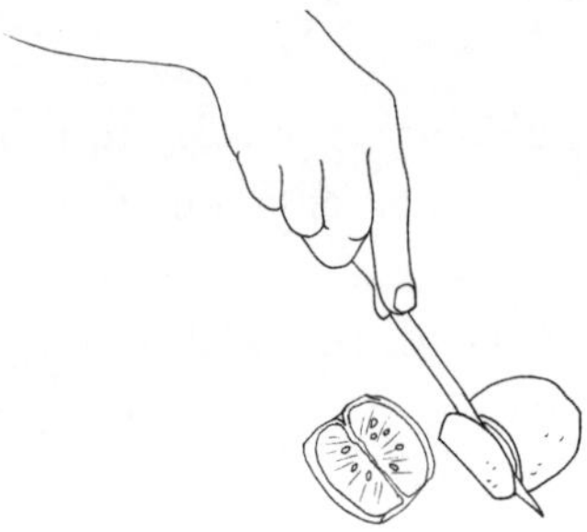

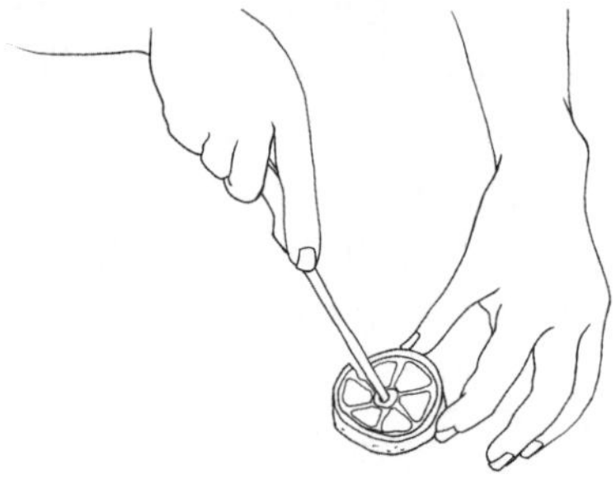

Twists: twists are used often in a variety of drinks, especially in those enduring, classic cocktails. Producing a twist requires a knife—ideally the U-shaped blade of a channel knife. To create a more dainty twist, hold the citrus in one hand, and with the channel knife in the other, cut a strip of peel about 3" long. The citrus peel is cut and emerges from the channel knife's center oval "window" so you can see the cut peel. Once you have the desired length of the peel, hold the peel over the surface of your cocktail, twist the peel into a tight spiral, and then release it into the drink, expressing the oils and adding a refreshing visual.

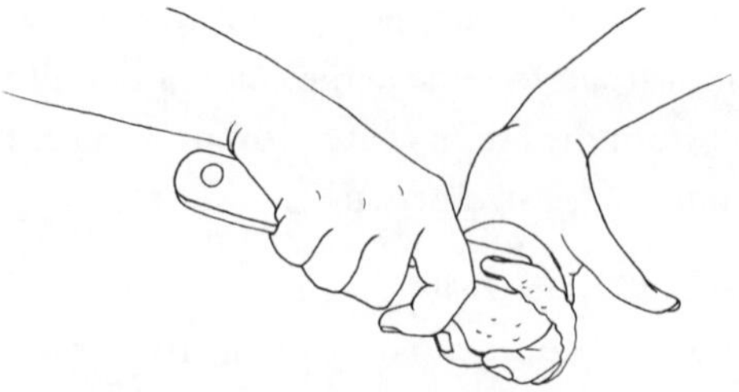

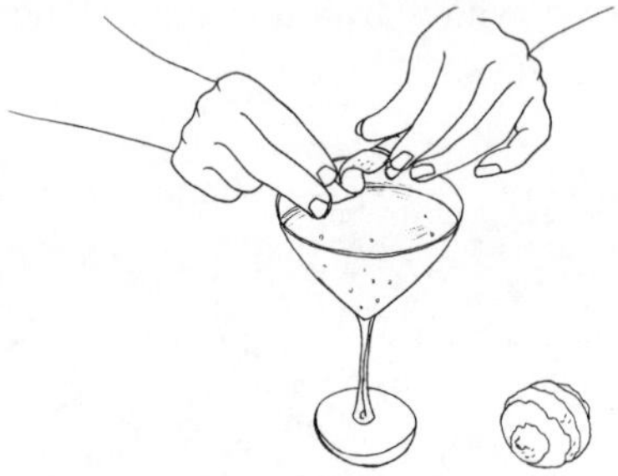

Tattoo: hold the citrus in one hand at a slight angle, and with the zester in the other hand score the fruit from top to bottom; repeat around the citrus. Cut the fruit at the midsection, and slice into wedges or wheels.

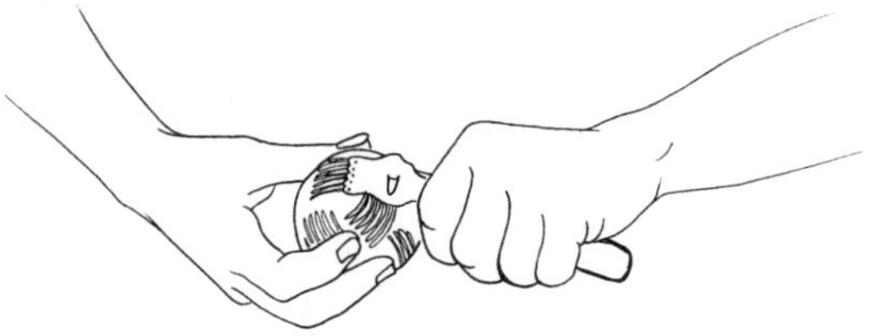

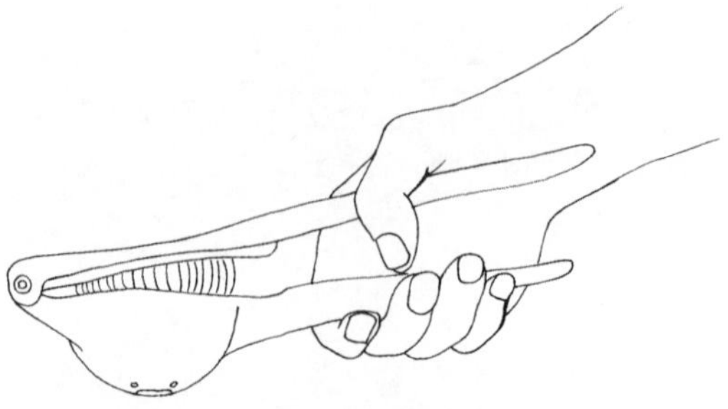

A tattooed citrus half is also the perfect vessel for a Flaming Citrus Shell—a dramatic garnish for tiki drinks. Use a citrus squeezer to remove the pulp from the tattooed citrus half and mold back into shape, smoothing out any fruit fiber. This is your vessel. Place a sugar cube or crouton soaked in overproof rum or lemon extract; the soaked cube serves as a wick. Float the citrus in the drink and light the cube.

Scored citrus: this designed wheel lends itself especially to oranges, grapefruits, and tangelos. Using a channel knife or a serrated knife, hold the fruit in one hand and remove a strip of peel from the citrus's top to bottom with the other hand. Repeat on the opposite side of the orange. Repeat this step three or more times so you have equidistant lines on the fruit. Slice the citrus at the midsection to create wheels or slices to garnish the cocktail glass—perfect in a Negroni, floating in a punch bowl, or posing on the rim of a pitcher of sangria.

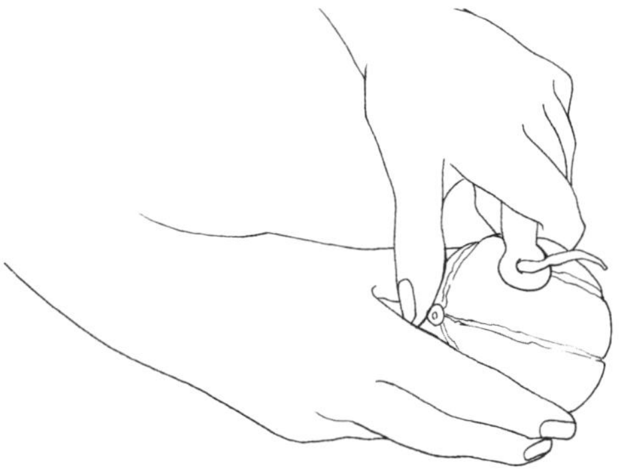

FRUIT GARNISHES

Gertrude Stein wrote "Rose is a rose is a rose"—when it comes to fruits, it may surprise you that cherries, raspberries, strawberries, apples, pears, quinces, apricots, peaches, watermelons, and cucumbers are all in the *Rosaceae* family. The quintessential English rose herself, The Queen of England, was gifted a specially made gin to mark her 90th birthday. Infused with red rose petals after distillation, the aptly named "English Rose" brand is a classic gin made with traditional botanicals. Fruit garnishes provide a kind of ballast to most every drink because they are beautiful, refreshing, and delicious. Moreover, fruit garnishes can be presented in a number of distinctive forms: freshly sliced, dehydrated, chopped, frozen, sugar-coated, or combined with other fruits, herbs, and flowers. Certain fruits, such as apples, strawberries, pineapples, and dragon fruit, can be shaped, cut, and made to take on fanciful, dreamy designs.

MARASCHINO CHERRIES

A staple of cocktail garnishes, maraschino cherries have a history that is wrapped in world politics and geography. A favorite of European aristocracy, the authentic maraschino—the marasca cherry—is grown only in the sandy soils found in the Croatia's Dalmatian mountains, with whole cherries preserved in Italy's maraschino liqueurs. Luxardo is the original maraschino cherry distillery on the Croatian coast, founded in 1821. The elegant import was soon embraced in the United States and served in fine bars and restaurants. With the ban on alcohol during the ill-fated Prohibition, liqueur-soaked cherries were also outlawed.

OLIVES

The rock star of garnishes has long been the olive (and yes, technically it is a fruit). Not unlike other classic garnishes, the olive was first used because of its myriad health benefits. Martini olives are preserved in brine, adding a salty taste to the cocktail. Brine-soaked olives likely came from a doctor at the Syrian Red Crescent, Dr. Ammar Martini. Cocktail legend has it that after the French left Syria, Martini went to Paris and managed a bar and café, and put an olive in the glass because Idlib province, where he was from, was known for particularly restorative olives. He was a doctor, after all. Most often, three very fresh, green olives are used for garnishing a Martini. It's a kind of tradition that at the first sip, one olive is consumed. The last olive or two are embraced with the last sip of martini. Olive garnishes can also include a stuffing of garlic, almonds, blue cheese, jalapeño, or anchovies.

Strawberries and pears make especially good fan garnishes, as do pickles.

To make a fan garnish, place the fruit on a cutting board. Cut several thin slices with a paring knife lengthwise through the fruit, leaving slices attached at the top, just below the hull or stem. Fan out or pull apart the slices. Keep all slices attached to the hull or stem. Float in a glass on top of the drink or rest on the side of the glass, one or two of the fans inside the glass and one perched on the outside.

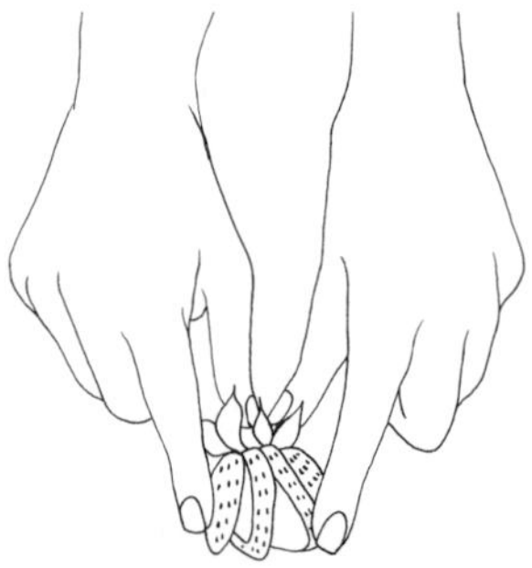

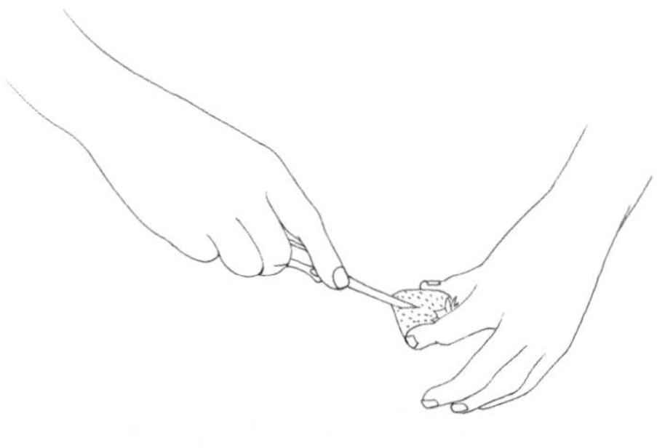

SHRUBS AND PICKLED FRUITS

Shrub cocktails hearken to the Colonial era when using vinegar to preserve fruits was essential. Shrubs—cold-infused simple syrups with vinegar added—have become increasingly popular. The classic shrub is extremely simple to prepare: just heat up equal parts sugar and vinegar until the former dissolves, pour over some cut-up fruit and let stand for a while; strain, bottle, and store.

A popular recipe is 2 cups sugar, 2 cups vinegar, and 1 pound fruit.

PICKLED STRAWBERRIES, APPLES, AND STONE FRUITS

Pickled fruits also make for tasty and dynamic garnishes; here is a basic recipe for 2 to 3 pounds of fruit:

1. Mix the fruit with 2 cups of sugar and 2 cups of salt, toss to coat, then allow to sit at room temperature for about 10 to 12 hours.

2. Strain out the fruit and transfer the liquid to a medium saucepan with ¾ cup red wine vin-

egar and ½ cup of simple syrup. (The pickled fruit is tangy, tart, and a bit sweet, so something like vanilla simple syrup is a considered flavor balance.)

3. Cook over high heat for 5 minutes, then pour over the fruit and let sit for another 12 hours.

4. Strain the fruit through a sieve, boil the liquid, and pour it over the fruit a few more times for a more refined syrup.

5. Add the fruit to clean mason jars and pour the cooled liquid over the fruit, pressing down until it's covered.

HERBS

Herbs intoxicate the nose and amplify a heady aroma or fragrance, and there is no shortage of options for how to work them into garnishes.

Float an herb leaf or sprig or bud to drink with the season. Indulge in the fragrance and the composition. Rosemary, lavender, and tarragon are lovely perched in the glass, when seen from a side angle.

Rim a glass with herbal simple syrup, balsamic vinegar infused with herbs (I especially love peach- and basil-infused balsamics), or roll the glass in dried herbs or herb-infused sugar for a kind of cocktail couture.

MUDDLING AND CRUSHING HERBS AND SPICES

Muddling herbs is the best option to release their essential oils. Use a muddler made of unvarnished wood, place the washed herbal leaves in a cocktail shaker or mixing glass, and press down with a few gentle twists to bruise the herbs and release their essences.

HERBAL BITTERS

You can readily create your own artisanal bitters and herbal tinctures made from botanicals—or source them from a plethora of award-winning homegrown purveyors including Modern Bar Cart, Hella Bitters, Regan's, Fee Brothers, and the classics: Peychaud's and Angostura.

HOW TO INFUSE SPIRITS WITH HERBS AND SPICES

As I posit in the chapter 2 introduction, vodka is the drink world's tofu—it blends well with almost anything. Tequila, rum, and gin work great too. Combine the spirit with crushed or muddled herbs and spices, such as ginger, cilantro, or angelica. Look for tastes that complement. For example, angelica with orange, rhubarb, or strawberry. Anise hyssop with blueberry, peach, or raspberry. Basils with limes, mints, or cinnamon. Cilantro with coconut, lemon, or mint. The possibilities are endless.

THE RIDDLE OF ICE

When I was a young boy, I was a fan of the movie *Conan the Barbarian* with Arnold Schwarzenegger. I had the books and while the movie was flawed, it still had its charms for a pre-teen boy.

Early in that movie (I'm going to spoil a few things for you, but it's been roughly 36 years since it was released so I'm thinking you've had plenty of time to take it in), before all the killing starts, before young Conan is orphaned, and before he becomes a heavily muscled brute bent on revenge, young Conan is seen sitting with his blacksmith father. The man (who has no name because he'll die horribly in the next 10 minutes), tells Conan "The Riddle of Steel." Conan's father tells him how giants stole the secret of steel from the god Crom and in the ensuing battle, the secret was left on the battlefield to be found by the race of men. Here is the important part, as it is almost the last thing this soon-to-be-deceased person says in the film: "And the secret of steel has always carried with it a mystery. You must learn its riddle, Conan, you must learn its discipline. For no one, no one in this world can you trust. Not men, not women, not beasts . . . this you can trust." As he says this, Conan's father points at the sword he made during the opening credits.

So why do I bring up a movie many of you probably haven't seen? Because I thought it would be a cool way to start the discussion on an important riddle in cocktails, The Riddle of Ice.

Everyone is familiar with ice as a substance. It cools down your drinks, many of you scrape it off of your car in the winter, some of you skate on it for fun. When it comes to cocktails, there are a few things you need to know.

While it is often overlooked, ice is one of the most important aspects of a cocktail. It is part presentation because everyone likes clean, clear cubes and spheres; part tool—either to cool down your drink as it is being shaken or stirred, or adding a little water to your creation as it melts. The same way that ice can be the finishing touch on your cocktail, bad ice can ruin it. High-end bars have expensive machines to make blocks of clear, perfect ice; if you go on YouTube and look up Japanese bartenders and ice, you will see bartenders wire-cut a chunk of ice from an almost transparent block and then chip at it with a three-pronged ice pick until it is a sphere that fits perfectly into a glass.

I'm going to make an assumption that most people reading this don't own a bar, aren't going to spend thousands of dollars on a machine that makes perfect ice, and don't have the time to hand-carve balls of ice for each drink, so the following tips are specifically for making better ice at home for your cocktails.

First off, use the best water you can get your hands on. This is pretty straightforward. The better the water, the better the ice. Filtering it is a good start. Spring or distilled water will also work if you prefer. Just add that to your party prep list and you'll be good to go.

Once you've sorted out the water, you need to put it in something so that you can freeze it. The standard trays can work in a pinch but you *may* (hint, hint) want to make a small investment in some silicone trays that produce larger cubes and spheres. The increased surface area of the bigger pieces of ice will melt slower so you avoid the dreaded "watery drink" phenomenon that will ruin the cocktail you worked so hard to create. Specialty stores and online retailers carry an array of styles and shapes, but my advice with the trays is to keep it simple.

Another thing to remember: ice trays take on the smells of the freezer (though metal trays do not hold odors as much as plastic and silicone trays). Since no one wants their ice smelling like that batch of stew you were saving for the right occasion, I suggest the following:

- Wash your ice trays before that big party—soap and water should be fine with regular trays; soap, water, and baking soda is the move with silicone trays because even though they make amazing ice, the silicone picks up more odors than a standard ice tray. In fact, with all of that in mind, giving the freezer a good cleaning before you start making ice for the big party wouldn't hurt.
- Have a party set of ice trays that is only used for cocktail ice—ice trays can't pick up freezer smells if they aren't in the freezer all the time. Keep this set in freezer bags in kitchen cabinets (though be sure to keep them away from the oven and stove since cooking will impart odors as well) to reduce the amount of odors your ice picks up.
- Make fresh ice for each party—the best way to avoid stinky, stale ice is to make fresh batches the day before or the day of the party. This minimizes the time the tray is in the freezer.
- If you need to make crushed ice, don't rely on a refrigerator's ice dispenser. Rather, get a Lewis bag and mallet. Back in the 19th century, these canvas sacks used to be a staple in bars. Ice is readily available today, of course, but crushing it to fit your cocktails is the way to go. Just add some of your freshly made cubes into the bag, give it a couple of whacks, and, voila, you have homemade crushed ice, perfect for cocktails, and stress relief.

Follow these tips and you will make better ice, and better cocktails.

And speaking of cocktails, you ready to make and drink some? The following pages (many, many pages) contain a bounty of recipes. They've been organized by base spirit, and are complemented by colorful photographs, intriguing histories, and expert insights. In the Appendix (page 809) you will find detailed instructions for the preparation of next-level garnishes; if you come across a term you don't recognize, or need a recipe for simple syrup or orgeat, check the Glossary (page 813).

Cheers!

VODKA

Vodka is one of the two clear core spirits covered in this book (the other being gin) and while they are similar in appearance there are differences, especially in how they work in cocktails.

Vodka can be made from anything that could be fermented to create alcohol. This includes grains such as rye, barley, and wheat, as well as vegetables like beets and potatoes. The location of the distillery and what the distillers have the easiest access to will generally govern what is used to create vodka. Many countries use grain to make their vodka, with potatoes being a close second. Each imparts different advantages since potatoes have a high level of starch that imparts a creamy, oily mouthfeel and a natural, light sweetness, while grains are thought to produce a cleaner spirit that is easier to pair with other ingredients.

Vodka is the tofu of spirits. While I'm not a huge fan of tofu, this comparison is not meant as an insult. Actually, it's a bit of a compliment. I have friends who love drinking vodka straight (and they are definitely not alone). They love vodka's lack of a strong taste and its relatively low-calorie count, and it is their spirit of choice for doing shots. I'm a fan of enjoying the flavor of my drinks, be they wine, whiskies, or cocktails, so the relative lack of a strong flavor is a negative for me. Also, as I've already mentioned, I'm not a huge fan of shots in general. That said, vodka's lack of a strong flavor profile makes it a perfect spirit for cocktails. You can pair it with damn near anything, hence its being a part of a diverse group of cocktails such as Martinis, Bloody Marys, and White Russians. Vodka goes well with most juices: you can literally add vodka to any type of fruit juice and voila . . . you have a cocktail—vodka and orange juice (a Screwdriver), vodka and cranberry juice (a Cape Cod), or vodka and grapefruit juice (a Greyhound). It plays well with many other spirits and complements whatever it is added to, which is not something you can say about other types of alcohol.

Since vodka looks like water, this brings to mind one of my favorite quotations from the actor, Bruce Lee:

"Empty your mind, be formless, shapeless—like water. Now you put water in a cup, it becomes the cup. You put water into a bottle, it becomes the bottle. You put it in a teapot, it becomes the teapot. Now water can flow, or it can crash. Be water, my friend."

Or in the case of vodka, with its ability to play well with other flavors and provide an ideal base for many a great cocktail, "Be tofu, my friend." *Favorite cocktail*: Greyhound—easy to make, always refreshing, and I love grapefruit.

A BRIEF OVERVIEW OF VODKA

The Russian love of vodka is undisputed. The same can't be said, however, for the country that can rightfully claim to have invented the potent spirit. There are historical records that allude to vodka being produced in Poland as early as the 8th century, and in Russia in the 9th century. Records that explicitly name vodka, which incidentally derives from the Slavic word for "water," *voda*, exist in Poland's Sandomierz Court Registry dating back to 1405, while any existing written record of vodka in Russia doesn't appear until 1751.

While potatoes are commonly a primary ingredient in vodka, the tubers didn't even show up in Europe until the 16th century, when the Spanish Conquistadors returned from South America with them. So the earliest vodkas were sugar- and grain-based. Vodka can also be made from grapes and whey, as well as carrots, beets, and several other ingredients; today, most commercial vodkas are made with fermented grains, like rice, wheat, rye, or sorghum.

Whatever the base starch being used, water and enzymes are added to it in order to convert the starch to sugar, before adding yeast to begin the fermentation process. In the early days of vodka production, wild airborne yeast was part of the equation (which was really more like magic, hence the associations with alchemy) but today it is all automated and regulated. The distillation process then begins, vaporizing the low ABV liquid as it moves through column stills and extracting impurities until the end result is a very high-percentage alcohol, which is then diluted and flavored before bottling.

Vodka is best stored in the freezer. With a minimum 40 percent ABV, the drink has a lot of "heat" to it, and when kept cold, the heat is tempered, allowing the body and depth of the vodka to be appreciated, whether one is doing shots or mixing cocktails.

GODMOTHER

Place both ingredients in a rocks glass filled with crushed ice and stir.

INGREDIENTS:

- 2 OZ. VODKA
- 1 OZ. AMARETTO

CAPE COD

GARNISH: 1 LIME WEDGE

Build in a chilled highball glass with ice cubes and garnish with the lime wedge.

INGREDIENTS:

- 1½ OZ. VODKA
- 5 OZ. CRANBERRY JUICE

GREYHOUND

Build in a highball glass with ice.

INGREDIENTS:

- 1 OZ. VODKA
- GRAPEFRUIT JUICE, TO TOP

VODKA GIMLET

GARNISH: 1 LIME WEDGE

Combine in a mixing glass filled with ice and strain into a cocktail glass. Garnish with a lime wedge.

INGREDIENTS:

- 1½ OZ. VODKA
- ½ OZ. FRESH LIME JUICE

SEX ON THE BEACH

Build in a Collins glass filled with ice by adding vodka and peach schnapps and topping off with equal parts orange juice and cranberry juice.

INGREDIENTS:

- ½ OZ. VODKA
- 1 OZ. PEACH SCHNAPPS
- 2 OZ. ORANGE JUICE
- 2 OZ. CRANBERRY JUICE

HARVEY WALLBANGER

GARNISH: 1 ORANGE SLICE

Pour vodka and orange juice into an ice-filled Collins glass. Float the Galliano on top and garnish with an orange slice.

INGREDIENTS:

- 1 OZ. VODKA
- 4 OZ. FRESH ORANGE JUICE
- ¼ OZ. GALLIANO

KAMIKAZE

Place the ingredients in a mixing glass filled with ice and stir to combine. Strain and serve as a cocktail or a shot.

INGREDIENTS:

- 1 OZ. VODKA
- ¼ OZ. TRIPLE SEC
- ¼ OZ. LIME JUICE

MELON BALL

Pour vodka into a Collins glass filled with ice and top with orange juice. Float the Midori on top.

INGREDIENTS:

- 1 OZ. VODKA
- ORANGE JUICE, TO TOP
- ½ OZ. MIDORI

SCREWDRIVER

Build in a highball glass filled with ice.

INGREDIENTS:

- 1 OZ. VODKA
- ORANGE JUICE, TO TOP

MIND ERASER

Layer in a double shot glass and drink through a straw.

INGREDIENTS:

- ¾ OZ. COFFEE LIQUEUR
- ¾ OZ. VODKA
- ¾ OZ. TONIC WATER

VARIATIONS ON VODKA MARTINIS

Whether or not you consider a Vodka Martini a "true" Martini, it's impossible to deny the incredible versatility of this delicious spirit and the riffs it inspires. The Vodka Martini has accrued a following of its own, with many taking after James Bond's example and settling into the familiar, comforting arms of this most popular of liquors.

While gin purists may turn up their noses, the truth is that the Vodka Martini is no less elegant, no less flavorful, and, frankly, no less perfect than its gin counterpart. It simply makes use of a different primary ingredient, one which lends itself to different strengths and weaknesses—particularly when it comes to flavored variants.

Even those who are not lovers of vodka will admit that it is the ideal liquor for a number of mixed drinks. This is because, perhaps more than any other type of alcohol, vodka takes on the flavor of anything it is mixed with. It adds bite to apple brandy. It grounds the sourness of lemon. It hides beneath the spice of a jalapeño, waiting to pounce. This quality makes vodka the perfect choice for many flavored Martini variants. Unlike gin, vodka imparts little flavor on its own—hence why I have dubbed it the "tofu of spirits." By not forcing the other ingredients to stand up to a bold flavor like juniper, vodka greatly expands your options when it comes to fun and whimsical takes on the Martini.

Even the most ardent of gin lovers would do well to sample Vodka Martini options. You may find that you prefer to remain loyal to the gin-centric classic. That's perfectly fine. Or you may find an entirely new reason to love the Martini. The opportunity to expand one's horizons is one that should never be turned down.

CLASSIC VODKA MARTINI

GARNISH: 1 LEMON TWIST

Place the vodka and vermouth in a mixing glass filled with ice and stir until thoroughly combined. Strain the resulting mixture into a cocktail glass and garnish with the twist of lemon.

INGREDIENTS:

- 4 PARTS SKYY VODKA
- 1 PART DRY VERMOUTH

BUDGET VODKA MARTINI

Place the vodka, vermouth, and lemon juice in a mixing glass filled with ice. Stir until thoroughly combined and strain the resulting mixture into a cocktail glass.

INGREDIENTS:

- 4 PARTS SVEDKA VODKA
- 1 PART DRY VERMOUTH
- DASH OF LEMON JUICE

PURIST'S VODKA MARTINI

GARNISH: 1 OLIVE

Place the vermouth into a cocktail shaker filled with ice and add the vodka. Stir or shake. Strain into a chilled cocktail glass and garnish with the olive.

INGREDIENTS:

- 2 DROPS OF DRY VERMOUTH
- 1¾ OZ. VODKA

THE DIRTY SPY

GARNISH: 1 PIMENTO-STUFFED GREEN OLIVE

Add the vodka, vermouth, and olive brine to a cocktail shaker filled with ice. Shake well, strain the resulting mixture into a cocktail glass, and garnish with the olive.

INGREDIENTS:

- 3 PARTS VODKA
- 1 PART DRY VERMOUTH
- SPLASH OF GREEN OLIVE BRINE

DRY VODKA MARTINI

GARNISH: 1 LEMON TWIST

Place the vodka and vermouth in a mixing glass filled with ice and stir until thoroughly combined. Strain the resulting mixture into a cocktail glass and garnish with the twist of lemon.

INGREDIENTS:

- 8 PARTS VODKA
- 1 PART DRY VERMOUTH

WET VODKA MARTINI

GARNISH: 1 LIME TWIST

Place the vodka and vermouth in a mixing glass filled with ice and stir until thoroughly combined. Strain the resulting mixture into a cocktail glass and garnish with the twist of lime.

INGREDIENTS:

- 2 PARTS VODKA
- 1 PART DRY VERMOUTH

PERFECT VODKA MARTINI

GARNISH: 1 LEMON TWIST

Place the vodka and vermouths in a mixing glass filled with ice and stir until thoroughly combined. Strain the resulting mixture into a cocktail glass and garnish with the twist of lemon.

INGREDIENTS:

- 4 PARTS VODKA
- 1 PART DRY VERMOUTH
- 1 PART SWEET VERMOUTH

DIRTY VODKA MARTINI

GARNISH: 3 PIMENTO-STUFFED OLIVES

Place the vodka, vermouth, and olive brine in a mixing glass filled with ice and stir until thoroughly combined. Strain the resulting mixture into a cocktail glass and garnish with the pimento-stuffed olives skewered on a toothpick.

INGREDIENTS:

- 4 PARTS VODKA
- 1 PART DRY VERMOUTH
- SPLASH OF OLIVE BRINE

MCCLURE'S PICKLE MARTINI

GARNISH: 1 PICKLE SLICE

Place the vodka and brine in a mixing glass and fill with ice. Stir until very cold, strain into a chilled cocktail glass, and garnish with the pickle slice.

INGREDIENTS:

- 2 OZ. VODKA
- 1 OZ. BRINE FROM A JAR OF MCCLURE'S PICKLES

VODKA MARTINI SHOOTER

GARNISH: 1 PIMENTO-STUFFED GREEN OLIVE

Place the vodka, vermouth, and olive brine in a cocktail shaker filled with ice and shake vigorously. Strain the resulting mixture into a shot glass and garnish by balancing an olive on a toothpick over the center of the glass.

INGREDIENTS:

- 1 OZ. VODKA
- ¼ OZ. DRY VERMOUTH
- DASH OF OLIVE BRINE

APPLETINI

GARNISH: 3 APPLE SLICES

Place the vodka, Sour Apple Pucker, and triple sec in a cocktail shaker filled with ice and shake vigorously. Strain the resulting mixture into a cocktail glass and garnish with three thin slices of apple skewered on a toothpick.

INGREDIENTS:

- 3 PARTS VODKA
- 1 PART SOUR APPLE PUCKER
- 1 PART TRIPLE SEC

LYCHEETINI

GARNISH: 1 LYCHEE

Place the vodka, triple sec, and lychee liqueur in a cocktail shaker filled with ice and shake vigorously. Strain the resulting mixture into a cocktail glass and garnish with a lychee skewered on a toothpick.

INGREDIENTS:

- 3 PARTS VODKA
- 1 PART TRIPLE SEC
- 2 PARTS LYCHEE LIQUEUR

ESPRESSO MARTINI

GARNISH: HANDFUL OF ESPRESSO BEANS

Place the vodka, Kahlua, and espresso in a cocktail shaker filled with ice. Shake vigorously, strain the resulting mixture into a cocktail glass, and garnish with the espresso beans.

INGREDIENTS:

- 3 PARTS VODKA
- 1 PART KAHLUA
- 2 PARTS ESPRESSO

FRENCH MARTINI DE NANCY

GARNISH: 1 STRIP OF GRAPEFRUIT ZEST

Place all of the ingredients in a cocktail shaker filled with ice and shake vigorously. Strain into a cocktail glass and garnish with the grapefruit zest.

INGREDIENTS:

- ½ OZ. GIFFARD CRÈME DE PAMPLEMOUSSE ROSE
- 1½ OZ. VODKA
- SQUEEZE OF LEMON JUICE
- 2 OZ. GRAPEFRUIT JUICE

SOUR CHERRY MARTINI

GARNISH: 1 LIME WHEEL & 1 MARASCHINO CHERRY

Place the vodkas, lime juice, and grenadine in a cocktail shaker filled with ice and shake vigorously. Strain the resulting mixture into a cocktail glass and garnish with the lime wheel and maraschino cherry.

INGREDIENTS:

- 1 PART VODKA
- 2 PARTS CHERRY VODKA
- 1 PART LIME JUICE
- DASH OF GRENADINE

BELLINI MARTINI

GARNISH: 1 PEACH SLICE

Place the vodka, peach schnapps, and simple syrup in a cocktail shaker filled with ice and shake vigorously. Place the Champagne in the cocktail shaker and gently stir. Strain the resulting mixture into a cocktail glass and garnish with the slice of peach.

INGREDIENTS:

- 2 PARTS VODKA
- 1 PART PEACH SCHNAPPS
- SPLASH OF SIMPLE SYRUP
- 1 PART CHAMPAGNE

RASPBERRY MARTINI

GARNISH: 3 RASPBERRIES

At the bottom of a cocktail shaker, muddle 5 raspberries and the simple syrup. Add ice, the vodkas, and triple sec and shake vigorously. Strain the resulting mixture into a cocktail glass and garnish with the 3 raspberries.

INGREDIENTS:

- 5 RASPBERRIES
- SPLASH OF SIMPLE SYRUP
- 2 PARTS VODKA
- 1 PART RASPBERRY VODKA
- 1 PART TRIPLE SEC

SPICY MARTINI

GARNISH: 2 JALAPEÑO-STUFFED OLIVES

Place the vodka, vermouth, and hot sauce in a cocktail shaker filled with ice and shake vigorously. Strain the resulting mixture into a cocktail glass and garnish with the jalapeño-stuffed olives skewered on a toothpick.

INGREDIENTS:

- 4 PARTS VODKA
- 1 PART DRY VERMOUTH
- DASH OF JALAPEÑO PEPPER HOT SAUCE

PICKLED MARTINI

GARNISH: 1 TO 2 CORNICHONS

Place the vodka, vermouth, and pickle juice in a mixing glass filled with ice. Stir until thoroughly combined, strain the resulting mixture into a cocktail glass, and garnish with 1 or more cornichons on a toothpick.

INGREDIENTS:

- 4 PARTS VODKA
- 1 PART DRY VERMOUTH
- SPLASH OF PICKLE JUICE

CLASSIC WHITE RUSSIAN

Let's get the word "Russian" out of the way first: this drink's connection to Russia is the vodka. It wasn't created in Russia or by a Russian. And the White Russian cannot be discussed without first examining the Black Russian, a vodka-and-Kahlua cocktail supposedly created in the late 1940s by bartender Gustave Tops in Brussels at the Hotel Metropole, in honor of the American ambassador to Luxembourg, Perle Mesta. The Oklahoma-born Mesta was a politically active socialite. Her support for Harry S. Truman's two presidential campaigns secured her overseas appointment and laid the foundation for the Irving Berlin musical *Call Me Madam*, starring Ethel Merman as a character largely based on Mesta. Neither the play nor the history books documents who added the cream to concoct the White Russian, though the cocktail's first known appearance in print can be traced back to 1965 ads for a coffee liqueur.

THE DUDE ABIDES

In the 1960s and '70s, the White Russian was a popular drink, but then in the '80s, perhaps because of trends in calorie counting, the adult milkshake went the way of leisure suits. But then in 1998, it began to make a comeback as the *Big Lebowski* went from cult favorite to bona fide classic. The Dude, the film's central character played by Jeff Bridges, drinks nothing but White Russians. In fact, the movie opens with the Dude meandering through the dairy section at the supermarket Ralphs, where he buys half-and-half, and only half-and-half (for which he writes out a check for 69 cents). The Dude isn't picky when it comes to his White Russians, powdered creamer will do just fine, thank you. And that is probably the best way to think about this drink today, so long as you can bolster the vodka with the rich flavors of Kahlua and cream or half-and-half.

INGREDIENTS:

1½ OZ. VODKA

½ OZ. KAHLUA

DASH OF CREAM

Add vodka and Kahlua to a rocks glass filled with ice. Stir and top with the dash of cream.

FANCY WHITE RUSSIAN

GARNISH: 1 CINNAMON STICK & DUSTING OF NUTMEG

Place the vodka, coffee liqueur, and milk in a cocktail shaker filled with ice and shake vigorously. Place ice in a rocks glass and strain the contents of the shaker into it. Garnish with the dusting of nutmeg and the cinnamon stick.

INGREDIENTS:

1 PART VODKA

1 PART COFFEE LIQUEUR

3 PARTS MILK

MASON JAR SCREWDRIVER

GARNISH: 1 ORANGE SLICE

Fill a mason jar with ice, add the vodka, and top off with orange juice. Dab a finger into the pomegranate juice, rub it along the edge of the jar, and garnish with the orange slice.

INGREDIENTS:

1 PART VODKA

2 PARTS ORANGE JUICE

DASH OF POMEGRANATE JUICE, FOR THE RIM

DEEP THROAT

Combine the coffee vodka and whipped cream vodka in a cocktail shaker filled with ice. Shake vigorously for 15 to 20 seconds, strain into shot glasses, and top them with the whipped cream. Drink without using your hands.

INGREDIENTS:

1 PART COFFEE VODKA

1 PART WHIPPED CREAM VODKA

DOLLOP OF WHIPPED CREAM

HAIRY NAVEL

GARNISH: 1 ORANGE SLICE

Fill a mason jar with the desired amount of ice, add the vodka and schnapps, and stir. Top with orange juice and a small splash of pineapple juice and garnish with the orange slice.

INGREDIENTS:

1½ OZ. VODKA

1½ OZ. PEACH SCHNAPPS

4 OZ. ORANGE JUICE

SPLASH OF PINEAPPLE JUICE

LEMONADE SHOCKER

GARNISH: 1 LEMON SLICE

Place the desired amount of ice in a mason jar. Add the vodka, blue curaçao, and lemon juice and stir. Top with the club soda and garnish with the lemon slice.

INGREDIENTS:

- 2 OZ. VODKA
- 1 OZ. BLUE CURAÇAO
- 2 OZ. LEMON JUICE
- 2 OZ. CLUB SODA

MINT MULE

GARNISH: 1 LIME WHEEL

Tear the mint leaves in half to release the flavor and place them at the bottom of a highball glass or copper mug. Add the lime juice and muddle. Add ice, and then pour in the vodka and ginger beer. Stir until thoroughly mixed and garnish with the lime wheel.

INGREDIENTS:

- 6 MINT LEAVES
- JUICE OF 1 LIME WEDGE
- 1 PART VODKA
- 2 PARTS GINGER BEER

BLUE LAGOON

GARNISH: 1 LEMON SLICE & 1 MARASCHINO CHERRY

Place the vodka and blue curaçao in a cocktail shaker filled with ice and shake vigorously. Place the desired amount of ice in a mason jar and strain the mixture into it. Top with the lemonade and the splash of lime juice. Garnish with the slice of lemon and maraschino cherry.

INGREDIENTS:

- 1 PART VODKA
- 1 PART BLUE CURAÇAO
- 4 PARTS LEMONADE
- SPLASH OF LIME JUICE

CITRUS SUNSET

GARNISH: 1 LIME SLICE

Place the desired amount of ice in a mason jar, and then add the vodka and grapefruit juice. Add the lime juice and the lemon juice and stir until mixed. Pour a small amount of grenadine into the middle of the drink and allow it to sink to the bottom, creating a subtle layering effect with the grapefruit juice. Garnish with the slice of lime.

INGREDIENTS:

- 1 PART VODKA
- 4 PARTS GRAPEFRUIT JUICE
- JUICE OF ½ LIME
- JUICE OF ¼ LEMON
- DASH OF GRENADINE

MOSCOW MULE

GARNISH: 1 LIME WEDGE & 1 SPRIG OF MINT (OPTIONAL)

Cocktail lore is full of cock-and-bull stories, but the history of the Moscow Mule is well documented and can be pinpointed to a day in 1941 when three lives converged at the Cock 'n' Bull pub on the Sunset Strip in Los Angeles. John Martin, the recently minted owner of the financially struggling Smirnoff Vodka distillery, was commiserating with his friend Jack Morgan, owner of the Cock 'n' Bull, who at the time was trying to launch his own brand of ginger beer. Enter Sophie Berezinski: the Russian immigrant had arrived in America with 2,000 copper mugs that she had designed and her father had stamped out on his press. Unable to sell the mugs in Russia, Sophie made the long trip to California, where her luck did not change, at first. But then one day she happened into Morgan's bar to find two men lamenting their entrepreneurial woes. Together Berezinski, Martin, and Morgan would develop a cocktail that married ginger beer, vodka, and the cooling properties of copper to make the Moscow Mule.

THE WASHINGTON WALLOP?

The Moscow Mule's popularity is largely the result of pure marketing genius, fusing a good drink with a unique package. But at the height of the Cold War, despite the cocktail's American roots and capitalist spirit, some suggested that the drink be given a new name: the Washington Wallop. At the time, a bartender at the Cock 'n' Bull decried the idea, declaring that changing the name would be like refusing to listen to Tchaikovsky. Luckily, the name stuck, and Mules are on more menus than ever.

INGREDIENTS:

- JUICE OF ½ LIME
- 1 PART VODKA
- 3 PARTS GINGER BEER

Place the lime juice in a copper mug and add the desired amount of ice. Add the vodka and top with ginger beer. Garnish with the lime wedge and, if desired, a sprig of mint.

MELON REFRESHER

GARNISH: LIME WHEELS

Place the desired amount of ice in a mason jar and then add the melon liqueur and vodka. Top with lemon-lime soda and garnish with a few lime wheels.

INGREDIENTS:

- 1 PART MELON LIQUEUR
- 1 PART VODKA
- 4 PARTS LEMON-LIME SODA

CHERRY BOMB

GARNISH: 1 MARASCHINO CHERRY

Place maraschino cherries in each shot glass. Combine the cherry vodka and Red Bull in a cocktail shaker filled with ice, shake vigorously for 15 to 20 seconds, and strain into the shot glasses.

INGREDIENTS:

- 1 PART CHERRY VODKA
- 1 PART RED BULL

CHERRY SWIZZLE

Combine the cherry vodka and lime juice in a cocktail shaker filled with ice. Shake vigorously for 15 to 20 seconds and strain into shot glasses, filling each glass ⅔ of the way. Top with the Diet 7UP.

INGREDIENTS:

- 2 PARTS SKINNYGIRL WHITE CHERRY VODKA
- 1 PART FRESH LIME JUICE
- 1 PART DIET 7UP

CHERRY TOOTSIE POP

Combine all of the ingredients in a cocktail shaker filled with ice. Shake vigorously for 15 to 20 seconds and strain into shot glasses.

INGREDIENTS:

- 1 PART CHOCOLATE VODKA
- 1 PART RED BULL
- DASH OF GRENADINE

CHOCOLATE CREAM & PEACHES

Combine all of the ingredients in a cocktail shaker filled with ice. Shake vigorously for 15 to 20 seconds and strain into shot glasses.

INGREDIENTS:

- 1 PART CHOCOLATE VODKA
- 1 PART PEACH VODKA
- 1 PART SKIM MILK

GINGERBREAD

Combine all of the ingredients in a cocktail shaker filled with ice. Shake vigorously for 15 to 20 seconds and strain into shot glasses.

INGREDIENTS:

- 1 PART RUMCHATA
- 1 PART DOMAINE DE CANTON
- 1 PART VANILLA VODKA

GRAPE CHILL

GARNISH: GREEN GRAPES (OPTIONAL)

Combine all of the ingredients in a cocktail shaker filled with ice. Shake vigorously for 15 to 20 seconds and strain into shot glasses. If desired, garnish with green grapes skewered on a toothpick.

INGREDIENTS:

- 2 PARTS GRAPE VODKA
- 1 PART VANILLA VODKA
- 1 PART PINEAPPLE JUICE

GRAPE SOURBALL

GARNISH: ORANGE SLICES (OPTIONAL)

Combine all of the ingredients in a cocktail shaker filled with ice. Shake vigorously for 15 to 20 seconds and strain into shot glasses.

Tip: This can also be great on the rocks or in a cocktail glass.

INGREDIENTS:

- 1 PART GRAPE VODKA
- 1 PART CRYSTAL LIGHT LEMONADE
- 1 PART ORANGE JUICE

GUMBALL

Combine all of the ingredients in a cocktail shaker filled with ice. Shake vigorously for 15 to 20 seconds and strain into shot glasses.

INGREDIENTS:

1 PART RASPBERRY VODKA

1 PART BANANA LIQUEUR

1 PART GRAPEFRUIT JUICE

HEAD RUSH

Combine all of the ingredients in a cocktail shaker filled with ice. Shake vigorously for 15 to 20 seconds and strain into shot glasses.

INGREDIENTS:

1 PART PEACH VODKA

1 PART PEAR VODKA

1 PART SAMBUCA

JOLLY RANCHER

Combine all of the ingredients in a cocktail shaker filled with ice. Shake vigorously for 15 to 20 seconds and strain into shot glasses.

INGREDIENTS:

1 PART APPLE VODKA

1 PART CHERRY VODKA

1 PART PEACH VODKA

1 PART DIET CRANBERRY JUICE

PINK LEMONADE

Wet the rims of the shot glasses and dip them into the sugar. Combine all of the ingredients in a cocktail shaker filled with ice. Shake vigorously for 15 to 20 seconds and strain into shot glasses.

INGREDIENTS:

SUGAR, FOR THE RIM

1 PART VODKA

1 PART LEMON JUICE

1 PART DIET CRANBERRY JUICE

PINK PETALS

Combine all of the ingredients in a cocktail shaker filled with ice. Shake vigorously for 15 to 20 seconds and strain into shot glasses.

INGREDIENTS:

1 PART SKINNYGIRL WHITE CHERRY VODKA
1 PART SKINNYGIRL COCONUT VODKA
DASH OF GRENADINE

POISON APPLE

Combine the ingredients in a cocktail shaker filled with ice. Shake vigorously for 15 to 20 seconds and strain into shot glasses.

INGREDIENTS:

1 PART SKINNYGIRL WHITE CHERRY VODKA
1 PART APPLE JUICE WITH NO SUGAR ADDED

PURPLE HOOTER

GARNISH: RASPBERRIES (OPTIONAL)

Combine the vodkas in a cocktail shaker filled with ice. Shake vigorously for 15 to 20 seconds and strain into shot glasses, filling each glass ⅔ of the way. Top off with the chilled Diet 7UP. If desired, garnish with raspberries.

INGREDIENTS:

1 PART RASPBERRY VODKA
1 PART SKINNYGIRL NAKED VODKA
1 PART DIET 7UP, CHILLED

STORM WARNING

Combine all of the ingredients in a cocktail shaker filled with ice. Shake vigorously for 15 to 20 seconds and strain into shot glasses.

INGREDIENTS:

1 PART SKINNYGIRL WHITE CHERRY VODKA
1 PART CHOCOLATE VODKA
1 PART IRISH CREAM

WOO SHOO

Combine the ingredients in a cocktail shaker filled with ice. Shake vigorously for 15 to 20 seconds and strain into shot glasses.

INGREDIENTS:

- 1 PART PEACH SCHNAPPS
- 3 PARTS CRANBERRY VODKA

ABSOLUT BITCH

Combine all of the ingredients in a cocktail shaker filled with ice. Shake vigorously for 15 to 20 seconds and strain into shot glasses.

INGREDIENTS:

- 1 PART ABSOLUT VODKA
- 1 PART IRISH CREAM
- 1 PART COFFEE LIQUEUR
- 1 PART TUACA

ANGEL'S KISS

Fill a shot glass halfway with the chocolate vodka. Place a bar spoon upside-down just barely above the vodka and touching the side of the glass. Slowly and carefully pour skim milk over the spoon and into the glass until the glass is full. Carefully add a few drops of grenadine into the center of the milk layer.

INGREDIENTS:

- 1 PART CHOCOLATE VODKA
- 1 PART SKIM MILK
- 3 DROPS OF GRENADINE

TEDDY BEAR

Combine the vodkas in a cocktail shaker filled with ice. Shake vigorously for 15 to 20 seconds and strain into shot glasses.

INGREDIENTS:

- 1 PART VANILLA VODKA
- 1 PART ROOT BEER VODKA

DANGEROUS GRANDMA

Combine all of the ingredients in a cocktail shaker filled with ice. Shake vigorously for 15 to 20 seconds and strain into shot glasses.

INGREDIENTS:

- 1 PART COFFEE VODKA
- 1 PART WHISK(E)Y
- 1 PART AMARETTO
- 1 PART ORANGE JUICE

VINEYARD SPLASH

GARNISH: 1 HANDFUL OF WATERMELON CUBES

If making the puree from scratch, place 4 oz. of fresh purple grapes in a food processor along with the juice from half of a lime. Add ¼ cup of fresh watermelon and blend until smooth.

Wet the rim of a mason jar, dip it into some sugar, and add the desired amount of ice. Add the lime juice and the vodka, and then pour in the puree. Add the 1 teaspoon of sugar and stir thoroughly. Top with the club soda and garnish with the watermelon cubes skewered on a toothpick.

INGREDIENTS:

- 1 PART PURPLE GRAPE-AND-WATERMELON PUREE
- 1 TEASPOON SUGAR, PLUS MORE FOR THE RIM
- JUICE OF ½ LIME
- 1 PART VODKA
- DASH OF CLUB SODA

VODKA SUNRISE

GARNISH: 1 ORANGE SLICE & 1 MARASCHINO CHERRY

Place ice in a pint glass, and then add the vodka and lemon juice. Stir, fill with orange juice, and top with a splash of grenadine. Do not stir, allowing the grenadine to slowly filter down through the orange juice and vodka. Garnish with the maraschino cherry and orange slice.

INGREDIENTS:

- 1 PART VODKA
- DASH OF LEMON JUICE
- 2 PARTS ORANGE JUICE
- SPLASH OF GRENADINE

HELL'S GATE

GARNISH: THIN SLICES OF CUCUMBER (OPTIONAL)

Combine all of the ingredients in a cocktail shaker filled with ice. Shake vigorously for 15 to 20 seconds and strain into shot glasses. If desired, garnish with thin slices of cucumber.

INGREDIENTS:

- 1 PART SKINNYGIRL CUCUMBER VODKA
- 3–4 DROPS OF TABASCO
- DASH OF WASABI PASTE

VANILLA PEAR

GARNISH: 1 PEAR SLICE

Wet the rim of a mason jar and dip it into the sugar. Place the pear juice and vanilla vodka in a cocktail shaker filled with ice, add the almond extract, and shake vigorously until combined. Strain into the mason jar and garnish with the slice of pear.

INGREDIENTS:

- SUGAR, FOR THE RIM
- 2 PARTS PEAR JUICE
- 1 PART VANILLA VODKA
- DROP OF ALMOND EXTRACT

MASON JAR MUDSLIDE

GARNISH: 1 SPRIG OF MINT

Place the vodka, coffee liqueur, Irish cream, heavy cream, and ice in a blender and puree until the desired consistency is achieved. For added chocolaty taste, add a dash of chocolate syrup to the blender before pureeing. Pour the cocktail into a mason jar, top with whipped cream, and drizzle chocolate syrup on top. Garnish with the sprig of mint.

INGREDIENTS:

- 1 OZ. VODKA
- 1 OZ. COFFEE LIQUEUR
- 1 OZ. IRISH CREAM
- 1 OZ. HEAVY CREAM
- 1 CUP ICE
- CHOCOLATE SYRUP, TO TASTE
- DOLLOP OF WHIPPED CREAM

BONA DEA

GARNISH: 1 LEMON TWIST

Combine the peach vodka and cranberry juice in a rocks glass filled with ice and stir. Top with sparkling wine and garnish with the lemon twist.

INGREDIENTS:

- 1 OZ. PEACH VODKA
- 1 OZ. CRANBERRY JUICE
- SPARKLING WINE, TO TOP

EARLY RISER

GARNISH: 1 STRIP OF ORANGE PEEL

Combine vodka and orange juice in a cocktail glass filled with ice and stir. Top off with the sweet vermouth and add a splash of club soda. Garnish with the strip of orange peel.

INGREDIENTS:

- 1 PART VODKA
- 3 PARTS ORANGE JUICE
- 1 PART SWEET VERMOUTH
- SPLASH OF CLUB SODA

RASPBERRY TWIST

GARNISH: 3 OR 4 RASPBERRIES

Place the desired amount of ice in a mason jar and add the raspberry vodka. Add the lemonade and sweetened iced tea, stir until thoroughly mixed, and garnish with the raspberries.

INGREDIENTS:

- 1 PART RASPBERRY VODKA
- 2 PARTS LEMONADE
- 2 PARTS SWEETENED ICED TEA

OCEAN BREEZE

Combine all ingredients, except the Sprite, in a punch bowl filled with ice and stir until thoroughly mixed. Top with the Sprite.

INGREDIENTS:

- 1 PART VODKA
- 1 PART GIN
- 1 PART GRAPEFRUIT JUICE
- 3 PARTS CRANBERRY JUICE
- 1 PART SPRITE

Q&A WITH SERGEY CHESNOKOV, HEAD BARTENDER AT STRELKA

In 2009, the Strelka Institute was founded "to change the cultural and physical landscapes of Russian cities." The bar's fusion of art deco and 1960s and 1970s Italian and Scandinavian design makes it an ideal embodiment of the institute's broader goals.

What can you tell us about how the bar started?

Our bar opened its doors eight years ago as the social heart of the Strelka Institute. At that time, there were not so many places in Moscow for trendy youngsters to gather, drink, or hold business lunches and dinners, dance and listen to good music. So Strelka became one of the first. For me, as chief barman, it was a great experience transferring the institute's ideas of progressiveness and diversity to the bar menu.

Can you tell us about the theme of the bar and its focus?

Our mission is to provide maximum comfort for our guests. For example, we don't play music loud during the day. But at parties we do, of course. There is nothing intrusive or pretentious in the bar; all in all the atmosphere is super relaxed. We examine our audience habits and behavior on an everyday basis, and that is the main thing that allows us to treat our guests best.

What does your team look for when creating a new cocktail for your menu?

Mix maximum different tastes to perfect balance. We make complicated things comprehensible.

How does the food and culture of Moscow influence the cocktails that you offer?

We use lots of local ingredients like northern berries, tea mushroom, black currant leaves, etc.

What are the best parts of running a cocktail bar in Moscow? Are there any downsides or things that make it difficult?

The main thing I really love is this endless action and progress, which can make you feel great, as you always are pushing the envelope, and at the same time bad because of fear of missing something.

Blue Hawaiian, Brandy Alexander, Pink Squirrel, Rusty Nail, Tom Collins, White Russian, Grasshopper, Rob Roy, Pink Lady: If you had to pick one of these classic cocktails to add to your cocktail menu how would you reimagine your choice to make it fit in with your style?

First of all, we make even the most ordinary and simple cocktails based on high-quality spirits. Of these cocktails you mentioned, I would go with minimalism, and avoid any extra flourishes.

Do you have a favorite cocktail?

Gimlet.

Do you have a favorite alcohol to work with when making cocktails?

Vodka and gin are perfect in terms of cleanliness and production technologies. There are no fermentation products. I prefer using them, as my main goal is to make people feel good when they wake up in the morning after visiting our bar.

STRELKA SPRITZ

All these ingredients we infuse on strawberries, blueberries, and Schisandra (10g each). Then we mix it in a wine glass with ice and Sprite.

INGREDIENTS:

- ¾ OZ. ROSÉ VERMOUTH
- ⅓ OZ. ORANGE LIQUEUR
- ⅓ OZ. CHERRY BRANDY
- DASH OF CAMPARI
- DASH OF AGAVE SYRUP
- DASH OF ALMOND SYRUP
- DASH OF ROSE WATER
- ⅓ OZ. PROSECCO
- ⅔ OZ. PIMM'S NO. 1
- ⅔ OZ. ABSOLUT RASPBERRY
- ⅔ OZ. ABSOLUT KURANT
- ⅓ OZ. AMARO RAMAZZOTTI
- ⅓ OZ. AMARO MONTENEGRO

STRELKA LEMONADE

All these ingredients we infuse on lime and elder leaves. And then we mix it with ice and Perrier.

INGREDIENTS:

- DASH OF GRAPEFRUIT CORDIAL
- DASH OF LUXARDO
- DASH OF ELDER SYRUP
- ½ OZ. ABSOLUT CITRON
- ½ OZ. ABSOLUT MANDARIN
- ½ OZ. ABSOLUT RASPBERRY

MANGO PUNCH

We make the cocktail by combining all of the ingredients, heating them with steam, and then decorate the cocktail with additional mango.

INGREDIENTS:

- 2½ OZ. MANGO
- 2½ OZ. ICE SAKE
- ½ OZ. HONEY
- SQUEEZE OF LIME JUICE

JUNGLE PUNCH

Combine vodka, Sprite, and fruit punch in a pitcher or punch bowl filled with ice. Stir until thoroughly mixed.

INGREDIENTS:

1 PART VODKA
1 PART SPRITE
3 PARTS FRUIT PUNCH

THE SLAMMER

Combine all ingredients in a large punch bowl and stir until thoroughly mixed. Do not add ice (though ice should be made available).

INGREDIENTS:

1 PART VODKA
1 PART AMARETTO
1 PART SOUTHERN COMFORT
3 PARTS ORANGE JUICE

SEA BREEZE

GARNISH: 1 LIME WEDGE & 1 CHERRY

Combine vodka and lime juice in a glass filled with ice, then add the remaining fruit juices. Stir to combine and garnish with a lime wedge and a cherry.

INGREDIENTS:

1 PART VODKA
DASH OF LIME JUICE
2 PARTS CRANBERRY JUICE
1 PART GRAPEFRUIT JUICE

CAPESCREW

GARNISH: 1 ORANGE WHEEL

Pour the vodka over ice into a highball glass and add a splash of triple sec. Add the orange juice and cranberry juice, stir until thoroughly mixed, and garnish with the orange wheel.

INGREDIENTS:

1 PART VODKA
SPLASH OF TRIPLE SEC
1 PART ORANGE JUICE
1 PART CRANBERRY JUICE

BLASTOFF

GARNISH: 1 ORANGE TWIST

Place the ingredients in a glass filled with ice, stir to combine, and garnish with the orange twist.

INGREDIENTS:

2 OZ. VODKA

1 OZ. GRAPEFRUIT JUICE

SQUEEZE OF LEMON JUICE

SQUEEZE OF LIME JUICE

CREAMSICLE

GARNISH: 1 ORANGE SLICE

Place all of the ingredients in a mixing glass filled with ice, stir, and strain over ice into a rocks glass. Garnish with the orange slice.

INGREDIENTS:

1 PART ORANGE JUICE

1 PART VODKA

1 PART HEAVY CREAM

SPLASH OF TRIPLE SEC

STRAWBERRIES AND CREAM

GARNISH: 1 STRAWBERRY

Pour the strawberry vodka and vanilla vodka over ice into a highball glass. Top with cream and stir until thoroughly mixed. Add the splash of grenadine and garnish with the strawberry.

INGREDIENTS:

1 PART STRAWBERRY VODKA

1 PART VANILLA VODKA

2 PARTS HEAVY CREAM

SPLASH OF GRENADINE

RING #4

GARNISH: 1 LEMON SLICE

Place ice in a highball glass and add the vodka and triple sec. Fill with lemonade and top with the splash of grenadine to add an inviting red hue to the drink. Garnish with the lemon slice.

INGREDIENTS:

1 PART RASPBERRY VODKA

SPLASH OF TRIPLE SEC

2 PARTS LEMONADE

SPLASH OF GRENADINE

BUDGET COSMOPOLITAN

GARNISH: 1 LIME WEDGE

Fill a cocktail shaker with ice and add the vodka, triple sec, cranberry juice, and lime juice. Shake vigorously, strain the resulting mixture into a cocktail glass, and garnish with the lime wedge.

INGREDIENTS:

- 2 PARTS SVEDKA VODKA
- 1 PART TRIPLE SEC
- 1 PART CRANBERRY JUICE
- SPLASH OF LIME JUICE

PERFECT COSMOPOLITAN

GARNISH: 1 LIME WEDGE

Fill a cocktail shaker with ice and add the vodka, triple sec, cranberry juice, and lime juice. Shake vigorously, strain the resulting mixture into a cocktail glass, and garnish with the lime wedge.

INGREDIENTS:

- 2 PARTS GREY GOOSE VODKA
- 1 PART TRIPLE SEC
- 1 PART CRANBERRY JUICE
- JUICE OF 1 LIME WEDGE

ROSE COSMO

GARNISH: 1 LIME WEDGE

Place all of the ingredients in a cocktail shaker filled with ice and shake until combined and very cold. Strain into a large, chilled cocktail glass.

INGREDIENTS:

- 2 OZ. DRAGON BLEU ROSE VODKA (OR PREFERRED ROSE-FLAVORED VODKA)
- ½ OZ. TRIPLE SEC OR COINTREAU
- ½ OZ. LIME JUICE
- ¾ OZ. CRANBERRY JUICE

BETTY'S COSMO

Add the vodka, cranberry juice cocktail, Cointreau, and Rose's lime juice to a cocktail shaker filled with ice. Shake vigorously, strain the resulting mixture into a cocktail glass, and top with the squeeze of fresh lime juice.

INGREDIENTS:

- 3 OZ. SKYY VODKA
- 3 OZ. CRANBERRY JUICE COCKTAIL
- 1 OZ. COINTREAU
- DASH OF ROSE'S LIME JUICE
- SQUEEZE OF FRESH LIME JUICE

CLASSIC COSMOPOLITAN

GARNISH: 1 LIME WHEEL

The stories behind classic cocktails are often lengthy meanderings through hearsay and hazy recollections, which is part of the reason why drinks attain the status of a classic—they can endure such vagaries. But the Cosmopolitan's origin story is fairly straightforward and only goes back to 1985. Cheryl Cook was tending bar at the Strand in Miami's South Beach when she came up with a Kamikaze made with Absolut Citron, triple sec, Rose's lime juice, and cranberry juice, which was added to make it look pretty. Variations on the drink made it to the northern climes of New York City, where celebs and trendsetters spread the word after hitting spots like the Odeon. Like its base spirit, the Cosmo can be done up any number of ways, so long as it looks, and tastes, good.

SEX AND THE CITY: THE COSMO BREAKS OUT

In July 1999, *The New York Times* ran the story, "For a Thirsty City, It's a Cocktail Summer," declaring: "New York has become a cocktail party of sexy, colorful fruit-filled drinks. Vacation-style drinks." *Sex and the City* was only into its second season, but Carrie Bradshaw and company had already glamorized the low-cal, colorful drinks, causing them to be ordered well beyond Lower Manhattan and Miami. It was a time where the cocktail renaissance was in its nascent stages, and exotic ingredients weren't quite the norm, though Carrie trying to order a Cosmo at a McDonald's drive-thru seemed just about perfect.

INGREDIENTS:

1 OZ. VODKA

¼ OZ. TRIPLE SEC

¼ OZ. LIME JUICE

DASH OF CRANBERRY JUICE

Combine all ingredients in a cocktail shaker filled with ice and shake vigorously. Strain into a cocktail glass and garnish with a lime wheel.

LIQUID APPLE PIE

GARNISH: 1 CINNAMON STICK

Add the vanilla vodka and brown sugar to your glass and stir them together. Pour the apple cider on top and finish with a dusting of cinnamon. Garnish with a cinnamon stick.

INGREDIENTS:

- 1 PART VANILLA VODKA
- DASH OF BROWN SUGAR
- 3 PARTS APPLE CIDER, WARMED
- DASH OF CINNAMON

PEACH TREE ICED TEA

Tear the mint leaves in half and place them at the bottom of a rocks glass. Add the peach schnapps and muddle. Add ice to the glass, and then pour in the vodka and iced tea. Stir until thoroughly mixed.

INGREDIENTS:

- 6 MINT LEAVES
- 1 PART PEACH SCHNAPPS
- 1 PART VODKA
- 2 PARTS ICED TEA

CHERRY LIME SPIKE

GARNISH: 1 LIME WHEEL

Pour the cherry vodka and lime juice into a highball glass and stir. Add ice, fill with the club soda, and top with a small dash of grenadine. Garnish with the lime wheel.

INGREDIENTS:

- 1 PART CHERRY VODKA
- 1 PART LIME JUICE
- 2 PARTS CLUB SODA
- DASH OF GRENADINE

THE ESSENTIAL BLOODY MARY

GARNISH: ANYTHING YOUR HEART DESIRES

Place the Worcestershire sauce and lemon juice in a glass and add ice. Pour in the vodka and tomato juice and stir until thoroughly mixed. Garnish with bacon, olives, lemon wedges, celery, pickles, or anything your heart desires.

INGREDIENTS:

- DASH OF WORCESTERSHIRE SAUCE
- DASH OF LEMON JUICE
- 1 PART VODKA
- 2 PARTS TOMATO JUICE

THE INCREDIBLE APICIUS BLOODY MARY

Place the cherry tomatoes in a cocktail shaker and crush them. Add the Tabasco Chipotle, balsamic reduction, cranberry juice, vodka, pepper, bitters, and celery salt. Shake vigorously for 20 seconds and double-strain into a chilled cocktail glass.

INGREDIENTS:

- 1 CUP CHERRY TOMATOES
- 4 DROPS OF TABASCO CHIPOTLE
- 2 DASHES OF WHITE BALSAMIC REDUCTION
- 1¾ OZ. CRANBERRY JUICE
- ¾ OZ. VODKA
- DASH OF BLACK PEPPER
- 3 DROPS OF THE BITTER END MEMPHIS BBQ BITTERS
- 3 PINCHES OF CELERY SALT

BEET BLOODY MARY

GARNISH: 1 DRIED APPLE RING

Chili-Infused Vodka: Combine 4 cups vodka, 3 sliced and seeded jalapeño peppers, and 5 seeded chipotle peppers in an airtight container, shake, and let sit for 2 to 3 days. Strain before using.

Place all of the ingredients in a cocktail shaker filled with ice and shake vigorously. Strain into a glass filled with ice and garnish with the dried apple ring.

INGREDIENTS:

- 2 OZ. CHILI-INFUSED VODKA
- 1½ OZ. BEET JUICE
- 1½ OZ. PRESSED APPLE JUICE
- ½ OZ. LEMON JUICE
- ½ OZ. FRESH PRESSED GINGER JUICE, WITH EQUAL PART SUGAR ADDED
- ¼ OZ. ORANGE JUICE
- PINCH OF SALT

THE ORIGINAL BLOODY MARY

Synonymous with hair-of-the-dog hangover cure, and ubiquitous as the beverage of choice for a brunch bender, the Bloody Mary is known by one and all, even those who don't like its tangy bite. Like with most classic cocktails, there is no certain origin story for the Bloody Mary, but Russians (and their vodka) fleeing the Revolution starting around 1920, and the growing popularity of American canned tomato juice, certainly serve as the seeds for the drink. In his autobiography, comedian George Jessel claims that in 1927 inspiration struck on one night in Palm Beach that lasted all morning. His far-fetched tale, involving having vodka on hand during Prohibition, and the presence of a woman named Mary who happened to be wearing a white dress and insisted she be called "Bloody Mary" after having the drink spill on her, is a great story that has never been corroborated. Ernest Hemingway also liked to tell of introducing the concoction in Hong Kong (dubious as that is, see below for Hemingway's opinionated take on the proper way to mix a Bloody Mary). We might never know exactly who came up with the drink, though most agree that famed bartender Ferdinand Petiot popularized early iterations of it, first at Harry's New York Bar in Paris, and then at the King Cole Bar at the St. Regis Hotel in Manhattan, where he served up something called the "Red Snapper," which included the spices and seasonings associated with the drink today.

PAPA'S PITCHER

"To make a pitcher of Blood Marys (any smaller amount is worthless) take a good sized pitcher and put in it as big a lump of ice as it will hold. (This to prevent too rapid melting and watering of our product.) Mix a pint of good Russian vodka and an equal amount of chilled tomato juice. Add a table spoon full of Worchester Sauce. Lea and Perrins is usual but can use A1 or any good beef-steak sauce. Stir. Then add a jigger of fresh squeezed lime juice. Stirr. Then add small amounts of celery salt, cayenne pepper, black pepper. Keep on stirring and taste to see how it is doing. If you get it too powerful weaken with more tomato juice. If it lacks authority add more vodka. Some people like more lime than others. For combating a really terrific hangover increase the amount of Worcester sauce—but don't lose the lovely color." *Letter from Ernest Hemingway to Bernard Peyton, April 5, 1947*

INGREDIENTS:

4 DASHES OF SALT
2 DASHES OF CAYENNE PEPPER
2 DASHES OF GROUND BLACK PEPPER
6 DASHES OF WORCESTERSHIRE SAUCE
JUICE OF ½ LEMON
2 OZ. VODKA
2 OZ. TOMATO JUICE

Place the salt, cayenne, and black pepper in a pint glass. Fill with ice and then add the Worcestershire, lemon, vodka, and tomato juice. Stir until combined. Be sure to use ground pepper instead of cracked pepper and do not add celery salt.

MASON JAR BLOODY MARY

GARNISH: 1 CELERY STALK, 3 OLIVES, OR COOKED BACON

Wet the rim of a mason jar with the lime wedge and then dip the glass into the Old Bay seasoning. Add ice, the vodka, olive brine, lime juice, and horseradish and then top with tomato juice, leaving enough space to stir. Stir until thoroughly combined. Add the Worcestershire sauce, hot sauce, pepper, and celery salt. Stir again until combined. Garnish with either a celery stalk, olives, or a rasher of bacon.

INGREDIENTS:

- JUICE OF 1 LIME WEDGE
- OLD BAY SEASONING, FOR THE RIM
- 2 OZ. VODKA
- ½ OZ. OLIVE BRINE
- 2 DASHES OF HORSERADISH
- TOMATO JUICE, TO TOP
- 3 DROPS OF WORCESTERSHIRE SAUCE
- 3 DASHES OF HOT SAUCE
- DASH OF BLACK PEPPER
- 2 DASHES OF CELERY SALT

PEAR PRESSURE

GARNISH: 1 THIN PEAR SLICE

Wet the rim of a rocks glass and dip it into the sugar. Place the liquid ingredients in a cocktail shaker filled with ice and shake vigorously. Strain the contents of the cocktail shaker into the glass and garnish with the pear slice.

INGREDIENTS:

- SUGAR, FOR THE RIM
- 1 PART VANILLA VODKA
- 1 PART PEAR JUICE
- SPLASH OF LIME JUICE

MOCHA MOCHA MOCHA

Place the vodka, liqueurs, and milk in a cocktail shaker filled with ice and shake vigorously. Strain the resulting mixture into a rocks glass filled with ice.

INGREDIENTS:

- 1 PART VODKA
- 1 PART CHOCOLATE LIQUEUR
- 1 PART COFFEE LIQUEUR
- 2 PARTS MILK

DRINK THE C

GARNISH: 1 MARASCHINO CHERRY

Place ice, the cherry vodka, and cola in a rocks glass and stir. Top with the splash of coconut rum and Cointreau and stir again. Garnish with the maraschino cherry.

INGREDIENTS:

- 1 PART CHERRY VODKA
- 2 PARTS COLA
- SPLASH OF COCONUT RUM
- SPLASH OF COINTREAU

GINGER BINGER

GARNISH: 1 LIME WHEEL & 1 SPRIG OF MINT (OPTIONAL)

Fill a highball glass with ice, and then add the vodka, triple sec, and grapefruit juice. Stir, top with ginger ale, and stir again. Garnish with the lime wheel and a sprig of mint, if desired.

INGREDIENTS:

- 1 PART VODKA
- SPLASH OF TRIPLE SEC
- 1 PART GRAPEFRUIT JUICE
- 2 PARTS GINGER ALE

LEMON DROP

GARNISH: 1 LEMON TWIST

Combine the vodka, triple sec, and lemon juice in a cocktail shaker filled with ice and shake vigorously. Wet the rim of a cocktail glass, and then dip it into the sugar. Strain the cocktail into the glass and garnish with the twist of lemon.

INGREDIENTS:

- 2 PARTS VODKA
- 1 PART TRIPLE SEC
- 1 PART LEMON JUICE
- SUGAR, FOR THE RIM

ROSE DE VARSOVIE

Place all of ingredients in a mixing glass filled with ice and stir for about 15 seconds. Strain into a chilled cocktail glass.

INGREDIENTS:

- 1¾ OZ. VODKA
- ½ OZ. PETER HEERING CHERRY LIQUEUR
- 4 DROPS OF COINTREAU
- 3–4 DROPS OF ANGOSTURA BITTERS

ROSE SALT DOG

Wet the rim of a highball glass and then dip it into the salt. Fill the glass with ice, add all of the ingredients, and stir until combined.

INGREDIENTS:

- HIMALAYAN PINK SEA SALT, FOR THE RIM
- 2 OZ. VODKA
- 2¼ OZ. FRESH GRAPEFRUIT JUICE
- ½ OZ. GIFFARD CRÈME DE PAMPLEMOUSSE ROSE
- 1 SPOONFUL OF LUXARDO

ALCHIMIA COCKTAIL

To make galangal syrup, add some slices of galangal to a basic simple syrup while it's boiling. Remove from heat and let stand for as long as possible. To make the infusion, place the fresh herbs, spices, and orange peel in boiling water and let it steep. The longer you steep it, the more fragrant the infusion; strain and let cool before using. Place all of the ingredients in a cocktail shaker filled with ice and shake vigorously. Strain into a cocktail glass.

INGREDIENTS:

- ½ OZ. GALANGAL SYRUP
- 1¼ OZ. INFUSION OF LEMON BALM, VERBENA, CINNAMON, AND ORANGE PEEL
- 1¾ OZ. RUSSIAN STANDARD PLATINUM VODKA
- ½ OZ. CRÈME DE CASSIS (PREFERABLY MICKAEL ANTOLIN BRAND)
- ¾ OZ. FRESH LEMON JUICE

100% WINTER VITAMIN

Place all of the ingredients in a cocktail shaker filled with ice and shake vigorously. Strain into a small carafe or bowl.

INGREDIENTS:

- 1¾ OZ. VODKA
- 2 TEASPOONS CYNAR
- 2 TEASPOONS APEROL
- 2 TEASPOONS HONEY
- 2 TEASPOONS LIME
- 2 SPOONFULS OF APRICOT/ YUZU JAM
- 1¾ OZ. FRESH CARROT-APPLE JUICE
- 2 DASHES OF CELERY BITTERS

BISOUS DU SOLEIL

GARNISH: 1 ORANGE TWIST

Combine the vodka, Cointreau, and the juices in a cocktail shaker filled with ice. Shake vigorously and strain into a champagne flute. Top with Champagne and garnish with the twist of orange.

INGREDIENTS:

- 1 OZ. VODKA
- DASH OF COINTREAU
- 1½ OZ. CRANBERRY JUICE
- JUICE OF ½ LIME
- JUICE OF 1 ORANGE WEDGE
- CHAMPAGNE, TO TOP

MISTINGUETTE

GARNISH: 1 GRAPEFRUIT TWIST

To make the honey syrup infused with horseradish, place 1 part water and 1 part honey in a saucepan, bring to a boil, and add some grated horseradish. Remove from heat, let cool, and strain. Place all of the cocktail ingredients in a cocktail shaker filled with ice and shake vigorously. Strain into a cocktail glass and garnish with the grapefruit twist.

INGREDIENTS:

- ½ OZ. HONEY SYRUP INFUSED WITH HORSERADISH
- ½ OZ. PINK GRAPEFRUIT JUICE
- 2 TEASPOONS FRESH LEMON JUICE
- 1 OZ. LILLET BLANC
- 1 OZ. VODKA
- DASH OF JAMAICAN JERK BITTERS

EQUISSE NO. 1

Place all of the ingredients in a cocktail shaker filled with ice and shake vigorously. Strain into a coupe.

INGREDIENTS:

- 1¾ OZ. GREY GOOSE PEAR
- 1½ OZ. WHITE CHARDONNAY GRAPE JUICE
- 4 TEASPOONS FRESH GRAPEFRUIT
- 4 TEASPOONS FRESH LIME
- 1½ TABLESPOONS VANILLA SYRUP (PREFERABLY HOMEMADE)

PINK PANTHER

Place all of the ingredients, except for the lemonade, in a cocktail shaker filled with ice and shake vigorously. Strain into a highball glass filled with ice and top with the lemonade.

INGREDIENTS:

- 2 OZ. GREY GOOSE VODKA
- 1 OZ. ST-GERMAIN
- JUICE FROM ½ GRAPEFRUIT
- JUICE FROM ½ LIME
- JUICE FROM ½ LEMON
- GRIOTTISSIMO CHERRY
- LORINA SPARKLING FRENCH BERRY LEMONADE, TO TOP

CHOCO PEAT

Place all of the ingredients in a mixing glass filled with ice, stir, and strain into a cocktail glass.

INGREDIENTS:

- ½ OZ. DARK CHOCOLATE LIQUEUR
- ¾ OZ. KAHLUA
- 1¼ OZ. STOLICHNAYA HOT VODKA (OR OTHER SPICY VODKA)
- ¾ OZ. THE PEAT MONSTER WHISKY

MR. FUNK

GARNISH: 1 LEMON TWIST

Place the vodka and cranberry juice in a rocks glass filled with ice and stir. Top with sparkling wine and garnish with a lemon twist.

INGREDIENTS:

- 1 OZ. PEACH VODKA
- 1 OZ. CRANBERRY JUICE
- SPARKLING WINE, TO TOP

LONG ISLAND EXPRESS

GARNISH: 1 LEMON SLICE

Add the ingredients to a highball glass filled with ice in the order they are listed, stir until combined, and garnish with the slice of lemon.

Variation: The Long Island Iced Tea traditionally contains vodka, rum, tequila, and gin. If you think it sounds better to make the Long Island Express with any of these instead of vodka, do not hesitate to make the substitution.

INGREDIENTS:

- JUICE OF ½ LEMON
- 1 PART VODKA
- SPLASH OF TRIPLE SEC
- 2 PARTS COLA

ZEITOUNI

Place the basil leaves and simple syrup in a cocktail shaker and muddle. Add the pineapple and apple and muddle until they release their juices. Pour the vodka and the olive oil into the shaker, and then add the pepper and salt. Add ice and shake vigorously. Strain and serve in a chilled coupe.

INGREDIENTS:

- 4 BASIL LEAVES
- 2 TEASPOONS SIMPLE SYRUP
- 1 ROUND OF FRESH PINEAPPLE
- 3 SLICES OF GRANNY SMITH APPLE
- 2 OZ. KETEL ONE CITROEN
- 1 TEASPOON OLIVE OIL
- PINCH OF BLACK PEPPER
- PINCH OF SALT

AMELIA

GARNISH: 1 CROWN OF MINT

Pour the vodka, puree, St-Germain, and juice into a cocktail shaker. Add large ice cubes, shake vigorously, and strain into a chilled cocktail glass. Place the crown of mint into your palm and smack it with your other hand to release the aroma. Gently place the mint on the surface of the cocktail.

BLACKBERRY PUREE

Place all of the ingredients in a blender and puree until smooth. Strain and store in the refrigerator for up to 4 days. Makes about 1 cup.

INGREDIENTS:

- 1½ OZ. VODKA
- 1 OZ. BLACKBERRY PUREE (SEE RECIPE BELOW)
- ¾ OZ. ST-GERMAIN
- ½ OZ. FRESH LEMON JUICE

BLACKBERRY PUREE:

- 1 CUP BLACKBERRIES, FRESH OR THAWED
- 2 TABLESPOONS CASTER SUGAR
- 2 TABLESPOONS WATER
- 2 TABLESPOONS FRESH LEMON JUICE

GREAT IDEA

GARNISH: 1 LEMON WEDGE

Place all of the ingredients in a highball glass and gently stir. Fill the glass with ice and garnish with the lemon wedge.

INGREDIENTS:

- 1 OZ. VODKA
- 1 OZ. JÄGERMEISTER
- ½ OZ. LEMON JUICE

CHILTON

GARNISH: 1 LEMON WHEEL

Wet the rim of a highball glass and then dip it into the salt. Fill the glass with ice, add the vodka and lemon juice, and top with Topo Chico. Stir and garnish with the lemon wheel.

INGREDIENTS:

- SALT, FOR THE RIM
- 1½ OZ. VODKA
- JUICE OF 2 LEMONS
- TOPO CHICO, TO TOP

BERRIES FROM THE WEST

GARNISH: 1 LEMON WHEEL & BLUEBERRIES

Combine all of the ingredients in a cocktail shaker filled with ice and shake vigorously. Strain into a rocks glass and garnish with the lemon wheel and blueberries.

INGREDIENTS:

- 2 OZ. WESTERN SON BLUEBERRY VODKA
- 1 OZ. SIMPLE SYRUP
- 1 OZ. FRESH LEMON JUICE

RUBY TWILITE

GARNISH: 1 CITRUS WEDGE

Keeping the look of a Texas sunset in mind, layer the vodka, lemonade, and beer in a pint glass and garnish with the wedge of citrus.

INGREDIENTS:

- 1 OZ. DEEP EDDY RUBY RED GRAPEFRUIT VODKA
- 4 OZ. LEMONADE
- SHINER RUBY REDBIRD BEER, TO FLOAT

WESTERN
SON
10X DISTILLED
PINEY WOODS
BLUEBERRY
FLAVORED VODKA
PILOT POINT, TEXAS

GIN

Gin, while similar in appearance to vodka, is definitely its own beast. The two spirits are paired together in the eternal fight over which makes for the better Martini, but gin deserves an entry in this book, if only for the Gin & Tonic. That drink is one of the greatest hot weather cocktails of all time in my not-so-humble opinion. Think about it: When it's hot, is there a quicker, more refreshing cocktail you can make?

The weird thing is that it wasn't more common among my family when I was a kid. I spent many a summer visiting family in Trinidad and Gin & Tonics were not "the drink," even though it was hot as hell. There was gin around (Gordon's, as I recall), but shandies and beer were more much common.

The reason I find this lack of gin weird is that Trinidad was a British colony, so you would think Gin & Tonics would be a thing. But rum drinks and the aforementioned shandies were the cocktails of choice with my aunts, uncles, and cousins during my visits.

Unlike vodka, gin is not meant to "go gentle into that good night," to cite Dylan Thomas. If gin is in your cocktail, you'll know it. In that way, it's vodka's polar opposite. It's not necessarily a difficult ingredient to work with (honestly, I think whisk(e)y is harder); it just doesn't disappear the way that vodka can. Just as vodka has a long lineup of cocktails, gin is no slouch. Gin has Martinis, the Negroni (the bartender's best friend), the Aviation, the Corpse Reviver No. 2, and the Bee's Knees, to name only a scant few.

Also, gin has probably benefitted the most from the local distilling boom. These days, most folks don't have to try too hard to find a great local source of gin that tastes better than the big-name options. It's certainly an excellent way to make homemade versions of classic gin cocktails stand out and support local distillers at the same time.

Favorite cocktail: For me it's a toss-up between the Corpse Reviver No. 2 and the Bee's Knees, and the Bee's Knees generally comes out on top because I don't always have absinthe in the house to make the Corpse Reviver. Let's face it—sometimes simplicity wins the day.

A BRIEF HISTORY OF GIN

The history of gin is nearly as muddled as that of a poorly made Martini. Although popular culture credits Franciscus Sylvius, a physician from the Netherlands, with creating the beverage in the 1600s, gin (or its clear precursor) has been recorded as far back as the 1200s.

First mentioned in an early encyclopedia known as the *Der Naturen Bloeme*, genever was the predecessor to what we today know as gin. Still popular in certain parts of the world (including the Netherlands), genever is a juniper-flavored beverage that shares many elements with its better-known contemporary. Genever was the drink of choice in the Dutch military in the late 1500s, and some believe that the term "Dutch courage" refers to the beverage being used to embolden soldiers before battle.

Gin began its rise to prominence in the 17th century as the Dutch became increasingly powerful on the world stage. William of Orange is credited with popularizing the drink in Great Britain, as Dutch gin was imported in much greater quantities during his occupation of England. Not surprisingly, the expansion of gin into new markets, and its steadily increasing popularity, led to new innovations in the distillation process, and gin began to slowly evolve into the form we recognize today.

The process of making gin is variable, depending on the type of still being used. Both

genever and early gins were made using copper pot stills, in which a grain mash was distilled and redistilled with flavoring botanicals. Due in large part to the inefficiency of these early pot stills, genever and early iterations of gin were generally low in alcohol content.

The introduction of column stills in the early 1800s made the production of gin more efficient and potent. Essentially a series of small pot stills, column stills allow for continuous distillation—eliminating the need for "batches" of gin—while distilling a higher concentration of consumable alcohol. This allowed for the production of stronger gin in greater quantities than had been previously possible.

As different types of both pot and column stills have been developed, methods for infusing the flavor of these botanicals have varied—though the stills themselves remain copper in all but the rarest cases. Distillers may prefer to use different stills depending on their preferred flavoring methods. Hendrick's, for instance, uses both the "Carter-Head" still—known for its long neck and vapor-driven infusion method—and the "Bennett" still—a small pot still that is rarely seen today but is famous for imparting robust flavors.

Today, many gins start with a neutral (flavorless) alcohol and add botanicals afterward, rather than the grain mash method used during gin's early days. Other gin producers elect to infuse their gin with essential oils, a method that allows for more affordable production, but is generally viewed as being less refined. Although the primary flavoring agent in gin will always be juniper, different gin makers have chosen to emphasize flavors that range from floral to herbal, offering drinkers a range of styles and flavor options—a variability that is reflected in the wide range of gins available today.

As is typical of many alcoholic beverages, gin consumption grew as regulations governing the production of alcohol were eased. Because gin could be produced with lower-quality barley than what is necessary to produce beer, it quickly gained popularity as an affordable alternative to other types of alcohol. This rapid rise in popularity, which occurred during the first half of the 18th century, would eventually become known as the "Gin Craze," and the glut of cheap gin available meant that it was accessible to even the poorest members of society. This accessibility led to a stigmatization of gin that has, in some form, lasted to this day, with phrases like "gin mill" and "gin joint" retaining negative connotations.

The centuries since the Gin Craze have been quieter, but the gin market has evolved considerably. At different times, changing regulations have led to the popularization of sweeter gins, dryer gins, more herbal gins, and other slight variations on the juniper theme. Many of these styles survive today, such as "London Dry" gin. This, the most popular style of gin, lacks the sweetness of other offerings and is usually high in alcohol content. London Dry gin is also known for the inclusion of citrus peel among its botanicals, an element often detectable in its aroma.

Today, you can walk into any liquor store in America and find an entire wall dedicated to gin. It's a testament not just to its staying power, but also to its tremendous flavor, which provides the foundation for classic and popular cocktails such as the Martini, the Negroni, and the Gin & Tonic.

THE ELDER FASHION

GARNISH: 1 GRAPEFRUIT TWIST

Place the cocktail ingredients in a mixing glass filled with ice and stir. Strain over ice into a rocks glass and garnish with the grapefruit twist.

INGREDIENTS:

- 2 OZ. PLYMOUTH GIN
- ½ OZ. ST-GERMAIN
- DASH OF ORANGE BITTERS

AVIATION

GARNISH: 1 CHERRY

Place the cocktail ingredients in a cocktail shaker filled with ice and shake until chilled. Strain into a chilled cocktail glass and garnish with the cherry.

INGREDIENTS:

- 2 OZ. GIN
- ½ OZ. LUXARDO
- ¼ OZ. FRESH LEMON JUICE

BLOOD ORANGE COCKTAIL

Place all of the ingredients in a cocktail shaker filled with ice, shake vigorously, and strain into a chilled cocktail glass.

INGREDIENTS:

- 1½ OZ. GIN
- ⅓ OZ. AMARO
- 1 OZ. FRESH BLOOD ORANGE JUICE

DIXIE COCKTAIL

Place all of the ingredients in a cocktail shaker filled with ice, shake vigorously, and strain into a chilled cocktail glass.

INGREDIENTS:

- 1 OZ. GIN
- 1 OZ. FRESH ORANGE JUICE
- 1 TABLESPOON SAMBUCA
- ½ OZ. DRY VERMOUTH

WATERMELON STAND

Place the watermelon and gin in a cocktail shaker and muddle. Add the remaining ingredients and shake until combined. Strain over crushed ice into a highball glass.

INGREDIENTS:

- 4 WATERMELON CHUNKS
- 1½ OZ. GIN
- ¾ OZ. LEMON JUICE
- ½ OZ. SIMPLE SYRUP
- ½ OZ. APEROL

GIN SOUR

GARNISH: 1 LEMON SLICE

Place all of the cocktail ingredients in a cocktail shaker filled with ice and shake vigorously. Strain into a sour glass and garnish with the slice of lemon.

INGREDIENTS:

- 2 OZ. GIN
- 1 OZ. FRESH LEMON JUICE
- 1 TEASPOON POWDERED SUGAR

GIN GIMLET

GARNISH: 1 LIME WEDGE

Place the cocktail ingredients in a mixing glass filled with ice and stir. Strain into a cocktail glass and garnish with the lime wedge.

INGREDIENTS:

- 1½ OZ. GIN
- ½ OZ. FRESH LIME JUICE

GREEN DRAGON

Place all of the ingredients in a cocktail shaker filled with ice, shake vigorously, and strain into a chilled cocktail glass.

INGREDIENTS:

- 1½ OZ. GIN
- ½ OZ. CARAWAY LIQUEUR
- ½ OZ. GREEN CRÈME DE MENTHE
- 1 OZ. LEMON JUICE
- 4 DASHES OF ORANGE BITTERS

QUICK COLLINS

GARNISH: 1 MARASCHINO CHERRY & 1 LEMON SLICE

Place the gin in a chilled highball glass and top with the Tom Collins mix. Garnish with the cherry and lemon slice.

INGREDIENTS:

- 1 OZ. GIN
- TOM COLLINS MIX

WHITE LADY

Place all of the ingredients in a cocktail shaker filled with ice, shake vigorously, and strain into a chilled cocktail glass.

INGREDIENTS:

- 2 OZ. GIN
- 1 OZ. COINTREAU
- ½ OZ. FRESH LEMON JUICE
- DASH OF EGG WHITE

PINK GIN

GARNISH: 1 STRIP OF LEMON ZEST

Place the gin and bitters in a rocks glass filled with ice and stir until chilled. Express the oils from the lemon peel over the cocktail and then garnish with the strip of lemon zest.

INGREDIENTS:

- 1½ OZ. GIN
- 2–3 DASHES OF ANGOSTURA BITTERS
- 1 LEMON PEEL

SILVER BULLET

Place all of the ingredients in a cocktail shaker filled with ice, shake vigorously, and strain into a chilled cocktail glass.

INGREDIENTS:

- 1 OZ. GIN
- 1 OZ. KÜMMEL
- 1 TABLESPOON FRESH LEMON JUICE

MAIDEN'S PRAYER

Combine the ingredients in a cocktail shaker filled with ice, shake vigorously for 15 to 20 seconds, and strain into shot glasses.

INGREDIENTS:

- 1 PART GIN
- 1 PART LILLET BLANC
- 1 PART APPLE JUICE WITH NO SUGAR ADDED

TOM COLLINS

GARNISH: 1 ORANGE SLICE & 1 MARASCHINO CHERRY

Place the gin, sugar, and juices in a cocktail shaker filled with ice and shake vigorously. Strain into a highball glass or mason jar, top with soda water, and stir until thoroughly combined. Garnish with the orange slice and the maraschino cherry.

INGREDIENTS:

- 2 PARTS GIN
- 1 TEASPOON SUGAR
- 1 PART LEMON JUICE
- 1 PART LIME JUICE
- 4 PARTS SODA WATER

MASON JAR GREYHOUND

GARNISH: 1 SPRIG OF ROSEMARY & 1 GRAPEFRUIT TWIST

Fill a mason jar with ice and add the gin. Top with grapefruit juice, stir, and garnish with the sprig of rosemary and the grapefruit twist.

INGREDIENTS:

- 1 PART GIN
- 2 PARTS GRAPEFRUIT JUICE

MASON JAR GIN FIZZ

GARNISH: 1 LEMON SLICE

Fill a cocktail shaker with ice, add the gin, lemon juice, and powdered sugar and shake vigorously. Strain the cocktail into a mason jar filled with ice, fill with the club soda, and top with the dash of grenadine. Garnish with the slice of lemon.

INGREDIENTS:

- 1½ OZ. GIN
- 1 OZ. LEMON JUICE
- 1 TEASPOON POWDERED SUGAR
- 4 OZ. CLUB SODA
- DASH OF GRENADINE

THE RAMBLE

Place the gin and lemon juice in a cocktail shaker with no ice, shake until combined, and strain over ice in a rocks glass. Muddle the raspberries and simple syrup and pour the mixture over the top of the drink.

INGREDIENTS:

- 2 OZ. PLYMOUTH GIN
- 1 OZ. LEMON JUICE
- 4–5 RASPBERRIES
- ¾ OZ. SIMPLE SYRUP

BRIGHT RUBY

GARNISH: 1 ORANGE SLICE

Fill a cocktail shaker with ice, add the gin, orange liqueur, and grapefruit juice, and shake vigorously. Strain the cocktail into a mason jar filled with ice, top with club soda, and add the dash of grenadine. Stir until combined and garnish with the orange slice.

INGREDIENTS:

- 1 PART GIN
- DASH OF ORANGE LIQUEUR
- 2 PARTS GRAPEFRUIT JUICE
- 2 PARTS CLUB SODA
- DASH OF GRENADINE

MASON JAR GIN & TONIC

GARNISH: 1 LIME WEDGE & 1 SPRIG OF ROSEMARY

Place the gin and rosemary leaves in a cocktail shaker filled with ice, shake vigorously, and strain into a mason jar filled with ice. Add the tonic water and garnish with the sprig of rosemary and the lime wedge.

INGREDIENTS:

- 2 OZ. GIN
- HANDFUL OF ROSEMARY LEAVES
- 4 OZ. TONIC WATER

SOUTH SIDE

GARNISH: 1 LEMON SLICE & 1 SPRIG OF MINT

Place the gin, limoncello, sugar, lemon juice, and mint leaves in a cocktail shaker filled with ice, shake vigorously, and strain into a mason jar filled with ice. Garnish with the slice of lemon and sprig of mint.

INGREDIENTS:

- 2 OZ. GIN
- DASH OF LIMONCELLO
- 2 TEASPOONS SUGAR
- JUICE OF 1 LEMON
- 4 MINT LEAVES

STRAWBERRY-BASIL LEMONADE

GARNISH: 1 STRAWBERRY

Place the strawberry slices and basil in a mason jar, muddle, and then add ice. Add the gin, vodka, and lemonade and stir until combined. Top with the club soda and garnish with the strawberry.

INGREDIENTS:

- 1 STRAWBERRY, SLICED
- 2 BASIL LEAVES
- 2 OZ. GIN
- DASH OF STRAWBERRY VODKA
- 3 OZ. LEMONADE
- SPLASH OF CLUB SODA

BLACKBERRY PUNCH-OUT

GARNISH: 1 BLACKBERRY

Place the 6 blackberries, mint, and simple syrup at the bottom of a cocktail shaker and muddle. Add ice, gin, lemonade, and grenadine, shake vigorously, and strain into a mason jar filled with ice. Garnish with the blackberry.

INGREDIENTS:

- 6 BLACKBERRIES
- 4 MINT LEAVES
- DASH OF SIMPLE SYRUP
- 2 OZ. GIN
- 3 OZ. LEMONADE
- DASH OF GRENADINE

CLASSIC GIN & TONIC

GARNISH: 1 LIME WEDGE

Fill a glass with ice, and then add the gin and tonic water. Stir until thoroughly mixed, top with the splash of lime juice, and garnish with the lime wedge.

INGREDIENTS:

- 1 PART TANQUERAY GIN
- 1 PART TONIC WATER
- SPLASH OF LIME JUICE

PERFECT GIN & TONIC

GARNISH: 1 LIME WHEEL

Place a lime wheel and the lime juice in glass, muddle, and add ice. Add the gin, top with tonic water, stir until thoroughly mixed, and garnish with another lime wheel.

INGREDIENTS:

- 1 LIME WHEEL
- SPLASH OF LIME JUICE
- 1 PART BOMBAY SAPPHIRE GIN
- 1 PART TONIC WATER

THE CHAMBER G&T

Fill a chilled mason jar or highball glass with ice cubes. Pour the gin and tonic water into the glass, express the lemon zest over the cocktail, and then drop the zest into the drink.

INGREDIENTS:

- 1½ OZ. CITADELLE GIN
- 4½ OZ. FEVER TREE TONIC WATER
- 1 STRIP OF LEMON ZEST

BUDGET GIN & TONIC

GARNISH: 1 LIME WEDGE

Fill a glass with ice and add the gin and tonic water. Stir until thoroughly mixed, top with the splash of lime juice, and garnish with the lime wedge.

INGREDIENTS:

- 1 PART SEAGRAM'S GIN
- 1 PART TONIC WATER
- SPLASH OF LIME JUICE

1505 G&T

Fill a tumbler about ¼ of the way with gin, and then add ice. Add the lime juice, top with tonic water, and stir until thoroughly mixed.

INGREDIENTS:

- 2 PARTS TANQUERAY GIN
- 1 PART FRESH LIME JUICE
- 4 PARTS TONIC WATER

PEACH GIN TEA

GARNISH: 2 TO 3 PEACH WEDGES

Place the iced tea, gin, peach puree, and sugar in a cocktail shaker filled with ice and shake until combined. Strain into a mason jar filled with ice and garnish with the peach wedges.

INGREDIENTS:

- 4 OZ. ICED TEA
- 2 OZ. GIN
- 2 OZ. PEACH PUREE
- 1 TEASPOON SUGAR

STRAWBERRY GIN MOJITO

GARNISH: 1 SPRIG OF MINT

Place the strawberries in a mason jar, muddle, and fill the glass with ice. Place the gin, simple syrup, and lime juice in a cocktail shaker filled with ice and shake vigorously. Strain into the mason jar and stir until thoroughly combined. Top with club soda, stir, and garnish with the sprig of mint.

INGREDIENTS:

- 2 STRAWBERRIES, HULLED AND SLICED
- 2 OZ. GIN
- ½ OZ. SIMPLE SYRUP
- JUICE OF ½ LIME
- 1 OZ. CLUB SODA

NOT-QUITE COLLINS

GARNISH: 1 ORANGE SLICE & 1 MARASCHINO CHERRY

Place the gin, sugar, and lemon juice in a cocktail shaker filled with ice and shake until thoroughly combined. Strain into a highball glass, top with club soda, and garnish with the orange slice and maraschino cherry.

INGREDIENTS:

- 1 PART GIN
- 1 TEASPOON SUGAR
- SPLASH OF LEMON JUICE
- 2 PARTS CLUB SODA

FRENCH NEGRONI

GARNISH: 1 ORANGE WHEEL

Add the cocktail ingredients to a rocks glass in the order they are listed. Fill the glass with ice and garnish with the orange wheel.

INGREDIENTS:

- 1½ OZ. GIN
- 1 OZ. SUZE
- 1 OZ. SWEET VERMOUTH

TEXAS NEGRONI

Place a large ice cube in a rocks glass, place the gin, Amaro, and vermouth in the glass, and stir to combine. Rub the rim of the glass with the grapefruit peel, discard, and float the additional gin on top.

INGREDIENTS:

- 2 OZ. REVOLUTION AUSTIN RESERVE GIN, PLUS MORE TO FLOAT
- 1 OZ. REVOLUTION AMICO AMARO
- 1 OZ. NOILLY PRAT ROUGE VERMOUTH
- 1 STRIP OF GRAPEFRUIT PEEL

BITTER NEGRONI

GARNISH: 1 ORANGE TWIST

Place the cocktail ingredients in a mixing glass filled with ice and stir until thoroughly combined. Strain over ice into a rocks glass and garnish with the orange slice.

INGREDIENTS:

- 1 PART GIN
- 1 PART CAMPARI
- 1 PART SWEET VERMOUTH
- DASH OF BITTERS

NEGRONI

GARNISH: 1 ORANGE TWIST

Don't let the ruby candy-like color of this Italian apertivo fool you; there is nothing sweet about this drink. Its bitter bite is intended to stir your appetite before a meal, and bitterness seems to be at the heart of a dispute over the origins of this drink. One claim has it that the drink is named for Count Camillo Negroni, who in 1919 requested that a bartender in Florence, Italy, fix him a more potent version of his favorite cocktail, an Americano. The bartender replaced soda water with gin, and lemon garnish with orange, and soon enough the count's new favorite became everyone's new favorite. In fact, so goes this version of the story, the cocktail's popularity resulted in the Negroni family starting an eponymous distillery in Treviso so they could produce a bottled version of their namesake beverage. But, according to Difford's Guide, one Colonel Hector Andres Negroni, responding to a book about the drink in an angry Amazon review, insists that there is no evidence of a Camillo Negroni in his family genealogy, and furthermore it was General Pascal Oliver Comte de Negroni, a Frenchman, who invented the drink, during the Franco-Prussian War, in 1870. Best not to take sides in this fight. Rather, enjoy a Negroni and remember what Kingsley Amis had to say on the matter: "This is a really fine invention. It has the power, rare with drinks and indeed with anything else, of cheering you up."

NEGRONI WEEK

With notable advocates like Kingsley Amis and Orson Welles, who also happened to be legendary drinkers, the Negroni's status as a classic has been secure for some time. But in 2013 *Imbibe* magazine and Campari teamed up for Negroni Week, using the cocktail as a vehicle for a full-blown international marketing campaign. But even cynics have to admit that this charitable event is a good thing: between 2013 and 2018 Negroni Week has grown to include 10,000 venues worldwide and raised $2 million.

INGREDIENTS:

1 OZ. CAMPARI

1 OZ. SWEET VERMOUTH

1 OZ. GIN

Place the cocktail ingredients in a rocks glass filled with ice, stir until combined, and garnish with a twist of orange.

SALTY MUTT

GARNISH: 1 GRAPEFRUIT WEDGE

INGREDIENTS:

- SALT, FOR THE RIM
- 1 PART GIN
- 1 PART GRAPEFRUIT JUICE
- 1 PART CRANBERRY JUICE

Wet the rim of a rocks glass and dip it into the salt. Place the gin, grapefruit juice, and cranberry juice in a cocktail shaker filled with ice and shake vigorously. Strain into the rocks glass and garnish with the grapefruit wedge.

SINGAPORE EXPRESS

GARNISH: 1 MARASCHINO CHERRY & 1 ORANGE SLICE

INGREDIENTS:

- 2 PARTS GIN
- 1 PART CHERRY LIQUEUR
- 1 PART TRIPLE SEC
- 3 PARTS PINEAPPLE JUICE

Place the gin, liqueur, triple sec, and pineapple juice in a cocktail shaker filled with ice and shake vigorously. Strain into a Hurricane glass filled with ice and garnish with the maraschino cherry and the slice of orange.

HINT OF MINT

GARNISH: 4 LEMON WHEELS

INGREDIENTS:

- 20 MINT LEAVES
- 1 PART GINGER ALE
- 2 PARTS LEMONADE
- 1 PART GIN

Tear the mint leaves in half and place them at the bottom of a pitcher. Add ice, the ginger ale, lemonade, and gin and stir until combined. Divide between four glasses and garnish each with a lemon wheel.

GIN ROSE

GARNISH: 1 MARASCHINO CHERRY

INGREDIENTS:

- 1 PART GIN
- 1 PART TRIPLE SEC
- 2 PARTS CLUB SODA
- SPLASH OF GRENADINE

Pour the gin and triple sec into a rocks glass filled with ice, fill with club soda, and stir until thoroughly combined. Top with the splash of grenadine and garnish with the maraschino cherry.

Nº TEN
FRESH CITRUS AND BOTANICALS
ROSE'S
GRENADINE
SYRUP
Rose's products are used around the world to add a special flavor to food and drink.
12 FL OZ (355 mL)

GIN AND JUICE

GARNISH: 1 LIME WHEEL & 1 MARASCHINO CHERRY

Place the gin, cranberry juice, triple sec, and lime juice in a cocktail shaker filled with ice and shake vigorously. Strain over ice into a rocks glass and garnish with the lime wheel and maraschino cherry.

INGREDIENTS:

- 1 PART GIN
- 1 PART CRANBERRY JUICE
- SPLASH OF TRIPLE SEC
- JUICE OF ½ LIME

CHERRY GIN SOUR

GARNISH: 1 MARASCHINO CHERRY & 1 ORANGE SLICE

Place the gin, cherry liqueur, lemon juice, and simple syrup in a cocktail shaker filled with ice and shake vigorously. Strain into a rocks glass filled with ice and garnish with the maraschino cherry and the orange slice.

INGREDIENTS:

- 1 PART GIN
- 1 PART CHERRY LIQUEUR
- 1 PART LEMON JUICE
- SPLASH OF SIMPLE SYRUP

CLASSIC GIMLET

GARNISH: 1 LIME WHEEL

Place the gin and lime juice in a cocktail shaker filled with ice and shake until thoroughly combined. Strain into a cocktail glass and garnish with the lime wheel.

INGREDIENTS:

- 4 OZ. TANQUERAY GIN
- JUICE OF ½ LIME

TWISTED GIMLET

GARNISH: 1 LIME WHEEL

Place the cocktail ingredients in a mixing glass filled with ice and stir until thoroughly mixed. Strain into a cocktail glass and garnish with the lime wheel.

INGREDIENTS:

- 2 PARTS GIN
- 1 PART TRIPLE SEC
- 1 PART LIME JUICE
- 2 DROPS OF ORANGE BITTERS

GIN WATERFALL

GARNISH: 20 LEMON WHEELS

Place all of the liquid ingredients in a large punch bowl and stir until thoroughly mixed. Add the lemon wheels, and then ladle the punch into highball glasses filled with ice.

INGREDIENTS:

- 1 PART GIN
- 1 PART CHAMPAGNE
- 2 PARTS SPRITE
- JUICE OF 5 LEMONS

GIN POM POM

GARNISH: 1 LIME WHEEL & POMEGRANATE SEEDS

Tear the mint leaves in half and place them in a cocktail shaker filled with ice. Add the gin, pomegranate juice, and lime juice and shake vigorously. Strain into a rocks glass filled with ice and garnish with the lime wheel and pomegranate seeds.

INGREDIENTS:

- 6 MINT LEAVES
- 1 PART GIN
- 1 PART POMEGRANATE JUICE
- JUICE OF 1 LIME WEDGE

FRENCH 75

GARNISH: 1 LEMON TWIST & 1 CHERRY

Place the sugar cube in a champagne flute and squeeze in the lemon juice. Pour in the gin, top with Champagne, and garnish with the lemon twist. Skewer the cherry with a toothpick and place it over the top of the champagne flute.

INGREDIENTS:

- 1 SUGAR CUBE
- JUICE OF 1 LEMON WEDGE
- 1 PART GIN
- 2 PARTS CHAMPAGNE

BLUEBERRY SPARKLER

GARNISH: 1 LEMON WHEEL & BLUEBERRIES

Blueberry Simple Syrup: Add ½ cup of blueberries to a basic simple syrup while it's boiling. Cook until the berries release their juices, remove from heat, and strain before using.

Place the gin, blueberry simple syrup, and lemon juice in a cocktail shaker filled with ice and shake vigorously. Strain into a rocks glass filled with ice, top with club soda, and garnish with a lemon wheel and blueberries.

INGREDIENTS:

- 1 OZ. BLUEBERRY SIMPLE SYRUP
- 2 OZ. GIN
- JUICE OF ½ LEMON
- 1 OZ. CLUB SODA

HISTORY OF THE MARTINI

"The proper union of gin and vermouth is a great and sudden glory; it is one of the happiest marriages on earth, and one of the shortest lived."—Bernard DeVoto, American historian

Cocktails are not complicated. Literally anyone can create one—and spirit-slinging establishments of all kinds festoon their menus with them on a daily basis. Walk into just about any bar or restaurant and you'll find a bevy of specialty cocktails, often named for local celebrities or peppered with puns. Some are good. Others are bad. But few have staying power. They are disposable recipes, designed to be purchased, enjoyed, and summarily forgotten.

What, then, makes a cocktail stand out? What elevates it to honored status? And what allows it to stand the test of time?

Enter the Martini.

H. L. Mencken once called the Martini "the only American invention as perfect as the sonnet." High praise from a man legendary for his lyrical prose, and a sentiment that echoes over a hundred years of acclaim heaped upon the revered cocktail.

The origin of the Martini is difficult to pin down. The name "Martini" is believed to derive from a brand of Italian vermouth named after its founder, Alessandro Martini. Some theories speculate that the cocktail was created by a bartender in Martinez, California, while others hypothesize that it simply adopted the name after becoming well known there. One popular theory even states that the drink originated when a miner during the California Gold Rush requested that the bartender create a brand-new cocktail to celebrate his striking it rich. Whether any version is true is up for debate, but the "Martinez Cocktail" does have several elements in common with the Martini, and has been documented as far back as 1887—one year before Harry Johnson's *New and Improved Bartender's Manual* first published the Martini name.

In truth, the true origin of the Martini is lost to history, and connoisseurs of the cocktail are each likely to have a favorite pet theory. Perhaps you're among those who believe that the Martini was first created in New York's Knickerbocker Hotel. Or perhaps you prefer the British theory that the drink was named for the Martini & Henry rifle, the strength of the cocktail mimicking the gun's infamous kick. Countless cities, hotels, publications, and individuals have clamored to take credit for the original Martini cocktail, and each theory has its own merits.

Whatever its origins, the Martini became wildly popular in the 1920s, and during that time it settled into a more consistent and recognizable form: gin and vermouth, in a ratio nearing 2:1 or 3:1. The drink was known for being served at the aforementioned Knickerbocker Hotel, a favorite haunt of industrialists like John D. Rockefeller, and as Rockefeller and other public figures made their love of the cocktail known, it began to soar in popularity.

Since its rise to prominence, the Martini has enjoyed the ebbs and flows of popularity that any fad must endure; however, it is perhaps the simplicity of the cocktail that ensures its periodic return to trendiness, along with its ample opportunity for variability. More than a drink, the Martini serves as the perfect metaphor for the country in which is was born: it is elegant, it is malleable, it is strong. Perhaps David Wondrich of Liquor.com puts it best: "As things stand, the Martini is another American legend, like Billy the Kid: a larger-than-life invention of the nation's collective will."

SHAKEN OR STIRRED?

James Bond's preference for a shaken Martini is well known, but the debate over whether the cocktail is better mixed by shaking or stirring is far from settled. Bartenders, Martini lovers, and even biochemists have weighed in over the years, each approaching the debate from a different angle.

When the Martini first rose to prominence, stirring was the prescribed mixing method. This fact alone leads many Martini lovers to adhere to the rule, as they believe the stirred version to be the drink's purest form. Others subscribe to the belief that shaking gin "bruises" the liquor, leaving it with a more bitter taste.

Some have speculated that 007's love of shaken Martinis derives from the fact that certain vodkas are made from potato rather than grain, giving them an oily quality. A shaken Martini is, anecdotally at least, better at dispersing the oil, which results in a smoother drink. Shaking also appears to incorporate the vermouth more thoroughly.

Of course, there is much more to the debate than the texture of the alcohol or the proper way to chill it. Scientists have even entered the fray, conducting studies, performing research, and identifying empirical, quantifiable differences between the shaken and stirred Martini.

John Hayes, a food science professor at Penn State University, once told NPR that shaking a Martini dilutes the drink, giving it a more watery quality. Unlike stirring, shaking a cocktail chips away at the ice, resulting in tiny flakes that melt as the drink warms. On the other hand, these tiny ice flakes help keep the drink cold for a longer period of time.

Hayes went on to speculate that Bond's preference for this slight dilution of the cocktail might be because it kept his head clearer, giving him a mental edge in the risky situations in which he typically found himself. However, not everyone is this generous in their interpretation. President Bartlet, of *The West Wing* fame, once said of his fictional counterpart, "Shaken, not stirred, will get you cold water with a dash of gin and dry vermouth. The reason you stir it with a special spoon is so not to chip the ice. James is ordering a weak martini and being snooty about it."

In 1999, a team of biochemists at the University of Western Ontario conducted their own study of the difference between shaken and stirred Martinis. They discovered that a shaken Martini contains slightly more antioxidants than a stirred Martini, although they were unable to determine what caused the disparity.

Whether antioxidants actually affect the taste of a Martini is a separate debate, but one chemist who participated in the study has continued researching other elements that impact the flavor of the cocktail. Darcy O'Neil agrees with the theory that potato vodka has an oily quality, and his tests confirm that shaking a Martini made with potato vodka successfully dissipates that oil. He also agrees that shaking a Martini will make it colder, but notes that after 20 shakes or so, a cocktail has generally gotten as cold as it's going to get.

Boston-based culinary scientist Dave Arnold has thoughts of his own on the matter. While he agrees with O'Neil that shaking a cocktail will make it colder, he points out that the ability to detect certain flavors is impeded when a drink becomes too cold. Sweetness, in particular, becomes more difficult to taste, and Arnold recommends adding additional sweetener to a drink if you plan to shake it.

If you've ever shaken a drink yourself, chances are you've encountered Arnold's next talking point: air bubbles. Egg whites are a common cocktail ingredient because, when shaken, the bubbles they generate create a beautiful foamy texture. The Martini lacks an ingredient that reacts this way, and the air bubbles generated by shaking it dissipate extremely quickly. Because of this, Arnold recommends making a smaller drink if you plan to shake it, so that you can consume it before the bubbles disappear, as they add a unique texture that should not be wasted.

So, what's the verdict?

Those in search of a classic Martini experience should order their drink stirred. Those who would like to be sure that the gin (or vodka) and vermouth are mixed as thoroughly as possible should order their drink shaken. Those looking for a colder Martini should shake it. Those looking for a sweeter Martini should stir it. In the end, the two methods produce different results, but which version is "better" is determined entirely by personal preference.

Try both versions and decide for yourself!

GIN MARTINIS AND VARIATIONS

Gin is the backbone of the Martini. Its fundamental ingredient. Whether you prefer your Martini dry or wet, with dry vermouth or sweet vermouth, shaken or stirred, every decision is made with gin in mind.

In a way, gin itself is a reflection of the Martini. It's simple, yet flavorful. The juniper is omnipresent, accented in small ways by different distillers, providing a fundamental flavor profile that sets it apart from other liquors. Like the Martini, gin can be an acquired taste, but those who enjoy it tend to love it.

With that in mind, these classic Martini recipes paint a picture of a devoted audience. There are many different ways to envision the Martini, and many different ways to enjoy it. But traditional Martinis stray little from the recipe that has endured since the turn of the century.

Sample one recipe or sample them all. Repeatedly return to your favorite or create something new. The Martini is revered for its simplicity, but also appreciated for its adaptability. The true beauty of the Martini lies in the fact that the perfect iteration rests in the eye of the beholder.

PICASSO MARTINI

Pour your favorite gin into a chilled cocktail glass and then add the vermouth ice cube.

INGREDIENTS:

- 2 OZ. GIN
- 1 ICE CUBE MADE WITH NOILLY PRAT VERMOUTH

ORANGE MARTINI

GARNISH: 1 ORANGE TWIST

Place the gin, vermouth, liqueur, and bitters in a mixing glass filled with ice and stir until thoroughly combined. Strain into a cocktail glass and garnish with the orange twist.

INGREDIENTS:

- 3 PARTS GIN
- 1 PART DRY VERMOUTH
- 1 PART ORANGE LIQUEUR
- DASH OF ORANGE BITTERS

WAKEUP MARTINI

GARNISH: 1 LEMON TWIST

Place the cocktail ingredients in a cocktail shaker filled with ice and shake vigorously to completely integrate the maple syrup. Strain into a cocktail glass and garnish with a lemon twist.

INGREDIENTS:

- 2 PARTS GIN
- 1 PART TRIPLE SEC
- SPLASH OF LEMON JUICE
- SPLASH OF MAPLE SYRUP

LE GRAND'S ORIGINAL DRY MARTINI

Place all of the ingredients in a mixing glass filled with ice, stir, and strain into a chilled cocktail glass.

INGREDIENTS:

- 1¼ OZ. NOILLY PRAT DRY VERMOUTH
- 1¼ OZ. TANQUERAY GIN
- 2 DASHES OF ORANGE BITTERS

VERDANT MARTINI

Place the green shiso cress, borage cress, and a pinch of Kona Sansho in a mixing glass. Add ice, the gin, and the vermouth and stir vigorously. Double-strain into a very cold cocktail glass.

INGREDIENTS:

- 4 GREEN SHISO CRESS
- 2 BORAGE CRESS
- KONA SANSHO (JAPANESE PEPPER)
- 2 OZ. GIN
- 2 DASHES OF NOILLY PRAT DRY VERMOUTH

CLASSIC MARTINI

GARNISH: 1 LEMON TWIST

The classic Martini is an astounding alchemy of gin and vermouth. It dates back to at least 1888, when the name was first used in *Harry Johnson's New and Improved Bartender's Manual*, and it remains one of the world's most popular cocktails. Simple, elegant, and flavorful, a traditional Martini has just two ingredients and can be enjoyed equally by both cocktail aficionados and the uninitiated. These elements, perhaps more than any other, have kept the Martini in the public eye. Easy to mix, the cocktail requires no special tools or expertise to create. Beautiful to look at, it lends an air of class to any occasion. And delicious to drink, it allows even novice drinkers to understand that a careful balance of flavors can create something that is more than the sum of its parts.

007 APPROVED

Of course, James Bond is likely more responsible for the current popularity of the Martini than any living, breathing individual. The beloved fictional spy, known for his suave demeanor, cool attitude, and hard-drinking lifestyle, was known to Ian Fleming's readers as a Martini lover. In 1953's *Casino Royale*, Fleming's first novel, 007 famously ordered a Vesper Martini (see page 170), with very specific instructions: "Three measures of Gordon's, one of vodka, half a measure of Kina Lillet. Shake it very well until it's ice-cold, then add a large thin slice of lemon peel." But it wasn't until Sean Connery delivered the famous "shaken, not stirred" line in the film *Dr. No* that the mantra became ingrained in the minds of the general public. Since then, the request has appeared in a majority of Bond films, and was named one of the 100 Best Movie Quotes of the past 100 years by the American Film Institute, underlining the cultural relevance of the famous secret agent's drink order.

INGREDIENTS:

- **4 PARTS TANQUERAY GIN**
- **1 PART DRY VERMOUTH**

Place the gin and vermouth in a mixing glass filled with ice and stir until thoroughly combined. Strain into a cocktail glass and garnish with the twist of lemon.

ORIGIN BAR, HONG KONG

Location: Hong Kong, China
Founded: 2012

Cultural Significance: The newest establishment on the list of places Martini lovers have to visit, Origin Bar was Hong Kong's first gin-focused bar. While the ingredients of the Martini originated in Europe and the drink itself rose to prominence in the United States, there are plenty of people and establishments in Asia that respect the Martini. Origin has placed the Martini and other gin-centric cocktails at the heart of their business, a move that has been met with great success.

Origin features globally recognized mixologists and boasts 15 unique gin infusions. The gin enthusiasts behind the bar have no shortage of modern tools at their disposal, and their infusion methods include "the use of a rotary evaporator for redistilling unique flavors into the gin, and a water bath and vacuum to slow-cook." Origin is dedicated to bringing a unique gin and Martini experience to the Hong Kong marketplace.

Why You Should Drink Your Martini Here: If you find yourself in Hong Kong, you won't find an establishment more dedicated to bringing out all the right flavors from gin. Origin offers gin options from dozens of different distillers to go with a carefully crafted menu featuring both respected classics and welcome innovations. Origin is a refreshingly modern take on the classic gin bar, and one you would do well to visit.

gin

HIGHBROW MARTINI

GARNISH: 1 LEMON TWIST

Place the gin and vermouth in a mixing glass filled with ice and stir until thoroughly combined. Strain into a cocktail glass and garnish with the twist of lemon.

INGREDIENTS:

- 4 PARTS BOMBAY SAPPHIRE GIN
- 1 PART DRY VERMOUTH

BRADFORD MARTINI

GARNISH: 1 LEMON TWIST

Place the gin and vermouth in a cocktail shaker filled with ice and shake well. Strain into a cocktail glass and garnish with the twist of lemon.

INGREDIENTS:

- 4 PARTS GIN
- 1 PART DRY VERMOUTH

DIRTY MARTINI

GARNISH: 3 PIMENTO-STUFFED OLIVES

Place the gin, vermouth, and olive brine in a mixing glass filled with ice and stir until thoroughly combined. Strain into a cocktail glass and garnish with the pimento-stuffed olives skewered on a toothpick.

INGREDIENTS:

- 4 PARTS GIN
- 1 PART DRY VERMOUTH
- SPLASH OF OLIVE BRINE

BUDGET MARTINI

Place the gin, vermouth, and lemon juice in a mixing glass filled with ice and stir until thoroughly combined. Strain into a cocktail glass.

INGREDIENTS:

- 4 PARTS NEW AMSTERDAM GIN
- 1 PART DRY VERMOUTH
- DASH OF LEMON JUICE

OBAN
Glenfiddich
15
Glenfiddich
21
LAPHROAIG
LAPHROAIG
LAPHROAIG
24
LEOPOLD'S
GIN MARE
BLACKWOOD'S
VINTAGE DRY GIN
60%
BOTANIST
PICON
AMER
BIERE
DOLIN
DEATH'S DOOR
BEEFEATER
BOMBAY
DRY GIN
BROKERS
LONDON
DRY
GIN
BROKERS
LONDON
DRY
GIN
PLYMOUTH
APEROL

GIN PALACE, MELBOURNE

Location: Melbourne, Australia
Founded: 1997

Cultural Significance: In the early days of gin, the term "gin palace" was used as a pejorative. Rather than run from that history, this Australian establishment has elected to lean into it, embracing the term's royal implications and turning what might once have been an insult into the highest of compliments.

In fact, Gin Palace is named after an old speakeasy in Melbourne, an establishment that rose to prominence under that very name. Although that establishment was shut down, its spirit lives on in today's Gin Palace, an establishment whose owners strive to capture the welcoming atmosphere and rebellious attitude of its namesake. Gin Palace prides itself on serving guests around the clock while creating a feeling of class and dignity.

Why You Should Drink Your Martini Here: At Gin Palace, it is, as you might expect, all about the gin. The establishment features an extensive Martini menu, and you'll find a staff well versed in not just the flavor of gin, but its history. Gin Palace is also famous for its raucous parties, and boasts about its fifth and tenth anniversaries to this day. You simply won't find a more perfect place to enjoy a Martini in Australia.

FILTHY MARTINI

GARNISH: 3 BLUE CHEESE–STUFFED OLIVES & BLUE CHEESE CRUMBLES

Place the gin, vermouth, and olive brine in a mixing glass filled with ice and stir until thoroughly combined. Strain into a cocktail glass, crumble a small amount of blue cheese over the drink, and garnish with the blue cheese–stuffed olives skewered on a toothpick.

INGREDIENTS:

- 4 PARTS GIN
- 1 PART DRY VERMOUTH
- SPLASH OF OLIVE BRINE

PERFECT MARTINI

GARNISH: 1 LEMON TWIST

Place the gin and vermouths in a mixing glass filled with ice and stir until thoroughly combined. Strain into a cocktail glass and garnish with the twist of lemon.

INGREDIENTS:

- 5 PARTS GIN
- 1 PART DRY VERMOUTH
- 1 PART SWEET VERMOUTH

LIME MARTINI

GARNISH: 1 LIME SLICE

Place the gin, dry vermouth, and lime juice in a mixing glass filled with ice and stir until thoroughly combined. Take the strip of lime peel and rub it along the rim of a cocktail glass. Discard the lime peel, strain the mixture from the cocktail shaker into the cocktail glass, and garnish with the slice of lime.

INGREDIENTS:

- 4 PARTS GIN
- 1 PART DRY VERMOUTH
- 1 PART LIME JUICE
- 1 STRIP OF LIME PEEL

CRANTINI

GARNISH: 1 LIME WHEEL

Place the gin, triple sec, and cranberry liqueur in a mixing glass filled with ice and stir until well combined. Strain into a cocktail glass and garnish with the lime wheel.

INGREDIENTS:

- 3 PARTS GIN
- 1 PART TRIPLE SEC
- 1 PART CRANBERRY LIQUEUR

BAR HEMINGWAY, PARIS

Location: Ritz Hotel, Paris, France
Founded: Disputed

Cultural Significance: Ernest Hemingway features prominently in the history of more than one cocktail, but his name appears frequently throughout the history of the Martini. Bar Hemingway, unsurprisingly, is named for the famous writer and drinker, and it is said that during his time in Paris, Hemingway spent more time at the bar than any other place. Hemingway was not the only American expatriate to make the bar his home away from home: Cole Porter, Gary Cooper, F. Scott Fitzgerald, and others were known to while away the hours at the famous establishment.

Although the tale is likely embellished, Hemingway was said to have personally "liberated" the Ritz Hotel from German occupation during his time as a war correspondent in World War II. According to legend, Hemingway commandeered a group of soldiers, and, determined to be the first to set foot inside the liberated Ritz, raced to clear it of Germans. Perhaps fortunately for Hemingway, he arrived to find that the Germans had long since left, and, denied his desired battle, settled in to drink a series of Dry Martinis.

Why You Should Drink Your Martini Here: If Ernest Hemingway's fervor for both the Ritz Hotel and its Dry Martinis doesn't fill you with the desire to visit the bar and try one for yourself, it seems likely that nothing will. The Ritz has received more than one makeover over the years, but it remains well known for its Martinis, and makes a worthy stop for any individual interested in the cultural cache of the Martini cocktail.

MATCH
HEMINGWAY
LIFE
THE CALL OF DANGER
NYPD

VESPER MARTINI

GARNISH: 1 STRIP OF LEMON PEEL

Place the gin, vodka, and Lillet in a cocktail shaker filled with ice and shake well. Strain into a cocktail glass and garnish with the strip of lemon peel.

INGREDIENTS:

- **6 PARTS GIN**
- **2 PARTS VODKA**
- **1 PART LILLET BLANC**

MINT MARTINI

GARNISH: 3 MINT LEAVES

Place 3 mint leaves and the crème de menthe in a cocktail shaker and muddle. Add ice, the gin, and the dry vermouth to the shaker and shake well. Strain into a cocktail glass and garnish with the additional mint leaves.

INGREDIENTS:

- **3 MINT LEAVES**
- **1 PART CRÈME DE MENTHE**
- **6 PARTS GIN**
- **1 PART DRY VERMOUTH**

FAVORITE MARTINI

GARNISH: 1 STRIP OF LEMON ZEST & 2 CASTELVETRANO OLIVES

Combine the gin and vermouth in a mixing glass filled with ice and stir. Strain into a cocktail glass and garnish with the lemon zest and olives.

INGREDIENTS:

- **2¼ OZ. TANQUERAY NO. TEN GIN**
- **¾ OZ. VERMOUTH BLEND (½ DOLIN BLANC AND ½ NOILLY PRAT ORIGINAL DRY)**

ROSEMARY MARTINI

GARNISH: 1 SPRIG OF ROSEMARY

Place gin, vermouth, and a rosemary sprig in a cocktail shaker filled with ice and shake vigorously. Strain the resulting mixture into a cocktail glass and garnish with an additional sprig of rosemary.

INGREDIENTS:

- 4 PARTS BOMBAY SAPPHIRE GIN
- 1 PART DRY VERMOUTH
- 1 SPRIG OF ROSEMARY

WHITE WINE MARTINI

GARNISH: 3 GRAPES

Place the gin and white wine in a mixing glass filled with ice and stir until well combined. Strain into a cocktail glass and garnish with the grapes skewered on a toothpick.

INGREDIENTS:

- 2 PARTS GIN
- 1 PART WHITE WINE

MARTINI SHOOTER

GARNISH: 1 PIMENTO-STUFFED OLIVE

Place the gin, vermouth, and olive brine in a cocktail shaker filled with ice and shake until well combined. Strain into a shot glass and drop a pimento-stuffed olive into the glass.

INGREDIENTS:

- 1 OZ. GIN
- ¼ OZ. DRY VERMOUTH
- DASH OF OLIVE BRINE

THE MARTINEZ

GARNISH: 1 MARASCHINO CHERRY & 1 LEMON SLICE

Place the gin, vermouth, maraschino liqueur, and bitters in a mixing glass filled with ice and stir until well combined. Strain into a cocktail glass and garnish with the maraschino cherry and the slice of lemon.

INGREDIENTS:

- 3 PARTS GIN
- 1 PART SWEET VERMOUTH
- 1 PART LUXARDO
- DASH OF BITTERS

VERBENA COCKTAIL

Gin Infusion: Combine 1 liter of gin with ¼ cup of lemon verbena leaves and let the mixture steep for at least 24 hours and up to 4 days. Strain before using.

Lavender Syrup: Place a handful of dried lavender leaves in a basic simple syrup as it is boiling. When the sugar is dissolved, remove from heat and let the mixture cool. Strain before using.

Place all of the ingredients in a rocks glass filled with ice and stir until combined.

INGREDIENTS:

- 1¾ OZ. BEEFEATER 24 GIN INFUSED WITH LEMON VERBENA LEAVES
- 1 TABLESPOON LAVENDER SYRUP
- 2 TEASPOONS VELVET FALERNUM
- 1 OZ. APPLE JUICE

OH MY DOG

GARNISH: 1 LIME WEDGE

Gin Infusion: Place ½ tablespoon of crushed white peppercorns in a 1-liter bottle of gin. Steep for 5 hours and strain before using.

Place the infused gin, La Grenade, and cordial in a cocktail shaker filled with ice and shake until chilled. Strain over ice into a tumbler, top with ginger ale, and garnish with the lime wedge.

INGREDIENTS:

- 1¾ OZ. GIN INFUSED WITH WHITE PEPPER
- ½ OZ. LA GRENADE LIQUEUR
- ½ TABLESPOON BELVOIR RASPBERRY-AND-ROSE CORDIAL
- GINGER ALE, TO TOP

PURPLE SKY

Place all of the ingredients in a cocktail shaker filled with ice, shake until chilled, and strain into a chilled cocktail glass.

INGREDIENTS:

- 1½ OZ. GIN
- ½ OZ. FRESH LEMON JUICE
- 2 DASHES OF CRÈME DE VIOLETTE
- ½ OZ. LUXARDO

LEA D'ASCO

GARNISH: 1 STRIP OF ORANGE ZEST

Place all of the cocktail ingredients in a mixing glass filled with ice and stir for 20 seconds. Strain into a chilled cocktail glass and garnish with the strip of orange zest.

INGREDIENTS:

- ½ OZ. BEEFEATER GIN
- 1 OZ. LILLET BLANC
- 1 TABLESPOON WHISK(E)Y
- 1 TABLESPOON ABSINTHE

FORUM COCKTAIL

Place all of the ingredients in a mixing glass filled with ice, stir until combined, and strain into a chilled cocktail glass.

INGREDIENTS:

- 1½ OZ. GIN
- 2 TEASPOONS NOILLY PRAT DRY VERMOUTH
- 4–5 DROPS OF GRAND MARNIER

THE SOIREE

GARNISH: 2 TO 4 PINK PEPPERCORNS & 1 LEMON TWIST

Place the cocktail ingredients in a mixing glass filled with ice and stir until well combined. Strain into a chilled coupe and garnish with the lemon twist and the pink peppercorns.

INGREDIENTS:

- 2 OZ. AUDEMUS PINK PEPPER GIN
- 1 OZ. GIFFARD CRÈME DE PAMPLEMOUSSE ROSE
- JUICE OF ½ LEMON

ROSEBUD

Place all of the ingredients, except for the tonic water, in a cocktail shaker filled with ice and shake vigorously. Strain over ice into a highball glass and top with tonic water.

INGREDIENTS:

- ¼ OZ. HENDRICK'S GIN
- ½ TABLESPOON SWEET VERMOUTH
- ½ OZ. COMBIER CRÈME DE ROSE
- ½ OZ. SIMPLE SYRUP
- ½ OZ. FRESH LEMON JUICE
- 2 DASHES OF CRANBERRY BITTERS
- TONIC WATER, TO TOP

SNOW BOWL

Place the gin, white chocolate liqueur, and crème de menthe in a cocktail shaker filled with ice and shake well. Strain into a rocks glass filled with ice and top with the nutmeg.

INGREDIENTS:

- 1 PART GIN
- 1 PART WHITE CHOCOLATE LIQUEUR
- SPLASH OF CRÈME DE MENTHE
- DUSTING OF NUTMEG

RUBY FIZZ

GARNISH: 1 GRAPEFRUIT WEDGE

Place your desired amount of ice in a highball glass and pour in the gin and grapefruit juice. Stir, fill with club soda, and stir again. Top with the splash of grenadine and garnish with the grapefruit wedge.

INGREDIENTS:

- 1 PART GIN
- 1 PART GRAPEFRUIT JUICE
- 1 PART CLUB SODA
- SPLASH OF GRENADINE

SINGAPORE SLING

Place all of the ingredients other than the soda water into a cocktail shaker filled with ice. Shake vigorously, strain over ice into a highball glass, and top with soda water.

INGREDIENTS:

- 1 OZ. GIN
- 1¾ TABLESPOONS CHERRY BRANDY
- 2 TEASPOONS COINTREAU
- 3 TEASPOONS BÉNÉDICTINE
- DASH OF GRENADINE
- 1⅓ TABLESPOONS LIME JUICE
- 1 OZ. PINEAPPLE JUICE
- SODA WATER, TO TOP

BRAMBLE & QUEEN

GARNISH: 3 BLACKBERRIES

Place the gin, lemon juice, simple syrup, ylang ylang water, and egg white in a cocktail shaker filled with ice and shake until chilled. Strain into a chilled cocktail glass and top with the Champagne and blackberry liqueur. Garnish with the blackberries skewered on a toothpick

INGREDIENTS:

- ½ OZ. GIN
- ½ OZ. FRESH LEMON JUICE
- ½ OZ. SIMPLE SYRUP
- 1 TEASPOON YLANG YLANG WATER
- DASH OF EGG WHITE
- CHAMPAGNE, TO TOP
- 1 TABLESPOON BLACKBERRY LIQUEUR

BOBO PARISIEN

Place all of the ingredients in a cocktail shaker filled with ice, shake until chilled, and strain into a cocktail glass.

INGREDIENTS:

- **1¾ OZ. GIN**
- **½ OZ. ST-GERMAIN**
- **½ OZ. KINA L'AVION D'OR**
- **DASH OF RHUBARB BITTERS**
- **1 EGG WHITE**
- **SPLASH OF CLUB SODA**

MAZARINETTE

Rhubarb Juice: Chop 1 bunch of fresh or frozen rhubarb into ¾-inch pieces. Place them in a saucepan, cover with water, and simmer for 30 minutes. Strain through a fine sieve and let cool before using. The juice can be stored in your refrigerator for up to a week.

Place all of the ingredients other than the Champagne in a cocktail shaker filled with ice and shake until chilled. Strain into a chilled cocktail glass and top with Champagne.

INGREDIENTS:

- **1 TABLESPOON HOMEMADE RHUBARB JUICE**
- **1 TABLESPOON LEMON JUICE**
- **1 OZ. GORDON'S SLOE GIN**
- **¾ OZ. GIN**
- **1 OZ. SIPSMITH SUMMER CUP**
- **CHAMPAGNE, TO TOP**

LE PULPEUX

Place all of the ingredients, except for the ginger beer, in a cocktail shaker filled with ice and shake vigorously. Strain over ice into a highball glass and top with ginger beer.

INGREDIENTS:

- **1½ OZ. BEEFEATER GIN**
- **½ OZ. THYME LIQUEUR**
- **½ OZ. GRAPEFRUIT JUICE**
- **½ OZ. FRESH LIME JUICE**
- **GINGER BEER, TO TOP**

HANKY PANKY

GARNISH: 1 ORANGE TWIST

Place all of the ingredients in a mixing glass filled with ice and stir until combined. Strain into a coupe, express the orange twist over the glass, and then arrange it on the surface of the drink.

INGREDIENTS:

- 1½ OZ. GIN
- 1 OZ. SWEET VERMOUTH
- 2 DASHES OF FERNET-BRANCA

BIJOU COCKTAIL

GARNISH: 1 STRIP OF LEMON ZEST OR 1 CHERRY

Place the cocktail ingredients in a mixing glass filled with ice and stir. Strain into a chilled coupe and garnish with a strip of lemon zest or a cherry.

INGREDIENTS:

- 1½ OZ. DRY GIN
- ¾ OZ. SWEET VERMOUTH
- ¾ OZ. CHARTREUSE
- DASH OF ORANGE BITTERS

FRENCH 75 SQUARED

GARNISH: 2 CHERRIES

Place the gin, lemon juice, sugar, and elderflower liqueur in a cocktail shaker filled with cracked ice. Shake, strain into an chilled coupe until the glass is about ⅔ full, and top with Champagne. Garnish with the cherries skewered on a toothpick.

INGREDIENTS:

- 2 OZ. GIN
- 1 OZ. LEMON JUICE
- 1 TEASPOON SUGAR
- 1 OZ. ST-GERMAIN
- CHAMPAGNE, TO TOP

MARGUERITE

GARNISH: 1 STRIP OF ORANGE ZEST OR 1 CHERRY

Place the cocktail ingredients in a mixing glass filled with ice and stir. Strain into a chilled coupe and garnish with the orange zest or a cherry.

INGREDIENTS:

- 2 OZ. GIN
- 1 OZ. DRY VERMOUTH
- 2 DASHES OF ORANGE BITTERS

BEE'S KNEES

GARNISH: 1 LEMON TWIST

Place the cocktail ingredients in a cocktail shaker filled with ice and shake vigorously. Strain into a chilled coupe and garnish with the lemon twist.

INGREDIENTS:

- 2 OZ. LONDON DRY GIN
- ¾ OZ. LEMON JUICE
- ¾ OZ. HONEY SYRUP

LANDRACE

GARNISH: 1 ORANGE TWIST

Blue Corn Gin: Combine 8 oz. landrace blue corn and 1 liter of Greenall's London Dry Gin and steep in a cool, dark place for 14 days while agitating daily. Strain before using.

Infused Vermouth: Combine 32 oz. of huitlacoche and 4 cups of Everclear and steep for 24 hours. Strain and combine 1 part of the resulting tincture with 5 parts dry vermouth.

Combine the gin, infused vermouth, Luxardo, and bitters in a mixing glass filled with ice and stir until combined. Strain into a chilled cocktail glass, express the orange peel over the drink and discard, and garnish with the orange twist.

Tip: Huitlacoche is a fungus known as corn soot that is utilized by some of the world's most inventive chefs. It adds a subtle but wonderful mushroom-y flavor to any preparation and is available online.

INGREDIENTS:

- 2 OZ. BLUE CORN GIN
- 1 OZ. HUITLACOCHE-INFUSED VERMOUTH
- 1 OZ. LUXARDO
- DASH OF REGAN'S ORANGE BITTERS
- DASH OF BITTERMENS SCARBOROUGH BITTERS
- 1 LARGE STRIP OF ORANGE PEEL

VICE VERSA

Place all of the ingredients except for the Cava in a cocktail shaker filled with ice and shake vigorously. Strain into a large coupe and top with the Cava.

INGREDIENTS:

- ¾ OZ. GRAPEFRUIT JUICE
- ½ OZ. LUXARDO BITTER
- ½ OZ. GIFFARD CRÈME DE PAMPLEMOUSSE ROSE
- 1 OZ. NY DISTILLING CO. DOROTHY PARKER GIN
- ROSÉ CAVA, TO TOP

STATE STREET COCKTAIL

Place the sugar, lemon juice, and lime juice in a cocktail shaker and stir until the sugar dissolves. Add the remaining ingredients and ice, shake until chilled, and strain into a rocks glass.

INGREDIENTS:

- 2 SPOONFULS OF WHITE SUGAR
- 1½ OZ. LEMON JUICE
- ½ OZ. LIME JUICE
- 1½ OZ. UNSWEETENED PINEAPPLE JUICE
- 1½ OZ. GIN
- 1 EGG WHITE

OBITUARY COCKTAIL

GARNISH: 1 LEMON TWIST

Place the cocktail ingredients in a mixing glass filled with ice and stir. Strain into a chilled cocktail glass and garnish with the lemon twist.

INGREDIENTS:

- 2 OZ. GIN
- 1 OZ. DRY VERMOUTH
- 1 SPOONFUL OF ABSINTHE

AUDEMUS
SPIRITS
CRÉATEUR DE SPIRITUEUX
PINK
PEPPER
GIN
500 ML
44% VOL

AUDEMUS CENTURY

Place all of the ingredients in a cocktail shaker filled with ice, shake vigorously, and strain into a chilled coupe.

INGREDIENTS:

- 1 OZ. AUDEMUS PINK PEPPER GIN
- ¾ OZ. COCCHI AMERICANO
- ¾ OZ. WHITE CHOCOLATE LIQUEUR
- ¾ OZ. LEMON JUICE

JOY DIVISION

GARNISH: 1 LEMON TWIST

Place all of the ingredients in a mixing glass filled with ice and stir. Strain into a coupe and garnish with the lemon twist.

INGREDIENTS:

- 2 OZ. BEEFEATER LONDON DRY GIN
- 1 OZ. DOLIN BLANC
- ½ OZ. TRIPLE SEC OR COINTREAU
- 3 DASHES OF ABSINTHE

THE BRONX COCKTAIL

GARNISH: 1 STRIP OF ORANGE PEEL

Place all of the ingredients in a cocktail shaker filled with ice and shake vigorously. Strain into a chilled cocktail glass, and double-strain if the juice is very pulpy. Garnish with the strip of orange peel.

INGREDIENTS:

- 1½ OZ. LONDON DRY GIN
- ½ OZ. SWEET VERMOUTH
- ½ OZ. EXTRA DRY VERMOUTH
- 1 OZ. FRESH ORANGE JUICE
- DASH OF REGAN'S ORANGE BITTERS NO. 6 (OPTIONAL)

GIN-GIN MULE

GARNISH: 1 LIME WHEEL, CANDIED GINGER, & 1 SPRIG OF MINT

Place the lime juice, simple syrup, and mint in a mixing glass and muddle. Add the ginger beer, gin, and ice and shake until chilled. Strain into a highball glass and garnish with an additional sprig of mint, the lime wheel, and the candied ginger.

INGREDIENTS:

- ¾ OZ. FRESH LIME JUICE
- 1 OZ. SIMPLE SYRUP
- 1 SPRIG OF MINT
- 1 OZ. GINGER BEER
- 1¾ OZ. TANQUERAY GIN

THE CLOVER CLUB COCKTAIL

GARNISH: 2 RASPBERRIES

Combine the cocktail ingredients in a cocktail shaker and dry shake for 20 seconds. Add ice and shake until chilled. Strain into a coupe and garnish with the raspberries skewered on a toothpick.

INGREDIENTS:

- **1½ OZ. DRY GIN**
- **½ OZ. DRY VERMOUTH**
- **½ OZ. LEMON JUICE**
- **½ OZ. RASPBERRY SYRUP (OR MUDDLE 5 RASPBERRIES IN ½ OZ. SIMPLE SYRUP)**
- **½ OZ. EGG WHITE**

THE SOUTHSIDE

GARNISH: MINT LEAVES

Mint Simple Syrup: Add several sprigs of mint while preparing a basic simple syrup recipe and strain before serving.

Place the cocktail ingredients in a cocktail shaker filled with ice and shake vigorously. Strain into a Collins glass and garnish with additional mint leaves.

INGREDIENTS:

- **4–5 MINT LEAVES**
- **2 OZ. GIN**
- **1 OZ. MINT SIMPLE SYRUP**
- **JUICE OF 1 LEMON**
- **SPLASH OF SODA**

CORPSE REVIVER NO. 2

GARNISH: 1 LEMON TWIST

Place the cocktail ingredients in a cocktail shaker filled with ice and shake until combined. Strain into a coupe and garnish with the lemon twist.

INGREDIENTS:

- ¾ OZ. LONDON DRY GIN
- ¾ OZ. LEMON JUICE
- ¾ OZ. COINTREAU
- ¾ OZ. COCCHI AMERICANO
- 1 TEASPOON ABSINTHE

GREEN GIANT

GARNISH: 1 SUGAR SNAP PEA

Place the 4 sugar snap peas, the tarragon, and the simple syrup in a cocktail shaker and muddle. Add ice and the remaining cocktail ingredients and shake until chilled. Double-strain over ice into a rocks glass and garnish with an additional sugar snap pea.

INGREDIENTS:

- 4 SUGAR SNAP PEAS, TRIMMED AND SNAPPED IN HALF
- 8–10 FRESH TARRAGON LEAVES
- ¾ OZ. SIMPLE SYRUP
- 2 OZ. GIN
- ½ OZ. DRY VERMOUTH
- ¾ OZ. LEMON JUICE

NORTHERN LIGHTS

GARNISH: 1 GRAPEFRUIT TWIST

Place the cocktail ingredients in a cocktail shaker filled with ice and shake vigorously. Strain into a coupe and garnish with the grapefruit twist.

INGREDIENTS:

- 1½ OZ. BOTANIST GIN OR TANQUERAY NO. TEN
- ¾ OZ. LILLET ROSE
- ½ OZ. PIERRE FERRAND DRY CURAÇAO OR RHUM CLÉMENT CRÉOLE SHRUBB
- 1 OZ. FRESH GRAPEFRUIT JUICE
- ¼ OZ. FRESH LIME

THE DUKE OF SUFFOLK

Sweet Tea: Place a bag of English breakfast and a bag of Earl Grey in 5 oz. of hot water. Steep for 5 minutes and then sweeten to taste with simple syrup.

Place the gin in a mug and stir in the sweet tea. Top with the dollop of whipped cream.

INGREDIENTS:

- 6 OZ. SWEET TEA, HOT
- 1¼ OZ. HENDRICK'S GIN OR FORDS GIN
- DOLLOP OF WHIPPED CREAM

PLEASANT DEMISE

GARNISH: 1 SPRIG OF THYME

Place the cocktail ingredients in a cocktail shaker filled with ice and shake vigorously. Double-strain into a chilled coupe and garnish with the sprig of thyme.

SPICED GRENADINE

Place 1½ cups of the pomegranate juice, the cinnamon sticks, cloves, and orange peel in a saucepan and simmer over medium heat until the liquid is reduced by half. Remove from heat, strain, and add the remaining pomegranate juice, pomegranate molasses, and sugar. Place the saucepan over medium heat and cook, while stirring, until the sugar is completely dissolved. Let cool before using.

INGREDIENTS:

- 1½ OZ. LONDON DRY GIN
- ½ OZ. ST. GEORGE SPICED PEAR LIQUEUR
- ½ OZ. FRESH LEMON JUICE
- ½ OZ. SPICED GRENADINE (SEE RECIPE BELOW)
- 4 DASHES OF PEYCHAUD'S BITTERS

SPICED GRENADINE:

- 3 CUPS 100% POMEGRANATE JUICE
- 3 CINNAMON STICKS
- ½ OZ. WHOLE CLOVES
- PEEL OF 1 ORANGE
- ½ OZ. POMEGRANATE MOLASSES
- 3 CUPS WHITE SUGAR

3L
2L
2L
3L
3L

WOOLYNESIA

GARNISH: 1 SPRIG OF MINT

Place all of the cocktail ingredients in a cocktail shaker with no ice and dry shake for 10 to 15 seconds. Add ice and shake for 15 more seconds. Strain over pellet ice into a tiki mug and garnish with the sprig of mint.

INGREDIENTS:

- 1½ OZ. GREENHOOK GINSMITHS OLD TOM GIN
- ¾ OZ. ANCHO REYES VERDE CHILE POBLANO LIQUEUR
- 1 OZ. LIME JUICE
- ½ OZ. APEROL
- ½ OZ. PASSION FRUIT JUICE
- 1 TEASPOON GINGER
- 1 TEASPOON CINNAMON
- 1 TEASPOON GIFFARD CRÈME PÊCHE DE VIGNE

CELERY GIMLET

GARNISH: 1 CELERY STALK & 1 LIME WHEEL

Celery Syrup: Add 1 cup of diced celery to a basic simple syrup recipe as it is boiling. When the sugar has dissolved, remove from heat, let cool, and strain before using.

Place the cocktail ingredients in a cocktail shaker filled with ice and shake vigorously. Strain over ice into a rocks glass and garnish with the celery stalk and lime wheel.

INGREDIENTS:

- ½ OZ. CELERY SYRUP
- 1½ OZ. NY DISTILLING CO. DOROTHY PARKER GIN
- ¼ OZ. CHARTREUSE
- ¼ OZ. ST-GERMAIN
- ¾ OZ. LIME JUICE
- ½ OZ. LIME SYRUP
- 5 DASHES OF VERJUS
- 2 DASHES OF CELERY BITTERS
- PINCH OF CITRUS SALT

PERFECT GIMLET

GARNISH: 2 LIME WHEELS

Place the cocktail ingredients in a cocktail shaker filled with ice and shake vigorously. Strain into a coupe and garnish with the lime wheels.

GINGER-LIME CORDIAL

Wash the limes with warm water and scrub with your hands or a vegetable brush. Set them on a dish towel to dry. When dry, peel the limes with a vegetable peeler, removing as little of the underlying white pith as possible. Place the peeled limes in the refrigerator to chill overnight. Place the peels in a non reactive container, and then add the sugar, making sure that the peels are covered with sugar. Cover the container and let rest for 8 to 12 hours.

The next day, cut your limes in half and juice them. Peel the ginger and cut it into small pieces. Combine the lime juice and ginger in a blender and pulse well to make a slurry. Add this mixture to the lime peel–and–sugar mixture and stir for several minutes, until the sugar is dissolved. Cover and refrigerate for at least 12 hours and up to 2 days. When ready, strain through a fine sieve and store in a clean, sterile covered container or a bottle. Place in the refrigerator for 1 more day before using. Makes roughly 4 cups.

Tip: A very ripe lime is puffy and feels heavier than a typical lime.

INGREDIENTS:

- 2 OZ. LONDON DRY GIN
- 1 OZ. GINGER-LIME CORDIAL (SEE RECIPE BELOW)
- ¾ OZ. FRESH LIME JUICE

GINGER-LIME CORDIAL:

- 18 VERY RIPE LIMES, AT ROOM TEMPERATURE
- 3 CUPS SUGAR
- 1 POUND FRESH GINGER

GIN BASIL SMASH

GARNISH: 1 BASIL LEAF

Place the syrup and the basil leaves in a cocktail shaker and muddle. Add the gin, lemon juice, and ice and shake for 10 seconds. Double-strain over ice into a rocks glass and garnish with the additional basil leaf.

INGREDIENTS:

- ½ OZ. LIBER & CO. CLASSIC GUM SYRUP
- 9 FRESH BASIL LEAVES
- 2 OZ. GIN
- ¾ OZ. LEMON JUICE

GIN 'N' ROSES

GARNISH: DRIED ROSEBUDS

Place all of the ingredients in a cocktail shaker and fill with ice. Shake until chilled, strain into a rocks glass filled with ice, and garnish with dried rosebuds.

INGREDIENTS:

- 1 OZ. MARTIN MILLER'S GIN
- 1 OZ. COCCHI ROSA
- ½ OZ. FRESH LEMON JUICE
- ½ OZ. GIFFARD BLACK ROSE LIQUEUR
- ¼ OZ. HONEY SYRUP (1:3 HONEY-TO-WATER RATIO)

SEITHENNIN (LOST TO THE SEA)

GARNISH: LAVER OIL & PICKLED WRACK SEAWEED

Wet the rim of a cocktail glass and dip it into the seaweed powder. Place the gin and Chartreuse in a mixing glass filled with ice and stir until chilled. Add the dash of kelp bitters to the cocktail glass, and then strain the gin-and-Chartreuse mixture into the glass. Garnish with the pickled seaweed and a few drops of laver oil.

INGREDIENTS:

- LAVER SEAWEED POWDER, FOR THE RIM
- 2 OZ. SIPSMITH VJOP GIN
- ½ OZ. CHARTREUSE
- DASH OF KELP BITTERS

GENTLEMAN CALLER

GARNISH: 1 STRIP OF LEMON PEEL

Place all of the ingredients in a mixing glass filled with ice and stir. Strain into a Nick & Nora glass and garnish with a strip of lemon peel.

INGREDIENTS:

- 1 OZ. GIN
- 1 OZ. FINO SHERRY
- ½ OZ. APEROL

TEXAS FIZZ

GARNISH: 1 ORANGE TWIST

Combine the cocktail ingredients, except for the Champagne, in a cocktail shaker filled with ice and shake vigorously. Strain into a chilled Collins glass, top with the Champagne, and garnish with the orange twist.

INGREDIENTS:

- 1½ OZ. LONDON DRY GIN
- ½ OZ. FRESH LEMON JUICE
- ¾ OZ. FRESH ORANGE JUICE
- ¼ OZ. GRENADINE
- 2–3 OZ. BRUT CHAMPAGNE, CHILLED

THE DITMARS

GARNISH: 1 ORANGE WHEEL

Place all of the ingredients in a cocktail shaker filled with ice. Gently roll the shaker (so as to avoid bruising the gin) until chilled. Strain into a coupe and float an orange wheel on top as garnish.

INGREDIENTS:

- 1½ OZ. QUEENS COURAGE NEW YORK OLD TOM GIN
- ¾ OZ. LICOR BEIRÃO
- ½ OZ. FRESH LIME JUICE
- 2 SPOONFULS OF FERNET-BRANCA

FAMOUS GIN FIZZ

Place all of the ingredients, except for the soda water, in a cocktail shaker and dry shake for 15 to 20 seconds. Fill the shaker one-quarter full with ice and whip shake for 3 to 5 minutes. Pour into a chilled Collins glass and top with soda water until a foamy head forms.

INGREDIENTS:

- 2 OZ. GIN
- 1 OZ. HALF-AND-HALF
- ¾ OZ. SIMPLE SYRUP
- ½ OZ. LEMON JUICE
- ½ OZ. LIME JUICE
- 2 DASHES OF ORANGE BLOSSOM WATER
- 1 EGG WHITE
- SODA WATER, TO TOP

PROVENÇALE GIN FIZZ

GARNISH: SPRIGS OF ROSEMARY & THYME

Honey-Lavender Syrup: In a small saucepan, steep 1 oz. lavender in 1 cup hot water. Strain into a small bowl, add 1 cup honey, and stir to combine. Store in an airtight container and refrigerate for up to 2 weeks.

Place the egg white, lemon juice, and honey-lavender syrup in a cocktail shaker and dry shake for 15 to 20 seconds. Add the gin, goat's milk, cream, and orange blossom water, and shake again. Double-strain into a Collins glass and gently top with soda. Garnish with the rosemary and thyme sprigs.

INGREDIENTS:

- ¾ OZ. HONEY-LAVENDER SYRUP
- 1 EGG WHITE
- ¾ OZ. LEMON JUICE
- 1½ OZ. GIN
- ¾ OZ. GOAT'S MILK
- ¼ OZ. HEAVY CREAM
- 2 DROPS OF ORANGE BLOSSOM WATER
- SODA WATER, TO TOP

ST. CLAUDE COCKTAIL

GARNISH: 3 DASHES OF ANGOSTURA BITTERS

Lemongrass Simple Syrup: Add 2 slightly crushed lemongrass stalks to a basic simple syrup as it boils. When the sugar has dissolved, remove from heat, let cool, and strain before using.

Place the gin and egg white in a cocktail shaker and dry shake. Add the remaining cocktail ingredients, shake, and strain into a coupe. Garnish with the Angostura Bitters.

INGREDIENTS:

- ¾ OZ. LEMONGRASS SIMPLE SYRUP
- 1 OZ. GIN
- 1 EGG WHITE
- 1 OZ. MANZANILLA SHERRY
- 1 OZ. LEMON JUICE
- ¾ OZ. UNSWEETENED PINEAPPLE JUICE
- ¼ OZ. SUZE

GARDEN PARTY

GARNISH: PINCH OF BLACK PEPPER

Place the lemon juice, simple syrup, and red bell pepper in a cocktail shaker and muddle. Add ice, gin, and Aperol and shake vigorously. Strain into a coupe and garnish with the black pepper.

INGREDIENTS:

- ¾ OZ. LEMON JUICE
- ½ OZ. SIMPLE SYRUP
- 2 STRIPS OF RED BELL PEPPER
- 2 OZ. GIN
- ¾ OZ. APEROL

WHAT REALLY HAPPENED

GARNISH: 1 STRIP OF LEMON PEEL

Combine the cocktail ingredients in a cocktail shaker filled with ice and shake vigorously. Pour the cocktail and the ice into a Collins glass, express the lemon peel over the drink, and then use it as a garnish.

INGREDIENTS:

- ¾ OZ. LONDON DRY GIN
- ¾ OZ. BARROW'S INTENSE GINGER LIQUEUR
- ¾ OZ. LEMON JUICE
- ¼ OZ. HONEY SYRUP

ROSE WATER SOUR

GARNISH: RED ROSE TINCTURE

Rose Water Mix: Combine 1 cup red wine and 1 cup white sugar and stir until the sugar is dissolved. Add a few drops of cardamom tincture and stir. Add ¾ cup Combier Liqueur de Rose and ¾ cup orgeat and stir until combined.

Place the cocktail ingredients in a cocktail shaker and dry shake for 15 to 20 seconds. Add ice, shake until chilled, and strain into a coupe. Garnish with a few drops of red rose tincture.

INGREDIENTS:

- ¾ OZ. ROSE WATER MIX
- 2 OZ. FLORAL GIN
- ¾ OZ. LEMON JUICE
- 1 EGG WHITE

SUMMER ON THE RIVIERA

GARNISH: 1 LEMON TWIST

Place the cocktail ingredients in a cocktail shaker filled with ice and shake vigorously. Strain into a coupe and garnish with the lemon twist.

INGREDIENTS:

- 2 OZ. CITADELLE GIN
- ½ OZ. BITTER TRUTH ELDERFLOWER LIQUEUR
- ½ OZ. LEMON JUICE
- ½ OZ. PIERRE FERRAND DRY CURAÇAO
- ¼ OZ. SIMPLE SYRUP

QUARTZ COMPOSER

GARNISH: 1 MEXICAN MINT MARIGOLD BLOSSOM

Canary Melon Syrup: Add ½ cup of canary melon chunks to a basic simple syrup recipe when it is boiling. Cook for 5 minutes, remove from heat, let cool, and strain before using.

Place the cocktail ingredients in a cocktail shaker filled with ice and shake until chilled. Strain over ice in a rocks glass and garnish with the Mexican mint marigold blossom.

INGREDIENTS:

- ¾ OZ. CANARY MELON SYRUP
- ¾ OZ. GENIUS OLD HIGHBORN TEXAS DRY GIN
- ¾ OZ. MEZCAL VAGO
- ¼ OZ. SAMBUCA
- ½ OZ. LIME JUICE

CORPSE IMBIBER

GARNISH: 1 STRIP OF GRAPEFRUIT PEEL

Place the gin, Cocchi Rosa, juices, and Gran Classico in a cocktail shaker filled with ice and shake until chilled. Mist a coupe with absinthe, strain the cocktail into it, and garnish with the strip of grapefruit peel.

INGREDIENTS:

- 1½ OZ. GENIUS STANDARD STRENGTH GIN
- ¾ OZ. COCCHI ROSA
- ¾ OZ. FRESH GRAPEFRUIT JUICE
- ¼ OZ. FRESH LEMON JUICE
- ¾ OZ. GRAN CLASSICO
- ABSINTHE MIST

EVERYBODY'S GIRL

GARNISH: 1 STRIP OF GRAPEFRUIT PEEL

Place the cocktail ingredients, except for the Prosecco, in a cocktail shaker filled with ice and shake vigorously. Strain into a Collins glass, top with Prosecco, and garnish with the strip of grapefruit peel.

INGREDIENTS:

- ¾ OZ. OLD HIGHBORN TEXAS DRY GIN
- ¾ OZ. ST-GERMAIN
- ¾ OZ. LUSTAU FINO SHERRY
- ¾ OZ. GRAPEFRUIT JUICE
- ¼ OZ. LEMON JUICE
- PROSECCO, TO TOP

AVIATION VARIATION

GARNISH: DRIED ROSEBUDS

Place the cocktail ingredients, except for the egg white, in a cocktail shaker and add ice. Shake until chilled, strain, discard the ice, and return the cocktail to the shaker. Add the egg white and dry shake until very frothy. Strain into a coupe and garnish with dried rosebuds.

INGREDIENTS:

- 1½ OZ. FORDS GIN
- ¾ OZ. PARFAIT AMOUR
- ¼ OZ. LUXARDO
- ¾ OZ. LEMON JUICE
- ¼ OZ. SIMPLE SYRUP
- 2 DASHES OF LAVENDER BITTERS
- 2 DROPS OF ROSE WATER
- 1 EGG WHITE

1000W THUMPER

GARNISH: 1 WATERMELON SPEAR

Combine the cocktail ingredients, except for the club soda, in a cocktail shaker filled with ice and shake vigorously. Strain into a Collins glass, top with the club soda, and garnish with the watermelon spear.

INGREDIENTS:

- ¾ OZ. FRESH LIME JUICE
- ½ OZ. MINERAL SIMPLE SYRUP (1 PART CRAZY WATER NO. 4 TO 1 PART SUGAR)
- 2 OZ. FRESH WATERMELON JUICE
- 1½ OZ. TANQUERAY GIN
- DASH OF ANGOSTURA BITTERS
- 2 DROPS OF MINERAL WATER SOLUTION (1 PART KOSHER SALT TO 9 PARTS CRAZY WATER NO. 4)
- 2 DROPS OF VIEUX PONTARLIER ABSINTHE
- ICE-COLD CLUB SODA, TO TOP

THE FLEUR DU MAL

GARNISH: DRIED ROSEBUDS

Place all of the ingredients, except for the orange blossom water, in a cocktail shaker and shake vigorously. Double-strain into a coupe, spritz with orange blossom water, and garnish with the dried rosebuds.

INGREDIENTS:

- 1 OZ. GIN
- 1 OZ. LILLET BLANC
- 1 OZ. ST-GERMAIN
- ½ OZ. LEMON JUICE
- ½ OZ. GRAPEFRUIT JUICE
- ¼ OZ. GRENADINE
- ¼ OZ. BRADLEY'S KINA TONIC
- SPRITZ OF ORANGE BLOSSOM WATER

HUSK FIZZ

GARNISH: 1 LIME LEAF

Coriander Syrup: Place ½ cup coriander seeds in a basic simple syrup as it is boiling. Remove from heat, let cool, and strain before using.

Place the gin, lime juice, coriander syrup, coconut milk, and torn lime leaf in a cocktail shaker filled with ice and shake until chilled. Strain into a chilled Collins glass and top with the club soda. Spritz with the orange blossom water and garnish with the additional lime leaf.

INGREDIENTS:

- ¾ OZ. CORIANDER SYRUP
- 1½ OZ. LONDON DRY GIN
- ½ OZ. LIME JUICE
- ¾ OZ. COCONUT MILK
- 1 LIME LEAF, TORN
- CLUB SODA, CHILLED, TO TOP
- SPRITZ OF ORANGE BLOSSOM WATER

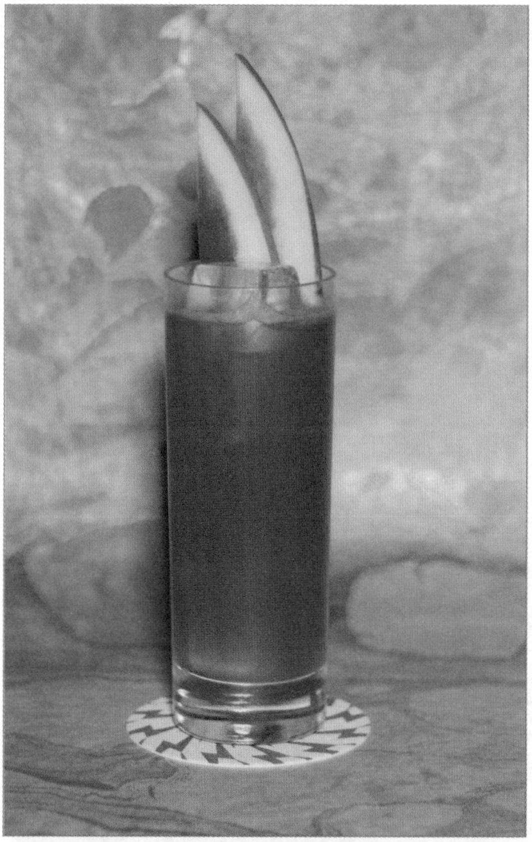

THE MISSIONARY

GARNISH: 1 STRIP OF GRAPEFRUIT PEEL

Place the cocktail ingredients in a cocktail shaker and shake vigorously. Strain into a rocks glass, add ice, and garnish with the strip of grapefruit peel.

INGREDIENTS:

- 1½ OZ. GIN
- 1 OZ. MIXED BERRY SHRUB (SEE PAGE 40)
- ¾ OZ. GRAPEFRUIT JUICE
- 2 CUCUMBERS, CHOPPED

SEERSUCKER

GARNISH: 1 LEMON TWIST

Place the gin, lemon juice, and simple syrup in a cocktail shaker filled with ice and shake vigorously. Strain into a champagne flute, top with the Prosecco or Champagne, and garnish with a lemon twist.

INGREDIENTS:

- 1 OZ. SEERSUCKER SOUTHERN STYLE GIN
- ½ OZ. LEMON JUICE
- ½ OZ. SIMPLE SYRUP
- PROSECCO OR CHAMPAGNE, CHILLED, TO TOP

LA BUENA VERBENA

GARNISH: 1 LEMON VERBENA LEAF

Place the ingredients in a chilled mixing glass filled with ice and stir until very cold. Strain into a chilled coupe glass and make a small slit in the lemon verbena leaf so you can place it on the rim.

INGREDIENTS:

- 1¼ OZ. GIN
- ½ OZ. KEY LIME JUICE
- 1 OZ. SWEET LEMON VERBENA TEA (SEE RECIPE BELOW)
- ¼ OZ. SAFFRON SYRUP (SEE RECIPE BELOW)

SWEET LEMON VERBENA TEA

Place the water and sugar in a small saucepan and bring to a boil. Add lemon verbena leaves, remove from heat, and let steep for 20 minutes. Strain and let cool completely.

SWEET LEMON VERBENA TEA:

- 1 CUP WATER
- 2 OZ. NATURAL CANE SUGAR
- 6 LARGE LEMON VERBENA LEAVES

SAFFRON SYRUP

Place the saffron, water, and sugar in a small saucepan and bring to a boil. Remove from heat, let cool completely, strain, and store in the refrigerator.

SAFFRON SYRUP:

- ⅛ TEASPOON SAFFRON THREADS, CRUSHED
- 1 CUP WATER
- 1 CUP NATURAL CANE SUGAR

Q&A WITH SAMUEL KWOK, BAR MANAGER AT QUINARY

Quinary's long bar in Hong Kong's SoHo neighborhood is more like a laboratory—Quinary cocktails are crafted using in-house gadgets like a rotary evaporator, and are acclaimed thanks to redistilling and slow cooking flavored spirts. Consistently included on lists of the world's best bars, the Quinary menu features reinventions of classic drinks made memorable thanks to unexpected combinations of flavors and aromas.

What can you tell us about how the bar started?

Quinary was founded by world-renowned mixologist Antonio Lai and Charlene Dawes in 2012. Being arguably one of the first places to kick-start the mixology trend in Hong Kong, particularly with what we call "multisensory mixology," Quinary has some of the most inventive cocktails in the city that subvert the five senses.

Can you tell us about the theme of the bar and what is the focus of your cocktails?

Quinary has the sophistication of a speakeasy without the elusive location. The bar itself is moodily lit and sleek without being over-the-top. Almost always busy, but you will never feel neglected.

We offer not only drinks, but an experience. We awaken the five senses with the use of multi dimensional flavors, as well as molecular elements by engaging caviar, air, smoke, and cream. All of which are notably found in the signature Earl Grey Caviar Martini, and another bestseller, Lavender Meringue Pie. You will see us even pairing unusual ingredients with progressive techniques and equipment, playing around with perception, flavor, and science. As *Drinks International* describes, we "might as well be working on the sixth [sense]."

What do you look for when creating a new cocktail for your menu?

Our way is to think out of the box and do things that have never been done before, to let our customers expect the unexpected. The bar team looks for creative and novel ways to create cocktails that are not only delicious, photo-worthy, and speedy to serve, given our high volume, but also are able to open up our customers to new experiences.

How does the food and culture of Hong Kong influence the cocktails that you offer?

Because Hong Kong is a multicultural melting pot, we are heavily influenced by both Eastern and Western cultures, especially food cultures. Like one of our signatures, Quinary Sour, we give it an unexpected oomph with Black Label whisky infused with monk fruit, a natural sweetener native to Southeast Asia that is commonly found in local markets, and homemade umami liquorice syrup, topped with a spritz of bitters and bonito flakes.

We are also inspired by the heritage of Hong Kong—from fishing village to major international metropolis. A perfect example is the Quinary Bloody Mary, a classic twist bursting with local cultures and flavors, with ingredients available at wet markets or the historical Dried Seafood Street in Sheung Wan. The dried scallop and shrimp garnishes call to mind the old fishing villages, while Chinese celery, spicy local vinegar, and homemade umami Shaoxing wine add a localized, exotic touch.

What are the best parts of running a cocktail bar in Hong Kong? Are there any downsides or things that make it difficult?

Best part is that Hong Kong is a dynamic metropolis. There are always novel food trends and new bar openings popping up around the corner, which allow us to observe, adapt, and reflect, and at the same time experiment and push our limits. We are lying if we tell you that running a bar business is easy, but we grow from challenges, and challenges are opportunities.

Blue Hawaiian, Brandy Alexander, Pink Squirrel, Rusty Nail, Tom Collins, White Russian, Grasshopper, Rob Roy, Pink Lady: If you had to pick one of these classic cocktails to add to your cocktail menu how would you reimagine your choice to make it fit in with your style?

I would recreate a Tom Collins. Like some of the most cherished timeless classics, it is a very simple cocktail—a basic combination of a base spirit, citrus, sugar, and bubbles—so straightforward it allows great capacity for a twist.

To serve it at Quinary, we would replace lemon juice with grapefruit juice, sugar with homemade jasmine tea syrup, and soda with elderflower-flavored soda. You can imagine it being more rounded and complex with a floral touch.

Do you have a favorite cocktail?

Boulevardier—whisky, vermouth, Campari.

Do you have a favorite alcohol to work with when making cocktails?

Bourbon and rye whiskies always come first to my mind.

COOL LAGOON

GARNISH: FROZEN GREEN GRAPES & 1 SPRIG OF BASIL

Pickled Jalapeño Pepper Syrup: Add 5 slices of pickled jalapeño and a dash of the brine to a basic simple syrup when it is boiling. After 1 minute, remove from heat, let cool, and strain before using.

Place the basil in a cocktail shaker and muddle. Add ice and the remaining ingredients and shake vigorously. Strain into a rocks glass filled with ice and garnish with the frozen grapes and sprig of basil.

INGREDIENTS:

- 1 OZ. PICKLED JALAPEÑO PEPPER SYRUP
- 6 THAI BASIL LEAVES
- 1 HANDFUL OF ITALIAN BASIL LEAVES
- 1½ OZ. IRON BALLS GIN
- 1 OZ. ITALICUS ROSOLIO DI BERGAMOTTO LIQUEUR
- ⅓ OZ. PAVAN LIQUEUR
- DASH OF THE BITTER TRUTH CUCUMBER BITTERS

LAVENDER MERINGUE PIE

GARNISH: 1 DRIED LEMON WHEEL

Combine all of the ingredients, except for the marshmallow foam, in a cocktail shaker filled with ice and shake vigorously. Strain into a coupe, top with marshmallow foam, and garnish with the dried lemon wheel. If desired, caramelize marshmallow foam with a blowtorch.

INGREDIENTS:

- 1½ OZ. LIMONCELLO
- ¾ OZ. LAVENDER GIN
- 1 OZ. FRESH LEMON JUICE
- 2 TEASPOONS EGG WHITE
- 2 TEASPOONS SIMPLE SYRUP
- MARSHMALLOW FOAM, FOR TOPPING

WHISK(E)Y

Whisk(e)y is the product of distillation and time, and when you see "whisk(e)y" it is meant to encompass all whiskies and the two spelling variants. The distillation process starts with the creation of a "beer." This beer doesn't taste like the ones you buy in the supermarket (but that's beside the point for purposes of this conversation). This beer is made from malted barley (scotch), corn (bourbon), rye, or a mix of all of the above. It is heated to a boil and, since alcohol reaches its boiling point before water, that alcohol can be captured (as steam), collected, and condensed back into a liquid form that we call whisk(e)y.

Whisk(e)y is my favorite spirit. While I have fondness for them all and truth be told, spirits like vodka and gin are probably more versatile as a cocktail ingredient, for me whiskies have a certain presence that is hard to beat.

So, what is that presence?

Whiskies are multifaceted creatures. Even within a category (let's say bourbon, for example), there are a variety of tastes and flavors that can be had. Evan Williams Single Barrel and Michter's are both bourbons but they do not taste the same. There are bourbons that will burn your face off (George T. Stagg, a cask-strength release that often tops 120 proof, comes to mind), while there are others that you would happily sip in your backyard. Journey into Scotch or Japanese whiskies and you will find yourself in a veritable forest of flavors. I've already accepted the fact that a lifetime is too short to accomplish the task of tasting all of the available options (but I'm still eager to try).

Maybe that wide variation in what you can get from each brand, style, and bottling is what draws me in. Gins don't tend to surprise me. The nose can tell you a lot, and most gins are variations on a theme, with some managing to play the song better than others. Vodkas are designed to fit in wherever you need them. But with whiskies, the nose can lie, and even when you taste the same pour with friends, you aren't necessarily getting the same flavors. This makes whisk(e)y some sort of Choose Your Own Adventure each time you switch bottles. Two bourbons can make wildly different cocktails, as can two scotches. Whiskies can be hard to work with in cocktails, but when you get it right they are quite the pleasure. Now you get the chance to chart your own path.

Favorite Cocktail: I'll be a traditionalist and go for the Old Fashioned. It's my default whisk(e)y cocktail; but, I always look over a bar's menu to see if there is an interesting homegrown creation that catches my eye.

A BRIEF OVERVIEW OF WHISK(E)Y

Unlike gin and vodka, which can be bottled quickly after distillation, whiskies are best when matured. This maturation takes place in oak casks. For bourbon, those casks have to be virgin oak (i.e., never used before). Other whiskies, like Irish, Scotch, and Japanese, have a bit more flexibility and can use oak casks that have already been used to age other spirits. Sherry and Port casks and used bourbon barrels are popular choices but rum, Sauternes, and other wine barrels have been used to great effect.

The name will tell you the geographic origin of the whisk(e)y in question. So Japanese whisky is made in Japan (and some Japanese "whisky" isn't really whisky, but that is a whole other topic, one that is covered in the excellent book *Whisky Rising* by Stefan van Eycken), Indian whiskies like Amrut and Paul John are from India, bourbons are from the United States (and do not have to be from Kentucky, as is sometimes thought), Canadian is from Canada, and scotch is from Scotland. Each country has specific rules about what counts as a whisk(e)y in their region, but so long as a manufacturer follows the rules for the region they are good.

Here are the basic defining, and legally binding, characteristics of the world's whiskies.

By its loosest definition, whisk(e)y is any spirit distilled from grain—usually from a "mash bill" of corn, rye, wheat, malted barley, or a combination thereof. Within this loose category, there are numerous varieties of whisk(e)y—scotch, Tennessee whiskey, bourbon, rye, and Irish whiskey, to name but a few. Each of these is distinguished by differences in their distillation process or the makeup of their mash bill, or both.

Tennessee whiskey shares a similar mash bill and distillation method with bourbon. However, Tennessee whiskey undergoes an additional "mellowing" known as the Lincoln County Process, where the unaged whiskey is slowly filtered through charcoal to give it a smoother flavor.

Named America's Native Spirit by Congress in 1964, bourbon is truly America's signature whiskey, and deeply intertwined with the history of its birthplace, Kentucky. Corn was a favorite crop of Kentucky's early pioneers, many of whom were Scottish and Scots-Irish immigrants.

Having brought the distillation techniques of their homeland with them, it was only a matter of time before they applied them to Kentucky corn. A 51 percent to 80 percent corn mash bill is now enshrined as one of bourbon's defining features, which is what makes it notably sweeter than most whiskies. Furthermore, bourbon must be aged in new, charred oak barrels, lending the spirit a smokiness, as well as notes of caramel and vanilla.

Like bourbon, rye is an entirely American invention. Once popular throughout the northeastern United States and even distilled by George Washington himself, rye whiskey was

almost wiped out by Prohibition. Long eclipsed by other whiskies, rye has recently enjoyed a renaissance, with more and more distilleries capitalizing on its surging popularity every year. Although its flavor profile varies somewhat from label to label, rye whiskey's minimum 51 percent rye grain mash bill makes it a dryer, spicier whisk(e)y, lending a bold, peppery quality to any drink.

Scotch is made and matured in Scotland using malted barley (whole grains of other cereals may be added). It must be aged in oak barrels for at least three years, and spirit caramel is allowed for color (unlike with bourbon). Scotch whisky does not include the *e*, and this naming practice is followed by the Japanese and Canadians.

The mistake that people make with whiskies in general is that they pigeonhole both the flavor and the spirit. They assume all scotch is smoky and that bourbon is too rough to enjoy on its own. There are a fair number of people whose only experience with whisk(e)y is as part of the beer-and-a-shot duo. Yes, it will get the job done (quick inebriation, if that's your thing), but it is akin to visiting Times Square in New York City or Piccadilly Circus in London and assuming you know the entire city. The universe of whisk(e)y is deep. If you are going to make a whisk(e)y cocktail, you need to know the back alleys along with the major thoroughfares.

Here is how it often plays out in a cocktail recipe, especially with scotches. A recipe will call for "scotch" as an ingredient. Fair enough, but how do you as know what type of scotch to use? Do you want a smoky single malt like an Ardbeg or a Laphroaig, or a sweeter one like a Balvenie or Glenmorangie? Perhaps a blend like Johnnie Walker, Compass Box, or Teacher's Highland Cream instead?

A simple rule of thumb is that if the other ingredients are sweet, you may want a scotch with a bit of smoke to cut the sweetness. Otherwise, you are pouring maple syrup on top of honey. Likewise, if the other ingredients are bitter or sour, a non-smoky scotch may be your best option. This is mainly an issue with scotch, but I'd recommend a quick taste of any whisk(e)y you are planning to use in order to familiarize yourself with the flavors you'll be working with. When in doubt, taste.

HOMEMADE IRISH CREAM

Place all of the ingredients in a blender and blend on high for 30 seconds to 1 minute. Pour into a resealable 1-quart container and store in the refrigerator for up to 2 months. Shake well before serving.

INGREDIENTS:

- $1\frac{1}{3}$ CUPS IRISH WHISKEY
- 1 CUP UNSWEETENED COCONUT MILK
- 2 TABLESPOONS SUGAR-FREE CHOCOLATE SYRUP
- 1 (14 OZ.) CAN OF FAT-FREE SWEETENED CONDENSED MILK
- 1 TEASPOON INSTANT COFFEE
- 1 TEASPOON VANILLA EXTRACT
- 1 TEASPOON ALMOND EXTRACT

WASHINGTON APPLE

Combine all ingredients, except for the Diet 7UP, in a cocktail shaker filled with ice. Shake vigorously for 15 to 20 seconds and strain into shot glasses, making sure to leave some space in each glass. Top each glass with Diet 7UP.

INGREDIENTS:

- 1 PART CROWN ROYAL
- 1 PART APPLE VODKA
- 1 PART CRANBERRY JUICE
- DIET 7UP, TO TOP

MASON JAR MINT JULEP

GARNISH: 1 SPRIG OF MINT

Place the mint, sugar, and water in the bottom of a mason jar and muddle. Fill the jar with ice, add the whiskey and the schnapps, and garnish with a mint sprig.

INGREDIENTS:

- 6 MINT LEAVES
- DASH OF POWDERED SUGAR
- 1 PART WATER
- 3 PARTS BOURBON
- DASH OF MINT SCHNAPPS

WHISKEY SUNSET

GARNISH: 1 LEMON WHEEL

Fill a mason jar with ice and add all of the liquid ingredients except the ginger ale. Stir thoroughly, top with the ginger ale, and garnish with the lemon wheel.

INGREDIENTS:

- 2 OZ. BOURBON
- 2 OZ. WHITE WINE
- 1 OZ. LEMONADE
- DASH OF SIMPLE SYRUP
- 3 OZ. GINGER ALE

MASH
VENT

THREE LEAF CLOVER

Fill a shot glass one-third full with Irish Mist. Place a bar spoon upside down so that it is just above the Irish Mist and touching the side of the glass. Slowly and carefully pour the Irish cream over the spoon and into the glass, making a layer that fills the second-third of the glass. Pour the Irish whiskey over the spoon to fill the remainder of the glass.

INGREDIENTS:

- 1 PART IRISH MIST LIQUEUR
- 1 PART IRISH CREAM
- 1 PART IRISH WHISKEY

BOURBON BENDER

Place all of the ingredients in a cocktail shaker filled with ice, shake vigorously for 15 to 20 seconds, and strain into shot glasses.

INGREDIENTS:

- 1 PART BOURBON
- 1 PART AMARETTO
- 1 PART FRESH LIME JUICE

IRISH NUT

Place all of the ingredients in a cocktail shaker filled with ice, shake vigorously for 15 to 20 seconds, and strain into shot glasses.

INGREDIENTS:

- 1 PART FRANGELICO
- 1 PART IRISH WHISKEY
- 1 PART IRISH CREAM

TOE TAG

Combine the ingredients in a shot glass and enjoy.

INGREDIENTS:

- 1 PART WILD TURKEY
- 1 PART JACK DANIEL'S

WHISKEY NUT

GARNISH: 1 ORANGE WHEEL & HANDFUL OF ROASTED PEANUTS

Fill a glass halfway with ice and add the whisk(e)y, orange liqueur, peanut extract, and cola. Stir and garnish with the orange wheel and a handful of peanuts.

INGREDIENTS:

- 2 OZ. WHISK(E)Y
- DASH OF ORANGE LIQUEUR
- 2 DROPS OF PEANUT EXTRACT
- 6 OZ. COLA

BROWN DERBY

GARNISH: 1 GRAPEFRUIT SLICE

Fill a cocktail shaker with ice and add the ingredients. Shake vigorously until thoroughly mixed. Strain into a mason jar filled with ice and garnish with the slice of grapefruit.

Variation: Replace the maple whisk(e)y with 2 oz. bourbon and add 2 drops maple syrup.

INGREDIENTS:

- 2 OZ. MAPLE WHISK(E)Y
- 2 OZ. GRAPEFRUIT JUICE
- ½ OZ. HONEY

RENEGADE LEMONADE

GARNISH: 4 SPRIGS OF MINT & 8 LEMON WHEELS

Place ice in a half-gallon pitcher and add the simple syrup. Add the lemon juice and whisk(e)y and top with the water. Stir until thoroughly mixed, pour into four mason jars filled with ice, and garnish each with a sprig of mint and 2 lemon wheels.

INGREDIENTS:

- 1 CUP SIMPLE SYRUP
- JUICE OF 6 LEMONS
- 1 CUP WHISK(E)Y
- 4 CUPS COLD WATER

SWEET TEA PUNCH

GARNISH: 2 TO 3 LEMON WHEELS

Place the lemon slice, mint leaves, and bourbon in a mixing glass and muddle. Place ice in a mason jar and strain the bourbon mixture into it. Top with the sweet tea and garnish with the lemon wheels.

INGREDIENTS:

- 1 LEMON SLICE
- 2 MINT LEAVES
- 1 PART BOURBON
- 4 PARTS SWEET TEA

THE RISE OF JAPANESE WHISKY

Discerning whisk(e)y connoisseurs started paying attention to Japanese whisky in 2001, after *Whisky Magazine* awarded a Yoichi single cask release "Best of the Best," the first time a non-Scottish whisky had taken the top prize at such a contest. Eyebrows were raised and curiosity was piqued, but interest in Japanese whisky was still a niche phenomenon and would remain so for another seven or eight years. The period between 2005 and 2009 was an exciting time to be discovering Japanese whisky. The quality of all but the bottom-shelf blends was top-notch, prices were low or reasonable, and there was very little competition from other interested parties. The fact that it was such an under-the-radar field—vastly underappreciated and completely uncharted—made it all the more appealing. That has changed considerably. One upside is that more bartenders in Japan are being rightfully recognized as top-notch mixologists, thanks in large part to the Japanese-made whiskies on hand.

BAMBOO LEAF MARTINI

GARNISH: 1 SMALL YUZU WEDGE

Take a bamboo leaf and cut a small incision along the axis of the leaf; take one end of the leaf and pull it through the incision to make a "cup." Place the leaf-cup in a cocktail glass. Fill a mixing glass with ice, add white crème de menthe, and swirl to rinse; discard the excess. Add the whisky, water, and bamboo leaf syrup. Stir to chill and strain into the leaf-cup in the cocktail glass. Squeeze a small piece of yuzu lightly outside the leaf-cup to add an accent to the cocktail.

INGREDIENTS:

- 1 BAMBOO LEAF
- WHITE CRÈME DE MENTHE, TO RINSE
- 1⅓ OZ. TAKETSURU PURE MALT WHISKY
- ⅔ OZ. SOFT WATER
- 1 TEASPOON BAMBOO LEAF SYRUP (SEE PAGE 308, SUBSTITUTE BAMBOO LEAVES FOR THE ROSEMARY)

TATAMI COCKTAIL

GARNISH: 1 LEMON TWIST

Mix the pineapple juice, simple syrup, apricot brandy, and lemon juice in a cobbler shaker; set aside. Mix the whisky and crème de cacao in a mixing glass; set aside. Take the lemongrass stalks and dip them into the bottle of Yamazaki whisky; set aside. Add ice to the cobbler shaker and shake lightly. Double-strain into a cocktail glass and carefully float the liquid in the mixing glass on top. Ignite the lemongrass with a lighter and shake to extinguish. Place the lemongrass stalks in the cocktail glass and garnish with the twist of lemon.

INGREDIENTS:

- 1 OZ. PINEAPPLE JUICE
- ⅓ OZ. SIMPLE SYRUP
- 1 TEASPOON APRICOT BRANDY
- 1 TEASPOON FRESH LEMON JUICE
- ½ OZ. SUNTORY YAMAZAKI 12 YEAR WHISKY
- 1 TEASPOON DARK CRÈME DE CACAO
- 2 (3 TO 4 INCH) STALKS OF LEMONGRASS

THE ZEN BARTENDER

Takayuki Suzuki started working as a bartender when he was around 20 years old. He spent some time barhopping his way from Vancouver to Miami, but returned to Japan because he couldn't get a work visa. Suzuki spent a little over two years working at a bar in Roppongi, Tokyo, and then returned to the U. S. to study at the International School of Bartending in New York. He worked at various bars around town but again couldn't get a work visa. On returning to Tokyo, he was asked to set up a bar at a small luxury hotel in the Nasu Highlands. In April 2003, he became manager of Bar Fifteen at the Shiba Park Hotel. In September of the same year, he set up the bar at the newly opened Park Hotel in Shiodome. He then moved to Nasu, opening what must be the smallest, most remote bar in Japan. The Black Tea Arbor is in the middle of a forest and seats only one person. He works to spread Japanese bartending philosophy through seminars all over the world. He is also the author of an exquisite collection of autobiographical short stories entitled *The Perfect Martini.*

RAINY SEASON

GARNISH: 1 SPRIG OF MINT

Put the whisky, lemon juice, and cucumber in a blender and puree until smooth. Add the umeboshi and blend some more; add the simple syrup and puree to incorporate. Add a small handful of ice and puree; repeat adding ice and pureeing until the mix has the consistency of a smoothie. Spoon into a Nick & Nora glass and garnish with the sprig of mint.

INGREDIENTS:

- 1⅓ OZ. SUNTORY HIBIKI 12 YEAR WHISKY
- 1 TEASPOON FRESH LEMON JUICE
- 4 CUCUMBER SLICES
- ½ TEASPOON UMEBOSHI
- ⅓ OZ. SIMPLE SYRUP

GREEN BREEZE

GARNISH: 2 TO 3 MINT LEAVES

Using a bar spoon, gently muddle the mint and the crème de menthe in a conical highball glass; discard the liqueur. Carve an ice sphere; the diameter should be such that the ice sphere sits in the glass without touching the bottom. Add the whisky, then just enough tonic water so that the mixture just covers the bottom of the ice sphere. Top up with soda. Spank a few mint leaves and use as a garnish.

INGREDIENTS:

- FRESH MINT LEAVES
- SPLASH OF WHITE CRÈME DE MENTHE
- 1 OZ. SUNTORY HAKUSHU 12 YEAR WHISKY
- TONIC WATER
- SODA WATER, TO TOP

JAPANESE RED PINE HIGHBALL

GARNISH: 1 BAMBOO LEAF (OPTIONAL)

Using a bar spoon, gently muddle the fresh mint and crème de menthe in a Riesling glass; discard most of the liqueur. Roll up a sheet of kyogi and insert it in the glass so that it lines the inside; pull one end up so it sticks out of the glass. Place two large ice cubes in the glass. Add the whisky and top up with soda. Garnish with the bamboo leaf, if desired.

**Kyogi is a paper-thin sheet of wood, commonly used to serve food.*

INGREDIENTS:

- FRESH MINT LEAVES, PREFERABLY JAPANESE
- SPLASH OF WHITE CRÈME DE MENTHE
- 1 SHEET OF KYOGI*
- 1½ OZ. SUNTORY YAMAZAKI DISTILLER'S RESERVE WHISKY
- SODA WATER, TO TOP

THE PRODIGY

Hiroyasu Kayama started tending bar when he was 20. Following short stints at various bars, he became head bartender at Bar Amber in Nishi-Azabu, Tokyo. After six years, he decided to strike out on his own. He opened a bar in the Nishi-Shinjuku area of Tokyo in July 2013 and named it BenFiddich (a reversed translation of his last name in Gaelic). Kayama is a keen botanist, so it was wonderfully appropriate that he won the first prize at The Botanist Foraged Cocktail Contest in Japan in July 2015.

GRAIN MARKET

In a cocktail shaker, crush the grapes with a muddler. Add the whisky and Madeira. Add ice, shake vigorously, and double-strain into a cocktail glass.

INGREDIENTS:

- 6–7 KYOHO GRAPES (OR CONCORD GRAPES)
- 1½ OZ. NIKKA COFFEY GRAIN WHISKY
- ⅔ OZ. MEDIUM-SWEET MADEIRA

MAPLE MARRIAGE

GARNISH: 1 STRIP OF YUZU PEEL (OPTIONAL)

Mix the whisky, maple syrup, yuzu juice, and egg white in a cocktail shaker using a hand blender. Add ice, shake until frothy, and strain into a coupe. Carefully add the bitters to the foam's surface in a circular pattern; use the tip of a toothpick to connect the droplets. Garnish with a strip of yuzu peel, if desired.

INGREDIENTS:

- 1⅔ OZ. ICHIRO'S MALT DOUBLE DISTILLERIES WHISKY
- ⅓ OZ. MAPLE SYRUP
- ⅓ OZ. YUZU JUICE
- 1 EGG WHITE
- 8 DROPS OF GINGER BITTERS

FOREST FLAVOR

GARNISH: 1 SAGE LEAF

Thoroughly muddle the sage leaves in a mortar with a pestle (preferably a Japanese mortar, a *suribachi*, with a wooden pestle, a *surikogi*). Add the whisky and muddle some more; add the honey and lime juice and muddle some more. Transfer to a French cocktail shaker, shake with ice to chill, and double-strain over ice into a highball glass. Top up with soda and stir gently; garnish with the additional sage leaf.

INGREDIENTS:

- 4 FRESH SAGE LEAVES
- 1½ OZ. SUNTORY HAKUSHU DISTILLER'S RESERVE WHISKY
- ⅓ OZ. HONEY
- ⅓ OZ. FRESH LIME JUICE
- CLUB SODA, TO TOP

JAPONISM

In a bowl, whisk the egg white until foamy. In another bowl, beat the yolk, shiro-an, and matcha powder until combined. Add the egg white foam and whisk a bit more to incorporate. Add the whisky and sake and whisk to incorporate. Transfer to a French cocktail shaker, shake with ice, and double-strain into a *guinomi* (Japanese earthenware sake cup).

**Shiro-an is white sweet bean paste.*

INGREDIENTS:

- 1 EGG, SEPARATED
- 1 OZ. SHIRO-AN*
- 2 TEASPOONS MATCHA POWDER
- 1½ OZ. FUJISANROKU 50° NON-CHILL FILTERED WHISKY
- ⅔ OZ. DRY SAKE

AROMATIC CHICHIBU

Combine all ingredients in a mixing glass filled with ice, stir, and strain into a Burgundy wine glass. Fill a stemless cocktail glass with crushed ice and place the bowl of the wine glass on the bed of ice.

INGREDIENTS:

- 1⅓ OZ. ICHIRO'S MALT CHICHIBU THE PEATED CASK STRENGTH WHISKY
- ⅔ OZ. BÉNÉDICTINE
- ⅓ OZ. SWEET VERMOUTH
- ⅓ OZ. FRESH BLACK CURRANT PUREE
- 1 TEASPOON FERNET-BRANCA

VENDOME
LOU. KY.

IRISH ROSE

GARNISH: 1 LIME WEDGE

Place the Irish whiskey and lemon-lime soda in a mason jar filled with ice. Squeeze the lemon and lime juices into the jar and add the grenadine. Stir until combined and garnish with the lime wedge.

INGREDIENTS:

- 2 PARTS IRISH WHISKEY
- 3 PARTS LEMON-LIME SODA
- JUICE OF 1 LEMON WEDGE
- JUICE OF 1 LIME WEDGE
- 1 PART GRENADINE

MASON JAR BOURBON PRESS

GARNISH: 1 LEMON SLICE

Place a few large ice cubes in a mason jar and add the bourbon and orange bitters. Fill with the ginger ale and club soda and garnish with the slice of lemon.

INGREDIENTS:

- 2 OZ. BOURBON
- DASH OF ORANGE BITTERS
- 2 OZ. GINGER ALE
- 2 OZ. CLUB SODA

WHISKEY SOUR

GARNISH: 1 MARASCHINO CHERRY

Place the ingredients in a rocks glass filled with ice, stir, and garnish with the maraschino cherry.

INGREDIENTS:

- 2 PARTS WHISK(E)Y
- 1 PART LEMON JUICE
- SPLASH OF WATER
- PINCH OF SUGAR

WHISKEY LEMONADE

Place the ingredients in a rocks glass filled with ice and stir.

INGREDIENTS:

- 3 PARTS PINK LEMONADE
- 1 PART WHISK(E)Y

WHISKEY AND COKE

Place the whisk(e)y and cola in a highball glass filled with ice, stir, and then add the lime juice.

INGREDIENTS:

1 PART WHISK(E)Y

3 PARTS COCA-COLA

JUICE OF 1 LIME

REDNECK LEMONADE

Place the whisk(e)y and hard lemonade in a highball glass filled with ice and stir.

INGREDIENTS:

1 PART WHISK(E)Y

3 PARTS HARD LEMONADE

WHISKEY DANGER

Place the whisk(e)y and lemonade in a rocks glass filled with ice, stir, and top with the cranberry juice.

INGREDIENTS:

1 PART WHISK(E)Y

3 PARTS LEMONADE

1 PART CRANBERRY JUICE

BOURBON SWEET TEA

Place the bourbon and sweet tea in a rocks glass filled with ice, stir, and top with the squeeze of lemon juice.

INGREDIENTS:

1 PART BOURBON

2 PARTS SWEET TEA

SQUEEZE OF LEMON JUICE

THOMPSON'S OLD FASHIONED

GARNISH: 1 STRIP OF ORANGE PEEL & 2 LUXARDO MARASCHINO CHERRIES

Combine the simple syrup and bitters in a rocks glass, fill with ice, and then add the rye. If desired, add the water or club soda. Rub the orange peel around the rim of the glass and use as a garnish along with the cherries.

INGREDIENTS:

- 1 OZ. SIMPLE SYRUP
- 3–4 DASHES OF AROMATIC BITTERS
- 2 OZ. WILLETT FAMILY ESTATE RYE
- SPLASH OF WATER OR CLUB SODA (OPTIONAL)

PERFECT OLD FASHIONED

GARNISH: 1 ORANGE SLICE & 1 MARASCHINO CHERRY

Place the sugar cube in a rocks glass and saturate with the bitters. Add the water and muddle. Fill the glass with ice and add the bourbon. Stir gently and garnish with the slice of orange and maraschino cherry.

INGREDIENTS:

- 1 SUGAR CUBE
- 2 DROPS OF BITTERS
- SPLASH OF WATER
- 2 OZ. WOODFORD RESERVE BOURBON

RED HOUSE OLD FASHIONED

GARNISH: 1 STRIP OF LEMON PEEL

Place the cardamom seed in a mixing glass, add ice and the remaining cocktail ingredients, and stir until chilled. Strain into a double rocks glass containing a sphere of ice and garnish with the strip of lemon peel.

INGREDIENTS:

- 1 CARDAMOM SEED
- 1 OZ. JIM BEAM RYE WHISKEY
- ½ OZ. BITTER TRUTH PIMENTO DRAM
- ½ OZ. DRAMBUIE

POISON GIRL OLD FASHIONED

GARNISH: 1 STRIP OF ORANGE PEEL

Place the cocktail ingredients in a mixing glass filled with ice and stir. Strain into a rocks glass containing one large ice cube and garnish with the strip of orange peel.

INGREDIENTS:

- 2 OZ. BOURBON
- 4 DASHES OF ANGOSTURA ORANGE BITTERS
- DASH OF FEE BROTHERS BLACK WALNUT BITTERS
- DASH OF ANGOSTURA BITTERS
- ½ OZ. SIMPLE SYRUP

CLASSIC OLD FASHIONED

GARNISH: 1 MARASCHINO CHERRY

The Old Fashioned is commonly attributed to James E. Pepper, bartender at the Pendennis Club in Louisville, Kentucky, circa 1880. Pepper's version used bourbon. But the name more accurately reflects a style of cocktail making that has existed since the concept of a mixed drink, namely, combining a spirit with some sugar, some water, and bitters. After Prohibition, a fruit garnish became part of the Old Fashioned preparation. Over time fruit has been muddled, different whiskies have been used, and garnishes from orange slices and maraschino cherries to pineapple pieces and pickled mushrooms have been deployed. A 1936 *New York Times* piece, laments such flourishes. Penned by "Old Timer," the article "Aftermath of Prohibition: Proper Mixing of Drinks Seems to Be All but a Lost Art" opines: "Consider, for instance, the Old-Fashioned cocktail. Time was when the affable and sympathetic bartender moistened a lump of sugar with Angostura bitter, dropped in a lump of ice, neither too large or too small, stuck in a miniature bar spoon and passed the glass to the client with a bottle of good bourbon from which said client was privileged to pour his own drink." Today, with mixology having rediscovered its appreciation for vintage cocktail recipes, the classic Old Fashioned has returned to its pared-down roots, relying on the quality of the ingredients—though there probably aren't any bartenders who will let you keep the bottle of bourbon.

IT'S A *MAD MEN* WORLD

The television series *Mad Men* romanticized the liquid lunch days of 1960s corporate America through the advertising executives whose boozy blue-skying was subsidized by expense accounts. Don Draper, the show's central character, taught viewers how to drink like it was their profession. Draper's appreciation for an Old Fashioned is established in the opening scene of the first season; Draper is introduced to the world sitting in a bar, working, and drinking his cocktail of choice. Over 7 seasons, many Old Fashioneds are consumed, though Draper is only seen making one (and a bastardized version at that) in season 3. But his fondness for an old drink in an era where everything seems to be changing says quite a bit about why fiction spurred a real-life resurrection of this cocktail, and why it has endured.

INGREDIENTS:

- PINCH OF SUGAR
- 1 STRIP OF ORANGE PEEL
- SPLASH OF WATER
- 2 DROPS OF BITTERS
- 2 OZ. BOURBON

Place the sugar, orange peel, water, and bitters in a rocks glass and muddle. Fill the glass with ice, add the bourbon, stir, and garnish with the maraschino cherry.

BUDGET OLD FASHIONED

Place the simple syrup, bitters, and maraschino cherry in a glass and muddle. Fill the glass with ice, add the bourbon, and stir gently.

INGREDIENTS:

- SPLASH OF SIMPLE SYRUP
- 2 DROPS OF BITTERS
- 1 MARASCHINO CHERRY
- 2 OZ. EVAN WILLIAMS BOURBON

THE FRENCH OLD FASHIONED

GARNISH: 1 ORANGE WHEEL & 1 MARASCHINO CHERRY

Place the whisky, bitters, sugar, and club soda in a rocks glass, stir to combine, and add ice. Garnish with the orange wheel and the maraschino cherry.

INGREDIENTS:

- 2 OZ. BASTILLE WHISKY
- 4 DASHES OF ANGOSTURA BITTERS
- 1 TEASPOON SUGAR
- SPLASH OF CLUB SODA

TRUFFLE OLD FASHIONED

GARNISH: FRESHLY SHAVED BLACK TRUFFLE

Smoked Mushroom Cordial: Dehydrate a handful of portobello peelings and stems. Put the completely dehydrated mushroom pieces in an airtight container, place applewood chips in a smoking gun, and add smoke to the container. Shake the container and let them smoke for 3 minutes.

Pour hot water over the mushrooms and then strain. Squeeze the mushrooms to remove all of the liquid. Add an equivalent amount of white sugar to the broth, stir to dissolve, and add a pinch of white truffle salt.

Place the cocktail ingredients in a mixing glass filled with ice and stir until chilled. Strain into a rocks glass filled with ice and garnish with the shaved black truffle.

Tip: To fat wash any liquor, combine 3 tablespoons of the chosen fat and 1 cup of liquor. Place mixture in freezer overnight and skim off fat before using.

INGREDIENTS:

- ¼ OZ. SMOKED PORTOBELLO MUSHROOM CORDIAL
- 2 OZ. CHIVAS REGAL 12, FAT WASHED WITH BLACK TRUFFLE BUTTER
- 2 DASHES OF SCRAPPY'S CHOCOLATE BITTERS

THE BROOKLYN

Place all of the ingredients in a mixing glass filled with ice, stir, and strain into a coupe.

INGREDIENTS:

- 1½ OZ. RYE WHISKEY
- 1½ OZ. DRY VERMOUTH
- ½ TEASPOON LUXARDO
- ½ TEASPOON AMER PICON

EMPLOYEES ONLY MANHATTAN

GARNISH: 1 LEMON TWIST

Place the rye, vermouth, Grand Marnier, and bitters in a mixing glass, add large ice cubes, and stir for 40 revolutions. Strain into a chilled cocktail glass and garnish with the lemon twist.

INGREDIENTS:

- 1½ OZ. RITTENHOUSE RYE
- 1¾ OZ. COCCHI VERMOUTH DI TORINO
- ½ OZ. GRAND MARNIER
- 3 DASHES OF ANGOSTURA BITTERS

THE ENABLER

Pour a gallon of iced tea into a 5-gallon jug. Add a gallon of whisk(e)y and alternate between the whisk(e)y and iced tea until the jug is full. Turn the jug over onto a water cooler and enjoy.

INGREDIENTS:

- 3 GALLONS ICED TEA
- 2 GALLONS WHISK(E)Y

CELTIC COFFEE

Place the Jameson in a mug and pour the coffee on top. Add the Baileys, stir, add the sugar, and stir again.

INGREDIENTS:

- 1 PART JAMESON IRISH WHISKEY
- 4 PARTS HOT COFFEE
- 1 PART BAILEYS IRISH CREAM
- SUGAR, TO TASTE

WAKEUP CIDER

Place the whisk(e)y and cider in a rocks glass filled with ice. Top with the sparkling cider and stir.

INGREDIENTS:

- 1 PART WHISK(E)Y
- 2 PARTS APPLE CIDER
- 1 PART SPARKLING CIDER

SIMPLE MANHATTAN

GARNISH: 1 MARASCHINO CHERRY

Place the cocktail ingredients in a mixing glass filled with ice and stir. Strain into a cocktail glass and garnish with the maraschino cherry.

INGREDIENTS:

- 3 PARTS RYE WHISKEY
- 1 PART SWEET VERMOUTH
- 2 DROPS OF BITTERS

GENTLEMAN'S MANHATTAN

GARNISH: 1 CHERRY OR LEMON TWIST

Place the cocktail ingredients in a cocktail shaker, add ice, and shake until chilled. Strain into a chilled cocktail glass and garnish with a cherry or a lemon twist.

INGREDIENTS:

- 2 PARTS GENTLEMAN JACK TENNESSEE WHISKEY
- ½ PART SWEET VERMOUTH
- ½ PART DRY VERMOUTH
- 2 DASHES OF BITTERS

SUMMER MANHATTAN

GARNISH: 1 LEMON TWIST

Place the rye, Dubonnet Rouge, and bitters in a mixing glass filled with ice and stir. Strain into a cocktail glass and garnish with the lemon twist.

INGREDIENTS:

- 2 OZ. OLD OVERHOLT RYE WHISKEY
- 1 OZ. DUBONNET ROUGE
- 3 DASHES OF REGAN'S ORANGE BITTERS NO. 6

SMOKY MANHATTAN

GARNISH: 1 CHERRY OR ORANGE TWIST

Place the rye, Amaro, and bitters in a mixing glass filled with ice and stir until chilled. Strain into a cocktail glass and garnish with a cherry or an orange twist.

INGREDIENTS:

- 2 OZ. OLD OVERHOLT RYE WHISKEY
- ¾ OZ. CAPPELLETTI AMARO SFUMATO RABARBARO
- 2 DASHES OF REGAN'S ORANGE BITTERS NO. 6

BUDGET SOUR

GARNISH: 1 LEMON SLICE

Place the whiskey and sour mix in a rocks glass filled with ice, stir until combined, and garnish with the lemon slice.

INGREDIENTS:

1 PART RYE WHISKEY

2 PARTS SOUR MIX

ROB ROY

GARNISH: 1 MARASCHINO CHERRY

Place the cocktail ingredients in a mixing glass filled with ice and stir gently to avoid bruising the drink. Place the cherry in a cocktail glass and strain the cocktail into the glass.

INGREDIENTS:

2 OZ. SCOTCH (EITHER A BLEND OR A SMOKY SINGLE MALT, DEPENDING ON YOUR PREFERENCE)

1 OZ. SWEET VERMOUTH

2 DROPS OF BITTERS

TWISTED JULEP

GARNISH: MINT LEAVES & BLUEBERRIES

Place the mint leaves and the brown sugar in a double rocks glass and muddle. Add the blueberries, muddle, and then add the peach nectar and bourbon. Stir, fill the glass with crushed ice, and garnish with the additional mint and blueberries.

INGREDIENTS:

4–6 MINT LEAVES

PINCH OF BROWN SUGAR

4 BLUEBERRIES

½ PART PEACH NECTAR

2 OZ. JIM BEAM BLACK

BLACKBERRY SAGE JULEP

GARNISH: 1 BLACKBERRY & 1 SPRIG OF SAGE

Place the blackberries in a cocktail shaker, muddle, and then add ice, the sage, syrup, and bourbon. Shake gently for 5 seconds, strain into a rocks glass, and cover with crushed ice. Garnish with the additional blackberry and sprig of sage.

INGREDIENTS:

2 BLACKBERRIES

1 SPRIG OF SAGE

½ OZ. TURBINADO OR DEMERARA SYRUP

2 OZ. FOUR ROSES SMALL BATCH BOURBON

Four Roses
BOURBON

CLASSIC MINT JULEP

GARNISH: 1 SPRIG OF MINT

When you think of this drink, Kentucky and bourbon come to mind, but the Mint Julep's origins have nothing to do with either association. The word "julep" derives from the Persian word for a sweet, rosewater syrup, *gulab*. In colonial America, it seems that the term was common among Virginia farmers who started their days with a mix of rum, water, sugar, and mint. The establishment of ice houses in the first half of the 19th century allowed a hot and humid part of the country to bask in the refreshing chill of a julep over crushed ice, colloquially called a "hail-storm julep" for a spell. With whisk(e)y ever more available after the Civil War, especially in the South, it, and in particular bourbon, became the spirit of choice for a julep. Kentucky senator Henry Clay is given much credit for helping spread the cocktail's notoriety, but freed slaves working in and running bars in the North likely did as much, if not more. The Kentucky Derby decreed the Mint Julep its official drink in 1938, and these days well over 100,000 of them are served up at Churchill Downs over the two days of races.

"ONE MINT JULEP"

"I'm through with flirtin' and drinkin' whiskey / I got six extra children from a-getting frisky": so sang The Clovers in the 1952 song "One Mint Julep." That one drink was the cause of all the trouble, and the start of a genre of drinking songs being made into pop tunes. Over the years scores of artists covered the original, including Louis Prima, Count Basie, and Sarah Vaughn. But Ray Charles's 1961 instrumental version, arranged by Quincy Jones, on *Genius + Soul = Jazz*, not only became a hit, but helped introduce listeners to the idea of soul music. Legendary producer Creed Taylor wanted to add the line "Just a little bit of soda," but Charles went with "Just a little bit of soul, now."

INGREDIENTS:

- 4 MINT LEAVES, TORN
- 1 TEASPOON POWDERED SUGAR
- SPLASH OF WATER
- 2 OZ. MAKER'S MARK BOURBON

Place the mint leaves, powdered sugar, and water at the bottom of a glass and muddle. Fill the glass with cracked ice, add the bourbon, stir gently, and garnish with the sprig of mint.

BUDGET MINT JULEP

GARNISH: 1 SPRIG OF MINT

Place the mint leaves, sugar, and water in a rocks glass and muddle. Fill with ice, add the bourbon, and stir gently. Garnish with the sprig of mint.

INGREDIENTS:

- 4 MINT LEAVES
- 1 TEASPOON SUGAR
- SPLASH OF WATER
- 2 OZ. EVAN WILLIAMS BOURBON

MADAME ROUGE

Place the whisky and Amaro in a mixing glass filled with ice, stir, and strain into a chilled champagne flute. Top with the sparkling wine.

INGREDIENTS:

- 2 OZ. BRENNE SINGLE MALT WHISKY
- 1 OZ. AMARO
- 2 OZ. BRUT SPARKLING WINE

THE BASTILLE CELEBRATION

Combine the whisky and elderflower liqueur in a chilled champagne glass and top with the Champagne.

INGREDIENTS:

- 2 OZ. BASTILLE WHISKY
- SPLASH OF ST-GERMAIN
- CHAMPAGNE, TO TOP

THE LAFAYETTE

Place all of the ingredients in a cocktail shaker filled with ice and shake until chilled. Strain over a few ice cubes into a highball glass.

INGREDIENTS:

- 5 MINT LEAVES, CRUSHED
- 1¾ OZ. BOURBON
- ¾ OZ. LEMON JUICE
- 1¼ OZ. GRAPEFRUIT JUICE
- ¾ OZ. MANDARIN LIQUEUR

THE BASTILLE SOUR

Place all of the ingredients in a cocktail shaker filled with ice, shake vigorously, and strain into a rocks glass.

INGREDIENTS:

- 2 OZ. BASTILLE WHISKY
- ¾ OZ. ST-GERMAIN
- JUICE OF ¾ LEMON
- 1 EGG WHITE

LE BON CHIC BON GENRE (BCBG)

Place the rosemary, orange zest, and agave nectar in a cocktail shaker and muddle. Add ice and the remaining ingredients and shake until chilled. Strain into a highball glass filled with ice.

INGREDIENTS:

- 1 SPRIG OF ROSEMARY
- 1 STRIP OF ORANGE ZEST
- DASH OF AGAVE NECTAR
- 2 OZ. BASTILLE WHISKY
- 2 OZ. DOMAINE DE CANTON
- 1 OZ. WHITE WINE
- 2 OZ. APPLE CIDER
- SPLASH OF FRESH LEMON JUICE

THE YEAR OF THE FRENCHMAN

Place all of the ingredients, except the hibiscus liqueur, in a cocktail shaker filled with ice and shake until chilled. Strain into a chilled coupe and float the hibiscus liqueur on top.

INGREDIENTS:

- 2 OZ. BRENNE SINGLE MALT WHISKY
- ½ OZ. AGAVE NECTAR
- ¾ OZ. FRESH LIME JUICE
- 3 DASHES OF CELERY BITTERS
- 1 TEASPOON SOREL (OR OTHER HIBISCUS LIQUEUR), TO FLOAT

BOXING ROOM'S HIGHBALL

GARNISH: 1 LEMON WEDGE

Place the cocktail ingredients in a Collins glass filled with ice, stir until chilled, and garnish with the lemon wedge.

INGREDIENTS:

- 1½ OZ. RYE WHISKEY (GEORGE DICKEL PREFERRED)
- 4 OZ. ROOT BEER (ABITA PREFERRED)
- 3 DASHES OF ABSINTHE

WHALEN SMASH

GARNISH: 1 LIME OR LEMON SLICE (OPTIONAL)

Juice the lemon wedges into a rocks glass and drop the squeezed wedges into the glass. Add the mint, muddle, and then add ice. Add the bourbon, top with the ginger beer, and stir. Garnish with a lime or lemon slice, if desired.

INGREDIENTS:

- ½ LEMON, CUT INTO THIRDS
- 4 MINT LEAVES
- 3 PARTS BOURBON
- 1 PART GINGER BEER

MISH MASH

Fill a glass with ice and add the bourbon, triple sec, and simple syrup. Stir until combined, and then add the splash of grenadine.

INGREDIENTS:

- 2 PARTS BOURBON
- 1 PART TRIPLE SEC
- 1 PART SIMPLE SYRUP
- SPLASH OF GRENADINE

1789

Place all of the ingredients in a mixing glass filled with ice, stir until combined, and strain into a cocktail glass.

INGREDIENTS:

- ½ OZ. BONAL GENTIANE-QUINA
- ½ OZ. LILLET BLANC
- 1⅓ OZ. BASTILLE WHISKY

14 JULLIET

Fig Syrup: Add 4 halved figs to a basic simple syrup recipe when it is boiling and press down on the figs to release their juices. When the sugar is dissolved, remove from heat, let cool, and strain before using.

Place the lime juice, whisky, and fig syrup in a cocktail glass filled with ice, stir, and top with the ginger beer.

INGREDIENTS:

- ½ TABLESPOON FIG SYRUP
- JUICE OF 4 LIME WEDGES
- 2 OZ. BASTILLE WHISKY
- GINGER BEER, TO TOP

BONAL
APÉRITIF
des Montagnes de la Grande
QUINQUINA VIN
MAISON FONDÉE EN
DISTILLERIE
PRODUIT DE

THE LAST CALL

Place the ingredients in a cocktail shaker filled with ice, shake until chilled, and strain into a chilled coupe.

INGREDIENTS:

2 OZ. BRENNE SINGLE MALT WHISKY

1 OZ. SOREL (OR OTHER HIBISCUS LIQUEUR)

YUZU CORN

GARNISH: 1 YUZU TWIST

Place the lemon cress leaves in a cocktail shaker and muddle. Add ice and the remaining cocktail ingredients and shake vigorously. Strain into a rocks glass containing a large sphere of ice and garnish with the twist of yuzu.

INGREDIENTS:

6 LEMON CRESS LEAVES

1¾ OZ. NIGORI YUZUSHU

1⅓ OZ. HUDSON NEW YORK CORN WHISKEY

½ OZ. FERNANDO DE CASTILLO ANTIQUE FINO

2 TEASPOONS LUXARDO

2 DASHES OF HONEY

DE LA BRETAGNE

Place all of the ingredients in a mixing glass without ice and use a small whisk to aerate the mixture. Swizzle to combine the mixture and pour into a coupe or cocktail glass.

INGREDIENTS:

1 OZ. RYE WHISKEY

¾ OZ. POMMEAU DE BRETAGNE

½ OZ. BÉNÉDICTINE

½ TABLESPOON HYDROMEL OR MEAD

4 DASHES OF ANISE EXTRACT

BLACK POINT A LA FRANCAISE

GARNISH: 1 DRIED ORANGE WHEEL

Place all of the ingredients in a mixing glass filled with ice and stir. Strain into a Nick & Nora glass and garnish with the dried orange wheel.

INGREDIENTS:

1½ OZ. JOHNNIE WALKER DOUBLE BLACK

½ TABLESPOON PICON CLUB ORANGE LIQUEUR BITTERS

½ TABLESPOON YELLOW CHARTREUSE

1 TEASPOON GRAND MARNIER

MOONFLOWER

Place all of the ingredients, except for the Perrier, in a mixing glass filled with ice and gently stir for 3 seconds. Strain into a Collins glass filled with ice, add the Perrier, and stir until well combined.

INGREDIENTS:

- 1½ OZ. CHIVAS REGAL 12
- 2 OZ. COLD-BREWED COFFEE
- ½ OZ. DUBONNET ROUGE
- 5 DROPS OF ST. GEORGE ABSINTHE VERT
- 1 TABLESPOON PERRIER

NIGHT BIRD

Place all of the ingredients in a mixing glass filled with ice, stir, and strain into a chilled cocktail glass.

INGREDIENTS:

- 1¾ OZ. TALISKER STORM
- 1 SPOONFUL OF CALVADOS GUM SYRUP
- 5 DASHES OF CRÈME DE VIOLETTE
- 2 DROPS OF DR. ADAM ELMEGIRAB'S TEAPOT BITTERS

BOBBY BURNS

GARNISH: 1 LEMON TWIST

Place all of the ingredients in a mixing glass filled with ice and stir for 30 seconds. Strain into a chilled coupe and garnish with the lemon twist.

INGREDIENTS:

- 2 OZ. SPENCERFIELD SPIRIT CO. SHEEP DIP OR JOHNNIE WALKER BLACK
- 1 OZ. DOLIN VERMOUTH DE CHAMBÉRY ROUGE
- ¼ OZ. BÉNÉDICTINE
- DASH OF REGAN'S ORANGE BITTERS NO. 6

PENICILLIN

Honey-Ginger Syrup: Add 1 part water, 1 part honey, and a 2-inch piece of fresh ginger to a saucepan. Bring to a boil, remove from heat, let cool, and remove the piece of ginger before using.

Place the blended scotch, lemon juice, and honey-ginger syrup in a cocktail shaker filled with ice and shake vigorously. Strain into a rocks glass filled with ice and pour the Islay scotch over the back of a spoon so that it floats delicately on top.

INGREDIENTS:

- ¾ OZ. HONEY-GINGER SYRUP
- 2 OZ. BLENDED SCOTCH
- ¾ OZ. FRESH LEMON JUICE
- ¼ OZ. SMOKY ISLAY SCOTCH (COMPASS BOX THE PEAT MONSTER, LAPHROAIG, OR LAGAVULIN RECOMMENDED), TO FLOAT

WHISKY SOUR CERISE

GARNISH: 2 LUXARDO MARASCHINO CHERRIES

Place the cocktail ingredients in a cocktail shaker filled with ice and shake until chilled. Strain into a rocks glass filled with ice and garnish with the Luxardo maraschino cherries.

INGREDIENTS:

- **1½ OZ. BRENNE SINGLE MALT WHISKY**
- **1–2 OZ. FRESH LEMON JUICE**
- **1½ TEASPOONS SIMPLE SYRUP**
- **1½ TEASPOONS LUXARDO**

BOULEVARDIER

GARNISH: 1 LEMON TWIST

Place the cocktail ingredients in a mixing glass filled with ice and stir. Strain into a coupe and garnish with the lemon twist.

INGREDIENTS:

- **1 OZ. RITTENHOUSE RYE**
- **1 OZ. OLD OVERHOLT RYE WHISKEY**
- **1 OZ. CAMPARI**
- **⅓ OZ. CARPANO ANTICA SWEET VERMOUTH**
- **⅔ OZ. CINZANO ROSSO**

NEW YORK SOUR

GARNISH: 1 LEMON WHEEL & 1 BRANDIED CHERRY

Place the scotch, simple syrup, and lemon juice in a cocktail shaker filled with ice and shake. Strain into a rocks glass filled with ice and gently pour the wine over the back of a spoon so that it floats delicately on top. Skewer the garnishes and balance them on the rim.

INGREDIENTS:

- **2 OZ. FAMOUS GROUSE SMOKY BLACK SCOTCH**
- **¾ OZ. SIMPLE SYRUP**
- **¾ OZ. FRESH LEMON JUICE**
- **¼ OZ. DRY RED WINE, TO FLOAT**

TRINIDAD SOUR

Place all of the ingredients in a cocktail shaker filled with ice, shake until chilled, and strain into a coupe.

INGREDIENTS:

- **1½ OZ. ANGOSTURA BITTERS**
- **½ OZ. RYE WHISKEY**
- **¾ OZ. LEMON JUICE**
- **1 OZ. ORGEAT**

BLOOD, LUST, AND DIAMONDS

GARNISH: 1 CHERRY

Place the cocktail ingredients in a cocktail glass filled with ice and stir until chilled. Strain into a coupe and garnish with the cherry.

INGREDIENTS:

- 2 OZ. RYE WHISKEY
- ¾ OZ. BONAL GENTIANE-QUINA
- ½ OZ. COGNAC
- DASH OF ANGOSTURA BITTERS
- DASH OF PEYCHAUD'S BITTERS
- DASH OF AMARETTO

LITTLE ITALY

GARNISH: 2 LUXARDO MARASCHINO CHERRIES

Place the rye, Cynar, and vermouth in a mixing glass and fill with ice. Stir, strain into a chilled cocktail glass, and garnish with the cherries.

INGREDIENTS:

- 2 OZ. RITTENHOUSE RYE
- ½ OZ. CYNAR
- ¾ OZ. MARTINI & ROSSI SWEET VERMOUTH

SFORZANDO

GARNISH: 1 ORANGE TWIST

Place the cocktail ingredients in a mixing glass filled with ice and stir. Strain into a cocktail glass and garnish with the orange twist.

INGREDIENTS:

- 1 OZ. RITTENHOUSE RYE
- ¾ OZ. DEL MAGUEY CHICHICAPA MEZCAL
- ½ OZ. BÉNÉDICTINE
- ½ OZ. DOLIN BLANC
- 2 DASHES OF BITTERMENS XOCOLATL MOLE BITTERS

LOUISIANA PURCHASE PUNCH

GARNISH: LEMON TWISTS

Place all of the ingredients in a large punch bowl and stir to combine. Add ice and stir until chilled. Garnish each glass with a lemon twist

OLEO SACCHARUM

Place the peels and the sugar in a large bowl and toss to combine. Using some serious elbow grease, use a muddler or the back of a heavy wooden spoon to pound the peels until they express their oils. Let sit for 30 minutes to 1 hour. Strain through a fine sieve and discard the peels.

INGREDIENTS:

- 4 CUPS DOMAINE DE CANTON
- 3 CUPS BOURBON
- 3 CUPS AMONTILLADO SHERRY
- 4 CUPS BREWED BLACK TEA
- 4 CUPS BLENHEIM HOT GINGER ALE
- 4 CUPS LEMON JUICE
- 2½ CUPS OLEO SACCHARUM (SEE RECIPE BELOW)

OLEO SACCHARUM:

- 8 LEMON PEELS
- 2 ORANGE PEELS
- 2½ CUPS GRANULATED SUGAR

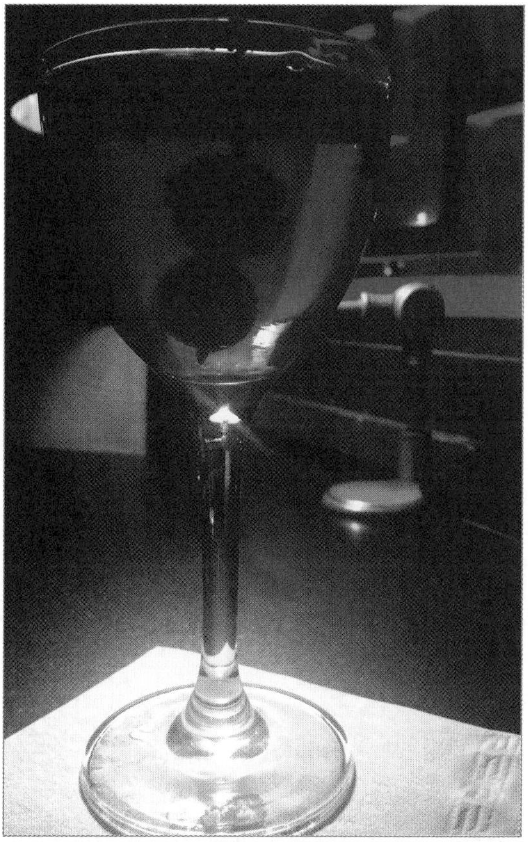

VIEUX CARRÉ (THE OLD QUARTER)

GARNISH: 1 LEMON TWIST

Place the cocktail ingredients in a mixing glass filled with ice and stir. Strain into a rock glass filled with ice and garnish with the lemon twist.

INGREDIENTS:

- ¾ OZ. RYE WHISKEY
- ¾ OZ. COGNAC
- ¾ OZ. SWEET VERMOUTH
- 1 SPOONFUL OF BÉNÉDICTINE
- DASH OF PEYCHAUD'S BITTERS
- DASH OF ANGOSTURA BITTERS

WHISKEY BUSINESS

GARNISH: 1 ANCHO CHILI POWDER–DUSTED LEMON WHEEL

Place the cocktail ingredients in a cocktail shaker filled with ice and shake until chilled. Strain into a rocks glass containing a large ice cube and garnish with the lemon wheel.

INGREDIENTS:

- 1 OZ. RITTENHOUSE RYE
- 1 OZ. ANCHO REYES
- ½ OZ. LEMON JUICE
- ½ OZ. CINNAMON SYRUP (SEE RECIPE BELOW)

CINNAMON SYRUP

Place all of the ingredients in a medium saucepan and bring to a simmer over low heat while stirring to dissolve the sugar. When the sugar is dissolved, remove from heat and let sit overnight. Strain before using.

CINNAMON SYRUP:

- 2 CUPS SUGAR
- 1 CUP WARM WATER
- 7 CINNAMON STICKS

MARGOT TENENBAUM

Place all of the ingredients in a cocktail shaker filled with ice, shake vigorously, and strain into a coupe.

INGREDIENTS:

- 2 OZ. BOURBON
- ¾ OZ. FRESH LEMON JUICE
- ½ OZ. HONEY SYRUP
- ½ OZ. ZUCCA RABARBARO AMARO

DON LOCKWOOD

GARNISH: 1 LONG ORANGE TWIST

Add the ingredients to a rocks glass in the order that they are listed. Add ice, stir 10 to 15 times, and garnish with the orange twist.

INGREDIENTS:

- DASH OF ANGOSTURA BITTERS
- 2 DASHES OF CHOCOLATE BITTERS
- ⅜ OZ. MAPLE SYRUP
- 1 OZ. ISLAY SCOTCH
- 1 OZ. BOURBON

BANKER'S PUNCH

GARNISH: GRATED NUTMEG

Place the cocktail ingredients in a cocktail shaker filled with ice and shake until chilled. Strain into a rocks glass containing a few large ice cubes and grate the nutmeg over the drink.

INGREDIENTS:

- 3 DASHES OF AROMATIC BITTERS
- ¾ OZ. LIME JUICE
- ¾ OZ. RASPBERRY CORDIAL
- ¾ OZ. GRAHAM'S LBV PORT
- ¾ OZ. REDBREAST 12 YEAR OLD
- ¾ OZ. DEAD RABBIT JAMAICAN RUM BLEND (¼ OZ. EACH OF LIGHT, GOLD, AND DARK RUM)

PSYCHO KILLER

Infused Campari: Place 1 cup Campari and 1 tablespoon of cacao nibs in a mason jar, shake, and let steep for 1 hour, while shaking the jar occasionally. Strain before using.

Place all of the ingredients in a mixing glass filled with ice and stir until chilled. Strain into a cocktail glass.

INGREDIENTS:

- ¾ OZ. CACAO NIB-INFUSED CAMPARI
- 2 DASHES OF ABSINTHE
- ½ OZ. CRÈME DE CACAO
- ½ OZ. GIFFARD BANANE DU BRESIL LIQUEUR
- 2 OZ. REDBREAST 12 YEAR OLD

MAXIMUM WAGE

GARNISH: 1 ORANGE TWIST

Add the ingredients to a rocks glass in the order that they are listed. Add ice, stir, and garnish with the orange twist.

INGREDIENTS:

- 2 OZ. ELIJAH CRAIG 12-YEAR-OLD BOURBON
- ⅜ OZ. BYRRH GRAND QUINQUINA
- ⅜ OZ. PIERRE FERRAND DRY CURAÇAO
- 2 DASHES OF ANGOSTURA BITTERS

HIGHLAND CREAM

Place all of the ingredients in a cocktail shaker filled with ice, shake vigorously, and strain into a cocktail glass.

INGREDIENTS:

- 1 OZ. GRANT'S SCOTCH WHISKY
- 2 OZ. COFFEE LIQUEUR
- 2 OZ. CRÈME DE CACAO
- 1 OZ. ESPRESSO
- 4 OZ. CRÈME FRAÎCHE

ANALOGUE

GARNISH: 1 LEMON TWIST

Place the cocktail ingredients in a mixing glass filled with ice and stir until chilled. Strain into a rocks glass containing a large ice cube and garnish with the lemon twist.

INGREDIENTS:

- 1 OZ. FOUR ROSES BOURBON
- 1½ OZ. DARK RUM
- ½ OZ. VELVET FALERNUM
- ¼ OZ. DOMAINE DE CANTON
- ¼ OZ. ST. ELIZABETH ALLSPICE DRAM
- 3 DASHES OF ANGOSTURA BITTERS

TENNESSEE BELLINI

Combine the whiskey and peach puree in a champagne flute, and then top with Champagne.

INGREDIENTS:

- 1 PART GENTLEMAN JACK TENNESSEE WHISKEY
- 1 PART PEACH PUREE
- CHAMPAGNE, TO TOP

THE SCOTCH CRINGE

Place the egg and lime juice in a cocktail shaker and dry shake. Add the remaining ingredients, briefly muddle the watermelon, and then add ice. Shake vigorously and strain into a Collins glass filled with ice.

INGREDIENTS:

- 1 EGG
- ¾ OZ. LIME JUICE
- 2 OZ. SCOTCH
- ¾ OZ. SIMPLE SYRUP
- 2 WATERMELON CUBES

NIGHTTRIPPER

GARNISH: 1 STRIP OF ORANGE PEEL

Place all of the ingredients in a mixing glass filled with ice and stir until chilled. Strain into a brandy snifter filled with ice and garnish with the strip of orange peel.

INGREDIENTS:

- 1¾ OZ. BOURBON
- ¾ OZ. AMARO
- ¼ OZ. STREGA
- 2 DASHES OF PEYCHAUD'S BITTERS

DORIAN GRAY

GARNISH: GRATED NUTMEG

Infused Maple Syrup: Place 1 sprig of rosemary and 1½ oz. maple syrup in a microwave-safe bowl and microwave on high for 30 seconds. Let cool and then discard the rosemary.

Place the cocktail ingredients in a cocktail shaker filled with ice and shake vigorously. Strain into a coupe and grate the nutmeg over the cocktail.

INGREDIENTS:

- ½ OZ. ROSEMARY-INFUSED MAPLE SYRUP
- 1½ OZ. BLACK BOTTLE SCOTCH
- ¾ OZ. PÜR LIKÖR WILLIAMS PEAR LIQUEUR
- ¾ OZ. FRESH LEMON JUICE
- ½ OZ. DRY VERMOUTH
- 2 DASHES OF ANGOSTURA BITTERS

MY OLD PIANO

Place the ingredients in a mixing glass filled with ice, stir, and strain into a cocktail glass.

INGREDIENTS:

- 1½ OZ. RITTENHOUSE RYE
- ¾ OZ. CARPANO ANTICA
- ½ OZ. MEZCAL
- ¼ OZ. KÜMMEL
- 2 DASHES OF APPLE BITTERS

PICTURING WILD FIELDS

GARNISH: 1 LEMON TWIST

Place the cocktail ingredients in a mixing glass filled with ice and stir. Strain into a chilled Nick & Nora glass and garnish with the lemon twist.

INGREDIENTS:

- 1 SPOONFUL OF ORGEAT
- ¼ OZ. PÜR LIKÖR ELDERFLOWER
- ½ OZ. SUZE
- ¾ OZ. LA DIABLADA ITALIA PISCO
- 1½ OZ. GLENFIDDICH 12 YEAR OLD SINGLE MALT SCOTCH WHISKY

SCREEN DOOR SLAM

GARNISH: 1 STRIP OF ORANGE PEEL

Infused Aperol: Split one fresh vanilla bean down the middle, place it in a bottle of Aperol, and steep for at least 3 days. Strain the mixture when you are ready to use it, or leave the bean inside the bottle if you prefer a stronger vanilla flavor.

Place all of the cocktail ingredients, other than the absinthe, in a mixing glass filled with ice and stir until well chilled. Rinse a rocks glass with the absinthe, discard the excess, and add a large ice cube. Strain the cocktail into the glass and garnish with the strip of orange peel.

INGREDIENTS:

- 1 OZ. VANILLA-INFUSED APEROL
- 2 OZ. MAKER'S MARK BOURBON
- ¼ OZ. RICH HONEY SYRUP (2:1 HONEY-TO-WATER RATIO)
- ABSINTHE, TO RINSE

GLASGOW MILK PUNCH

GARNISH: 1 LEMON TWIST

Place the cocktail ingredients in a cocktail shaker filled with ice and shake vigorously. Strain into a rocks glass containing a few ice cubes and garnish with the lemon twist.

INGREDIENTS:

- 1½ OZ. COMPASS BOX GREAT KING STREET GLASGOW BLEND
- ½ OZ. COMPASS BOX ORANGERIE
- ½ OZ. OLEO SACCHARUM (SEE PAGE 258)
- 2¼ OZ. WHEY (CLARIFIED MILK WITH LEMON)

THE THIN VEIL

GARNISH: 1 CHERRY

Place the cocktail ingredients in a mixing glass filled with ice and stir. Strain into a coupe and garnish with the cherry.

INGREDIENTS:

- 1½ OZ. BOURBON
- 1 OZ. OLOROSO SHERRY
- ½ OZ. PETER HEERING CHERRY LIQUEUR
- ½ OZ. CRUZAN BLACK STRAP RUM
- ¼ OZ. CYNAR
- 1 SPOONFUL OF NOCINO WALNUT LIQUEUR
- DASH OF BITTERMENS BURLESQUE BITTERS

BIG IRON

GARNISH: 1 ORANGE OR LEMON TWIST

Place the cocktail ingredients in a mixing glass filled with ice and stir. Strain into a rocks glass filled with ice and garnish with your preferred twist.

INGREDIENTS:

- 2 OZ. MISTER KATZ'S ROCK & RYE
- DASH OF ANGOSTURA BITTERS
- DASH OF ORANGE BITTERS

INNUENDO

GARNISH: 1 STRIP OF LEMON PEEL

Peach Syrup: Place 1 cup water and 1 cup sugar in a saucepan and bring to a boil. Add 1 sliced peach to the saucepan, stir, and reduce heat so that the syrup simmers. Cook for 25 minutes, remove from heat, and let cool. Strain before using.

Place the cocktail ingredients in a cocktail shaker filled with ice and shake vigorously. Strain into a rocks glass filled with ice and garnish with the strip of lemon peel.

INGREDIENTS:

- ¾ OZ. PEACH SYRUP
- 2 OZ. CORSAIR TRIPLE SMOKE WHISKEY
- 1 OZ. TEA
- ¼ OZ. LEMON JUICE

BOURBON

WHISKEY SLING

GARNISH: 1 LEMON WHEEL

Place the ingredients in a cocktail shaker filled with ice and shake vigorously. Strain into a rocks glass filled with ice and garnish with a lemon wheel.

INGREDIENTS:

- 4 OZ. GENTLEMAN JACK TENNESSEE WHISKEY
- 1 OZ. LEMON JUICE
- 1½ OZ. SIMPLE SYRUP
- 2 DASHES OF ORANGE BITTERS

JACK & COLA

GARNISH: 1 LIME WHEEL

Place the whiskey and cola in a highball glass filled with ice, stir, and garnish with the lime wheel.

INGREDIENTS:

- 1 PART JACK DANIEL'S OLD NO. 7
- 3 PARTS COLA

JACK & GINGER

GARNISH: 1 LEMON OR LIME SLICE

Place the whiskey and ginger ale in a highball glass filled with ice, stir, and garnish with a slice of lemon or lime.

INGREDIENTS:

- 1 PART JACK DANIEL'S OLD NO. 7
- 3 PARTS GINGER ALE

JACK'S OLD HAUNT

Place the ingredients in a rocks glass, add ice, and stir until chilled.

INGREDIENTS:

- ¾ OZ. JACK DANIEL'S TENNESSEE RYE
- ¾ OZ. COGNAC
- ¾ OZ. NOILLY PRAT ROUGE VERMOUTH
- ¼ TEASPOON BÉNÉDICTINE
- 2 DASHES OF PEYCHAUD'S BITTERS
- 2 DASHES OF ANGOSTURA BITTERS

JACK DANIEL'S
LYNCHBURG, TENNESSEE
JACK DANIEL'S

JACK DANIEL'S

Jack Daniel's, located in Lynchburg, Tennessee, is the best-selling whisk(e)y in the world—moving even more product than Johnnie Walker, which it recently surpassed.

Jasper Newton "Jack" Daniel, born in 1850, was of Irish, Scottish, and Welsh descent. The youngest of 10 children, he learned how to make whiskey in the 1850s from Reverend Dan Call and Call's slave and distiller, Nathan "Nearest" Green. Green became a mentor to Jack, and was instrumental in helping him develop his whiskey. In 1875, Daniel and Call established a distillery. Now a free man, Green was hired as its head distiller. By 1884, Daniel owned the company outright and purchased the land where the distillery now resides.

Daniel died in Lynchburg on October 10, 1911. While there is an apocryphal tale that his death resulted from an infection that sprouted after he kicked the safe in his office, this is not true. He died of blood poisoning. His nephew, Lemuel "Lem" Motlow, ran Jack Daniel's for the next 36 years and built it into one of the biggest brands in the country. The company was sold to the Brown-Forman Corporation in 1956, and at last made it onto the National Register of Historic Places in 1972.

The current distillery is a truly massive operation. Jack Daniel's has six constantly working stills, four column stills and two pot stills, all of which are 100 percent copper. The distillery also has its very own burn station where the charcoal for the "mellowing process" is made in a carefully controlled setting. It is only once the spirit is slowly filtered through charcoal tanks that it becomes Tennessee whiskey. The distillery fills roughly 2,000 barrels of whiskey a day, which will age in one of the 89 rickhouses throughout Lynchburg.

Fact: One-third of all scotch is aged in former Jack Daniel's barrels.

TENNESSEE MULE

GARNISH: 1 LIME WHEEL & 1 SPRIG OF MINT

Place the cocktail ingredients in a copper mug filled with ice, stir, and garnish with the lime wheel and the sprig of mint.

INGREDIENTS:

- 1 PART JACK DANIEL'S OLD NO. 7
- SQUEEZE OF FRESH LIME JUICE
- 3 PARTS GINGER BEER

JACK JULEP

GARNISH: 1 SPRIG OF MINT

Place the cocktail ingredients in a cocktail shaker filled with ice and shake vigorously. Strain into a double rocks glass filled with crushed ice and garnish with an additional sprig of mint.

INGREDIENTS:

- 2 PARTS JACK DANIEL'S OLD NO. 7
- DASH OF SUGAR
- 1 SPRIG OF MINT

SELECT AND STAVE

GARNISH: 1 STRIP OF ORANGE PEEL

Place the cocktail ingredients in a cocktail shaker, add ice, and shake until chilled. Strain into a cocktail glass and garnish with the strip of orange peel.

INGREDIENTS:

- 1 PART JACK DANIEL'S SINGLE BARREL SELECT
- ¾ PART SWEET VERMOUTH
- ¾ PART PETER HEERING CHERRY LIQUEUR
- 1 PART FRESH ORANGE JUICE

JAVA JACK SHOT

Combine the ingredients in a mixing glass and pour into shot glasses or a chilled cocktail glass.

INGREDIENTS:

- 1 PART JACK DANIEL'S OLD NO. 7
- 1 PART COFFEE LIQUEUR

DEAL BREAKER

GARNISH: 1 ORANGE SLICE

Place the whiskey, honey, and bitters in a mixing glass filled with ice and stir. Rinse a cocktail glass with the absinthe and rhubarb bitters, strain the cocktail into it, and garnish with the orange slice.

INGREDIENTS:

- 2 OZ. CORSAIR QUINOA WHISKEY
- ½ OZ. HONEY
- 2 DASHES OF PEYCHAUD'S BITTERS
- ABSINTHE, TO RINSE
- DASH OF RHUBARB BITTERS, TO RINSE

SOUTHERN CHARM

GARNISH: MINT LEAVES

Place the watermelon cubes in a cocktail shaker, muddle, and pour out the juice. Add ice, the bourbon, watermelon syrup, pomegranate liqueur, bitters, lime juice, and mint, shake vigorously, and double-strain into a rocks glass containing crushed ice. Place the cucumber and the soda in a dry cocktail shaker, muddle, and shake vigorously. Double-strain the mixture on top of the cocktail and garnish with additional mint leaves.

INGREDIENTS:

- 3 WATERMELON CUBES
- 2 OZ. FOUR ROSES BOURBON
- 1 OZ. MONIN WATERMELON SYRUP
- ½ OZ. PAMA POMEGRANATE LIQUEUR
- 4–5 DROPS OF BITTERMENS HOPPED GRAPEFRUIT BITTERS
- ½ OZ. LIME JUICE
- 8 MINT LEAVES
- 3 HALF-MOONS OF CUCUMBER
- 1 OZ. MR. Q. CUMBER SODA

BLACK FOREST

GARNISH: 1 STRIP OF LEMON PEEL

Place the cocktail ingredients in a mixing glass filled with ice and stir until chilled. Strain into a snifter and garnish with the strip of lemon peel.

INGREDIENTS:

- 2 OZ. CORSAIR TRIPLE SMOKE WHISKEY
- ½ OZ. HÜNERKOPF ALT (GERMAN HALF-BITTER)
- ¼ OZ. RICH SORGHUM SYRUP (2:1 SORGHUM-TO-WATER RATIO)
- PINCH OF SALT

DARK SIDE

GARNISH: 1 LIME WHEEL

Place the cocktail ingredients in a cocktail shaker, add ice, and shake vigorously. Double-strain into a Collins glass filled with ice and garnish with the lime wheel.

INGREDIENTS:

- 2 OZ. HARTFIELD & CO. WHISKEY
- ¾ OZ. SIMPLE SYRUP
- 1 OZ. BONAL GENTIANE-QUINA
- ¾ OZ. FRESH LIME JUICE
- 7 DASHES OF REGAN'S ORANGE BITTERS NO. 6

BUFFALO BOWTIE

GARNISH: 1 LIME BOW TIE

Combine the bourbon and peach syrup in a highball glass filled with ice, top with ginger ale, and garnish with a lime bow tie.

INGREDIENTS:

- 1½ OZ. BUFFALO TRACE BOURBON
- 1 OZ. PEACH SYRUP (SEE PAGE 266)
- GINGER ALE, TO TOP

POMEGRANATE SMASH

GARNISH: POMEGRANATE SEEDS

Place the cocktail ingredients in a cocktail shaker filled with ice and shake vigorously for 10 seconds. Strain over ice into a rocks glass and garnish with the pomegranate seeds.

INGREDIENTS:

- 2 PARTS MAKER'S MARK 46 BOURBON
- 1 PART POM WONDERFUL POMEGRANATE JUICE
- ½ PART HONEY
- ½ PART FRESH LEMON JUICE

PUNCH 415

GARNISH: MINT LEAVES

Combine the cocktail ingredients in a cocktail shaker filled with ice and shake until chilled. Strain into a rocks glass filled with ice and garnish with the mint leaves.

INGREDIENTS:

- 1½ OZ. FOUR ROSES SINGLE BARREL BOURBON
- ¾ OZ. FRESH LIME JUICE
- ½ OZ. MONIN ORGEAT
- 2 OZ. PINEAPPLE JUICE
- 5 DASHES OF ANGOSTURA BITTERS

THUNDER PUNCH

Place the lemon wheels at the bottom of a Hurricane glass and fill the glass with ice. Place the remaining ingredients, except for the ginger beer, in a cocktail shaker filled with ice and shake for 10 seconds. Strain into the glass and top with the ginger beer.

INGREDIENTS:

- 2–3 LEMON WHEELS
- 1½ OZ. FOUR ROSES YELLOW LABEL BOURBON
- ½ OZ. FINEST CALL PEACH PUREE
- ½ OZ. STIRRINGS BLOOD ORANGE COCKTAIL BITTERS
- ¼ OZ. FINEST CALL LEMON JUICE
- 1½ OZ. REGATTA GINGER BEER

SUMMER CITRUS

GARNISH: 1 LEMON TWIST

Place the cocktail ingredients in a cocktail shaker filled with ice and shake vigorously. Strain into a rocks glass filled with ice and garnish with the lemon twist.

INGREDIENTS:

- 1¼ OZ. FOUR ROSES YELLOW LABEL BOURBON
- ¾ OZ. CLOVER HONEY SYRUP
- ½ OZ. LEMON JUICE
- ½ OZ. GRAPEFRUIT JUICE
- DASH OF ANGOSTURA BITTERS

FOUR ROSES COLLINS

GARNISH: 1 STRIP OF LEMON PEEL & CHERRIES

Place the bourbon, lemon juice, and sugar in a highball glass filled with ice. Top with the club soda, stir, and garnish with the lemon peel and cherries.

INGREDIENTS:

- 1½ OZ. FOUR ROSES BOURBON
- JUICE OF 1 LEMON
- 1 TEASPOON SUGAR
- CLUB SODA, TO TOP

DERBY SEASON

GARNISH: 1 STRIP OF LEMON PEEL

Place the bourbon, lemon juice, and simple syrup in a mixing glass filled with ice and stir. Strain into a wine glass filled with ice, top with the Rosé, and garnish with the strip of lemon peel.

INGREDIENTS:

- 2 OZ. JIM BEAM BLACK
- ¾ OZ. LEMON JUICE
- ¾ OZ. SIMPLE SYRUP
- ½ OZ. DRY ROSÉ

SILVER 75

GARNISH: 1 STRIP OF LEMON PEEL

Place the bourbon, lemon juice, and simple syrup in a mixing glass filled with ice and stir. Strain into a wine glass or coupe and top with the sparkling wine. Express the strip of lemon peel over the glass, and then set it on top of the cocktail.

INGREDIENTS:

- ¾ OZ. FOUR ROSES BOURBON
- ½ OZ. SIMPLE SYRUP
- ½ OZ. LEMON JUICE
- 4 OZ. SPARKLING WINE

MAKER'S MULE

GARNISH: 1 LIME WEDGE & 1 SPRIG OF MINT

Place the bourbon and lime juice in a copper mug filled with ice. Fill with the ginger beer and garnish with the lime wedge and sprig of mint.

INGREDIENTS:

- 1½ PARTS MAKER'S MARK BOURBON
- SPLASH OF LIME JUICE
- GINGER BEER, CHILLED, TO TOP

BUFFALO SMASH

GARNISH: 1 BLACKBERRY & 1 SPRIG OF MINT

Place the blackberries, mint leaves, and the honey syrup in a cocktail shaker and muddle. Add ice, lemon juice, and bourbon and shake vigorously. Double-strain into a rocks glass containing crushed ice, top with the splash of soda water, and garnish with the additional blackberry and the mint sprig.

INGREDIENTS:

- 2 BLACKBERRIES
- 6–8 MINT LEAVES
- 1 PART HONEY SYRUP
- 2 PART LEMON JUICE
- 6 PARTS BUFFALO TRACE BOURBON
- SPLASH OF SODA WATER

KENTUCKY MAID

GARNISH: 1 ENGLISH CUCUMBER SLICE & 1 SPRIG OF MINT

Place the cucumbers in a cocktail shaker and muddle. Add ice and the remaining cocktail ingredients and shake vigorously. Double-strain into a rocks glass filled with ice, stick the sprig of mint through the additional cucumber slice, and garnish the drink with it.

INGREDIENTS:

- 2 ENGLISH CUCUMBER SLICES
- 2 OZ. BUFFALO TRACE BOURBON
- 6 FRESH MINT LEAVES
- ¾ OZ. FRESH LIME JUICE
- ¾ OZ. SIMPLE SYRUP

FAMILY MEAL

GARNISH: 1 STRIP OF LEMON PEEL

Place the coffee concentrate and the bourbon in a rocks or highball glass, add ice, and stir gently. Top with the cola, express the lemon peel over the cocktail, and use it as a garnish.

INGREDIENTS:

- ¼ PART COLD BREW COFFEE CONCENTRATE
- 1½ PARTS MAKER'S MARK BOURBON
- MEXICAN COCA-COLA, TO TOP

AUTUMN LEAVES

GARNISH: 1 STRIP OF LEMON PEEL

Place the cocktail ingredients in a mixing glass filled with ice and stir. Strain into a double rocks glass filled with ice, express the lemon peel over the cocktail, and discard.

INGREDIENTS:

- 1¼ OZ. FOUR ROSES SINGLE BARREL BOURBON
- ¼ OZ. CARPANO ANTICA
- ½ OZ. RAMAZZOTTI AMARO
- DASH OF ANGOSTURA BITTERS

HEARTS ON FIRE

GARNISH: 2 BRANDY-SOAKED CHERRIES

Place the cocktail ingredients in a cocktail glass, stir, and garnish with the brandy-soaked cherries.

INGREDIENTS:

- 2 OZ. BUFFALO TRACE BOURBON
- ¾ OZ. CHAMBORD
- ½ OZ. LUXARDO
- 2 DASHES OF BITTERMENS HELLFIRE HABANERO SHRUB

RISIN' OUTLAW

GARNISH: 1 STRIP OF LEMON PEEL

Add the cocktail ingredients to a rocks glass in the order that they are listed, stir, express the lemon peel over the cocktail, and discard.

INGREDIENTS:

- 1 OZ. FOUR ROSES SINGLE BARREL BOURBON
- 1 OZ. VIDA MEZCAL
- ½ OZ. COCCHI AMERICANO
- ½ OZ. DOLIN BLANC
- ⅛ OZ. DEMERARA SYRUP
- ⅛ OZ. WATER
- 7 DROPS OF ORANGE BITTERS

A DARK ART

GARNISH: 1 JASMINE BLOSSOM (OPTIONAL)

Black Sesame Syrup: Place ½ cup of black sesame seeds in a skillet and toast for 1 to 2 minutes. Remove from the saucepan and set aside. Combine 3 cups sugar and 2 cups hot water and stir until dissolved. Place the sesame seeds and syrup in a blender or food processor and puree for 1 to 2 minutes. Let the mixture sit for 3 to 12 hours, and then strain it through 2 to 3 layers of cheesecloth while squeezing the mixture to remove all of the liquid. Discard the solids, add 2 tablespoons of vodka and ½ teaspoon of orange blossom water, stir, and transfer the syrup to an airtight container. The syrup will keep for approximately 2 weeks.

Combine the cocktail ingredients in a cocktail shaker filled with ice and shake vigorously. Strain into a coupe containing ice and, if desired, garnish with the jasmine blossom.

INGREDIENTS:

- ½ OZ. BLACK SESAME SYRUP
- 1½ OZ. MAKER'S MARK 46 BOURBON
- JUICE OF 1 LIME
- 13 DASHES OF ANGOSTURA BITTERS
- PINCH OF ACTIVATED CHARCOAL

A COWBOY'S BREAKFAST

GARNISH: 2 STRIPS OF CANDIED BACON

Infused Maple Syrup: Combine ½ cup of maple syrup and ½ cup of crispy bacon pieces in a mason jar and let stand for at least 1 hour. Strain before using.

Candied Bacon: Preheat the oven to 400°F. Combine ⅓ cup of brown sugar and a tablespoon of maple syrup in a bowl and dredge 8 to 10 slices of bacon in the mixture. Place the bacon on a baking sheet and place in the oven. Bake for 15 to 20 minutes while flipping the bacon over halfway through. Remove from the oven and let cool before using.

Place the bourbon, tequila, bacon-infused maple syrup, egg white, cherry bark bitters, and liquid smoke in a cocktail shaker and dry shake. Add ice and shake until chilled. Strain into a coupe and garnish with the candied bacon.

INGREDIENTS:

- ½ OZ. BACON-INFUSED MAPLE SYRUP
- 1½ OZ. BUFFALO TRACE BOURBON
- ½ OZ. CAZADORES TEQUILA
- 1 EGG WHITE
- 3 DASHES OF CHERRY BARK BITTERS
- 2 DASHES OF LIQUID SMOKE

BLACK DOG

Place the ingredients in a cocktail shaker filled with ice and shake until chilled. Strain into a small tumbler or a coupe.

INGREDIENTS:

- 3 PARTS BOURBON
- 1 PART SWEET VERMOUTH
- 1 PART BLACKBERRY BRANDY

FOUR ROSES SKYSCRAPER

Fill a mixing glass with cracked ice and add the bourbon and vermouth. Stir until chilled, strain into a glass filled with ice, and top with the soda water.

INGREDIENTS:

- 3 PARTS FOUR ROSES BOURBON
- 1 PART SWEET VERMOUTH
- SODA WATER, TO TOP

BLACK MANHATTAN

GARNISH: 1 MARASCHINO CHERRY

Place the bourbon, bitters, and vermouth in a mixing glass filled with ice and stir until the glass is frosted. Strain into a coupe and garnish with the maraschino cherry.

INGREDIENTS:

- 1½ OZ. FOUR ROSES SMALL BATCH BOURBON
- 2–3 DASHES OF BLACK WALNUT BITTERS
- 1 OZ. SWEET VERMOUTH

CORSAIR
GRAINIAC
9 GRAIN BOURBON

SPRING MANHATTAN

Place all of the ingredients in a mixing glass filled with ice, stir until chilled, and strain into a chilled cocktail glass.

INGREDIENTS:

- 2 OZ. JIM BEAM BLACK
- ½ OZ. APERITIF WINE
- ½ OZ. SWEET VERMOUTH

FASHIONABLY OLD

GARNISH: 1 STRIP OF ORANGE PEEL

Place the ingredients in a mixing glass filled with cracked ice and stir for 30 to 45 seconds. Strain into a rocks glass filled with ice and garnish with the strip of orange peel.

INGREDIENTS:

- 2 OZ. CORSAIR GRAINIAC 9 GRAIN BOURBON
- ¼ OZ. DEMERARA SUGAR
- 3 DASHES OF BARREL-AGED BITTERS

THE O. G. O. F.

GARNISH: 1 TORCHED ORANGE TWIST

Place the cocktail ingredients in a mixing glass filled with ice and stir until chilled. Strain into a rocks glass and garnish with the torched orange twist.

INGREDIENTS:

- 2 OZ. MAKER'S MARK CASK STRENGTH BOURBON
- ¼ OZ. COCKTAIL & SONS SPICED DEMERARA SYRUP
- 2 DASHES OF ANGOSTURA BITTERS
- 2 DASHES OF BITTERMENS XOCOLATL MOLE BITTERS

SPICED PUNCH

GARNISH: LEMON WHEELS, CINNAMON STICKS, WHOLE CLOVES, STAR ANISE PODS, & ALLSPICE BERRIES

Peel the lemons and set the fruit aside. Place the lemon peels and the sugar in a bowl, mash to combine, and let stand for 1 hour. Juice the lemons and strain to remove all pulp.

Place the tea bags in the boiling water and steep for 5 minutes. Remove the tea bags and discard them. Add the sugar-and-lemon peel mixture to the tea and stir until the sugar is dissolved. Strain and discard the solids. Add the bourbon and the lemon juice, stir to combine, and chill the punch in the refrigerator.

Add the ginger beer before serving and garnish each drink with lemon wheels and the spices.

INGREDIENTS:

- 6 LEMONS
- 1 CUP GRANULATED SUGAR
- 8 BAGS OF CHAI TEA
- 4 CUPS BOILING WATER
- 1 CUP FOUR ROSES BOURBON
- 1 (12 OZ.) BOTTLE OF GINGER BEER

HOT APPLE CIDER

GARNISH: 3 ORANGE PEELS & 30 TO 40 WHOLE CLOVES

Place the apple cider, bourbon, and cinnamon sticks in a slow cooker and cook on low for 2 hours, making sure the mixture does not boil. Cut the orange peels into rectangles and press the cloves into them. Garnish each glass with a clove-studded square of orange peel.

INGREDIENTS:

- 8 CUPS APPLE CIDER
- 4 CUPS FOUR ROSES YELLOW LABEL BOURBON
- 5 CINNAMON STICKS

HOT BUTTERED BOURBON

GARNISH: GRATED NUTMEG OR 1 CINNAMON STICK

Hot Buttered Mix: Place ½ stick of room-temperature butter, 1½ cups brown sugar, 1 teaspoon cinnamon, ½ teaspoon grated nutmeg, ¼ teaspoon ground cloves, and ¼ teaspoon salt in a mixing bowl and stir until well combined.

Fill a mug with boiling water and let sit for 45 seconds. Dump out the water and fill two-thirds of the way with hot water. Add the hot buttered mix and stir vigorously. Add the bourbon and bitters and add more water if needed. Stir briefly, garnish with grated nutmeg or a tall cinnamon stick, and serve with a spoon in the mug.

INGREDIENTS:

- 1 OZ. HOT BUTTERED MIX
- VERY HOT WATER (170°F), PLUS MORE AS NEEDED
- 1½ OZ. FOUR ROSES BOURBON
- DASH OF ANGOSTURA BITTERS

Four Roses
BOURBON

SEAHORSE

GARNISH: THICK SLICES OF BOURBON-SOAKED STAR FRUIT & LUXARDO MARASCHINO CHERRIES AND SYRUP

Combine the cocktail ingredients in a large punch bowl and chill in the refrigerator for at least 1 hour. Garnish each drink with a slice of the bourbon-soaked star fruit, Luxardo cherries, and a drizzle of Luxardo syrup.

Tip: You can use any bourbon you want to soak the slices of star fruit, but Noah's Mill, a small batch bourbon produced by Willett, is recommended.

INGREDIENTS:

- 1 (750 ML) BOTTLE OF OLD BARDSTOWN BOTTLED IN BOND BOURBON
- 1 GALLON ORANGE JUICE
- 2 CUPS LEMON JUICE
- 1 CAPFUL OF BLOOD ORANGE BITTERS
- 1 CUP SIMPLE SYRUP

RYE SOUR

GARNISH: 1 MARASCHINO CHERRY & 1 LEMON SLICE

Add the whiskey, lemon juice, and simple syrup to a cocktail shaker filled with ice. Shake vigorously. Strain the resulting mixture into a glass filled with ice and garnish with a maraschino cherry and a slice of lemon.

INGREDIENTS:

- 2½ OZ. RYE WHISKEY
- 1 OZ. LEMON JUICE
- ⅓ OZ. SIMPLE SYRUP

THE SMOKING GUN

GARNISH: 2 LUXARDO MARASCHINO CHERRIES

Place the cocktail ingredients in a mixing glass filled with ice and stir until chilled. Strain into a decanter and use a smoking gun filled with cherry wood to infuse the cocktail with smoke. Swirl the decanter, slowly pour into a rocks glass containing 1 large ice cube, and garnish with the Luxardo maraschino cherries.

INGREDIENTS:

- ½ OZ. ORGEAT
- 3 DASHES OF ANGOSTURA BITTERS
- OILS FROM 1 ORANGE PEEL
- ½ OZ. WATER
- 2 OZ. VANILLA-INFUSED BOURBON
- ½ OZ. AVERNA AMARO

FALCON SMASH

GARNISH: 2 BASIL LEAVES

Place all of the ingredients in a rocks glass and muddle the basil leaves. Add ice and garnish with additional basil leaves.

INGREDIENTS:

- 2 OZ. CORSAIR RYEMAGEDDON WHISKEY
- 1 OZ. LEMON JUICE
- 6 BASIL LEAVES
- 1 OZ. SIMPLE SYRUP

WATER FOR ELEPHANTS RYE SWIZZLE

GARNISH: 1 LIME WEDGE (OPTIONAL)

Place the ingredients in a Collins glass, fill the glass with ice, and use the swizzle method to combine. If desired, garnish with a lime wedge.

INGREDIENTS:

- 1–2 OZ. WILLETT FAMILY ESTATE SMALL BATCH RYE
- JUICE FROM 1 LIME
- 3–4 DASHES OF AROMATIC BITTERS
- 1 OZ. TIPPLEMAN'S DOUBLE FALERNUM SYRUP

WAX AND WANE

GARNISH: 1 FIRE & FLAVOR CEDAR WRAP & 1 SPRIG OF ROSEMARY

Place the cocktail ingredients in a cocktail shaker filled with ice, shake vigorously, and double-strain into a Collins glass. Light the cedar wrap on fire and quickly extinguish it. Add it and the sprig of rosemary to the cocktail.

INGREDIENTS:

- 2 OZ. CORSAIR RYEMAGEDDON WHISKEY
- ¼ OZ. FRESH LEMON JUICE
- ¼ OZ. DEMERARA SYRUP
- 4 DASHES OF ANGOSTURA BITTERS
- 1 EGG WHITE
- 6 BASIL LEAVES

PREAKNESS

Place the ingredients in a cocktail shaker filled with ice, shake until chilled, and strain into a rocks glass.

INGREDIENTS:

- 4 PARTS RYE WHISKEY
- 1 PART BÉNÉDICTINE
- 1 PART SWEET VERMOUTH
- 4 DASHES OF ANGOSTURA BITTERS

SOUTH OF NY SOUR

GARNISH: CRACKED PINK PEPPERCORNS

Place all of the cocktail ingredients, except for the Malbec, in a cocktail shaker without ice and dry shake. Add ice to the shaker and shake until chilled. Strain into a rocks glass filled with ice, top with the Malbec, and garnish with the cracked pink peppercorns.

INGREDIENTS:

- 2 OZ. CORSAIR TRIPLE SMOKE WHISKEY
- 1 OZ. LEMON
- 1 OZ. SIMPLE SYRUP
- 1 EGG WHITE
- 5 DROPS OF THE BITTER END MEMPHIS BBQ BITTERS
- 1 OZ. MALBEC

CORSAIR
AMERICAN RYE WHISKEY

CORSAIR
SMALL BATCH

VANILLA

FRISCO

Place the ingredients in a cocktail shaker filled with ice, shake until chilled, and strain into a cocktail glass.

INGREDIENTS:

- 2 PARTS RYE WHISKEY
- 1 PART LEMON JUICE
- SPLASH OF BÉNÉDICTINE

KENTUCKY VANILLA DROP

Lemon Sour: Place 2 cups water, 1½ cups sugar, ¼ cup corn syrup, and 2 tablespoons lemon zest in a small saucepan and cook, while stirring, over medium heat. When the sugar has dissolved, remove the pan from the stove and add ½ cup lemon juice and ½ cup lime juice. Stir and let cool completely before using.

Combine the ingredients in a cocktail shaker filled with ice and shake vigorously. Strain into shot glasses or a chilled coupe.

INGREDIENTS:

- 1 PART LEMON SOUR
- 1 PART JIM BEAM VANILLA

VANILLA SMASH

Place the lemon wedges and the mint in a double rocks glass and muddle. Fill the glass with ice, and then add the Jim Beam Vanilla.

INGREDIENTS:

- 2 LEMON WEDGES
- 6–8 MINT LEAVES
- 1 PART JIM BEAM VANILLA

BOURBON BALL MILKSHAKE

GARNISH: CHOCOLATE SYRUP, DOLLOP OF WHIPPED CREAM, & CANDIED PECANS (OPTIONAL)

Place the ice cream, bourbon cream, and chocolate fudge in a blender and puree until smooth. Line the inside of a frozen glass with drizzles of chocolate syrup and pour the cocktail into the glass. Pour milkshake into glass and top with additional chocolate syrup, whipped cream, and, if desired, candied pecans.

INGREDIENTS:

- 4 SCOOPS OF VANILLA ICE CREAM
- 2 OZ. BUFFALO TRACE BOURBON CREAM
- 2 OZ. CHOCOLATE FUDGE
- CHOCOLATE SYRUP, TO DRIZZLE

VANILLA FIZZ

GARNISH: 1 STRIP OF ORANGE PEEL

Place all of the cocktail ingredients, except for the club soda, in a cocktail shaker filled with ice and shake vigorously for as long as you can. Strain into a chilled Collins glass, add the splash of club soda, and garnish with the strip of orange peel.

INGREDIENTS:

- 1 PART JIM BEAM VANILLA
- 2 PARTS HALF & HALF
- 1 PART LEMON SOUR (SEE PAGE 295)
- 1 PART EGG WHITE
- SPLASH OF CLUB SODA

CHARBONNEAU WAY

GARNISH: 1 SPRIG OF THYME

Place all of the cocktail ingredients, except for the absinthe mist, in a cocktail shaker filled with ice and shake vigorously. Mist a coupe with the absinthe, strain the cocktail into the glass, and garnish with the sprig of thyme.

INGREDIENTS:

- 2 OZ. RYE WHISKEY
- ½ OZ. LEMON JUICE
- ½ OZ. MAPLE SYRUP
- ¼ OZ. SUZE
- ABSINTHE MIST

SCOTCH AND SALT

GARNISH: 1 STRIP OF ORANGE PEEL

Smoked Salt Tincture: In a small bowl, dissolve 2 teaspoons of hickory-smoked salt in 4 oz. water.

Place all of the ingredients in a double rocks glass, stir, and garnish with a strip of orange peel.

INGREDIENTS:

- 4 DROPS OF SMOKED SALT TINCTURE
- 1½ OZ. SCOTCH
- ¾ OZ. COCCHI AMERICANO
- ¾ OZ. COCCHI STORICO VERMOUTH DI TORINO
- ½ OZ. WHITE GRAPEFRUIT JUICE

CHAI TODDY

Place the chai concentrate in a tea kettle and warm according to the manufacturer's instructions. Place the bourbon in a mug, pour the hot chai on top, and finish with the splash of hot water.

INGREDIENTS:

- 6 OZ. CHAI CONCENTRATE
- 2 OZ. BOURBON
- SPLASH OF HOT WATER

JIM BEAM
VANILLA

BRIGHT LIGHTS, BIG CITY

GARNISH: 1 MARASCHINO CHERRY

Place the cocktail ingredients in a mixing glass filled with ice and stir gently. Place the maraschino cherry in a cocktail glass and strain the cocktail over it.

INGREDIENTS:

- 2 OZ. WHISTLEPIG STRAIGHT RYE WHISKEY
- ⅔ OZ. SWEET VERMOUTH
- 2 DROPS OF BITTERS

KNIGHT TAKES BISHOP

GARNISH: 1 SPRIG OF TARRAGON

Place all of the ingredients in a cocktail shaker filled with ice and shake vigorously. Strain the cocktail, discard the ice, return the cocktail to the shaker, and dry shake for 20 seconds. Strain into a rocks glass filled with ice and garnish with the sprig of tarragon.

INGREDIENTS:

- 2 OZ. IRISH WHISKEY (TULLAMORE DEW PREFERRED)
- ¾ OZ. LEMON JUICE
- ½ OZ. HONEY SYRUP
- ½ OZ. APRICOT LIQUEUR
- ½ OZ. SHERRY (PALO CORTADO PREFERRED)
- 1 EGG WHITE

PARIS BETWEEN THE WARS

GARNISH: 1 STRIP OF GRAPEFRUIT PEEL

Place all of the cocktail ingredients, with the exception of the cider, in a cocktail shaker filled with ice and shake vigorously. Strain into a Collins glass filled with ice, add the cider, express the strip of grapefruit peel over the cocktail, and discard.

INGREDIENTS:

- 1 OZ. SCOTCH (SMOKY BLEND PREFERRED)
- ¾ OZ. CAMPARI
- ¾ OZ. LEMON JUICE
- ½ OZ. HONEY SYRUP (2:1 HONEY-TO-WATER RATIO)
- 3 OZ. DRY PEAR CIDER

STRAWBERRY-BASIL SODA, ADVANCED TIGER STYLE

GARNISH: 1 SPRIG OF THAI BASIL & 1 COCKTAIL UMBRELLA

Place all of the cocktail ingredients, except for the soda water, in a cocktail shaker filled with ice and shake until chilled. Strain into a Collins glass filled with ice, top with the soda water, and garnish with the Thai basil and the cocktail umbrella.

INGREDIENTS:

- 1 OZ. THAI BASIL-STRAWBERRY SHRUB (SEE PAGE 623)
- 2 OZ. BOURBON
- 1 OZ. LEMON JUICE
- DASH OF HONEY
- SODA WATER, TO TOP

ARNAUD'S SPECIAL COCKTAIL

GARNISH: 1 ORANGE TWIST

Place the ingredients in a cocktail shaker and shake until combined. Strain into a rocks glass and garnish with the orange twist.

INGREDIENTS:

- 2 OZ. SCOTCH
- 1 OZ. DUBONNET ROUGE
- 3 DASHES OF ORANGE BITTERS

ABERDEEN

GARNISH: 1 STRIP OF ORANGE PEEL

Lapsang Souchong Syrup: Place two bags of lapsang souchong in a standard simple syrup recipe as it comes to a boil. Remove from heat, steep until cool, and strain.

Add the cocktail ingredients to a rocks glass in the order that they are listed. Add ice, stir, express the orange peel over the drink, and then place it in the glass.

INGREDIENTS:

- ½ OZ. LAPSANG SOUCHONG SYRUP
- 2 DASHES OF JACK RUDY AROMATIC BITTERS
- 2 OZ. BLACK BOTTLE SCOTCH

BARRELED DATE
BATCH NUMBER
MASH BILL
DISTILLED BY
CHATTANOOGA WHISKEY Co.
58
CHATTANOOGA WHISKEY Co.

SoBou

THE BIG CHIEF

GARNISH: 1 TORCHED STRIP OF ORANGE PEEL

Place all of the ingredients in a mixing glass filled with ice and stir until chilled. Strain into a Nick & Nora glass, express the torched orange peel over the cocktail, and then use it as a garnish.

INGREDIENTS:

- 2 OZ. BOURBON
- ½ OZ. AMARO
- ½ OZ. PUNT E MES VERMOUTH

STREETCAR NAMED DESIRE

GARNISH: 1 SPRIG OF MINT

Place all of the cocktail ingredients, except for the bitters, in a cocktail shaker filled with ice and shake vigorously. Strain into a rocks glass filled with ice, top with the bitters, and garnish with the mint sprig.

INGREDIENTS:

- 1½ OZ. BOURBON
- ¾ OZ. COCKTAIL & SONS MINT AND LEMON VERBENA SYRUP
- ¾ OZ. LEMON JUICE
- 4 DASHES OF ANGOSTURA BITTERS

DIRTY WATER

GARNISH: 1 LEMON WEDGE

Place all of the cocktail ingredients in a cocktail shaker filled with ice and shake vigorously. Do not strain, but pour the contents of the shaker into a Collins glass filled halfway with ice and garnish with the lemon wedge.

INGREDIENTS:

- 1½ OZ. GREEN MINT TEA, CHILLED
- 3–4 SPRIGS OF MINT
- 1 OZ. BOURBON
- ½ OZ. SIMPLE SYRUP

THE ZEMURRAY

GARNISH: 1 LUXARDO MARASCHINO CHERRY

Place all of the cocktail ingredients in a mixing glass filled with ice and stir until chilled. Strain into a chilled cocktail glass and garnish with the Luxardo maraschino cherry.

INGREDIENTS:

- 2 OZ. BOURBON
- ¼ OZ. BANANA LIQUEUR
- ¼ OZ. PALO CORTADO SHERRY
- 2 DASHES OF PEYCHAUD'S BITTERS
- DASH OF ANGOSTURA BITTERS

WHISKEYDENNIS

Place all of the ingredients in a cocktail shaker filled with ice, shake vigorously, and double-strain into a chilled coupe.

INGREDIENTS:

- 2 OZ. BOURBON
- ½ OZ. APRICOT LIQUEUR
- ½ OZ. APRICOT PRESERVES
- ¼ OZ. PEYCHAUD'S APERITIVO
- ¼ OZ. LEMON JUICE
- ¼ OZ. LIME JUICE
- 2 DASHES OF ANGOSTURA BITTERS

BERRY WHITE

GARNISH: 1 LONG STRIP OF LEMON PEEL & MIXED BERRIES

Wild Berry Cordial: Combine 2 pints blueberries, 1 pint blackberries, 1 pint raspberries, 3 cups brown sugar, and 1 cup bourbon in a large saucepan and bring to a boil over medium-high heat. Cook until the berries began to pop, remove from heat, and chill in the refrigerator. Double-strain before using.

Place the cocktail ingredients in a cocktail shaker filled with ice and shake vigorously. Double-strain into a wine glass, skewer the lemon peel on a cocktail pick, and garnish the cocktail with this and the mixed berries.

INGREDIENTS:

- 1 OZ. WILD BERRY CORDIAL
- ½ OZ. RICH DEMERARA SYRUP (3:1 SUGAR-TO-WATER RATIO)
- 2 OZ. BOURBON
- ¾ OZ. FRESH ORANGE JUICE
- ½ OZ. FRESH LEMON JUICE

PASSING DEADLINE

GARNISH: DUSTING OF CINNAMON & 1 CINNAMON STICK

Place all of the cocktail ingredients in a mixing glass filled with ice and stir until chilled. Strain into a rocks glass filled with ice and garnish with the dusting of cinnamon and the cinnamon stick.

INGREDIENTS:

- 1½ OZ. BOURBON
- ½ OZ. COCCHI STORICO VERMOUTH DI TORINO
- ½ OZ. LUSTAU EAST INDIA SOLERA SHERRY
- ½ OZ. SALERS GENTIANE
- 1 SPOONFUL OF TURBINADO SYRUP
- DASH OF ANGOSTURA BITTERS
- DASH OF BITTERMENS XOCOLATL MOLE BITTERS

THE BARRINGER

GARNISH: 1 LEMON WHEEL

Place all of the cocktail ingredients in a mixing glass filled with ice and stir. Double-strain into a coupe and garnish with the lemon wheel.

INGREDIENTS:

- 1½ OZ. WHISK(E)Y
- ¾ OZ. DRY CURAÇAO
- ½ OZ. TURBINADO SYRUP
- ½ OZ. FRESH LEMON JUICE

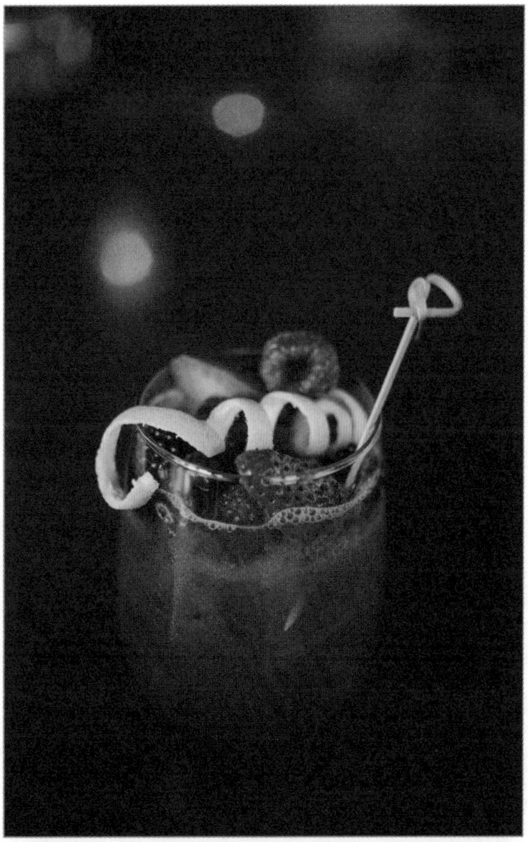

THE COLT .45

GARNISH: 1 ORANGE TWIST

Place all of the cocktail ingredients in a mixing glass filled with ice and stir. Strain into a rocks glass filled with ice and garnish with an orange twist.

INGREDIENTS:

- 2 OZ. WHITMEYER'S BOURBON
- ½ OZ. COFFEE LIQUEUR
- 2 DASHES OF ORANGE BITTERS

JOHNNY'S BOILERMAKER SHOTS

GARNISH: 1 ANGOSTURA-SOAKED ORANGE SLICE

Orange-Cherry Syrup: Place 1 cup of syrup from a jar of Luxardo maraschino cherries and the peel of 1 orange in a medium saucepan and bring to a gentle simmer. Remove from heat, let cool, and strain before using.

Place the cocktail ingredients in a container, stir until thoroughly combined, and refrigerate for up to 1 month. When ready to serve, rim a chilled shot glass with salt and sugar, pour the cocktail into the glass, and garnish with the soaked orange slice.

INGREDIENTS:

- 1 CUP ORANGE-CHERRY SYRUP
- 4 CUPS INEXPENSIVE, HIGH-PROOF WHISK(E)Y
- 1¼ CUPS PURIFIED WATER
- 1 OZ. ANGOSTURA BITTERS
- SALT, FOR THE RIM
- SUGAR, FOR THE RUM

WOOSTER'S SOUR

GARNISH: DASH OF ANGOSTURA BITTERS

Place all of the ingredients in a cocktail shaker and dry shake for 10 seconds. Add ice, shake for 30 seconds, and double-strain into a rocks glass. Top with the dash of Angostura Bitters and use a straw to articulate the foam into a design.

INGREDIENTS:

- 1 OZ. OLD OVERHOLT RYE WHISKEY
- 1 OZ. FRESH LEMON JUICE, STRAINED
- ¾ OZ. MATHILDE PÊCHE CORDIAL
- ½ OZ. PUNCH ALLA FIAMMA
- ½ OZ. TURBINADO SYRUP
- 1 EGG WHITE

THIRD COAST MULE

GARNISH: 1 STRIP OF LEMON PEEL

Place the whiskey, lemon juice, and simple syrup in a cocktail shaker filled with ice and shake vigorously. Strain into a Collins glass filled with ice, top with the ginger beer and coconut water, express the strip of lemon peel over the cocktail, and then use it as a garnish.

INGREDIENTS:

- 1½ OZ. YELLOW ROSE BLENDED WHISKEY
- ¾ OZ. LEMON JUICE
- ¾ OZ. SIMPLE SYRUP
- 2 OZ. GINGER BEER
- 2 OZ. COCONUT WATER

THROWING SHADE

Combine all of the ingredients in a cocktail shaker filled with ice, shake vigorously, and double-strain into a chilled coupe.

INGREDIENTS:

- 1½ OZ. JAPANESE WHISKY
- ¾ OZ. FRESH GRAPEFRUIT JUICE
- ½ OZ. RABARBARO ZUCCA AMARO
- ½ OZ. GINGER SYRUP (SEE PAGE 255, REPLACE HONEY WITH SUGAR)
- DASH OF PEYCHAUD'S BITTERS

TARRAGUEUR

GARNISH: 1 SPRIG OF TEXAS TARRAGON & 1 STRIP OF GRAPEFRUIT PEEL

Place the cocktail ingredients in a cocktail shaker containing one large ice cube and shake vigorously. Strain into a Nick & Nora glass and garnish with the sprig of tarragon and the additional strip of grapefruit peel.

INGREDIENTS:

- 1½ OZ. WHISK(E)Y
- 1 OZ. TEXAS RUBY RED GRAPEFRUIT JUICE
- ½ OZ. HONEY SYRUP
- 1 SMALL STRIP OF GRAPEFRUIT PEEL
- 8–10 TEXAS TARRAGON LEAVES
- DASH OF SALINE SOLUTION (1:10 SALT-TO-WATER RATIO)

GOMA FASHION

GARNISH: 1 LUXARDO MARASCHINO CHERRY

Place the ingredients in a rocks glass filled with ice, stir for 20 seconds, and garnish with the Luxardo maraschino cherry.

INGREDIENTS:

- 2 OZ. RYE WHISKEY, FAT WASHED WITH TOASTED SESAME OIL (SEE PAGE 238)
- ½ OZ. GIFFARD VANILLE DE MADAGASCAR
- ¼ OZ. TURBINADO SYRUP
- 3 DASHES OF ANGOSTURA BITTERS
- 3 DASHES OF ORANGE BITTERS

HILL COUNTRY HIGHBALL

GARNISH: 1 SPRIG OF ROSEMARY & 1 STRIP OF GRAPEFRUIT PEEL

Rosemary Simple Syrup: Place 1 cup sugar, 1 cup water, and 2 to 3 sprigs of rosemary in a small saucepan and simmer for 10 to 15 minutes. Remove from heat, strain, and let cool before using.

Place the whiskey and syrup in a highball glass filled with ice and stir. Top with the sparkling water and garnish with the sprig of rosemary and strip of grapefruit peel.

INGREDIENTS:

- ¾ OZ. ROSEMARY SIMPLE SYRUP
- 2 OZ. TREATY OAK DISTILLING WHISKEY
- WATERLOO SPARKLING WATER, TO TOP

TX

GRAPES OF WRATH

GARNISH: 1 ORANGE WHEEL & 1 CHERRY

Place the whiskey, syrup, lemon juice, and egg white in a cocktail shaker and dry shake for 20 seconds. Double-strain into a rocks glass, add ice, and float the wine on top. Garnish with the orange wheel and the cherry.

INGREDIENTS:

- 1¾ OZ. FIRESTONE & ROBERTSON TX BLENDED WHISKEY
- ¾ OZ. SIMPLE SYRUP
- ¾ OZ. LEMON JUICE
- 1 OZ. EGG WHITE
- ¾ OZ. CHATEAU STE. MICHELLE SYRAH, TO FLOAT

WHITE ROCK WITCH

GARNISH: 1 STRIP OF ORANGE PEEL

Cappillaire Syrup: Place several fronds of fresh maidenhair ferns in a bowl and bring 2 cups water to boil. Pour the water over the ferns, let stand for 30 minutes, and then add 1 oz. orange blossom water and 1½ cups sugar. Stir until the sugar is dissolved and reheat if necessary.

Place the cocktail ingredients in a cocktail shaker filled with ice and shake vigorously. Strain into a highball glass filled with ice and garnish with the strip of orange peel.

INGREDIENTS:

- ¾ OZ. CAPPILLAIRE SYRUP
- 1½ OZ. DEVILS RIVER WHISKEY
- ¾ OZ. REVOLUTION SPIRITS AMICO AMARO
- ¾ OZ. LEMON JUICE

THE FRIENDLY STRANGER IN THE BLACK SEDAN

GARNISH: BITTER CHERRY FOAM & 1 STRIP OF ORANGE PEEL

Bitter Cherry Foam: Place 3 oz. egg whites, 3 dashes of black walnut bitters, and a splash of Peter Heering Cherry Liqueur in a mixing bowl and whip until firm.

Place the cocktail ingredients in a mixing glass, add ice, and stir. Strain into a chilled coupe, garnish with the bitter cherry foam, express the orange peel over the cocktail, and discard.

INGREDIENTS:

- 2½ OZ. OLD FORESTER STATESMAN BOURBON
- ½ OZ. GRAND MARNIER
- ½ OZ. PETER HEERING CHERRY LIQUEUR
- SPLASH OF WATER

SMOKEY THE PEAR

GARNISH: 1 TORCHED SPRIG OF ROSEMARY

Place the pear, lemon juice, and simple syrup in a cocktail shaker and muddle. Add ice, the whisk(e)y, and the Grand Marnier and shake vigorously. Place the torched rosemary sprig in a rocks glass containing one large ice cube and double-strain the cocktail into the glass.

INGREDIENTS:

- ¼ CUP PEAR, CHOPPED
- 1 OZ. LEMON JUICE
- ½ OZ. ROSEMARY SIMPLE SYRUP (SEE PAGE 308)
- 2 OZ. WHISK(E)Y
- ¾ OZ. GRAND MARNIER

CLEAN-CUT KID

GARNISH: 1 STRIP OF LEMON PEEL

Lemon-Coriander Tincture: Fill a mason jar three-quarters of the way with equal parts cilantro and lemon and cover with 80 proof vodka. Store in a cool, dark place for 6 weeks and strain before using.

Place the cocktail ingredients in a mixing glass filled with ice and stir until chilled. Strain into a chilled cocktail glass, express the strip of lemon peel over the cocktail, and discard.

INGREDIENTS:

- 3 DASHES OF LEMON-CORIANDER TINCTURE
- 2½ OZ. RYE WHISKEY
- ⅜ OZ. SUZE
- 2 DASHES OF BLACK WALNUT BITTERS
- ¼ OZ. AGED COCONUT WHITE BALSAMIC VINEGAR

TEXAS GENTLEMAN

GARNISH: 1 STRIP OF ORANGE PEEL

Add the cocktail ingredients to a rocks glass filled with ice in the order they are listed and garnish with the orange peel.

INGREDIENTS:

- 2 OZ. FIRESTONE & ROBERTSON TX BLENDED WHISKEY
- ½ OZ. CAFFE DEL FUEGO
- 3 DASHES OF FEE BROTHERS AZTEC CHOCOLATE BITTERS

SOUTHERN SHIPWRECK

Wet the rim of a coupe and dip it into the sugar. Place the remaining ingredients in a cocktail shaker filled with ice, shake vigorously, and strain into the coupe.

INGREDIENTS:

- SUGAR, FOR THE RIM
- 1 OZ. SMITH AND CROSS JAMAICAN RUM
- 1 OZ. WHISK(E)Y
- ¾ OZ. LIME JUICE
- ¾ OZ. ORGEAT
- ¼ OZ. BROWN SUGAR SYRUP
- 5 DASHES OF SCRAPPY'S CHOCOLATE BITTERS

SHRUB YOU THE RIGHT WAY

GARNISH: 1 SPRIG OF MINT

Peach Shrub: Combine equal parts peach puree, sugar, and sherry vinegar.

Place the cocktail ingredients in a cocktail shaker filled with ice and shake until chilled. Strain into a rocks glass and garnish with the sprig of mint.

INGREDIENTS:

- ¾ OZ. PEACH SHRUB
- 2 OZ. MAKER'S MARK BOURBON
- ½ OZ. FRESH LEMON JUICE
- ½ OZ. CRÈME DE NOYAUX ALMOND CREAM LIQUEUR
- DASH OF PEACH BITTERS

PEACHY KEANE

GARNISH: 1 DRIED PEACH & 1 PIECE OF GINGER CANDY

Place the cocktail ingredients in a cocktail shaker and dry shake for 10 seconds. Add ice, shake for 30 seconds, and double-strain into a rocks glass filled with ice. Garnish with the dried peach and the piece of ginger candy.

INGREDIENTS:

- 1 OZ. OLD FORESTER CLASSIC 86 PROOF BOURBON
- ½ OZ. GIFFARD CRÈME DE PÊCHE DE VIGNE
- ½ OZ. THE KING'S GINGER LIQUEUR
- ¾ OZ. HONEY
- ¾ OZ. LEMON JUICE
- 1 EGG WHITE

LITTLE RYE LIES

GARNISH: 1 SPRIG OF MINT & 1 STRIP OF ORANGE PEEL

Infused Simple Syrup: Bring 1 cup water to boil, remove from heat, and add 4 bags of your preferred black tea. Steep for 5 minutes, remove tea bags, and bring the mixture to a gentle boil over medium heat. Add 1 cup sugar and stir until it is dissolved. Remove from heat and let cool before using.

Place the cocktail ingredients in a mixing glass filled with ice and stir until chilled. Strain into a rocks glass containing one large cube and garnish with the sprig of mint and the strip of orange peel.

INGREDIENTS:

- ½ OZ. BLACK TEA–INFUSED SIMPLE SYRUP
- 2 OZ. OLD OVERHOLT RYE WHISKEY
- 2 DASHES OF REGAN'S ORANGE BITTERS NO. 6
- DASH OF ANGOSTURA BITTERS

KILL GIL

GARNISH: 1 STRIP OF ORANGE ZEST

Place the cocktail ingredients in a mixing glass filled with ice and stir until chilled. Strain into a rocks glass containing one large cube, express the strip of orange zest over the cocktail, and then use it as a garnish.

INGREDIENTS:

- 2 OZ. GENTLEMAN JACK TENNESSEE WHISKEY
- ¼ OZ. BÉNÉDICTINE
- ¾ OZ. TEMPUS FUGIT GRAN CLASSICO

KAMEHAMEHA

GARNISH: 1 LEMON TWIST

Add the cocktail ingredients to a rocks glass containing one large ice cube in the order they are listed and garnish with the lemon twist.

INGREDIENTS:

- 1 OZ. SUNTORY TOKI WHISKY
- ½ OZ. TAKARA SHOCHU
- ½ OZ. RITTENHOUSE RYE
- ½ OZ. PUNT E MES VERMOUTH
- 2 DASHES OF ANGOSTURA BITTERS

BOURBON COBBLER

GARNISH: 1 LEMON TWIST

Place the cocktail ingredients in a mixing glass and stir until combined. Add a bit of ice, gently stir, strain into a wine goblet filled with ice, and garnish with the lemon twist.

INGREDIENTS:

- 1⅔ OZ. EAGLE RARE BOURBON
- ⅔ OZ. LUXARDO
- ½ OZ. SIMPLE SYRUP
- 3 STRIPS OF LEMON PEEL
- 3 STRIPS OF ORANGE PEEL
- 3 STRIPS OF GRAPEFRUIT PEEL

OLD TIMER

GARNISH: 1 ORANGE TWIST

Place all of the cocktail ingredients, except for the club soda, in a cocktail shaker filled with ice and shake vigorously. Double-strain into a Collins glass filled with ice, top with club soda, and garnish with the orange twist.

INGREDIENTS:

- 1½ OZ. BOURBON
- ½ OZ. CYNAR
- ½ OZ. PUNT E MES VERMOUTH
- ½ OZ. LEMON JUICE
- ¼ OZ. SIMPLE SYRUP
- 2–4 DASHES OF ANGOSTURA BITTERS
- CLUB SODA, TO TOP

THE OLD WORLD

GARNISH: 1 PEACH SLICE

Place the peach slices, brown sugar, and peach bitters in a rocks glass and muddle. Add the St-Germain and the bourbon and stir. Add ice and garnish with an additional slice of peach.

INGREDIENTS:

- 2 PEACH SLICES
- SPOONFUL OF BROWN SUGAR
- 2 DASHES OF PEACH BITTERS
- ½ OZ. ST-GERMAIN
- 1½ OZ. BULLEIT BOURBON

REV'S HILL COUNTRY DONKEY

GARNISH: 1 LIME WEDGE

Fill a copper mug with crushed ice, add the bourbon and lime juice, and top with ginger beer. Garnish with the lime wedge.

INGREDIENTS:

- 2½ OZ. GARRISON BROTHERS TEXAS STRAIGHT SMALL BATCH BOURBON WHISKEY
- JUICE OF ½ LIME
- GINGER BEER, TO TOP

WITHOUT A TRACE

GARNISH: 1 STRIP OF ORANGE PEEL

Place all of the ingredients, except for the absinthe, in a mixing glass filled with ice and stir. Rinse a rocks glass with absinthe, discard the excess, and gently place a large ice cube in the glass. Strain the cocktail into the glass and garnish with the strip of orange peel.

INGREDIENTS:

- 1½ OZ. BUFFALO TRACE BOURBON
- ½ OZ. AMARO NONINO QUINTESSENTIA
- ½ OZ. HONEY SYRUP
- ½ OZ. FRESH LEMON JUICE
- ABSINTHE, TO RINSE

JOE BUCK

GARNISH: 1 CAYENNE-DUSTED LEMON WHEEL

Dijon Syrup: Place 4 cups honey, 3 teaspoons of smoked paprika, 1 cup Dijon mustard, and ½ cup hot water in a bowl and whisk until thoroughly combined.

Place the whiskey, syrup, and lemon juice in a cocktail shaker filled with ice and shake vigorously. Pour the cocktail into a copper mug, add more ice, and top with the ginger beer. Utilize the swizzle method to combine and garnish with the cayenne-dusted lemon wheel.

INGREDIENTS:

- ½ OZ. DIJON SYRUP
- 1½ OZ. BALCONES BABY BLUE WHISKEY
- ½ OZ. LEMON JUICE
- GINGER BEER, TO TOP

TONIQUE'S SAZERAC

GARNISH: 1 STRIP OF LEMON PEEL

Rinse the inside of a chilled rocks glass with the Herbsaint and discard the excess. Place the remaining cocktail ingredients in a mixing glass filled with ice and stir. Strain into the glass, express the strip of lemon peel over the cocktail, and then use as a garnish.

INGREDIENTS:

- ⅛ OZ. HERBSAINT ANISE-FLAVORED LIQUEUR
- 2 OZ. RYE WHISKEY
- ¼ OZ. GOMME SYRUP
- 9 DASHES OF PEYCHAUD'S BITTERS

TAYLOR BIRD SAZERAC

GARNISH: 1 LEMON TWIST

Place all of the cocktail ingredients, except for the absinthe mist, in a mixing glass filled halfway with ice and stir. Mist a rocks glass with the absinthe, strain the cocktail into it, and garnish with the lemon twist.

INGREDIENTS:

- ¼ OZ. STEEN'S SYRUP
- 1 OZ. COGNAC
- 1 OZ. RYE WHISKEY
- 2 DASHES OF ORANGE BITTERS
- 6 DASHES OF PEYCHAUD'S BITTERS
- ABSINTHE MIST

LANE

SAZERAC

LEXINGTON

GARNISH: 1 STRIP OF LEMON PEEL

Rinse the inside of a chilled jam jar or rocks glass with Herbsaint and discard excess. Place the remaining ingredients in a mixing glass filled with ice, stir until chilled, strain into the glass, and garnish with the strip of lemon peel.

INGREDIENTS:

- ⅛ OZ. HERBSAINT ANISE-FLAVORED LIQUEUR
- 1¼ OZ. RYE WHISKEY
- ¾ OZ. SWEET VERMOUTH
- ½ OZ. GINGER LIQUEUR
- DASH OF ANGOSTURA BITTERS

THE BAUDIN

GARNISH: 1 STRIP OF LEMON PEEL

Place all of the cocktail ingredients in a cocktail shaker filled with ice and shake vigorously. Strain into a rocks glass filled with ice and garnish with the strip of lemon peel.

INGREDIENTS:

- 1½ OZ. BOURBON
- ¾ OZ. HONEY SYRUP
- ½ OZ. LEMON JUICE
- DASH OF HOT SAUCE (TABASCO PREFERRED)

IRONROOT ICED TODDY

GARNISH: 1 STRIP OF LEMON PEEL

Place all of the cocktail ingredients in a cocktail shaker filled with ice and shake vigorously. Strain into a rocks glass filled with ice and garnish with the strip of lemon peel.

INGREDIENTS:

- 1 OZ. IRONROOT HARBINGER BOURBON
- 1 OZ. LEMONADE
- 1 OZ. HONEY SYRUP
- ¼ OZ. FRESH LEMON JUICE

JACK SAZERAC

GARNISH: 1 STRIP OF LEMON PEEL

Add the ingredients to a rocks glass in the order they are listed and garnish with the strip of lemon peel.

INGREDIENTS:

- 1½ OZ. JACK DANIEL'S SINGLE BARREL RYE
- 2 DASHES OF PEYCHAUD'S BITTERS
- DASH OF ANGOSTURA BITTERS
- 1 SPOONFUL OF ABSINTHE

MAGGIE BAILEY

GARNISH: 1 SPRIG OF THYME

Place the cocktail ingredients in a cocktail shaker filled with ice and shake vigorously. Strain into a rocks glass filled with ice and garnish with the thyme sprig.

ROASTED CORN SYRUP

Preheat the oven to 400°F. Place the corn, oil, salt, and pepper in a bowl and toss until combined. Spread into one even layer on a baking sheet and bake, while turning the corn over a few times, until golden brown, about 12 to 15 minutes. Remove the corn from the oven and transfer to a saucepan. Add the thyme and water and simmer for 15 to 20 minutes, until the mixture takes on a slightly milky appearance. Strain, add an equivalent amount of sugar to the mixture, and stir until dissolved.

INGREDIENTS:

- 2 OZ. WHITE WHISKEY
- ½ OZ. DOLIN BLANC
- ¾ OZ. HEAVY CREAM
- ¾ OZ. ROASTED CORN SYRUP (SEE RECIPE BELOW)

ROASTED CORN SYRUP:

- 2 CUPS CORN KERNELS
- 1 TEASPOON VEGETABLE OIL
- 1 TEASPOON SALT
- 1 TEASPOON GROUND BLACK PEPPER
- 1 CUP FRESH THYME
- 3 CUPS WATER
- 1–2 CUPS SUGAR

THE PEACEFUL PEOPLE

Place the ingredients in a cocktail shaker filled with ice, shake vigorously, and strain into a rocks glass or a clay cup.

TOASTED BUTTER PECAN SYRUP

Preheat the oven to 350°F. Place the pecans on a baking sheet and place them in the oven for 5 minutes. Remove from the oven, let cool slightly, and then pulse in a food processor. Combine the pecans and the water and let stand for 2 hours. Place the mixture in a food processor or blender, puree until smooth, and strain through cheesecloth while gently squeezing to remove as much liquid as possible. Add the caster sugar, stir until dissolved, and then add the melted butter and, if using, the xanthan gum. Stir to combine.

INGREDIENTS:

- 1½ OZ. BALCONES BABY BLUE WHISKEY
- 1 TEASPOON MEZCAL
- ¾ OZ. TOASTED BUTTER PECAN SYRUP (SEE RECIPE BELOW)
- ½ OZ. LEMON JUICE
- 3 DASHES OF COFFEE BITTERS

TOASTED BUTTER PECAN SYRUP:

- ½ CUP PECANS
- 1¼ CUPS WATER
- 1 CUP CASTER SUGAR
- 2 TEASPOONS BUTTER, MELTED
- 1 TEASPOON XANTHAM GUM (OPTIONAL)

SAZERAC

GARNISH: 1 STRIP OF LEMON PEEL

The quintessential New Orleans drink serves as a microcosm for the city's history, straddling French traditions and New World innovation. Pharmacist Amedie Peychaud (yes, of bitters fame) liked to mix his family recipe for bitters with brandy and other spirits. Peychaud sold his bitters around town, and at the Merchant's Exchange House a cocktail was created using the bitters and a French Cognac, Sazerac-du-Forge et Fils, which the bar's owner, Sewell T. Taylor, imported. The drink became the house specialty, and when Thomas H. Handy took over the establishment, around 1870, he changed the name to the Sazerac Coffee House. Somewhere along the line absinthe was thrown into the mix. When a grape blight broke the Cognac supply chain between France and the U. S., Handy turned to rye in order to keep pumping out Sazeracs. By the 1890s, a Sazerac Cocktail was being bottled and sold by the Sazerac Company, making it the first branded cocktail. When absinthe was outlawed in the U. S. in 1912, the Sazerac Company developed a replacement, Herbsaint. Today, this cousin to the Old Fashioned is popular well beyond the Crescent City.

TO YOUR HEALTH

Both bitters and absinthe were considered medicinal products in the 19th century; mixing them with spirits and sugar was intended to help the medicine go down. It was believed that absinthe (not dubbed the "devil in the bottle" until the 20th century) aided digestion and bitters were a cure-all. So it makes sense that the Sazerac started in an apothecary.

- 1 SUGAR CUBE
- 3 DASHES OF PEYCHAUD'S BITTERS
- 1½ OZ. SAZERAC RYE WHISKEY
- ¼ OZ. HERBSAINT ANISE-FLAVORED LIQUEUR

Fill a rocks glass with ice. Drop the sugar cube into a mixing glass, add bitters, muddle the sugar, and then add rye. Discard the ice from the rocks glass, rinse with Herbsaint, then pour the rye mixture into the chilled glass. Garnish with the strip of lemon peel.

Q&A WITH LIAM DEEGAN OF BARREL PROOF

"We stopped counting at 300 whiskies" pretty much sums up all you need to know about Barrel Proof, and why this neighborhood bar in New Orleans has a national reputation. Its relaxed Lower Garden District vibe begs to be the backdrop for a long night of sipping drinks.

What can you tell us about how the bar started?

It was basically a place where the owners of Sylvain, where I was running the bar at the time, wanted to open based on how we drank. We liked shots of whisk(e)y and beer. We enjoyed cocktails, and making them, but at the end of the night, and frequently during the night, we just drank whisk(e)y. Barrel Proof came from a blend of being a bit geeky about booze, but also being casual and not letting it dominate the conversation. We wanted a place that was first and foremost fun to hang out at, but also offered good stuff to drink.

Can you tell us about the theme of the bar and its influences on your cocktails?

Barrel Proof has always been a whisk(e)y bar, in a neighborhood setting. Sometimes it's a neighborhood bar, with a giant whisk(e)y list. It all depends on the day, but we pride ourselves on never alienating the neighborhood aspect of the bar in a building that's housed saloons for about 100 years.

What does your team look for when creating a new cocktail?

Typically we always include at least one whisk(e)y cocktail, but we try to offer some non-whisk(e)y options so people don't feel forced to drink whisk(e)y. We have a lot of tequila and gin drinkers come into the bar, and lots of people who are just cocktail enthusiasts, who know they can get a solid cocktail from us, but don't necessarily need to nerd out on bourbon.

How does the food and culture of New Orleans influence the cocktails that you offer?

We have a strict Sazerac recipe that never changes.

What are the best parts of running a cocktail bar in New Orleans? Are there any downsides or things that make it difficult?

It's a very small community and everyone drinks at everyone else's bars, sends guests around town, and workshops and tastes drinks with each other.

You live and work in a world-class cocktail city. What are some bars that you enjoy and draw inspiration from?

Every dive bar I go to is more an inspiration than most cocktail bars. The hospitality and sentimental aesthetic and design of those bars is something I always learn from. Cutting-edge cocktail bars, I learn about new products, taste some things, and see interesting techniques employed. But at the end of the day, I find I take away the most from neighborhood joints.

Blue Hawaiian, Brandy Alexander, Pink Squirrel, Rusty Nail, Tom Collins, White Russian, Grasshopper, Rob Roy, Pink Lady: If you had to pick one of these classic cocktails to add to your menu how would you reimagine your choice to make it fit in with your style?

The Grasshopper that Paul Gustings does at Tujague's is one of my favorites. Basically the same recipe, but he adds a bit of brandy for a kick and extra backbone. The White Russian on the menu at Longway Tavern, our sister bar/restaurant, has more vodka to make the drink more balanced and less cloying. Obviously, adding more booze is something I lean toward. Green Chartreuse in a Piña Colada never hurt.

Do you have a favorite cocktail?

Sidecar, underrated and delicious.

Do you have a favorite alcohol to work with when making cocktails?

Brandy, Cognac specifically, is always a favorite.

TEQUILA *and* MEZCAL

For years, my nickname for tequila was the "mind eraser." Let's go back to 2003 and I'll tell you a story so you understand why.

I was at a birthday party with a few friends in Manhattan's West Village. I did two shots of tequila. *(Before you start to call me a hypocrite after I bemoaned shots in the beginning of this book, please note that despite my own personal rule against shots, I will break that rule for certain friends during their birthdays. It is also quite possible that I instituted my rule after this night. Perhaps we should just move on.)*

Next thing I know, I was waking up in my room at the Hotel Chelsea, fully clothed with the TV and AC on. The fact that I was living there at all is a story in and of itself, but I might need to know you a bit better before I dive into those details. I called a friend who was with me that night and asked her if she'd brought me back to my room. She said no. I asked her if she remembered how I'd left the bar; she told me that I hailed a cab.

So, apparently, I took a cab, got back to my room, turned on the TV and air conditioner, and had no recollection of any of it. Most impressive. Hence the name—mind eraser. It was like I'd been the guinea pig in a bold tequila experiment. Needless to say, I've been very cautious ever since.

This is not to say that I avoid tequila, that would be a lie. It's just that I make sure to show it proper respect. I'm too old at this point for a repeat of what happened in 2003.

Tequila is for more than shots. It's the core spirit in the ever popular Margarita and aged tequila can be sipped, just like my beloved whisk(e)y. The cocktails that follow include a lot of Margarita recipes but you will learn, as did I, that tequila is capable of much more.

Favorite cocktail: Paloma Plus, tequila and grapefruit—yes please!

A BRIEF OVERVIEW OF TEQUILA AND MEZCAL

All tequila is mezcal. But not all mezcal is tequila. The same as all bourbon is whisk(e)y, but not all whisk(e)y is bourbon.

Both tequila and mezcal are made by distilling the core of the agave plant, known as the *piña*. There are about 30 different varietals of agave plant that can be used to make mezcals. But only blue agave can be used for tequila. Tequila and mezcal primarily come from different regions of Mexico. Tequila makers can be found in Michoacán, Guanajuato, Nayarit, Tamaulipas, and Jalisco, which is where the town of Tequila is located. Oaxaca is where 85 percent of mezcal is produced, though it is also made in Durango, Guanajuato, Guerrero, San Luis Potosí, Tamaulipas, Zacatecas, Michoacán, and Puebla.

Keep an eye out for *mixtos*, which are not 100 percent pure blue agave. Most people experience mixtos when they are introduced to tequila, since there are more mixto brands on the market than pure agave brands. Legally, these mixto tequilas must be made with at least 51 percent pure blue agave sugar. The other half of the sugars can be from non-agave sources, like sugarcane, which will affect the taste and experience of the spirit in a negative fashion. So, in order to make sure you're getting the best experience, carefully read the label of any tequila bottle before you purchase, and remember: say no to mixtos.

MAKING AND AGING TEQUILA AND MEZCAL

To make tequila, the agave is steamed in ovens before being distilled in copper pots. For mezcal, the agave is cooked over charcoal in lava rock-lined pits dug in the ground and distillation happens in clay vessels; this is why mezcals have a smoky flavor. Once distilled, both tequila and mezcal are aged in oak barrels. The amount of time spent in the barrel determines the type of tequila or mezcal that is bottled:

Plata (no more than 2 months): also called blanco, silver, joven, or white tequila, this is the purest form of distilled blue agave. Once it has been distilled, it is immediately bottled and distributed. Plata should taste fresh and fruity, with a clean, herbaceous hint. The best way to imbibe plata is on the rocks with a squeeze of fresh lime.

Reposado (2 to 12 months): extra time in the barrel lets this "rested" tequila mellow out, and imparts a hint of flavor, ranging from oak to vanilla, baking spices, and fruit.

Añejo (1 to 3 years): this tequila has more depth and complexity than both plata and reposado, featuring notes of wood, nuts, and chocolate. While each brand is unique in terms of wood used and resting time, all añejo is going to be soft, smooth, and distinct on the palate.

Extra Añejo (minimum of 3 years): this "extra aged" variety is a relative newcomer to the scene, only becoming an official classification in March 2006.

Tequila, like Champagne, is a designated Appellation of Origin (AO). It is tended to by individuals known as *jimadors*, who have taken great pains to learn this centuries-old art, which is still largely done by hand. In order to get a product that is saleable, these jimadors have to plant the agave, care for the plants, and harvest them when they are perfectly ripe. A huge amount of time, energy, and passion gets put into every bottle of pure blue agave tequila. That's even more the case when the tequila is aged.

FLAVORED TEQUILAS

There are all sorts of flavored and infused tequilas on the market: espresso, cucumber, pomegranate, cinnamon, strawberry, coconut, and habanero, just to name a few. If you can think of something that might go well with tequila, there's a good chance that flavor of tequila exists. Some of these are good when making cocktails, but be cautious, and always make sure to taste the tequila on its own first. Not all of the flavored tequilas are great. If you have the time, making your own infused tequila is a cool experiment. Once you get it down, they make for great gifts and are also welcome at any party.

TEQUILA TROPIC

GARNISH: 1 ORANGE WHEEL

Place the sugar, juices, and tequila in a cocktail shaker filled with ice and shake until thoroughly mixed. Fill a rocks glass halfway with ice, strain the cocktail into it, and garnish with an orange wheel.

INGREDIENTS:

- 1 TEASPOON SUGAR
- 4 OZ. ORANGE JUICE
- JUICE OF ½ LEMON
- JUICE OF ½ LIME
- 2 OZ. SILVER TEQUILA

EL DIABLO

GARNISH: 2 TO 3 RASPBERRIES, 2 TO 3 BLACKBERRIES, & 1 LIME SLICE

Fill a cocktail shaker with ice and add the tequila, black currant liqueur, and lime juice. Shake until chilled, add ice to your glass as desired, and strain the mixture into it. Top with the ginger beer and garnish with the slice of lime, blackberries, and raspberries.

Variation: For a Blue Diablo, substitute blue curaçao for the black currant liqueur and add a dash of lemon juice to lighten the flavor.

Tip: Ginger beer has a harsher taste than most carbonated beverages, making it a challenging cocktail component. Unlike club soda or even ginger ale, ginger beer runs the risk of overpowering the flavor of anything you add to it. If you're looking to create some unique cocktails for yourself, make sure your other ingredients are assertive enough to stand out against the ginger beer before you use it. Or just substitute ginger ale.

INGREDIENTS:

- 1½ OZ. SILVER TEQUILA
- 1 OZ. BLACK CURRANT LIQUEUR
- JUICE OF 1 LIME
- GINGER BEER, TO TOP

PEPINO

GARNISH: 1 LIME WEDGE & 1 PINEAPPLE SLICE

Place the simple syrup, cilantro, and cucumber slices in a cocktail shaker and muddle. Add the remaining cocktail ingredients and some ice and shake vigorously. Place your desired amount of ice in a glass and strain the cocktail into the glass. Garnish with the lime wedge and pineapple slice.

Variation: Some versions call for the inclusion of egg white, which you should only do if you feel comfortable with the risks of ingesting raw egg. Most other variations are cosmetic, such as the addition of a dash of agave nectar.

INGREDIENTS:

- 1 OZ. SIMPLE SYRUP
- 3 CILANTRO LEAVES
- 3 CUCUMBER SLICES
- 2 OZ. SILVER TEQUILA
- 1 OZ. ORANGE LIQUEUR
- 1 OZ. PINEAPPLE JUICE
- JUICE OF ½ LIME

MASON JAR PALOMA

GARNISH: 1 LIME SLICE

Add the tequila and grapefruit soda to a mason jar filled with ice. Add the lime juice, stir, and garnish with the lime slice.

Variations: If you're not a fan of grapefruit soda, you can replace it with a mixture of grapefruit juice, club soda, and lime juice.

As with many tequila-based cocktails, coating the rim of your glass with salt is an option.

CROWD PLEASER

To turn this cocktail into a punch, squeeze the juice of a few limes into your punch bowl, and then add as much tequila and grapefruit soda as you want. The joy of the Paloma is its simplicity—and it's that same simplicity that makes it the perfect large batch drink.

INGREDIENTS:

- 1 PART TEQUILA
- 3 PARTS GRAPEFRUIT SODA
- SPLASH OF LIME JUICE

FIRE WALK WITH ME

Place the lime juice, orgeat, and jalapeño in a cocktail shaker and muddle. Add ice, the tequila, and the falernum, shake vigorously, and strain into a coupe.

INGREDIENTS:

- ½ OZ. LIME JUICE
- ½ OZ. ORGEAT
- 2 JALAPEÑO PEPPER SLICES
- 2 OZ. REPOSADO TEQUILA
- ½ OZ. FALERNUM

PINEAPPLE LEAP

Place the ingredients in a cocktail shaker filled with ice, shake vigorously, and strain into a Collins glass filled with crushed ice.

INGREDIENTS:

- 1¼ OZ. TEQUILA
- 2 OZ. PINEAPPLE JUICE
- 1 OZ. FRESH LEMON JUICE
- ¼ OZ. GRENADINE

RUDE COSMOPOLITAN

GARNISH: 1 STRIP OF ORANGE PEEL

Place the cocktail ingredients in a cocktail shaker filled with ice and shake vigorously. Strain into a chilled cocktail glass and garnish with the strip of orange peel.

INGREDIENTS:

- 1¼ OZ. TEQUILA
- ¼ OZ. GRAND MARNIER
- JUICE OF 1 LIME
- 1 OZ. CRANBERRY JUICE

SHADY LADY

Place the ingredients in a cocktail shaker filled with ice, shake vigorously, and strain into a short tumbler.

INGREDIENTS:

- 2 OZ. TEQUILA
- 1 OZ. MELON LIQUEUR
- 5 OZ. FRESH GRAPEFRUIT JUICE

JALISCO SOUR

GARNISH: DUSTING OF NUTMEG, 2 TO 4 DASHES OF ANGOSTURA BITTERS, & 1 LIME WEDGE OR TWIST

Place the cocktail ingredients in a cocktail shaker filled halfway with crushed ice and shake vigorously. Strain into a rocks glass and garnish with the nutmeg, bitters, and lime component.

INGREDIENTS:

1 OZ. SILVER TEQUILA

1 OZ. PISCO

¾ OZ. FRESH LIME JUICE

¾ OZ. SIMPLE SYRUP

1 EGG WHITE

RANCH WATER

GARNISH: 1 LIME WEDGE

After pouring out 2 oz. of the Topo Chico, add the tequila and lime juice to the bottle, and garnish with the lime wedge.

INGREDIENTS:

1 (12 OZ.) BOTTLE OF TOPO CHICO

1½ OZ. SILVER TEQUILA

¼ OZ. FRESH LIME JUICE

TEQUILA-GRAPEFRUIT COCKTAIL

GARNISH: 1 ORANGE WHEEL

Place the cocktail ingredients in a glass filled with ice, stir until chilled, and garnish with the orange wheel.

INGREDIENTS:

1 PART GOLD TEQUILA

1 PART GINGER ALE

2 PARTS GRAPEFRUIT JUICE

DASH OF ORANGE LIQUEUR

THE BRAVE

GARNISH: 1 TORCHED STRIP OF ORANGE PEEL

Place the mezcal, tequila, Amaro, and curaçao in a wine glass and swirl. Mist the inside of the glass above the cocktail with the bitters and garnish with the torched strip of orange peel.

INGREDIENTS:

1 OZ. DEL MAGUEY CHICHICAPA MEZCAL

1 OZ. TEQUILA CABEZA

½ OZ. AMARO AVERNA

¼ OZ. ROYAL COMBIER CURAÇAO

3 MISTS OF ANGOSTURA BITTERS

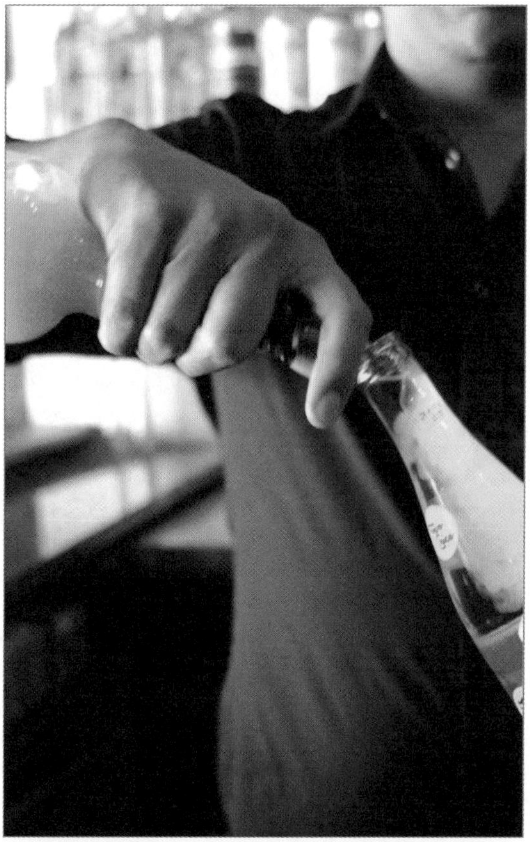

LOVEJOY

GARNISH: 1 GRAPEFRUIT SLICE

Place the cocktail ingredients in a cocktail shaker filled with ice and shake vigorously. Strain into a highball glass filled with pebble ice and garnish with the grapefruit slice.

INGREDIENTS:

- 1 OZ. OLMECA ALTOS TEQUILA
- ¾ OZ. EL SILENCIO MEZCAL
- ¾ OZ. FRESH LIME JUICE
- ¾ OZ. WATERMELON & PRICKLY PEAR SHRUB (SEE PAGE 40)
- 6 DROPS OF SALINE SOLUTION (SEE PAGE 308)

THE HATCHBACK

GARNISH: 1 GRAPEFRUIT SLICE

Place all of the cocktail ingredients, except for the Topo Chico, in a cocktail shaker and shake vigorously. Strain into a mason jar filled with ice, top with the Topo Chico, and garnish with the grapefruit slice.

INGREDIENTS:

- 1½ OZ. SILVER TEQUILA
- ¾ OZ. CAMPARI
- ½ OZ. FRESH LIME JUICE
- ½ OZ. FRESH TEXAS RUBY RED GRAPEFRUIT JUICE
- ½ OZ. SIMPLE SYRUP
- TOPO CHICO, TO TOP

HOT MESS

GARNISH: 1 LEMON WHEEL

Serrano Grenadine: Place 1 cup of pomegranate juice and 2 diced serrano peppers in a saucepan and cook until the mixture is syrupy. Remove from heat, let cool, and strain before using.

Place the cocktail ingredients in a cocktail shaker filled with ice and shake vigorously. Strain into a rocks glass filled with ice and garnish with the lemon wheel.

INGREDIENTS:

- ½ OZ. SERRANO GRENADINE
- ⅓ OZ. CHOLULA HOT SAUCE
- 1¾ OZ. REPOSADO TEQUILA (OLMECA ALTOS PREFERRED)
- ¾ OZ. FRESH LEMON JUICE

GINGER PALOMA

GARNISH: 1 GRAPEFRUIT WEDGE

Place the tequila, juices, and syrup in a cocktail shaker containing 2 tablespoons of crushed ice and shake vigorously. Strain into a chilled Collins glass filled with ice, top with the seltzer and the salt, and garnish with the grapefruit wedge.

INGREDIENTS:

- 2 OZ. TEQUILA OCHO
- 1 OZ. FRESH RUBY RED GRAPEFRUIT JUICE
- ½ OZ. FRESH LIME JUICE
- ¼ OZ. GINGER SYRUP (SEE PAGE 255, SUBSTITUTE SUGAR FOR THE HONEY)
- 2½ OZ. SELTZER WATER
- PINCH OF KOSHER SALT

TORONHA

GARNISH: PREFERRED FRUIT

Place the cocktail ingredients in a blender and puree until smooth. Pour into a mason jar and garnish with whatever fruit you prefer.

INGREDIENTS:

- 2 OZ. SILVER TEQUILA
- ½ OZ. ORANGE LIQUEUR
- 2 OZ. GRAPEFRUIT JUICE
- DASH OF ORANGE JUICE
- DASH OF GRENADINE
- 1 CUP ICE

PEACEFUL MULE

GARNISH: 1 GRAPEFRUIT WHEEL

Place the cocktail ingredients in a mason jar filled with ice, gently stir, and garnish with the grapefruit wheel.

INGREDIENTS:

- 4 OZ. JALAPEÑO LIME SOCO GINGER BEER
- 2 OZ. SILVER TEQUILA
- 2 OZ. FRESH GRAPEFRUIT JUICE
- ½ OZ. AGAVE NECTAR

CARDS ON THE TABLE

GARNISH: CRACKED BLACK PEPPER

Cardamom Tincture: Combine ½ cup of high-proof vodka with 1 tablespoon of lightly crushed cardamom pods in a mason jar, cover, and store in a cool, dark place for 3 to 5 days, while shaking every day. When the flavor is to your liking, strain and store in a cool, dark place for up to 1 year.

Combine the cocktail ingredients in a cocktail shaker filled with ice and shake vigorously. Strain into a coupe and garnish with the black pepper.

INGREDIENTS:

- 2 DASHES OF CARDAMOM TINCTURE
- 2 OZ. STRAWBERRY TEQUILA
- ¾ OZ. LEMON JUICE
- ¾ OZ. SIMPLE SYRUP

DARK PALOMA

GARNISH: 1 GRAPEFRUIT WHEEL

Place all of the cocktail ingredients, except for the Topo Chico, in a cocktail shaker filled with ice and shake vigorously. Strain into a Collins glass filled with ice, top with the Topo Chico, and garnish with the grapefruit wheel.

INGREDIENTS:

- 1 OZ. FRESH GRAPEFRUIT JUICE
- ½ OZ. FRESH LIME JUICE
- ½ OZ. AGAVE NECTAR
- 1½ OZ. SILVER TEQUILA
- TOPO CHICO, TO TOP

SILK STOCKING

Place the ingredients in a cocktail shaker filled with ice, shake vigorously, and strain into a chilled cocktail glass.

INGREDIENTS:

- 2 OZ. TEQUILA
- 1 OZ. HEAVY CREAM
- 1 OZ. CRÈME DE CACAO
- 1 TEASPOON CHAMBORD

YOU HAD ME AT HIBISCUS

GARNISH: DEHYDRATED HIBISCUS

Place the cocktail ingredients in a cocktail shaker filled with ice and shake vigorously. Double-strain into a coupe and garnish with the dehydrated hibiscus.

INGREDIENTS:

- ½ OZ. HIBISCUS SYRUP (SEE PAGE 664)
- ¾ OZ. LEMON JUICE
- ¼ OZ. LUXARDO
- 1½ OZ. REPOSADO TEQUILA

TRUE ROMANCE

GARNISH: 1 LIME TWIST & PINCH OF SALT

Place the cocktail ingredients in a rocks glass and stir. Add one large ice cube and garnish with the lime twist and the pinch of sea salt.

INGREDIENTS:

- 1½ OZ. MEZCAL
- 1 OZ. YELLOW CHARTREUSE
- ¾ OZ. AMARO AVERNA

BLESSING OF AGAVE

GARNISH: 1 STRIP OF GRAPEFRUIT PEEL

Combine the cocktail ingredients in a cocktail shaker and dry shake for 10 seconds. Add ice and shake for 30 seconds. Double-strain into a coupe and garnish with the strip of grapefruit peel.

INGREDIENTS:

- 1½ OZ. TEQUILA CABEZA
- ½ OZ. APEROL
- ¾ OZ. FRESH GRAPEFRUIT JUICE
- ¼ OZ. LIME JUICE
- ½ OZ. AGAVE NECTAR
- 1 EGG WHITE

MEXICAN MARTINI

GARNISH: 1 JALAPEÑO-STUFFED OLIVE

Wet the rim of a cocktail glass and dip it into the salt. Place the cocktail ingredients in a cocktail shaker filled with ice and shake vigorously. Strain into the cocktail glass and garnish with the olive.

INGREDIENTS:

- SALT, FOR THE RIM
- 3 OZ. REPOSADO TEQUILA
- 1½ OZ. COINTREAU
- 1½ OZ. FRESH LIME JUICE
- ½ OZ. 1888 DIRTIEST MARTINI MIX

PALOMA REYNA

GARNISH: 1 STRIP OF ORANGE PEEL & 1 SPRIG OF THYME

Grapefruit-Thyme Cordial: Peel 2 ruby red grapefruits, discard the peels, and juice them into a small saucepan. Add the juice of 2 large lemons to the saucepan, add a handful of thyme leaves and an equal amount of sugar, and cook over low heat while stirring. Once the sugar has dissolved, allow the mixture to simmer for 30 minutes before removing from heat. Strain before using.

Combine the tequila, cordial, and lime juice in a cocktail shaker filled with ice and shake vigorously. Strain into a Collins glass filled with ice, top with the Topo Chico, and garnish with the strip of orange peel and the thyme sprig.

INGREDIENTS:

- ¾ OZ. GRAPEFRUIT-THYME CORDIAL
- 1½ OZ. TEQUILA
- ½ OZ. LIME JUICE
- TOPO CHICO, TO TOP

1888

THUNDER GUN EXPRESS

Place the orange wedges in a cocktail shaker and muddle. Add ice and the remaining ingredients, shake vigorously, and strain into a rocks glass filled with ice.

INGREDIENTS:

- 4 ORANGE WEDGES
- 2 DASHES OF CARDAMOM BITTERS
- ¾ OZ. WILDFLOWER HONEY SYRUP
- ¾ OZ. AMARO MONTENEGRO
- 1 OZ. DEL MAGUEY VIDA MEZCAL

THE ONLY WORD

GARNISH: 1 LIME WHEEL

Place the cocktail ingredients in a cocktail shaker filled with ice and shake vigorously. Strain into a coupe and garnish with the lime wheel.

INGREDIENTS:

- ¾ OZ. TEQUILA
- ¾ OZ. LIME JUICE
- ¾ OZ. CHARTREUSE
- ¾ OZ. LUXARDO
- ¼ OZ. MEZCAL
- DASH OF CELERY BITTERS

BURNING IN EFFIGY

GARNISH: 1 ABUELITA HOT CHOCOLATE TABLET, GRATED, & 1 STRIP OF LEMON PEEL

Place the cocktail ingredients in a cocktail shaker filled with ice and shake until chilled. Double-strain into a coupe and garnish with the grated chocolate and the lemon peel.

INGREDIENTS:

- 2 OZ. SILVER TEQUILA
- ½ OZ. STREGA
- ½ OZ. LEMON JUICE
- ¼ OZ. ANCHO REYES
- ¼ OZ. CRÈME DE CACAO

DISTRITO FEDERAL

GARNISH: 1 STRIP OF GRAPEFRUIT PEEL

Place the cocktail ingredients in a mixing glass filled with ice and stir until thoroughly combined. Strain into a rocks glass containing one large piece of ice, express the strip of grapefruit peel over the cocktail, and then use it as a garnish.

INGREDIENTS:

- 2 OZ. ARETTE AÑEJO TEQUILA
- ¾ OZ. COCCHI STORICO VERMOUTH DI TORINO
- 1 SPOONFUL OF WAHAKA MEZCAL ESPADÍN
- 2 DASHES OF BITTERMENS XOCOLATL MOLE BITTERS
- DASH OF ANGOSTURA BITTERS

PITAYA-RITA

GARNISH: 1 DRAGON FRUIT SLICE

Place the cocktail ingredients in a cocktail shaker filled with ice and shake vigorously. Strain into a rocks glass and garnish with the slice of dragon fruit.

INGREDIENTS:

- 1½ OZ. PATRÓN REPOSADO TEQUILA
- 1 OZ. DRAGON FRUIT PUREE
- 1¼ OZ. LEMON JUICE
- ¾ OZ. AGAVE NECTAR
- ¾ OZ. GRAND MARNIER

DESERT SPOON

GARNISH: 1 SPRIG OF ROSEMARY

Place the cocktail ingredients in a cocktail shaker filled with ice and shake vigorously. Strain into a coupe and garnish with the rosemary sprig.

INGREDIENTS:

- 2 OZ. HACIENDA DE CHIHUAHUA SOTOL REPOSADO
- ½ OZ. COINTREAU
- 2 OZ. RUBY RED GRAPEFRUIT JUICE
- 1 OZ. LIME JUICE
- ½ OZ. AGAVE NECTAR

COOPER'S CAFÉ

GARNISH: 1 STRIP OF ORANGE PEEL

Place the cocktail ingredients in a cocktail shaker filled with ice and shake vigorously. Strain into a Nick & Nora glass and garnish with the strip of orange peel.

INGREDIENTS:

- 1 SHOT OF ESPRESSO (MEXICAN COFFEE BEAN PREFERRED), AT ROOM TEMPERATURE
- 1½ OZ. DEL MAGUEY CREMA DE MEZCAL
- ½ OZ. DEL MAGUEY VIDA MEZCAL
- ½ OZ. CINNAMON SYRUP (SEE PAGE 260)

AMY JO JOHNSON

GARNISH: 1 STRAWBERRY & 1 BASIL LEAF

Place the strawberry and basil in a cocktail shaker and muddle. Add ice and the remaining ingredients and shake vigorously. Strain into a rocks glass and garnish with the additional strawberry and basil.

INGREDIENTS:

- 1 STRAWBERRY
- 3 BASIL LEAVES
- 1½ OZ. MEZCAL
- ¾ OZ. LIME JUICE
- ¾ OZ. SIMPLE SYRUP
- 1 TEASPOON UME SHRUB (2 PARTS UMESHU PLUM WINE AND 1 PART BALSAMIC VINEGAR)

TEQUILA SUNRISE

GARNISH: 1 MARASCHINO CHERRY & 1 ORANGE SLICE

This drink might have originated in the desert heat of the Arizona Biltmore Hotel in the 1930s or '40s and featured crème de cassis, lime juice, and soda water, but the version that is popular today comes from the Trident, a restaurant in Sausalito, California. That's where legendary concert promoter Bill Graham threw a party for the Rolling Stones to help launch the band's 1972 tour of the States. Mick Jagger and company took a liking to the potency of the sweet, citrusy drink, going so far as to dub their American dates the "cocaine and Tequila Sunrise tour."

INGREDIENTS:

1 PART TEQUILA

DASH OF LEMON JUICE

ORANGE JUICE, TO TOP

SPLASH OF GRENADINE

Place ice in a glass and add the tequila and lemon juice. Stir, top with the orange juice, and add the splash of grenadine. Do not stir the drink; instead, allow the grenadine to slowly filter down through the orange juice and tequila. Garnish with the maraschino cherry and orange slice.

Variations:

Florida Sunrise: Made with equal parts orange juice and pineapple juice.

Tequila Sunset: Substitute dark rum or blackberry brandy for the grenadine.

PAN BY QUINARY

GARNISH: HOMEMADE PEAR SORBET, 1 SPRIG OF DILL, & 1 PIECE OF GINGER

Place all of the ingredients in a cocktail shaker filled with ice and shake vigorously. Strain into a glass and garnish with the sorbet, dill, and ginger.

INGREDIENTS:

- 30 ML DON JULIO BLANCO
- 10 ML BIANCO VERMOUTH
- 10 ML LEMONGRASS SIMPLE SYRUP (SEE PAGE 195)
- 20 ML PEAR PURÉE

DARK WINGS

GARNISH: HANDFUL OF BLACKBERRIES

Place the tequila, blackberry liqueur, and lime juice in a cocktail shaker filled with ice and shake until chilled. Strain into a highball glass filled with ice, top with the ginger beer, and garnish with the handful of blackberries.

INGREDIENTS:

- 1 PART SILVER TEQUILA
- 1 PART BLACKBERRY LIQUEUR
- JUICE OF 1 LIME
- 2 PARTS GINGER BEER

PALOMA PLUS

GARNISH: 1 GRAPEFRUIT WEDGE

Add the tequila, grapefruit juice, and lime juice to a highball glass filled with ice and stir. Top with the grapefruit soda, stir again, and garnish with the grapefruit wedge.

INGREDIENTS:

- 1 PART TEQUILA
- SPLASH OF GRAPEFRUIT JUICE
- JUICE OF 1 LIME WEDGE
- 2 PARTS GRAPEFRUIT SODA

TIA MIA

GARNISH: 1 LIME WHEEL, 1 ORCHID BLOSSOM, & 1 SPRIG OF MINT

Place the cocktail ingredients in a cocktail shaker filled with ice and shake vigorously. Strain over crushed ice into a rocks glass and garnish with the sprig of mint, lime wheel, and orchid blossom.

INGREDIENTS:

- 1 OZ. DEL MAGUEY VIDA MEZCAL
- 1 OZ. APPLETON SIGNATURE RUM
- ¾ OZ. LIME JUICE
- ½ OZ. TOASTED ALMOND ORGEAT
- ½ OZ. PIERRE FERRAND DRY CURAÇAO

TIJUANA SWIZZLE

Black Pepper Syrup: Place 10 black peppercorns in a basic simple syrup when it is boiling. After 1 minute, remove from heat, let cool, and strain before using.

Place the coffee beans in a highball glass and muddle. Add the remaining ingredients, except for the bitters, fill the glass with crushed ice, use the swizzle method to combine, and then place the bitters on top.

Serving suggestion: While you do not have to garnish this drink at all for it to stand out, the place where it originated—the Park Hyatt Paris-Vendôme—garnishes this drink with a strip of lime peel, a star anise pod, a cinnamon stick, a coffee bean, and a small red pepper.

INGREDIENTS:

- 1 TABLESPOON BLACK PEPPER SYRUP
- 4 COFFEE BEANS
- 2 OZ. DEL MAGUEY VIDA MEZCAL
- ¾ OZ. APRICOT JUICE
- ¾ OZ. LIME JUICE
- 1 TABLESPOON BÉNÉDICTINE
- 1 TABLESPOON GINGER CORDIAL
- 5 DASHES OF ANGOSTURA BITTERS

JENNIFER'S SLIPPER

GARNISH: 2 MARASCHINO CHERRIES

Place the cocktail ingredients in a cocktail shaker filled with crushed ice and shake until chilled. Strain into a chilled cocktail glass and garnish with the maraschino cherries.

Tip: There are some quality sour mixes available at the store, but homemade will always be better. If you're interested, combine 1 cup sugar and 1 cup water in a medium saucepan and simmer, while stirring, until the sugar dissolves. Remove from heat, add 2 cups lime juice and 2 cups lemon juice (no pulp in either), and let sit until cool. Store in the refrigerator for up to 2 weeks.

INGREDIENTS:

- 1 OZ. TEQUILA
- ½ OZ. MIDORI
- 2 OZ. SOUR MIX

ANTICUADO

GARNISH: 1 TORCHED LIME TWIST

Place the tequila, lime, and bitters in a cocktail shaker and muddle. Add the orange juice, agave nectar, and ice and shake vigorously. Double-strain the cocktail into a coupe and garnish with the torched twist of lime.

How to torch a citrus peel: When it comes to garnishes for tequila cocktails, you can always add a wedge of fresh lime and be done with it. If you are feeling a little more adventurous, or you just want to have a fun party trick up your sleeve, try introducing some fire to your garnish. Heating the peel, or even singeing it slightly with a flame, will add even more flavor.

Intrigued? Here's how: Peel a twist from a citrus peel, light a match, and hold the match under the twist until it is lightly brown and fragrant. You can use this technique for herbs like rosemary or thyme as well.

INGREDIENTS:

- 1½ OZ. REPOSADO TEQUILA
- ½ LIME, CUT INTO THIRDS
- 4 DASHES OF AROMATIC BITTERS
- 1 OZ. FRESH ORANGE JUICE
- ½ OZ. AGAVE NECTAR

SMOKE ON THE BEACH

GARNISH: 1 STRIP OF ORANGE PEEL

Place the cocktail ingredients in a cocktail shaker filled halfway with ice and shake vigorously. Double-strain into a coupe, express the strip of orange peel over the cocktail, and then use it as a garnish.

INGREDIENTS:

- 1 OZ. MEZCAL
- 1 OZ. SILVER TEQUILA
- 1 OZ. FRESH LIME JUICE
- 1 OZ. PINEAPPLE JUICE
- ½ OZ. AGAVE NECTAR

FROZEN TEQUILA REFRESHER

GARNISH: 1 LIME WHEEL

Place the cocktail ingredients in a blender and puree until the desired consistency is achieved. Pour into a Hurricane glass and garnish with the lime wheel.

INGREDIENTS:

- 1 CUP WATERMELON, SEEDED AND CUBED
- 1 OZ. SIMPLE SYRUP
- 2 OZ. SILVER TEQUILA
- JUICE OF ½ LIME
- 1 CUP ICE

MEXICAN MULE

GARNISH: 1 LIME WHEEL

Place the tequila, triple sec, and lime juice in a highball glass filled with ice, top with the ginger beer, and stir until thoroughly mixed. Garnish with the lime wheel.

INGREDIENTS:

- 1 PART TEQUILA
- SPLASH OF TRIPLE SEC
- JUICE OF 1 LIME WEDGE
- 2 PARTS GINGER BEER

TEQUILA LEMONADE

GARNISH: 1 LEMON WHEEL

Place the lemon juice and sugar in a mason jar and stir until the sugar has mostly dissolved. Add your desired amount of ice and rub one of the mint leaves around the rim of the glass. Tear all of the leaves in half and add them to the glass. Add the tequila and water, stir until combined, and garnish with the lemon wheel.

INGREDIENTS:

- JUICE OF 2 LEMONS
- 1 TEASPOON SUGAR
- 4 MINT LEAVES
- 2 OZ. SILVER TEQUILA
- 6 OZ. WATER

L'ORANGE PASSION

GARNISH: 1 LIME WEDGE & 1 STRIP OF LEMON PEEL

Place the cocktail ingredients in a cocktail shaker filled with ice and shake until chilled. Strain into a highball glass filled with ice and garnish with the lime wedge and strip of lemon peel.

INGREDIENTS:

- 1 OZ. TEQUILA
- ½ OZ. LILLET BLANC
- ½ OZ. COINTREAU OR PREFERRED ORANGE LIQUEUR
- ORANGE JUICE, TO TASTE
- PASSION FRUIT JUICE, TO TASTE
- SQUEEZE OF LIME JUICE

BAJA LEMONADE

GARNISH: 1 LEMON WHEEL

Place the rosemary, tequila, and coconut rum in a cocktail shaker filled with ice and shake vigorously. Strain into a highball glass filled with ice, top with the lemonade, and garnish with the lemon wheel.

INGREDIENTS:

- 1 SPRIG OF ROSEMARY
- 1 PART TEQUILA
- SPLASH OF COCONUT RUM
- 2 PARTS LEMONADE

APPLE TART

GARNISH: 1 LIME WHEEL

Place the cocktail ingredients in a cocktail shaker filled with ice and shake vigorously. Strain into a highball glass filled with ice and garnish with the lime wheel.

Tip: This recipe will also work well as a punch.

INGREDIENTS:

- 2 OZ. TEQUILA
- 1 OZ. APPLE SCHNAPPS
- 1 OZ. APPLE JUICE
- JUICE OF 1 LIME

FUEGO DE COLIMA

Place all of the ingredients in a cocktail shaker filled with ice, shake vigorously, and strain into a rocks glass.

GINGER-AND-LEMONGRASS CORDIAL

Place the ingredients in a saucepan and simmer, while stirring occasionally, for 20 minutes. Remove from heat, let cool, and strain before using. It will keep in the fridge for 2 to 4 weeks.

INGREDIENTS:

- 1¾ OZ. CALLE 23 TEQUILA (OR ANY OTHER GOOD TEQUILA)
- ¾ OZ. GINGER-AND-LEMONGRASS CORDIAL (SEE RECIPE BELOW)
- 2 TEASPOONS CHAIRMAN'S RESERVE SPICED RUM
- 1 TABLESPOON SIMPLE SYRUP

GINGER-AND-LEMONGRASS CORDIAL:

- 1 LARGE PIECE OF GINGER, PEELED AND SLICED
- 1 LEMONGRASS STALK, WHITE PART ONLY, CRUSHED
- 2 CUPS WATER
- 1½ CUPS SUGAR

TEQUILA SOUR

GARNISH: 1 SPRIG OF MINT

Place the lemon juice, tequila, and sugar in a cocktail shaker filled with ice and shake vigorously. Place the blueberries and lemon wheel in a highball glass and add ice. Strain the cocktail into the glass and garnish with the mint sprig.

INGREDIENTS:

- JUICE OF 1 LEMON
- 2 OZ. TEQUILA
- 1 TEASPOON SUGAR
- HANDFUL OF BLUEBERRIES
- 1 LEMON WHEEL

LA CONQUISTADOR

GARNISH: 1 LIME WEDGE

Wet the rim of a rocks glass and dip it into the spicy salt. Combine the remaining ingredients in a cocktail shaker filled with ice and shake vigorously. Strain into the rocks glass and garnish with the lime wedge.

INGREDIENTS:

- SPICY SALT, FOR THE RIM
- ½ OZ. OLMECA ALTOS TEQUILA REPOSADO
- ½ OZ. OLMECA ALTOS TEQUILA PLATA
- 1 TABLESPOON GIFFARD CRÈME DE CACAO (WHITE)
- ½ OZ. FRESH LIME JUICE
- 1 TEASPOON AGAVE SYRUP
- 5–7 DASHES OF FEE BROTHERS AZTEC CHOCOLATE BITTERS

OAXACA OLD FASHIONED

GARNISH: 1 TORCHED ORANGE TWIST

Place the cocktail ingredients in a rocks glass containing one large ice cube, stir until chilled, and garnish with the torched orange twist.

INGREDIENTS:

- 1½ OZ. EL TESORO REPOSADO TEQUILA
- ½ OZ. DEL MAGUEY SAN LUIS DEL RIO MEZCAL
- 2 DASHES OF ANGOSTURA BITTERS
- 1 SPOONFUL OF AGAVE NECTAR

NAKED AND FAMOUS

Place all of the ingredients in a cocktail shaker filled with ice, shake until chilled, and strain into a coupe.

INGREDIENTS:

- ¾ OZ. DEL MAGUEY CHICHICAPA MEZCAL
- ¾ OZ. YELLOW CHARTREUSE
- ¾ OZ. APEROL
- ¾ OZ. LIME JUICE

MIDNIGHT MARAUDER

Place all of the ingredients in a mixing glass, add ice, and stir briskly. Strain into a chilled Nick & Nora glass or a coupe.

INGREDIENTS:

- 1 OZ. DEL MAGUEY VIDA MEZCAL
- 1 OZ. BONAL GENTIANE-QUINA
- 1 OZ. CYNAR
- DASH OF BITTERMENS XOCOLATL MOLE BITTERS

BLOODY MARIA

GARNISH: 1 CELERY STALK & 1 LEMON WEDGE

Wet the rim of a pint glass or mason jar and dip it into the black pepper. Add ice, the tequila, olive brine, lime juice, and horseradish, top with tomato juice, and stir until thoroughly mixed. Add the Worcestershire sauce, hot sauce, and celery salt, season with black pepper, stir again, and garnish with the celery stalk and the lemon wedge.

Tip: As with the Bloody Mary, there are too many possibilities with the Bloody Maria to even know where to begin. Once you have a general sense of what you like, do what every bartender in the world does: experiment with new ingredients until you find something that works for you.

INGREDIENTS:

- CRACKED BLACK PEPPER, FOR THE RIM, PLUS MORE TO TASTE
- 2 OZ. GOLD TEQUILA
- ½ OZ. OLIVE BRINE
- JUICE OF 1 LIME WEDGE
- 2 DASHES OF HORSERADISH
- TOMATO JUICE, TO TOP
- 3 DROPS OF WORCESTERSHIRE SAUCE
- 3 DASHES OF HOT SAUCE
- 2 DASHES OF CELERY SALT

COFFEE IN CHIHUAHUA

Infused Tequila: Place 3 spoonfuls of coffee in a filter, tie it closed, and place it in 6 oz. of tequila. Steep for 4 hours and remove the coffee before using.

Light the cinnamon stick so that it smolders on one end, place it on a plate, and cover with a rocks glass so that the smoke accumulates in the glass. Place the remaining ingredients in a mixing glass filled with ice and stir until chilled. Discard the cinnamon stick, strain the cocktail into the rocks glass, and add a few ice cubes.

INGREDIENTS:

- 2 OZ. COFFEE-INFUSED REPOSADO TEQUILA
- 1 CINNAMON STICK
- 1 SPOONFUL OF AGAVE NECTAR
- 3 DASHES OF ANGOSTURA BITTERS

NO SAY

GARNISH: 1 MAKRUT LIME LEAF

Place the cocktail ingredients in a cocktail shaker filled with ice and shake vigorously. Strain into a rocks glass filled with ice and garnish with the makrut lime leaf.

INGREDIENTS:

- 1¾ OZ. ILEGAL MEZCAL
- ¾ OZ. APEROL
- ¼ OZ. RHUM CLÉMENT MAHINA COCO
- 1 OZ. LIME JUICE
- ½ OZ. PINEAPPLE JUICE
- ¾ OZ. LEMONGRASS SIMPLE SYRUP (SEE PAGE 195)

DOPE

GARNISH: 1 STRIP OF GRAPEFRUIT PEEL

Place the egg and mezcal in a cocktail shaker and dry shake for 10 seconds. Add ice and the remaining cocktail ingredients and shake for 20 seconds. Double-strain into a rocks glass, express the strip of grapefruit peel over the cocktail, and discard.

INGREDIENTS:

- 1 EGG
- 1 OZ. MEZCAL (DEL MAGUEY VIDA PREFERRED)
- 1 OZ. GALLIANO
- 1 OZ. PINEAPPLE JUICE
- DASH OF LACTART (ACID OF MILK)

AGUARDIENTE DOLAR

GARNISH: 1 LIME WHEEL

Infused Mezcal: Place 2 cinnamon sticks in a mason jar filled with mezcal and store in a cool, dark place for at least 2 days. Strain before using.

Place the infused mezcal, liqueur, lime juice, and ginger syrup in a cocktail shaker filled with ice and shake vigorously. Shake, strain into a Collins glass, and top with the ginger ale. Add the bitters and garnish with the lime wheel.

INGREDIENTS:

- 1¾ OZ. CINNAMON-INFUSED MEZCAL (DEL MAGUEY VIDA PREFERRED)
- ¼ OZ. AMARGO-VALLET LIQUEUR
- ¾ OZ. LIME JUICE
- ¾ OZ. GINGER SYRUP (SEE PAGE 255, SUBSTITUTE SUGAR FOR THE HONEY)
- GINGER ALE, TO TOP
- 6 DASHES OF ANGOSTURA BITTERS

CROSSEYED AND PAINLESS

GARNISH: 1 LEMON TWIST

Place all of the ingredients, except for the Herbsaint, in a mixing glass filled with ice and stir. Rinse a coupe with the Herbsaint and discard the excess. Strain the cocktail into the glass and garnish with the lemon twist.

INGREDIENTS:

- ¾ OZ. SLOE GIN
- ¾ OZ. TEQUILA
- ¾ OZ. DRY CURAÇAO
- ¾ OZ. LILLET ROUGE
- DASH OF ANGOSTURA BITTERS
- ⅛ OZ. HERBSAINT ANISE-FLAVORED LIQUEUR

SORCIÈRE

Place all of the ingredients in a cocktail shaker filled with ice and shake vigorously. Double-strain into a rocks glass.

INGREDIENTS:

- ¼ OZ. CINNAMON SYRUP (SEE PAGE 260)
- ½ OZ. FRESH LEMON JUICE
- ½ OZ. AQUAVIT
- ¾ OZ. SILVER TEQUILA
- 1 OZ. MASTIHA LIQUEUR

CULTURE VULTURE

GARNISH: 1 SPRIG OF MINT

Pepita Orgeat: Place 1 cup pumpkin seeds in a large saucepan and toast over medium heat. Add 2 cups water, bring to a boil, remove from heat, and let cool. When cool, pulse in a blender until the mixture is a coarse meal, and then strain the liquid through cheesecloth. Discard the solids, transfer the liquid to a small pot, and add an equal amount of sugar. Simmer until the sugar dissolves, add 1½ oz. vodka and 1 teaspoon orange blossom water, stir, and let cool before using.

Place all of the cocktail ingredients, except for the bitters, in a cocktail shaker and dry shake. Strain into a double rocks glass containing cracked ice, top with the bitters, and garnish with the sprig of mint.

INGREDIENTS:

- ¾ OZ. PEPITA ORGEAT
- 1½ OZ. MEZCAL (EL BUHO PREFERRED)
- ½ OZ. AÑEJO TEQUILA (SIEMBRA AZUL PREFERRED)
- ¾ OZ. LIME JUICE
- 3 DROPS OF ORANGE BLOSSOM WATER
- 2 MINT LEAVES
- 14 DROPS OF ANGOSTURA BITTERS

SHADYSIDE FIZZ

GARNISH: 3 DROPS OF ANGOSTURA BITTERS

Place the egg white and lime juice in a cocktail shaker and dry shake. Add ice, the tequila, bitters, and simple syrup, and shake vigorously. Strain into a Collins glass filled with ice, top with Sprite, and garnish with the additional drops of bitters.

INGREDIENTS:

- 1 EGG WHITE
- ¾ OZ. LIME JUICE
- 1 OZ. SILVER TEQUILA (HERRADURA PREFERRED)
- 1 OZ. ANGOSTURA BITTERS
- ¾ OZ. SIMPLE SYRUP
- SPRITE, TO TOP

BERLIN IN '77

GARNISH: 1 ORANGE WHEEL

Place all of the cocktail ingredients, except for the bitters, in a cocktail shaker filled with ice and shake vigorously. Strain into a double rocks glass, add the bitters, and garnish with the orange wheel.

INGREDIENTS:

- 1 OZ. MEZCAL (DON AMADO PREFERRED)
- 1 OZ. TEQUILA (CABEZA BLANCO PREFERRED)
- 1 OZ. ORANGE JUICE
- ½ OZ. LEMON JUICE
- ½ OZ. CINNAMON SYRUP (SEE PAGE 260)
- DASH OF AROMATIC BITTERS

PARKWAY FLOAT

GARNISH: DOLLOP OF SWEETENED CREAM

Sweetened Cream: Place 2 oz. heavy cream and 1 tablespoon sugar in a mason jar and shake until combined.

Place the tequila and Fernet-Branca in a Collins glass filled halfway with ice and stir. Add the root beer and top with the sweetened cream.

INGREDIENTS:

- 2 OZ. AÑEJO TEQUILA (EL TESORO PREFERRED)
- ¾ OZ. FERNET-BRANCA
- 2 OZ. ROOT BEER

SLEEPING TIGER

GARNISH: 1 LIME WHEEL, DASH OF CAYENNE PEPPER, & DASH OF DEMERARA SUGAR

Place the cocktail ingredients in a cocktail shaker filled with ice and shake vigorously. Double-strain into a rocks glass filled with ice and garnish with the lime wheel, cayenne, and sugar.

INGREDIENTS:

- 1½ OZ. DEL MAGUEY VIDA MEZCAL
- ¾ OZ. LIME JUICE
- ¼ OZ. GINGER SYRUP (SEE PAGE 255, SUBSTITUTE SUGAR FOR THE HONEY)
- ¼ OZ. HONEY SYRUP
- ½ OZ. PINEAPPLE JUICE

THIRD PLAYER

GARNISH: 1 CINNAMON STICK

Place all of the ingredients in a cocktail shaker, fill with ice, and shake vigorously. Strain into a rocks glass filled with crushed ice and garnish with the cinnamon stick.

TOASTED BLACK CARDAMOM-AND-CINNAMON MAPLE SYRUP

Place the cinnamon sticks in a skillet, toast over medium heat until they release their aroma and begin to crackle, and remove from the pan. Place the cinnamon sticks, cardamom pods, syrup, and water in a small saucepan and cook over medium heat for 5 minutes. Remove from heat, let cool to room temperature, strain, and store in the refrigerator for up to 1 month.

INGREDIENTS:

- ¾ OZ. BUENBICHO MEZCAL JOVEN
- ½ OZ. YAGUARA CACHAÇA
- ½ OZ. TOASTED BLACK CARDAMOM-AND-CINNAMON MAPLE SYRUP (SEE RECIPE BELOW)
- ½ OZ. FRESH LIME JUICE
- ¼ OZ. MACCHU PISCO
- ¼ OZ. ROTHMAN & WINTER ORCHARD APRICOT LIQUEUR
- ¼ OZ. ANCHO REYES
- ½ OZ. ORGEAT
- ¼ OZ. VELVET FALERNUM
- 2 DASHES OF BITTERMENS XOCOLATL MOLE BITTERS
- PINCH OF SALT

TOASTED BLACK CARDAMOM-AND-CINNAMON MAPLE SYRUP:

- 2 CINNAMON STICKS, SMASHED
- 3 BLACK CARDAMOM PODS, SMASHED
- 1 CUP MAPLE SYRUP
- ½ CUP WATER

649

RASPBERRY MARGARITA

GARNISH: HANDFUL OF RASPBERRIES

Wet the rim of a mason jar and dip it into the salt. Fill a cocktail shaker with ice, add the cocktail ingredients, and shake until chilled. Place ice in the glass, strain the cocktail into it, and garnish with the raspberries.

INGREDIENTS:

- SALT, FOR THE RIM
- 3 PARTS TEQUILA
- 2 PARTS ORANGE LIQUEUR
- 1 PART RASPBERRY LIQUEUR
- 1 PART LIME JUICE

APPLE PIE MARGARITA

GARNISH: 1 APPLE SLICE

Wet the rim of a glass and dip it into the cinnamon-sugar mixture. Fill a cocktail shaker with ice, add the cocktail ingredients, and shake until chilled. Place ice in the glass, strain the cocktail into it, and garnish with the slice of apple.

INGREDIENTS:

- CINNAMON-SUGAR MIXTURE, FOR THE RIM
- 2 PARTS CINNAMON TEQUILA
- 1 PART ORANGE LIQUEUR
- 2 PARTS APPLE CIDER

CLASSIC MARGARITA

GARNISH: 1 LIME SLICE

In Spanish, "margarita" means "daisy," and this cocktail's origins reach back to a style of drink popular during the 1930s and '40s. A Daisy, the combination of a spirit, citrus juice, and grenadine served over shaved ice, came in gin and whisk(e)y varieties, so it is no surprise that a tequila iteration—calling for tequila, orange liqueur, lime juice, and a splash of soda—came to be. Though exactly who thought up the Margarita as we know it today remains a matter of debate. One story has it that Mexican restaurant owner Carlos Herrera devised the drink in 1938, as a way to impress Ziegfeld showgirl Marjorie King, who happened to be allergic to all alcohol other than tequila, which she didn't like to drink straight. Herrera supposedly solved the problem by adding salt and lime to create the world's first Margarita. But there is also the story of socialite Margaret Sames and a party she hosted at her Acapulco villa in 1948. Wanting to impress her guests, she reportedly stirred up a drink that featured her favorite spirits: Cointreau and tequila. No matter who mixed it first, the Margarita is now the most popular mixed drink in the United States, even beating out the Martini.

WASTIN' AWAY AGAIN IN MARGARITAVILLE

In his most famous song, Jimmy Buffett sings about "booze in the blender" and "that frozen concoction that helps me hang on," but his ideal Margarita is served on the rocks, the same as the one he had back in Austin, Texas, in 1977. On his way to the airport he and a friend stopped at a Mexican restaurant, had the house Margarita, and then he wrote "Margaritaville" on the spot in 5 minutes. In June 2018, he explained his take on drinking Margaritas to *InStyle*: "I've had great ones and I've had bad ones over the years. But the very best Margarita? That will always be the one that somebody else buys for you."

INGREDIENTS:

SALT, FOR THE RIM
2 PARTS SILVER TEQUILA
1 PART TRIPLE SEC
1 PART LIME JUICE

Wet the rim of a glass and dip it into the salt. Place the tequila, triple sec, and lime juice in a cocktail shaker filled with ice and shake until chilled. Strain into the glass and garnish with the slice of lime.

PERFECT MARGARITA

GARNISH: 1 LIME WHEEL

Wet the rim of a glass and dip it into the salt. Place the tequila, Grand Marnier, and lime juice in a cocktail shaker filled with ice and shake until chilled. Strain into the glass and garnish with the lime wheel.

INGREDIENTS:

- SALT, FOR THE RIM
- 2 PARTS JOSE CUERVO 1800 SILVER TEQUILA
- 1 PART GRAND MARNIER
- 1 PART LIME JUICE

CRANBERRY MARGARITA

GARNISH: 1 LIME WHEEL & HANDFUL OF CRANBERRIES

Wet the rim of a glass and dip it into the salt. Place the cocktail ingredients in a cocktail shaker filled with ice and shake vigorously. Place ice in the glass, strain the cocktail into it, and garnish with the lime wheel and handful of cranberries.

INGREDIENTS:

- SALT, FOR THE RIM
- 1 PART LIME JUICE
- 2 PARTS TEQUILA
- 1 PART ORANGE LIQUEUR
- 2 PARTS CRANBERRY JUICE

EARLY NIGHT

GARNISH: 1 MARASCHINO CHERRY & 1 STAR FRUIT SLICE

Place the cocktail ingredients in a highball glass filled with ice, stir until chilled, and garnish with the slice of star fruit and a cherry.

Variations: If cherry isn't your favorite flavor, feel free to substitute melon liqueur or limoncello. And if star fruit feels a touch too fancy, an orange wheel will do the trick.

INGREDIENTS:

- 1 PART TEQUILA
- 1 PART LUXARDO
- JUICE OF ½ LIME
- 2 PARTS ORANGE JUICE

BUDGET MARGARITA

GARNISH: 1 LIME WEDGE

Wet the rim of a glass and dip it into the salt. Place the tequila and margarita mix in a cocktail shaker filled with ice and shake until chilled. Strain into the glass and garnish with the lime wedge.

INGREDIENTS:

- SALT, FOR THE RIM
- 1 PART JOSE CUERVO GOLD TEQUILA
- 1 PART MARGARITA MIX

END OF THE LIME

GARNISH: 1 LIME WEDGE

Place the tequila and lime juice in a rocks glass filled with ice, top with the soda, and garnish with the lime wedge.

INGREDIENTS:

- 1 PART TEQUILA
- JUICE OF ½ LIME
- 2 PARTS LEMON-LIME SODA

WHAT'S NEW

GARNISH: 1 STRIP OF ORANGE PEEL

Place the syrup, bitters, and tequila in a chilled rocks glass and stir. Add 1 to 2 medium ice cubes to the glass, stir for 30 to 45 seconds, and garnish with the twist of lime.

INGREDIENTS:

- ½ OZ. SIMPLE SYRUP
- 2–3 DASHES OF ORANGE BITTERS
- 2 OZ. AÑEJO TEQUILA

BLOODY MARIA EXPRESS

GARNISH: ANYTHING YOUR HEART DESIRES

Place the Worcestershire sauce and lemon juice in a pint glass and then add ice. Add the tequila and tomato juice and stir until chilled. Garnish with anything you want—lemon, lime, cilantro, olives, or even bacon.

INGREDIENTS:

- DASH OF WORCESTERSHIRE SAUCE
- DASH OF LEMON JUICE
- 1 PART TEQUILA
- 2 PARTS TOMATO JUICE

BERRY BURSTER

GARNISH: 1 KIWI SLICE

Reserve a slice of the kiwi for a garnish. Place the rest of the kiwi and the strawberries in a rocks glass and muddle. Add ice, the tequila, and the juice, stir, and garnish with the reserved slice of kiwi.

INGREDIENTS:

- 1 KIWI, SLICED
- 4 STRAWBERRIES, SLICED
- 1 PART TEQUILA
- 1 PART STRAWBERRY-KIWI JUICE

TEQUILA SPARKLER

GARNISH: 1 LIME WEDGE

Place the tequila and lime juice in a champagne flute, top with the Champagne, and garnish with a lime wedge.

INGREDIENTS:

1 PART TEQUILA
SPLASH OF LIME JUICE
3 PARTS CHAMPAGNE

TEQUILA LIME SODA

GARNISH: 1 LIME WHEEL

Place the tequila and lime juice in a rocks glass filled with ice and gently stir. Top with the club soda and garnish with the lime wheel.

INGREDIENTS:

1 PART SILVER TEQUILA
1 PART LIME JUICE
3 PARTS CLUB SODA

TEQUILA SIDECAR

GARNISH: 1 CITRUS TWIST

Place the cocktail ingredients in a cocktail shaker filled halfway with ice and shake until chilled. Strain into a coupe or cocktail glass and garnish with the twist of citrus.

Tip: Any añejo tequila will work, but if you can find one that has been aged in old cognac barrels, that is even better.

INGREDIENTS:

1½ OZ. AÑEJO TEQUILA
1 OZ. SIMPLE SYRUP
1 OZ. ORANGE LIQUEUR
½ OZ. FRESH LIME JUICE

LEMON-LIME MARGARITA

GARNISH: 1 LIME OR LEMON WEDGE

Wet the rim of a rocks glass and dip it into the salt. Place the cocktail ingredients in a cocktail shaker filled halfway with ice and shake vigorously. Fill the glass with ice, strain the cocktail into the glass, and garnish with a wedge of lime or lemon.

INGREDIENTS:

SEA SALT, FOR THE RIM
2 OZ. SILVER TEQUILA
½ OZ. FRESH LIME JUICE
½ OZ. FRESH LEMON JUICE
1 OZ. SIMPLE SYRUP

LEMON MARGARITA

GARNISH: 1 LIME WEDGE OR 1 LEMON WHEEL

Wet the rim of a rocks glass and dip it into the salt. Place the cocktail ingredients in a cocktail shaker filled halfway with ice and shake vigorously. Fill the glass with ice, strain cocktail into it, and garnish with the lime wedge or lemon wheel.

INGREDIENTS:

- SEA SALT, FOR THE RIM
- 2 OZ. SILVER TEQUILA
- 1 OZ. FRESH LEMON JUICE
- 1 OZ. ORANGE LIQUEUR
- 1 OZ. SIMPLE SYRUP

BLACK PEPPER MARGARITA

GARNISH: 1 LIME SLICE & JALAPEÑO PEPPER SLICES (OPTIONAL)

Wet the rim of a rocks glass and dip it into the salt and the pepper. Place the cocktail ingredients in a cocktail shaker filled with ice and shake vigorously. Fill the glass with ice, strain the cocktail into the glass, and garnish with the slice of lime and, if desired, the jalapeño.

INGREDIENTS:

- SEA SALT, FOR THE RIM
- BLACK PEPPER, FOR THE RIM
- 2 OZ. SILVER TEQUILA
- ½ OZ. FRESH LIME JUICE
- ½ OZ. FRESH LEMON JUICE
- 1 OZ. BLACK PEPPER SYRUP (SEE PAGE 354)

MONGOOSE MARGARITA

GARNISH: 1 LIME WEDGE

Wet the rim of a rocks glass and dip it into the salt. Place the cocktail ingredients in a cocktail shaker filled with ice and shake vigorously. Fill the glass with ice, strain the cocktail into the glass, and garnish with the lime wedge.

INGREDIENTS:

- SALT, FOR THE RIM
- 2 OZ. RASPBERRY TEQUILA
- 1 OZ. LIME JUICE
- ½ OZ. COINTREAU
- ½ OZ. AGAVE NECTAR

PEAR-CINNAMON MARGARITA

GARNISH: 1 PEAR SLICE & 1 STAR ANISE POD (OPTIONAL)

Wet the rim of a rocks glass and dip it into the cinnamon. Place the ginger and lemon juice in a cocktail shaker and muddle. Add ice, the tequila, pear puree, and ginger liqueur and shake vigorously. Fill the glass with ice, strain the cocktail into the glass, and top with the splash of seltzer. Garnish with the pear slice and, if desired, a star anise pod.

INGREDIENTS:

- CINNAMON, FOR THE RIM
- 1-INCH PIECE OF GINGER, PEELED
- 1 OZ. FRESH LEMON JUICE
- 2 OZ. REPOSADO TEQUILA
- 1½ OZ. FRESH PEAR PUREE
- 1 OZ. DOMAINE DE CANTON
- SPLASH OF SELTZER WATER

ON THE ROCKS

"On the rocks" is a classic phrase in the spirits world, especially when it comes to Margaritas. Before making your way through these recipes, please keep in mind that the "rocks," or ice, can make or break your drink. If you don't use thick ice cubes directly from the freezer, your drink will become diluted too quickly. Once this happens, it doesn't matter how good your other ingredients are—all that quality will be washed away.

POMEGRANATE MARGARITA

GARNISH: POMEGRANATE SEEDS & 1 LIME WEDGE

Wet the rim of a rocks glass and dip it into the salt. Place the cocktail ingredients in a cocktail shaker filled halfway with ice and shake vigorously. Fill the glass with ice, strain the cocktail into it, and garnish with the lime wedge and pomegranate seeds.

INGREDIENTS:

- SEA SALT, FOR THE RIM
- 2 OZ. REPOSADO OR POMEGRANATE TEQUILA
- 1½ OZ. POMEGRANATE JUICE
- 1 OZ. FRESH LIME JUICE
- ⅔ OZ. SIMPLE SYRUP OR GRENADINE

MEXICAN GIMLET

GARNISH: 1 LIME WEDGE

Place the tequila and lime juice in a cocktail shaker filled with ice and shake until chilled. Strain into a cocktail glass or a coupe and top with a splash of seltzer, if desired. Garnish with the lime wedge.

INGREDIENTS:

- 3 OZ. SILVER TEQUILA
- 1½ OZ. FRESH LIME JUICE
- SPLASH OF SELTZER (OPTIONAL)

THE TEQUILA DAISY

Place all of the ingredients, except for the seltzer, in a cocktail shaker filled halfway with ice and shake until chilled. Strain into a coupe or cocktail glass and top with the splash of seltzer.

INGREDIENTS:

- 2 OZ. SILVER OR REPOSADO TEQUILA
- 1 OZ. FRESH LEMON JUICE
- ½ OZ. GRENADINE
- ½ OZ. SIMPLE SYRUP
- SPLASH OF SELTZER

PINK MARGARITA

GARNISH: 1 LIME WHEEL & 1 LEMON TWIST

Wet the rim of a coupe and dip it into the salt. Place the tequila, syrup, and sour mix in a cocktail shaker filled with ice and shake vigorously. Strain into the coupe and garnish with the lime wheel and the lemon twist.

INGREDIENTS:

- PINK HIMALAYAN SEA SALT, FOR THE RIM
- 1½ OZ. REPOSADO TEQUILA
- ¾ OZ. MONIN WILDBERRY SYRUP
- 3 OZ. SOUR MIX

KEY LIME MARGARITA

GARNISH: 1 KEY LIME WEDGE

Wet the rim of a rocks glass and dip it into the salt. Place the cocktail ingredients in a cocktail shaker filled with ice and shake vigorously. Fill the glass with ice, strain the cocktail into the glass, and garnish with the key lime wedge.

Tip: A key lime is ripe when it is almost completely yellow. You may find them green at the store, so make sure you let them ripen before using.

INGREDIENTS:

- SEA SALT, FOR THE RIM
- 2 OZ. SILVER TEQUILA
- 1 OZ. FRESH KEY LIME JUICE
- 1 OZ. ORANGE LIQUEUR
- 1 OZ. SIMPLE SYRUP

BLOOD ORANGE MARGARITA

GARNISH: 1 BLOOD ORANGE WEDGE

Wet the rim of a rocks glass or a cocktail glass and dip it into the salt. Place the cocktail ingredients in a cocktail shaker filled with ice and shake vigorously. Fill the glass with ice, strain the cocktail into the glass, and garnish with the blood orange wedge.

INGREDIENTS:

- SEA SALT, FOR THE RIM
- 2 OZ. SILVER TEQUILA
- 2 OZ. FRESH BLOOD ORANGE JUICE
- ½ OZ. ORANGE LIQUEUR
- 1 OZ. SIMPLE SYRUP

STRAWBERRY MARGARITA

GARNISH: 1 SMALL STRAWBERRY & 1 LIME WEDGE

Wet the rim of a rocks glass and dip it into the salt. Place the cocktail ingredients in a cocktail shaker filled with ice and shake vigorously. Fill the glass with ice, strain the cocktail into the glass, and garnish with the lime wedge and strawberry.

INGREDIENTS:

- SEA SALT, FOR THE RIM
- 2 OZ. SILVER TEQUILA
- 1 OZ. STRAWBERRY TEQUILA
- 2 OZ. FRESH STRAWBERRY JUICE
- 1 OZ. FRESH LIME JUICE
- 1 OZ. SIMPLE SYRUP

BLACKBERRY MARGARITA

GARNISH: 1 LIME WEDGE & 1 BLACKBERRY

Wet the rim of a rocks glass and dip it into the salt. Place the cocktail ingredients in a cocktail shaker, muddle, fill with ice, and shake vigorously. Fill the glass with ice, strain the cocktail into the glass, garnish with the lime wedge and the blackberry, and top with a splash of seltzer, if desired.

INGREDIENTS:

- SEA SALT, FOR THE RIM
- 2 OZ. SILVER TEQUILA
- 1 OZ. MEZCAL
- 1 OZ. FRESH LIME JUICE
- 1 OZ. SIMPLE SYRUP
- 4–5 BLACKBERRIES
- SPLASH OF SELTZER (OPTIONAL)

COCONUT MARGARITA

GARNISH: 1 LIME WHEEL

Wet the rim of a tumbler and dip it into the shredded coconut. Place the cocktail ingredients in a cocktail shaker filled with ice and shake vigorously. Fill the glass with ice, strain the cocktail into the glass, and garnish with the lime wheel.

INGREDIENTS:

- SHREDDED COCONUT, FOR THE RIM
- 2 PARTS TEQUILA
- 1 PART COCONUT RUM
- 1 PART LIME JUICE
- 1 OZ. CREAM OF COCONUT

CHERRY LIMEADE MARGARITA

GARNISH: 1 LIME WHEEL

Wet the rim of a coupe and dip it into the salt. Place the cocktail ingredients in a cocktail shaker filled with ice and shake vigorously. Fill the coupe with ice, strain the cocktail into the glass, and garnish with the lime wheel.

INGREDIENTS:

- SALT, FOR THE RIM
- 2 PARTS TEQUILA
- 1 PART LUXARDO
- 1 PART LIME JUICE

WATERMELON MARGARITA

GARNISH: 1 WATERMELON CHUNK & 1 SPRIG OF MINT

Wet the rim of a rocks glass and dip it into the salt. Place the cocktail ingredients in a cocktail shaker filled with ice and shake vigorously. Fill the glass with ice, strain the cocktail into the glass, and garnish with the watermelon chunk and the sprig of mint.

INGREDIENTS:

- SEA SALT, FOR THE RIM
- 2 OZ. SILVER TEQUILA
- 1 OZ. FRESH LIME JUICE
- 1½ OZ. WATERMELON PUREE
- ½ OZ. SIMPLE SYRUP
- 1 OZ. ORANGE LIQUEUR

BASIL MARGARITA

GARNISH: 1 LIME WEDGE & BASIL LEAVES

Basil Syrup: Add 5 to 7 basil leaves to a standard simple syrup when it is boiling. After 1 minute, remove the saucepan from heat and allow the basil leaves to cool with the syrup. Strain before using.

Wet the rim of a rocks glass and dip it into the salt. Place the cocktail ingredients in a cocktail shaker filled with ice and shake vigorously. Fill the glass with ice, strain the cocktail into the glass, and garnish with the lime wedge and the basil leaves.

INGREDIENTS:

- ¾ OZ. BASIL SYRUP
- SEA SALT, FOR THE RIM
- 2 OZ. SILVER TEQUILA
- 1 OZ. FRESH LIME JUICE
- 1 OZ. ORANGE LIQUEUR

LAVENDER MARGARITA

GARNISH: 1 SPRIG OF LAVENDER OR 1 LEMON SLICE

Wet the rim of a rocks glass and dip it into the sugar. Place the tequila, liqueur, syrup, and lime juice in a cocktail shaker filled with ice and shake vigorously. Fill the glass with ice, strain the cocktail into the glass, top with the splash of seltzer, if desired, and garnish with a lavender sprig or a lemon slice.

INGREDIENTS:

- SUGAR, FOR THE RIM
- 2 OZ. SILVER TEQUILA
- ½ OZ. ORANGE LIQUEUR
- 1 OZ. LAVENDER SYRUP (SEE PAGE 174)
- 1 OZ. FRESH LIME JUICE
- SPLASH OF SELTZER (OPTIONAL)

THYME MARGARITA

GARNISH: 1 SPRIG OF THYME OR 1 LIME WEDGE

Combine the salt and the thyme leaves in a small dish. Wet the rim of a rocks glass and dip it into the mixture. Place the cocktail ingredients in a cocktail shaker filled with ice and shake vigorously. Fill the glass with ice, strain the cocktail into the glass, and garnish with the sprig of thyme or the lime wedge.

INGREDIENTS:

- 1 TEASPOON SEA SALT
- 1 TEASPOON THYME LEAVES, FINELY CHOPPED
- 2 OZ. SILVER TEQUILA
- ½ OZ. YELLOW CHARTREUSE
- 1 OZ. THYME SYRUP (SEE PAGE 459)
- 1 OZ. FRESH LIME JUICE

ROSEMARY MARGARITA

GARNISH: 1 LIME WEDGE & 1 SPRIG OF ROSEMARY

Wet the rim of a rocks glass and dip it into the sugar. Place the cocktail ingredients in a cocktail shaker filled with ice and shake vigorously. Fill the glass with ice, strain the cocktail into the glass, and garnish with the lime wedge and sprig of rosemary.

INGREDIENTS:

- SUGAR, FOR THE RIM
- 2 OZ. REPOSADO TEQUILA
- ½ OZ. YELLOW CHARTREUSE
- 1 OZ. ROSEMARY SYRUP (SEE PAGE 308)
- ½ OZ. FRESH LIME JUICE
- ½ OZ. FRESH LEMON JUICE

MOJITO-RITA

GARNISH: MINT LEAVES & 1 LIME WEDGE

Wet the rim of a Collins glass and dip it into the salt. Place the tequila, lime juice, and mint leaves in a cocktail shaker and muddle. Add ice and the syrup or agave nectar and shake vigorously. Fill the glass with ice, strain the cocktail into the glass, and top with the seltzer, if desired. Garnish with additional mint leaves and the lime wedge.

INGREDIENTS:

- SEA SALT, FOR THE RIM
- 4 OZ. REPOSADO TEQUILA
- 2 OZ. FRESH LIME JUICE
- 2 OZ. MINT SIMPLE SYRUP (SEE PAGE 308, SUBSTITUTE MINT FOR THE ROSEMARY) OR AGAVE NECTAR
- 1 OZ. ORANGE LIQUEUR
- 5–7 MINT LEAVES
- SPLASH OF SELTZER (OPTIONAL)

THE MAINE MARGARITA

GARNISH: MINT LEAVES

Wet the rim of a rocks glass and then dip it in the sea salt. Place the tequila, lime juice, and blueberries in a cocktail shaker and muddle. Add ice, agave nectar, and bitters and shake vigorously. Fill the glass with ice, strain the cocktail into the glass, and garnish with the mint.

INGREDIENTS:

- SEA SALT, FOR THE RIM
- 2 OZ. AÑEJO TEQUILA
- 1½ OZ. FRESH LIME JUICE
- 2 TABLESPOONS FRESH BLUEBERRIES
- 1 OZ. AGAVE NECTAR
- 2–3 DASHES OF ORANGE BITTERS

CUCUMBER-MINT MARGARITA

GARNISH: MINT LEAVES & 1 LIME WEDGE

Wet the rim of a rocks glass, and then dip it in the sea salt. Add the tequila, mint leaves, and cucumber to a cocktail shaker and muddle. Add ice, lime juice, and syrup or agave nectar and shake vigorously. Fill the glass with ice, strain the cocktail into the glass, and garnish with additional mint and the lime wedge.

INGREDIENTS:

- SEA SALT, FOR THE RIM
- 4 OZ. REPOSADO TEQUILA
- 5–7 MINT LEAVES
- 1 TABLESPOON CUCUMBER, DICED
- 2 OZ. FRESH LIME JUICE
- 2 OZ. MINT SYRUP (SEE PAGE 308, SUBSTITUTE MINT FOR THE ROSEMARY) OR AGAVE NECTAR

ROSEMARY-GINGER MARGARITA

GARNISH: 1 LEMON SLICE & 1 SPRIG OF ROSEMARY

Wet the rim of a rocks glass and dip it into the salt. Place the cocktail ingredients in a cocktail shaker and muddle. Add ice and shake vigorously. Fill the glass with ice, strain the cocktail into the glass, and garnish with the slice of lemon and the rosemary.

INGREDIENTS:

- SEA SALT, FOR THE RIM
- 2 OZ. REPOSADO TEQUILA
- 1 OZ. DOMAINE DE CANTON
- ½ OZ. ROSEMARY SYRUP (SEE PAGE 308)
- 1–2 SMALL PIECES OF FRESH GINGER ROOT, PEELED
- ½ OZ. FRESH LIME JUICE
- ½ OZ. FRESH LEMON JUICE

ELDERFLOWER MARGARITA

GARNISH: 1 WHITE FLOWER OR 1 LIME WEDGE

Wet the rim of a cocktail glass and dip it into the salt. Place the tequila, St-Germain, and lime juice in a cocktail shaker and shake until chilled. Fill the glass with ice, strain the cocktail into the glass, top with the seltzer, if desired, and garnish with a white flower or a lime wedge.

INGREDIENTS:

- SEA SALT, FOR THE RIM
- 2 OZ. SILVER TEQUILA
- 2 OZ. ST-GERMAIN
- 1⅓ OZ. FRESH LIME JUICE
- SPLASH OF SELTZER (OPTIONAL)

MARASCHINO CHERRY MARGARITA

GARNISH: 2 MARASCHINO CHERRIES

Wet the rim of a cocktail glass or a coupe and dip it into the salt. Place all of the cocktail ingredients in a cocktail shaker and shake vigorously. Fill the glass with ice, strain the cocktail into the glass, and garnish with the maraschino cherries.

INGREDIENTS:

- SEA SALT, FOR THE RIM
- 2 OZ. SILVER TEQUILA
- 1½ OZ. MARASCHINO CHERRY SYRUP
- ½ OZ. LUXARDO
- ½ OZ. GINGER SYRUP (SEE PAGE 255, SUBSTITUTE SUGAR FOR THE HONEY)
- 1 OZ. FRESH LIME JUICE

SHERRY MARGARITA

GARNISH: 1 LIME WEDGE & 1 GRAPEFRUIT WEDGE

Wet the rim of a rocks glass and dip it into the salt. Place the cocktail ingredients in a cocktail shaker and shake vigorously. Fill the glass with ice, strain the cocktail into the glass, and garnish with the lime wedge and grapefruit wedge.

INGREDIENTS:

- SEA SALT, FOR THE RIM
- 1 OZ. SILVER TEQUILA
- 1 OZ. FINO SHERRY
- ¾ OZ. FRESH GRAPEFRUIT JUICE
- ½ OZ. FRESH LIME JUICE
- ¼ OZ. AGAVE NECTAR
- 1–2 DASHES OF ORANGE BITTERS

CUTIES MARGARITA

GARNISH: 1 CLEMENTINE WEDGE

Wet the rim of a coupe and dip it into the salt. Place the tequila, juice, liqueur, and, if using, syrup, in a cocktail shaker filled with ice and shake vigorously. Strain the cocktail into the glass and garnish with the clementine wedge.

INGREDIENTS:

- SEA SALT, FOR THE RIM
- 2 OZ. SILVER TEQUILA
- 2 OZ. FRESH CLEMENTINE JUICE
- ½ OZ. ORANGE LIQUEUR
- ½ OZ. SIMPLE SYRUP (OPTIONAL)

STRAIGHT UP

Asking a bartender to serve you a cocktail "straight up" is simply requesting that they serve it in the proper glass, with no ice. As these cocktails focus more on the simple flavors of the actual booze, it is essential that the materials used are of the highest quality, since there is no melted ice to dilute the flavors. And sure, there is no "second drink" once the ice melts. But trust me—the first one will do the trick.

For the Margaritas in this section it is essential that you use a chilled glass. So make sure you place your glassware in the freezer a half hour before you're going to use them.

HIBISCUS MARGARITA

GARNISH: 1 LIME WEDGE OR TWIST

Wet the rim of a cocktail glass or a coupe and dip it into the salt. Place all of the cocktail ingredients, except for the seltzer, in a cocktail shaker filled with ice and shake vigorously. Strain the cocktail into the glass, top with the seltzer, and garnish with a lime wedge or twist.

INGREDIENTS:

- SEA SALT, FOR THE RIM
- 2 OZ. SILVER TEQUILA
- 1½ OZ. HIBISCUS TEA
- 1 OZ. FRESH LIME JUICE
- 1 OZ. ORANGE LIQUEUR
- ½ OZ. AGAVE NECTAR
- SPLASH OF SELTZER

MORNING MARGARITA

GARNISH: 1 LIME WEDGE OR 1 ORANGE TWIST

Wet the rim of a rocks glass and dip it into the salt. Place all of the cocktail ingredients, except for the seltzer, in a cocktail shaker and shake vigorously. Strain the cocktail into the glass, add the seltzer, if using, and garnish with a lime wedge or an orange twist.

INGREDIENTS:

- SEA SALT, FOR THE RIM
- 2 OZ. REPOSADO TEQUILA
- 2 TEASPOONS ORANGE MARMALADE
- 1 OZ. FRESH LIME JUICE
- ½ OZ. SIMPLE SYRUP
- ½ OZ. ORANGE LIQUEUR
- SPLASH OF SELTZER WATER (OPTIONAL)

SMOKY MARGARITA

GARNISH: 1 LIME WEDGE

Ancho Chili Syrup: Add two ancho chilies to a standard simple syrup recipe when it is boiling. After 1 minute, remove the saucepan from the heat and allow the chilies to cool with the syrup. Strain before using.

Combine the sea salt and paprika, wet the rim of a rocks glass, and dip it into the mixture. Place the syrup and the remaining ingredients in a cocktail shaker filled halfway with ice and shake vigorously. Strain the cocktail into the glass and garnish with the lime wedge.

INGREDIENTS:

- 1 OZ. ANCHO CHILI SYRUP
- 1 TABLESPOON SMOKED SEA SALT
- 1 TEASPOON SMOKED PAPRIKA
- 2 OZ. REPOSADO TEQUILA
- 1 OZ. FRESH LIME JUICE
- ½ OZ. ORANGE LIQUEUR

HONEY MARGARITA

GARNISH: 1 SPRIG OF MINT

Wet the rim of a cocktail glass and dip it into the bee pollen and salt. Place the cocktail ingredients in a cocktail shaker filled with ice and shake until chilled. Strain the cocktail into the glass and garnish with the mint.

INGREDIENTS:

- BEE POLLEN, FOR THE RIM
- SEA SALT, FOR THE RIM
- 3 OZ. AÑEJO TEQUILA
- 2½ OZ. HONEY SYRUP
- ½ OZ. ORANGE LIQUEUR
- 1 OZ. FRESH LIME JUICE

PINK PEPPERCORN & GRAPEFRUIT MARGARITA

GARNISH: 1 GRAPEFRUIT WEDGE

Pink Peppercorn Syrup: Add three tablespoons of pink peppercorns to a standard simple syrup recipe while it is boiling. After 1 minute, remove the saucepan from heat and allow the peppercorns to cool with the syrup. Strain before using.

Combine the sea salt and ground pink peppercorns in a small bowl, wet the rim of a cocktail glass or a coupe, and dip it into the mixture. Place the syrup, tequila, and juice in a cocktail shaker filled halfway with ice and shake vigorously. Strain the cocktail into the glass, top with a splash of seltzer, if desired, and garnish with the wedge of grapefruit.

INGREDIENTS:

- 1 OZ. PINK PEPPERCORN SYRUP
- SEA SALT, FOR THE RIM
- GROUND PINK PEPPER, FOR THE RIM
- 2 OZ. SILVER TEQUILA
- 3 OZ. FRESH GRAPEFRUIT JUICE
- SPLASH OF SELTZER (OPTIONAL)

PEAR-CILANTRO MARGARITA

GARNISH: 1 SPRIG OF CILANTRO

Wet the rim of a coupe and dip it into the salt. Place the cocktail ingredients in a cocktail shaker filled with ice and shake vigorously. Strain the cocktail into the glass and garnish with the sprig of cilantro.

INGREDIENTS:

- SEA SALT, FOR THE RIM
- 1½ OZ. REPOSADO TEQUILA
- 1½ OZ. PEAR NECTAR
- ½ OZ. AGAVE NECTAR
- 1 OZ. FRESH LIME JUICE
- 6–8 CILANTRO LEAVES, MINCED

BEET MARGARITA

GARNISH: 1 LIME WEDGE & SKEWERED PICKLED BEETS

Wet the rim of a cocktail glass and dip it into the salt. Place the cocktail ingredients in a cocktail shaker filled with ice and shake vigorously. Strain the cocktail into the glass and garnish with the lime wedge and skewered beets.

INGREDIENTS:

- SEA SALT, FOR THE RIM
- 3 OZ. REPOSADO TEQUILA
- 2 OZ. PICKLED BEET JUICE
- 2 OZ. FRESH LIME JUICE
- ⅔ OZ. SIMPLE SYRUP

AMARO MARGARITA

GARNISH: 1 LIME SLICE

Place the cocktail ingredients in a cocktail shaker filled with ice and shake until it is very cold. Double-strain into a cocktail glass or a coupe and garnish with the slice of lime.

INGREDIENTS:

- 1½ OZ. REPOSADO TEQUILA
- ½ OZ. MEZCAL
- ¾ OZ. AMARO NONINO QUINTESSENTIA
- ¾ OZ. FRESH LIME JUICE
- ½ OZ. AGAVE NECTAR

PORT WINE MARGARITA

GARNISH: 1 LIME WEDGE OR TWIST

Wet the rim of a cocktail glass or coupe and dip it into the salt. Place the cocktail ingredients in a cocktail shaker filled with ice and shake vigorously. Strain into the glass and garnish with a lime wedge or a lime twist.

INGREDIENTS:

- SEA SALT, FOR THE RIM
- 1 OZ. RUBY PORT
- 2 OZ. SILVER TEQUILA
- ½ OZ. FRESH LIME JUICE
- 1 OZ. ORANGE LIQUEUR
- ½ OZ. AGAVE NECTAR
- ½ OZ. FRESH ORANGE JUICE

LYCHEE MARGARITA

GARNISH: 1 LYCHEE OR 1 LIME WEDGE

Lychee Puree: Pour the fruit from an 8 oz. can of lychees and one-third of the syrup into a blender and puree until smooth.

Wet the rim of a cocktail glass or a coupe and dip it into the sugar or salt. Place the lychee puree, tequila, and lime juice in a cocktail shaker filled with ice and shake until chilled. Strain the cocktail into the glass and top with the splash of seltzer, if desired. Garnish with the lychee or the lime wedge.

INGREDIENTS:

- 1 OZ. LYCHEE PUREE
- SUGAR OR SALT, FOR THE RIM
- 2 OZ. SILVER TEQUILA
- 1 OZ. FRESH LIME JUICE
- SPLASH OF SELTZER WATER (OPTIONAL)

GUAVA MARGARITA

GARNISH: 1 LIME TWIST OR WHEEL

Wet the rim of a cocktail glass or a coupe and dip it into the salt. Place the cocktail ingredients in a cocktail shaker filled with ice and shake vigorously. Strain the cocktail into the glass and garnish with a twist of lime or a lime wheel.

INGREDIENTS:

- SEA SALT, FOR THE RIM
- 2 OZ. SILVER TEQUILA
- 2 OZ. GUAVA JUICE OR NECTAR
- 1 OZ. FRESH LIME JUICE
- 1 OZ. ORANGE LIQUEUR
- ½ OZ. AGAVE NECTAR

MAPLE MARGARITA

GARNISH: 1 LIME OR ORANGE TWIST

Wet the rim of a cocktail glass or a coupe and dip it into the salt. Place the cocktail ingredients in a cocktail shaker filled with ice and shake vigorously. Strain the cocktail into the glass and garnish with a lime or orange twist.

INGREDIENTS:

- SEA SALT, FOR THE RIM
- 1½ OZ. SILVER TEQUILA
- ½ OZ. ORANGE LIQUEUR
- ¼ OZ. MEZCAL
- 1¼ OZ. PURE MAPLE SYRUP
- 1 OZ. FRESH LIME JUICE

FRENCH MARGARITA

GARNISH: 1 LIME TWIST

Place the cocktail ingredients in a cocktail shaker filled with ice and shake until it is very cold. Strain into a chilled cocktail glass and garnish with the lime twist.

INGREDIENTS:

- 2 OZ. SILVER TEQUILA
- ½ OZ. PINEAPPLE JUICE
- ½ OZ. FRESH LIME JUICE
- ¼ OZ. CHAMBORD
- ¼ OZ. DRY VERMOUTH

CHOCOLATE-ESPRESSO MARGARITA

GARNISH: CHOCOLATE SHAVINGS & 1 ORANGE TWIST

Wet the rim of a cocktail glass or a coupe and dip it into the cocoa powder. Place the heavy cream in a bowl and whisk until it has thickened but is not the consistency of whipped cream. Place the tequilas, the orange liqueur, coffee component, and ice in a mixing glass and stir until chilled. Strain into the glass, float the cream on top, and garnish with the chocolate shavings and the orange twist.

INGREDIENTS:

- COCOA POWDER, FOR THE RIM
- 2 OZ. HEAVY CREAM
- ½ OZ. COFFEE TEQUILA
- 1 OZ. SILVER TEQUILA
- ½ OZ. ORANGE LIQUEUR
- 1 OZ. ESPRESSO OR STRONG COFFEE, CHILLED

THE ORIGINAL FROZEN MARGARITA

GARNISH: 1 LIME WHEEL

Wet the rim of a coupe and dip it into the sea salt. Place the cocktail ingredients in a blender and puree until smooth. Pour the cocktail into the glass and garnish with the lime wheel.

INGREDIENTS:

- SEA SALT, FOR THE RIM
- 3 OZ. SILVER TEQUILA
- 1½ OZ. LIME JUICE
- 1 OZ. SIMPLE SYRUP
- 1½ OZ. ORANGE LIQUEUR
- 1 CUP ICE

FROZEN COCONUT MARGARITA

GARNISH: 1 LIME WHEEL

Wet the rim of a coupe and dip it into the shredded coconut. Place the cocktail ingredients in a blender and puree until smooth. Pour the cocktail into the glass and garnish with the lime wheel.

INGREDIENTS:

- SHREDDED COCONUT, FOR THE RIM
- 2 OZ. AÑEJO TEQUILA
- 2 OZ. COCONUT PUREE
- 1 OZ. FRESH LIME JUICE
- ¼ OZ. AGAVE NECTAR
- ½ OZ. ORANGE LIQUEUR
- 1 CUP ICE

FROZEN STRAWBERRY AND ORANGE MARGARITA

GARNISH: 1 ORANGE WHEEL & 1 STRAWBERRY

Wet the rim of a coupe and dip it into the sea salt. Place the cocktail ingredients in a blender and puree until smooth. Pour the cocktail into the glass and garnish with the orange wheel and a strawberry.

INGREDIENTS:

- 3 OZ. SILVER TEQUILA
- 1 OZ. FRESH LIME JUICE
- 1½ OZ. FRESH ORANGE JUICE
- ½ CUP FRESH STRAWBERRIES, DICED
- 1 OZ. SIMPLE SYRUP
- 1½ OZ. ORANGE LIQUEUR
- 1 CUP ICE

HONEYDEW AND MINT MARGARITA

GARNISH: 1 SPRIG OF MINT

Wet the rim of a cocktail glass and dip it into the sea salt. Place the cocktail ingredients in a blender and puree until smooth. Pour the cocktail into the glass and garnish with the sprig of mint.

INGREDIENTS:

- SEA SALT, FOR THE RIM
- 3 OZ. SILVER TEQUILA
- ¾ CUP FRESH HONEYDEW MELON, DICED
- 4–5 MINT LEAVES
- 2 OZ. FRESH LIME JUICE
- 1 OZ. ORANGE LIQUEUR
- ¾ CUP ICE

FROZÉE MARGARITA

GARNISH: 1 LIME WEDGE

Wet the rim of a coupe and dip it into the sea salt. Place the cocktail ingredients in a blender and puree until smooth. Pour the cocktail into the glass and garnish with the lime wedge.

INGREDIENTS:

- PINK HIMALAYAN SEA SALT, FOR THE RIM
- 2½ OZ. SILVER TEQUILA
- ¼ CUP ROSÉ
- 2 OZ. FRESH LIME JUICE
- 1 OZ. ORANGE LIQUEUR
- 1 CUP ICE

FROZEN MARGARITAS

Frozen beverages first rose to prominence in the United States during the 1950s, when people everywhere started to find that the Margarita and its frozen kin were the perfect way to spend their leisure time—whether it be the beach or a backyard barbeque. Most people use blenders to make the frozen Margarita, but if you are going to be cranking them out for a big crowd all summer long, it might be wise to invest in a slushy machine.

WATERMELON-BASIL MARGARITA

GARNISH: 1 LIME WEDGE

Wet the rim of a coupe and dip it into the sea salt. Place the cocktail ingredients in a blender and puree until smooth. Pour the cocktail into the glass and garnish with the lime wedge.

INGREDIENTS:

- SEA SALT, FOR THE RIM
- 3 OZ. SILVER TEQUILA
- 1½ OZ. FRESH LIME JUICE
- 1 CUP FRESH WATERMELON, DICED
- 3–4 BASIL LEAVES
- 1 OZ. SIMPLE SYRUP
- 1½ OZ. ORANGE LIQUEUR
- 1 CUP ICE

THE HAWAIIAN

GARNISH: 1 LIME WEDGE

Wet the rim of a coupe and dip it into the sea salt. Place the cocktail ingredients in a blender and puree until smooth. Pour the cocktail into the glass and garnish with the lime wedge.

INGREDIENTS:

- SEA SALT, FOR THE RIM
- 3 OZ. REPOSADO TEQUILA
- 3 OZ. PASSION FRUIT NECTAR
- 1 OZ. FRESH LIME JUICE
- ½ OZ. ORANGE LIQUEUR
- ½ OZ. AGAVE NECTAR
- 1 CUP ICE

FROZEN PINEAPPLE MARGARITA

GARNISH: 1 LIME WEDGE

Wet the rim of a coupe and dip it into the sea salt. Place the cocktail ingredients in a blender and puree until smooth. Pour the cocktail into the glass and garnish with the lime wedge.

INGREDIENTS:

- SEA SALT, FOR THE RIM
- 2 OZ. SILVER TEQUILA
- 1 OZ. MEZCAL
- 3 OZ. PINEAPPLE JUICE
- 1 CUP ICE
- ¼ CUP FRESH PINEAPPLE, CUBED
- 1½ OZ. ORANGE LIQUEUR
- 2 OZ. FRESH LIME JUICE

PINEAPPLE AND TAMARIND MARGARITA

GARNISH: 1 PINEAPPLE CHUNK

Wet the rim of a coupe and dip it into the sea salt. Place the cocktail ingredients in a blender and puree until smooth. Pour the cocktail into the glass and garnish with the pineapple chunk.

INGREDIENTS:

- SEA SALT, FOR THE RIM
- 3 OZ. REPOSADO TEQUILA
- 3 OZ. PINEAPPLE JUICE
- ¼ CUP FRESH PINEAPPLE, CUBED
- 1 OZ. TAMARIND NECTAR
- 1 OZ. ORANGE LIQUEUR
- 2 OZ. FRESH LIME JUICE
- 1 CUP ICE

FROZEN APPLE-CINNAMON MARGARITA

GARNISH: 1 CINNAMON STICK

Combine the salt, sugar, and cinnamon in a small bowl, wet the rim of a coupe, and dip it into the mixture. Place the cocktail ingredients in a blender and puree until smooth. Pour the cocktail into the glass and garnish with the cinnamon stick.

INGREDIENTS:

- 1 TEASPOON SEA SALT
- 1 TABLESPOON SUGAR
- 1 TEASPOON CINNAMON
- 1½ OZ. MEZCAL
- 1 OZ. SILVER TEQUILA
- ½ CUP APPLE CIDER
- 1 OZ. FRESH LEMON JUICE
- 1 OZ. CINNAMON SYRUP (SEE PAGE 260)
- ½ OZ. ORANGE LIQUEUR
- ¾ CUP ICE

CANTALOUPE-BASIL MARGARITA

GARNISH: 1 SPRIG OF BASIL

Wet the rim of a coupe and dip it into the sea salt. Place the cocktail ingredients in a blender and puree until smooth. Pour the cocktail into the glass and garnish with the basil.

INGREDIENTS:

- SEA SALT, FOR THE RIM
- 3 OZ. REPOSADO TEQUILA
- ¾ CUP FRESH CANTALOUPE, DICED
- 3–4 BASIL LEAVES
- 2 OZ. FRESH LIME JUICE
- 1 OZ. ORANGE LIQUEUR
- ¾ CUP ICE

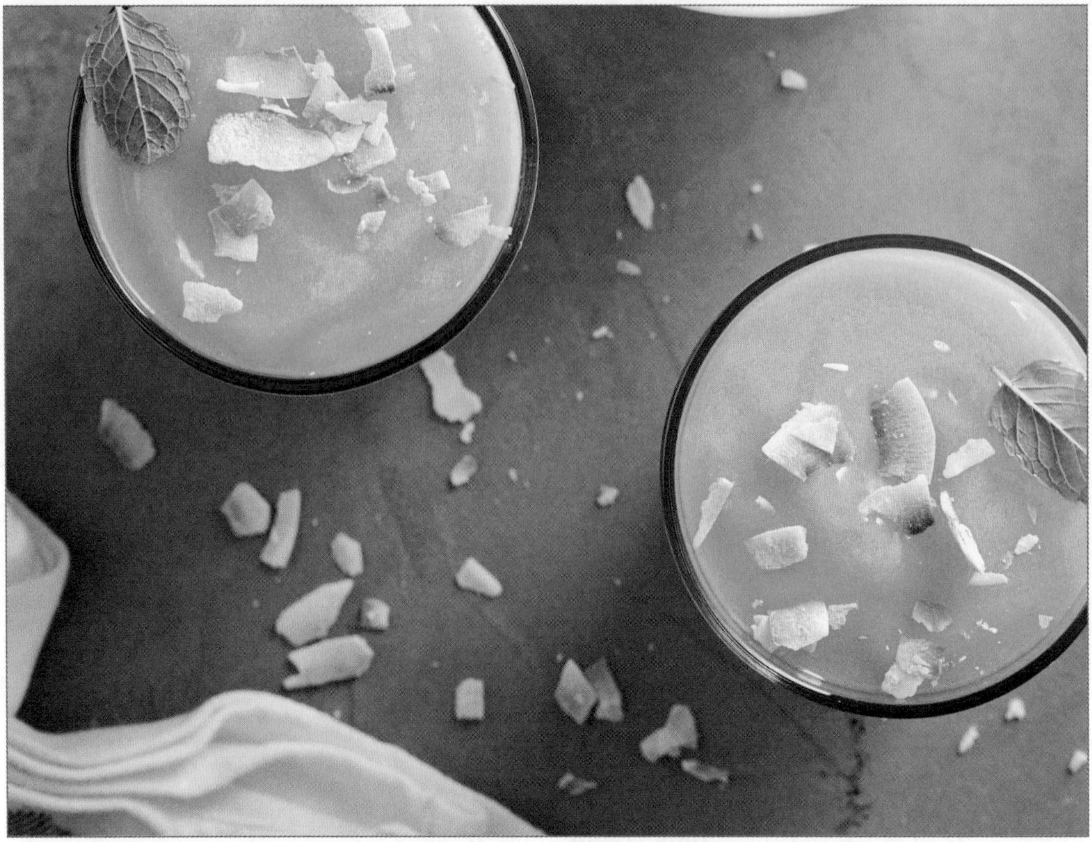

ORANGE-COCONUT MARGARITA

GARNISH: 1 ORANGE TWIST

Wet the rim of a coupe and dip it into the sea salt. Place the cocktail ingredients in a blender and puree until smooth. Pour the cocktail into the glass and garnish with the orange twist.

INGREDIENTS:

- 2½ OZ. AÑEJO TEQUILA
- 2 OZ. COCONUT PUREE
- 2 OZ. FRESH ORANGE JUICE
- ½ OZ. FRESH LIME JUICE
- 1 CUP ICE
- ½ OZ. AGAVE NECTAR
- 1 OZ. ORANGE LIQUEUR

ANCHO CHILI MARGARITA

GARNISH: 1 LIME WEDGE

Combine the smoked sea salt and chili powder in a small dish, wet the rim of a rocks glass, and dip it into the mixture. Place the tequila, syrup, lime juice, and liqueur in a cocktail shaker filled with ice and shake vigorously. Fill the glass with ice, strain the cocktail into the glass, and garnish with the lime wedge.

INGREDIENTS:

- 1 TABLESPOON SMOKED SEA SALT
- ½ TEASPOON ANCHO CHILI POWDER
- 2 OZ. REPOSADO TEQUILA
- 1 OZ. ANCHO CHILI SYRUP (SEE PAGE 399)
- 1 OZ. FRESH LIME JUICE
- ¾ OZ. ORANGE LIQUEUR

CUCUMBER-JALAPEÑO MARGARITA

GARNISH: 1 LIME WEDGE, CUCUMBER, & JALAPEÑO

Jalapeño Syrup: Add a diced jalapeño pepper to a standard simple syrup when it is boiling. After 1 minute, remove the saucepan from heat, let cool, and strain before using.

Wet the rim of a highball glass and dip it into the sea salt. Place the tequila, lime juice, syrup or agave nectar, 1 tablespoon of the cucumber, and 2 to 3 slices of jalapeño in a cocktail shaker and muddle. Add ice and shake vigorously. Fill the glass with ice, strain the cocktail into it, and garnish with the lime wedge and the remaining cucumber and jalapeño.

INGREDIENTS:

- 2 OZ. JALAPEÑO SYRUP OR AGAVE NECTAR
- SEA SALT, FOR THE RIM
- 4 OZ. REPOSADO TEQUILA
- 2 OZ. FRESH LIME JUICE
- 1 JALAPEÑO PEPPER, CUT INTO THIN ROUNDS
- 1¼ TABLESPOONS CUCUMBER, DICED

PINEAPPLE-JALAPEÑO MARGARITA

GARNISH: 1 LIME WEDGE & PINEAPPLE

Wet the rim of a rocks glass and dip it into the sea salt. Place the tequila, lime juice, syrup or agave nectar, pineapple juice, jalapeño, and 1 tablespoon of the pineapple in a cocktail shaker and muddle. Add ice and shake vigorously. Fill the glass with ice, strain the cocktail into it, and garnish with the lime wedge and the remaining pineapple.

INGREDIENTS:

- SEA SALT, FOR THE RIM
- 4 OZ. REPOSADO TEQUILA
- 2 OZ. FRESH LIME JUICE
- 1 OZ. JALAPEÑO SYRUP (SEE PAGE 411) OR AGAVE NECTAR
- 1 OZ. PINEAPPLE JUICE
- 2–3 THIN SLICES OF JALAPEÑO PEPPER
- 1¼ TABLESPOONS PINEAPPLE, DICED

HABANERO MARGARITA

GARNISH: 1 BASIL LEAF, 1 HABANERO SLICE, & 1 LIME WEDGE

Habanero Syrup: Add half of a diced habanero pepper to a standard simple syrup when it is boiling. After 1 minute, remove the saucepan from heat, let cool, and strain before using.

Wet the rim of a rocks glass and dip it into the sea salt. Place the syrup, tequila, lime juice, and orange liqueur in a cocktail shaker filled with ice and shake vigorously. Fill the glass with ice, strain the cocktail into it, and garnish with the lime wedge, slice of habanero, and basil leaf.

Variation: If you're looking for even more heat, muddle a small piece of the habanero in the shaker with the lime juice before adding ice and the other ingredients.

INGREDIENTS:

- ¾ OZ. HABANERO SYRUP
- SEA SALT, FOR THE RIM
- 2 OZ. SILVER TEQUILA
- 1 OZ. FRESH LIME JUICE
- 1 OZ. ORANGE LIQUEUR

SPICY MARGARITAS

I have been a spicy food lover for a long time now, and once you get into the world of spicy food you can never really go back. But I only recently discovered that my beloved heat was not limited to food. There are spicy drinks! To my taste buds, spice is flavor. If you're a little wary of venturing into this part, here's some great news—you can easily control how much spice goes into your drink. If spicy isn't your thing, I recommend cutting the spicy ingredients by half. And if you're one of those people who can't get enough, then by all means add as many chilies or as much hot sauce as you damn well please.

MATCHA MARGARITA

GARNISH: 2 TO 3 JALAPEÑO PEPPER SLICES

Combine 2 teaspoons of the matcha powder and the salt, wet the rim of a rocks glass, and dip it into the mixture. Place the piece of jalapeño and the lime juice in a cocktail shaker and muddle. Add the tequila, green tea, simple syrup, orange liqueur, remaining matcha powder, and ice to the shaker and shake vigorously. Fill the glass with ice, strain the cocktail into the glass, and garnish with the slices of jalapeño.

INGREDIENTS:

- 2¼ TEASPOONS MATCHA POWDER
- 1 TEASPOON FINE SEA SALT
- ½-INCH PIECE OF FRESH JALAPEÑO PEPPER
- 1 OZ. FRESH LIME JUICE
- 2 OZ. SILVER TEQUILA
- 3 OZ. FRESHLY BREWED GREEN TEA, CHILLED
- ½ OZ. SIMPLE SYRUP
- ½ OZ. ORANGE LIQUEUR

SRIRACHA MARGARITA

GARNISH: 1 LIME WHEEL

Wet the rim of a rocks glass and dip it into the sea salt. Place the cocktail ingredients in a cocktail shaker filled with ice and shake vigorously. Fill the glass with ice, strain the cocktail into it, and garnish with the lime wheel.

INGREDIENTS:

- 2 OZ. SILVER TEQUILA
- 1 OZ. FRESH LIME JUICE
- 1 TEASPOON SRIRACHA
- ¾ OZ. SIMPLE SYRUP
- 1 OZ. ORANGE LIQUEUR

MICHELADA MARGARITA

GARNISH: 1 LIME WHEEL

Combine the sea salt and pepper in a small dish, wet the rim of a pint glass, and dip it into the mixture. Place the cocktail ingredients in a mixing glass filled with ice and stir. Fill the pint glass with ice, strain the cocktail into the glass, and garnish with lime wheel.

INGREDIENTS:

- 1 TEASPOON SEA SALT
- 1 TEASPOON FRESHLY GROUND BLACK PEPPER
- 1 (12 OZ.) CAN OF TECATE (OR PREFERRED LAGER)
- 2 OZ. SILVER TEQUILA
- 1 OZ. FRESH LIME JUICE
- ½ OZ. ORANGE LIQUEUR
- ½ OZ. HOT SAUCE
- ⅛ OZ. WORCESTERSHIRE SAUCE
- ⅛ OZ. SOY SAUCE

BLOODY MARGARITA

GARNISH: 1 LIME WEDGE, 1 LEAFY CELERY STALK, & PICKLED JALAPEÑOS

Combine the sea salt, 1 teaspoon of the black pepper, chili powder, and celery salt in a small dish, wet the rim of a rocks glass, and dip it into the mixture. Place the tequila, orange juice, lime juice, jalapeño brine, tomato juice, hot sauce, horseradish, and remaining black pepper in a cocktail shaker, add ice, and shake until chilled. Fill the glass with ice, strain the cocktail into the glass, and garnish with the lime wedge, celery stalk, and pickled jalapeños.

INGREDIENTS:

- 1 TABLESPOON SEA SALT
- 1⅛ TEASPOON FRESHLY GROUND BLACK PEPPER
- 1 TEASPOON CHILI POWDER
- 1 TEASPOON CELERY SALT
- 2 OZ. REPOSADO TEQUILA
- 1 OZ. FRESH ORANGE JUICE
- ½ OZ. FRESH LIME JUICE
- ¼ OZ. PICKLED JALAPEÑO PEPPER BRINE
- 2 OZ. TOMATO JUICE
- DASH OF HOT SAUCE
- ⅛ TEASPOON HORSERADISH

BLOODY KIMCHI MARGARITA

GARNISH: 1 LIME WEDGE, 1 LEAFY CELERY STALK, PICKLED JALAPEÑOS, & 1 PIECE OF KIMCHI

Combine the sea salt, 1 teaspoon of the black pepper, the celery salt, and the chili powder in a small dish, wet the rim of a rocks glass, and dip the rim into the mixture. Place the kimchi and its juice in a food processor or blender and puree until smooth. Place the kimchi puree, the tequila, orange juice, lime juice, jalapeño brine, tomato juice, horseradish, and remaining black pepper in a cocktail shaker, add ice, and shake vigorously. Fill the glass with ice, strain the cocktail into it, and garnish with additional kimchi, the lime wedge, celery stalk, and pickled jalapeños.

INGREDIENTS:

- 1 TABLESPOON SEA SALT
- 1⅛ TEASPOON FRESHLY GROUND BLACK PEPPER
- 1 TEASPOON CELERY SALT
- 1 TEASPOON CHILI POWDER
- 1½ OZ. KIMCHI
- 2 OZ. REPOSADO TEQUILA
- 1 OZ. FRESH ORANGE JUICE
- ½ OZ. FRESH LIME JUICE
- ¼ OZ. PICKLED JALAPEÑO PEPPER BRINE
- 2 OZ. TOMATO JUICE
- ⅛ TEASPOON HORSERADISH

TEX-MEX MULE

GARNISH: 1 LIME WEDGE

Place the cocktail ingredients in a cocktail shaker filled with ice and shake vigorously. Fill a copper mug with ice, strain the cocktail into it, and garnish with the lime wedge.

INGREDIENTS:

- 2½ OZ. REPOSADO TEQUILA
- 2 OZ. FRESH LIME JUICE
- ½ OZ. DOMAINE DE CANTON
- ½ OZ. ORANGE LIQUEUR
- 5 OZ. GINGER BEER

JULEP MARGARITA

GARNISH: 1 SPRIG OF MINT

Place the mint leaves and powdered sugar in the bottom of a rocks glass and muddle. Add the tequila, ½ oz. of seltzer, and the lime juice and fill glass with crushed ice. Top with another small splash of seltzer, stir, and garnish with the sprig of mint.

INGREDIENTS:

- 4–5 MINT LEAVES
- 1 TEASPOON POWDERED SUGAR
- 2 OZ. AÑEJO TEQUILA
- ½ OZ. SELTZER WATER, PLUS A SMALL SPLASH
- SQUEEZE OF LIME JUICE

CAVA MARGARITA

GARNISH: 1 LIME WEDGE

Wet the rim of a champagne flute and dip it into the sea salt. Place the tequila, lime juice, simple syrup, and orange liqueur in a cocktail shaker filled with ice and shake vigorously. Strain the cocktail into the champagne flute, top with the Cava, and garnish with the lime wedge.

INGREDIENTS:

- SEA SALT, FOR THE RIM
- 2 OZ. SILVER TEQUILA
- 1 OZ. FRESH LIME JUICE
- ¾ OZ. SIMPLE SYRUP
- 1 OZ. ORANGE LIQUEUR
- 6 OZ. CAVA

BLACKBERRY-SAGE MARGARITA

GARNISH: 1 LIME WEDGE & 1 SAGE LEAF

Wet the rim of a rocks glass and dip it into the salt. Place the tequila, blackberries, and sage leaves in a cocktail shaker and muddle. Add ice, the lime juice, and simple syrup and shake vigorously. Fill the glass with ice, strain the cocktail into the glass, top with the splash of seltzer, and garnish with the lime wedge and the additional sage leaf.

INGREDIENTS:

- SEA SALT, FOR THE RIM
- 2½ OZ. SILVER TEQUILA
- 4–5 BLACKBERRIES
- 2–3 SAGE LEAVES
- 1 OZ. FRESH LIME JUICE
- 1 OZ. SIMPLE SYRUP
- SPLASH OF SELTZER WATER

DARK AND STORMY MARGARITA

Wet the rim of a highball glass and dip it into the salt. Place the remaining ingredients, except for the splash of ginger beer, in a cocktail shaker filled with ice and shake until chilled. Fill the glass with ice, strain the cocktail into the glass, and top with the splash of ginger beer.

INGREDIENTS:

- SEA SALT, FOR THE RIM
- 2 OZ. REPOSADO TEQUILA
- ¾ OZ. AMARO
- ¾ OZ. FRESH LIME JUICE
- 2–3 DASHES OF ORANGE BITTERS
- 2 OZ. GINGER BEER, PLUS A SMALL SPLASH

SPARKLING MARGARITAS

Whether it's beer, Cava, Prosecco, Champagne, cider, tonic, soda, or seltzer, bubbles sell. Carbonation is whimsical and exciting, and puts everyone in the mind to celebrate and have a good time. Because of this, a sparkling cocktail can brighten up a cocktail party—or even a random weeknight. I truly don't believe I have ever seen a frown upon a person's face while they're holding a fizzy drink. It's hard to improve on the Margarita's festive reputation, but adding a little effervescence does just that.

THINK PINK

GARNISH: 1 LIME WEDGE OR TWIST

Wet the rim of a rocks glass and dip into the salt. Place the cocktail ingredients, except for the small splash of Rosé, in a cocktail shaker filled with ice and shake vigorously. Strain the cocktail into the glass, garnish with a twist of lime or a lime wedge, and top with the splash of Rosé.

Tip: Don't be afraid to try different kinds of salts and spices for the rim of your Margarita's glass. Plain old sea salt will always work fine, but there are also pink Himalayan and Hawaiian sea salts, black Icelandic salt, smoked sea salt, fleur de sel, and sel gris. Each of these will bring different flavors and aesthetic qualities to your Margarita. For the Margaritas that require a sugar rim, try switching it up between granulated, turbinado, light and dark brown sugar, and powdered sugar. You can also try muddling an herb or spice with the sugar to see if they will enhance your cocktail.

INGREDIENTS:

PINK HIMALAYAN OR HAWAIIAN SEA SALT, FOR THE RIM
2 OZ. SILVER TEQUILA
1 OZ. FRESH LIME JUICE
1 OZ. FRESH RUBY RED GRAPEFRUIT JUICE
3 OZ. SPARKLING ROSÉ, PLUS A SMALL SPLASH
¾ OZ. SIMPLE SYRUP
1 OZ. ORANGE LIQUEUR

CORONARITA

GARNISH: 1 LIME WEDGE

Wet the rim of a large coupe and dip it into the sea salt. Place the tequila, lime juice, simple syrup, and orange liqueur in a cocktail shaker filled with ice and shake vigorously. Fill the glass with ice, strain the cocktail into the glass, carefully flip the mini-bottle of Corona into the glass, and garnish with the lime wedge.

INGREDIENTS:

SEA SALT, FOR THE RIM
2 OZ. SILVER TEQUILA
1 OZ. FRESH LIME JUICE
¾ OZ. SIMPLE SYRUP
1 OZ. ORANGE LIQUEUR
1 (7 OZ.) MINI-BOTTLE OF CORONA

GINGER ALE MARGARITA

GARNISH: 1 LIME WEDGE

Wet the rim of a large coupe and dip it into the salt. Place the tequila, lime juice, ginger liqueur, and orange liqueur in a cocktail shaker filled with ice and shake until chilled. Fill the glass with ice, strain the cocktail into the glass, carefully flip the bottle of ginger ale into the glass, and garnish with the lime wedge.

INGREDIENTS:

- SEA SALT, FOR THE RIM
- 2 OZ. SILVER TEQUILA
- 1 OZ. FRESH LIME JUICE
- ¾ OZ. DOMAINE DE CANTON
- 1 OZ. ORANGE LIQUEUR
- 1 (12 OZ.) BOTTLE OF GINGER ALE

HARD APPLE CIDER MARGARITA

GARNISH: 1 LIME WEDGE

Wet the rim of a large coupe and dip it into the sea salt. Place the tequila, lime juice, ginger liqueur, and orange liqueur in a cocktail shaker filled with ice and shake until chilled. Fill the glass with ice, strain the cocktail into it, carefully flip the bottle of cider into the glass, and garnish with the lime wedge.

INGREDIENTS:

- SEA SALT, FOR THE RIM
- 2 OZ. SILVER TEQUILA
- 1 OZ. FRESH LIME JUICE
- ¾ OZ. DOMAINE DE CANTON
- 1 OZ. ORANGE LIQUEUR
- 1 (12 OZ.) BOTTLE OF HARD APPLE CIDER

PINEAPPLE UPSIDE-DOWN MARGARITA

GARNISH: 1 MARASCHINO CHERRY & 1 GRILLED PINEAPPLE WEDGE

Combine the sea salt and brown sugar in a small dish, wet the rim of a coupe, and dip it into the mixture. Place the cocktail ingredients in a cocktail shaker filled with ice and shake vigorously. Strain into the glass and garnish with the maraschino cherry and the grilled pineapple wedge.

INGREDIENTS:

- 1 TABLESPOON SEA SALT
- 1 TABLESPOON BROWN SUGAR
- 1½ OZ. REPOSADO TEQUILA
- ¾ OZ. MEZCAL
- ¾ OZ. LUXARDO
- 1 OZ. PINEAPPLE NECTAR
- ½ OZ. FRESH LIME JUICE
- ½ OZ. AGAVE NECTAR

SMOKY AND SPICY MARGARITA

GARNISH: 1 DEHYDRATED ORANGE WHEEL

Place the cocktail ingredients in a cocktail shaker filled with ice and shake vigorously. Double-strain into a chilled cocktail glass and garnish with the dehydrated orange wheel.

INGREDIENTS:

- 1⅓ OZ. DEL MAGUEY VIDA MEZCAL
- ½ TABLESPOON ISLAY SCOTCH WHISKY
- 1 OZ. FRESH LIME JUICE
- ⅓ OZ. HABANERO SYRUP (SEE PAGE 412)
- ½ TABLESPOON CAMPARI
- 3 DASHES OF THE BITTER END THAI COCKTAIL BITTERS

KIWI MARGARITA

GARNISH: 1 LIME WEDGE OR 1 KIWI SLICE

Wet the rim of a coupe and dip it into the sea salt. Place the cocktail ingredients in a cocktail shaker filled with ice and shake vigorously. Strain the cocktail into the glass and garnish with a lime wedge or a slice of kiwi.

INGREDIENTS:

- SEA SALT, FOR THE RIM
- 3 OZ. REPOSADO TEQUILA
- 1½ OZ. FRESH LIME JUICE
- ½ CUP RIPE KIWI, DICED
- 1 OZ. SIMPLE SYRUP
- 1½ OZ. ORANGE LIQUEUR

THE HIGH ROLLER

GARNISH: 1 LIME TWIST

Wet the rim of a rocks glass and dip it into the salt. Place the tequila, Grand Marnier, and lime juice in a cocktail shaker filled with ice and shake until chilled. Fill the rocks glass with ice, strain the cocktail into the glass, carefully flip the split of Champagne into the glass, and garnish with the twist of lime.

INGREDIENTS:

- FLEUR DE SEL, FOR THE RIM
- 2 OZ. PREMIUM SILVER TEQUILA
- 1 OZ. GRAND MARNIER
- 1 OZ. FRESH LIME JUICE
- 1 (187 ML) SPLIT OF YOUR FAVORITE CHAMPAGNE

BLOODY SECRET

GARNISH: 2 BAY LEAVES, 1 PICKLED SHALLOT, & 2 SMALL, DRIED RED PEPPERS

Magic Copper Bay Potion: Combine Worcestershire, Tabasco, diced jalapeño, BBQ and Cajun spices, horseradish, and smoked paprika according to your taste.

Add the cocktail ingredients to a highball glass containing 4 large cubes of ice in the order they are listed, stirring between each addition. Garnish with the bay leaves, pickled shallot, and dried red peppers and serve with the bottle of tomato juice.

INGREDIENTS:

- ½ TABLESPOON MAGIC COPPER BAY POTION
- 1⅓ OZ. TEQUILA
- ¾ OZ. FRESH LEMON JUICE
- 6 DASHES OF ROASTED GARLIC BITTERS
- 1 BOTTLE OF HIGH QUALITY TOMATO JUICE (GRANNY'S SECRET PREFERRED), FOR SERVING

MANGO-HABANERO MARGARITA

GARNISH: 1 LIME WEDGE & 1 BASIL LEAF

Combine the chili powder and sea salt in a small dish, wet the rim of a rocks glass, and dip the rim into the mixture. Place the cocktail ingredients in a cocktail shaker filled with ice and shake vigorously. Fill the rocks glass with ice, strain the cocktail into the glass, and garnish with the lime wedge and basil leaf.

INGREDIENTS:

- 1 TEASPOON CHILI POWDER
- 1 TEASPOON SEA SALT
- 3 OZ. REPOSADO TEQUILA
- 1 OZ. FRESH LIME JUICE
- 2 OZ. FRESH MANGO PUREE
- 1 OZ. ORANGE LIQUEUR
- ¾ OZ. HABANERO SYRUP (SEE PAGE 412)

SERRANO AND MINT MARGARITA

GARNISH: 1 LIME WEDGE OR TWIST & SERRANO PEPPER SLICES

Wet the rim of a cocktail glass or coupe and dip it into the salt. Place the cocktail ingredients in a cocktail shaker filled with ice and shake vigorously. Strain the cocktail into the glass and garnish with a few slices of serrano pepper and a twist of lime or a lime wedge.

INGREDIENTS:

- SEA SALT, FOR THE RIM
- 2 OZ. SILVER TEQUILA
- 1 OZ. FRESH LIME JUICE
- ¾ OZ. SIMPLE SYRUP
- ½ SERRANO PEPPER
- 1 OZ. ORANGE LIQUEUR

Q&A WITH BENJAMIN WOOD OF BEATNIK

"The 1950s were a time of immense change in American culture and around the world, a period of incredible economic growth and prosperity when the status quo was challenged by a new generation, whose eccentric, bohemian and unconventional spirit inspired Beatnik. Here we reach out into the past and into the wider world, as the Beat Generation did in their own time, to bring uncommon and cosmopolitan stories to Chicago."
– Daniel Alonso, founder and designer of Beatnik

Can you tell us a bit about yourself and something about how this bar was started?

I grew up in what was once a small farming community in Arizona. Although I am now a city dweller, a bit of cowboy luster endures, lending slivers of grit and mettle to the person I strive to be. I have been fortunate to develop some meaningful relationships in my travels and one of those relationships started on a trip to Lapostolle Winery in Chile, where I met Daniel Alonso.

Dani is the founder and managing partner of Bonhomme Hospitality Group (owners of Beatnik, Beatnik on the River, Black Bull, Bordel, Cafe Bonhomme, Celeste, and Disco). Over a few years, I developed a friendship with Dani and we connected on many levels related to the food and beverage industry. This paved the way for my involvement in Beatnik. I cannot take any credit for how this bar started as I arrived in Chicago a month after opening. It was all the brainchild of Dani and his partners Nader, Fadi, and Rafid (aka the Bonhommies).

The extravagant design of Beatnik was inspired by the bohemian lifestyle and aesthetic sensibility of the 1950s in America and Europe. Designed and built by Bonhomme Hospitality Group, Beatnik captures the worldly spirit of this era by taking guests on a voyage through the bucolic splendor of a Mediterranean farmhouse, the colorful opulence of Moorish architecture, and the tropical lushness of Bali. The words best-suited to describe the timeless grandeur of Beatnik are "eclectic," "unconventional," "eccentric," and "personal." Antiques from around the globe are paired with customized creations to capture the kind of spontaneity one could find in the home or atelier of an artist.

What is the focus of your cocktails and what are your influences? As you've had extensive experience with building bars in New York City, how did

those experiences help with the development of Beatnik?

The cocktails themselves are built around the desire to create drinks that are fun, creative, beautiful, and unstuffy while incorporating practices inspired by the anti-waste movement. To that end, the bar team constantly collaborates with the culinary team to cross-utilize and repurpose all perishables, from the kitchen to the bar and vice versa.

Although I have been involved in the food and beverage industry for many years now, the mecca that is New York City has evolved and influenced me both personally and as a professional in this industry on a large scale. I had the opportunity to work alongside and learn from some of the best in the business. Inspired by the intention, respect, skill, and love for beverage by mentors and friends such as Dale DeGroff, Steve Olson, Tim Cooper, Richie Boccato, and Willy Shine, to name just a few, my fire was lit. New York itself also forces people to rise up—you cannot survive there if you don't. Simply put, the creation of our bar program at Beatnik would not have been possible, for me, without the experiences I had in New York. The things I learned from my comrades, the processes of building bars and restaurants, the fact that the food and beverage scene in New York is the rule with regard to being the catalyst for new, inventive, the first, the best.

What do you look for when creating new cocktails for your menu?

This isn't a question easily answered for me. The manifestation always starts with an idea and that idea could be born out of excitement over a new or underutilized or forgotten flavor, an ingredient, a style, a vessel, a technique, a gap, a trend, a story, or the desire to give guests what they want.

I'll often start with a chart of variants to make sure that the menu has diversity. Variance in spirit, flavor, texture, ABV, presentation, preparation, technique, vessel, ice, color, and narrative are all important, and they have to be economic. I then focus on a particular and research likes and dislikes, see if there are examples that have worked in the past, look for creative inspiration, and use any help I can get to develop a base to start development. Then I apply the scientific method through experimentation, which can sometimes be very intentional and other times more akin to the act of throwing things against a wall to see what sticks.

How does the food and culture of Chicago influence the cocktails that you offer?

For Beatnik in particular, the food has been a major influence. Every time we have approached something new, one of the first things I do is ask our Executive Chef Marcos Campos if there are any products we could mutually benefit from cross-utilizing. For example, when developing our house Bloody Mary, the kitchen was using a Moroccan-style preserved lemon, but only the fruit itself. The juice that was left over has a stunningly complex and vibrant flavor, so we incorporated it into our Bloody Mary mix. We ended up creating an imbalance of need for juice to fruit, so we found a way to incorporate the lemons into a cocktail on our dinner menu to close the loop and eliminate waste, creating a natural circle. This was also something I was familiar with from my time at Distilled in New York.

I would also say that the space itself normally has more influence than the city. Beatnik is gorgeous, and women especially tend to gravitate toward the space. Being cognizant that the majority of guests are female, we do our best to provide offerings that account for this. However, I did find out that Chicagoans were not immediately attracted to fresh ginger—the spice was too aggressive. That has since changed, and people seem to be more welcoming of the ginger spice.

What are the best parts of running a cocktail bar in Chicago? Are there any downsides or things that make it difficult?

Although the modern craft cocktail renaissance has been seeping into every nook and cranny of the industry for years now, it still gives me hope and energy when I get involved with a community outside of New York. Chicago has had a cocktail culture for many years now and the talent and skills that exist within this city are the best part. Going through the creative process with new people in new places is always a real treat. If pushed to find a difficulty, I would have to say the sourcing and availability of goods and products. New York can spoil bartenders as most things are readily available 24 hours a day.

Blue Hawaiian, Brandy Alexander, Pink Squirrel, Rusty Nail, Tom Collins, White Russian, Grasshopper, Rob Roy, Pink Lady: If you had to pick one of these classic cocktails to add to your cocktail menu how would you reimagine your choice to make it fit in with your style?

I have recently put a cocktail on our menu that is a play on a Tom Collins. The cocktail itself is an ode within an ode, if that's possible. While in the idea process, I recalled a cocktail that my dear friend John Lermayer had put on a menu at The Florida Room in Miami some years before. His cocktail is called the Red Bell Pepper Daisy, which could have been an ode to the Jerry Thomas version. I set out to make a cocktail that would be an ode to John and fit our concept. Tragically, John passed about a month after we put the cocktail on our menu, and naturally it is one of our most popular. We take a whole red bell pepper and break it down. We use a portion of it to infuse a blanco (silver) tequila, we take the core and bits and make a red bell pepper agave, then we take what is left and dehydrate it into slivers to make a sustainable garnish and prepare in the style of a Collins. Only slightly different from John and Jerry's original versions, but it is a zero-waste, closed-loop, refreshing, light, and delightful version that uses a spirit our community gravitates toward.

Do you have a favorite cocktail?

I really don't have a favorite—at best I have a favorite spirit category: mezcal. I do love to teach the Old Fashioned, though. I think it affords the bartender the opportunity for the perfect representation of that immeasurable quotient, which is love or caring to the guest in cocktail form.

Do you have a favorite alcohol to work with when making cocktails?

Although my loves have been known to wax and wane, right now I am almost overbearingly in love with Sherry in everything. All expressions.

MÁMÙ VIDA

GARNISH: 1 SZECHUAN FLOWER ("BUZZ BUTTON") & SAL DE GUSANO*

One of Beatnik's signature cocktails is the Mámù Vida. The Szechuan peppercorns and the numbing Szechuan "buzz buttons" are standout ingredients for the spicy, yet smoky cocktail. When eaten, the peppercorns provoke a multisensory experience, including mouth tingling, numbness, and increased salivation, making it an unusual, yet exciting surprise in the drink.

"The Szechuan peppercorns and buzz buttons are somewhat difficult to source, but we have been able to source them from local purveyors around Chicago. The global origins of the ingredients—from Mexico to China to Brazil—fit within Beatnik's narrative of pulling and sourcing ingredients from other regions around the world. The name of the cocktail itself is a combination of the Chinese Szechuan peppercorn and Mexican mezcal and chipotle ingredients—Mámù meaning 'numb' in Mandarin and Vida meaning 'life' in Spanish."—Benjamin Wood

INGREDIENTS:

- ¾ OZ. SZECHUAN-CHIPOTLE HONEY
- ¾ OZ. FRESH LEMON JUICE
- 2 OZ. DEL MAGUEY VIDA MEZCAL (BRAND IS IMPORTANT)

Szechuan-Chipotle Honey: Chop or rip 4½ oz. of chipotle Meco into halves and set aside. In a saucepan, toast ½ oz. of Szechuan peppercorns until fragrant. Add the chipotle and 2 cups of water and bring to a boil. Reduce the heat and simmer for 5 minutes. Strain out all solids through a fine sieve and combine the liquid with an equivalent amount of Grade B honey, making a 1:1 syrup. Let sit until cool.

Place the cocktail ingredients in a cocktail shaker, add cubed ice, shake, and strain into a double rocks glass. Garnish with a Szechuan flower or "buzz button" and sal de gusano.

**Both ingredients can be easily sourced online. For easier garnish preparation, feel free to substitute a lemon wheel and a pinch of salt per cocktail.*

WINE, BRANDY, COGNAC, *and* VERMOUTH

Wine, along with beer, is among the oldest alcoholic beverages we'll discuss in this book. Humans have been consuming wine in one form or another for thousands of years. The wine that you use to toast an event with your friends is not so far removed from what the Romans would have used to celebrate their triumphs. It has held its favored place at our tables for several reasons. It is relatively easy to produce as compared to whiskies and gins. This allows for production all over the world, encompassing small family concerns to multimillion-dollar businesses. It is versatile—pairing well with most varieties of food and serving as an important ingredient in many recipes. It is also diverse, with many styles, types, and flavor options to be tried and enjoyed—sweet whites like Muscat, medium-bodied reds like Cabernet Franc, or dessert wines like Port and Sherry.

Wine is even important to the whisk(e)y industry. We discuss this further in the whisk(e)y section, but many whiskies are aged or finished in wine barrels previously used to store Sauternes, Port, and Sherries (primarily Pedro Ximenez and Oloroso) and it is undeniable that these barrels play an important part in the flavor of many popular whiskies.

The versatility of wine's role in the cooking sphere follows it into cocktails. Wine can be the base of a cocktail, or it can play a part and still make its presence felt.

Last but not least, wine is accessible. It is easy to acquire and there is an enjoyable wine for every budget. As mentioned above, there are lots of options for any flavor palate to enjoy. That accessibility is hard to beat. Digging into the vagaries of exotic tequilas and whiskies can be expensive and depending on where you live, near impossible, but wine, like a good friend, is always around.

Since brandies, Cognacs, piscos, and vermouths are all wine-based and we didn't want sangrias to have all the fun in the wine category, those spirits will be covered here as well.

Favorite cocktail: Original French 75—I decided against sangria because of sweetness and the difficulty in making a single serving; a French 75 is easy to make, and tasty.

A BRIEF OVERVIEW OF WINE

Fermenting fruit to produce alcohol has been going on for as long as there has been fruit and microbes, so there is no way to really know when humans began making wine from grape juice. Evidence of rice and honey wine has been discovered on shards of 9,000-year-old pottery in Central China; and in the Caucuses, 7,400-year-old grape residue has been documented. In terms of viticulture—the cultivation of grapevines—as we know it today, the Phoenicians are a good reference point; around 1200 BCE they started transporting both wine and grapevines in Southern Europe and North Africa. With the rise of the Roman Empire, the making of wine spread throughout Europe and was bolstered by the Emperor Constantine's conversion to Christianity in 312 AD as well as the use of wine as a holy sacrament. Fast-forward several centuries and wine made it back to Asia and across the Atlantic.

A multivolume encyclopedia dedicated to wine would still fall short of recording all there is to say about this hopped-up grape juice, so we won't go too deep into it here. For one thing, while mixing wine cocktails you'll definitely want to use wines you enjoy drinking, but you most certainly don't want to uncork that $100 bottle you've been saving and pour it into a pitcher of sangria.

But we can be cursory and informative, so it is worth mentioning *terroir*, which is a French term that refers to all the elements that feed into where specific grapes grow, ranging from soil profile to climate, elevation, and exposure to sun. These factors flavor the grapes, and are reflected in the flavor of the wine that is produced. Human intervention, like when the grapes are picked and how the wine is aged also influence a wine's taste but should not be considered dynamics of terroir. And it is worth noting that even in wine-growing regions, whether Bordeaux, France, or Napa, California, several different terroirs exist.

Wines are named one of two ways. A varietal wine is named after the grape that it is made from (or in the case of multiple grapes being used, the primary grape); so a California Chardonnay is made from Chardonnay grapes, Cabernet Sauvignon is made from grapes of the same name. Other wines, mostly European ones, are named for the region where the grapes are grown, like Bordeaux.

The first decision in the wine-making process is when to pick the grapes; this determines the acidity and sweetness of the wine. The harvested grapes are then sorted and the maceration process begins, allowing tannins, coloring agents, and flavors to become must, the combination of solids like skins, seeds, and pulp with the grape juice. Maceration times vary, as do the techniques (e.g., pump overs vs. punch downs) to manage fermentation. Once fermented, the wine is clarified by filtering out all the solids and then racking the wine, before either bottling it or aging it in barrels. Simple as that!

The recipes that follow utilize red and white wines as well as other zippy grape-based libations. Brandy is distilled from wine or fruit juice; Cognac is a type of brandy from the Cognac region of Western France; pisco is another type of brandy that comes from Peru. Sherry is a fortified wine from Southern Spain; other fortified wines include Port, Madeira, and Moscatel, to name a few.

DOVER CLUB

GARNISH: 2 RASPBERRIES

Place the 4 raspberries and simple syrup in a cocktail shaker and muddle. Add the remaining cocktail ingredients and dry shake for 10 seconds. Add ice and shake for 30 seconds. Strain into a wine glass and garnish with the additional raspberries.

INGREDIENTS:

- 4 RASPBERRIES
- ½ OZ. SIMPLE SYRUP
- 3 OZ. PINOT NOIR
- 1½ OZ. ORANGE JUICE
- 1 TEASPOON RASPBERRY PRESERVES
- 1 EGG WHITE

MISS BEHAVIN'

GARNISH: 1 PEAR SLICE

Place the lemon juice, apple brandy, eau de vie, and simple syrup in a cocktail shaker filled with ice and shake vigorously. Strain into a champagne flute, top with Champagne, and garnish with the pear slice.

INGREDIENTS:

- ¾ OZ. LEMON JUICE
- ¾ OZ. LAIRD'S STRAIGHT APPLE BRANDY BOTTLED IN BOND
- ¾ OZ. PEAR EAU DE VIE
- 1 OZ. SIMPLE SYRUP
- CHAMPAGNE, TO TOP

DE WALLEN

GARNISH: 1 GRIOTTINE (CHERRY IN KIRSCH) & 1 STRAWBERRY

Place the strawberry and grenadine in a cocktail shaker and muddle. Add ice, the Sherry, and the Muscat and shake vigorously. Strain into a small snifter, top with Champagne, and garnish with the Griottine and the additional strawberry.

INGREDIENTS:

- 1 STRAWBERRY
- ¾ OZ. PINK HOUSE ALCHEMY DARK CHERRY GRENADINE
- 1½ OZ. PEDRO XIMENEZ SHERRY
- 1½ OZ. MUSCAT
- CHAMPAGNE, TO TOP

BELLINI

Place the peach nectar in a champagne flute and top with Champagne.

INGREDIENTS:

- 1 OZ. PEACH NECTAR
- CHAMPAGNE, TO TOP

BUCK'S FIZZ

Fill a champagne flute two-thirds of the way with Champagne and top with the orange juice.

INGREDIENTS:

- 2 OZ. CHAMPAGNE
- 1 OZ. ORANGE JUICE

RED BUCK'S FIZZ

Fill a champagne flute two-thirds of the way with Prosecco and top with the blood orange juice.

INGREDIENTS:

- 2 OZ. PROSECCO
- 1 OZ. BLOOD ORANGE JUICE

RED WINE MIMOSA

Place the red wine and orange juice in a wine glass filled with ice. Top with the splash of club soda and stir until chilled.

INGREDIENTS:

- 1 PART RED WINE
- 1 PART ORANGE JUICE
- SPLASH OF CLUB SODA

LE PÊCHE ROYALE

Place the lambic in a white wine glass, pour the Champagne on top, and then float the St-Germain on the surface of the cocktail.

INGREDIENTS:

- 4 OZ. LINDEMAN'S PÊCHE LAMBIC
- 4 OZ. CHAMPAGNE
- ¼ OZ. ST-GERMAIN

LA VIE EN ROSE

GARNISH: 2 TO 3 STRAWBERRIES

Strawberry and Gin Reduction: Place 2 oz. gin and 4 strawberries in a food processor and puree until smooth. Strain into a small saucepan through a fine sieve and cook over medium heat until the mixture has reduced by half.

Place the red wine and reduction in a wine glass and stir. Top with Champagne and garnish with the strawberries.

INGREDIENTS:

- 1 OZ. STRAWBERRY AND GIN REDUCTION
- 3 OZ. RED WINE
- CHAMPAGNE, TO TOP

MIMOSA

GARNISH: 1 ORANGE SLICE & 1 SPRIG OF LAVENDER

Place the orange juice in a champagne flute, top with Champagne, and garnish with the orange slice and lavender.

INGREDIENTS:

- 1½ OZ. ORANGE JUICE
- 1½ OZ. CHAMPAGNE

JUICE BOX

GARNISH: ASSORTED DICED FRUIT

Place the brandy, wine, juices, and Sprite in a wine glass filled halfway with ice, stir until chilled, and garnish with the assortment of diced fruit.

INGREDIENTS:

- 1 PART BRANDY
- 2 PARTS RED WINE
- 1 PART CRANBERRY JUICE
- 2 PARTS ORANGE JUICE
- 1 PART SPRITE

MÉNAGE À TROIS

Place all of the ingredients, except for the seltzer water, in a large pitcher or container. Cover and refrigerate for 4 or more hours. When ready to serve, add ice and the seltzer water and stir.

INGREDIENTS:

- 1 (750 ML) BOTTLE OF DRY RED WINE
- 2 ORANGES, SLICED THIN
- 1 PEACH, PITTED AND SLICED THIN
- 1 CUP RED GRAPES, FROZEN
- ¼ CUP PEACH BRANDY
- 2 CUPS SELTZER WATER

OASIS

Place all of the ingredients, except for the seltzer water, in a large pitcher or container. Cover and refrigerate for 4 or more hours. When ready to serve, add ice and the seltzer water and stir.

INGREDIENTS:

- 1 (750 ML) BOTTLE OF DRY RED WINE
- 2 LIMES, SLICED VERY THIN
- 1 CUP BLACKBERRIES, FROZEN
- 1 CUP GREEN GRAPES, HALVED AND FROZEN
- 2 CUPS POMEGRANATE JUICE
- ¼ CUP BRANDY
- 2 CUPS LEMON-LIME SELTZER WATER

CLASSIC RAZZ

Place all of the ingredients, except for the seltzer water, in a large pitcher or container. Cover and refrigerate for 4 or more hours. When ready to serve, add ice and the seltzer water and stir.

INGREDIENTS:

- 1 (750 ML) BOTTLE OF DRY RED WINE
- 2 GRANNY SMITH APPLES, CORED, SEEDED, AND DICED
- 1 ORANGE, SLICED THIN
- 1 CUP RASPBERRIES, FROZEN
- ¼ CUP RASPBERRY VODKA
- 2 CUPS SELTZER WATER

BERRY ORANGE-Y

In a small saucepan, combine the blueberries and sugar and cook over medium heat until the blueberries start to burst, about 10 minutes. Simmer, while stirring constantly, for 2 minutes, remove from heat, and stir until well combined and slightly cool. Place the blueberry-and-sugar mixture in a pitcher, stir in the wine, orange slices, orange juice, and Grand Marnier, cover, and refrigerate for at least 4 hours. When ready to serve, add ice and the seltzer water and stir.

INGREDIENTS:

- 2 CUPS BLUEBERRIES
- ¼ CUP SUGAR
- 1 (750 ML) BOTTLE OF DRY RED WINE
- 1 ORANGE, SLICED THIN
- 1 CUP ORANGE JUICE
- ¼ CUP GRAND MARNIER
- 1 CUP SELTZER WATER

RED HEAD

Place the wine, sugar, and white grape juice in a large pitcher and stir until sugar has dissolved. Add the brandy, cherries, and grapes, stir, cover the pitcher, and refrigerate for at least 4 hours. When ready to serve, add ice and the seltzer water and stir.

INGREDIENTS:

- 1 (750 ML) BOTTLE OF DRY RED WINE
- ½ CUP SUGAR
- ½ CUP WHITE GRAPE JUICE
- ¼ CUP BRANDY
- 2 CUPS CHERRIES
- 1 CUP SEEDLESS GRAPES, HALVED AND FROZEN
- 1 CUP SELTZER WATER

RUM RUNNER WITH A TWIST

Place all of the ingredients in a large pitcher or container and stir. Cover and refrigerate for 4 or more hours. When ready to serve, add ice and stir.

INGREDIENTS:

- 1 (750 ML) BOTTLE OF DRY RED WINE
- 2 ORANGES, SLICED THIN
- 2 LEMONS, SLICED THIN
- 1 LIME, SLICED THIN
- 1 CUP ORANGE JUICE
- ½ CUP DARK RUM

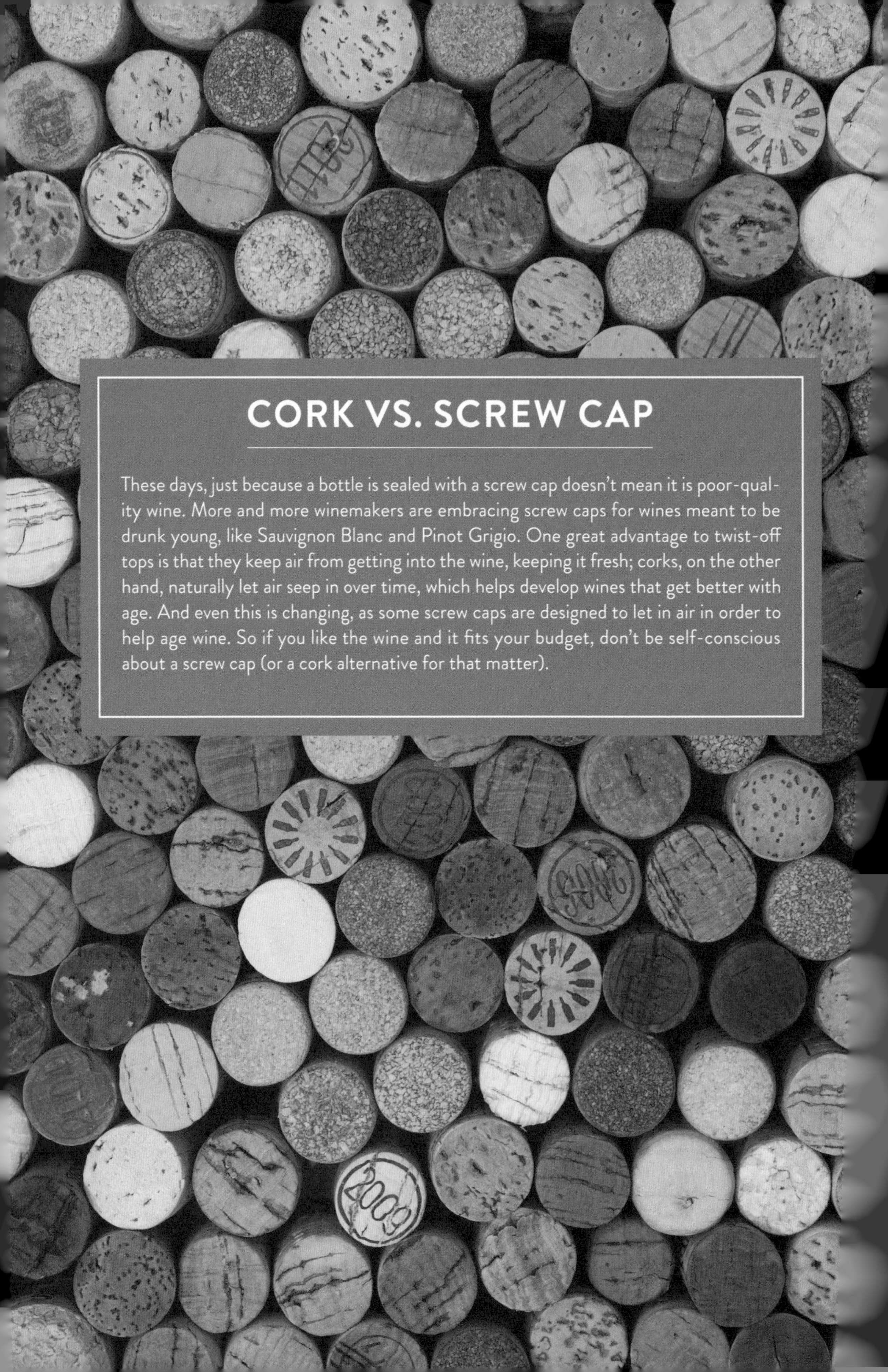

CORK VS. SCREW CAP

These days, just because a bottle is sealed with a screw cap doesn't mean it is poor-quality wine. More and more winemakers are embracing screw caps for wines meant to be drunk young, like Sauvignon Blanc and Pinot Grigio. One great advantage to twist-off tops is that they keep air from getting into the wine, keeping it fresh; corks, on the other hand, naturally let air seep in over time, which helps develop wines that get better with age. And even this is changing, as some screw caps are designed to let in air in order to help age wine. So if you like the wine and it fits your budget, don't be self-conscious about a screw cap (or a cork alternative for that matter).

SPICY ISLAND

Place all of the ingredients, except for the seltzer water, in a large pitcher or container. Cover and refrigerate for 4 or more hours. When ready to serve, add ice and the seltzer water and stir.

INGREDIENTS:

- 1 (750 ML) BOTTLE OF DRY RED WINE
- 1 CUP PINEAPPLE, DICED AND FROZEN
- 1 JALAPEÑO PEPPER, SEEDED AND SLICED THIN
- 1 CUP PINEAPPLE JUICE
- DASH OF HOT SAUCE
- 2 CUPS SELTZER WATER

SUMMER DAY

Place all of the ingredients, except for the seltzer water, in a large pitcher or container. Cover and refrigerate for 4 or more hours. When ready to serve, add ice and the seltzer water and stir.

INGREDIENTS:

- 1 (750 ML) BOTTLE OF DRY RED WINE
- 1 GRANNY SMITH APPLE, SEEDED, CORED, AND DICED
- 1 CUP BLUEBERRIES, FROZEN
- 1 CUP STRAWBERRIES, SLICED THIN AND FROZEN
- ¼ CUP BRANDY
- 2 CUPS SELTZER WATER

CHERRY POM-POM

Place all of the ingredients, except for the seltzer water, in a large pitcher or container. Cover and refrigerate for 4 or more hours. When ready to serve, add ice and the seltzer water and stir.

INGREDIENTS:

- 1 (750 ML) BOTTLE OF DRY RED WINE
- 2 CUPS CHERRIES, PITTED AND HALVED
- 1 LEMON, SLICED THIN
- 1 CUP CHERRY JUICE
- ½ CUP POMEGRANATE JUICE
- 2 CUPS LEMON SELTZER WATER

MELBA MEDLEY

Place all of the ingredients, except for the seltzer water, in a large pitcher or container. Cover and refrigerate for 4 or more hours. When ready to serve, add ice and the seltzer water and stir.

INGREDIENTS:

- 1 (750 ML) BOTTLE OF DRY RED WINE
- 2 CUPS CHERRIES, PITTED AND HALVED
- 1 CUP BLACKBERRIES
- 1 PEACH, PITTED, SLICED THIN, AND FROZEN
- ½ CUP PEACH VODKA
- 2 CUPS SELTZER WATER

PURPLE PASSION

Place all of the ingredients, except for the seltzer water, in a large pitcher or container. Cover and refrigerate for 4 or more hours. When ready to serve, add ice and the seltzer water and stir.

INGREDIENTS:

- 1 (750 ML) BOTTLE OF DRY RED WINE
- 1 PLUM, PITTED, SLICED THIN, AND FROZEN
- ½ CUP CHERRIES, PITTED AND HALVED
- ½ CUP BLACKBERRIES
- ¼ CUP GRAND MARNIER
- 2 CUPS SELTZER WATER

CHERRY SODA SIZZLE

Place all of the ingredients, except for the soda, in a large pitcher or container. Cover and refrigerate for 4 or more hours. When ready to serve, add ice and the soda and stir.

INGREDIENTS:

- 1 (750 ML) BOTTLE OF DRY RED WINE
- 2 PEARS, CORED, SEEDED, AND DICED
- 1 JALAPEÑO PEPPER, SEEDED AND SLICED THIN
- ¼ CUP BRANDY
- 2 CUPS BLACK CHERRY SODA

PLUMDEMONIUM

Place all of the ingredients, except for the seltzer water, in a large pitcher or container. Cover and refrigerate for 4 or more hours. When ready to serve, add ice and the seltzer water and stir.

INGREDIENTS:

- 1 (750 ML) BOTTLE OF DRY RED WINE
- 2 PLUMS, PITTED, SLICED THIN, AND FROZEN
- 1 APRICOT, PITTED AND DICED
- 1 CUP CRANBERRY JUICE
- ¼ CUP BRANDY
- 1 CUP SELTZER WATER
- ½ CHERRIES, PITTED AND HALVED (OPTIONAL)

GET FIGGY WITH IT

GARNISH: SPRIGS OF THYME

Place all of the ingredients, except for the seltzer water, in a large pitcher or container. Cover and refrigerate for 4 or more hours. When ready to serve, add ice and the seltzer water, stir, and garnish each glass with a sprig of thyme.

INGREDIENTS:

- 1 (750 ML) BOTTLE OF DRY RED WINE
- 1 CUP FRESH RASPBERRIES
- 2–3 FIGS, DICED AND FROZEN
- 1 CUP FIG JUICE
- ½ CUP POMEGRANATE JUICE
- 1 CUP SELTZER WATER

BOUGH DOWN

Place all of the ingredients, except for the soda, in a large pitcher or container. Cover and refrigerate for 4 or more hours. When ready to serve, add ice and the soda and stir.

INGREDIENTS:

- 1 (750 ML) BOTTLE OF DRY RED WINE
- 1 PEACH, PITTED, SLICED THIN, AND FROZEN
- 1 PLUM, PITTED, SLICED THIN, AND FROZEN
- 1 GRANNY SMITH APPLE, CORED, SEEDED, AND DICED
- ¼ CUP BRANDY
- 2 CUPS LEMON-LIME SODA

CHERRY KISS

Chocolate Simple Syrup: Stir ⅓ cup unsweetened cocoa powder into a standard simple syrup after it has been removed from heat. Let the mixture sit for 3 hours and strain before using.

Place all of the ingredients, except for the soda, in a large pitcher or container. Cover and refrigerate for 4 or more hours. When ready to serve, add ice and the soda and stir.

INGREDIENTS:

- ½ CUP CHOCOLATE SIMPLE SYRUP
- 1 (750 ML) BOTTLE OF DRY RED WINE
- 1 CUP CHERRIES, PITTED AND HALVED
- 1 (12 OZ.) CAN OF BLACK CHERRY SODA

FALL FARMER

GARNISH: POMEGRANATE SEEDS

Place all of the sangria ingredients in a large pitcher or container. Cover and refrigerate for 4 or more hours. When ready to serve, add ice, stir, and garnish with the pomegranate seeds.

INGREDIENTS:

- 1 (750 ML) BOTTLE OF DRY RED WINE
- 2 APPLES, CORED, SEEDED, AND DICED
- 1 ORANGE, SLICED THIN
- ¼ CUP APPLE VODKA
- 1 CUP APPLE CIDER
- DASH OF CINNAMON

FLAVOR FIESTA

Place all of the ingredients, except for the seltzer water, in a large pitcher or container. Cover and refrigerate for 4 or more hours. When ready to serve, add ice and the seltzer water and stir.

INGREDIENTS:

- 1 (750 ML) BOTTLE OF DRY RED WINE
- 2 GRANNY SMITH APPLES, CORED, SEEDED, AND DICED
- ½ CUP MANGO, DICED AND FROZEN
- 1 CUP STRAWBERRIES, SLICED THIN AND FROZEN
- 1 CUP WHITE GRAPE JUICE
- ¼ CUP GIN
- 1 CUP SELTZER WATER

SANGRIA BLANCA

Place all of the ingredients, except for the seltzer water, in a large pitcher or container. Cover and refrigerate for 4 or more hours. When ready to serve, add ice and the seltzer water and stir.

INGREDIENTS:

- 1 (750 ML) BOTTLE OF DRY WHITE WINE
- 1 CUP SEEDLESS GREEN GRAPES, HALVED
- ½ CUP SEEDLESS RED GRAPES, HALVED
- 2 CUPS WHITE GRAPE JUICE
- ¼ CUP BRANDY
- 2 CUPS SELTZER WATER

SWEET PEACH

Place all of the ingredients, except for the seltzer water, in a large pitcher or container. Cover and refrigerate for 4 or more hours. When ready to serve, add ice and the seltzer water and stir.

INGREDIENTS:

- 1 (750 ML) BOTTLE OF DRY WHITE WINE
- 2 PEACHES, PITTED AND DICED
- ½ CUP BLUEBERRIES, FROZEN
- 1 CUP PEACH NECTAR
- ¼ CUP PEACH SCHNAPPS
- 2 CUPS SELTZER WATER

LEMON-LIME TIME

Place all of the ingredients, except for the soda, in a large pitcher or container. Cover and refrigerate for 4 or more hours. When ready to serve, add ice and the soda and stir.

INGREDIENTS:

- 1 (750 ML) BOTTLE OF DRY WHITE WINE
- 1 LARGE ORANGE, SLICED THIN AND CHOPPED
- ½ LEMON, SLICED THIN
- ½ LIME, SLICED THIN
- ¼ CUP TRIPLE SEC
- 2 CUPS LEMON-LIME SODA

JUICY MELON

Place all of the ingredients, except for the seltzer water, in a large pitcher or container. Cover and refrigerate for 4 or more hours. When ready to serve, add ice and the seltzer water and stir.

INGREDIENTS:

- 1 (750 ML) BOTTLE OF DRY WHITE WINE
- 1 LARGE ORANGE, SLICED THIN
- 1 CUP HONEYDEW MELON, DICED
- ½ CUP MIDORI
- 2 CUPS SELTZER WATER

BERRY BLUE

Place all of the ingredients, except for the seltzer water, in a large pitcher or container. Cover and refrigerate for 4 or more hours. When ready to serve, add ice and the seltzer water and stir.

INGREDIENTS:

- 1 (750 ML) BOTTLE OF DRY WHITE WINE
- ½ CUP RASPBERRIES, FROZEN
- ½ CUP BLACKBERRIES, FROZEN
- ½ CUP BLUEBERRIES, FROZEN
- ½ CUP BERRY VODKA
- 1 CUP RASPBERRY JUICE
- 2 CUPS SELTZER WATER

LAVENDER LIFT

GARNISH: SPRIGS OF LAVENDER

Place the ingredients for the sangria, except for the seltzer water, in a large pitcher or container. Cover and refrigerate for 4 or more hours. When ready to serve, add ice and the seltzer water, stir, and garnish each glass with a sprig of lavender.

INGREDIENTS:

- 1 (750 ML) BOTTLE OF DRY WHITE WINE
- ¼ CUP GIN OR VODKA
- 1 CUP BLUEBERRIES, FROZEN
- 1 KIWI, PEELED, DICED, AND FROZEN
- 1 CUP LAVENDER SIMPLE SYRUP (SEE PAGE 174)
- 1½ CUPS BLUEBERRY SELTZER WATER

MELON MARVEL

GARNISH: FRESH BASIL LEAVES & LIME SLICES

Place the wine, watermelon, watermelon juice, and basil syrup in a large pitcher or container. Cover and refrigerate for 4 or more hours. When ready to serve, add ice and the seltzer water, stir, and garnish each glass with basil and a slice of lime.

INGREDIENTS:

- 1 (750 ML) BOTTLE OF DRY WHITE WINE
- 2 CUPS WATERMELON, SEEDED, CUBED, AND FROZEN
- 1 CUP WATERMELON JUICE
- 1 CUP BASIL SYRUP (SEE PAGE 391)
- 1 CUP SELTZER WATER

PIÑA-GRIA

Place all of the ingredients, except for the seltzer water, in a large pitcher or container. Cover and refrigerate for 4 or more hours. When ready to serve, add ice and the seltzer water and stir.

INGREDIENTS:

- 1 (750 ML) BOTTLE OF DRY WHITE WINE
- 1 CUP PINEAPPLE, DICED AND FROZEN
- 1 CUP PINEAPPLE JUICE
- ½ CUP CREAM OF COCONUT
- ½ CUP COCONUT VODKA
- 1 CUP SELTZER WATER

SASSY & SAVORY

GARNISH: SPRIGS OF ROSEMARY

Place all of the sangria ingredients, except for the seltzer water, in a large pitcher or container. Cover and refrigerate for 4 or more hours. When ready to serve, add ice and the seltzer water, stir, and garnish each glass with a sprig of rosemary.

INGREDIENTS:

- 1 (750 ML) BOTTLE OF DRY WHITE WINE
- 1 GRAPEFRUIT, PEELED, SEEDED, AND SECTIONS CUT INTO THIRDS
- 2 CUPS BLUEBERRIES, FROZEN
- ¼ CUP GRAPEFRUIT VODKA
- ½ CUP SIMPLE SYRUP
- 2 CUPS SELTZER WATER

BLACK-EYED PEACH

Place all of the ingredients, except for the seltzer water, in a large pitcher or container. Cover and refrigerate for 4 or more hours. When ready to serve, add ice and the seltzer water and stir.

INGREDIENTS:

- 1 (750 ML) BOTTLE OF DRY WHITE WINE
- 1 LARGE OR 2 MEDIUM PEACHES, PITTED, DICED, AND FROZEN
- ½ CUP BLACKBERRIES
- 1 CUP PEACH NECTAR
- ¼ CUP PEACH SCHNAPPS
- 2 CUPS SELTZER WATER

PEAR-FECT

Place all of the ingredients, except for the soda, in a large pitcher or container. Cover and refrigerate for 4 or more hours. When ready to serve, add ice and the soda and stir.

INGREDIENTS:

- 1 (750 ML) BOTTLE OF DRY RED WINE
- 2 PEARS, CORED, SEEDED, AND DICED
- 1 CUP SEEDLESS GRAPES, FROZEN
- 1 CUP ORANGE JUICE
- 1 (12 OZ.) CAN OF CREAM SODA

OH MY DARLIN'

Place the wine and sugar in a large pitcher and stir until the sugar is dissolved. Add the clementine sections, basil, and Grand Marnier, cover, and refrigerate for at least 4 hours. When ready to serve, add ice and the seltzer water and stir.

INGREDIENTS:

- 1 (750 ML) BOTTLE OF DRY RED WINE
- ½ CUP SUGAR
- 2 CLEMENTINES, PEELED AND SECTIONS HALVED
- 6–8 BASIL LEAVES, CHOPPED
- ¼ CUP GRAND MARNIER
- 2 CUPS ORANGE SELTZER WATER

FLORAL ON THE FINISH

Place all of the ingredients, except for the seltzer water, in a large pitcher or container. Cover and refrigerate for 4 or more hours. When ready to serve, add ice and the seltzer water and stir.

INGREDIENTS:

- 1 (750 ML) BOTTLE OF DRY RED WINE
- ½ CUP LAVENDER SYRUP (SEE PAGE 174)
- 2 PEARS, CORED AND DICED
- ¼ CUP FRAMBOISE
- 2 CUPS SELTZER WATER

PEPPER PEACH

Place all of the ingredients, except for the seltzer water, in a large pitcher or container. Cover and refrigerate for 4 or more hours. When ready to serve, add ice and the seltzer water and stir.

INGREDIENTS:

- 1 (750 ML) BOTTLE OF DRY WHITE WINE
- ½ CUP MANGO, DICED AND FROZEN
- 1 JALAPEÑO PEPPER, SEEDED AND SLICED THIN
- 1 LARGE PEACH, PITTED, DICED, AND FROZEN
- 2 CUPS PEACH JUICE
- 1 CUP SELTZER WATER

RASPBERRY ROMANCE

In a saucepan, combine the raspberries and sugar and cook, while stirring constantly, for 5 minutes. Remove from heat and stir until the mixture has cooled slightly. Stir in the unsweetened cocoa powder and transfer the mixture to a large pitcher or container. Stir in the wines and refrigerate for 4 or more hours. When ready to serve, add ice and the sparkling water and stir.

INGREDIENTS:

- 2 CUPS RASPBERRIES
- ½ CUP SUGAR
- 1 TABLESPOON UNSWEETENED COCOA POWDER
- 1 (750 ML) BOTTLE OF DRY RED WINE
- ½ CUP CHOCOLATE WINE
- 1 CUP RASPBERRY SPARKLING WATER

SÍ SEÑORA

Place all of the ingredients, except for the seltzer water, in a large pitcher or container. Cover and refrigerate for 4 or more hours. When ready to serve, add ice and the seltzer water and stir.

INGREDIENTS:

- 1 (750 ML) BOTTLE OF DRY WHITE WINE
- 1 CUP SEEDLESS GREEN GRAPES, HALVED
- 2 WHITE PEACHES, PITTED AND DICED
- 2 CUPS WHITE GRAPE JUICE
- ½ CUP PEACH VODKA
- 2 CUPS SELTZER WATER

SLEEK HEAT

Place all of the ingredients, except for the seltzer water, in a large pitcher or container. Cover and refrigerate for 4 or more hours. When ready to serve, add ice and the seltzer water and stir.

INGREDIENTS:

- 1 (750 ML) BOTTLE OF DRY WHITE WINE
- 1 CUP SEEDLESS GREEN GRAPES, HALVED AND FROZEN
- 2 PLUMS, PITTED, DICED, AND FROZEN
- ½ CUP GINGER SYRUP (SEE PAGE 255, SUBSTITUTE SUGAR FOR THE HONEY)
- 1 CUP SELTZER WATER

HONEY PLUM

Place all of the ingredients, except for the soda, in a large pitcher or container. Cover and refrigerate for 4 or more hours. When ready to serve, add ice and the soda and stir.

INGREDIENTS:

- 1 (750 ML) BOTTLE OF DRY WHITE WINE
- 1 NECTARINE, PITTED, DICED, AND FROZEN
- 2 PLUMS, PITTED, DICED, AND FROZEN
- ½ CUP HONEY VODKA
- 1 (12 OZ.) CAN OF LEMON-LIME SODA

TROUBLE IN THE TROPICS

Place all of the ingredients, except for the soda, in a large pitcher or container. Cover and refrigerate for 4 or more hours. When ready to serve, add ice and the soda and stir.

INGREDIENTS:

- 1 (750 ML) BOTTLE OF DRY WHITE WINE
- 1 CUP PINEAPPLE, DICED AND FROZEN
- 1 JALAPEÑO PEPPER, SEEDED AND SLICED THIN
- 1 (12 OZ.) CAN OF LEMON-LIME SODA

SÍ SEÑOR

Place all of the ingredients, except for the seltzer water, in a large pitcher or container. Cover and refrigerate for 4 or more hours. When ready to serve, add ice and the seltzer water and stir.

INGREDIENTS:

- 1 (750 ML) BOTTLE OF DRY WHITE WINE
- 1 CUP SEEDLESS RED GRAPES, HALVED
- 1 GRANNY SMITH APPLE, CORED, SEEDED, AND DICED
- ½ ORANGE, SLICED
- 2 CUPS APPLE JUICE
- ½ CUP BRANDY
- 2 CUPS SELTZER WATER

FALL FRUIT FIESTA

GARNISH: POMEGRANATE SEEDS & CINNAMON STICKS

Place all of the sangria ingredients, except for the soda, in a large pitcher or container. Cover and refrigerate for 4 or more hours. When ready to serve, add ice and the soda, stir, and garnish with the pomegranate seeds and cinnamon sticks.

INGREDIENTS:

- 1 (750 ML) BOTTLE OF DRY WHITE WINE
- 1 RED DELICIOUS APPLE, CORED, SEEDED, AND DICED
- 1 CUP SEEDLESS GREEN GRAPES, HALVED
- 1 CUP POMEGRANATE JUICE
- JUICE OF 1 LIME
- ¼ CUP BRANDY
- 1 (12 OZ.) CAN OF LEMON-LIME SODA

LEMON THYME

GARNISH: SPRIGS OF THYME

Thyme Syrup: Add 4 sprigs of thyme to a standard simple syrup when it is boiling. After 1 minute, remove from heat, let sit for 2 hours, and strain before using.

Place all of the sangria ingredients, except for the seltzer water, in a large pitcher or container. Cover and refrigerate for 4 or more hours. When ready to serve, add ice and the seltzer water, stir, and garnish each glass with a sprig of thyme.

INGREDIENTS:

- ½ CUP THYME SYRUP
- 1 (750 ML) BOTTLE OF DRY WHITE WINE
- 1 LEMON, SLICED THIN AND CHOPPED
- ½ CUP LIMONCELLO
- 2 CUPS SELTZER WATER

BERRY'D ALIVE

Place all of the ingredients, except for the seltzer water, in a large pitcher or container. Cover and refrigerate for 4 or more hours. When ready to serve, add ice and the seltzer water and stir.

INGREDIENTS:

- 1 (750 ML) BOTTLE OF DRY WHITE WINE
- 1½ CUP STRAWBERRIES, CHOPPED
- 1 CUP BLACKBERRIES
- 2 CUPS BLUEBERRY-POMEGRANATE JUICE
- ½ CUP PREFERRED BERRY-FLAVORED VODKA
- 1 CUP MIXED BERRY SELTZER WATER

BERRY BUBBLY

Place the thawed strawberries, their juice, the blueberries, and lime juice in a bowl and stir gently. Divide the mixture between the serving glasses and top with the sparkling wine.

INGREDIENTS:

- 1 CUP SLICED, FROZEN STRAWBERRIES, THAWED, JUICE RESERVED
- 1 CUP BLUEBERRIES, FROZEN
- 1 TABLESPOON FRESH LIME JUICE
- 1 (750 ML) BOTTLE OF SPARKLING WINE, VERY COLD

NUTTY CHERRY

Place the cherries, nectarine, and liqueur in a bowl, cover, and chill in the refrigerator for anywhere from 2 to 6 hours. When ready to serve, divide the mixture between the serving glasses and top with the sparkling wine.

INGREDIENTS:

- 1 CUP CHERRIES, PITTED AND HALVED
- 1 CUP NECTARINE, DICED
- ¼ CUP AMARETTO
- 1 (750 ML) BOTTLE OF SPARKLING WINE, VERY COLD

APPLE & SPICE

Place the apples, cranberries, cranberry juice, apple cider, apple vodka, and nutmeg in a bowl, stir to combine, cover, and refrigerate for anywhere from 2 to 6 hours. When ready to serve, strain the juice into a measuring cup. Divide the fruit and the juice between the serving glasses and top with the sparkling wine.

INGREDIENTS:

- 1 GRANNY SMITH APPLE, PEELED, CORED, SEEDED, AND DICED
- 1 EMPIRE APPLE, PEELED, CORED, SEEDED, AND DICED
- ½ CUP FRESH CRANBERRIES
- ¼ CUP CRANBERRY JUICE
- ¼ CUP APPLE CIDER
- ¼ CUP APPLE VODKA
- DASH OF NUTMEG
- 1 (750 ML) BOTTLE OF SPARKLING WINE, VERY COLD

BERRY PROVENÇAL

Place the raspberries, blueberries, and lavender syrup in a bowl, stir to combine, cover, and refrigerate for 1 hour. Divide the mixture between the serving glasses and top with sparkling wine.

INGREDIENTS:

- 1 PINT RASPBERRIES, FROZEN
- 1 CUP BLUEBERRIES, FROZEN
- ¾ CUP LAVENDER SYRUP (SEE PAGE 174)
- 1 (750 ML) BOTTLE OF SPARKLING WINE, VERY COLD

BERRY BANILLA

Place all of the ingredients, except for the soda, in a large pitcher or container. Cover and refrigerate for 2 hours. Remove the vanilla bean and refrigerate for 2 or more hours. When ready to serve, add ice and the soda and stir.

INGREDIENTS:

- 1 (750 ML) BOTTLE OF DRY WHITE WINE
- 2 PEARS, CORED, SEEDED, DICED, AND FROZEN
- 1 CUP BLUEBERRIES, FROZEN
- 1 VANILLA BEAN
- ½ CUP VANILLA VODKA
- 1 (12 OZ.) CAN OF CREAM SODA

SCHEHERAZADE

Place all of the ingredients, except for the seltzer water, in a large pitcher or container. Cover and refrigerate for 4 or more hours. When ready to serve, add ice and the seltzer water and stir.

INGREDIENTS:

- 1 (750 ML) BOTTLE OF DRY WHITE WINE
- 1 GRANNY SMITH APPLE, CORED, SEEDED, AND DICED
- 1 CUP FRESH CHERRIES, PITTED, HALVED, AND FROZEN
- ½ CUP FRANGELICO (OR OTHER HAZELNUT LIQUEUR)
- 1 CUP SELTZER WATER

HELLO, HONEY!

Place the grape halves, melon pieces, and Midori in a bowl and stir gently. Divide the mixture between the serving glasses and top with the sparkling wine.

INGREDIENTS:

- ½ CUP SEEDLESS RED GRAPES, HALVED
- ½ CUP SEEDLESS GREEN GRAPES, HALVED
- 1 CUP HONEYDEW MELON, DICED
- 2 TABLESPOONS MIDORI
- 1 (750 ML) BOTTLE OF SPARKLING WINE, VERY COLD

FRUITY DOWN UNDER

Place 2 cups of the watermelon and the sugar in a blender and puree until smooth. Place the puree in a bowl, add the remaining watermelon and the kiwi, and stir to combine. Divide the mixture between the serving glasses and top with the sparkling wine.

INGREDIENTS:

- **3 CUPS WATERMELON, SEEDED, DICED, AND FROZEN**
- **¼ CUP SUGAR**
- **½ CUP KIWI, DICED AND FROZEN**
- **1 (750 ML) BOTTLE OF SPARKLING WINE, VERY COLD**

HOT TROPIXX

Place the pineapple, mango, mango juice, jalapeño, lime juice, and vodka in a bowl, cover, and refrigerate for up to 2 hours. When ready to serve, strain the juice into a measuring cup. Divide the fruit and the juice between the serving glasses and top with the sparkling wine.

INGREDIENTS:

- **1 CUP PINEAPPLE, DICED**
- **¾ CUP DICED, CANNED MANGO**
- **½ CUP JUICE FROM A CAN OF MANGO**
- **1 JALAPEÑO PEPPER, SLICED THIN**
- **¼ CUP FRESH LIME JUICE**
- **¼ CUP VODKA**
- **1 (750 ML) BOTTLE OF SPARKLING WINE, VERY COLD**

THYME ON THE FARM

GARNISH: SPRIGS OF THYME (OPTIONAL)

Place the strawberries, melon, syrup, and vodka in a bowl, stir to combine, cover, and refrigerate for 1 hour. Divide the mixture between the serving glasses, top with sparkling wine, and garnish with the sprigs of thyme, if desired.

INGREDIENTS:

- **1 CUP STRAWBERRIES, SLICED THIN**
- **½ CUP HONEYDEW MELON, DICED**
- **½ CUP THYME SYRUP (SEE PAGE 459)**
- **¼ CUP VODKA**
- **1 (750 ML) BOTTLE OF SPARKLING WINE, VERY COLD**

GREEN WITH ENVY

Place the apples, grapes, juice, vodka, and syrup in a bowl, stir, cover, and refrigerate for anywhere from 2 to 6 hours. When ready to serve, strain the juice into a measuring cup. Divide the fruit and the juice between the serving glasses and top with the sparkling wine.

INGREDIENTS:

- 2 GRANNY SMITH APPLES, CORED, SEEDED, AND DICED
- ½ CUP SEEDLESS GREEN GRAPES, HALVED AND FROZEN
- ½ CUP WHITE GRAPE JUICE
- ¼ CUP APPLE VODKA
- ½ CUP ROSEMARY SYRUP (SEE PAGE 308)
- 1 (750 ML) BOTTLE OF SPARKLING WINE, VERY COLD

ORANGE YOU PRETTY

Reserve six slices of orange and place the rest in a bowl. Add the lemon juice and Grand Marnier, stir to combine, cover, and refrigerate for 1 hour. Divide this mixture, the reserved orange slices, and the raspberries between the serving glasses and top with the sparkling wine.

INGREDIENTS:

- ½ NAVEL ORANGE, SLICED THIN
- 2 TABLESPOONS FRESH LEMON JUICE
- ¼ CUP GRAND MARNIER
- 4–6 RASPBERRIES
- 1 (750 ML) BOTTLE OF SPARKLING WINE, VERY COLD

MIXED BAG

Place the berries, their juice, the simple syrup, and vodka in a bowl, stir to combine, cover, and refrigerate for 1 hour. Divide the mixture between the serving glasses and top with the sparkling wine.

INGREDIENTS:

- 1½ CUPS FROZEN MIXED BERRIES, THAWED
- ½ CUP JUICE FROM THAWED BERRIES
- ½ CUP SIMPLE SYRUP
- ½ CUP STRAWBERRY OR BLUEBERRY VODKA
- 1 (750 ML) BOTTLE OF SPARKLING WINE, VERY COLD

STRAWBERRY LEMONADE

Place all of the ingredients in a large pitcher or container. Cover and refrigerate for 4 or more hours. When ready to serve, add ice and stir.

INGREDIENTS:

- 1 (750 ML) BOTTLE OF BLUSH WINE
- 2 CUPS STRAWBERRIES, SLICED
- 1 (12 OZ.) CAN OF FROZEN LEMONADE CONCENTRATE
- 1½ CUPS WATER

4TH OF JULY

GARNISH: APPLE SLICES (OPTIONAL)

Place all of the sangria ingredients, except for the seltzer water, in a large pitcher or container. Cover and refrigerate for 4 or more hours. When ready to serve, add ice and the seltzer water, stir, and garnish each glass with apple slices, if desired.

INGREDIENTS:

- 1 (750 ML) BOTTLE OF SWEET WHITE WINE
- ½ CUP BLUEBERRIES, FROZEN
- ½ CUP RASPBERRIES, FROZEN
- ½ CUP CHERRIES, PITTED, HALVED, AND FROZEN
- ½ CUP VODKA
- 1 CUP MIXED BERRY SELTZER WATER

BASIL-BERRY SANGRIA

GARNISH: BASIL LEAVES

Place all of the ingredients, except for the seltzer water, in a large pitcher or container. Cover and refrigerate for 2 hours. When ready to serve, add ice and the seltzer water, stir, and garnish each glass with basil leaves.

INGREDIENTS:

- 1 (750 ML) BOTTLE OF DRY ROSÉ
- 1 CUP STRAWBERRIES, SLICED
- 1 CUP MIXED BERRY VODKA
- ½ CUP BASIL SYRUP (SEE PAGE 391)
- 2 CUPS STRAWBERRY SELTZER WATER

MAUREEN'S ROSÉ

GARNISH: BASIL LEAVES & STRAWBERRIES (OPTIONAL)

Open the bottle of Rosé and slide the cucumber pieces inside. Put the cork back in the bottle and refrigerate overnight. Strain the wine into a pitcher, dice half of the cucumber, and discard the rest. Place the diced cucumber in the pitcher, add the lemon juice and the St-Germain, stir, and serve over ice. If desired, garnish each glass with basil leaves and strawberries.

INGREDIENTS:

- 1 (750 ML) BOTTLE OF DRY ROSÉ
- ½ CUCUMBER, PEELED AND SLICED LENGTHWISE
- 2 TEASPOONS LEMON JUICE
- 2 TABLESPOONS ST-GERMAIN

MINTY MELON

GARNISH: 1 WATERMELON WEDGE & SPRIG OF MINT

Place all of the ingredients, except for the seltzer water, in a large pitcher or container. Cover and refrigerate for 2 hours. When ready to serve, add ice and the seltzer water and stir.

INGREDIENTS:

- 1 (750 ML) BOTTLE OF DRY ROSÉ
- 2 CUPS WATERMELON, DICED AND FROZEN
- ½ CUP TEQUILA
- 6–8 LARGE MINT LEAVES
- ½ CUP MINT SYRUP (SEE PAGE 308, SUBSTITUTE MINT FOR THE ROSEMARY)
- 1 CUP WATERMELON SELTZER WATER

SLUSH BERRY

Place all of the ingredients in a blender and puree until smooth, working in batches if necessary. Divide the mixture between the serving glasses.

INGREDIENTS:

- 1 (750 ML) BOTTLE OF SWEET RED WINE
- 1 CUP BLUEBERRIES
- 1 CUP RASPBERRIES
- 1 CUP STRAWBERRIES
- 1 CUP ORANGE JUICE
- ¼ CUP TRIPLE SEC
- 1 CUP ICE

FROZEN BERRY-ADE SANGRIA

GARNISH: 1 LEMON OR LIME, SLICED THIN

Fill an ice cube tray with some of the wine and another with the lemonade. Put the trays in the freezer and freeze for anywhere from 4 hours to overnight. Place the wine and lemonade cubes in a blender along with the strawberries, rum, and any remaining wine. Puree until smooth, divide between the serving glasses, and garnish each glass with slices of lemon or lime.

INGREDIENTS:

- 1 (750 ML) BOTTLE OF SWEET WHITE OR BLUSH WINE
- 2 CUPS LEMONADE
- 1 CUP FRESH STRAWBERRIES, SLICED
- ½ CUP DARK RUM

CHEATIN' EASY

Place all of the ingredients in a large pitcher, stir to combine, and serve over ice.

INGREDIENTS:

- 1 (750 ML) BOTTLE OF FRUITY, DRY RED WINE
- 2 CUPS BERRY-PINEAPPLE-PASSION FRUIT JUICE
- 1 CUP FROZEN BLUEBERRIES
- ¼ CUP BERRY VODKA
- 2 CUPS LIME SELTZER WATER

PASSIONATE CHEAT

GARNISH: 1 SMALL BUNCH OF MINT

Place the sangria ingredients in a large pitcher and stir to combine. Divide between the serving glasses and garnish with the bunch of mint.

INGREDIENTS:

- 1 (750 ML) BOTTLE OF DRY WHITE WINE
- 2 CUPS PEACH-PASSION FRUIT JUICE
- ½ CUP TRIPLE SEC OR GRAND MARNIER
- 2 CUPS PEACH SELTZER WATER

CHEATIN' HEART

Place all of the ingredients in a large pitcher, stir to combine, and serve over ice.

INGREDIENTS:

- 1 (750 ML) BOTTLE OF BOLD, DRY RED WINE
- 1½ CUPS BLUEBERRY-POMEGRANATE JUICE
- 1 CUP STRAWBERRIES, SLICED
- ¼ CUP VODKA
- 2 CUPS BLUEBERRY SELTZER WATER

SPIKED NICE

GARNISH: LIME OR LEMON WEDGES

Place the sangria ingredients in a large pitcher and stir to combine. Divide between the serving glasses and garnish with lime or lemon wedges.

INGREDIENTS:

- 1 (750 ML) BOTTLE OF BOLD, DRY RED WINE
- 2 PEACHES, PITTED AND DICED
- 1 (12 OZ.) CAN OF SPIKEDSELTZER CAPE COD CRANBERRY
- ¼ CUP TEQUILA

APPLE OF MY CHEATING EYE

Place the ingredients in a large pitcher, stir to combine, and divide between the serving glasses.

INGREDIENTS:

- 1 (750 ML) BOTTLE OF DRY WHITE WINE
- 2 CUPS ORANGE-PINEAPPLE-APPLE JUICE
- 1 APPLE, CORED, SEEDED, AND DICED
- ½ CUP TRIPLE SEC
- 2 CUPS GREEN APPLE SELTZER WATER

CAUGHT RED-HANDED

GARNISH: LIME WEDGES

INGREDIENTS:

- 12 OZ. CHILI-LIME MANGO
- 1 CUP WELCH'S MANGO TWIST
- 1 (750 ML) BOTTLE OF DRY WHITE WINE
- ½ CUP GIN
- 2 CUPS LIME SELTZER WATER

Chili-Lime Mango: Place ½ tablespoon maple syrup, ½ teaspoon salt, 1 teaspoon chili powder, and the zest and juice of 1 lime in a bowl and stir to combine. Add 2 pitted and diced mangoes and toss to coat.

Place all of the sangria ingredients, except for the seltzer water, in a pitcher, stir to combine, and let sit for at least 1 hour. When ready to serve, stir in the seltzer water, serve over ice, and garnish with the lime wedges.

CHEATING ON THE BEACH

GARNISH: MARASCHINO CHERRIES

INGREDIENTS:

- 1 (750 ML) BOTTLE OF DRY WHITE WINE
- 2 CUPS PINEAPPLE, DICED (CANNED OR FRESH)
- ½ CUP DARK RUM
- 2 CUPS COCONUT SELTZER WATER

Place the sangria ingredients in a large pitcher and stir to combine. Serve over ice and garnish with the maraschino cherries.

CHEATIN' DOWN UNDER

INGREDIENTS:

- 1 (750 ML) BOTTLE OF SEMI-DRY SPARKLING WINE
- 1½ CUPS STRAWBERRIES, SLICED
- 2 CUPS STRAWBERRY-KIWI JUICE
- ½ CUP VODKA

Place the ingredients in a large pitcher, stir to combine, and divide between the serving glasses.

PORCH SWING

Place all of the ingredients, except for the seltzer water, in a large pitcher or container. Cover and refrigerate for 4 or more hours. When ready to serve, add ice and the seltzer water and stir.

INGREDIENTS:

- 1 (750 ML) BOTTLE OF BLUSH WINE
- 1 LARGE PEACH, PITTED, DICED, AND FROZEN
- 1 GRANNY SMITH APPLE, CORED, SEEDED, AND DICED
- ½ CUP APPLE VODKA
- 1 CUP SELTZER WATER

COLORS OF SUNSET

Place all of the ingredients, except for the soda, in a large pitcher or container. Cover and refrigerate for 4 or more hours. When ready to serve, add ice and the soda and stir.

INGREDIENTS:

- 1 (750 ML) BOTTLE OF BLUSH WINE
- 1 CUP CHERRIES, PITTED, HALVED, AND FROZEN
- 1 LEMON, SLICED THIN
- ½ CUP GIN
- 1 (12 OZ.) CAN OF BLACK CHERRY SODA

BLUE LAGOON

Place all of the ingredients, except for the seltzer water, in a large pitcher or container. Cover and refrigerate for 4 or more hours. When ready to serve, add ice and the seltzer water and stir.

INGREDIENTS:

- 1 (750 ML) BOTTLE OF SWEET WHITE WINE
- 2 CUPS WATERMELON, DICED AND FROZEN
- ½ CUP BLUE CURAÇAO
- 2 CUPS PLAIN OR WATERMELON SELTZER WATER

AHHH SO GOOD

Place all of the ingredients, except for the seltzer water, in a large pitcher or container. Cover and refrigerate for 4 or more hours. When ready to serve, add ice and the seltzer water and stir.

INGREDIENTS:

- 1 (750 ML) BOTTLE OF SWEET WHITE WINE
- 2 NECTARINES, PITTED, DICED, AND FROZEN
- 1 PEAR, CORED, DICED, AND FROZEN
- JUICE OF ½ LIME
- 2 CUPS SELTZER WATER

WHAT'S LOVE GOT TO DO WITH IT?

Place all of the ingredients, except for the soda, in a large pitcher or container. Cover and refrigerate for 4 or more hours. When ready to serve, add ice and the soda and stir.

INGREDIENTS:

- 1 (750 ML) BOTTLE OF SWEET RED WINE
- 1 NECTARINE, PITTED AND DICED
- 1 PLUM, PITTED AND DICED
- ½ CUP SEEDLESS GREEN GRAPES, HALVED
- ¼ CUP VODKA
- 1 (12 OZ.) CAN OF LEMON-LIME SODA

BASIC RED WINE SANGRIA

Place all of the ingredients, except for the seltzer water, in a large pitcher or container. Cover and refrigerate for 4 or more hours. When ready to serve, add ice and the seltzer water and stir.

INGREDIENTS:

- 1 (750 ML) BOTTLE OF DRY RED WINE
- 2 ORANGES, SLICED THIN
- 2 GRANNY SMITH APPLES, CORED, SEEDED, AND DICED
- ¼ CUP BRANDY OR TRIPLE SEC
- 1 CUP LEMON SELTZER WATER

CLASSIC SANGRIA

Even though it means "bleeding" in Spanish, sangria is not always made with red wine. One of the drink's hallmarks is its adaptability. This trait dates back to the *hippocras* of antiquity, a drink made from wine and whatever spices and other ingredients were on hand. Grapes have been grown in Spain for so long it is unclear when wine was first made there. But when the Phoenicians arrived in the southern port of Cadiz in 1100 BCE they brought with them viticulture techniques and tippling tendencies. Traditionally, red wines like Rioja and Tempranillo were used to make sangria, but as the concept spread across Europe, and the Atlantic, white and sparkling wines were used, too, as well as an array of fruits. The American thirst for sangria was incited at the Spain pavilion during the 1964 World's Fair in New York. Serving up a recipe of Spanish red, brandy, sugar, and chopped fruit sold the public on sangria but had the unintended consequence of associating Spanish wine as sweet and inferior to French and Italian wines. Spain's wine reputation has recovered, and pitchers of sangria remain crowd-pleasers.

SANGRIA SONGS

Sangria has been a foil in English-language pop music for decades, with everyone from Ed Sheeran to Tyler the Creator citing the beverage to evoke atmosphere and turn a phrase. Lou Reed's seminal 1972 album *Transformer* included "Perfect Day" with the line "Just a perfect day / Drink Sangria in the park." His longtime partner Laurie Anderson sang about sipping from "a little jug of red sangria" in "Beautiful Red Dress." Country star Blake Shelton had a hit in 2014 with "Sangria," a song about a woman whose lips taste like, you guessed it, sangria. And the 2018 collaboration between Camila Cabello and Pharrell Williams, "Sangria Wine," has a beat that nods to Jamaican dancehall behind lines like "Let's float around like the fruit on the top."

INGREDIENTS:

- 1 BOTTLE (750 ML) DRY RED WINE
- 2 ORANGES, SLICED THIN IN WHOLE OR HALF-MOONS
- 2 GRANNY SMITH APPLES, CORED AND SEEDED, CUT INTO BITE-SIZED CHUNKS
- ¼ CUP BRANDY
- 1 CUP LEMON SELTZER

Combine all ingredients, except the seltzer, in a large pitcher or container. Cover and refrigerate for 4 or more hours. When ready to serve, add ice and seltzer and stir.

CLASSIC RED WINE SANGRIA

Divide the fruit equally between 2 pitchers. Add 2 cups of pomegranate juice to each pitcher and stir. Add ¾ cup of brandy to each pitcher. Next, add 4 bottles of wine to each of the pitchers (you'll add the remaining bottles when you combine the pitchers). Stir to combine, cover with plastic wrap or foil, and refrigerate the pitchers overnight. An hour before the sangria is to be served, combine the 2 pitchers in a large punch bowl. Add the remaining 4 bottles of wine and stir. Cover the punch bowl and place it in a cool spot. When you're ready to serve the sangria, slowly add the soda and gently stir it so you don't lose too much of the soda's carbonation. Serve with lots of ice on the side so that guests can fill their glasses as they see fit, and then ladle the sangria into the glasses.

INGREDIENTS:

- 5 APPLES, CORED, SEEDED, AND DICED
- 5 ORANGES, SLICED THIN AND CHOPPED
- ½ CUP POMEGRANATE SEEDS
- 4 CUPS POMEGRANATE JUICE
- 1½ CUPS BRANDY
- 12 (750 ML) BOTTLES OF DRY RED SPANISH WINE
- 4 (12 OZ.) CANS OF LEMON-LIME SODA

CLASSIC RED WINE SANGRIA II

Divide the fruit equally between 2 pitchers. Add 2 cups of apple juice and 1 cup of peach nectar to each pitcher and stir. Add ¼ cup of brandy to each pitcher. Next, add 4 bottles of wine to each of the pitchers (you'll add the remaining bottles when you combine the pitchers). Stir to combine, cover with plastic wrap or foil, and refrigerate the pitchers overnight. An hour before the sangria is to be served, combine the 2 pitchers in a large punch bowl. Add the remaining 4 bottles of wine and stir. Cover the punch bowl and place it in a cool spot. When you're ready to serve the sangria, slowly add the seltzer water and gently stir it so you don't lose too much of the carbonation. Serve with lots of ice on the side so that guests can fill their glasses as they see fit, and then ladle the sangria into the glasses.

INGREDIENTS:

- 4 CUPS SEEDLESS RED GRAPES, HALVED
- 5 APPLES, CORED, SEEDED, AND DICED
- 4 RIPE PEACHES, PITTED AND DICED
- 4 CUPS APPLE JUICE
- 2 CUPS PEACH NECTAR
- ½ CUP BRANDY
- 12 (750 ML) BOTTLES OF LIGHT-BODIED, DRY RED WINE
- 6 CUPS SELTZER WATER

CLASSIC RED WINE SANGRIA III

Divide the fruit and strawberry juice equally between 2 pitchers. Add ½ cup of brandy to each pitcher. Next, add 4 bottles of wine to each of the pitchers (you'll add the remaining bottles when you combine the pitchers). Stir to combine, cover with plastic wrap or foil, and refrigerate the pitchers overnight. An hour before the sangria is to be served, combine the 2 pitchers in a large punch bowl. Add the remaining 4 bottles of wine and stir. Cover the punch bowl and place it in a cool spot. When you're ready to serve the sangria, slowly add the seltzer water and gently stir it so you don't lose too much of the carbonation. Serve with lots of ice on the side so that guests can fill their glasses as they see fit, and then ladle the sangria into the glasses.

INGREDIENTS:

- 3 CUPS FRESH OR FROZEN STRAWBERRIES, HALVED, JUICE RESERVED
- 3 CUPS FRESH OR FROZEN BLUEBERRIES
- 2 CUPS FRESH OR FROZEN BLACKBERRIES
- 1 CUP BRANDY
- 6 (750 ML) BOTTLES OF DRY RED WINE
- 6 (750 ML) BOTTLES OF SWEET RED WINE
- 6 CUPS PLAIN OR UNSWEETENED BERRY SELTZER WATER, OR 3 CUPS OF EACH

SANGRIA BLANCA

Divide the fruit, peach nectar, and juice equally between 2 pitchers. Add ¾ cup of raspberry liqueur to each pitcher. Next, add 4 bottles of wine to each of the pitchers (you'll add the remaining bottles when you combine the pitchers). Stir to combine, cover with plastic wrap or foil, and refrigerate the pitchers overnight. An hour before the sangria is to be served, combine the 2 pitchers in a large punch bowl. Add the remaining 4 bottles of wine and stir. Cover the punch bowl and place it in a cool spot. When you're ready to serve the sangria, slowly add the seltzer water and gently stir it so you don't lose too much of the carbonation. Serve with lots of ice on the side so that guests can fill their glasses as they see fit, and then ladle the sangria into the glasses.

INGREDIENTS:

- 6 PEACHES, PITTED AND DICED
- 2 GRANNY SMITH APPLES, CORED, SEEDED, AND DICED
- 2 CUPS FRESH OR FROZEN RASPBERRIES
- 3 CUPS PEACH NECTAR
- 2 CUPS APPLE JUICE
- 1½ CUPS RASPBERRY LIQUEUR
- 12 (750 ML) BOTTLES OF LIGHT-BODIED, DRY WHITE WINE
- 6 CUPS SELTZER WATER

MAS SANGRIA BLANCA

Divide the fruit and their juices equally between 2 pitchers. Add ½ cup of brandy to each pitcher. Next, add 4 bottles of wine to each of the pitchers (you'll add the other bottles when you combine the pitchers). Stir to combine, cover the pitchers with plastic wrap or foil, and refrigerate overnight. An hour before the sangria is to be served, combine the 2 pitchers in a large punch bowl. Add the remaining 4 bottles of wine and stir. Cover the punch bowl and place it in a cool spot. When you're ready to serve the sangria, slowly add the soda and gently stir it so you don't lose too much of the carbonation. Serve with lots of ice on the side so that guests can fill their glasses as they see fit, and then ladle the sangria into the glasses.

INGREDIENTS:

- 6 ORANGES, HALVED AND SLICED THIN, JUICE RESERVED
- 4 LEMONS, HALVED AND SLICED THIN, JUICE RESERVED
- 3 LIMES, HALVED AND SLICED THIN, JUICE RESERVED
- 1 CUP BRANDY
- 12 (750 ML) BOTTLES OF FRUITY, DRY WHITE WINE
- 6 CUPS LEMON-LIME SODA

SUMMER DAY STRAWBERRY SANGRIA

Divide the frozen lemonade and water between 2 pitchers and stir. Divide the lemon and strawberries between the pitchers. Next, add 4 bottles of wine to each of the pitchers (you'll add the other bottles when you combine the pitchers). Stir, cover the pitchers with plastic wrap or foil, and refrigerate overnight. An hour before the sangria is to be served, combine the 2 pitchers into a large punch bowl. Add the remaining 4 bottles of wine and stir. Cover the punch bowl and place it in a cool spot. When you're ready to serve the sangria, slowly add the seltzer water and gently stir it so you don't lose too much of the carbonation. Serve with lots of ice on the side so that guests can fill their glasses as they see fit, and then ladle the sangria into the glasses.

INGREDIENTS:

- 4 (12 OZ.) CANS OF FROZEN PINK LEMONADE CONCENTRATE
- 6 CUPS WATER
- 2 LEMONS, HALVED AND SLICED
- 6 CUPS STRAWBERRIES, SLICED THIN
- 12 (750 ML) BOTTLES OF SWEET BLUSH WINE
- 6 CUPS SELTZER WATER

RAINBOW SANGRIA

Place all of the fruit in a glass in the order listed and fill with white wine.

INGREDIENTS:

- ¼ CUP GRAPES
- ¼ CUP BLUEBERRIES
- ¼ CUP KIWI, SLICED
- ¼ CUP MANGO, SLICED
- ¼ CUP ORANGE, SLICED
- ¼ CUP STRAWBERRIES, SLICED
- WHITE WINE, TO FILL

MEMORABLE MOSCATO-GRIA

In a large bowl, combine the nectarine pieces, raspberries, and lime juice. Stir gently to combine. Pour the Grand Marnier over the mixture, cover, and refrigerate overnight. When ready to serve, transfer the marinated fruit to a large punch bowl and slowly add the Moscato d'Asti, pouring down the side so that it stays bubbly. Serve with lots of ice on the side.

INGREDIENTS:

- 6 NECTARINES, PITTED AND CUT INTO BITE-SIZED PIECES
- 4 CUPS RASPBERRIES
- JUICE OF 2 LIMES
- 1½ CUPS GRAND MARNIER
- 12 (750 ML) BOTTLES OF MOSCATO D'ASTI

SANGRIA BLANCA TROPICA

Divide the pineapple and grapefruits between 2 pitchers. Add ½ cup of rum to each pitcher and stir. Next, add 4 bottles of wine to each of the pitchers (you'll add the other bottles when you combine the pitchers), and stir these ingredients together. Add 1 cup of kiwi to each pitcher and gently press down on them to release their juices. Cover the pitchers with plastic wrap or foil and refrigerate overnight. Put the remaining cup of kiwi pieces in a plastic bag and freeze them. An hour before the sangria is to be served, combine the 2 pitchers in a large punch bowl. Add the remaining 4 bottles of wine and the bag of frozen kiwi and stir. Cover the punch bowl and place it in a cool spot. When you're ready to serve the sangria, slowly add the seltzer water and gently stir it so you don't lose too much of the carbonation. Serve with lots of ice on the side so that guests can fill their glasses as they see fit, and then ladle the sangria into the glasses.

INGREDIENTS:

- 4 CUPS FRESH OR FROZEN PINEAPPLE, DICED
- 3 LARGE RED GRAPEFRUITS, PEELED AND DICED
- 1 CUP DARK RUM
- 12 (750 ML) BOTTLES OF FRUITY, DRY WHITE WINE
- 3 CUPS KIWI, PEELED AND DICED
- 6 CUPS SELTZER WATER

SHERRY CHERIE

Tamarind Water: Place ¾ pound of shelled dried tamarind pods, 1 cup sugar, and 8 cups water in a large saucepan and bring to a boil over medium-high heat. Reduce heat to medium and cook, while occasionally stirring and mashing, for 30 minutes. Remove from heat, strain, and cool to room temperature before using.

Add the ingredients to a rocks glass filled with ice in the order that they are listed and gently stir.

INGREDIENTS:

- 1 OZ. TAMARIND WATER
- 1½ OZ. AMONTILLADO SHERRY
- 1 TABLESPOON DRY CURAÇAO
- 2 TEASPOONS SIMPLE SYRUP
- BRUT CHAMPAGNE, CHILLED, TO TOP

ROSÉ-PAMP

Place the liqueur and wine in a chilled wine glass and stir to combine.

INGREDIENTS:

- 1 OZ. GIFFARD CRÈME DE PAMPLEMOUSSE ROSE
- 4 OZ. ROSÉ, CHILLED

MOLOKAI MISHAP

Place the ingredients in a double rocks glass containing two large ice cubes and stir to combine.

INGREDIENTS:

- 1 OZ. COCCHI AMERICANO
- 1 OZ. PEACH LIQUEUR
- 1 OZ. PINEAPPLE JUICE
- 1 OZ. WHITE RHUM AGRICOLE
- 8 DROPS OF BITTERMENS ELEMAKULE TIKI BITTERS

RARE STAMPS

GARNISH: 1 LEMON TWIST

Place the cocktail ingredients in a mixing glass filled with ice and stir until chilled. Strain into a coupe and garnish with the lemon twist.

INGREDIENTS:

- 1½ OZ. COCCHI AMERICANO
- 1 OZ. DARK RUM (RON DEL BARRILITO PREFERRED)
- ½ OZ. CARDAMARO APERITIF WINE

THE RIGHT SIDE OF JACKSON

Place the Sherry and Grand Marnier in a mixing glass filled with ice, gently stir, and strain into a brandy snifter.

INGREDIENTS:

- 2 OZ. FINO SHERRY
- ¾ OZ. GRAND MARNIER

SHERRY COBBLER

GARNISH: SEASONAL BERRIES & 1 SPRIG OF MINT

Place the sugar and orange in a cocktail shaker and muddle. Add ice and the Sherry and shake vigorously. Strain into a highball glass filled with crushed ice and garnish with the berries and sprig of mint.

INGREDIENTS:

- 1 TABLESPOON SUGAR
- 2–3 ORANGE SLICES
- 3½ OZ. AMONTILLADO OR OLOROSO SHERRY

SUNDAY MORNING COMING DOWN

GARNISH: 1 SPRIG OF MINT

Place the mint leaves in the bottom of a julep cup and gently muddle. Add the remaining cocktail ingredients, fill with crushed ice, and stir until chilled. Add more crushed ice until it is above the rim and garnish with the sprig of mint.

INGREDIENTS:

- 3–4 MINT LEAVES
- 1½ OZ. MADEIRA
- 1 OZ. RUM
- ¼ OZ. RICH DEMERARA SYRUP (2:1 SUGAR-TO-WATER RATIO

SAKURA MARTINI

GARNISH: 1 CHERRY BLOSSOM

Place the sake, gin, and Luxardo in a mixing glass filled with ice and stir until chilled. Strain into a cocktail glass and garnish with the cherry blossom.

INGREDIENTS:

- 2½ OZ. DRY SAKE
- 1 OZ. GIN
- ¼ TEASPOON LUXARDO

LIPSTICK & ROUGE

GARNISH: 1 LEMON TWIST

Place the Aperol, Luxardo Amaretto di Saschira, and lemon juice in a cocktail shaker filled with ice and shake vigorously. Strain into a champagne flute, top with the Prosecco, and garnish with the lemon twist.

INGREDIENTS:

- ¾ OZ. APEROL
- ¾ OZ. LUXARDO AMARETTO DI SASCHIRA
- ¾ OZ. LEMON JUICE
- 3 OZ. PROSECCO

THE LITTLEJOHN COBBLER

GARNISH: 1 SPRIG OF MINT, 1 STRAWBERRY SLICE, 1 KUMQUAT SLICE, & DUSTING OF POWDERED SUGAR

Kumquat-Strawberry Cordial: Combine 3 cups sliced strawberries and 3 tablespoons sugar in a bowl and let sit for 1 hour, mashing occasionally so that the strawberries release all of their juice. Stir in 1 cup of kumquat juice and ¾ cup vodka and strain before using.

Place the cocktail ingredients in a cocktail shaker filled with ice and shake vigorously. Strain into a julep cup filled with ice and garnish with the sprig of mint, the strawberry, kumquat slice, and dusting of powdered sugar.

INGREDIENTS:

- 1½ OZ. KUMQUAT-STRAWBERRY CORDIAL
- ¾ OZ. PX SHERRY
- ¾ OZ. OLOROSO SHERRY
- ¾ OZ. PLANTATION O.F.T.D RUM
- ¼ OZ. FRESH LIME JUICE

THREE EMMAS COCKTAIL

GARNISH: 2 BASIL LEAVES

Beer & Rose Cordial: Combine 2 bottles of lager and 3 cups sugar in a medium saucepan and cook over low heat. Stir until the sugar has dissolved, making sure the mixture does not come to a boil. Remove from heat and let cool completely. Stir in a 8 ½ oz. bottle of East India Company Rose Cordial and ½ oz. rose water and store in the refrigerator.

Place the cocktail ingredients in a cocktail shaker filled with ice and shake vigorously. Strain into a Nick & Nora glass filled with crushed ice and garnish with the basil leaf.

INGREDIENTS:

- 1 OZ. BEER & ROSE CORDIAL
- 1 OZ. AMONTILLADO SHERRY
- ¾ OZ. THE BOTANIST GIN
- ½ OZ. LEMON JUICE
- ½ OZ. GRAPEFRUIT JUICE

BANANA PUNCH

GARNISH: ½ BANANA, SLICED & 2 SPRIGS OF MINT

Pour the brandy, vodka, and lime juice into a Collins glass filled with crushed ice. Top with club soda, stir, and garnish with the banana slices and sprigs of mint.

INGREDIENTS:

- 1½ OZ. APRICOT BRANDY
- 1 OZ. VODKA
- ½ OZ. FRESH LIME JUICE
- CLUB SODA, TO TOP

VELVET CLUB

Place the Cognac, Lillet, and crème de cacao in a mixing glass filled with ice and stir until chilled. Strain into a coupe and top with the Champagne.

INGREDIENTS:

- 1 OZ. COGNAC
- ½ OZ. LILLET BLANC
- ½ OZ. CRÈME DE CACAO
- CHAMPAGNE, TO TOP

APPLE BRANDY SOUR

GARNISH: 1 LEMON SLICE & 1 MARASCHINO CHERRY

Place the cocktail ingredients in a cocktail shaker filled with ice and shake vigorously. Strain into a chilled cocktail glass and garnish with the slice of lemon and maraschino cherry.

INGREDIENTS:

- 1 OZ. FRESH LIME JUICE
- ½ TEASPOON SIMPLE SYRUP
- 2 OZ. APPLE BRANDY

APRICOT FUZZ

Place the brandy, juices, and simple syrup in a cocktail shaker filled with ice and shake vigorously. Strain into a highball glass filled with ice, top with club soda, and gently stir.

INGREDIENTS:

- 2 OZ. APRICOT BRANDY
- 1 OZ. LEMON JUICE
- ½ OZ. LIME JUICE
- 1 TEASPOON SIMPLE SYRUP
- CLUB SODA, TO TOP

PULP FICTION

GARNISH: 1 APPLE SLICE

Place the Cognac, liqueur, and apple juice in a cocktail shaker filled with ice and shake vigorously. Strain into a highball glass filled halfway with ice, top with the lemonade, and garnish with an apple slice.

INGREDIENTS:

2 OZ. COGNAC

1 OZ. APPLE LIQUEUR

2 OZ. APPLE JUICE

LEMONADE, TO TOP

EXCLUSIF-TINI

GARNISH: 1 ORANGE WEDGE

Infused Exclusif: Combine a 750 ml bottle of the Cognac and the zest from 4 oranges in a large container and store in a cool, dark place for 1 week. Strain before using.

Place the cocktail ingredients in a cocktail shaker filled with ice and shake vigorously. Strain into a cocktail glass and garnish with the orange wedge.

INGREDIENTS:

1½ OZ. ORANGE-INFUSED COURVOISIER VSOP EXCLUSIF

1½ OZ. BLACK TEA

½ OZ. SIMPLE SYRUP

2 DASHES OF BLOOD ORANGE BITTERS

CHERRY SLING

GARNISH: 1 LEMON TWIST

Place the brandy and lemon juice in a rocks glass filled with ice, stir, and garnish with the lemon twist.

INGREDIENTS:

2 OZ. CHERRY BRANDY

1 OZ. LEMON JUICE

BRANDY ALEXANDER

Place the ingredients in a cocktail shaker filled with ice, shake vigorously, and strain into a chilled cocktail glass.

INGREDIENTS:

½ OZ. BRANDY

½ OZ. CRÈME DE CACAO

½ OZ. HEAVY CREAM

RITZ SIDECAR

GARNISH: 1 LEMON TWIST

Place the cocktail ingredients in a mixing glass filled with ice and stir until chilled. Strain into a rocks glass filled with ice and garnish with the lemon twist.

INGREDIENTS:

- 2½ OZ. COGNAC
- 1½ OZ. TRIPLE SEC OR COINTREAU
- 1 OZ. LEMON JUICE

ORIGINAL FRENCH 75

GARNISH: 1 STRIP OF LEMON PEEL (OPTIONAL)

Place the Cognac, lemon juice, and simple syrup in a cocktail shaker and shake vigorously. Strain into a champagne flute and top with Champagne. If desired, garnish with the strip of lemon peel.

INGREDIENTS:

- 1 OZ. DUDOGNON RESERVE 10 YEAR COGNAC (OR YOUR FAVORITE COGNAC)
- ½ OZ. FRESH LEMON JUICE
- ¼ OZ. SIMPLE SYRUP
- CHAMPAGNE, TO TOP

CHERRY HOOKER

GARNISH: 1 LIME WHEEL

Place the cocktail ingredients in a mason jar filled with ice, stir until chilled, and garnish with the lime wheel.

Variation: One popular variation, known as the Cherry Sunrise, involves adding a dash of grenadine syrup at the very end. It doesn't do much to the taste, but the added aesthetics make it worth taking a look at.

INGREDIENTS:

- 3 OZ. CHERRY BRANDY
- ORANGE JUICE, TO TOP
- DASH OF LIME JUICE

PERUVIAN SHRUB

GARNISH: 1 BLACKBERRY & 1 SPRIG OF THYME

Red Fruits Shrub: Combine ½ cup sugar, ½ cup white wine vinegar, and ½ cup of a mixture of strawberries and raspberries in a small saucepan and simmer over medium heat until the fruit releases its juices. Strain into a jar and store in the refrigerator for 3 days before using.

Place the cocktail ingredients in a cocktail shaker filled with ice and pour them into a mixing glass. Pour the cocktail back and forth between the shaker and the glass until combined. Strain into a rocks glass and garnish with the raspberries, strawberries, and mint leaves.

Tip: This method of mixing is known as the Cuban roll method. It allows you to mix the ingredients without diluting the cocktail as much as a standard shake.

INGREDIENTS:

- 1 OZ. RED FRUITS SHRUB
- 1¾ OZ. PISCO
- ½ OZ. FRESH APPLE JUICE
- 2 TEASPOONS PETER HEERING CHERRY LIQUEUR
- DASH OF RHUBARB BITTERS
- ½ OZ. CORONA

FALUKA

GARNISH: PAN MASALA

Jallab Syrup: Combine 3 tablespoons of date molasses, 2 teaspoons of rose water, and 1 tablespoon pine nuts.

Place the cocktail ingredients in a cocktail shaker filled with ice and shake vigorously. Strain into a rocks glass filled with ice and garnish with the pan masala.

Tip: Pan masala is a combination of betel leaf and arcea nut that is widely consumed in Southern and Southeastern Asia. It is a stimulant that is noted for its psychoactive properties.

INGREDIENTS:

- ½ OZ. JALLAB SYRUP
- 1¾ OZ. PISCO
- ⅓ OZ. FRESH LIME JUICE
- 1 EGG WHITE

ÈMILE ZOLA (J'ACCUSE)

GARNISH: 1 BASIL LEAF

Place the ingredients in a mixing glass filled with ice and stir until chilled. Strain into a coupe and garnish with the basil leaf.

INGREDIENTS:

- 1½ OZ. CANDOLINI GRAPPA BIANCA
- ¾ OZ. CALVADOS
- ½ OZ. DRY VERMOUTH
- 4 DASHES OF BITTERCUBE BLACKSTRAP BITTERS

IGGY

GARNISH: 1 STRIP OF GRAPEFRUIT PEEL

Eucalyptus Syrup: Combine 2 cups of water and 2 cups of sugar in a medium saucepan and bring to a boil. Reduce heat to a simmer, cook for 1 minute, add ⅓ cup of eucalyptus leaves, and remove from heat. Let sit until cool and strain before using.

Place the cocktail ingredients in a cocktail shaker filled with ice and shake vigorously. Strain into a chilled cocktail glass and garnish with the strip of grapefruit peel.

INGREDIENTS:

- 1 TABLESPOON EUCALYPTUS SYRUP
- 1½ OZ. DOLIN BLANC VERMOUTH
- ¾ OZ. MERLET BROTHERS BLEND COGNAC
- 4 DASHES OF AMARO
- DASH OF SALINE SOLUTION (SEE PAGE 308)

PEACE TREATY

GARNISH: 1 LEMON TWIST

Place the cocktail ingredients in a mixing glass filled with ice and stir until chilled. Strain into a chilled coupe, express the lemon twist over the cocktail, and then use it as a garnish.

INGREDIENTS:

- 2 OZ. MANZANILLA SHERRY
- 1 OZ. LA QUINTINYE VERMOUTH ROYALE BLANC
- ½ OZ. LUXARDO
- 2 DASHES OF ORANGE BITTERS

NEW JACK CITY

GARNISH: 1 GINKGO LEAF

Place the cocktail ingredients in a mixing glass, add ice, and stir until chilled. Strain into a coupe or a cocktail glass and garnish with the ginkgo leaf.

INGREDIENTS:

- 1¼ OZ. UMESHU (JAPANESE PLUM WINE)
- ¾ OZ. RYE WHISKEY
- ¾ OZ. APPLEJACK
- 4 TEASPOONS SWEET VERMOUTH

VERMOUTH

Fortified wines were being prepared in China prior to 1000 BCE, and these are the earliest predecessors of what we now call vermouth. Among the earliest herbal additions to these wines was wormwood, a bitter herb known in Germany as wermut, and from which vermouth takes its name. "Wormwood wines" from Italy, Germany, and France became increasingly popular, and the sweet and dry forms of vermouth began to take shape. Italy is generally considered to be the first country to produce vermouth in its current form, and it was in Turin, Italy, that the beverage was first popularized as an aperitif rather than a medicinal tonic.

Turin's Antonio Benedetto Carpano is generally considered the first to commercialize the modern form of the drink, and it wasn't long before other vermouth makers began to appear in the region—including Martini & Rossi, which remains a popular brand today. Indeed, many of today's best-known vermouth makers are Italian. The renaissance of vermouth makers in Turin quickly brought the spirit to prominence, and by the 1700s the drink was readily available as far away as England.

Although the red color of sweet vermouth and the clear color of dry vermouth might lead the uninitiated to believe that red and white wines, respectively, are used to create each concoction, the truth is that both the sweet and dry versions contain a similar wine base. Sweet vermouth takes on a reddish-brown hue from the caramel that is added. If red and white wines were the basis for sweet and dry vermouth, respectively, their colors would likely be reversed, since it is red wine that is typically considered "dry" and white wine that is considered "sweet."

Following vermouth's transition from medicinal liquor to popular aperitif, it wasn't long before it began appearing in cocktails, most notably in the Martini.

MORNING GLORY COCKTAIL

GARNISH: 1 STRIP OF LEMON PEEL

Place the cocktail ingredients, except for the club soda, in a mixing glass filled with ice and stir until chilled. Strain into a chilled cocktail glass and top with the club soda. Express the strip of lemon peel over the cocktail, and then use it as a garnish.

INGREDIENTS:

- 1 OZ. RYE WHISKEY
- 1 OZ. VSOP COGNAC
- 1 TEASPOON SIMPLE SYRUP
- ½ TEASPOON GRAND MARNIER
- 2 DASHES OF ANGOSTURA BITTERS
- DASH OF ABSINTHE
- 1 OZ. CLUB SODA

AMOUR À LA FRANÇAISE

GARNISH: 1 LEMON TWIST

Place the cocktail ingredients in a cocktail shaker filled with ice and shake vigorously. Strain into a Nick & Nora glass and garnish with the lemon twist.

INGREDIENTS:

- 1⅓ OZ. BRANDY
- ¾ OZ. GINGER LIQUEUR
- 1 TABLESPOON LEMON JUICE
- 1 TABLESPOON SIMPLE SYRUP
- 4 DASHES OF CRÈME DE CASSIS
- 1 EGG WHITE

LE METRO

GARNISH: 2 GRIOTTINES (CHERRIES IN KIRSCH)

Place the cocktail ingredients in a cocktail shaker filled with ice and shake until chilled. Strain into a chilled cocktail glass and garnish with the Griottines.

INGREDIENTS:

- 2 OZ. HIGH-QUALITY FRENCH BRANDY OR COGNAC
- 1 OZ. CRÈME DE CASSIS
- ½ OZ. LEMON JUICE
- 3 DASHES OF PEYCHAUD'S BITTERS

MARCONI WIRELESS

GARNISH: 1 GRAPEFRUIT TWIST

Place the cocktail ingredients in a mixing glass filled with ice and stir until chilled. Strain into a coupe and garnish with the grapefruit twist.

INGREDIENTS:

- 1½ OZ. LAIRD'S STRAIGHT APPLE BRANDY BOTTLED IN BOND
- ¾ OZ. CARPANO ANTICA FORMULA
- ¾ OZ. COCCHI TORINO
- DASH OF PEYCHAUD'S BITTERS

APPLE TODDY

GARNISH: 1 LONG LEMON TWIST & 4 CLOVES

Fill a mug with hot water. When the mug is warm, discard the water, place the cocktail ingredients in the mug, and stir to combine. Garnish with the long lemon twist and the cloves.

INGREDIENTS:

- 2 OZ. CALVADOS
- 1 TEASPOON MAPLE SYRUP
- 3 OZ. HOT CINNAMON-APPLE TEA

B & B

Place the ingredients in a rocks glass filled with ice and stir until combined.

INGREDIENTS:

- 1 PART BÉNÉDICTINE
- 1 PART BRANDY

OLD HICKORY

GARNISH: 1 LEMON TWIST

Place the cocktail ingredients in a rocks filled halfway with ice, stir until chilled, and garnish with the lemon twist.

INGREDIENTS:

- 1½ OZ. DRY VERMOUTH
- 1½ OZ. SWEET VERMOUTH
- 2 DASHES OF PEYCHAUD'S BITTERS
- DASH OF ORANGE BITTERS (REGAN'S NO. 6 PREFERRED)

Q&A WITH JULIÁN DÍAZ, CO-OWNER OF 878 BAR

Named after its street number, *ocho-siete-ocho*, and hidden behind a big decorative wooden door, this Buenos Aires spot is known for its relaxed mood and incredible cocktails.

What can you tell us about how the bar started?

I opened the bar with Florencia Capella, in 2004. We both had been working in the industry. We were both 22 years old back then, so we've grown up together with the bar.

Can you tell us about the theme of the bar and its focus?

Designed as a local bar, we wanted to use local products, natural juices, first-class products. We think this is a bar from Villa Crespo to the world, the neighborhood and this city represent us. When we started all bars in Buenos Aires were very influenced by European and U. S. bar tendencies, and we wanted to be different and keep it Argentinian.

What does your team look for when creating a new cocktail for your menu?

We don't like to make our customers wait, so that's why we create easy cocktails, representative of our culture, with seasonal and fresh products. Our menu offers a wide selection of cocktails for every person and for every moment.

How does the food and culture of Argentina influence the cocktails that you offer?

Argentina has great culinary and cocktail traditions. We like bitters so much. We are the primary consumers of bitters in the world, so these and aperitifs are the main ingredients in most Argentinian cocktails. And our wine culture is more than 200 years old. Vermouth and other products that immigrants have brought with them have infiltrated the DNA of our palates and our gastronomic culture.

What are the best parts of running a cocktail bar in Buenos Aires? Are there any downsides or things that make it difficult?

Right now we are going through a crisis. Everything is harder and the future uncertain. We've been dealing with inflation for a long time, so we don't have stable prices, and for foreign visitors this can be frightening. But, somehow, we as a people have gotten used to living, working, and developing under such problematic conditions. The best part is that we don't need a license to serve and sell alcohol here, so everyone is able to open a bar. Argentinian people love to spend time with friends in bars.

Blue Hawaiian, Brandy Alexander, Pink Squirrel, Rusty Nail, Tom Collins, White Russian, Grasshopper, Rob Roy, Pink Lady: If you had to pick one of these classic cocktails to add to your cocktail menu how would you reimagine your choice to make it fit in with your style?

878 is more than 14 years old. We are always renewing the classics. The Rusty Nail is one of my favorites from the list. We prepared it with top-shelf National Whisky, cane liqueur, and honey. It was a very South American Rusty Nail. When using local ingredients to reinvent a classic cocktail it is very important to respect the drink's origins but be open to new flavors and combinations.

Do you have a favorite cocktail?

Our company name is Old Fashioned SRL. This always has been one of my favorite cocktails, and since opening it has been one of our signature drinks. Before *Mad Men* and the incoming boom we were the second bar in Argentina to make an Old Fashioned. And I also love cocktails that use aperitifs, like the Cynar Julep, our national Julep, which represents the new cocktail generation in Buenos Aires.

Do you have a favorite alcohol to work with when making cocktails?

I am a sommelier. I love wine, so I think because of this I love vermouth. It affords the possibility of creating different styles of cocktails, with low levels of alcohol, so we can continue drinking another wine after the cocktail. Today we have an upsurge of new high-quality vermouth, and I love watching these producers grow. There's a lot to discover yet. So I toast for vermouth!

BRANDY MILK PUNCH

GARNISH: GRATED NUTMEG

Place the cocktail ingredients in a cocktail shaker filled with ice and shake vigorously. Strain into a chilled rocks glass and garnish with the nutmeg.

INGREDIENTS:

- 3 OZ. WHOLE MILK
- 1 OZ. HALF-AND-HALF
- 2 OZ. BRANDY
- 1 OZ. SIMPLE SYRUP
- ½ TEASPOON VANILLA EXTRACT

CENTRAL STANDARD THYME

GARNISH: 1 LEMON WHEEL & 1 SPRIG OF THYME

Place the lime juice, simple syrup, lemon-thyme water, and pisco in a rocks glass and stir. Add ice, top with ginger beer, and garnish with the lemon wheel and the sprig of thyme.

INGREDIENTS:

- ¾ OZ. LIME JUICE
- ½ OZ. SIMPLE SYRUP
- ¾ OZ. LEMON-THYME WATER
- 2 OZ. CUATRO G'S MOSTO VERDE ACHOLADO PISCO
- GINGER BEER, TO TOP

OLGA BREESKIN

GARNISH: 1 ANCHO CHILI PEPPER

Place the cocktail ingredients in a cocktail shaker and dry shake for 10 seconds. Add ice and shake for 30 seconds. Double-strain into a coupe and garnish with the ancho chili pepper.

INGREDIENTS:

- 2 OZ. PISCO
- ¾ OZ. LEMON
- ¾ OZ. ANCHO CHILI DEMERARA SYRUP (SEE PAGE 399)
- ½ OZ. EGG WHITE

SERENDIPITI

Place the brandy and mint in a rocks glass and muddle. Add ice and the apple juice, top with Champagne, and gently stir.

INGREDIENTS:

- 1 OZ. CALVADOS (OR YOUR PREFERRED APPLE BRANDY)
- 1 SPRIG OF MINT
- 1 OZ. APPLE JUICE
- CHAMPAGNE, TO TOP

BERGDORF LUNCH

GARNISH: 2 TO 3 GRANNY SMITH APPLE SLICES

Apple-Pear Juice: Juice two Granny Smith apples and one Bartlett pear in a juicer. Add 1 tablespoon of Vitamin C powder to the mixture to preserve color.

Place the juice, St-Germain, and pisco in a cocktail shaker filled with ice and shake vigorously. Strain into a tiki glass filled with crushed ice, add the orange blossom water, and garnish with the apple slices.

INGREDIENTS:

- 2 OZ. APPLE-PEAR JUICE
- ¾ OZ. ST-GERMAIN
- 1½ OZ. MACCHU LA DIABLADA PISCO
- SPLASH OF ORANGE BLOSSOM WATER

SADE'S TABOO

Place the ingredients in a mixing glass filled with ice, stir until chilled, and strain into a coupe.

INGREDIENTS:

- 2 OZ. HIGH-QUALITY COGNAC (HINE PREFERRED)
- ¾ OZ. COCCHI AMERICANO
- ¾ OZ. SWEET VERMOUTH (DOLIN PREFERRED)
- DASH OF BITTERMENS HOPPED GRAPEFRUIT BITTERS

BRANDY CRUSTA

GARNISH: 1 LEMON PEEL

Wet the rim of a chilled cocktail glass and dip it into the sugar. Place the cocktail ingredients in a cocktail shaker filled with ice and shake until chilled. Strain into the glass and garnish with an entire lemon peel.

INGREDIENTS:

- SUGAR, FOR THE RIM
- 1¾ OZ. COGNAC
- ¾ OZ. LEMON JUICE
- ½ OZ. DRY CURAÇAO
- ¼ OZ. LUXARDO
- 2 DASHES OF ANGOSTURA BITTERS

FROZEN COOKIE MILK PUNCH

GARNISH: CHOCOLATE SHAVINGS

Place the cocktail ingredients in a blender and puree until smooth. Pour into a Collins glass and garnish with the chocolate shavings.

INGREDIENTS:

- 1 CUP VANILLA ICE CREAM
- 2 MEDIUM CHOCOLATE CHIP COOKIES, CRUSHED
- 1½ OZ. COGNAC

ST. CHARLES PUNCH

GARNISH: 2 LEMON WEDGES

Place the lemon juice, Cognac, simple syrup, and dry curaçao in a cocktail shaker filled with ice and shake vigorously. Strain into a Collins glass filled with ice, top with the Port, and garnish with the lemon wedges.

INGREDIENTS:

- 1½ OZ. LEMON JUICE
- 1 OZ. COGNAC
- ½ OZ. SIMPLE SYRUP
- DASH OF DRY CURAÇAO
- 1½ OZ. PORT

ST. CHARLES PUNCH V. 2.0

Place the Cognac, lemon juice, orgeat, and dry curaçao in a cocktail shaker filled with ice and shake vigorously. Strain into a Collins glass filled with ice and top with the Port.

INGREDIENTS:

- 2 OZ. COGNAC
- 1 OZ. LEMON JUICE
- ½ OZ. ORGEAT
- ¼ OZ. DRY CURAÇAO
- ¼ OZ. PORT

ROFFIGNAC

Place the shrub, Cognac, and simple syrup in a cocktail shaker filled with ice and shake vigorously. Strain into a highball glass filled halfway with ice and top with the club soda.

INGREDIENTS:

- 1½ OZ. RASPBERRY SHRUB (SEE PAGE 40)
- 2 OZ. COGNAC
- ½ OZ. SIMPLE SYRUP
- CLUB SODA, TO TOP

YELLOW PARROT

GARNISH: 1 LEMON TWIST

Place the cocktail ingredients in a mixing glass filled with ice and stir until chilled. Strain into a rocks glass containing 3 large ice cubes and garnish with the lemon twist.

INGREDIENTS:

- 1 OZ. APRICOT BRANDY (MARIE BRIZARD APRY PREFERRED)
- 1 OZ. YELLOW CHARTREUSE
- 1 OZ. ABSINTHE (VIEUX PONTARLIER PREFERRED)

SON OF STAN

GARNISH: DASH OF GROUND CINNAMON & 1 CINNAMON STICK

Place the brandy, Bénédictine, Dolin Blanc, and apple juice in a cocktail shaker filled with ice and shake vigorously. Strain into a Collins glass filled with ice, top with the splash of soda, and garnish with the ground cinnamon and cinnamon stick.

INGREDIENTS:

- 1½ OZ. LAIRD'S APPLE BRANDY
- ¾ OZ. BÉNÉDICTINE
- SPLASH OF DOLIN BLANC
- 1 OZ. APPLE JUICE
- SPLASH OF CLUB SODA

SIDECAR

GARNISH: 1 LEMON TWIST

If desired, wet the rim of a coupe and dip it into the sugar. Place the cocktail ingredients in a cocktail shaker filled with ice and shake until chilled. Strain into the coupe and garnish with the lemon twist.

INGREDIENTS:

- SUGAR, FOR THE RIM (OPTIONAL)
- 1½ OZ. COGNAC
- ¾ OZ. COINTREAU
- ¾ OZ. LEMON JUICE

TOM THUMB'S BLUES

GARNISH: 1 LEMON TWIST

Place the cocktail ingredients in a mixing glass filled with ice and stir until chilled. Strain into a coupe and garnish with the lemon twist.

INGREDIENTS:

- 2 OZ. SWEET VERMOUTH
- 1 OZ. OLD TOM GIN
- ½ TEASPOON LUXARDO
- 2 DASHES OF ANGOSTURA BITTERS

THE HARDEST WALK

GARNISH: 1 ORANGE TWIST

Place the cocktail ingredients in a mixing glass filled with ice and stir until chilled. Strain into a double rocks glass and garnish with the orange twist.

INGREDIENTS:

- 2 OZ. PUNT E MES VERMOUTH
- 1 OZ. OVERPROOF RUM (PLANTATION PREFERRED)
- ½ TEASPOON GRAN CLASSICO
- 14 DROPS OF ORANGE BITTERS (REGAN'S NO. 6 PREFERRED)

RUM

Being of Caribbean descent, I have been around rum all of my life, from the rum raisin ice cream that was a favorite of my father's to the rum punches and fruitcakes that were holiday traditions. Basically, eggnog got kicked to the curb in our house. That said, as an adult, it wasn't the spirit I drifted toward as my go-to (that was whisk(e)y, see page 210). It's not that I don't enjoy rum. It is a must-have in any well-stocked bar. But something about it drove me to look for something new.

That something could be the sweetness that rum is known for, and considering how it's made, you can't get away from this element of its flavor profile. There is also my dislike of additional flavoring being added to spirits. I prefer, if you haven't guessed, spirits in their natural guises. For my personal sipping purposes, a simple white rum wins over any of the spiced and flavored rums that are so popular. I am a huge fan of the aged rums—20- and 40-year-old rums are a bargain compared to their whisk(e)y equivalents—that have become more common of late.

When it comes to cocktails, though, rum is a beast. It has the tropical vacation drink of choice crown on lockdown. Besides the aforementioned rum punches, rum is the base for such cocktails as the Cuba Libre, the Daiquiri, Piña Coladas, and Mojitos. It's hard at this point to have those drinks and not think of sun and sand, even in the dead of winter. It's been said of my beloved whisk(e)y that it is "sunlight, held together by water." That may be even more true of rum.

Favorite cocktail: I have a soft spot for Mojitos, but the Daiquiri wins. A well-made Daiquiri is one of my favorite cocktails, period. End of story.

A BRIEF HISTORY OF RUM

Rum conjures up the tropics and good times. But the spirit's history is not so cheery, running through empire building, slavery, and even Cold War politics. Rum rose from the sticky dregs of the sugar industry, which flourished in the Caribbean after Christopher Columbus brought sugarcane to the New World. Hundreds of sugar refineries were established in places like Mexico and Brazil by the 17th century, with slavery being the industry's fuel. Slaves handled every aspect of the sugar-making process, from farming, harvesting, and milling the cane to boiling the extracted juice to create crystalized sugar. Molasses, the dark, syrupy by-product of making sugar, was fed to the slaves and livestock (and a great deal of it was just dumped into the sea). But it was only a matter of time before fermented molasses was imbibed, and eventually distilled to create rum.

The inventor of rum will never be known. In fact, spirits expert David Wondrich cites a document written in Persian, dating back to the late 16th century, that references sugarcane extract being fermented and distilled somewhere in the realm of the Moghul Emperor of India (comprising what we know today as northern India, and parts of Afghanistan and Iran). Considering this evidence, and the fact that explorers, traders, and military expeditions from Europe crisscrossed the globe with bits and pieces of what they found here and there, it seems more than reasonable to believe that the idea for making rum has roots in Asia.

There is no arguing, however, that the spirit became a popular product in the New World. A 1647 record of a party on Barbados documents a feast that included "kill-devil," one of rum's early names; the *Oxford English Dictionary* cites the etymological origins of the word as relating to "rumbustion," British slang for an uproar, no doubt the result of drinking these early batches of rum. British sailors received a daily ration of rum. In the American colonies, it was more popular than whisk(e)y. George Washington, running for the Virginia House of Burgesses in 1758, plied voters with the stuff. Before the Boston Tea Party, the Portsmouth Molasses Party in 1771 stormed the *Resolution* to rescue impounded smuggled molasses and defy the taxes levied on the product by King George III's Sugar Act of 1764. As the 19th century saw American distillers taking advantage of abundant corn crops to make more and more whisk(e)y, rum's popularity waned, but never faded, and in other parts of the world it continued to flourish.

BACARDI AND CUBA

Bacardi was the first rum sold worldwide in the modern era. Don Facundo Bacardí Massó, a wine merchant born in Spain, emigrated to Cuba in 1830. In those days, rum was not a refined drink, and was often made with low standards for local consumption. It was Facundo who began systematizing the process, creating a proprietary strain of yeast to make the base product from which the rum was distilled. Facundo was also credited with aging rum in white oak barrels to mellow the final product. This is how he manufactured the first clear, or "white," rum in the world.

Facundo and his brother José first established the distillery in Santiago de Cuba in 1862. Bats soon made their home in the far recesses of the factory, and the company's instantly recognizable bat logo was born. Emilio Bacardi, Facundo's eldest son, was appointed mayor of Santiago de Cuba in 1899 by U. S. general Leonard Wood, after the Cuban war for independence from Spain, which ended in 1898. Emilio had been a leader in the Free Cuba movement, helping to establish the family, and its business.

The most famous symbol of rum's rise in Cuba is the Bacardi Building, which is still considered one of the crowning achievements of Cuban architecture. As the company became more international in scope, with offices around the world, a new main office befitting their cosmopolitan status was built in 1930, as the third generation entered the business. The executives "branded Cuba as the home of rum, and Bacardi as the king of rums." The headquarters, as it still stands today, became known as the "Cathedral of Rum." The Bacardi Building in Havana is regarded as one of the finest Art Deco buildings in Latin America.

But in 1960, Bacardi was forced to leave Cuba after Fidel Castro took over all of country's distilleries. The company set up shop in Puerto Rico and other surrounding countries. However, the label still states: "Company founded in Santiago de Cuba in 1862."

RUM VS. RHUM

The distinctions between "rum" and "rhum" are about much more than an *h*. The best way to start thinking about it is to remember, once again, how all scotch is whisk(e)y, but not all whisk(e)y is scotch. All rhum is rum, but not all rum is rhum—a little more confusing when the words sound the same, but read on for clarification.

Demerara rum derives from fermented molasses, which is why rum tends to be sweeter and darker. Rhum agricole, a French term because most rhum is made on Caribbean islands colonized by the French, is made from sugarcane juice; the juice is fed directly into the fermenter before being distilled, resulting in a drier, vegetal, and lighter spirit.

Both rum and rhum, like all distillates, are clear after distillation. White rum is typically watered down and bottled. Any color present in white rums derives from the amount of time they are left to age in oak barrels.

DARK & STORMY

GARNISH: 1 LIME WEDGE

Place the rum and ginger beer in a rocks glass filled with ice, stir until chilled, and garnish with the lime wedge.

INGREDIENTS:

- 2 OZ. DARK RUM
- 4 OZ. GINGER BEER

MAI TAI

GARNISH: 1 SPRIG OF FRESH MINT & 1 LIME WHEEL

Place the cocktail ingredients in a cocktail shaker filled with ice and shake vigorously. Strain into a rocks glass filled with ice and garnish with the lime wheel and sprig of fresh mint.

INGREDIENTS:

- 2 OZ. 17-YEAR-OLD J. WRAY & NEPHEW JAMAICAN RUM
- ½ OZ. ORGEAT
- ½ OZ. DEKUYPER ORANGE CURAÇAO
- ¼ OZ. RICH SIMPLE SYRUP (2:1 SUGAR-TO-WATER RATIO)
- JUICE OF 1 LIME

BAHAMA MAMA

GARNISH: 1 STRAWBERRY OR 1 CHERRY

Place the cocktail ingredients in a mixing glass filled with ice and stir until chilled. Strain into a highball glass filled with ice and garnish with a strawberry or a cherry.

INGREDIENTS:

- ½ OZ. DARK RUM
- ½ OZ. COCONUT LIQUEUR
- ¼ OZ. 151 PROOF RUM
- ¼ OZ. KAHLUA
- JUICE OF ½ LEMON
- 4 OZ. PINEAPPLE JUICE

IMPROVED PIÑA COLADA

GARNISH: 1 ORANGE SLICE

Place all of the ingredients, except for the Campari, in a blender and puree until smooth. Pour into a Hurricane glass, and then pour the Campari over the back of a spoon so that it floats on top of the drink. Garnish with the orange slice.

INGREDIENTS:

- 2 OZ. SPICED RUM
- 1½ OZ. PINEAPPLE JUICE
- 2 OZ. COCO LOPEZ CREAM OF COCONUT
- ½ OZ. PASSION FRUIT PURÉE
- 1 CUP ICE
- CAMPARI, TO FLOAT

HOMEMADE SPICED RUM

15 whole cloves
3 cinnamon sticks
20 whole allspice berries
2 tablespoons dark brown sugar
1 (750 ml) bottle of white rum
1 whole vanilla bean

In a small saucepan, place the cloves, cinnamon sticks, and allspice and cook over medium-low heat until they begin to release their aroma. Shake the pan periodically so that the aromatics do not burn. Remove from heat, add the dark brown sugar and about a tablespoon of rum, and stir until the sugar has dissolved. Split the vanilla bean in half, scrape out the seeds, and add the seeds and the pod to the mixture. Stir to combine and let cool to room temperature. Add enough rum that the mixture is easy to pour, pour it into a large container, and add the remaining rum. Store in a cool, dark place and keep in mind that the longer you let the rum steep, the stronger the flavor will be. Strain before using.

RUNAWAY RUM RUNNER PUNCH

Fill a punch bowl or another large container with ice, add the rum and orange juice, and then top with the cranberry-raspberry juice. Do not stir and serve immediately.

INGREDIENTS:

- 1 PART SPICED RUM
- 2 PARTS ORANGE JUICE
- 1 PART CRANBERRY-RASPBERRY JUICE

THE PADDINGTON

GARNISH: 1 GRAPEFRUIT TWIST

Rinse a coupe with absinthe and dump out any excess. Place the cocktail ingredients in a cocktail shaker filled with ice and shake vigorously. Strain into the coupe and garnish with the grapefruit twist.

INGREDIENTS:

- ABSINTHE, TO RINSE
- 1½ OZ. WHITE RUM
- ½ OZ. LEMON JUICE
- ½ OZ. GRAPEFRUIT JUICE
- ½ OZ. LILLET BLANC
- 1 SPOONFUL OF ORANGE MARMALADE

GOLDEN FRIENDSHIP

GARNISH: 1 ORANGE SLICE & 1 CHERRY

Add the cocktail ingredients to a Collins glass filled with ice in the order they are listed and garnish with the orange slice and cherry.

INGREDIENTS:

- 1 OZ. AMARETTO
- 1 OZ. SWEET VERMOUTH
- 1 OZ. WHITE RUM
- 1 OZ. GINGER ALE

KILL DEVIL PUNCH

GARNISH: 1 LIME WHEEL

Place the sugar cubes, club soda, and raspberries in a large coupe and muddle. Add the lemon juice, pineapple juice, rum, and ice and stir. Top with the Champagne and garnish with the lime wheel.

INGREDIENTS:

- 4 SUGAR CUBES
- 1 OZ. CLUB SODA
- 4 RASPBERRIES
- 1 OZ. LEMON JUICE
- 2 OZ. PINEAPPLE JUICE
- 2 OZ. APPLETON ESTATE V/X RUM
- 1½ OZ. CHAMPAGNE

PAIN REMOVER

GARNISH: 1 MARASCHINO CHERRY (OPTIONAL)

Place the ingredients in cocktail shaker filled with ice, shake vigorously, and pour into a plastic cup. If desired, garnish with a maraschino cherry.

INGREDIENTS:

- 1½ OZ. RUM
- ½ OZ. CREAM OF COCONUT
- 2 OZ. ORANGE JUICE
- 12 OZ. PINEAPPLE JUICE

VANILLA FLOAT

Pour the spiced rum and cola into a pint glass, add a scoop of vanilla ice cream, and serve with a long spoon.

Variation: Substituting root beer or orange soda for the cola are tasty takes on this simple cocktail.

INGREDIENTS:

- 1 PART SPICED RUM
- 2 PARTS COLA
- 1 SCOOP OF VANILLA ICE CREAM

DEVIL'S KISS

Place the ingredients in a cocktail shaker filled with ice, shake until chilled, and strain into shot glasses.

INGREDIENTS:

- 1 PART SPICED RUM
- 1 PART COFFEE LIQUEUR
- 1 PART GRAND MARNIER

MAI KINDA GAI

GARNISH: 2 SPRIGS OF MINT, 1 ORANGE SLICE, & 1 CHERRY

Banana-Cashew Orgeat: In a saucepan, bring 1 cup of cashew milk to a simmer. Place 2 cups of granulated sugar in a container, pour the heated milk over it, and then stir until the sugar is fully dissolved. Let cool, and then add 4 oz. of Giffard Banane du Bresil liqueur. Stir until blended, label, and store.

Combine all of the cocktail ingredients, except for the Ron Zacapa rum, in a cocktail shaker filled with ice and shake vigorously. Strain into a rocks glass filled with ice, float the Ron Zacapa rum on top, and garnish with the mint sprigs, orange slice, and cherry.

INGREDIENTS:

- ¾ OZ. BANANA-CASHEW ORGEAT
- 1½ OZ. HAMILTON 86 DEMERARA RUM
- ½ OZ. MANDARINE NAPOLÉON LIQUEUR
- 1 OZ. FRESH LIME JUICE
- ½ OZ. RON ZACAPA RUM, TO FLOAT

Monty's

THE
ANDERSON

THE PINK FLAMINGO

Fernet-Branca Reduction: In a saucepan, combine equal parts Fernet–Branca and sugar and cook over medium heat until the mixture has been reduced to a syrup.

Place all of the ingredients, except for the reduction, in a blender and puree until smooth. Place the Fernet-Branca reduction in a Daiquiri glass and add the contents of the blender.

INGREDIENTS:

- SPLASH OF FERNET-BRANCA REDUCTION
- 1½ OZ. BANKS 5 ISLAND RUM
- ½ OZ. LIBER & CO. PINEAPPLE GUM SYRUP
- 1 OZ. HIBISCUS TEA
- ½ OZ. CONDENSED MILK
- ½ OZ. CREAM OF COCONUT
- ½ CUP ICE

COCONUT CREAM PIE

Place the ingredients in a cocktail shaker filled with ice, shake until chilled, and strain into shot glasses.

INGREDIENTS:

- 1 PART COCONUT RUM
- 1 PART WHIPPED CREAM VODKA
- DASH OF FRESH LIME JUICE

SCOOBY SNACK

Place the ingredients in a cocktail shaker filled with ice, shake until chilled, and strain into shot glasses.

INGREDIENTS:

- 1 PART COCONUT RUM
- 1 PART BANANA LIQUEUR
- 1 PART MELON LIQUEUR
- 1 PART PINEAPPLE JUICE
- 1 PART SKIM MILK

VANILLA ICE CREAM

Place the ingredients in a cocktail shaker filled with ice, shake until chilled, and strain into shot glasses.

INGREDIENTS:

- 1 PART RUMCHATA
- 1 PART VANILLA RUM

PLANTER'S PUNCH

GARNISH: 1 ORANGE SLICE, 1 LEMON SLICE, & 1 PINEAPPLE SLICE

Place the rums, bitters, and juices in a Collins glass filled with ice and stir. Float the triple sec and grenadine on top and garnish with the slices of orange, lemon, and pineapple.

INGREDIENTS:

- 2 OZ. LIGHT RUM
- 1 OZ. DARK RUM
- 2 DASHES OF BITTERS
- 2 OZ. ORANGE JUICE
- 1 TEASPOON PINEAPPLE JUICE
- ¾ OZ. TRIPLE SEC
- DASH OF GRENADINE

MASON JAR MOJITO

GARNISH: 2 TO 3 LIME WHEELS & 2 SPRIGS OF MINT

Place the sugar and fresh lime juice in a mason jar and stir until the sugar has dissolved. Add one-quarter of the crushed ice, rub the mint leaves around the rim of the jar, tear each one in half, and place on top of the ice. Stir again. Add the rum, club soda, and remaining ice, stir, and garnish with the lime wheels and sprigs of mint.

Variations: As with many popular drinks, there are countless variations of the Mojito, most centering around the alcohol. A few popular takes are the Mexican Mojito, which substitutes tequila for rum; the English Mojito, which substitutes gin; and the Dirty Mojito, which substitutes spiced rum.

INGREDIENTS:

- 1 TABLESPOON SUGAR
- JUICE OF ½ LIME
- ½ CUP CRUSHED ICE
- 10 MINT LEAVES
- 2 OZ. WHITE RUM
- 6 OZ. CLUB SODA

MASON JAR MANGO TANGO

GARNISH: 1 MANGO SLICE

Place the cocktail ingredients in a blender and puree until smooth. Pour into a mason jar and garnish with the slice of mango.

Variation: Some individuals claim that it isn't a true Mango Tango unless a Frozen Strawberry Daiquiri (see page 566) is layered into the drink.

INGREDIENTS:

- 1 OZ. DARK RUM
- 1 OZ. COCONUT RUM
- 1 OZ. ORANGE LIQUEUR
- JUICE OF ½ LIME
- 4 OZ. MANGO JUICE
- 2 OZ. PINEAPPLE JUICE
- 1 CUP ICE

SUNSET

GARNISH: 1 GRAPEFRUIT TWIST

Place the cocktail ingredients in a mason jar filled with ice, stir until combined, and garnish with the grapefruit twist.

INGREDIENTS:

1 PART COCONUT RUM
1 PART PINEAPPLE JUICE
2 PARTS GRAPEFRUIT JUICE

HURRICANE

GARNISH: 1 ORANGE WHEEL & 1 MARASCHINO CHERRY

Place the cocktail ingredients in a cocktail shaker filled with ice and shake vigorously. Strain into a Hurricane glass filled with ice and garnish with the orange wheel and maraschino cherry.

INGREDIENTS:

1 PART DARK RUM
1 PART WHITE RUM
1 PART PASSION FRUIT SYRUP
1 PART ORANGE JUICE
DASH OF POMEGRANATE JUICE
JUICE OF ½ LIME

TOM AND JERRY

GARNISH: 1 CINNAMON STICK

Place the cocktail ingredients in a mason jar in the order they are listed, stir, and garnish with a cinnamon stick.

Tip: If you're feeling lazy, you can replace the egg white and simple syrup with a bit of warm eggnog.

INGREDIENTS:

DASH OF EGG WHITE, BEATEN
1 OZ. SIMPLE SYRUP
1 OZ. DARK RUM
1 OZ. BRANDY
2 OZ. WARM MILK

CARIBBEAN CRANBERRY

GARNISH: 1 ORANGE SLICE

Place the cocktail ingredients in a highball glass filled with ice, stir until chilled, and garnish with the orange slice.

INGREDIENTS:

1 PART COCONUT RUM
1 PART ORANGE JUICE
1 PART CRANBERRY JUICE

MOJITO

GARNISH: 3 TO 6 MINT SPRIGS & 2 OR 3 LIME WHEELS

The predecessor to the Mojito was the El Draque, supposedly devised by the infamous English sea captain Sir Francis Drake, who used the mint and lime he crossed the Atlantic with—the mint relieved seasickness, the lime helped prevent scurvy—to improve the taste of the potent sugarcane spirits he encountered in the New World. With lime and sugar readily available in Cuba, it only makes sense that Cubans took to using them to flavor their rum. And as these things go, it only makes sense that local customs became exotic novelties in the bars of Havana, especially with visiting Americans during Prohibition. Why the drink came to be known as the "Mojito" is unclear, though. Bacardi claims the "mojo" is an African word, meaning "to cast a little spell"; others say that the drink's name stems from the Cuban word "mojo," referring to a sour citrus sauce. Regardless of where the name came from, it stuck, and its popularity extended well beyond Cuba after the likes of Nat King Cole, Pablo Neruda, and, of course, Ernest Hemingway heralded this classic cocktail after falling for the version served at Havana's El Bodeguita del Medio.

MOJITO IN POP CULTURE

Ernest Hemingway lived on a plantation he called *Finca Vigia*, or "Lookout Farm," in San Francisco de Paula, Cuba, from mid-1939 to 1960. One of Cuba's most internationally famous residents, he was known to stay out late drinking in the many saloons. Especially endearing to the Cuban people was the fact that, even after the Cuban Revolution, Hemingway retained good relations with the Cuban government. He was a fan of Mojitos and Daiquiris. But at La Bodeguita, Hemingway had his own version of the former, which substituted sparkling wine for the club soda (see page 535).

INGREDIENTS:

- 1 TABLESPOON SUGAR
- JUICE OF ½ LIME
- 1 CUP CRUSHED ICE
- 2 OZ. WHITE RUM
- 6 OZ. CLUB SODA
- 10 MINT LEAVES

Add the sugar and fresh lime juice to a Collins glass and stir until the sugar has dissolved. Add one-quarter of the crushed ice, then take 10 mint leaves, rub them over the rim of the glass, then tear each one in half and add on top of the ice. Stir again. Add the rum, club soda, and remaining ice. Stir one last time, then add a few mint sprigs and lime wheels for garnish and enjoy. Stick the lime wheels into the drink itself for a little extra visual flair.

Hemingway's signed quote: "My mojito in the Bodeguita del Medio and my daiquiri in the Floridita"

HEMINGWAY'S MOJITO

GARNISH: 1 LIME TWIST

Place the lime juice, sugar, and mint leaves in a highball glass and muddle. Add the rum and sparkling wine, stir gently, and garnish with the lime twist.

INGREDIENTS:

- JUICE OF 1 LIME
- 2 TEASPOONS NATURAL CANE SUGAR
- 5 MINT LEAVES
- 1½ OZ. CUBAN RUM
- 3 OZ. SPARKLING WINE

PINEAPPLE-CITRUS REFRESHER

GARNISH: 1 SPRIG OF MINT

Place the simple syrup and the pineapple slices in a mason jar and muddle. Add ice, rub the mint leaves on the jar's rim, and then tear them in half and place them in the jar. Add the lime juice, rum, and soda, stir, and garnish with the sprig of mint.

INGREDIENTS:

- 2 OZ. SIMPLE SYRUP
- 2–3 PINEAPPLE SLICES
- HANDFUL OF MINT LEAVES
- JUICE OF ½ LIME
- 2 OZ. WHITE RUM
- 4 OZ. LEMON-LIME SODA

CUBA LIBRE

Fill a highball glass with lime juice, the twist of lime, and ice, add the rum, and top with cola.

INGREDIENTS:

- ½ OZ. LIME JUICE
- 1 LIME TWIST
- 2 OZ. WHITE RUM
- COLA, TO TOP

CARIBBEAN RUM PUNCH

GARNISH: 2 TO 3 PINEAPPLE CHUNKS

Add the cocktail ingredients into a mason jar filled with ice, stir until chilled, and garnish with the pineapple chunks.

Variation: This can easily be turned into a punch that is meant for a large crowd. To do this, add the lime juice and bitters to taste and keep the proportions of all the other ingredients the same.

INGREDIENTS:

- 1 PART WHITE RUM
- 1 PART COCONUT RUM
- JUICE OF ½ LIME
- DASH OF BITTERS
- 2 PARTS ORANGE JUICE
- 2 PARTS PINEAPPLE JUICE

PIÑA COLADA

GARNISH: 1 PINEAPPLE CHUNK

Place the cocktail ingredients in a blender and puree until smooth. Pour into a glass and garnish with the pineapple chunk and maraschino cherry.

INGREDIENTS:

- 1 PART WHITE RUM
- 1 PART CREAM OF COCONUT
- 3 PARTS PINEAPPLE JUICE
- ½ CUP ICE

BANANA CREAM PIE

GARNISH: 1 BANANA SLICE & DUSTING OF NUTMEG

Remove a slice from the banana and reserve for a garnish. Place the rest of the banana in a blender and puree until smooth. Add the puree, rums, and cream to a cocktail shaker filled with ice and shake vigorously for 30 seconds. Strain into a glass filled with ice and garnish with the nutmeg and reserved slice of banana.

INGREDIENTS:

- 1 BANANA
- 1 PART VANILLA RUM
- 1 PART BANANA RUM
- 1 PART HEAVY CREAM

STRAWBERRY LEMONADE SPLASH

GARNISH: 1 KIWI SLICE

Place the strawberries, lemon juice, and sugar in a blender and puree until smooth. Place ice in a mason jar, add the puree and the rum, and top with the water. Stir until combined and garnish with the slice of kiwi.

INGREDIENTS:

- 4 FRESH STRAWBERRIES
- JUICE OF ¼ LEMON
- ½ TEASPOON SUGAR
- 1 OZ. RUM
- 3 OZ. WATER

PRIVATEER

GARNISH: 1 LIME WHEEL

Squeeze the juice of the lime wedges into a glass, and then drop the squeezed wedges in. Add ice, the rum, and cola, stir, and garnish with the lime wheel.

INGREDIENTS:

- ½ LIME, HALVED
- 1 PART COCONUT RUM
- 3 PARTS COLA

TROPICAL STORM

GARNISH: 1 LIME WEDGE

Place the cocktail ingredients in a cocktail shaker filled with ice and shake vigorously. Strain into a Hurricane glass and garnish with the lime wedge.

INGREDIENTS:

- 1 PART WHITE RUM
- 1 PART DARK RUM
- 1 PART PASSION FRUIT SYRUP
- JUICE OF ½ LEMON
- SPLASH OF GRENADINE

RUM CHOCOLATE

Pour the hot chocolate into a mug, add the dark rum, and top with the handful of marshmallows.

INGREDIENTS:

- 3 PARTS HOT CHOCOLATE
- 1 PART DARK RUM
- HANDFUL OF MARSHMALLOWS

RUM AND COCONUT

GARNISH: 1 LEMON WEDGE

Wet the rim of a rocks glass and dip it into the shredded coconut. Add ice, the rum, and coconut water, stir, and garnish with the lemon wedge.

INGREDIENTS:

- SHREDDED COCONUT, FOR THE RIM
- 1 PART COCONUT RUM
- 3 PARTS COCONUT WATER

YOUR TAI

GARNISH: 1 ORANGE SLICE

Place the cocktail ingredients in a cocktail shaker filled with ice and shake until chilled. Strain into a highball glass filled with ice and garnish with the orange slice.

INGREDIENTS:

2 PARTS WHITE RUM
1 PART DARK RUM
1 PART CURAÇAO
JUICE OF ½ LIME

CARIBBEAN CRANBERRY TWIST

GARNISH: 1 ORANGE SLICE

Place the rum, orange juice, and cranberry juice in a highball glass filled with ice and stir until chilled. Top with the splash of triple sec and garnish with the orange slice.

INGREDIENTS:

1 PART COCONUT RUM
1 PART ORANGE JUICE
1 PART CRANBERRY JUICE
SPLASH OF TRIPLE SEC

RED RUM FIZZ

GARNISH: 1 MARASCHINO CHERRY & 1 ORANGE SLICE

Place the rum and orange juice in a highball glass filled with ice, stir, and top with the club soda. Float the grenadine on top and garnish with a maraschino cherry and an orange slice.

INGREDIENTS:

1 PART RUM
1 PART ORANGE JUICE
CLUB SODA, TO TOP
SPLASH OF GRENADINE

SUNBURST

GARNISH: 1 GRAPEFRUIT TWIST

Place the cocktail ingredients in a highball glass filled with ice in the order they are listed and garnish with the grapefruit twist.

INGREDIENTS:

1 PART COCONUT RUM
1 PART PINEAPPLE JUICE
JUICE OF 1 LEMON WEDGE
2 PARTS GRAPEFRUIT JUICE

ONE DARK NIGHT

GARNISH: 1 LIME WEDGE

Place the rum, ginger beer, and lime juice in a highball glass filled with ice and stir until thoroughly mixed. Float the splash of orgeat on top and garnish with the lime wedge.

INGREDIENTS:

- 1 PART DARK RUM
- 2 PARTS GINGER BEER
- JUICE OF ½ LIME
- SPLASH OF ORGEAT

CIDERMEISTER

GARNISH: 1 CINNAMON STICK

Place the coconut rum, Jägermeister, and apple cider in a highball glass filled with ice and stir until chilled. Top with the cinnamon and garnish with the cinnamon stick.

INGREDIENTS:

- 1 PART COCONUT RUM
- 1 PART JÄGERMEISTER
- 4 PARTS FRESH APPLE CIDER
- DUSTING OF CINNAMON

COOL SUMMER

GARNISH: LEMON WHEELS

Tear the mint leaves in half and place them in a pitcher. Add the lime juice and muddle. Add ice, rum, and lemonade and stir until chilled. When serving, fill each glass with ice and garnish with lemon wheels.

INGREDIENTS:

- 20 MINT LEAVES
- JUICE OF 4 LIME WEDGES
- 1 PART WHITE RUM
- 2 PARTS LEMONADE

AFTER DARK

GARNISH: 1 MARASCHINO CHERRY & 1 ORANGE SLICE

Add the dark rum and club soda to a rocks glass filled with ice. Add the splash of grenadine, let it settle, and top with the bitters. Garnish with the maraschino cherry and orange slice.

INGREDIENTS:

- 1 PART DARK RUM
- 2 PARTS CLUB SODA
- SPLASH OF GRENADINE
- 2 DROPS OF AROMATIC BITTERS

CARIBBEAN COFFEE

Place the coconut rum and coffee in a mug, top with the splash of coconut milk, add sugar, if desired, and stir.

INGREDIENTS:

- 1 PART COCONUT RUM
- 4 PARTS HOT COFFEE
- SPLASH OF COCONUT MILK
- SUGAR, TO TASTE (OPTIONAL)

PPR

GARNISH: 1 STRIP OF GRAPEFRUIT PEEL & 1 MARASCHINO CHERRY

Place the cocktail ingredients in a highball glass filled with ice, stir until chilled, and garnish with the strip of grapefruit peel and maraschino cherry.

INGREDIENTS:

- 2½ OZ. RUM
- ¾ OZ. GIFFARD CRÈME DE PAMPLEMOUSSE ROSE
- ¾ OZ. LEMON JUICE
- 1 SPOONFUL OF LUXARDO
- 3 DASHES OF PEYCHAUD'S BITTERS

CAPRI C'EST FINI

GARNISH: 1 MOZZARELLA BALL, 1 CHERRY TOMATO, & 1 BASIL LEAF

Place the tomatoes and basil leaves in a cocktail shaker and muddle. Add ice and the remaining cocktail ingredients and shake vigorously. Double-strain into a chilled coupe and garnish with the mozzarella ball, basil leaf, and cherry tomato.

INGREDIENTS:

- 4 CHERRY TOMATOES
- 2 BASIL LEAVES
- ½ OZ. FRESH LEMON JUICE
- ½ OZ. SIMPLE SYRUP
- ½ TEASPOON BALSAMIC VINEGAR
- ½ OZ. PLANTATION 3 STARS RUM

FAÇON MARIA

Place the ingredients in a mixing glass filled with ice, stir until chilled, and strain into a rocks glass.

INGREDIENTS:

- 1¾ OZ. SAINT LUCIA DISTILLERS CHAIRMAN'S RESERVE SPICED ORIGINAL RUM
- 3 DASHES OF ANGOSTURA BITTERS
- 1 TEASPOON VIRGIN SUGARCANE HONEY

WHEN YOU'RE A JET

GARNISH: 1 STRIP OF LIME PEEL

Place the cocktail ingredients in a mixing glass filled with ice and stir until chilled. Strain into a cocktail glass, express the strip of lime peel over the cocktail, twist, and use as a garnish.

INGREDIENTS:

- 1½ OZ. AGED DARK RUM (7 TO 12 YEARS PREFERRED)
- ½ OZ. DRY VERMOUTH
- ½ OZ. GIFFARD BIGALLET CHINA-CHINA LIQUEUR
- 2 DASHES OF CHOCOLATE OR MOLE BITTERS

BEHIND GOD'S BACK

GARNISH: 1 SPRIG OF MINT

Place the cocktail ingredients in a pilsner or Hurricane glass filled with crushed ice and use the swizzle method to combine. Add more ice, float the bitters on top, and garnish with the sprig of mint.

INGREDIENTS:

- ¼ OZ. SIMPLE SYRUP
- ¼ OZ. CINNAMON SYRUP (SEE PAGE 260)
- ¼ OZ. ORGEAT
- ½ OZ. PINEAPPLE JUICE
- ¾ OZ. LIME JUICE
- 2 OZ. SAINT CHAIRMAN'S RESERVE RUM
- 2 DASHES OF PEYCHAUD'S BITTERS
- 2 DASHES OF ANGOSTURA BITTERS

02
Cap

DULCINEA

GARNISH: 1 BRANDY-SOAKED CHERRY

Place the cocktail ingredients in a mixing glass filled with ice and stir until chilled. Strain into a chilled coupe and garnish with the brandy-soaked cherry.

INGREDIENTS:

- 2 DASHES OF BITTERMENS XOCOLATL MOLE BITTERS
- ½ OZ. DEL MAGUEY CREMA DE MEZCAL
- 1 OZ. CREAM SHERRY
- 1½ OZ. ZACAPA 23 CENTENARIO RUM

MARY PICKFORD

Place the ingredients in a cocktail shaker filled with ice, shake until chilled, and strain into a chilled cocktail glass.

INGREDIENTS:

- ½ OZ. WHITE RUM (HAVANA CLUB OR BANKS 5 ISLAND BLEND PREFERRED)
- 1½ OZ. PINEAPPLE JUICE
- 1 TEASPOON GRENADINE
- 6 DROPS OF LUXARDO

OLD CUBAN

Place all of the ingredients, except for the Champagne and bitters, in a cocktail shaker filled with ice and shake vigorously. Strain into a chilled cocktail glass and top with the Champagne and bitters.

INGREDIENTS:

- 6 MINT LEAVES
- ½ OZ. LIME JUICE
- 1⅓ OZ. HAVANA CLUB 3 YEARS RUM (OR YOUR FAVORITE PREMIUM WHITE RUM)
- ½ OZ. SIMPLE SYRUP
- 1 TEASPOON GINGER-LIME CORDIAL (SEE PAGE 190)
- BILLECART-SALMON BRUT CHAMPAGNE, TO TOP
- 2 DASHES OF ANGOSTURA BITTERS

OVERSIZED TOOL

GARNISH: 3 LUXARDO MARASCHINO CHERRIES

Place the cocktail ingredients in a cocktail shaker filled with ice and shake vigorously. Strain into a Collins glass filled with crushed ice and garnish with the cherries skewered on a toothpick.

INGREDIENTS:

- ¾ OZ. WHITE RUM
- ¾ OZ. AMBER RUM
- ¾ OZ. SYRUP FROM JAR OF LUXARDO MARASCHINO CHERRIES
- 1 OZ. FRESH LIME JUICE

PAPA DOUBLE

GARNISH: 1 LIME WHEEL

Place the cocktail ingredients in a blender and puree on high until smooth. Pour into a Hurricane glass and garnish with the lime wheel.

INGREDIENTS:

- JUICE OF 1 LIME
- JUICE OF ½ GRAPEFRUIT
- ½ CUP SHAVED ICE
- 3½ OZ. WHITE RUM
- ½ OZ. LUXARDO

THE RATTLE AND THE RHYTHM

GARNISH: MINT LEAVES

Place the cocktail ingredients in a cocktail shaker filled with ice and shake vigorously. Strain into a rocks glass and garnish with additional mint.

INGREDIENTS:

- 1½ OZ. WHITE RUM
- ¾ OZ. LIME JUICE
- ¾ OZ. SIMPLE SYRUP
- ¾ OZ. JICAMA JUICE
- 3–4 MINT LEAVES
- PINCH OF SMOKED SEA SALT
- 2 DASHES OF COFFEE BITTERS

ROSES FOR ALEX

GARNISH: 1 MARASCHINO CHERRY

Place the white rum and triple sec in a rocks glass filled with ice and stir until chilled. Top with the club soda and grenadine and garnish with the maraschino cherry.

INGREDIENTS:

- 1 PART WHITE RUM
- 1 PART TRIPLE SEC
- 2 PARTS CLUB SODA
- SPLASH OF GRENADINE

ISLAND PUNCH

GARNISH: 1 PINEAPPLE SLICE

Place the cocktail ingredients in a cocktail shaker filled with ice and shake until chilled. Strain into a glass filled with ice and garnish with the slice of pineapple.

INGREDIENTS:

- 1 PART DARK RUM
- 1 PART PINEAPPLE JUICE
- 1 PART ORANGE JUICE
- 2 DROPS OF AROMATIC BITTERS

HAITIAN DIVORCE

GARNISH: 1 ORANGE TWIST & 1 LIME TWIST

Place the cocktail ingredients in a rocks glass filled with large ice cubes, stir until chilled, and garnish with the orange and lime twists.

INGREDIENTS:

- 1½ OZ. BARBANCOURT 5 STAR RHUM
- ¾ OZ. DEL MAGUEY VIDA MEZCAL
- ½ OZ. PEDRO XIMENEZ SHERRY
- 2 DASHES OF ANGOSTURA BITTERS

CUBAN REDHEAD

GARNISH: 1 SPRIG OF MINT

Place the rum, coffee liqueur, and Irish cream in a cocktail shaker filled with ice and shake until chilled. Strain into a rocks glass filled with ice, top with the crème de menthe, and garnish with the sprig of mint.

INGREDIENTS:

- 1 PART WHITE RUM
- 1 PART COFFEE LIQUEUR
- 1 PART IRISH CREAM
- DASH OF CRÈME DE MENTHE

BAC
PUERTO

BALL
&
CHAIN

LAWYERS, GUNS, AND MONEY

GARNISH: 1 ORANGE TWIST & DUSTING OF SPICY CHOCOLATE MIXTURE

Spicy Chocolate Mixture: Combine equal parts cocoa powder, chili powder, and sugar in a small dish.

Place the cocktail ingredients in a cocktail shaker filled with ice and shake vigorously. Strain into a rocks glass filled with ice and garnish with the orange twist and the spicy chocolate mixture.

INGREDIENTS:

- 2 DASHES OF AMARGO CHUNCHO BITTERS
- 2 DASHES OF BITTERMENS HELLFIRE HABANERO SHRUB
- ¼ OZ. TEMPUS FUGIT CRÈME DE CACAO
- ½ OZ. RUBY PORT
- ½ OZ. PEDRO XIMENEZ SHERRY
- ½ OZ. BARBANCOURT FIVE STAR RHUM
- 1½ OZ. COTES DU RHONE

BLACKTAIL RUM & COLA

GARNISH: 1 LEMON TWIST

Place all of the cocktail ingredients, except for the Champagne, in a highball glass filled with ice and stir. Top with Champagne and garnish with the lemon twist.

INGREDIENTS:

- DASH OF DR. ADAM ELMEGIRAB'S ORINOCO AROMATIC BITTERS
- ½ TEASPOON FERNET-BRANCA
- ¾ OZ. COLA SYRUP
- 1 OZ. BACARDI FACUNDO NEO SILVER RUM
- 4 OZ. CHAMPAGNE

CALLE OCHO OLD FASHIONED

GARNISH: 1 DRIED TOBACCO LEAF

Tobacco-Infused Bitters: Steep 1 or 2 tobacco leaves in a 6.7 oz. bottle of Angostura Bitters for 3 to 5 hours. Strain and store.

Place the cocktail ingredients in a mixing glass filled with ice and gently stir until chilled. Strain into a rocks glass filled with ice and garnish with a dried tobacco leaf.

INGREDIENTS:

- 3 DASHES OF TOBACCO-INFUSED BITTERS
- 2 OZ. BACARDI OCHO
- ¼ OZ. DEMERARA SYRUP

THE ESCAPE

GARNISH: 1 PINEAPPLE CHUNK & 1 MARASCHINO CHERRY

Place the rum, pineapple juice, and cream of coconut in a cocktail shaker filled with ice and shake until chilled. Strain into a goblet, float the vermouth on top, and garnish with the pineapple chunk and the maraschino cherry skewered on a toothpick.

INGREDIENTS:

- 2 OZ. EL DORADO DARK RUM
- 1 OZ. PINEAPPLE JUICE
- 1 OZ. COCO LOPEZ CREAM OF COCONUT
- ¾ OZ. SWEET VERMOUTH, TO FLOAT

HEADLESS HORSEMAN

Pumpkin Syrup: Add 1 cup of pumpkin puree to a standard simple syrup recipe when it is boiling. After 1 minute, remove from heat, let cool, and strain before using.

Coconut Blend: Combine equal parts Coco Lopez cream of coconut and coconut milk.

Place all of the ingredients, except for the lime wheel and the 151 proof rum, in a blender and puree until smooth. Pour into a tiki mug or a double rocks glass filled with ice. Place the lime wheel on top of the cocktail, carefully set the dash of 151 proof rum on top, and use a match to light it on fire. Wait until the fire has gone out to enjoy the cocktail.

INGREDIENTS:

- 1½ OZ. PUMPKIN SYRUP
- 1½ OZ. COCONUT BLEND
- 1½ OZ. UNAGED CACHAÇA
- ¾ OZ. ORANGE JUICE
- ½ OZ. ST. ELIZABETH ALLSPICE DRAM
- ¾ OZ. CINNAMON SYRUP (SEE PAGE 260)
- ¾ OZ. LIME JUICE
- 1 CUP ICE
- 1 LIME WHEEL
- DASH OF 151 PROOF RUM

MUTINY OF CLOWNS

Place all of the ingredients, except for the orange slice and the 151 proof rum, in a cocktail shaker filled with ice and shake vigorously for 10 seconds. Double-strain into a double rocks glass containing no ice. Place the orange slice on top of the cocktail, carefully set the dash of 151 proof rum on top, and use a match to light it on fire. Wait until the fire has gone out to enjoy the cocktail.

INGREDIENTS:

- ¾ OZ. CRUZAN BLACK STRAP RUM
- ¾ OZ. CYNAR
- ¾ OZ. FRESH LIME JUICE
- ½ OZ. GINGER SYRUP (SEE PAGE 255, SUBSTITUTE SUGAR FOR THE HONEY)
- ¼ OZ. DEMERARA SYRUP
- 1 ORANGE SLICE
- DASH OF 151 PROOF RUM

ROMEO À RIO

GARNISH: DASH OF SMOKED PAPRIKA

Red Fruit Syrup: Add ½ cup of raspberries and ½ cup strawberries to a standard simple syrup recipe, bring the mixture to a simmer, and use a wooden spoon to break up the berries. Cook for 5 minutes, remove from heat, let cool, and strain before using.

Place the cocktail ingredients in a cocktail shaker without ice and dry shake for 10 seconds. Add ice, shake vigorously, and strain into a chilled cocktail glass. Garnish with the dash of smoked paprika.

INGREDIENTS:

- ½ OZ. RED FRUIT SYRUP
- ½ OZ. FRESH LEMON JUICE
- 1¾ OZ. CACHAÇA
- 1 TEASPOON CRÈME DE VIOLETTE
- 2–3 SPRIGS OF MINT
- 1 EGG WHITE

ICED TEA PEYI

GARNISH: 1 LIME WHEEL

Place all of the cocktail ingredients in a cocktail shaker filled with ice and shake vigorously. Strain into a rocks glass filled with ice and garnish with the lime wheel.

INGREDIENTS:

- 1½ OZ. RHUM AGRICOLE OR AVUÁ PRATA CACHAÇA (OR YOUR FAVORITE RUM)
- 1¾ OZ. AGUA DE JAMAICA (ICED HIBISCUS TEA)
- 2 TEASPOONS GOMME SYRUP OR SIMPLE SYRUP
- 1 TABLESPOON LIME JUICE
- 1 TABLESPOON VELVET FALERNUM
- DASH OF PEYCHAUD'S BITTERS

CAIPIRINHA

Place the lime wedges and sugar cubes in a highball glass and muddle. Fill the glass with crushed ice, top with the cachaça, and stir until chilled.

INGREDIENTS:

- 1 LIME, CUT INTO 8 WEDGES
- 2 BROWN SUGAR CUBES
- 2 OZ. CACHAÇA

LE WOODY WOOD

GARNISH: 1 WALNUT HALF & 1 CINNAMON STICK

Infused Cachaça: Place ½ cup of walnuts in 1 cup of cachaça and let sit for 1 hour. Strain before using.

Place the cocktail ingredients in a wine glass filled with ice, stir until chilled, and garnish with the walnut half and cinnamon stick.

INGREDIENTS:

- 1½ OZ. WALNUT-INFUSED CACHAÇA
- ½ OZ. CALVADOS
- 1 TABLESPOON BÉNÉDICTINE
- 1 TABLESPOON ORANGE CURAÇAO

TUXEDO SITUATION

GARNISH: 1 SATSUMA TWIST & 1 CILANTRO LEAF

Place all of the cocktail ingredients, except for the Prosecco, in a cocktail shaker filled with ice and shake vigorously. Double-strain into a champagne flute, top with the Prosecco, and garnish with the satsuma twist and additional cilantro leaf.

INGREDIENTS:

- 8 CILANTRO LEAVES
- 1 OZ. SATSUMA JUICE, STRAINED
- 1½ OZ. CACHAÇA (AVUÁ PREFERRED)
- ½ OZ. SIMPLE SYRUP
- PROSECCO, TO TOP

CACHAÇA

Brazil's national drink, often called the "Brazilian rum," cachaça is made from raw sugarcane, and holds on to the cane's grassy, unrefined flavor. Like rhum agricole, it can only be distilled from sugarcane juice; but, like rum, that juice must be fermented. The taste of cachaça can be earthy and vegetal, but terroir does inform the flavor, as do the dozens of varieties of wood used to age it in. The ABV of cachaça is lower than rum's.

NERTZ!

GARNISH: 1 STRIP OF ORANGE PEEL

Place the cocktail ingredients in a cocktail shaker filled with ice and shake until chilled. Double-strain into a chilled coupe, express the strip of orange peel over the cocktail, and then use as a garnish.

INGREDIENTS:

- 1½ OZ. CACHAÇA (AVUÁ PREFERRED)
- ¾ OZ. PINEAPPLE JUICE
- ½ OZ. LEMON JUICE
- ½ OZ. GRENADINE
- 2 DASHES OF ORANGE BITTERS (REGAN'S NO. 6 PREFERRED)
- DASH OF ANGOSTURA BITTERS

HAWAIIAN WAR CHANT

GARNISH: 1 ORANGE TWIST

Place the cocktail ingredients in a mixing glass filled with ice and stir until chilled. Strain into a rocks glass filled with ice and garnish with the orange twist.

INGREDIENTS:

- 2 OZ. QUALITY AGED RUM (PLANTATION ORIGINAL DARK DOUBLE AGED PREFERRED)
- ¼ OZ. GRAPEFRUIT LIQUEUR (GIFFARD CRÈME DE PAMPLEMOUSSE ROSE PREFERRED)
- ¼ OZ. CINNAMON SYRUP (SEE PAGE 260)
- DASH OF ANGOSTURA BITTERS
- DASH OF ABSINTHE

THE MOONTOWER

GARNISH: 1 STRIP OF LIME PEEL

Pineapple Syrup: Place 1 pineapple that has been cut into 1-inch cubes and 1 quart of sugar in a larger container and let sit for 4 hours. Place in a blender, puree, and strain through a chinois before using.

Place the cocktail ingredients in a mixing glass filled with ice and stir until chilled. Strain into a coupe, express the strip of lime peel over the cocktail, and discard.

INGREDIENTS:

- ¼ OZ. PINEAPPLE SYRUP
- 2 OZ. STIGGINS' FANCY PLANTATION PINEAPPLE RUM
- 1½ OZ. WÖLFFER ESTATE VERJUS
- ¼ OZ. SMITH & CROSS RUM

MONKEY'S UNCLE

GARNISH: 1 LEMON TWIST

Place the cocktail ingredients in a mixing glass filled with ice and stir until chilled. Strain into a chilled double rocks glass containing one large ice cube and garnish with the lemon twist.

INGREDIENTS:

- 1 OZ. EL DORADO 12-YEAR RUM
- 1 OZ. SANTA TERESA 1796 RUM
- ½ OZ. AMARO SIBILLA
- ½ OZ. GIFFARD BANANE DU BRESIL
- 2 DASHES OF BITTERMENS ELEMAKULE TIKI BITTERS

WHO CAN IT BE NOW: MEN AT WORK

GARNISH: 1 LIME TWIST

Place the cocktail ingredients in a cocktail shaker filled with ice and shake vigorously. Strain into a rocks glass filled with ice and garnish with the lime twist.

INGREDIENTS:

- 1½ OZ. DAMOISEAU RHUM AGRICOLE 110
- ½ OZ. AMARO
- ¾ OZ. SIMPLE SYRUP
- 1 OZ. LIME JUICE

NACIONAL

GARNISH: GRATED NUTMEG

Nacional Biz: Combine ¼ oz. each of banana liqueur, Suze, and Blume Marillen Apricot Eau-de-Vie.

Place the cocktail ingredients in a cocktail shaker filled with ice and shake vigorously. Strain into a double rocks glass filled with large ice cubes and garnish with the grated nutmeg.

INGREDIENTS:

- ¾ OZ. NACIONAL BIZ
- ¾ OZ. LIME JUICE
- ½ OZ. PINEAPPLE JUICE
- ½ OZ. YUZU SYRUP
- ¼ OZ. BANANA SYRUP
- 2 OZ. WHITE RUM

DAIQUIRI

GARNISH: 1 LIME WHEEL

At the tail end of the 19th century, Cuba was finally extricating itself from Spanish rule, but little could Cubans have known how their partnership with the United States would become of such geopolitical import over the course of the 20th century. As soon as the peace treaty with Spain was signed, U. S. exploratory expeditions were sent into the iron ore mines of the Sierra Maestra Mountains, where there just so happens to be a town called Daiquri. It was in this town that engineer Stockton Cox first saw the locals mixing Bacardi Carta Blanca with their coffee. Stockton began toying around with various combinations until landing on rum, lime juice, and sugar. He and his cohorts took to drinking them in the morning, and one fine day they collectively decided to name the drink after the place where they first drank it.

MORE THAN A PREMADE MIX

For too long, the frozen Daiquiri suffered the undeserved reputation of being a packaged blender drink that only kids and the elderly sipped through straws. But the frozen Daiquiri came to life at Floridita in Havana when bartender Constantino Ribalaigua Vert whipped one up using shaved ice and a blender. Ernest Hemingway liked what he tasted the first time he sampled this innovation, but truly fell for it after having Vert make some adjustments, namely losing the sugar (on account of Papa's diabetes) and doubling the amount of rum. It is rumored that Hemingway once downed 15 such frozen Daiquiris in one sitting.

INGREDIENTS:

- 2 OZ. LIGHT RUM
- ½ OZ. LIME JUICE
- 1 TEASPOON SUGAR

Combine all ingredients in a cocktail shaker filled with ice and shake vigorously. Strain into a chilled coupe and garnish with a lime wheel.

FROZEN HEMINGWAY DAIQUIRI

GARNISH: 1 LIME WEDGE

Place the cocktail ingredients in a blender and puree until smooth. Pour into a coupe and garnish with the lime wedge.

INGREDIENTS:

- 2 OZ. WHITE RUM
- ¼ OZ. CHERRY LIQUEUR
- 1 OZ. GRAPEFRUIT JUICE
- JUICE OF ½ LIME
- 1 CUP SHAVED ICE

FROZEN PINEAPPLE DAIQUIRI

GARNISH: 1 PINEAPPLE CHUNK

Place the cocktail ingredients in a blender and puree at a slow speed until smooth. Pour into a coupe and garnish with the additional pineapple chunk.

INGREDIENTS:

- 1 TABLESPOON LIME JUICE
- 4 PINEAPPLE CHUNKS
- 1½ OZ. LIGHT RUM
- ½ TEASPOON SUGAR
- 1 CUP ICE

FROZEN STRAWBERRY DAIQUIRI

GARNISH: 2 STRAWBERRIES

Wet the rim of a mason jar or a coupe and dip it into the sugar. Place the cocktail ingredients in a blender and puree until smooth. Pour the cocktail into the glass and garnish with the additional strawberries.

INGREDIENTS:

- SUGAR, FOR THE RIM
- 1½ OZ. WHITE RUM
- ½ OZ. ORANGE LIQUEUR
- ¼ OZ. SIMPLE SYRUP
- JUICE OF ½ LIME
- ½ CUP FRESH STRAWBERRIES, HULLED AND SLICED
- 1 CUP ICE

LYCHEE DAIQUIRI

GARNISH: 1 LIME WHEEL

Lychee Syrup: Remove the skin and seeds from 8 oz. of lychees and puree. Pour puree into a saucepan, add 1 cup sugar and 1 cup water, and cook over medium heat, while stirring, until desired consistency is reached. Remove from heat, let cool, and store in an airtight container.

Place the cocktail ingredients in a cocktail shaker filled with ice and shake until chilled. Strain into a coupe and garnish with the lime wheel.

INGREDIENTS:

- ¾ OZ. LYCHEE SYRUP
- 2 OZ. WHITE RUM
- 1 OZ. FRESH LIME JUICE
- 2 DASHES OF BITTERCUBE JAMAICAN #2 BITTERS

CUBAN SAZERAC

GARNISH: 1 LEMON TWIST

Rinse the inside of a rocks glass with the Herbsaint and discard the excess. Place the cocktail ingredients in a mixing glass filled with ice and stir until chilled. Strain into the glass and garnish with the lemon twist.

INGREDIENTS:

- ⅛ OZ. HERBSAINT ANISE-FLAVORED LIQUEUR
- 2 OZ. RUM (MATUSALEM GRAN RESERVA 18 PREFERRED)
- ¼ OZ. BANANA SYRUP
- 2 DASHES OF PEYCHAUD'S BITTERS

SEA BEAST

Place all of the ingredients in a cocktail shaker filled with ice, shake vigorously, and strain into a highball glass filled with ice.

Tip: If you cannot track down the Rhum Clément Sirop de Canne, you can substitute a rich simple syrup with a 2:1 sugar-to-water ratio.

INGREDIENTS:

- ¾ OZ. LIME JUICE
- ¾ OZ. PASSION FRUIT PURÉE
- ¾ OZ. FERNET-BRANCA
- 1 OZ. RHUM CLÉMENT SIROP DE CANNE
- 1½ OZ. RUM (RHUM CLÉMENT VSOP PREFERRED)

DAIQUIRI TWIST

GARNISH: 1 LIME WHEEL

Wet the rim of a cocktail glass and dip it into the sugar. Place the cocktail ingredients in a cocktail shaker filled with ice and shake vigorously. Strain the cocktail into the glass and garnish with the lime wheel.

INGREDIENTS:

- SUGAR, FOR THE RIM
- 2 PARTS WHITE RUM
- 1 PART LIME JUICE
- 1 PART TRIPLE SEC
- SPLASH OF SIMPLE SYRUP

BOSS COLADA

GARNISH: 3 DASHES OF PEYCHAUD'S BITTERS & 1 LIME WHEEL

Place the cocktail ingredients in a cocktail shaker filled with ice and shake vigorously. Strain into a pilsner glass filled with pebble ice and garnish with the bitters and lime wheel.

INGREDIENTS:

- 1 OZ. BITTERMENS BÄSKA SNAPS
- ½ OZ. RUM (BANKS 7 ISLAND PREFERRED)
- 1½ OZ. PINEAPPLE JUICE
- ½ OZ. LIME JUICE
- ½ OZ. ORGEAT

WHAT A ASPIRIN IS

GARNISH: 1 ORANGE SLICE, 1 CINNAMON STICK, & GRATED NUTMEG

Place the cocktail ingredients in a cocktail shaker filled with crushed ice and shake until chilled. Pour into a large tiki mug or Collins glass and fill with ice. Garnish with the orange slice, cinnamon stick, and grated nutmeg.

INGREDIENTS:

- 2½ OZ. DARK RUM
- 1 OZ. CREAM OF COCONUT (COCO LOPEZ PREFERRED)
- 1 OZ. ORANGE JUICE
- 4 OZ. PINEAPPLE JUICE

LITTLE BLACK STAR

GARNISH: 1 STAR ANISE POD

Place the cocktail ingredients in a cocktail shaker filled with ice and shake vigorously. Strain into a coupe and garnish with the star anise.

COFFEE SYRUP

Combine all of the ingredients in a medium saucepan and bring to a boil over high heat. Reduce heat to medium and stir until the mixture is thick enough to coat the back of a wooden spoon. Remove from heat, let cool, and store in an airtight container for up to 1 week.

INGREDIENTS:

- 1½ OZ. RUM (TREATY OAK BARREL RESERVE PREFERRED)
- ½ OZ. COFFEE SYRUP (SEE RECIPE BELOW)
- ½ OZ. FRESH LIME JUICE
- ¼ OZ. CURAÇAO (PIERRE FERRAND PREFERRED)
- ⅛ OZ. LUXARDO

COFFEE SYRUP:

- 2 CUPS SUGAR
- 1 CUP WATER
- 2¼ OZ. ESPRESSO (BUSTELO PREFERRED)
- DASH OF CINNAMON
- DASH OF CHILI POWDER

CARIBBEAN MILK PUNCH

GARNISH: GRATED NUTMEG

Vanilla Syrup: Add 1 oz. of vanilla extract to a standard simple syrup after removing the syrup from heat and stir to combine.

Place the cocktail ingredients in a cocktail shaker filled with ice and shake vigorously. Strain into a coupe and garnish with the nutmeg.

INGREDIENTS:

- 1 OZ. VANILLA SYRUP
- 1 OZ. RUM (PREFERABLY SMITH & CROSS OR MT. GAY BLACK BARREL)
- ½ OZ. BOURBON (BUFFALO TRACE PREFERRED)
- 1 OZ. HEAVY CREAM

FJORDIAN SLIP

GARNISH: 1 LEMON WHEEL

Place the cocktail ingredients in a cocktail shaker filled with ice and shake vigorously. Double-strain into a coupe and garnish with the lemon wheel.

INGREDIENTS:

- 1½ OZ. RUM (CAÑA BRAVA PREFERRED)
- ¾ OZ. FOSS BJORK BIRCH LIQUEUR
- ½ OZ. HONEY SYRUP
- ½ OZ. LEMON JUICE

NEW ORLEANS PRESIDENTE

Place all of the ingredients in a cocktail shaker filled halfway with ice, shake until chilled, and strain into a cocktail glass.

INGREDIENTS:

- ½ OZ. GRENADINE
- 1½ OZ. RUM
- ½ OZ. ORANGE JUICE

JEAN LAFITTE COCKTAIL

Place the sugar, absinthe, and curaçao in a cocktail shaker and muddle. Add ice and the remaining ingredients, shake vigorously, and strain into a chilled coupe.

INGREDIENTS:

- 1 TEASPOON WHITE SUGAR
- 2 DASHES OF ABSINTHE
- 2 DASHES OF CURAÇAO
- 1½ OZ. RUM
- 1 EGG YOLK

BARATARIA BUCCANEER

GARNISH: 3 DASHES OF PEYCHAUD'S BITTERS

Place the cocktail ingredients in a cocktail shaker, add ice, and shake until chilled. Strain the cocktail, discard the ice, return the cocktail to the shaker, and dry shake for 5 to 7 seconds. Pour into a chilled cocktail glass and garnish with the additional dashes of bitters.

INGREDIENTS:

- 1 OZ. RUM (CAÑA BRAVA 7 YEAR PREFERRED)
- 1 OZ. GALLIANO
- ¼ OZ. HERBSAINT ANISE-FLAVORED LIQUEUR
- ¼ OZ. ORANGE JUICE
- ¼ OZ. LEMON JUICE
- ¼ OZ. RICH DEMERARA SYRUP (2:1 SUGAR-TO-WATER RATIO)
- 3 DASHES OF PEYCHAUD'S BITTERS
- 1 EGG WHITE

DESERT LILY

GARNISH: 1 FABBRI AMARENA CHERRY

Place the cocktail ingredients in a blender and puree until smooth. Pour into a large plastic cup and garnish with the cherry.

INGREDIENTS:

- 2 OZ. RUM (CAÑA BRAVA PREFERRED)
- 1 OZ. ALOE VERA JUICE
- ¾ OZ. LIME JUICE
- ¾ OZ. SIMPLE SYRUP
- ½ OZ. PRICKLY PEAR PURÉE
- ¼ OZ. LEMON JUICE
- 2–3 DROPS OF FEE BROTHERS LAVENDER FLOWER WATER
- 1 CUP ICE

OLD SPICED CUP

GARNISH: 1 CUCUMBER WHEEL

Hot Sauce Shrub: Combine 1 cup of your preferred hot sauce with 2 cups sugar in a small saucepan and cook over low heat, while stirring, until the mixture has reduced by one-third. Remove from heat, let cool, and store in an airtight container.

Place the rum, shrub, and lemon juice in a mixing glass filled with ice and stir until chilled. Strain into a Collins glass filled halfway with ice, top with the soda water, and garnish with the cucumber wheel.

INGREDIENTS:

- ½ OZ. HOT SAUCE SHRUB
- 1½ OZ. OLD NEW ORLEANS CAJUN SPICE RUM
- ½ OZ. FRESH LEMON JUICE
- SODA WATER, TO TOP

NEW ORLEANS BUCK

GARNISH: 1 ORANGE TWIST

Place the ingredients, except for the ginger beer, in a cocktail shaker containing 1 or 2 ice cubes and shake vigorously (this is also known as a whip shake). Strain into a Collins glass filled with ice, top with the ginger beer, and garnish with the orange twist.

INGREDIENTS:

- 2 OZ. WHITE RUM
- 1 OZ. ORANGE JUICE
- ½ OZ. LIME JUICE
- DASH OF ANGOSTURA BITTERS
- GINGER BEER, TO TOP

BURNT SAGE SOUR

GARNISH: 3 TORCHED SAGE LEAVES

Burnt Sugar Syrup: Place 1 cup brown sugar in a saucepan and cook, while stirring, over low heat until melted. Cook for 1 more minute, remove from heat, and slowly stir in 1 cup of boiling water. Return to the stove and cook over medium heat for 2 minutes. Let cool before storing.

Place the ingredients in a cocktail shaker filled with ice and shake vigorously. Double-strain into a Nick & Nora glass, torch the sage leaves, and use them as a garnish.

INGREDIENTS:

- 1 OZ. BURNT SUGAR SYRUP
- 1 OZ. ANCHO REYES
- 1 OZ. PLANTATION O.F.T.D. RUM
- 1 OZ. PINEAPPLE JUICE
- ½ OZ. LIME JUICE

HURACÁN

GARNISH: 1 LUXARDO MARASCHINO CHERRY, 1 LIME WHEEL, & 1 EDIBLE ORCHID BLOSSOM

Place all of the cocktail ingredients, except for the chicory-pecan bitters, in a cocktail shaker filled with ice and shake vigorously. Strain into a Hurricane glass filled with crushed ice, top with the chicory-pecan bitters, and garnish with the maraschino cherry, lime wheel, and orchid blossom.

INGREDIENTS:

- 2 OZ. AGED RUM (MOCAMBO PREFERRED)
- 1 OZ. LIME CORDIAL (EL GUAPO PREFERRED)
- 1 OZ. PASSION FRUIT PURÉE
- 2 DASHES OF EL GUAPO FUEGO BITTERS
- 3 DASHES OF EL GUAPO CHICORY-PECAN BITTERS

MO'S MAI TAI

GARNISH: 1 SPENT LIME HALF & 1 SPRIG OF MINT

Place the cocktail ingredients in a cocktail shaker filled with ice and shake vigorously. Strain into a rocks glass filled with ice and garnish with the spent lime half and sprig of mint.

INGREDIENTS:

- 1½ OZ. APPLETON ESTATE SIGNATURE RUM
- ½ OZ. LA FAVORITE RHUM AGRICOLE BLANC
- ½ OZ. SIMPLE SYRUP
- ½ OZ. GIFFARD ORGEAT
- ½ OZ. CURAÇAO

CLASSIC HURRICANE

GARNISH: 1 ORANGE WHEEL

Place the cocktail ingredients in a cocktail shaker filled with ice and shake vigorously. Strain into a Hurricane glass containing ice and garnish with the orange wheel.

INGREDIENTS:

- 2 OZ. WHITE RUM
- 2 OZ. DARK RUM
- 1 OZ. LIME JUICE
- 2 OZ. PASSION FRUIT JUICE
- ½ OZ. SIMPLE SYRUP
- ½ OZ. ORANGE JUICE
- ½ OZ. GRENADINE

BALINESE ROOM #2

GARNISH: 1 LIME WHEEL & 1 STAR ANISE POD

Rinse a chilled Daiquiri glass with the absinthe and discard the excess. Place the cocktail ingredients in a cocktail shaker filled with ice and shake vigorously. Double-strain into the Daiquiri glass and garnish with the lime wheel and star anise.

INGREDIENTS:

- ABSINTHE, TO RINSE
- 1 OZ. PLANTATION GRANDE RÉSERVE BARBADOS RUM
- 1 OZ. DIMMI LIQUORE DI MILANO
- 1 OZ. YELLOW CHARTREUSE
- 1 OZ. FRESH LIME JUICE
- DASH OF ANGOSTURA BITTERS

¡SIN MAÍZ NO HAY PAÍS!

GARNISH: 1 SPRIG OF MINT & GRATED NUTMEG

Combine the rum, lime juice, pineapple juice, orange juice, and sherry in a mixing bowl. Place the whole milk, cream of coconut, and corn in a large saucepan and bring to a boil. Slowly add the rum mixture to the saucepan and stir constantly to combine. Strain the mixture at least three times, changing out the catch container each time. When the liquid is at the desired level of clarity, bottle it and chill. Serve in rocks glasses containing a large ice cube and garnish with a sprig of mint and nutmeg.

INGREDIENTS:

- 4 QUARTS HAMILTON JAMAICAN POT STILL GOLD RUM
- 1 QUART LIME JUICE
- 3 QUARTS PINEAPPLE JUICE
- 2 QUARTS ORANGE JUICE
- 1 QUART SHERRY MIXTURE (EQUAL PARTS FINO, OLOROSO, AND PALO CORTADO)
- 4 QUARTS WHOLE MILK
- 2 CUPS CREAM OF COCONUT
- 4 CUPS CORN

MANIGORDO

GARNISH: 1 PINEAPPLE LEAF, GRATED NUTMEG, & 1 ORANGE WEDGE

Chamomile Syrup: In a saucepan, bring 1 cup of water to a boil, and then add 2 cups of sugar. Stir until sugar is dissolved, add 5 bags of chamomile tea, remove from heat, and let steep. When cooled down, strain into an airtight container.

Place the cocktail ingredients in a cocktail shaker filled with ice and shake vigorously. Strain into a tiki mug over ice and garnish with the pineapple leaf, nutmeg, and orange wedge.

INGREDIENTS:

- ½ OZ. CHAMOMILE SYRUP
- ½ OZ. PLANTATION 3 STARS RUM
- ½ OZ. PLANTATION PINEAPPLE RUM
- ½ OZ. PLANTATION O.F.T.D. RUM
- ½ OZ. FRESH LIME JUICE
- ½ OZ. BERGAMOT LIQUEUR
- 3 DASHES OF ANGOSTURA BITTERS
- 1 OZ. PINEAPPLE JUICE

THE RUM DIARY

GARNISH: 1 STRIP OF LEMON PEEL

Place the cocktail ingredients in a mixing glass, add ice, and stir until chilled. Strain into a coupe and garnish with the strip of lemon peel.

INGREDIENTS:

- 2 OZ. BRUGAL 1888 RUM
- ½ OZ. AMARO NONINO QUINTESSENTIA
- ½ OZ. APEROL
- 2 DASHES OF ANGOSTURA BITTERS

RHUM RHUM ROOM PUNCH

Place all of the ingredients in a large punch bowl containing a block of ice and stir until combined.

INGREDIENTS:

- 2 CUPS LIME JUICE
- 2 CUPS ORANGE JUICE
- 2 CUPS PINEAPPLE JUICE
- 2 CUPS ALIZÉ RED PASSION LIQUEUR
- 1 CUP SMITH & CROSS RUM
- 2 CUPS DARK JAMAICAN RUM (MYERS'S ORIGINAL DARK PREFERRED)
- 1 CUP BACARDI 151 RUM
- 1 CUP SIMPLE SYRUP
- 1 CUP HONEY

GRAMPS OLD FASHIONED

GARNISH: 1 STRIP OF ORANGE PEEL

Black Pepper Syrup: In a saucepan, combine 1 cup Demerara sugar, 1 cup water, and ½ oz. crushed black peppercorns. Cook over medium heat until sugar is dissolved. Remove from heat and let sit for 2 hours.

Place the cocktail ingredients in a mixing glass filled with ice and stir until chilled. Strain into a rocks glass filled with ice and garnish with the strip of orange peel.

INGREDIENTS:

- ¼ OZ. BLACK PEPPER SYRUP
- 2 OZ. AÑEJO RUM
- 2 DASHES OF ANGOSTURA BITTERS
- 2 DASHES OF ORANGE BITTERS

EL PURO

GARNISH: 1 TORCHED CINNAMON STICK

Place all of the ingredients in a mixing glass filled with ice and stir until chilled. Strain into a coupe and garnish with the torched cinnamon stick.

INGREDIENTS:

- 2 OZ. ZAFRA RUM
- ½ OZ. CINNAMON SYRUP (SEE PAGE 260)
- 2 DASHES OF ANGOSTURA ORANGE BITTERS
- 2 DASHES OF BITTERCUBE BLACKSTRAP BITTERS

THE PROJECT

GARNISH: 1 TORCHED ORANGE TWIST & COFFEE BEANS

Place the cocktail ingredients in a cocktail shaker filled with ice and shake vigorously. Double-strain over an ice sphere in a rocks glass and garnish with the torched orange twist and the coffee beans.

INGREDIENTS:

- 2 OZ. SANTA TERESA 1796 RUM
- ¼ OZ. CYNAR
- 1 OZ. APEROL
- ¼ OZ. COFFEE SYRUP (SEE PAGE 570)

SALTY DOUG

Grapefruit Salt: Spread 1 cup of grapefruit pulp on a sheet in a food dehydrator and run until completely dry. Grind dried pulp in a spice grinder until fine, and then combine with 1 quart of kosher salt.

Wet the rim of a Collins glass and dip it into the grapefruit salt. Place the liquid ingredients in the juicer cup of a juicer, turn the juicer on high, and add the grapefruit chunks. Swirl to combine the mixture, place ice in the glass, and pour the cocktail into it.

INGREDIENTS:

- GRAPEFRUIT SALT, FOR THE RIM
- 1½ OZ. DIPLOMATICO MANTUANO RUM
- ½ OZ. FRESH LIME JUICE
- ½ OZ. AGAVE NECTAR
- 3–4 FRESH GRAPEFRUITS, PEEL AND PITH REMOVED, CUT INTO CHUNKS

ALOHA

BE MY WINE

GARNISH: 2 TO 3 PANSIES

White Wine Reduction: In a saucepan, combine 1 cup of dry white wine with ½ cup of sugar and simmer until reduced by half.

Place the cocktail ingredients in a mixing glass filled with ice and stir until chilled. Double-strain into a brandy snifter and garnish with the pansies.

INGREDIENTS:

- ¾ OZ. WHITE WINE REDUCTION
- 1½ OZ. DON Q RUM
- ¾ OZ. VELVET FALERNUM
- 1 SPRAY OF LAVENDER OIL

KAMA'AINA

GARNISH: 1 ORCHID BLOSSOM

#9: Combine 2 oz. Reàl Ginger Syrup with 1 oz. almond paste. Add 1 teaspoon of Alamea Pimento Liqueur and stir to combine.

Place all of the cocktail ingredients, except for the bitters, in a cocktail shaker filled with crushed ice and shake vigorously. Pour without straining into a tiki glass, add bitters, and garnish with the orchid blossom.

INGREDIENTS:

- ½ OZ. #9
- 1 OZ. ALAMEA SPICED RUM
- 1 OZ. RHUM AGRICOLE
- 1 OZ. GUAVA NECTAR
- ½ OZ. REÀL CREAM OF COCONUT
- ½ OZ. FRESH LIME JUICE
- 2 DASHES OF ANGOSTURA BITTERS

DAN'S PINA PARADISE

GARNISH: DUSTING OF CINNAMON & 1 STRIP OF ORANGE PEEL

Place the cocktail ingredients in a blender and puree until smooth. Pour into a brandy snifter and garnish with the dusting of cinnamon and the orange peel.

INGREDIENTS:

- 2 OZ. BACARDI AÑEJO CUATRO RUM
- ½ OZ. PLANTATION PINEAPPLE RUM
- 1½ OZ. CITRUS MIX (EQUAL PARTS LIME, GRAPEFRUIT, AND ORANGE JUICE)
- 1 OZ. #9 (RECIPE ABOVE)
- 4 PINEAPPLE CHUNKS
- 1 CUP ICE

TROPIC PUNCH

GARNISH: GRATED NUTMEG & 1 ORANGE WHEEL

Place the cocktail ingredients in a cocktail shaker filled with ice and shake vigorously. Strain into a highball glass filled with ice and garnish with the nutmeg and the orange wheel.

INGREDIENTS:

- 2 OZ. DARK RUM
- ½ OZ. APEROL
- 1 OZ. PINEAPPLE JUICE
- 1 OZ. ORANGE JUICE
- ½ OZ. FRESH LIME JUICE
- ½ OZ. AGAVE NECTAR
- DASH OF EGG WHITE

AVELLINO

GARNISH: 2 TO 3 GREEN APPLE SLICES & 1 CARDAMOM POD

Pistachio-Cardamom Powdered Sugar: Combine equal parts ground cardamom, powdered sugar, and crushed pistachios in a small dish.

Pineapple Syrup: Add ½ cup pineapple juice to a standard simple syrup when it is boiling. After 1 minute, remove from heat and let cool before using.

Wet the rim of a Nick & Nora glass and dip it into the pistachio-cardamom powdered sugar. Place a large ice cube in the glass. Muddle the syrup and green apple in a cocktail shaker, and then add ice. Add all of the remaining ingredients, except the IPA, and shake vigorously. Double-strain into the glass, top with the IPA, and garnish with the slices of green apple and cardamom pod.

INGREDIENTS:

- PISTACHIO–CARDAMOM POWDERED SUGAR, FOR THE RIM
- ½ OZ. PINEAPPLE SYRUP
- ½ GREEN APPLE, CHOPPED
- ½ OZ. YUZU JUICE
- ½ OZ. PINEAPPLE JUICE
- ½ OZ. CHARTREUSE
- 1½ OZ. PLANTATION PINEAPPLE RUM
- LAGUNITAS IPA, TO TOP

RHUM SWIZZLE

GARNISH: 1 WATERMELON SLICE

Watermelon Shrub: Combine the juice from 1 pressed watermelon with 2 cups of apple cider vinegar and 2 cups of sugar.

Place all of the ingredients and some pebble ice in a tiki glass, stir until chilled, add more ice, and garnish with the slice of watermelon.

INGREDIENTS:

- 1 OZ. WATERMELON SHRUB
- 1½ OZ. RHUM JM 100 PROOF
- ½ OZ. FRESH LIME JUICE
- ½ OZ. SIMPLE SYRUP
- ½ OZ. PINEAPPLE JUICE

BANANA DAIQUIRI

GARNISH: 3 DASHES OF ANGOSTURA BITTERS & 1 BANANA CHIP

Place the cocktail ingredients in a blender and puree until smooth. Pour into a coupe and top with 3 dashes of Angostura Bitters and a banana chip.

INGREDIENTS:

- 2 OZ. PARCE 3–YEAR RUM
- 1½ OZ. BANANA PUREE
- ½ OZ. SIMPLE SYRUP
- ½ OZ. FRESH LIME JUICE
- ½ CUP ICE

ROCKAWAY DAIQUIRI

GARNISH: GRATED NUTMEG

Place the cocktail ingredients in a cocktail shaker filled with ice and shake vigorously. Double-strain into a coupe and garnish with freshly grated nutmeg.

INGREDIENTS:

- 1 OZ. JAMAICAN RUM
- 1 OZ. VENEZUELAN RUM
- 2 OZ. FRESH PINEAPPLE JUICE
- ½ OZ. LICOR 43
- ½ OZ. AGAVE NECTAR
- 2 DROPS OF AROMATIC BITTERS

THE ARMANDE

Add the ingredients to a rocks glass in the order they are listed, add ice, and briefly stir to combine.

INGREDIENTS:

- 2 DASHES OF BITTERMENS XOCOLATL MOLE BITTERS
- 2 TEASPOONS TEMPUS FUGIT CRÈME DE CACAO
- 1 OZ. APPLETON ESTATE RARE BLEND 12 YEAR OLD RUM
- 1 OZ. OLD FORESTER SIGNATURE 100 PROOF BOURBON
- SALT, TO TASTE

OTHER SPIRITS *and* BEER

You are probably wondering: If vodka, gin, whisk(e)y, wine, tequila, and rum are "core spirits," what are "other spirits"? It is well past time that I explain the terms. Core spirits are the ones you will commonly find in the smallest of stores that sell spirits. You may have to hunt far and wide for the store that sells absinthe or applejack in your area, but will have no problem finding a bottle of rum.

While the spirits utilized in the recipes in this chapter are those that you might have a little trouble coming across, they are also spirits that you should be on the lookout for—they might very well be carried at your favorite liquor store and it just so happens you've never noticed. There are many amazing cocktails made with these other spirits, and once you have familiarized yourself with them, you'll be able to use them to create your own unique recipes.

For example, a friend of mine was over one Saturday and wanted to go for a walk in my neighborhood, grab some brunch, and seize a bit of the day. This was in direct opposition to my habit of spending many a weekend day cleaning and doing all of the tedious life tasks that everyone else seems to manage during the week, but I relented. During the course of this "mandatory" fun (and fun was had) we came across the Port Morris Distillery (see page 793). Now, I had heard about this place but never had been there. This is ridiculous on a number of levels, as Port Morris is at best a long walk from my apartment and I've traveled to distilleries in Japan, but apparently these things happen, especially to me.

One of the owners, Rafael Barbosa, was there that day and generously gave us a taste of all of the things he'd been cooking up under my nose, as well as a few cocktails to boot. It was here that I got my first taste of *pitorro*, considered to be the moonshine of Puerto Rico (and I didn't even have to go all the way to Puerto Rico). Pitorro is created in a fashion similar to a rum but, as it is aged for a short time in wood, had my friend fooled into thinking that it was a craft whisk(e)y. Hopefully you see how this "other spirit" thing works and how it can play into some interesting recipes. If you get a chance, track down some of these bottles and get mixing.

This collection of recipes also contains those that utilize beer as a base. Beer is not a spirit, but you may be surprised by the delicious cocktails it is capable of creating.

Favorite cocktail: Pimm's Cup—one of the other cocktails my friend Leslie introduced me to in college, and which I had the pleasure of drinking in Hong Kong at the World Rugby Sevens Series.

KITCHEN SINK

GARNISH: 1 LEMON SLICE

Place the cocktail ingredients in a cocktail shaker filled with ice and shake until chilled. Strain into a hurricane glass over ice and garnish with the slice of lemon.

INGREDIENTS:

- ½ OZ. VODKA
- ½ OZ. GIN
- ½ OZ. RUM
- ½ OZ. TEQUILA
- ½ OZ. BLUE CURAÇAO
- 2 OZ. PINEAPPLE JUICE
- SPLASH OF SPRITE

PERSEPHONE

Place all of the ingredients in a mixing glass filled with ice, stir, and pour into a chilled coupe.

INGREDIENTS:

- 1 OZ. APPLEJACK
- ½ OZ. LEMON JUICE
- ½ OZ. SIMPLE SYRUP
- ½ OZ. SLOE GIN
- ¾ OZ. DOLIN VERMOUTH DE CHAMBÉRY

BLUE-EYED BLONDE SHOOTER

Add the ingredients to a shot glass in the order they are listed.

INGREDIENTS:

- ½ OZ. BLUE CURAÇAO
- ½ OZ. IRISH CREAM
- ½ OZ. BANANA LIQUEUR

MINI GUINNESS

Fill a shot glass three-quarters of the way with coffee liqueur. Pour the Irish cream carefully over the back of a spoon so that it sits atop the coffee liqueur.

INGREDIENTS:

- 3 PARTS COFFEE LIQUEUR
- 1 PART IRISH CREAM

SCHNAPPS

In the United States, schnapps is often associated with youthful indiscretion and a nasty hangover. But that's because bad schnapps is little more than grain alcohol and fruit flavoring. The good stuff from Austria and Germany is distilled directly from seasonal fruit and is fruit brandy that is often taken as a shot.

OATMEAL COOKIE

Place all of the ingredients in a cocktail shaker filled with ice, shake vigorously for 15 to 20 seconds, and strain into shot glasses.

INGREDIENTS:

- 2 PARTS IRISH CREAM
- 1 PART CINNAMON SCHNAPPS
- 1 PART COFFEE LIQUEUR
- 1 PART FRANGELICO
- 1 PART SKIM MILK

WOO WOO

Place the ingredients in a cocktail shaker filled with ice, shake vigorously for 15 to 20 seconds, and strain into shot glasses.

INGREDIENTS:

- 1 PART PEACH SCHNAPPS
- 3 PARTS DIET CRANBERRY JUICE

AFTER FIVE

Fill a shot glass one-third of the way with coffee liqueur. Pour the Irish cream carefully over the back of a spoon so that it sits atop the coffee liqueur. Utilize the same technique with the peppermint schnapps.

INGREDIENTS:

- 1 PART COFFEE LIQUEUR
- 1 PART IRISH CREAM
- 1 PART PEPPERMINT SCHNAPPS

STILETTO

Place the ingredients in a cocktail shaker filled with ice, shake vigorously for 15 to 20 seconds, and strain into shot glasses.

INGREDIENTS:

- 1 PART GOLD TEQUILA
- 1 PART COFFEE VODKA
- 1 PART PEPPERMINT SCHNAPPS

LONG ISLAND ICED TEA

GARNISH: 1 LEMON WHEEL

Add the cocktail ingredients to a mason jar filled with ice in the order they are listed in and garnish with the lemon wheel.

INGREDIENTS:

½ OZ. VODKA
½ OZ. GIN
½ OZ. RUM
½ OZ. TEQUILA
½ OZ. TRIPLE SEC
DASH OF SOUR MIX
COLA, TO TOP

SNAKE BITE

Add the ingredients to a tall shot glass in the order they are listed.

INGREDIENTS:

1 PART APPLE VODKA
1 PART LIGHT BEER
1 PART APPLE CIDER

GRAND SLAM

GARNISH: 1 LIME WEDGE

Add the ingredients to a mason jar filled with ice in the order they are listed and garnish with the lime wedge.

INGREDIENTS:

½ OZ. VODKA
½ OZ. RUM
½ OZ. TEQUILA
½ OZ. ORANGE LIQUEUR
JUICE OF 1 LIME WEDGE
4 OZ. COLA

SNOWBALL

GARNISH: DOLLOP OF WHIPPED CREAM & 1 MARASCHINO CHERRY

Place the advocaat and lime juice in a cocktail shaker filled with ice and shake until chilled. Strain the mixture into a mason jar and add the maple syrup. Top with the lemonade and garnish with the whipped cream and maraschino cherry.

INGREDIENTS:

2 OZ. ADVOCAAT
DASH OF LIME JUICE
DASH OF MAPLE SYRUP
LEMONADE, TO TOP

ALABAMA SLAMMER

GARNISH: 1 ORANGE SLICE & 1 MARASCHINO CHERRY

Place the alcoholic ingredients in a mason jar filled with ice, top with the orange juice and grenadine, and garnish with the orange slice and maraschino cherry.

INGREDIENTS:

- ¾ OZ. PEACH LIQUEUR
- ¾ OZ. AMARETTO
- ¾ OZ. SLOE GIN
- ¾ OZ. VODKA
- 6 OZ. ORANGE JUICE
- DASH OF GRENADINE

RAPHAEL

GARNISH: 1 STRAWBERRY

Place the strawberry puree, manzana verde, and lime juice in a cocktail shaker filled with ice and shake vigorously. Strain into a champagne flute, top with Champagne, and garnish with the strawberry.

Tip: If you are unsure where to turn for quality manzana verde, both Briottet and Giffard are good choices.

INGREDIENTS:

- 2 OZ. STRAWBERRY PUREE
- ½ OZ. MANZANA VERDE APPLE LIQUEUR
- 1 TABLESPOON FRESH LIME JUICE
- BRUT CHAMPAGNE, TO TOP

DANGER

Place the ingredients in a cocktail glass filled with ice and stir to combine.

INGREDIENTS:

- 1 PART EVERCLEAR
- 1 PART GINGER ALE
- 4 PARTS HAWAIIAN PUNCH

PIMM'S CUP

GARNISH: 1 LEMON WHEEL

Place the Pimm's, soda, and Luxardo in a rocks glass filled with ice and stir until chilled. Place the cucumber wheels on top of the cocktail and garnish with the lemon wheel.

INGREDIENTS:

1 OZ. PIMM'S NO. 1

2 OZ. LEMON-LIME SODA

½ OZ. LUXARDO

2 CUCUMBER WHEELS

MACARONI COCKTAIL

Place the ingredients in a cocktail shaker filled with ice, shake until chilled, and strain into a very cold tea cup.

INGREDIENTS:

1 OZ. PASTIS

½ OZ. SWEET VERMOUTH

KIR ST. LOUIS

GARNISH: 1 LONG GRAPEFRUIT TWIST

Pour the liqueurs into a champagne flute, top with Champagne, and garnish with a long twist of grapefruit.

INGREDIENTS:

½ OZ. ST-GERMAIN

1 OZ. GIFFARD CRÈME DE PAMPLEMOUSSE ROSE

CHAMPAGNE, TO TOP

SWEET PEA

Place the liqueur and lemon juice in a highball glass filled with ice and top with the tonic water.

INGREDIENTS:

- 3 OZ. PERNOD OR ANOTHER ANISE-FLAVORED LIQUEUR
- 1 OZ. LEMON JUICE
- TONIC WATER, TO TOP (FEVER TREE PREFERRED)

FRENCH OPEN PIMM'S CUP

Place the cucumber, fruit, and mint in a pitcher filled with ice and stir. Add the Pimm's and lemonade, stir, and chill in the refrigerator. Pour into highball glasses filled with ice, making sure that everyone gets cucumber, the fruit, and mint in their glass.

INGREDIENTS:

- 1 ENGLISH CUCUMBER, SLICED THIN LENGTHWISE
- 1 LEMON, SLICED
- 1 LIME, SLICED
- 1 GREEN APPLE, DICED
- 8 SPRIGS OF MINT, CRUSHED
- 2 CUPS PIMM'S NO. 1
- 4 CUPS LORINA SPARKLING LEMONADE

CERISE SOIR

GARNISH: 2 GRIOTTINES

Place the cocktail ingredients in a cocktail shaker filled with ice and shake until chilled. Strain into a chilled Nick & Nora glass and garnish with the Griottines.

INGREDIENTS:

- 1 TEASPOON SIMPLE SYRUP
- DASH OF FRESH LEMON JUICE
- 1 TEASPOON LIQUID FROM JAR OF GRIOTTINES (CHERRIES IN KIRSCH)
- 1 OZ. RHUM CLÉMENT CRÉOLE SHRUBB

UMAMI MARTINI

GARNISH: 1 TO 2 OLIVES

Rinse a chilled martini glass with the vermouth and discard the excess. Add the Umami and garnish with 1 or 2 olives.

INGREDIENTS:

- DRY VERMOUTH, TO RINSE
- 2 OZ. AUDEMUS UMAMI

BLOODY UMAMI

GARNISH: 1 STRIP OF LEMON PEEL, 1 CELERY STALK, 1 TO 2 OLIVES, & 1 PICKLED GREEN BEAN

Add the cocktail ingredients to a rocks glass filled with ice in the order they are listed, stir, and garnish with the strip of lemon peel, celery stalk, pickled green bean, and 1 or 2 olives.

INGREDIENTS:

- 2 DASHES OF WORCESTERSHIRE SAUCE
- DASH OF TABASCO
- DASH OF CELERY BITTERS
- SALT AND PEPPER, TO TASTE
- 1½ OZ. AUDEMUS UMAMI
- ¾ CUP TOMATO JUICE

BARON OF BROOKLYN

GARNISH: 1 LONG LEMON TWIST

Place the cocktail ingredients in a mixing glass filled with ice and stir until chilled. Strain into a brandy snifter containing a large ice cube and garnish with the long twist of lemon.

INGREDIENTS:

- DASH OF MOLE
- DASH OF ANGOSTURA BITTERS
- ½ OZ. SUZE
- ½ OZ. GIFFARD BANANE DU BRESIL
- 1½ OZ. TAWNY PORT
- 1½ OZ. AVUÁ CACHAÇA

THE LAST WORD

GARNISH: 1 LIME TWIST

Place the cocktail ingredients in a cocktail shaker filled with ice and shake until chilled. Strain into a chilled coupe and garnish with the lime twist.

INGREDIENTS:

- ½ OZ. CHARTREUSE
- ½ OZ. LUXARDO
- ½ OZ. GIN
- ½ OZ. LIME JUICE

AUDEMUS
SPIRITS
CRÉATEUR DE SPIRITUEUX
UMAMI
500 ML
42% VOL

CORPSE REVIVER

Place the lemon juice and the liqueur in a cocktail glass containing a piece of ice and top with the Champagne.

INGREDIENTS:

- JUICE OF ¼ LEMON
- 2 OZ. PERNOD
- CHAMPAGNE, TO TOP

FLIRTBIRD

GARNISH: 1 WHOLE SHISO LEAF

Wet the rim of a rocks glass and dip it into the plum powder. Place the cocktail ingredients in a cocktail shaker filled with ice and shake vigorously. Place a large ice cube in the glass, strain the cocktail into the glass, and garnish with the whole shiso leaf.

INGREDIENTS:

- LI HING MUI PLUM POWDER, FOR THE RIM
- 1½ OZ. MIZU SAGA BARLEY SHOCHU
- 1 OZ. YUZU JUICE
- ½ OZ. AGAVE NECTAR
- 1 SHISO LEAF, TORN

VALENTINE'S GRAPEFRUIT

GARNISH: 1 GRAPEFRUIT TWIST

Place all of the ingredients, except for the club soda, in a Collins glass and stir to combine. Add ice, top with the club soda, and garnish with the grapefruit twist.

INGREDIENTS:

- ¾ OZ. CARPANO BIANCO
- ¾ OZ. GRAN CLASSICO
- ¾ OZ. FERNET-BRANCA
- 2 DASHES OF SCRAPPY'S GRAPEFRUIT BITTERS
- CLUB SODA, TO TOP

DRAGON'S BREATH

GARNISH: 1 LEMON TWIST & 1 PICKLED WALNUT

INGREDIENTS:

- 5 DROPS OF TABASCO
- 1 OZ. APRICOT LIQUEUR
- 1 OZ. DRY VERMOUTH
- 1 OZ. CALVADOS

Place the cocktail ingredients in a mixing glass filled with ice and stir until chilled. Strain into a chilled coupe, garnish with the lemon twist, and serve with the pickled walnut on the side.

Tip: Opies Pickled Walnuts are a good option if you don't want to go through the trouble of pickling the walnuts yourself.

DISAPPEARING ACT

GARNISH: 1 LEMON TWIST

INGREDIENTS:

- 1 OZ. LILLET BLANC
- ½ OZ. LINIE AQUAVIT
- ½ OZ. LEMON JUICE
- ½ OZ. SIMPLE SYRUP
- 1 TEASPOON GIFFARD CRÈME DE PÊCHE DE VIGNE
- SPARKLING WINE, TO TOP

Place all of the cocktail ingredients, except for the sparkling wine, in a cocktail shaker filled with ice and shake until chilled. Strain into a coupe, top with the sparkling wine, and garnish with the lemon twist.

ALABAZAM

GARNISH: 1 LEMON WHEEL

INGREDIENTS:

- 1 OZ. COGNAC VSOP
- 1 OZ. GRAND MARNIER
- JUICE OF ½ LEMON
- ½ OZ. RICH SIMPLE SYRUP (2:1 SUGAR-TO-WATER RATIO)
- DASH OF ORANGE BITTERS
- SODA WATER, TO TOP

Place all of the cocktail ingredients, except for the soda water, in a cocktail shaker filled with ice and shake vigorously. Strain into a Collins glass filled with crushed ice, top with the soda water, and garnish with the lemon wheel.

MACE

GARNISH: 2 MISTS OF MACE TINCTURE

Place the cocktail ingredients in a cocktail shaker filled with ice and shake vigorously. Double-strain into a coupe and spray the mace tincture on top.

INGREDIENTS:

- 1 OZ. LINIE AQUAVIT
- 1 OZ. APEROL
- ½ OZ. FRESH ORANGE JUICE
- ½ OZ. FRESH BEET JUICE
- ¾ OZ. SYRUP FROM CAN OF YOUNG COCONUT MEAT

MR. OCTOBER

GARNISH: GRATED NUTMEG

Place the cocktail ingredients in a cocktail shaker filled with ice and shake vigorously. Double-strain into a chilled coupe and garnish with the nutmeg.

INGREDIENTS:

- 1½ OZ. LAIRD'S APPLEJACK
- ¾ OZ. CINNAMON SYRUP (SEE PAGE 260)
- ¾ OZ. FRESH LEMON JUICE
- ½ OZ. GALLIANO
- 2 DASHES OF ST. ELIZABETH ALLSPICE DRAM

ROME WITH A VIEW

GARNISH: 1 ORANGE WHEEL & 1 LIME TWIST

Place all of the cocktail ingredients, except for the soda water, in a cocktail shaker filled with ice and shake vigorously. Strain into a Collins glass filled with ice, top with the soda water, and garnish with the orange wheel and lime twist.

INGREDIENTS:

- 1 OZ. CAMPARI
- 1 OZ. DRY VERMOUTH
- ½ OZ. LIME JUICE
- ¼ OZ. SIMPLE SYRUP
- SODA WATER, TO TOP

CAMPARI

In 1860, in Novara, Italy, Gaspare Campari created this iconic *apertivo*, the exact recipe for which remains a mystery to this day (though we do know that around 2005 the company stopped using cochineal bug dye to achieve the liqueur's crimson-colored hue; the reasoning for this decision is not so clear and theories range from making it vegan-friendly to accommodating those rare cases of allergic reactions to the dye). Campari is herbal and bitter, and there is no mistake when it is used in a cocktail.

GARIBALDI

GARNISH: 1 ORANGE WEDGE

Place 2 ice cubes in a Collins glass, add Campari, add a splash of orange juice, and stir to combine. Add 1 more ice cube, fill the glass with juice, and garnish with the orange wedge.

INGREDIENTS:

- 1½ OZ. CAMPARI
- FRESH ORANGE JUICE, TO TOP

ABSENT STARS

GARNISH: 1 ORANGE TWIST

Place the cocktail ingredients in a cocktail shaker filled halfway with ice and shake vigorously. Strain into a chilled double rocks glass filled with ice, rub the orange twist on the rim of the glass, and then use it as a garnish.

INGREDIENTS:

- 1 OZ. CAMPARI
- 1 OZ. WHITE RHUM AGRICOLE (LA FAVORITE BLANC PREFERRED)
- ¾ OZ. LEMON JUICE
- ½ OZ. PASSION FRUIT SYRUP
- ½ OZ. APRICOT BRANDY (MARIE BRIZARD APRY PREFERRED)
- 5 DROPS OF SALINE SOLUTION (SEE PAGE 308)
- 10 DROPS OF BITTERMENS HOPPED GRAPEFRUIT BITTERS

PINK CAMPARI

GARNISH: 1 LIME TWIST & 2 RASPBERRIES

Place the raspberries, juices, and sour mix in a cocktail shaker and muddle. Add ice, the Campari, and rye and shake vigorously. Strain into a chilled cocktail glass and garnish with the additional raspberries and lime twist skewered on a cocktail pick.

INGREDIENTS:

- 4–5 FRESH RASPBERRIES
- SPLASH OF PEAR JUICE
- SPLASH OF CRANBERRY JUICE
- SPLASH OF SOUR MIX
- 1 OZ. CAMPARI
- 1 OZ. HERMAN MARSHALL TEXAS RYE WHISKEY

AMERICANO

GARNISH: 1 LEMON SLICE

Place the Campari and sweet vermouth in a rocks glass filled with ice, top with the club soda, and garnish with the lemon slice.

INGREDIENTS:

- 1 OZ. CAMPARI
- 1 OZ. SWEET VERMOUTH
- 1 OZ. CLUB SODA

PAJARO DEL FUEGO

GARNISH: 1 LIME WEDGE

Place the cocktail ingredients in a cocktail shaker filled with ice and shake vigorously. Strain into a Collins glass filled with ice and garnish with the lime wedge.

INGREDIENTS:

- 1½ OZ. CAFFE DEL FUEGO
- 1½ OZ. PINEAPPLE SHRUB (SEE PAGE 40)
- ¾ OZ. CAMPARI
- ¾ OZ. LIME JUICE

CAMPARI COLADA

GARNISH: 1 ORANGE SLICE & 1 BRANDY-SOAKED CHERRY

Place the cocktail ingredients in a cocktail shaker and dry shake for 10 seconds. Pour into a tall tiki glass filled with crushed ice and use the swizzle method to combine. Garnish with the orange slice and the brandy-soaked cherry.

INGREDIENTS:

- 3 OZ. FRESH PINEAPPLE JUICE
- 1 OZ. CREAM OF COCONUT
- 1 OZ. HEAVY CREAM
- 2 OZ. CAMPARI

ABSINTHE SUISSESSE

Place all of the ingredients in a cocktail shaker and dry shake for 10 to 15 seconds. Add ice, shake until chilled, and strain into a chilled wine glass.

INGREDIENTS:

- 1 OZ. ABSINTHE
- ½ OZ. HERBSAINT ANISE-FLAVORED LIQUEUR
- ½ OZ. CRÈME DE MENTHE
- 1 OZ. HEAVY CREAM
- ¼ OZ. SIMPLE SYRUP
- DASH OF ORANGE BLOSSOM WATER
- 1 EGG WHITE

ABSINTHE FRAPPE

GARNISH: 1 SPRIG OF MINT

Place the cocktail ingredients in a cocktail shaker filled halfway with ice and shake vigorously. Strain into a julep cup filled with crushed ice and garnish with the sprig of mint.

INGREDIENTS:

- 1½ OZ. ABSINTHE
- ¼ OZ. SIMPLE SYRUP
- 2 OZ. SODA WATER
- DASH OF ANISETTE

THE IMPROVED COCKTAIL

GARNISH: 1 STRIP OF LEMON PEEL

Place the cocktail ingredients in a rocks glass and stir to combine. Add a large ice cube and stir until chilled. Express the strip of lemon peel over the cocktail, and then use it as a garnish.

INGREDIENTS:

- 2 OZ. BRANDY
- ¼ OZ. SIMPLE SYRUP
- 2 DASHES OF LUXARDO
- DASH OF ABSINTHE
- 2 DASHES OF AROMATIC BITTERS

ABSINTHE

It is hard to think of a spirit that has been as vilified and romanticized as absinthe. Its main ingredient, wormwood, has a long history of being used for medicinal purposes. Hippocrates administered a wine or spirit infused with wormwood as a remedy for multiple ailments, including jaundice and rheumatism. Starting in 1830, French soldiers fighting to colonize North Africa carried wormwood, adding it to their drinking water and wine to fight off fever and dysentery. Soon *une verte* was popular in France, and through a combination of national pride and rumors of its hallucinatory effects, the country was home to 29 absinthe distilleries by 1849. And here the opinions of absinthe diverge. Writers like Arthur Rimbaud praised the liberating, creative powers of "the green fairy"; while Edouard Manet painted "The Absinthe Drinker," a good-for-nothing wrapped in his indifference, glass of green next to him, and an empty bottle on its side at his feet. Much of the hype around absinthe, however, had to do more with larger cultural shifts in France, and it was used as a scapegoat while wine, which is as intoxicating, was never subjected to such scrutiny.

DAUPHIN

GARNISH: CACAO NIBS & 1 STAR ANISE POD

Place a glass in a bowl and add the cocktail ingredients to the glass in the order they are listed. Add pebble ice to the bowl and the glass, stir the cocktail, and garnish with the cacao nibs and star anise.

- 2 DASHES OF MIRACLE MILE BITTERS CO. CHOCOLATE CHILI BITTERS
- ½ OZ. DEMERARA SYRUP
- ½ OZ. ANCHO REYES
- 1 OZ. ABSINTHE
- 1¼ OZ. TOASTED COCONUT ALMOND MILK

MAISON ABSINTHE COLADA

GARNISH: 1 SPRIG OF MINT

Place the cocktail ingredients in a cocktail shaker filled with ice and shake vigorously. Strain into a Hurricane glass and garnish with the sprig of mint.

INGREDIENTS:

- 1 OZ. ABSINTHE
- ½ OZ. RHUM JM
- 1 TEASPOON CRÈME DE MENTHE
- 1 OZ. PINEAPPLE JUICE
- ½ OZ. LEMON JUICE
- 1 OZ. COCONUT SYRUP

GREEN GODDESS PUNCH

GARNISH: 1 SPRIG OF MINT, 1 LIME WHEEL, OR 1 CUCUMBER SLICE

Place the absinthe, lime juice, and simple syrup in a Collins glass filled with ice and stir. Top with the Topo Chico and garnish with a sprig of mint, a lime wheel, or a slice of cucumber.

INGREDIENTS:

- ½ OZ. VIOLET CROWN SPIRITS EMERALD ABSINTHE
- 1 OZ. LIME JUICE
- 1 OZ. SIMPLE SYRUP
- 4 OZ. TOPO CHICO

ABSINTHE DRIP

Pour the absinthe into a rocks glass. Place a slotted or absinthe spoon on top of the glass and place the sugar cube on top of the spoon. Drip the ice water very slowly over the cube and into the glass until the sugar cube is mostly dissolved and the absinthe begins to look cloudy. Place any remaining sugar in the cocktail and stir until dissolved.

INGREDIENTS:

- 1 OZ. ABSINTHE
- 1 SUGAR CUBE
- 4–5 OZ. ICE WATER

THE START AND FINISH

GARNISH: 1 ORANGE TWIST

Place the cocktail ingredients in a mixing glass filled with ice and stir until chilled. Strain into a rocks glass filled with ice and garnish with the orange twist.

INGREDIENTS:

- 1½ OZ. AMARO (AVERNA PREFERRED)
- ½ OZ. LILLET BLANC
- ½ OZ. DRY VERMOUTH
- ½ OZ. ABSINTHE
- DASH OF ORANGE BITTERS

ROLLO RAIDERS

GARNISH: 2 STRIPS OF LEMON PEEL & CARAWAY SEEDS

Place all of the ingredients in a cocktail shaker filled with ice and shake until chilled. Double-strain into a rocks glass filled with crushed ice and garnish with the strips of lemon peel and caraway seeds.

INGREDIENTS:

- ¾ OZ. PLAIN FULL-FAT YOGURT
- ½ OZ. ORGEAT
- ¾ OZ. LEMON JUICE
- ¾ OZ. AQUAVIT
- ¾ OZ. KÜMMEL
- ½ OZ. GIN (BEEFEATER PREFERRED)

GRASSHOPPER

Place the ingredients in a cocktail shaker filled with ice, shake until chilled, and strain into a chilled cocktail glass.

INGREDIENTS:

- 1 OZ. GREEN CRÈME DE MENTHE
- 1 OZ. BOLS CRÈME DE CACAO
- 1 OZ. HEAVY CREAM

DRINK OF LAUGHTER AND FORGETTING

GARNISH: 14 DROPS OF ANGOSTURA BITTERS

Place the cocktail ingredients in a cocktail shaker filled with ice and shake vigorously. Strain into a cocktail glass and garnish with the bitters.

INGREDIENTS:

- 1½ OZ. CYNAR
- ½ OZ. CHARTREUSE
- ¾ OZ. LIME JUICE
- ½ OZ. RICH DEMERARA SYRUP (2:1 SUGAR-TO-WATER RATIO)

THE VELLOCET

GARNISH: 1 SPRIG OF MINT

Place the cocktail ingredients in a Collins glass filled with crushed ice and use the swizzle method to combine. When the outside of the glass is frosted, garnish with the sprig of mint.

INGREDIENTS:

- 2 OZ. CHARTREUSE
- 1¼ OZ. PINEAPPLE JUICE
- ¾ OZ. LIME JUICE
- ½ OZ. FALERNUM
- 2 DASHES OF ANGOSTURA BITTERS
- 2 DASHES OF PEYCHAUD'S BITTERS

CARONDELET

GARNISH: 1 LEMON TWIST

Place the cocktail ingredients in a mixing glass filled with ice and stir. Strain over 3 large ice cubes in a rocks glass and garnish with the lemon twist.

INGREDIENTS:

- 1 OZ. ABSINTHE
- 1 OZ. APRICOT BRANDY
- 1 OZ. YELLOW CHARTREUSE

GRASSHOPPER: AN OVERLOOKED CLASSIC

Beverage program consultant Michał Maziarz is the former head bartender at the Four Seasons Hotel London at Ten Trinity Square.

What can you tell us about how you got into making cocktails?

There is a little story behind it. When I was rather young, around 6 years old, my father was a captain, spending 8 months a year on the sea. My mother worked full time. So I spent a lot of my early childhood with my grandparents. One day, after discovering my favorite superhero I pulled on my grandfather's trousers, went to him, and stated that I wanted to play Batman. He didn't have any clue about Batman and thought I said "Barman." He looked at me worried and suspicious, but nonetheless pulled out a stool, a few soda and juice bottles, a very old shaker, pourers, and openers and invited me to play. And there I was, bartending for the first time, at 6 years of age!

Honestly though, I did not like my first beer. I wanted to drink with my friends, however, so being a natural born solution seeker I looked for alternatives in my father's home bar. Since he was well traveled, he'd collected quite few bottles from all the places he visited. So I had plenty of options. This, combined with playing Barman, quickly escalated to creating cocktails and exploring the wide world of spirits.

Blue Hawaiian, Brandy Alexander, Pink Squirrel, Rusty Nail, Tom Collins, White Russian, Grasshopper, Rob Roy, Pink Lady: If you had to pick one of these cocktails to add to a menu how would you reimagine your choice to make it fit in with your style?

Grasshopper! I think it is one of the most overlooked classic cocktails. Everyone loves mint and chocolate. They are wonderful flavors to play with, and can take on any additional spirit if you balance it properly. How would I twist it? Perhaps an addition of Nikka Coffey Malt and rice koji milk instead of double cream? With a pinch of matcha powder on the top, or white chocolate, matcha Kit-Kat as a garnish. Ha!

SPIRITS
2012
DOUBLE GOLD
FESTLIG
AQUAVIT
KROGSTAD
DISTILLED FROM GRAIN

EARLY START

GARNISH: 1 FRENCH SORREL LEAF

Place the cocktail ingredients in a cocktail shaker filled with ice and shake vigorously. Double-strain into a coupe and garnish with the French sorrel leaf.

INGREDIENTS:

- 1½ OZ. KROGSTAD AQUAVIT
- ½ OZ. LIME JUICE
- ½ OZ. ORGEAT
- 1 EGG WHITE

A PROMISE'S GHOST

GARNISH: 1 LONG LEMON TWIST

Thai Basil-Strawberry Shrub: In a large saucepan, combine 2 pounds strawberries, 8 cups granulated sugar, 2 quarts water, and 1 cup of firmly packed Thai basil leaves. Bring to a boil over medium-high heat and cook until mixture is reduced by one-quarter. Turn off heat and allow mixture to cool to room temperature. Strain through a fine sieve into a large bowl, add 2 cups of rice wine vinegar, and stir until combined. Store in an airtight container and refrigerate for 2 weeks.

Place all of the cocktail ingredients, except for the sparkling wine, in a cocktail shaker and shake until chilled. Double-strain into a champagne flute, top with the sparkling wine, and garnish with the long twist of lemon.

INGREDIENTS:

- ¾ OZ. THAI BASIL-STRAWBERRY SHRUB
- 1 OZ. PIMM'S NO. 1
- ¾ OZ. PISCO (MACCHU PREFERRED)
- ¼ OZ. LEMON JUICE
- 2 OZ. SPARKLING WINE

APPLE BLOSSOM

Place the applejack, St-Germain, and lime juice in a Collins glass filled with ice, stir until chilled, and top with seltzer water.

INGREDIENTS:

- 1½ OZ. APPLEJACK
- ½ OZ. ST-GERMAIN
- ½ OZ. LIME JUICE
- SELTZER WATER, TO TOP

BOLIVIAN BIBLE THUMPER

GARNISH: DASH OF ANGOSTURA BITTERS

Place the ingredients in a cocktail shaker and dry shake for 10 seconds. Add ice and shake for 30 seconds. Double-strain into a coupe and top with the dash of Angostura.

INGREDIENTS:

- 1½ OZ. RUJERO SINGANI
- ¼ OZ. CHAREAU ALOE LIQUEUR
- ¼ OZ. DEMERARA SYRUP
- ¾ OZ. GRAPEFRUIT JUICE
- 1 EGG WHITE

ONE OF THESE NIGHTS

GARNISH: 1 TORCHED STAR ANISE POD

Place the cocktail ingredients in a cocktail shaker filled with ice and shake vigorously. Double-strain into a coupe and garnish with the torched star anise.

INGREDIENTS:

- 1¼ OZ. AMARO LUCANO
- ¾ OZ. HENNESSY V.S COGNAC
- ¼ OZ. PIERRE FERRAND DRY CURAÇAO
- ¼ OZ. LEMON JUICE
- ½ OZ. ORGEAT
- ¾ OZ. COLD BREW COFFEE
- DASH OF PEYCHAUD'S BITTERS

PURPLE RAIN

GARNISH: 1 STRIP OF GRAPEFRUIT PEEL

Place the cocktail ingredients in a mixing glass filled with ice and stir until chilled. Pour the cocktail into a double rocks glass, express the strip of grapefruit peel over the cocktail, and then use it as a garnish.

INGREDIENTS:

- 1 OZ. ZUCCA AMARO OR AMARO SFMUATO RABARBARO
- 1 OZ. COCCHI ROSA
- 2 DASHES OF LAVENDER BITTERS
- 4 OZ. ICED COFFEE (MEDIUM OR LIGHT ROAST PREFERRED)

BEER BASICS

True, beer isn't technically a spirit. But making cocktails with beer is all the rage. So here is a crash course on beer: typically, beer is made from four core ingredients: water, yeast, malt, and hops. There are two different types of beer: ales and lagers. Ales are made with top-fermenting yeasts; lagers use bottom-fermenting yeasts. There are myriad styles of beer, from India Pale Ale to stout, and porter to lambic and saison. While beer is commonly considered a stand-alone beverage, its use as an ingredient in a mixed drink dates back to the advent of cocktails. Monks of yore drank Posset, a precursor to Classic Eggnog (see page 655), which was spiced milk curdled with wine or ale. Works by literary titans William Shakespeare and Charles Dickens mention Purl (in the 17th and 19th centuries, respectively), a drink made from herbs and beer, and Flip was a hot drink of sugar, rum, eggs, and beer popular with sailors during the 18th century.

Beer styles vary, of course, depending on the hops, flavoring, body, aroma, and color, and all of these elements should be taken into account when using beer as a cocktail recipe ingredient. Here is a rundown on some popular beer styles and complementary spirits:

India Pale Ale: the hoppy bite, bold citrus, and herbal flavors go well with spirits that are floral and assertive, like tequila, pisco, and Campari.

Wheat beer (e.g., hefeweizen, Belgian witbier): the grain affects mouthfeel more than flavor, and tends to make for an effervescent beer light in flavor, which is why they are often served with a slice of lemon or orange; these beers play well with spirits typically enhanced by citrus, like gin, rum, and Aperol.

Porter: the balanced hops and burnt, caramelized flavor invite a sweet, syrupy spirit like Port or amaretto to be folded right in.

Stout: the rich, malty depth of a stout is a perfect companion to barrel-aged spirits like whisk(e)y and bourbon.

Saison: mildly tart, fruity, and spicy, spirits like vermouth and Aperol tame saisons (and other sour beers).

Pilsner: its crisp, malty sweetness and clean finish are very conducive to cocktails involving vodka.

Of course, this is a far from definitive list of beer styles, but it's enough for you to make informed decisions about how to concoct beery, spirited cocktails.

In the recipes that follow, when the style of beer or even the brand name makes a difference, it has been noted.

GINGER SHANDY

GARNISH: 1 LEMON SLICE

Rub the mint leaves along the rim of a mason jar or pint glass, tear them in half, and place them in the jar. Add ice, the beer, and the ginger beer and garnish with the slice of lemon.

INGREDIENTS:

- HANDFUL OF MINT LEAVES
- 2 PARTS BEER (WHEAT BEER PREFERRED)
- 1 PART GINGER BEER

EMERALD ISLE

Fill a pint glass three-quarters of the way with the Guinness. Fill a shot glass with the whiskey and the Irish cream, drop the shot glass into the pint glass, and, since the Irish cream will curdle, drink as fast as you can.

INGREDIENTS:

- 12 OZ. GUINNESS
- ¾ OZ. IRISH WHISKEY
- ¾ OZ. IRISH CREAM

THE ROCK

Place the ingredients in a pint glass and stir to combine.

INGREDIENTS:

- 6 OZ. MILWAUKEE'S BEST (OR OTHER INEXPENSIVE BEER)
- 1 OZ. WHISK(E)Y
- 1 OZ. RUM

BLACK VELVET

Pour the Champagne into a mason jar or pint glass and add the splash of sparkling cider. Pour the stout over the back of a spoon to layer it on top of the Champagne.

INGREDIENTS:

- 1 PART CHAMPAGNE
- SPLASH OF SPARKLING CIDER
- 1 PART STOUT

LEMON COOLER

GARNISH: 1 LEMON SLICE

Place the ingredients in a mason jar filled with ice, stir until combined, and garnish with the slice of lemon.

INGREDIENTS:

- 8 OZ. MASON JAR SHANDY (SEE PAGE 632)
- 1 OZ. WHISK(E)Y
- SPOONFUL OF HONEY
- DASH OF LEMON JUICE

CRANBERRY SHANDY

Place the syrup and beer in a pilsner glass and stir gently until combined.

CRANBERRY SHANDY SYRUP

Place all of the ingredients in a medium saucepan and bring to a boil over medium-high heat. After mixture begins to boil, reduce heat to a simmer and stir continuously with a wooden spoon, while gently pressing down on the cranberries until they have broken down. Cook until mixture has reduced by half and remove from heat. Strain through cheesecloth, let cool, and store in the refrigerator for up to 1 week.

INGREDIENTS:

- 2 OZ. CRANBERRY SHANDY SYRUP (SEE RECIPE BELOW)
- 12 OZ. BEER (IPA PREFERRED)

CRANBERRY SHANDY SYRUP:

- 12 OZ. FRESH CRANBERRIES
- 1½ CUPS WATER
- ¾ CUP WHITE SUGAR
- ¼ CUP LIME JUICE
- 1 LEMON PEEL

MASON JAR SHANDY

GARNISH: 1 LEMON WEDGE

Place the beer in a mason jar and top with the lemonade. Add ice, if desired, and garnish with the lemon wedge.

Tip: Wheat beers, lagers, and pilsners are the best choices for this particular preparation.

INGREDIENTS:

- 2 PARTS BEER
- 1 PART LEMONADE

FALL SHANDY

GARNISH: DUSTING OF NUTMEG

Place the beer and apple cider in a pint glass or mason jar, gently stir to combine, and garnish with the nutmeg.

INGREDIENTS:

- 2 PARTS PUMPKIN BEER
- 1 PART APPLE CIDER

BERMUDA BEER RUM

GARNISH: 1 LEMON WHEEL & 1 CHERRY

Place all of the cocktail ingredients, except for the pale ale, in a cocktail shaker filled with ice and shake vigorously. Strain into a highball glass filled with ice, top with the pale ale, and garnish with the lemon wheel and cherry skewered on a cocktail pick.

INGREDIENTS:

- 1½ OZ. GOSLING'S DARK RUM
- ½ OZ. AMARO DI ANGOSTURA
- ½ OZ. LEMON JUICE
- ½ OZ. CARPANO ANTICA
- ½ OZ. SIMPLE SYRUP
- THE BRONX BREWERY PALE ALE (OR YOUR FAVORITE PALE ALE), TO TOP

BOILERMAKER

It doesn't get much simpler than a shot and a beer, unless you drop the shot in the beer and drink it all at once, and if the shot is of whisk(e)y, then it's a Boilermaker. There are two popular, competing stories about the drink's origin. Both have to do with steam-powered locomotion, which makes sense. First, there is the tale of inventor Richard Trevitchik in Cornwall, England; legend has it that after a successful evening of testing out a steam-powered vehicle that he'd built, he went to celebrate at the pub, but in his haste neglected to extinguish the fire in his vehicle's boiler and when he returned everything had burned. A more plausible, and general, story is that factory workers fresh off their shifts ordered a shot of whisk(e)y and a pint of beer at their local, and the combination was named after what these hardworking men spent all day making.

THE BUTTERMAKER

In the opening scene of the 1976 classic *The Bad News Bears*, down-and-out Morris Buttermaker, played by Walter Matthau, parks his beat-up Cadillac convertible, opens a can of Budweiser, and adds some Jim Beam before taking a sip of what today pop culture has dubbed a Buttermaker Boilermaker. Over the course of the movie, the kids on the team Buttermaker coaches call him "Boilermaker." Between the casual treatment of alcoholism and the overall inappropriateness of the interactions between kids and adults, this movie could never be made today, but it's well worth watching, and it doesn't hurt to hoist a Buttermaker or two while taking it in.

INGREDIENTS:

1 (12 OZ.) CAN OF BEER

1 OZ. WHISK(E)Y

Pour the beer into a pint glass, drop a shot glass containing the whisk(e)y in, and drink immediately.

IPA OVER ICE

GARNISH: 1 ORANGE WEDGE

Place the juice, Campari, and simple syrup in a cocktail shaker filled with ice and shake vigorously. Strain into a pint glass filled with ice, top with the beer, and garnish with the orange wedge.

INGREDIENTS:

- 3 OZ. GRAPEFRUIT JUICE
- 1 OZ. CAMPARI
- DASH OF SIMPLE SYRUP
- 8 OZ. IPA

VEZA SUR SHOOT THE MOON

GARNISH: 1 MINT LEAF

Campari Syrup: In a saucepan, combine 1 cup water and 1 cup sugar. Cook over medium heat, while stirring occasionally, until all of the sugar is dissolved. Bring to a boil, and then reduce to a simmer for 5 minutes. Remove from heat and add 1 tablespoon Campari. Cool to room temperature and store in the refrigerator.

Place the syrup, lemon juice, guava puree, and mint leaves in a pint glass and muddle. Add ice and the beer, stir to combine, and garnish with the additional mint leaf.

INGREDIENTS:

- ¾ OZ. CAMPARI SYRUP
- ½ OZ. FRESH LEMON JUICE
- ¼ OZ. GUAVA PUREE
- 8 MINT LEAVES
- 8 OZ. SOUR BEER

STOUT 'N' CIDER

Place the hard cider in a pint glass and then slowly pour the stout over the back of a spoon to layer it on top.

INGREDIENTS:

- 8 OZ. HARD CIDER
- 8 OZ. STOUT

HAZE FOR DAYS

GARNISH: 1 ORANGE SLICE

Place the cocktail ingredients in a pint glass, stir to combine, and garnish with the orange slice.

INGREDIENTS:

- 8 OZ. PREFERRED NEW ENGLAND IPA
- 1 OZ. WHITE RUM
- 1 OZ. TRIPLE SEC

VEZA
SUR

FESTIVE DRINKS

As you may have guessed, I'm currently located in the Northeast of the United States. Specifically, I'm in New York City. Warm drinks for me have generally been of the Irish Coffee variety, except during the holidays where other drinks, like Hot Buttered Rum, might pop up at a party or family gathering. So this chapter combines warm drinks with holiday cocktails (since all of these recipes will warm the souls of you and yours, which is what the holidays are all about).

As the Northeast of the U. S. has some iteration of the four seasons (I must say that in my "old age" I've noticed that spring and fall seem shorter somehow, and perhaps these seasons are a figment of my imagination at this point), warm drinks have tended to be a thing I look forward to in cooler weather. They are also something I don't drink alone, with the exception of the Hot Toddy, which is good any time of year because as we all know, colds suck. I'm quite happy to consider the Hot Toddy as much a part of getting rid of a cold as any another medicine. They certainly taste better than Theraflu and Mucinex.

That said, warm drinks are more than pouring whisk(e)y into your hot chocolate. I mean, it's a warm drink if you pour brandy into your coffee, but is it the best warm drink you can make?

That's where we come in. The recipes that follow will help you improve your warm drink skills. They will give you a few new twists on old favorites or hip you to drinks you've never heard of that will soon become new favorites.

Favorite cocktail: I have to go with the Hot Toddy. It's an angel of mercy in my times of need.

WARM DRINKS

Romans started the tradition of heating up wine to fend off a cold back in the 2nd century, bestowing to the world, through hostile takeovers, the worthy tradition of mulled wine. Easy to make for a large group and wonderfully adaptable, it seems that various spices were added to the drink throughout Europe during the Middle Ages. Claret—Rhen wine, sugar, honey, and spices—and Lutendrank—wine, milk, and spices—became hugely popular in Sweden. In England, in the 1700s, mulled wine was politicized in the form of hot drinks called "ecclesiastics." Using ecclesiastical titles these hot drinks, not-so-subtle rebukes of the Roman Catholic Church, had names like the Smoking Bishop and the Smoking Pope, depending on the type of wine called for (the more expensive and rare, the higher up the hierarchy).

HOT TODDY

GARNISH: 1 LEMON SLICE & 1 CINNAMON STICK

Place the bourbon, honey, and lemon juice in a mug, pour the boiling water over it, and stir to combine. Garnish with the slice of lemon.

INGREDIENTS:

- 1 OZ. BOURBON
- 1 TABLESPOON HONEY
- 2 TEASPOONS LEMON JUICE
- ½ CUP BOILING WATER

APPLE PIE TODDY

GARNISH: GRATED NUTMEG

Place the simple syrup, applejack, and baked apple half in a mug, top with the boiling water, and garnish with the nutmeg.

INGREDIENTS:

- 1 TEASPOON SIMPLE SYRUP
- 6 OZ. APPLEJACK
- ½ OF A BAKED APPLE
- BOILING WATER, TO TOP

HOT TODDY MARGARITA

GARNISH: 1 CINNAMON STICK & 1 TO 2 WHOLE CLOVES

Combine the tequila, orange liqueur, agave nectar, lime juice, and orange juice in an insulated glass. Top with the hot water and garnish with the cinnamon stick and cloves.

INGREDIENTS:

- 2 OZ. AÑEJO TEQUILA
- ¾ OZ. ORANGE LIQUEUR
- ½ OZ. AGAVE NECTAR
- ¼ OZ. FRESH LIME JUICE
- ¼ OZ. FRESH ORANGE JUICE
- 1 OZ. VERY HOT WATER (170°F)

LADY MACBETH'S SECRET RECIPE

GARNISH: 1 LEMON TWIST

Earl Grey Syrup: Place 3 teabags of Earl Grey in a standard simple syrup after it removing it from heat. Let steep for 20 minutes and remove the tea bags before using.

Place the whiskey, cider, syrup, and lemon juice in a warm mug and stir. Add the splash of hot water, stir, top with the sparkling wine, and garnish with the lemon twist.

INGREDIENTS:

- ½ OZ. EARL GREY SYRUP
- 1½ OZ. KNAPPOGUE CASTLE 12 YEAR OLD SINGLE MALT IRISH WHISKEY
- 3 OZ. APPLE CIDER
- ½ OZ. LEMON JUICE
- SPLASH OF VERY HOT WATER (170°F)
- 2 OZ. SPARKLING WINE

HOT BUTTERED RUM

GARNISH: 1 CINNAMON STICK

Muddle the butter, brown sugar, cinnamon, nutmeg, and orange zest in the bottom of an Irish coffee glass to create a spiced butter mixture. Make sure the ingredients are thoroughly mixed, then add the vanilla extract. Add the hot water, rum, and allspice, stir to combine, and garnish with the cinnamon stick.

Variations:

✦ Some variations eliminate the allspice, while others forgo the vanilla extract and orange zest. It's simply a matter of how complex you want the flavor of the drink to be. If you're happy with nothing more than butter and cinnamon, then by all means go for it.

✦ Some prefer to make the spiced butter mixture in large batches and refrigerate it for later. This will allow you to easily make Hot Buttered Rum at a moment's notice, rather than having to mix butter and spices for every drink. Hold off on the vanilla extract, and you'll be ready to go in either of two ways: Hot Buttered Rum or Virgin Hot Buttered Rum (see page 711).

INGREDIENTS:

- 1 PAT OF BUTTER
- 1 TEASPOON BROWN SUGAR
- DASH OF CINNAMON
- DASH OF NUTMEG
- DASH OF ORANGE ZEST
- SPLASH OF VANILLA EXTRACT
- 6 OZ. VERY HOT WATER (170°F)
- 2 OZ. DARK RUM
- DASH OF ALLSPICE

BRENNE CHAI TODDY

GARNISH: 1 CINNAMON STICK & 1 STAR ANISE POD

Place the whisky, tea, and honey in a mug, stir to combine, and garnish with the cinnamon stick and star anise.

INGREDIENTS:

- 2 OZ. BRENNE SINGLE MALT WHISKY
- ¼ CUP CHAI TEA, HOT
- ½ TABLESPOON HONEY

ARCTIC WARMER

GARNISH: 1 OR 2 CINNAMON STICKS

Use a bag of your favorite tea to make a serving of tea in a mason jar. Add the butter. When the butter is melted, add the vodka, tequila, and cinnamon and stir until thoroughly combined. Garnish with a cinnamon stick or two.

INGREDIENTS:

4 PARTS HOT TEA
BUTTER, TO TASTE
2 PARTS VODKA
1 PART TEQUILA
DASH OF CINNAMON

MRS. CLAUS'S APPLE CIDER

GARNISH: MINT LEAVES

Place the cocktail ingredients in a cocktail shaker filled with crushed ice and shake until chilled. Strain into a shot glass and garnish with the mint leaves, if desired.

INGREDIENTS:

1 OZ. SPICED RUM
½ OZ. APPLE SCHNAPPS
½ OZ. CINNAMON SCHNAPPS
SPLASH OF LEMON-LIME SODA

VIN CHAUD

GARNISH: CINNAMON STICKS

Place all of the cocktail ingredients, except for the Cognac, in a saucepan and bring to a simmer. Remove from heat, add the Cognac, pour into mugs, and garnish with cinnamon sticks.

Tip: If you'd prefer something other than Cognac, pear eau de vie and Calvados are solid alternatives.

INGREDIENTS:

1 (750 ML) BOTTLE OF INEXPENSIVE RED WINE (COTES DU RHONE OR BORDEAUX PREFERRED)
1 STAR ANISE POD
2 PIECES OF GINGER (FRESH OR CANDIED)
3 CLOVES
2 CARDAMOM PODS
1 TABLESPOON ORANGE ZEST
1 TABLESPOON LEMON ZEST
½ CUP HONEY
½ CUP COGNAC

'TIS THE SEASONTINI

GARNISH: DUSTING OF CINNAMON (OPTIONAL)

Cinnamon Water: Place a cinnamon stick and 1 teaspoon of sugar in a cup of boiling water and steep for 30 minutes. Discard the cinnamon stick before using.

Place the cocktail ingredients in a cocktail shaker filled with ice and shake until chilled. Strain into a cocktail glass and garnish with the dusting of cinnamon, if desired.

INGREDIENTS:

- 1 TEASPOON CINNAMON WATER
- 1½ OZ. QUALITY VODKA
- 1 OZ. FRESH LIME JUICE
- 1 OZ. FRESH ORANGE JUICE
- ¼ OZ. GRAND MARNIER

CANCUN COFFEE

Add tequila and coffee liqueur to an Irish Coffee glass. Top with coffee. Finish with a splash of cream liqueur and stir until thoroughly mixed.

INGREDIENTS:

- 1 PART TEQUILA
- 1 PART COFFEE LIQUEUR
- 2 PARTS COFFEE
- SPLASH OF CREAM LIQUEUR

CUBAN COFFEE

Pour the rum and coffee into an Irish Coffee glass. Add a spoonful of sugar and the cream liqueur. Stir again until thoroughly mixed.

INGREDIENTS:

- 1 PART DARK CUBAN RUM
- 3 PARTS COFFEE
- 1 SPOONFUL OF SUGAR
- SPLASH OF CREAM LIQUEUR

CRANBERRY SPICE

GARNISH: 2 FRESH CRANBERRIES (OPTIONAL)

Place the cocktail ingredients in a cocktail shaker filled with ice and shake until chilled. Strain into a shot glass and garnish with cranberries, if desired.

INGREDIENTS:

- ¼ OZ. CHAMBORD
- ½ OZ. DOMAINE DE CANTON
- ¼ OZ. CABERNET SAUVIGNON
- 1 OZ. CRANBERRY JUICE

LEMON CHAMPAGNE FIZZ

GARNISH: 1 LEMON WEDGE

Combine the gin, lemon juice, and sugar in a cocktail shaker filled with crushed ice and shake vigorously. Strain into a shot glass, top with the Champagne, and garnish with the lemon wedge.

INGREDIENTS:

- ½ OZ. GIN
- ⅓ OZ. LEMON JUICE
- PINCH OF CASTER SUGAR
- 1 OZ. CHAMPAGNE

CHRISTMAS CRANBERRY MARGARITA SHOTS

GARNISH: CRANBERRIES

Wet the rims of shot glasses and dip them into a dish of sugar. Place the remaining ingredients in a large blender and puree until smooth. Pour the mixture into the shot glasses and garnish with the additional cranberries.

Tip: If you don't have a blender that will fit all of the ingredients at once, combine them in a bowl and add the mixture to your blender in batches.

INGREDIENTS:

- ½ CUP SUGAR, PLUS MORE FOR THE RIMS
- ¾ CUP TEQUILA
- ½ CUP GRAND MARNIER OR ANOTHER ORANGE LIQUEUR
- 1½ CUPS CRANBERRY JUICE
- ¾ CUP FRESH LIME JUICE
- 1½ CUPS FROZEN CRANBERRIES, RINSED
- 1 CUP ICE

EVERGREEN PINE

Pour the Dr. Pepper into a pint glass, drop a shot glass containing the gin into the glass, and drink immediately.

INGREDIENTS:

- 1 (12 OZ.) CAN OF DR. PEPPER
- 1 OZ. LONDON DRY GIN

THE TWELFTH NIGHT

GARNISH: MINT LEAVES

Place the vodka, triple sec, and white cranberry juice in a cocktail shaker filled with crushed ice and shake until chilled. Strain into a tall shot glass, add the lime juice and the soda, and garnish with the mint leaves.

INGREDIENTS:

- 1 OZ. ABSOLUT CITRON
- ½ OZ. TRIPLE SEC
- ½ OZ. WHITE CRANBERRY JUICE
- SPLASH OF FRESH LIME JUICE
- SPLASH OF LEMON-LIME SODA

SANTA'S SUIT

Wet the rim of a shot glass and dip it into the sugar. Place the remaining ingredients in a cocktail shaker filled with ice, shake until chilled, and strain into the shot glass.

INGREDIENTS:

- SUGAR, FOR THE RIM
- ½ OZ. COINTREAU
- ½ OZ. CHAMBORD
- ½ OZ. CRANBERRY JUICE

NEW YEAR'S DAY MIMOSA

Pour half of the orange liqueur into a bowl. Dip the rims of shot glasses or champagne flutes into the liqueur, and then dip them into the sugar. Place the remaining orange liqueur, Champagne, and orange juice in a pitcher, stir gently, and pour it into the rimmed glasses.

INGREDIENTS:

- ½ CUP GRAND MARNIER
- SUGAR, FOR THE RIMS
- 1 (750 ML) BOTTLE OF BRUT CHAMPAGNE, CHILLED
- 1 CUP FRESH ORANGE JUICE

AULD LANG SHOOTER

Place the ingredients in a cocktail shaker filled with ice, shake until chilled, and strain into a shot glass.

INGREDIENTS:

- ½ OZ. CHAMPAGNE, CHILLED
- ½ OZ. COINTREAU
- ½ OZ. BRANDY
- ½ OZ. SODA WATER, CHILLED

THREE WISE MEN

Place the ingredients in a cocktail shaker filled with ice, shake until chilled, and strain into a shot glass.

Variation: Add ½ oz. Wild Turkey bourbon to make this the popular Three Wise Men Go Hunting.

INGREDIENTS:

- ½ OZ. JIM BEAM BOURBON
- ½ OZ. JACK DANIEL'S OLD NO. 7
- ½ OZ. JOHNNIE WALKER SCOTCH WHISKY

BRANDIED EGGNOG

GARNISH: GRATED NUTMEG

Place the cocktail ingredients in a cocktail shaker filled with ice and shake vigorously. Strain into four shot glasses and garnish with the nutmeg.

INGREDIENTS:

- ¼ OZ. SIMPLE SYRUP
- 1½ OZ. BRANDY
- ¼ OZ. TAWNY PORT
- 3½ OZ. MILK
- ¾ OZ. HEAVY CREAM
- 1 EGG YOLK

COFFEE EGGNOG

GARNISH: DUSTING OF CINNAMON

Combine the cocktail ingredients in a blender and puree until smooth. Pour into a chilled Hurricane glass or divide between shot glasses, and then garnish with the cinnamon.

INGREDIENTS:

- 1 TEASPOON SIMPLE SYRUP
- 2 OZ. SCOTCH WHISKY
- 1 OZ. KAHLUA
- 6 OZ. MILK
- 1 OZ. HALF-AND-HALF
- ½ TEASPOON INSTANT COFFEE
- 1 EGG
- 1 CUP ICE

BALTIMORE EGGNOG

GARNISH: GRATED NUTMEG

Place the egg yolks and sugar in a bowl and beat until the mixture is thick. Stir in the Cognac, rum, peach brandy or Madeira, milk, and cream. Refrigerate until thoroughly chilled. Right before serving, beat the egg whites until they are stiff. Transfer the egg yolk-and-alcohol mixture to a chilled punch bowl and then fold in the egg whites. Do not stir. Serve in cocktail glasses or shot glasses and garnish with the nutmeg.

INGREDIENTS:

- 12 EGGS, YOLKS AND WHITES SEPARATED
- 2 CUPS CASTER SUGAR
- 2 CUPS COGNAC
- 1 CUP DARK RUM
- 1 CUP PEACH BRANDY OR MADEIRA
- 6 CUPS MILK
- 2 CUPS HEAVY CREAM

GENERAL HARRISON'S EGGNOG

GARNISH: GRATED NUTMEG & MARASCHINO CHERRIES (OPTIONAL)

Place the cocktail ingredients in a blender and puree until smooth. Pour into a Hurricane glass or divide between four shot glasses. Garnish with nutmeg and, if desired, maraschino cherries.

INGREDIENTS:

- 1 TEASPOON SIMPLE SYRUP
- 1 EGG
- 1 CUP HARD CIDER
- 1 CUP ICE

CLASSIC EGGNOG

GARNISH: GRATED NUTMEG

Eggnog is one of those drinks you either love or hate. But no matter your personal preference, all can agree that the holiday season is when folks break out their punch bowls to serve up some spiced and spiked milky goodness. The origins of eggnog reach back to the 13th century, when British monks regularly drank Posset, which, according to the *Oxford English Dictionary*, was "a drink made of hot milk curdled with ale, wine, or the like, often sweetened and spiced." It is likely that the monks also came up with the idea of adding eggs. Versions of such eggy concoctions spread from there. In Holland, *advocaat* (often called Dutch Eggnog) featured brandy and vodka, and while served in a glass the custardy creation is better suited for being eaten with a spoon. Unsurprisingly, Germans added beer to the mix for *biersuppe*. Spanish explorers brought their own takes to the New World, where they were further adapted; in Puerto Rico *coquito* is served with coconut milk and in Mexico *rompope* incorporates almonds. The abundance of chickens and cows on farms in the American colonies solidified the core ingredients of eggnog as we know it today, especially since Sherry and brandy were not as easy to come by as whiskey and rum. The role of eggnog in holiday festivities is likely tied to the fact that spices like nutmeg and vanilla were exotic ingredients only used for special occasions.

THE EGGNOG RIOT

At West Point, it had been a tradition amongst the cadets to celebrate Christmas with homemade eggnog, which previous superintendents ignored, happy to let their students unwind from the rigors of military education. But in 1826, the newly installed Colonel Sylvanus Thayer strictly forbade the cadets from possessing, let alone consuming, alcoholic beverages. Approximately 70 cadets decided to challenge their commanding officer's orders and had such a rip-roaring good time that 2 officers were assaulted and the windows of the North Barracks were smashed. The so-called "Eggnog Riot" resulted in 19 court-martials; of those cadets, some were expelled and ultimately only 2 remained at West Point. For the history buffs out there, both Robert E. Lee and Jefferson Davis were at West Point at this time, and both testified on behalf of their fellow cadets (though only Davis had indulged in the festivities).

INGREDIENTS:

- 6 EGGS, BEATEN UNTIL FROTHY
- ½ TEASPOON VANILLA EXTRACT
- ¼ TEASPOON NUTMEG, GRATED
- 1 CUP SUGAR, PLUS 1 TABLESPOON
- ¾ CUP BRANDY
- ⅓ CUP DARK RUM
- 2 CUPS HEAVY CREAM
- 2 CUPS MILK

Whisk the vanilla, nutmeg, sugar, brandy, rum, cream, and milk into the beaten eggs. When thoroughly combined, chill in the refrigerator until ready to serve. Pour into rocks glasses or shot glasses and garnish with the additional nutmeg when serving.

PISTE VERTE

GARNISH: MINT LEAVES

Place the cocktail ingredients in a cocktail shaker filled with ice and shake vigorously. Strain into a wine glass and garnish with the mint leaves.

INGREDIENTS:

- 2 TEASPOONS HONEY SYRUP
- 1 OZ. MAMONT VODKA
- 1 OZ. LIQUEUR DE SAPIN DOLIN
- 1 OZ. FRESH CLEMENTINE JUICE
- ½ OZ. FRESH LEMON JUICE

CHARTREUSE MULE

Pour the Chartreuse and lemon juice into a rocks glass filled with ice and top with the splash of ginger beer.

INGREDIENTS:

- 1 OZ. CHARTREUSE
- 2 TEASPOONS FRESH LEMON JUICE
- SPLASH OF GINGER BEER

CRANBERRY SPARKLER

GARNISH: 1 TO 2 CRANBERRIES

Place the liqueur and Cocchi Americano in a mixing glass filled with ice and stir until chilled. Strain into a chilled champagne flute, top with the Champagne or Crémant, and garnish with 1 or 2 cranberries.

INGREDIENTS:

- ½ OZ. BRIOTTET CRANBERRY LIQUEUR
- 2 TEASPOONS COCCHI AMERICANO
- 2 OZ. CHAMPAGNE OR CRÉMANT

FELIZ NAVIDAD

GARNISH: 4 TO 5 POMEGRANATE SEEDS

Place the cocktail ingredients in a cocktail shaker filled with ice and shake until chilled. Strain into a chilled rocks glass filled with ice and garnish with the pomegranate seeds.

INGREDIENTS:

- ½ OZ. EDMOND BRIOTTET LIQUER DE GRENADE (POMEGRANATE LIQUEUR)
- 1 OZ. TEQUILA OCHO PLATA
- 1 TABLESPOON ORANGE LIQUEUR
- 2 TEASPOONS LIME JUICE

EDUCATION SENTIMENTALE

GARNISH: 2 TO 3 APPLE SLICES

Chestnut-Honey Syrup: Add ½ pound of peeled, whole chestnuts to a standard honey syrup after it has come to a boil. Reduce heat so that the mixture simmers and cook until the chestnuts are translucent but still firm, about 25 minutes. Remove from heat, let cool completely, and strain before using.

Place all of the cocktail ingredients, except for the hard cider, in a cocktail shaker filled with ice and shake vigorously. Strain into a brandy snifter filled with crushed ice, top with the cider, and add more ice so that the glass is nearly overflowing. Garnish with a few slices of apple.

Tip: If you do not have any Domaine de Canton on hand, a piece of crushed ginger will suffice.

INGREDIENTS:

- ½ OZ. CHESTNUT-HONEY SYRUP
- 1¾ OZ. HIGH-QUALITY CALVADOS (CHRISTIAN DROUIN PREFERRED)
- ½ OZ. FRESH LEMON JUICE
- 1 TABLESPOON DOMAINE DE CANTON
- PINCH OF CINNAMON POWDER
- HARD CIDER, TO TOP

AND A PARROT IN A PALM TREE

GARNISH: 1 CINNAMON STICK & 1 ORCHID BLOSSOM

Spiced Coconut Syrup: In a small saucepan, combine 1 cup coconut water, 1 cup demerara sugar, 3 cinnamon sticks, 5 cloves, 5 allspice berries, and 3 cardamom pods. Cook over low heat, while stirring, until the sugar has dissolved and the mixture is thick enough to coat the back of a wooden spoon. Remove from heat, let cool, and strain before using.

Place the cocktail ingredients in a cocktail shaker filled with ice and shake vigorously. Strain into a highball glass filled with crushed ice and garnish with the cinnamon stick and orchid blossom.

INGREDIENTS:

- 2 OZ. SPICED COCONUT SYRUP
- 1½ OZ. REPOSADO TEQUILA
- ½ OZ. ILEGAL MEZCAL JOVEN
- ½ OZ. PIERRE FERRAND DRY CURAÇAO
- 1 OZ. LIME JUICE

CHRISTMAS MARTINI

GARNISH: 1 PEPPERMINT

Place the gin, vermouth, and schnapps in a mixing glass filled with ice and stir until well combined. Wet the rim of the cocktail glass, and then dip it into the crumbled candy cane. Strain the contents of the cocktail shaker into the cocktail glass and garnish with a peppermint.

INGREDIENTS:

- 3 PARTS GIN
- 1 PART DRY VERMOUTH
- 1 PART PEPPERMINT SCHNAPPS
- CANDY CANE CRUMBLES, FOR THE RIM

CHRISTMAPOLITAN

Place the ingredients in a cocktail shaker filled with ice and shake vigorously. Strain into a coupe and tie the red ribbon around the stem.

INGREDIENTS:

- 1½ OZ. VODKA
- 1 OZ. ST-GERMAIN
- 1 OZ. CRANBERRY SAUCE
- ½ OZ. FRESH LIME JUICE
- 2 DASHES OF FIG BITTERS
- DASH OF TABASCO
- 1 RED RIBBON, FOR THE STEM

GIN CHRISTMAS

GARNISH: 1 PEPPERMINT STICK & 1 LEMON SLICE

Add the gin, cranberry simple syrup, and lemon juice to a mason jar and stir. Add the tea, stir, and garnish with the peppermint stick and slice of lemon.

INGREDIENTS:

- 2 OZ. GIN
- 1 OZ. CRANBERRY SIMPLE SYRUP (SEE PAGE 149, SUBSTITUTE CRANBERRIES FOR BLUEBERRIES)
- JUICE OF ½ LEMON
- 6 OZ. MINT TEA, HOT

CLOVER CLUB

LA PERLA ROSA

GARNISH: 2 SPRIGS OF MINT & 1 LEMON TWIST

Place the cocktail ingredients in a blender and puree until smooth. Pour into a highball glass and garnish with the additional sprigs of mint and the lemon twist.

INGREDIENTS:

- 1½ OZ. SILVER TEQUILA
- ¾ OZ. LEMON JUICE
- 1 OZ. PEACH NECTAR
- HANDFUL OF SPRIGS OF MINT
- 2 DASHES OF ANGOSTURA BITTERS
- 1 CUP ICE

REMEMBER THE MAINE

GARNISH: 1 LEMON TWIST

Place the cocktail ingredients in a mixing glass filled with ice and stir until chilled. Strain into a chilled coupe and garnish with the lemon twist.

INGREDIENTS:

- 1½ OZ. RYE WHISKEY
- ¾ OZ. SWEET VERMOUTH
- 1 TEASPOON PETER HEERING CHERRY LIQUEUR
- DASH OF ABSINTHE
- DASH OF PEYCHAUD'S BITTERS

PENNY LANE

GARNISH: 3 BRANDY-SOAKED CHERRIES

Place the cocktail ingredients in a cocktail shaker filled with ice and shake vigorously. Strain into a chilled glass and garnish with the brandy-soaked cherries skewered on a cocktail pick.

INGREDIENTS:

- 1½ OZ. TEELING IRISH WHISKEY
- 1 OZ. SIMPLE SYRUP
- ½ OZ. OLOROSO SHERRY
- ½ OZ. FRESH LEMON JUICE
- ¼ OZ. CAPPELLETTI APERITIVO AMERICANO ROSSO
- ¼ OZ. LUXARDO
- 2 DASHES OF ORANGE BLOSSOM WATER
- 2 DASHES OF GRAPEFRUIT BITTERS

THE SPICY STANDISH

GARNISH: TANGERINE SLICES & LEMON WHEELS

Spiced Syrup: In a small saucepan, combine 1 cup water, 1 cup demerara sugar, 3 cinnamon sticks, 5 cloves, 5 allspice berries, and 3 cardamom pods. Cook over low heat, while stirring, until the sugar has dissolved and the mixture is thick enough to coat the back of a wooden spoon. Remove from heat, let cool, and strain before using.

Place the ingredients for the punch in a large punch bowl, stir until combined, and garnish with the tangerine slices and lemon wheels. Just before serving, add a large block of ice. Ladle into rocks glasses or teacups.

INGREDIENTS:

- 1/3 CUP SPICED SYRUP
- 4 (12 OZ.) BOTTLES OF PEAR CIDER
- 2 CUPS BRANDY
- 3/4 CUP AGED RUM
- 2 (12 OZ.) BOTTLES OF SPICY GINGER BEER
- 2 DASHES OF PEYCHAUD'S BITTERS

GATH'RING WINTER FUEL

GARNISH: CRANBERRIES AND RASPBERRIES

Hibiscus Syrup: In a small saucepan, combine 1 cup water, ½ cup hibiscus flowers (if you cannot locate dried hibiscus, remove the tea from 6 bags of hibiscus tea), 1 cinnamon stick, 5 whole cloves, 5 allspice berries, and 1 vanilla pod (split) and bring to a boil over medium heat. Remove from heat and let steep for 15 to 20 minutes. Strain, discard the solids, and return the liquid to the pan. Bring to a boil over medium heat, add an equal part sugar, and stir until the sugar is dissolved. Reduce to a simmer and cook until the mixture is syrupy. Remove from heat, let cool, and store in the refrigerator for up to 10 days.

Place the ingredients for the punch in a large punch bowl and stir to combine. Just before serving, add a large block of ice and the berries. Ladle into wine glasses or champagne flutes.

INGREDIENTS:

- 4 OZ. HIBISCUS SYRUP, PLUS MORE TO TASTE
- 2 (750 ML) BOTTLES OF SPARKLING WINE
- 1 (375 ML) BOTTLE OF AGED RUM OR COGNAC
- 6 OZ. ORANGE LIQUEUR
- 2–3 DASHES OF PEYCHAUD'S BITTERS

BATCH COCKTAILS

Making batch cocktails is an art, so heed this advice: start by using the recipe to make a drink for yourself (bartender's privilege) before you make the batch. That way you can tweak the recipe as needed for your taste and for your event and you won't waste any ingredients.

FLASK COCKTAILS

I've been a proud owner of a flask for over a decade. My first one was picked up at a rummage sale and since then I've acquired a few as gifts from friends. I love them just like I love cars and computers and just like those two possessions, they can be a pain in the ass—especially when it comes to maintaining them. It's hard to clean the nooks and crannies of a flask and there are times when soap and water and hard shakes don't quite cut it.

I often take a flask to parties. It's going to be hard not to sound like a snob so I won't even try to avoid it. My take is that since you rarely know what is going to be poured at a party, it seems a wise decision to bring a little something as backup. If the drink options are great, that flask might just be a warming nip of something on my way home. If the drink options are substandard, well . . . at least I can start the night with something nice.

That said, take this bit of wisdom from a longtime flask owner—the contents of a flask can and should be shared. Truth be told, I'd rather share the contents with cool folks at a party than take a nip alone.

So as a public service, we hip you (pun intended) to how to maintain your flask and better ways to put it to use. I can honestly say that I wish I had this info when I got my first one.

Favorite cocktail: It's between the Frisco and the Sidecar. Both are perfect for my flask usage—they'll help you keep warm when outside in the winter, and they have some lemon (need that citrus). But if I had to choose—Sidecar.

A BRIEF HISTORY OF THE FLASK

In a broad sense, a flask is anything that can be used to transport liquids, meaning flasks have been around since cavemen decided it was a good idea to carry water with them while hunting. Early flasks were made of animal skins and bladders (sometimes literally the bladder, and sometimes the stomach). The skins would be cured and sealed using beeswax to make them sturdy and keep them watertight.

In pre-Christian times, many temples and holy sites had a special spring or pool visitors could bathe in or drink from to help with health, wealth, or other cosmic issues. Available for purchase were small ceramic flasks with an image of the patron god or goddess so that visitors could bring some of those special waters home with them. The temple gained a source of income from the souvenir flasks. The worshippers would display their empty flasks to show their devotion. Roman coliseums had an even more direct income stream from flasks. They would sell molded wine-filled clay flasks adorned with images of famous gladiators. Not too different from commemorative cup day at the ballpark.

Around the 1600s, the clothing styles of the day provided men with internal pockets so that instead of carrying a purse tied to the belt, valuables could be kept hidden and more secure. As luck would have it, it was around this time that distilled alcohol was leaving the alchemist's laboratory and making its way to the common man. The improved distillation techniques made distilled alcohol safer and cheaper, and popular beverages such as whisk(e)y, vodka, rum, and gin started to appear. Since this newfangled "hard liquor" was concentrated in its effects,

not as much volume was needed as would be the case with wine or beer. Soldiers were one large group eager to have a simple way to carry liquid courage with them at all times. Liquor could provide bravery before battle, could calm the nerves after battle, and could even be used as a disinfectant. In the days of muzzle-loading muskets, soldiers carried powder flasks, which were small metal or bone containers used to carry gunpowder. Soldiers must have quickly realized that an extra powder flask filled with gin was a welcome ration.

Flasks as we think of them today started to take shape in the 19th century. In the early 1800s, there was a sharp increase in glass production in the United States. Molten glass could be blown into metal molds to quickly produce flasks of different designs, colors, and sizes, all at very reasonable prices. These flasks had thick sides and were shaped like flattened eggs, which made it easy to fit them in a pocket. Also popular were flasks that rounded and curved to lie better against the hip or leg, giving rise to the hip flasks we recognize today. Glass flasks could be purchased at taverns or general stores filled with whisk(e)y and then refilled from the shopkeeper's barrel. Flasks from this era were embossed with popular designs like patriotic eagles, flags, and stars, as well as images of famous people. These glass flasks were so cheap that they were often given out (filled of course!) to advertise anything from a liquor brand to a presidential candidate.

But now that flasks were so cheap, what was a poor aristocrat to do to show his status and wealth? The upper crust of society abandoned glass flasks in exchange for ones made from metal, the more precious the better. Even then, gold was deemed a bit too ostentatious, but silver was perfect. Silver also had the added benefit of improving the taste of the liquor. The rich led the charge in inventing flask elements that we take for granted today, including screw tops instead of corks to prevent leaks, and hinged tops so the screw cap didn't get lost. Even with such improvements, flasks were still considered an optional accessory. Sales of higher-end models stagnated until January 1920 when an event that made criminals out of many Americans occurred, giving them a very good reason to keep their liquor close and hidden.

Before Prohibition, the United States had a drinking problem. In the 1830s when glass flasks filled with whiskey were being handed out left and right, the average American over the age of 15 was drinking the equivalent of 90 bottles of 80 proof liquor per year, or an average of four shots a day. Something needed to be done, and for better or worse the idea at the time was an outright ban on the sale, production, and transportation of alcohol. The fabric of American culture changed almost overnight. Speakeasies became places where all Americans, including high-ranking government officials, came together over a shared passion for drinking. It is also remembered as the golden age of the flask. The *Washington Herald* reported in 1922: "Wholesale and retail dealers in silverware say that one bright spot in their business has been the demand for silver hip flasks. Hundreds of thousands have been bought for Christmas presents." Flasks became essential for anyone who wanted to consume alcohol outside the privacy of their own home. As Frank Kelly Rich writes in "Pocket Full of Joy: The Hip Flask Manifesto": "In the early days of Prohibition, before speakeasies began blossoming like desert roses, a flask wasn't just a thing to get you from one party to another, it was the party." Flasks also changed from the flashy display item a gentleman could casually produce to something that had to stay truly hidden. Thus, the start of the "novelty flask" or the flask that looked like anything but a flask. Flasks were being used by so many people that by the late 1920s local police could no longer

W. C. Fields made his career playing a hard-drinking scoundrel and apparently imitated the character he played in real life as well. Fields started his career as a vaudeville juggler and did not drink at all since it would interfere with his act. But his role as beer-guzzling, gyro pilot Professor Henry Quail in the 1933 movie *International House* gave him a reputation as a heavy drinker, and Fields began to inhabit the role in his personal life. Phil Silvers, who had minor roles in some of Fields's movies, tells a story of a flask-related incident during the filming of *Tales of Manhattan* in 1942 where the producers pleaded with Fields not to drink during shooting. Fields responded, "Gentlemen, this is only lemonade. For a little acid condition afflicting me." He then handed a flask to Silvers; it was pure gin.

be bothered to arrest someone they suspected of carrying one. It was assumed that everyone had a flask, so what was the point?

By 1933, it became clear that Prohibition was causing more problems than it solved, and it was repealed that December. After the repeal, there was no longer any reason to carry liquor around hidden in a flask. Flasks started to fade in popularity in all but a few small groups. Soldiers of course kept their flasks. On the silver screen, a private eye could be seen dragging out a flask and pouring a nip into his coffee. But the average American had left the flask behind. The cocktail or mixed drink had sprung up during Prohibition to mask the taste of poor quality liquor. Americans were exploring the cocktail craze, with elaborate Polynesian concoctions and various other mixed drinks utilizing the dizzying array of alcoholic products being introduced.

Many people are convinced that the flask is only for straight spirits: gin, vodka, bourbon, scotch, Cognac, brandy, etc. This was the tradition for many years, and may still possibly be the right thing for you. But today, one can make almost anything—there are no rules! One can make cocktails in a shaker, for instance, and pour the resulting drink into a flask. How about making yourself a Dirty Martini—just put in a few ice chips or leave

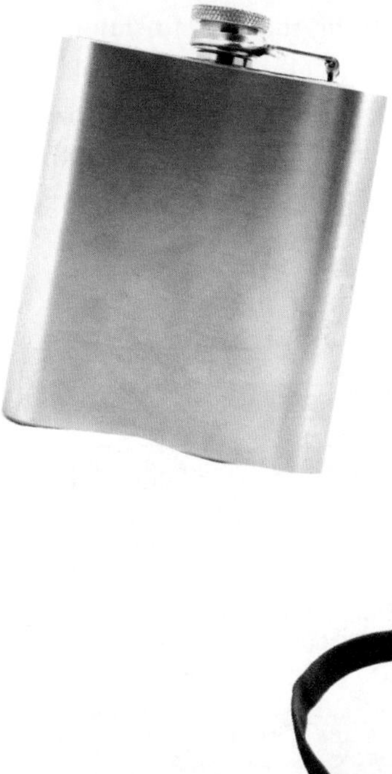

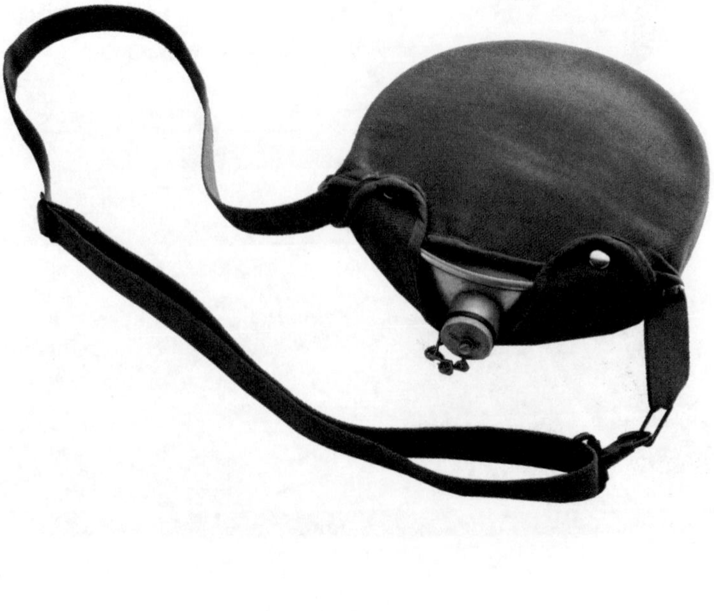

it near an ice pack while you travel. Or how about a Rob Roy, Manhattan, or Cosmo? Your imagination is the only thing stopping you.

FUNNELS

If you use a flask, you need to fill it and for that you will need a funnel. Some flasks come with funnels built in as part of the base or as part of a carrying case. Other models will include a small metal funnel with the purchase of the flask but the funnel is not attached or stored with the flask. Of course, a funnel can be quickly and easily crafted from a square of aluminum foil if a premade funnel is not available. The most ingenious funnels are the ones that not only are included with the flask but also are threaded so that they screw onto the top in place of the cap. These are great because the funnel won't tilt to the side or fall out while being used. But the best funnel is a simple, cheap one from a dollar store.

PAPA'S PET

Ernest Hemingway had a tall silver flask that he referred to by the name of "Jinny." Many have speculated that Jinny referred to Jinny Pfeiffer, the younger sister of Hemingway's second wife, Pauline. It was rumored that Hemingway was having an affair with Jinny, but there were also rumors that Jinny preferred the company of women. Hemingway writes of Jinny (his flask) in his semi-fictional biography *True at First Light*: "The Jinny flask was in one pocket of the old Spanish double cartridge pouches. It was a pint bottle of Gordon's we had bought at Sultan Hamud and it was named after another old famous silver flask that had finally opened its seams at too many thousand feet during a war and had caused me to believe for a moment that I had been hit in the buttocks."

ADMIRAL COCKTAIL

Combine ingredients in a cocktail shaker filled with ice, shake vigorously, and utilize a funnel to strain into a flask.

INGREDIENTS:

- 2 PARTS DRY GIN
- 1 PART PETER HEERING CHERRY LIQUEUR
- 1 PART FRESH LIME JUICE

ALASKA COCKTAIL

Combine ingredients in a cocktail shaker filled with ice, shake vigorously, and utilize a funnel to strain into a flask.

INGREDIENTS:

- 2 PARTS GIN
- 1 PART YELLOW CHARTREUSE
- 3 DASHES OF ORANGE BITTERS

AMERICANO

Place the Campari and vermouth in a mixing glass filled with ice, stir, and utilize a funnel to strain it into a flask. Top with the club soda.

INGREDIENTS:

- 1 PART CAMPARI
- 1 PART SWEET VERMOUTH
- 1 PART CLUB SODA

ASTORIA

Combine ingredients in a cocktail shaker filled with ice, shake vigorously, and utilize a funnel to strain into a flask.

INGREDIENTS:

- 1 PART GIN
- 1 PART DRY VERMOUTH
- 4 DASHES OF CAMPARI

B & B

Using a funnel, fill your flask halfway with Bénédictine, and then top it off with your favorite brandy.

INGREDIENTS:

1 PART BÉNÉDICTINE

1 PART BRANDY

BAT JUICE

Combine ingredients in a cocktail shaker filled with ice, shake vigorously, and utilize a funnel to strain into a flask.

INGREDIENTS:

4 PARTS CRANBERRY JUICE

1 PART BACARDI BLACK RUM

BLACK DOG

Combine ingredients in a cocktail shaker filled with ice, shake vigorously, and utilize a funnel to strain into a flask.

INGREDIENTS:

3 PARTS BOURBON

1 PART SWEET VERMOUTH

1 PART BLACKBERRY BRANDY

BLUE KAMIKAZE

Combine ingredients in a cocktail shaker filled with ice, shake vigorously, and utilize a funnel to strain into a flask.

INGREDIENTS:

1 PART BLUE CURAÇAO

1 PART VODKA

1 PART FRESH LIME JUICE

HIGH END

In March 2016, the Norman C. Heckler auction house sold a rare Masonic flask for $56,160, thought to be one of the highest prices ever paid for an antique flask. It featured the square and star Masonic symbol as well as a "crossed keys" Masonic symbol, and was made between 1820 and 1830 by Covington Glassworks in Connecticut. At the same auction, a rare flask bearing a portrait of George Washington sold for $49,140.

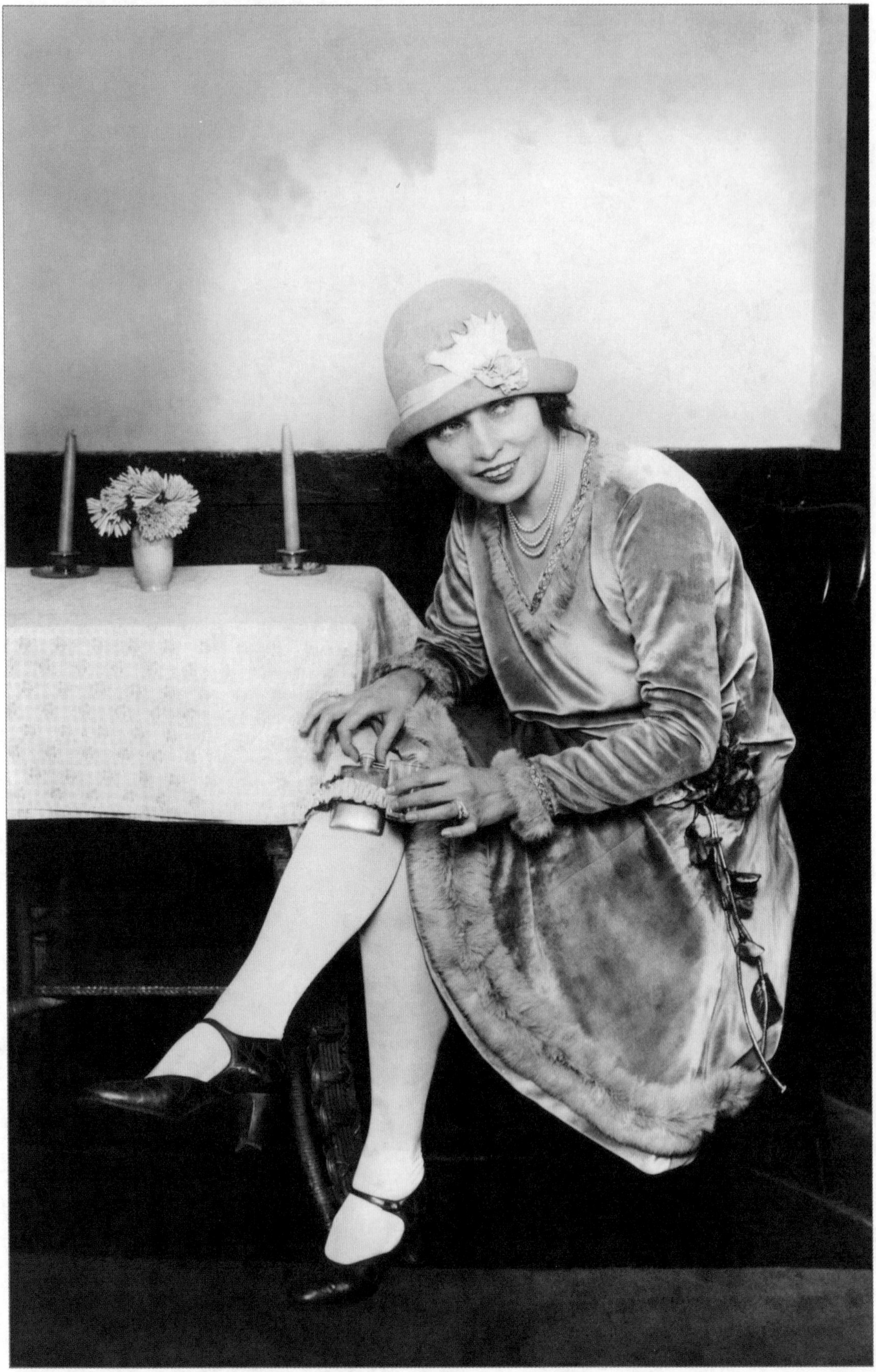

BOURBON BENDER

Combine ingredients in a cocktail shaker filled with ice, shake vigorously, and utilize a funnel to strain into a flask.

INGREDIENTS:

- 1 PART BOURBON
- 1 PART AMARETTO
- 1 PART FRESH LIME JUICE

CACTUS JACK

Combine ingredients in a cocktail shaker filled with ice, shake vigorously, and utilize a funnel to strain into a flask.

INGREDIENTS:

- 1 PART WHISK(E)Y
- 1 PART PINEAPPLE VODKA
- 1 PART ORANGE JUICE

CASINO

Combine ingredients in a cocktail shaker filled with ice, shake vigorously, and utilize a funnel to strain into a flask.

INGREDIENTS:

- 4 PARTS GIN
- 1 PART LUXARDO
- 1 PART LEMON JUICE
- 4 DASHES OF ORANGE BITTERS

CLASSIC GIN & TONIC

Pour gin and tonic into a flask using a funnel. Top with the lime juice.

INGREDIENTS:

- 1 PART TANQUERAY GIN
- 1 PART TONIC WATER
- SQUEEZE OF FRESH LIME JUICE

CLOISTER

Using a funnel, fill your flask halfway with gin, and then top it off with grapefruit juice.

INGREDIENTS:

- 1 PART GIN
- 1 PART GRAPEFRUIT JUICE

CORPSE REVIVER NO. 2

Pour the dash of absinthe into the flask, swish it around to coat the inside, and pour it out. Combine the remaining ingredients in a cocktail shaker filled with ice, shake vigorously, and utilize a funnel to strain into the flask.

INGREDIENTS:

- DASH OF ABSINTHE
- 1 PART GIN
- 1 PART COINTREAU
- 1 PART LILLET BLANC
- 1 PART LEMON JUICE

COSMOPOLITAN

Combine ingredients in a cocktail shaker filled with ice, shake vigorously, and utilize a funnel to strain into the flask.

INGREDIENTS:

- 2 PARTS VODKA
- 1 PART COINTREAU
- 1 PART CRANBERRY JUICE
- 1 PART LIME JUICE

FLASK-O-HAPPINESS

Combine ingredients, except the 7UP, in a cocktail shaker filled with ice, shake vigorously, and utilize a funnel to strain into a flask. Top off with a splash of 7UP.

INGREDIENTS:

- 1 PART RASPBERRY, BLACKBERRY, OR STRAWBERRY VODKA
- 1 PART PINEAPPLE JUICE
- 1 PART LIME JUICE
- SPLASH OF 7UP

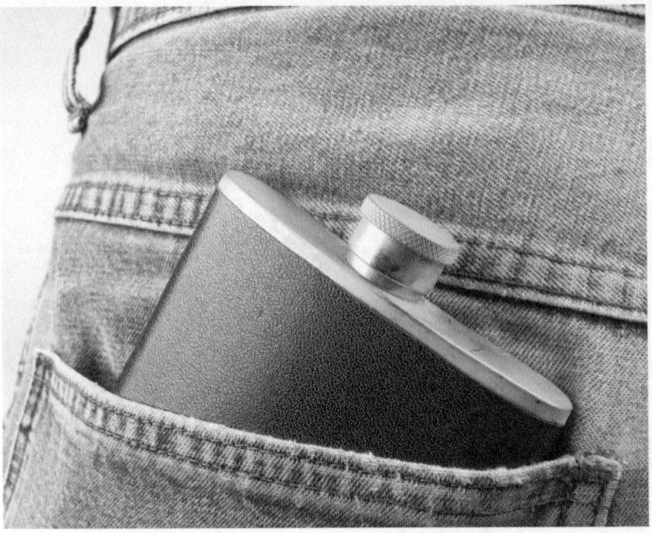

FRISCO

Combine ingredients in a cocktail shaker filled with ice, shake vigorously, and utilize a funnel to strain into a flask.

INGREDIENTS:

- 2 PARTS RYE WHISKEY
- 1 PART LEMON JUICE
- SPLASH OF BÉNÉDICTINE

GODFATHER

Combine ingredients in a cocktail shaker filled with ice, shake vigorously, and utilize a funnel to strain into a flask.

INGREDIENTS:

- 2 PARTS SCOTCH
- 1 PART AMARETTO

GODMOTHER

Combine ingredients in a cocktail shaker filled with ice, shake vigorously, and utilize a funnel to strain into a flask.

INGREDIENTS:

- 2 PARTS VODKA
- 1 PART AMARETTO

GRAPE CHILL

Combine ingredients in a cocktail shaker filled with ice, shake vigorously, and utilize a funnel to strain into a flask.

INGREDIENTS:

- 2 PARTS GRAPE VODKA
- 1 PART VANILLA VODKA
- 1 PART PINEAPPLE JUICE

GRAPE SOURBALL

Combine ingredients in a cocktail shaker filled with ice, shake vigorously, and utilize a funnel to strain into a flask.

INGREDIENTS:

1 PART GRAPE VODKA

1 PART CRYSTAL LIGHT LEMONADE

1 PART ORANGE JUICE

MANHATTAN

Combine ingredients in a cocktail shaker filled with ice, shake vigorously, and utilize a funnel to strain into a flask.

INGREDIENTS:

2 PARTS RYE WHISKEY

1 PART SWEET VERMOUTH

MARTINI

Combine ingredients in a cocktail shaker filled with ice, shake vigorously, and utilize a funnel to strain into a flask.

INGREDIENTS:

3 PARTS DRY GIN

1 PART DRY VERMOUTH

NEGRONI

Combine ingredients in a cocktail shaker filled with ice, shake vigorously, and utilize a funnel to strain into a flask.

INGREDIENTS:

2 PARTS GIN

1 PART CAMPARI

1 PART DRY VERMOUTH

2 DASHES OF ORANGE BITTERS

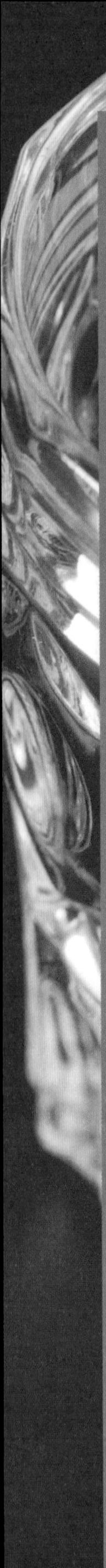

FLASK MATERIALS AND MAINTENANCE

STAINLESS STEEL

Steel is by far the most common material used today to make flasks. Steel is strong, inexpensive, and resists corrosion. Stainless steel also won't retain flavors or odors, so with a quick rinse you can change the contents of your flask without a hint of what was in it yesterday.

SILVER

Silver is considered to be the best material for flasks. Like stainless steel, it will not corrode and does not retain odors. Pure silver is thought by some to enhance the flavors of spirits such as whisk(e)y, gin, and vodka. One drawback to silver is its tendency to tarnish, so extra effort will be required to keep the flask looking like new.

PEWTER

Pewter, sometimes called "poor man's silver," is a mixture of tin, copper, and antimony. Earlier versions of pewter contained lead but once the adverse effects of lead poisoning became known, antimony was employed. Pewter flasks from before the 20th century are collectible but should be for display only. Modern pewter flasks are perfectly safe and combine the shine and elegance of silver for a fraction of the cost.

GOLD PLATED

For something really flashy, there are gold-plated flasks. Considering that a flask should be kept out of sight, the purpose of gold plating is questionable. It has been said that, like silver, gold enhances the flavor of the spirit.

PLASTIC

Flasks made from plastic or Nalgene are becoming more popular. Plastic flasks allow outside alcohol to be brought into concerts and onto cruise ships undetected. They are also cheap, do not retain odors, and do not affect the taste of the liquor.

Notes on Storage

Flasks are not meant to replace liquor bottles as a place to store booze. Liquor should not be kept in a flask for more than three days. After that, it starts to take on a metallic taste. Some suggest that the liquor left in the flask at the end of the day should be consumed as a nightcap before going to bed.

Cleaning Metal Flasks

Never use soap to clean the inside of a flask. Soap, even dish soap, can leave a residue that imparts a soapy flavor to anything put in it later. Here are the three simple, common products that work best to clean a metal flask:

1. Water

A rinse with plain water is the simplest and easiest way to clean out a flask. Fill the flask halfway with the hottest water you can stand. Close the cap and shake the flask for a few seconds before dumping out the water, then repeat at least twice more. Once the flask is well rinsed, allow it to air-dry upside down with the cap open.

2. White Vinegar

If the flask has a funky odor or funny taste, a rinse with white vinegar might help clean it out. Plain white vinegar can be found almost anywhere and is safe to drink, although very acidic. Fill the flask halfway with vinegar, close the cap and shake for 30 seconds to a minute, and then dump out the vinegar. Afterward, rinse multiple times with water, letting the flask dry upside down with the cap open.

3. Lemon Juice

Lemon juice can be used instead of vinegar. It is not as acidic, but has a much more pleasant smell if any residue is left in the flask. Fresh lemon juice should be used instead of the bottled kind. The bottled juice frequently has added sugar, which can lead to the growth of mold or mildew in the flask. Fill the flask halfway with lemon juice, close the cap, shake for 30 seconds to a minute, and then dump out the juice. Afterward, rinse multiple times with water, letting the flask dry upside down with the cap open.

Cleaning Glass-Lined Flasks

If you happen to have a vintage glass-lined flask, a great trick for cleaning it is to use a denture cleanser tablet. Put one tablet in the flask, breaking it into smaller pieces if it won't fit through the opening. Then, fill the flask about three-quarters full with warm water and allow the denture cleaner to work its magic. As the bubbles begin to die down, fill the flask to the top. Do not close the cap while cleaning this way. The bubbles will cause pressure to build up inside the flask and it could burst.

PRAIRIE WILDLIFE

Funnel the tequila into a flask and top with the Tabasco.

INGREDIENTS:

1 PART TEQUILA
TABASCO, TO TASTE

ROB ROY

Combine ingredients in a cocktail shaker filled with ice, shake vigorously, and utilize a funnel to strain into a flask.

INGREDIENTS:

2 PARTS SCOTCH
1 PART SWEET VERMOUTH

RUSTY NAIL

Combine ingredients in a cocktail shaker filled with ice, shake vigorously, and utilize a funnel to strain into a flask.

INGREDIENTS:

3 PARTS SCOTCH
1 PART DRAMBUIE

SIDECAR

Combine ingredients in a cocktail shaker filled with ice, shake vigorously, and utilize a funnel to strain into a flask.

INGREDIENTS:

2 PARTS BRANDY
1 PART LEMON JUICE
1 PART TRIPLE SEC

SNAKE BITE

Combine ingredients in a cocktail shaker filled with ice, shake vigorously, and utilize a funnel to strain into a flask.

INGREDIENTS:

- 4 PARTS CANADIAN WHISKY
- 1 PART FRESH LIME JUICE

SPITFIRE

Combine ingredients in a cocktail shaker filled with ice, shake vigorously, and utilize a funnel to strain into a flask.

INGREDIENTS:

- 1 PART WHISK(E)Y
- 1 PART DARK RUM
- 1 PART CHERRY VODKA

STINGER

Combine ingredients in a cocktail shaker filled with ice, shake vigorously, and utilize a funnel to strain into a flask.

INGREDIENTS:

- 3 PARTS BRANDY
- 1 PART WHITE CRÈME DE MENTHE

TEMPTATION

Combine ingredients in a cocktail shaker filled with ice, shake vigorously, and utilize a funnel to strain into a flask.

INGREDIENTS:

- 2 PARTS RYE WHISKEY
- 1 PART DUBONNET BLONDE
- 1 PART TRIPLE SEC
- 1 PART PERNOD

THE ULTIMATE NIGHTCAP

Frank Sinatra is rumored to be buried with a flask of his favorite drink, Jack Daniel's, in his pocket. He was also supposedly buried with a pack of Camels, his Zippo lighter, and 10 dimes. He had carried 10 dimes in his pocket since the kidnapping of his son in 1963, saying that he always wanted them handy in case he needed to make a phone call. His daughter Tina placed the dimes in his pocket. The whiskey was placed by Tina's sister Nancy.

THIRD RAIL

Combine ingredients in a cocktail shaker filled with ice, shake vigorously, and utilize a funnel to strain into a flask.

INGREDIENTS:

- 1 PART LIGHT RUM
- 1 PART CHERRY BRANDY
- 1 PART CALVADOS
- DASH OF PERNOD

TROPICAL STORM

Combine ingredients in a cocktail shaker filled with ice, shake vigorously, and utilize a funnel to strain into a flask.

INGREDIENTS:

- 1 PART WHITE RUM
- 1 PART DARK RUM
- 1 PART PASSION FRUIT SYRUP
- SPLASH OF LEMON JUICE

TWISTED GIMLET

Combine ingredients in a cocktail shaker filled with ice, shake vigorously, and utilize a funnel to strain into a flask.

INGREDIENTS:

- 2 PARTS GIN
- 1 PART TRIPLE SEC
- 2 DROPS OF ORANGE BITTERS

WALDORF

Combine ingredients in a cocktail shaker filled with ice, shake vigorously, and utilize a funnel to strain into a flask.

INGREDIENTS:

- 2 PARTS BOURBON
- 1 PART PERNOD
- 1 PART SWEET VERMOUTH
- 3 DASHES OF ANGOSTURA BITTERS

NONALCOHOLIC DRINKS

I consider my drinking life to have begun when I turned 21 and started to care enough about wine, beer, and spirits to have some decent opinions about what I chose to drink. For much of that time, I've had one very clear feeling about nonalcoholic beer: *What's the point?* This wasn't to diminish anyone's attempt to drink less or to live a sober life because those are goals that certainly don't need my validation. It's just that for me, especially in the case of beer, it never tasted so good that I wanted to drink its nonalcoholic equivalent. Personally, I'd rather just have coffee, tea, water, seltzer, or juice. But hey, that's me.

Taste was never the issue with nonalcoholic cocktails. There was always a plethora of refreshing nonalcoholic options for one to partake in, and we've tried to include a lot of them in the following pages. We have the variants for most of the standard cocktails and I'm very happy that we made this a big part of this book. These pages contain plenty of alcoholic cocktail recipes for you to work with. I don't think it would be a complete guide without the inclusion of healthy, nonintoxicating options.

This chapter is divvied up into two sections: mocktails and infusions. Whether you want to make the kids feel grown up (see Shirley Temple on page 712), don't drink alcohol, or are just not in the mood for booze, these mocktails offer something for everyone. Not only are they much more interesting to drink than soda, they also offer the wide range of flavor profiles that makes the world of cocktails so dynamic.

Experiment with these mocktails and infusions, find your favorites, and make them part of your routine. While I wouldn't suggest that you wake up with a Margarita or Old Fashioned (that would be spirit malpractice on my part and we can't have that), I have no problem with the thought of people hitting the drinks in this chapter hard first thing in the morning.

Favorite infusion: Strawberry and Lemon Water

Favorite mocktail: Lemon-Lime Spritzer

MOCKTAILS

These are often thought of as a lesser creation than the standard cocktail, but is it really? Everyone has finished a cocktail that was less than great, perhaps even bad, because at least there was some alcohol in it that could help them unwind. For a mocktail, there is no such saving grace. A mocktail lives and dies on taste alone. Otherwise, what's the point? The following pages contain a few that we thought were worth the bother.

VIRGIN PIÑA COLADA

GARNISH: 1 PINEAPPLE SLICE

Place the cocktail ingredients in a blender and puree until smooth. Pour into a Hurricane glass and garnish with the pineapple slice.

INGREDIENTS:

- 1 PART CREAM OF COCONUT
- 3 PARTS PINEAPPLE JUICE
- ¾ CUP ICE

FUZZLESS NAVEL

GARNISH: 1 MARASCHINO CHERRY & 1 ORANGE SLICE

Place the peach nectar and orange juice in a chilled highball glass, stir to combine, and garnish with the slice of orange and the maraschino cherry.

INGREDIENTS:

- 1 OZ. PEACH NECTAR
- 3 OZ. ORANGE JUICE

VIRGIN MUDSLIDE

GARNISH: DOLLOP OF WHIPPED CREAM & 1 MARASCHINO CHERRY

Wet the rim of a Hurricane glass or a mason jar and dip it into the chocolate shavings. Place the cream, ice cream, and syrups in a blender and puree until smooth. Pour into the glass and garnish with the whipped cream and maraschino cherry.

INGREDIENTS:

- CHOCOLATE SHAVINGS, FOR THE RIM
- 1 OZ. HEAVY CREAM
- 2–3 SCOOPS OF VANILLA ICE CREAM
- DASH OF MONIN AMARETTO SYRUP
- CHOCOLATE SYRUP, TO TASTE

LIME RICKEY

GARNISH: 1 LIME WEDGE

Place the simple syrup, lime juice, and spent lime half in a highball glass and stir to combine. Add ice, top with club soda, and garnish with the lime wedge.

INGREDIENTS:

- 1 OZ. SIMPLE SYRUP
- JUICE OF 1 LIME, 1 SPENT LIME HALF RESERVED
- 4 OZ. CLUB SODA

VIRGIN MULE

GARNISH: 1 LIME WEDGE

Place the lime juice in a mason jar or copper mug filled with ice, top with the ginger beer, and garnish with the lime wedge.

INGREDIENTS:

- JUICE OF ½ LIME
- 6 OZ. GINGER BEER

NOJITO

GARNISH: 3 TO 6 SPRIGS OF MINT & 1 LIME WHEEL

Place the sugar and lime juice in a mason jar and stir until the sugar is dissolved. Add the mint leaves, muddle, and then add the ice and ginger ale. Stir to combine and garnish with the sprigs of mint and the lime wheel.

INGREDIENTS:

- 1 TABLESPOON SUGAR
- JUICE OF ½ LIME
- HANDFUL OF MINT LEAVES
- 1 CUP CRUSHED ICE
- 8 OZ. GINGER ALE

VIRGIN MARY

GARNISH: 1 CELERY STALK & HANDFUL OF RED CHILI PEPPERS

Wet the rim of a pint glass or mason jar and dip it into a dish of black pepper. Place ice, the lime juice, olive brine, horseradish, Worcestershire sauce, hot sauce, dash of black pepper, and celery salt in the glass, top with the tomato juice, and stir. Garnish with the celery stalk and a handful of red chili peppers.

INGREDIENTS:

- DASH OF BLACK PEPPER, PLUS MORE FOR THE RIM
- JUICE OF 1 LIME WEDGE
- ½ OZ. OLIVE BRINE
- 2 DASHES OF HORSERADISH
- 3 DROPS OF WORCESTERSHIRE SAUCE
- 3 DASHES OF HOT SAUCE
- 2 DASHES OF CELERY SALT
- TOMATO JUICE, TO TOP

VIRGIN STRAWBERRY DAIQUIRI

GARNISH: STRAWBERRIES

Place the ingredients in a blender and puree until smooth. Pour into a Hurricane glass and garnish with the additional strawberries.

INGREDIENTS:

- 2 OZ. LEMON-LIME SODA
- ½ OZ. ORANGE JUICE
- ¼ OZ. SIMPLE SYRUP
- JUICE OF ½ LIME
- ½ CUP STRAWBERRIES, HULLED
- 1 CUP ICE

CHERRY LIMEADE

GARNISH: 1 MARASCHINO CHERRY & 1 LIME WEDGE

Homemade Grenadine: Place 4 cups of pomegranate juice in a medium saucepan and bring to a simmer over medium-low heat. Simmer until reduced by half, add 2 cups of sugar, and stir until sugar has dissolved. Remove from heat, let cool, and store in the refrigerator for up to 1 month.

Place the lime juice, sugar, and water in a mason jar and stir until the sugar has dissolved. Add the homemade grenadine, stir until well combined, and garnish with the maraschino cherry and lime wheel.

INGREDIENTS:

- 2 OZ. HOMEMADE GRENADINE
- JUICE OF 1 LIME
- 1 TABLESPOON SUGAR
- 1 CUP WATER

VIRGIN PRIVATEER

GARNISH: 1 LIME WEDGE

Juice the lime into a mason jar, drop the spent lime half in, and add ice, the cola, and the coconut syrup. Stir to combine and garnish with the lime wedge.

INGREDIENTS:

- JUICE OF ½ LIME, SPENT HALF RESERVED
- 1 CUP COLA
- 1 OZ. COCONUT SYRUP

VIRGIN SOUR

GARNISH: 1 LEMON SLICE & 1 MARASCHINO CHERRY

Place the lemon juice and sugar in a rocks glass, stir until the sugar has dissolved, and then add the ginger ale. Stir, add the grenadine, and garnish with the lemon slice and maraschino cherry.

INGREDIENTS:

- JUICE OF 1 LEMON
- 1 TEASPOON SUGAR
- 2 OZ. GINGER ALE
- DASH OF GRENADINE

VIRGIN APPLE PIE

GARNISH: DOLLOP OF ICE CREAM, 1 CINNAMON STICK, & 1 STAR ANISE POD

Place the apple cider and cream soda in a glass, and then add the cinnamon. Stir until well combined and garnish with the ice cream, cinnamon stick, and star anise.

INGREDIENTS:

- ¾ CUP APPLE CIDER
- ¼ CUP CREAM SODA
- DASH OF CINNAMON

NON ISLAND ICED TEA

GARNISH: 1 LEMON WEDGE

Place the iced tea, lemonade, and cola in a mason jar filled with ice, stir to combine, and garnish with the lemon wedge.

INGREDIENTS:

- 1 PART UNSWEETENED ICED TEA
- 1 PART LEMONADE
- 1 PART COLA

VIRGIN COSMOPOLITAN

GARNISH: 1 LIME WHEEL

Place the cranberry juice and lime juice in a cocktail glass and stir. Top with the Sprite and garnish with the lime wheel.

INGREDIENTS:

- 4 OZ. CRANBERRY JUICE
- JUICE OF 1 LIME WEDGE
- SPLASH OF SPRITE

VIRGIN MARGARITA

GARNISH: 1 ORANGE WEDGE

Wet the rim of a coupe and dip it into the salt. Place the juices and the simple syrup in a cocktail shaker filled with ice and shake vigorously. Strain into the coupe and garnish with the orange wedge.

Tip: To make a frozen version of this recipe, place the ingredients and 1 cup of ice in a blender and puree until smooth.

INGREDIENTS:

- SALT, FOR THE RIM
- 1 OZ. LEMON JUICE
- 1 OZ. LIME JUICE
- 1 OZ. ORANGE JUICE
- 1 OZ. SIMPLE SYRUP

FROZEN WATERMELON-LIME REFRESHER

GARNISH: 1 LIME WHEEL

Place the simple syrup, watermelon, lime juice, and ice in a blender and puree until smooth. Pour into a mason jar or a Hurricane glass and garnish with the lime wheel.

INGREDIENTS:

- 1 OZ. SIMPLE SYRUP
- 1½ CUPS WATERMELON, SEEDED AND CUBED
- JUICE OF 1 LIME
- 1 CUP ICE

VIRGIN MINT JULEP

GARNISH: 1 SPRIG OF MINT

Place the mint, sugar, lemon juice, and water in a rocks glass and muddle. Add ice and the ginger ale and garnish with the sprig of mint.

INGREDIENTS:

- 6 MINT LEAVES
- DASH OF POWDERED SUGAR
- JUICE OF ½ LEMON
- 1 OZ. WATER
- 3 OZ. GINGER ALE

THORNLESS ROSE

GARNISH: 1 LIME WEDGE

Place the juices, grenadine, and club soda in a rocks glass filled with ice, stir until chilled, and garnish with the lime wedge.

INGREDIENTS:

- JUICE OF ½ LEMON
- JUICE OF ½ LIME
- 1 OZ. GRENADINE
- 3 OZ. CLUB SODA

VIRGIN SANGRIA

GARNISH: 1 SLICED LEMON & 1 SLICED LIME

Place all of the ingredients for the sangria, except for the club soda, in a large airtight container and seal. Store in the refrigerator for 24 hours. When ready to serve, pour the mixture into a punch bowl, add the club soda, and garnish with the sliced lemon and lime.

INGREDIENTS:

- 1¼ CUPS GRAPE JUICE
- 6 OZ. APPLE JUICE
- 4 OZ. ORANGE JUICE
- 2 OZ. LEMON JUICE
- 2 OZ. LIME JUICE
- 1 APPLE, PEELED, CORED, AND DICED
- 1 ORANGE, PEELED AND SLICED THIN
- 1 CUP BLACKBERRIES
- 4 OZ. CLUB SODA

VIRGIN PIMM'S CUP

GARNISH: 2 CUCUMBER SLICES & 1 LEMON WHEEL

Place the mint leaves in a mason jar and gently muddle. Add ice and the liquid ingredients, stir to combine, and garnish with the cucumber slices and lemon wheel.

INGREDIENTS:

- 4 MINT LEAVES
- 4 OZ. LEMON-LIME SODA
- 2 OZ. GINGER ALE
- 1 OZ. COLA
- 1 OZ. ORANGE JUICE
- JUICE OF ½ LEMON
- 2 DROPS OF AROMATIC BITTERS

EXPRESS VIRGIN MARY

GARNISH: ANYTHING YOUR HEART DESIRES

Place the tomato juice, Worcestershire sauce, lemon juice, and black pepper in a pint glass filled with ice, stir to combine, and garnish with anything you please.

INGREDIENTS:

- 1 CUP TOMATO JUICE
- DASH OF WORCESTERSHIRE SAUCE
- DASH OF LEMON JUICE
- DASH OF BLACK PEPPER

VIRGIN BUTTERED RUM

GARNISH: 1 CINNAMON STICK

Place the butter, brown sugar, cinnamon, nutmeg, and orange zest in a mug and muddle. Add the ice cream, top with the hot water, and stir to combine. Season to taste and garnish with the cinnamon stick.

INGREDIENTS:

- 1 PAT OF BUTTER
- 1 TEASPOON BROWN SUGAR
- DASH OF CINNAMON, PLUS MORE TO TASTE
- DASH OF NUTMEG, PLUS MORE TO TASTE
- DASH OF ORANGE ZEST, PLUS MORE TO TASTE
- 2 OZ. VANILLA ICE CREAM
- HOT WATER (NEAR BOILING), TO TOP

SHIRLEY TEMPLE

GARNISH: 1 MARASCHINO CHERRY

Born in 1928, Shirley Temple was already under contract at the Fox Film Corporation by 1933. By the time she was 7, Temple was a Hollywood star, her likeness was being used on all matter of products, and she was feted everywhere she went. But all the attention lavished on her didn't make up for the fact that when out to restaurants where adults were sipping cocktails, there wasn't a special drink for her. So a quick-thinking bartender—likely at a Hollywood hot spot like Chasen's or the Brown Derby, but perhaps at the Royal Hawaiian Hotel—mixed grenadine and lime juice with ginger ale in an effort to appease the starlet. Temple never really cared for the drink, and in general fought to stop the unauthorized use of her name, but that did nothing to stop the drink from becoming popular with kids at restaurants.

INGREDIENTS:

6 OZ. GINGER ALE
DASH OF GRENADINE
DASH OF LIME JUICE

Place the ginger ale, grenadine, and lime juice in a highball glass filled with ice, stir gently, and garnish with the maraschino cherry.

ROY ROGERS

GARNISH: 1 MARASCHINO CHERRY

Roy Rogers's life as an entertainer started in the early 1930s as a singer, but he became a celebrity when he rivaled Gene Autry in films as a singing cowboy, starting in the late '30s, when Shirley Temple's film career was already petering out. No one really seems to know the origin of the nonalcoholic drink named after him. He didn't drink, but it is possible that some enterprising restaurateur came up with the idea in the name of keeping little boys happy by creating a faux cocktail that wasn't named after a cute little girl. The only meaningful difference in the two drinks is the cola in the Roy Rogers, though over time ginger ale, cola, and 7UP have become interchangeable as the carbonated base of the drink.

INGREDIENTS:

6 OZ. COLA
DASH OF GRENADINE
DASH OF LIME JUICE

Place the cola, grenadine, and lime juice in a pint glass filled with ice and garnish with the maraschino cherry.

LEMON-LIME SPRITZER

GARNISH: 1 LIME WEDGE OR 1 LEMON WEDGE

Wet the rim of a rocks glass and dip it into the sea salt. Place the lime juice, lemon juice, and simple syrup in a cocktail shaker filled with ice and shake vigorously. Fill the glass with ice and strain the contents of the shaker into the glass. Add the lemon-lime soda or seltzer, stir, and garnish with a lime or lemon wedge.

INGREDIENTS:

- SEA SALT, FOR THE RIM
- ½ OZ. FRESH LIME JUICE
- ½ OZ. FRESH LEMON JUICE
- 1 OZ. SIMPLE SYRUP
- 4 OZ. LEMON-LIME SODA OR SELTZER

CUCUMBER-CANTALOUPE SLUSH

GARNISH: 1 CUCUMBER SLICE

Place the cucumber and cantaloupe in a blender and puree until smooth. Add the club soda and ice and puree until the desired consistency is achieved. Pour into a mason jar and garnish with the cucumber slice.

INGREDIENTS:

- ½ CUCUMBER, DICED
- 2 CANTALOUPE SLICES, RIND REMOVED
- 3 OZ. CLUB SODA
- 1 CUP ICE

VANILLA-PEACH SPRITZER

GARNISH: 1 ORANGE SLICE

Place the seltzer water, peach slices, and vanilla in a glass, stir to combine, and chill in the refrigerator for 1 hour. When ready to serve, garnish with an orange slice.

INGREDIENTS:

- 1 CUP SELTZER WATER
- 1 PEACH, SLICED
- 1 TEASPOON PURE VANILLA EXTRACT

VIRGIN MIMOSA

GARNISH: 1 ORANGE SLICE

Pour the orange juice into a champagne flute, top with the Sprite or ginger ale, and garnish with the orange slice.

INGREDIENTS:

- 3 OZ. ORANGE JUICE
- 3 OZ. SPRITE OR GINGER ALE

VIRGIN SUNRISE

GARNISH: 1 ORANGE WHEEL

Place the orange juice in a Hurricane glass filled with ice, add the splash of grenadine, and do not stir. Garnish with the orange wheel.

INGREDIENTS:

- 1 CUP ORANGE JUICE
- SPLASH OF GRENADINE

CRIMSON LEMONADE

Pour the lemonade into a mason jar filled with ice, top with the splash of grenadine, and do not stir.

INGREDIENTS:

- 1 CUP LEMONADE
- SPLASH OF GRENADINE

VIRGIN BAJA LEMONADE

GARNISH: 1 LEMON WHEEL

Place the lemonade, syrups, and rosemary in a cocktail shaker filled with ice and shake vigorously. Strain into a glass filled with ice and garnish with the lemon wheel.

INGREDIENTS:

- 5 OZ. LEMONADE
- 1 OZ. COCONUT SYRUP
- SPLASH OF AGAVE NECTAR
- 1 SPRIG OF ROSEMARY

MATCHA MOCKARITA

GARNISH: 2 TO 3 JALAPEÑO SLICES & LIME WEDGE

Combine the sea salt and 2 teaspoons of the matcha powder in a small dish. Wet the rim of a rocks glass and then dip it into the matcha-and-salt mixture. Place the jalapeño pepper and lime juice in a cocktail shaker and muddle. Add the ginger tea, green tea, remaining matcha powder, simple syrup, orange juice, and ice and shake vigorously. Fill the rocks glass with ice, strain the contents of the shaker into it, and garnish with the lime wheel and additional jalapeño.

INGREDIENTS:

- 1 TEASPOON SEA SALT
- 2¼ TEASPOONS MATCHA POWDER
- ½-INCH PIECE OF JALAPEÑO PEPPER
- 1 OZ. FRESH LIME JUICE
- 2 OZ. FRESHLY BREWED GINGER TEA, CHILLED
- 3 OZ. FRESHLY BREWED GREEN TEA, CHILLED
- ½ OZ. SIMPLE SYRUP
- ½ OZ. FRESH ORANGE JUICE

FROZEN KIWI MOCKTAIL

GARNISH: 1 KIWI SLICE

Wet the rim of a coupe and dip it into the sea salt. Place the remaining ingredients in a blender and puree until smooth. Pour into the coupe and garnish with the additional kiwi.

INGREDIENTS:

- SEA SALT, FOR THE RIM
- 3 OZ. APPLE JUICE
- 1½ OZ. FRESH LIME JUICE
- ½ CUP KIWI, DICED
- 1 OZ. SIMPLE SYRUP
- 1½ OZ. FRESH ORANGE JUICE
- 1 CUP ICE

FROZEN PASSION FRUIT MOCKTAIL

GARNISH: 1 LIME WEDGE & 1 SPRIG OF MINT

Wet the rim of a coupe and dip it into the salt. Place the remaining ingredients in a blender and puree until smooth. Pour into the coupe and garnish with the lime wedge and sprig of mint.

INGREDIENTS:

- SEA SALT, FOR THE RIM
- 3 OZ. LEMON-LIME SELTZER
- 3 OZ. PASSION FRUIT NECTAR
- 1 OZ. FRESH LIME JUICE
- ½ OZ. FRESH ORANGE JUICE
- ½ OZ. AGAVE NECTAR
- 1 CUP ICE

CUCUMBER-MINT MOCKTAIL

GARNISH: 1 LIME WEDGE & MINT LEAVES

Wet the rim of a rocks glass and dip it into the salt. Place the mint leaves and cucumber in a cocktail shaker and muddle. Add ice, the lime juice, and mint syrup and shake vigorously. Fill the rocks glass with ice and strain the cocktail into it. Add the tonic water, stir, and garnish with the additional mint and the lime wedge.

INGREDIENTS:

- SEA SALT, FOR THE RIM
- 2 MINT LEAVES
- 1 TABLESPOON CUCUMBER, DICED
- 2 OZ. FRESH LIME JUICE
- 2 OZ. MINT SYRUP (SEE PAGE 308, SUBSTITUTE MINT SPRIGS FOR THE ROSEMARY)
- 4 OZ. TONIC WATER

CHOCOLATE-ESPRESSO MOCKTAIL

GARNISH: 2 TO 3 CHOCOLATE-COVERED ESPRESSO BEANS & 1 ORANGE TWIST

While the coffee component is still hot, stir the honey into it and place the mixture in the refrigerator until chilled. When you are ready to prepare the cocktail, wet the rim of a cocktail glass or a coupe and dip it into the cocoa powder. Place the heavy cream in a cocktail shaker, shake until it has thickened slightly, and set aside. Place the coffee-and-honey mixture and chocolate syrup in a mixing glass filled with ice and stir until chilled. Strain into the glass and then top with the thickened cream. Garnish with the chocolate-covered espresso beans and the orange twist.

INGREDIENTS:

- 3 OZ. ESPRESSO OR STRONG COFFEE
- 1 TEASPOON HONEY
- COCOA POWDER, FOR THE RIM
- 2 OZ. HEAVY CREAM
- 1 TEASPOON CHOCOLATE SYRUP

MANGO-LIME MOCKTAIL

GARNISH: 1 LIME WEDGE

Combine the chili powder and sea salt in a small dish, wet the rim of a rocks glass, and dip it into the mixture. Place the mango puree, orange juice, and lime juice in a cocktail shaker filled with ice and shake until chilled. Fill the glass with ice and strain the contents of the shaker into the glass. Top with the seltzer and garnish with the lime wedge.

INGREDIENTS:

- 1 TEASPOON CHILI POWDER
- 1 TEASPOON SEA SALT
- 3 OZ. FRESH MANGO PUREE
- 2 OZ. FRESH ORANGE JUICE
- 2 OZ. FRESH LIME JUICE
- 2 OZ. SELTZER

THE BRUNCH MOCKTAIL

GARNISH: 1 ORANGE TWIST OR 1 LIME WEDGE

Wet the rim of a rocks glass and dip it into the salt. Place the tonic, orange marmalade, lime juice, orange juice, and simple syrup in a cocktail shaker filled with ice and shake vigorously. Fill the rocks glass with ice and strain the contents of the shaker into the glass. Top with a splash of seltzer and garnish with a lime wedge or an orange twist.

INGREDIENTS:

- SEA SALT, FOR THE RIM
- 2 OZ. TONIC WATER
- 2 TEASPOONS ORANGE MARMALADE
- 1 OZ. FRESH LIME JUICE
- ½ OZ. FRESH ORANGE JUICE
- ½ OZ. SIMPLE SYRUP
- SPLASH OF SELTZER WATER

INFUSIONS

Infusion is pretty simple. When you infuse water with fruit, vegetables, herbs, or edible flowers, you're essentially taking the oils and aromas from the plants and adding them to your water. The result is water that tastes amazing. It won't taste artificial like the flavored bottled water available at the store. It'll taste like the actual ingredients you're using.

Almost any fruit, vegetable, or herb can be used to infuse water. Some produce is more suitable, such as citrus or cucumbers, but with a bit of effort, you can infuse almost anything.

You want to start with the freshest produce possible. Frozen, dried, or freeze-dried fruits and vegetables do not work well for infusing water, so stick to fresh. While you may not regularly buy organic produce, you should at least consider it for your infusions, since soaking the fruits and vegetables will release their oils and essences into the water.

Whether organic or conventional, you should thoroughly wash any produce you're going to infuse, even if you think it's already been washed.

ESPRESSO OLD FASHIONED

YIELD: 1 ORANGE TWIST

INGREDIENTS:

- 2 OZ. ESPRESSO, AT ROOM TEMPERATURE
- 2 DASHES OF AROMATIC BITTERS
- ¼ OZ. RICH SIMPLE SYRUP (2:1 SUGAR-TO-WATER RATIO)

Place the ingredients in a mixing glass filled with ice and stir until chilled. Strain into a double rocks glass containing one large ice cube and garnish with the orange twist.

CITRUS AND ROSEMARY WATER

YIELD: MAKES 8 SERVINGS

INGREDIENTS:

- 1 ORANGE, SLICED THIN
- ½ GRAPEFRUIT, SLICED THIN
- 1 SPRIG OF ROSEMARY
- 8 CUPS COLD, FILTERED WATER

Place the orange, grapefruit, and rosemary in a half-gallon pitcher or jar and cover with the water. Let sit for 1 to 2 hours at room temperature for a quick infusion, or refrigerate for anywhere from 4 hours to overnight. Enjoy within 2 days for optimum results.

CHERRY-LIMEADE FIZZ

YIELD: MAKES 8 SERVINGS
GARNISH: LIME SLICES

INGREDIENTS:

- 8 CUPS CHERRY-LIME SPRITZER (SEE PAGE 731)
- 1 CUP FRESH LIME JUICE
- 1 (10 OZ.) JAR OF MARASCHINO CHERRIES AND THE SYRUP
- SIMPLE SYRUP, TO TASTE

Place the spritzer, lime juice, the cherries and their syrup, and the simple syrup in a large pitcher and stir to combine. Serve over ice and garnish each glass with the lime slices.

BASIL-PINEAPPLE LEMONADE

YIELD: MAKES 8 SERVINGS

INGREDIENTS:

- 4 CUPS COLD, FILTERED WATER
- 4 CUPS PINEAPPLE JUICE
- 1 CUP FRESH LEMON JUICE
- BASIL SYRUP (SEE PAGE 391), TO TASTE

Place the water, pineapple juice, lemon juice, and syrup in a large pitcher and stir to combine. Store in the refrigerator until chilled and serve over ice.

CITRUS FIZZ

YIELD: MAKES 8 SERVINGS

Place the sliced fruit in a half-gallon pitcher or jar, cover with the seltzer water, and let the mixture steep in the refrigerator for 2 to 4 hours.

Tip: If you're not going to drink water made with citrus within 2 days, be sure to remove the rind in order to prevent the water from becoming too bitter.

INGREDIENTS:

- 2 LIMES, SLICED THIN
- 1 ORANGE, SLICED THIN
- 1 LEMON, SLICED THIN
- 8 CUPS SELTZER WATER

STRAWBERRY AND LEMON WATER

YIELD: MAKES 8 SERVINGS

Place the strawberries and lemon in a half-gallon pitcher or jar and cover with the water. Let sit for 1 to 2 hours at room temperature for a quick infusion, or refrigerate for anywhere from 4 hours to overnight. Drink within 2 days for optimum results.

INGREDIENTS:

- 1 PINT STRAWBERRIES, HULLED AND SLICED
- 1 LEMON, SLICED THIN
- 8 CUPS COLD, FILTERED WATER

BLACKBERRY AND LIME WATER

YIELD: MAKES 8 SERVINGS

Place the berries in a half-gallon pitcher or jar and muddle. Add the lime slices and cover with the water. Let sit for 1 to 2 hours at room temperature for a quick infusion, or refrigerate for anywhere from 4 hours to overnight. Drink within 2 days for optimum results.

Tip: When using in-season fruit, such as berries, always taste them before adding them to your water. If they are sweet and juicy, they are perfect. Sour, moldy, or astringent berries will make your water taste just like that—which is not good, especially alongside tart fruit like citrus.

INGREDIENTS:

- 1 PINT BLACKBERRIES
- 2 LIMES, SLICED THIN
- 8 CUPS COLD, FILTERED WATER

CHERRY-LIME SPRITZER

YIELD: MAKES 8 SERVINGS

Place the fruit in a half-gallon pitcher or jar and cover with the seltzer water. Steep in the refrigerator for 2 to 4 hours. Drink within 2 days for optimum results.

INGREDIENTS:

- 1 CUP SWEET CHERRIES, PITTED AND HALVED
- 2 LIMES, SLICED THIN
- 8 CUPS SELTZER WATER

ORANGE-GINGER SPRITZER

YIELD: MAKES 8 SERVINGS

Place the orange and ginger in a half-gallon pitcher or jar and cover with the seltzer water. Steep in the refrigerator for 2 to 4 hours. Drink within 2 days for optimum results.

INGREDIENTS:

- 1 ORANGE, SLICED THIN
- 2-INCH PIECE OF GINGER, PEELED AND SMASHED
- 8 CUPS SELTZER WATER

STRAWBERRY AND GRAPEFRUIT WATER

YIELD: MAKES 8 SERVINGS

Place the fruit in a half-gallon pitcher or jar and cover with the water. Let sit for 1 to 2 hours at room temperature for a quick infusion, or refrigerate for anywhere from 4 hours to overnight. Drink within 2 days for optimum results.

INGREDIENTS:

- 1 PINT STRAWBERRIES, HULLED AND SLICED
- 1 GRAPEFRUIT, PEEL AND PITH REMOVED
- 8 CUPS COLD, FILTERED WATER

ORANGE AND MANGO WATER

YIELD: MAKES 8 SERVINGS

Place the fruit in a half-gallon pitcher or jar and cover with the water. Let sit for 1 to 2 hours at room temperature for a quick infusion, or refrigerate for anywhere from 4 hours to overnight. Drink within 2 days for optimum results.

INGREDIENTS:

- 1 ORANGE, SLICED THIN
- 1 MANGO, PEELED, PITTED, AND DICED
- 8 CUPS COLD, FILTERED WATER

BLUEBERRY AND ORANGE WATER

YIELD: MAKES 8 SERVINGS

Place the blueberries and orange slices in a half-gallon pitcher or jar and cover with the water. Let sit for 1 to 2 hours at room temperature for a quick infusion, or refrigerate for anywhere from 4 hours to overnight.

INGREDIENTS:

- 1 PINT FRESH BLUEBERRIES, LIGHTLY MASHED
- 1 ORANGE, SLICED THIN
- 8 CUPS COLD, FILTERED WATER

BLACKBERRY AND GRAPEFRUIT WATER

YIELD: MAKES 8 SERVINGS

Place the blackberries in a half-gallon pitcher or jar and muddle. Add the grapefruit and cover with the water. Let sit for 1 to 2 hours at room temperature for a quick infusion, or refrigerate for anywhere from 4 hours to overnight.

INGREDIENTS:

- 1 PINT BLACKBERRIES
- 1 GRAPEFRUIT, PEEL AND PITH REMOVED
- 8 CUPS COLD, FILTERED WATER

PINEAPPLE COCONUT WATER

YIELD: MAKES 4 SERVINGS

Place the coconut water and pineapple in a jar and let the mixture steep in the refrigerator for 2 to 4 hours, or overnight.

INGREDIENTS:

- 4 CUPS PURE COCONUT WATER
- 1 CUP PINEAPPLE, DICED

CHERRY AND ALMOND WATER

YIELD: MAKES 8 SERVINGS

Place the cherries and almond extract in a half-gallon pitcher or jar and cover with the water. Let sit for 1 to 2 hours at room temperature for a quick infusion, or refrigerate for anywhere from 4 hours to overnight.

INGREDIENTS:

- 1 CUP SWEET CHERRIES, PITTED AND HALVED
- ½ TEASPOON PURE ALMOND EXTRACT
- 8 CUPS COLD, FILTERED WATER

STRAWBERRY-WATERMELON FIZZ

YIELD: MAKES 8 SERVINGS

Place the strawberries and watermelon in a half-gallon pitcher or jar, cover with the seltzer water, and let the mixture steep in the refrigerator for 2 to 4 hours.

INGREDIENTS:

1 PINT STRAWBERRIES, HULLED AND SLICED

1 CUP WATERMELON, CUBED

8 CUPS SELTZER WATER

TROPICAL SPRITZER

YIELD: MAKES 8 SERVINGS

Place the fruit in a half-gallon pitcher or jar, cover with the seltzer water, and let the mixture steep in the refrigerator for 2 to 4 hours.

INGREDIENTS:

1 CUP PINEAPPLE

½ CUP MANGO

½ CUP PAPAYA

8 CUPS SELTZER WATER

STONE FRUIT BLEND

YIELD: MAKES 8 SERVINGS

Place the fruit in a half-gallon pitcher or jar and cover with the water. Let sit for 1 to 2 hours at room temperature for a quick infusion, or refrigerate for anywhere from 4 hours to overnight.

INGREDIENTS:

2 CUPS STONE FRUIT MIXTURE (PEACHES, CHERRIES, PLUMS, APRICOTS), PITTED AND CHOPPED

8 CUPS COLD, FILTERED WATER

RASPBERRY-JALAPEÑO SPARKLER

YIELD: MAKES 8 SERVINGS

Place the jalapeño and raspberries in a half-gallon pitcher or jar and muddle. Cover with the seltzer water and let the mixture steep in the refrigerator for 2 to 4 hours.

INGREDIENTS:

1–2 JALAPEÑO PEPPERS, STEMMED, SEEDED, AND HALVED LENGTHWISE

1 PINT RASPBERRIES

8 CUPS SELTZER WATER

JALAPEÑO, CILANTRO, AND LIME WATER

YIELD: MAKES 8 SERVINGS

Place the jalapeño in a half-gallon pitcher or jar and muddle. Add the cilantro and lime and cover with the water. Let sit for 1 to 2 hours at room temperature for a quick infusion, or refrigerate for anywhere from 4 hours to overnight. Drink within 2 days for optimum results.

INGREDIENTS:

- 1–2 JALAPEÑO PEPPERS, STEMMED, SEEDED, AND HALVED LENGTHWISE
- 3 SPRIGS OF CILANTRO
- 1 LIME, SLICED THIN
- 8 CUPS COLD, FILTERED WATER

APPLE AND FENNEL WATER

YIELD: MAKES 8 SERVINGS

Place the fennel and apple in a half-gallon pitcher or jar and cover with the water. Let sit for 1 to 2 hours at room temperature for a quick infusion, or refrigerate for anywhere from 4 hours to overnight.

INGREDIENTS:

- ½ SMALL FENNEL BULB, SLICED THIN
- 1 APPLE, CORED AND SLICED THIN
- 8 CUPS COLD, FILTERED WATER

STRAWBERRY AND HIBISCUS WATER

YIELD: MAKES 8 SERVINGS

Place the hibiscus flowers and strawberries in a half-gallon pitcher or jar and cover with the water. Let sit for 1 to 2 hours at room temperature for a quick infusion, or refrigerate for anywhere from 4 hours to overnight.

INGREDIENTS:

- 3–4 HIBISCUS BLOSSOMS (FRESH OR DRIED)
- 1 PINT STRAWBERRIES, HULLED AND SLICED
- 8 CUPS COLD, FILTERED WATER

MANGO SPARKLER

YIELD: MAKES 6 SERVINGS

Place the mango and water in a blender and puree until smooth. Strain the puree through a fine sieve, discard the solids, and transfer the liquid to a pitcher. Add the seltzer and simple syrup, stir, and serve over ice.

INGREDIENTS:

- 2 MANGOES, PEELED, PITTED, AND DICED
- 2 TABLESPOONS WATER
- 6 CUPS SELTZER WATER
- SIMPLE SYRUP, TO TASTE

CUCUMBER, GINGER, AND LEMONGRASS WATER

YIELD: MAKES 8 SERVINGS

Place the cucumber, ginger, and lemongrass in a half-gallon pitcher or jar and cover with the water. Let sit for 1 to 2 hours at room temperature for a quick infusion, or refrigerate for anywhere from 4 hours to overnight.

INGREDIENTS:

- ½ CUCUMBER, SEEDED AND SLICED THIN
- 1-INCH PIECE OF GINGER, PEELED AND SMASHED
- 2 LEMONGRASS STALKS, BRUISED
- 8 CUPS COLD, FILTERED WATER

BLUEBERRY AND LAVENDER WATER

YIELD: MAKES 8 SERVINGS

Place the lavender and blueberries in a half-gallon pitcher or jar and muddle. Cover with the water and let sit for 1 to 2 hours at room temperature for a quick infusion, or refrigerate for anywhere from 4 hours to overnight. Strain before serving.

Tip: Less is definitely more when it comes to lavender, especially dried. If you use too much, it will make your water taste like soap.

INGREDIENTS:

- 1–2 SPRIGS OF LAVENDER OR ½ TEASPOON DRIED LAVENDER BUDS
- 1 CUP BLUEBERRIES
- 8 CUPS COLD, FILTERED WATER

LEMON AND ROSE WATER

YIELD: MAKES 8 SERVINGS

Place the rose component and lemon slices in a half-gallon pitcher or jar and cover with the water. Let sit for 1 to 2 hours at room temperature for a quick infusion, or refrigerate for anywhere from 4 hours to overnight.

INGREDIENTS:

- ½ CUP ROSE PETALS OR 1 TEASPOON ROSE WATER EXTRACT
- 1 LEMON, SLICED THIN
- 8 CUPS COLD, FILTERED WATER

VANILLA, LEMON, AND VIOLET WATER

YIELD: MAKES 8 SERVINGS

Place the violet petals, lemon slices, and vanilla component in a half-gallon pitcher or jar and cover with the water. Let sit for 1 to 2 hours at room temperature for a quick infusion, or refrigerate for anywhere from 4 hours to overnight.

INGREDIENTS:

½ CUP VIOLET PETALS

1 LEMON, SLICED THIN

1 VANILLA BEAN, HALVED LENGTHWISE OR 1 TEASPOON PURE VANILLA EXTRACT

8 CUPS COLD, FILTERED WATER

LEMON AND LAVENDER WATER

YIELD: MAKES 8 SERVINGS

Place the lavender and lemon in a half-gallon pitcher or jar and cover with the water. Let sit for 1 to 2 hours at room temperature for a quick infusion, or refrigerate for anywhere from 4 hours to overnight. Strain before serving.

INGREDIENTS:

1–2 SPRIGS OF LAVENDER OR ½ TEASPOON DRIED LAVENDER BUDS

1 LEMON, SLICED THIN

8 CUPS COLD, FILTERED WATER

APPLE AND CINNAMON WATER

YIELD: MAKES 8 SERVINGS

Place the apple and cinnamon sticks in a half-gallon pitcher or jar and cover with the water. Refrigerate for anywhere from 4 hours to overnight.

INGREDIENTS:

1 LARGE APPLE, CORED AND SLICED THIN

2 CINNAMON STICKS

8 CUPS COLD, FILTERED WATER

PEAR AND ANISE WATER

YIELD: MAKES 8 SERVINGS

Place the star anise and pear in a half-gallon pitcher or jar and cover with the water. Let sit for 1 to 2 hours at room temperature for a quick infusion, or refrigerate for anywhere from 4 hours to overnight.

INGREDIENTS:

2–3 STAR ANISE PODS

1 PEAR, CORED, STEMMED, AND SLICED THIN

8 CUPS COLD, FILTERED WATER

STRAWBERRY-BASIL LEMONADE

YIELD: MAKES 8 SERVINGS

INGREDIENTS:

- 3–4 BASIL LEAVES
- 1 PINT STRAWBERRIES, HULLED AND SLICED
- 1 LEMON, SLICED THIN
- 8 CUPS COLD, FILTERED WATER

Place the basil in a half-gallon pitcher or jar and lightly muddle. Add the strawberries and lemon and cover with the water. Let sit for 1 to 2 hours at room temperature for a quick infusion, or refrigerate for anywhere from 4 hours to overnight.

VANILLA, CINNAMON, AND ORANGE WATER

YIELD: MAKES 8 SERVINGS

INGREDIENTS:

- 1 VANILLA BEAN, HALVED LENGTHWISE
- 1 ORANGE, SLICED THIN
- 1 CINNAMON STICK
- 8 CUPS COLD, FILTERED WATER

Scrape the seeds out of the vanilla bean and add them and the pod to a half-gallon pitcher or jar. Add the orange and cinnamon stick and cover with the water. Let sit for 1 to 2 hours at room temperature for a quick infusion, or refrigerate for anywhere from 4 hours to overnight.

WATERMELON-MINT SPARKLER

YIELD: MAKES 8 SERVINGS

INGREDIENTS:

- 2 SPRIGS OF FRESH MINT
- 1 CUP WATERMELON, SEEDED AND CUBED
- 8 CUPS SELTZER WATER

Place the mint in a half-gallon pitcher or jar and gently muddle. Add the watermelon, cover with the seltzer water, and let the mixture steep in the refrigerator for 2 to 4 hours.

CINNAMON AND GRAPE WATER

YIELD: MAKES 8 SERVINGS

INGREDIENTS:

- 1 CUP GRAPES, HALVED AND SEEDED
- 1 CINNAMON STICK
- 8 CUPS COLD, FILTERED WATER

Place the grapes and cinnamon stick in a half-gallon pitcher or jar and cover with the water. Let sit for 1 to 2 hours at room temperature for a quick infusion, or refrigerate for anywhere from 4 hours to overnight.

KIWI, HONEYDEW, AND THYME WATER

YIELD: MAKES 8 SERVINGS

Place the kiwi in a half-gallon pitcher or jar and muddle. Add the melon and thyme and cover with the water. Let sit for 1 to 2 hours at room temperature for a quick infusion, or refrigerate for anywhere from 4 hours to overnight.

INGREDIENTS:

- 1 KIWI, PEELED AND SLICED
- 1 CUP HONEYDEW MELON, CUBED
- 1 SPRIG OF THYME
- 8 CUPS COLD, FILTERED WATER

CUCUMBER AND MINT WATER

YIELD: MAKES 8 SERVINGS

Place the mint and cucumber in a half-gallon pitcher or jar and cover with the water. Let sit for 1 to 2 hours at room temperature for a quick infusion, or refrigerate for anywhere from 4 hours to overnight.

INGREDIENTS:

- 2–3 SPRIGS OF MINT
- 1 CUCUMBER, SEEDED AND SLICED
- 8 CUPS COLD, FILTERED WATER

CUCUMBER, PEAR, AND ROSEMARY WATER

Place the cucumber, pear, and rosemary in a half-gallon pitcher or jar and cover with the water. Let sit for 1 to 2 hours at room temperature for a quick infusion, or refrigerate for anywhere from 4 hours to overnight.

INGREDIENTS:

- 1 CUCUMBER, SEEDED AND SLICED
- 1 MEDIUM RIPE PEAR, CORED AND THINLY SLICED
- 1 SPRIG OF ROSEMARY
- 8 CUPS COLD, FILTERED WATER

CHOCOLATE AND MINT WATER

YIELD: MAKES 8 SERVINGS

Place the mint and chocolate extract in a half-gallon pitcher or jar and cover with the water. Let sit for 1 to 2 hours at room temperature for a quick infusion, or refrigerate for anywhere from 4 hours to overnight.

INGREDIENTS:

- 2–3 SPRIGS OF MINT
- 1 TEASPOON PURE CHOCOLATE EXTRACT
- 8 CUPS COLD, FILTERED WATER

PINEAPPLE AND MINT WATER

YIELD: MAKES 8 SERVINGS

Place the pineapple and mint in a half-gallon pitcher or jar and cover with the water. Let sit for 1 to 2 hours at room temperature for a quick infusion, or refrigerate for anywhere from 4 hours to overnight.

INGREDIENTS:

- 1 CUP PINEAPPLE, DICED
- 2–3 SPRIGS OF MINT
- 8 CUPS COLD, FILTERED WATER

LEMON VERBENA AND THYME WATER

YIELD: MAKES 8 SERVINGS

Place the thyme and lemon verbena in a half-gallon pitcher or jar and cover with the water. Let sit for 1 to 2 hours at room temperature for a quick infusion, or refrigerate for anywhere from 4 hours to overnight.

INGREDIENTS:

- 1 SPRIG OF THYME
- 2–3 SPRIGS OF LEMON VERBENA
- 8 CUPS COLD, FILTERED WATER

CITRUS, SAGE, AND PINEAPPLE WATER

YIELD: MAKES 8 SERVINGS

Place the lemon, orange, pineapple, and sage in a half-gallon pitcher or jar and cover with the water. Let sit for 1 to 2 hours at room temperature for a quick infusion, or refrigerate for anywhere from 4 hours to overnight.

INGREDIENTS:

- ½ LEMON, SLICED THIN
- ½ ORANGE, SLICED THIN
- 1 CUP PINEAPPLE, DICED
- 4–5 SAGE LEAVES
- 8 CUPS COLD, FILTERED WATER

LEMON-BLACKBERRY-MINT SPRITZER

YIELD: MAKES 8 SERVINGS

Place the blackberries in a half-gallon pitcher or jar and muddle. Add the lemon and mint, cover with the seltzer, and let the mixture steep in the refrigerator for 2 to 4 hours.

INGREDIENTS:

- 1 PINT BLACKBERRIES
- 1 LEMON, SLICED THIN
- 2–3 SPRIGS OF MINT
- 8 CUPS SELTZER WATER

GRAPEFRUIT-ROSEMARY SPARKLER

YIELD: MAKES 4 SERVINGS
GARNISH: SPRIGS OF ROSEMARY

INGREDIENTS:

- 2 CUPS GRAPEFRUIT JUICE
- 2 CUPS SELTZER WATER
- ROSEMARY SYRUP (SEE PAGE 308), TO TASTE

Place the grapefruit juice, seltzer water, and rosemary syrup in a pitcher filled with ice and stir to combine. Garnish each glass with a sprig of rosemary.

BASIL-PEACH LEMONADE

YIELD: MAKES 6 SERVINGS

INGREDIENTS:

- 4 RIPE PEACHES, PEELED AND PITTED
- 2 CUPS COLD, FILTERED WATER, PLUS 2 TABLESPOONS
- 1 CUP LEMON JUICE
- 1 SMALL BUNCH OF BASIL, STEMMED
- BASIL SYRUP (SEE PAGE 391), TO TASTE

Place the peaches and the 2 tablespoons of water in a blender or food processor and puree until smooth. Strain the puree through a fine sieve, discard the solids, and transfer the liquid to a pitcher. Add the lemon juice, remaining water, basil, and basil syrup and stir to combine.

BLOOD ORANGE-STRAWBERRY SODA

YIELD: MAKES 8 SERVINGS

INGREDIENTS:

- 1 CUP FRESH STRAWBERRIES, HULLED
- 2 TABLESPOONS WATER
- 1 CUP FRESH BLOOD ORANGE JUICE
- 6 CUPS SELTZER WATER
- SIMPLE SYRUP, TO TASTE

Place the strawberries and water in a blender and puree until smooth. Strain through a fine sieve, discard the solids, and transfer to a pitcher. Add the blood orange juice, seltzer, and simple syrup and stir to combine.

CHAI CIDER

YIELD: MAKES 4 SERVINGS

Place all of the ingredients in a medium saucepan and bring to a boil. Reduce to a gentle simmer and cook for 15 to 20 minutes. Remove from heat and strain into a pitcher.

INGREDIENTS:

- 4 CUPS APPLE CIDER
- 1-INCH PIECE OF GINGER, PEELED
- 2 CINNAMON STICKS
- 4 WHOLE CLOVES
- 4 CARDAMOM PODS, SMASHED
- 4 WHOLE PEPPERCORNS
- 1 STAR ANISE POD

TWISTED TEMPLE

YIELD: MAKES 8 SERVINGS

Place the ingredients in a half-gallon pitcher or jar, stir to combine, and serve over ice.

INGREDIENTS:

- 1½ OZ. GRENADINE
- 8 CUPS CITRUS FIZZ (SEE PAGE 728)
- SIMPLE SYRUP, TO TASTE

CUCUMBER-MINT LEMONADE

YIELD: MAKES 10 SERVINGS

Place all of the ingredients in a half-gallon pitcher or jar filled with ice, stir to combine, and place in the refrigerator until ready to serve.

INGREDIENTS:

- 8 CUPS COLD, FILTERED WATER
- 1 SMALL CUCUMBER, SEEDED AND SLICED
- 1 BUNCH OF MINT LEAVES
- 2 CUPS LEMON JUICE
- SIMPLE SYRUP, TO TASTE

BERRY PUNCH

YIELD: MAKES 10 SERVINGS
GARNISH: ORANGE SLICES

Place the ingredients for the punch in a large pitcher or punch bowl and stir to combine. Serve over ice and garnish each glass with an orange slice.

INGREDIENTS:

- 4 CUPS MIXED BERRY SELTZER
- 4 CUPS TROPICAL SPRITZER (SEE PAGE 735)
- 1 CUP CRANBERRY JUICE
- 1 CUP ORANGE JUICE
- SIMPLE SYRUP, TO TASTE

SPARKLING WATERMELON LIMEADE

YIELD: MAKES 8 SERVINGS
GARNISH: LIME WEDGES

Place the watermelon and water in a blender and puree until smooth. Strain through a fine sieve, discard the solids, and transfer to a pitcher. Add the seltzer, lime juice, and simple syrup and stir to combine. Store in the refrigerator until chilled and garnish each glass with a lime wedge.

INGREDIENTS:

- 1 CUP WATERMELON, SEEDED AND CUBED
- 2 TABLESPOONS WATER
- 4 CUPS SELTZER WATER
- 1 CUP LIME JUICE
- SIMPLE SYRUP, TO TASTE

GINGER-LIME SPRITZER

YIELD: MAKES 8 SERVINGS

Place the ingredients in a half-gallon pitcher, stir to combine, and serve over ice.

INGREDIENTS:

- 4 CUPS GINGER ALE
- 4 CUPS ORANGE-GINGER SPRITZER (SEE PAGE 731)
- 1 CUP LIME JUICE
- SIMPLE SYRUP, TO TASTE

CITRUS-CRANBERRY PUNCH

YIELD: MAKES 8 SERVINGS

Place all of the ingredients in a large pitcher or punch bowl, stir to combine, and serve over ice.

INGREDIENTS:

- 4 CUPS CRANBERRY JUICE
- 4 CUPS CITRUS FIZZ (SEE PAGE 728)
- 1 CUP ORANGE JUICE
- SIMPLE SYRUP, TO TASTE

VANILLA-BERRY SPRITZER

YIELD: MAKES 10 SERVINGS
GARNISH: STRAWBERRIES, BLACKBERRIES, & RASPBERRIES

Place the berries, vanilla, and water in a blender and puree until smooth. Strain into a large pitcher through a fine sieve, discard the solids, add the seltzer and simple syrup, and stir. Serve over ice and garnish each glass with additional berries.

INGREDIENTS:

- ½ CUP STRAWBERRIES, SLICED
- ½ CUP BLACKBERRIES
- ½ CUP RASPBERRIES
- 1 TEASPOON VANILLA EXTRACT
- 3 TABLESPOONS WATER
- 8 CUPS SELTZER WATER
- SIMPLE SYRUP, TO TASTE

LAVENDER-COCONUT LEMONADE

YIELD: MAKES 6 SERVINGS
GARNISH: LAVENDER BUDS & LEMON SLICES

Place the coconut water, lemon juice, and syrup in a pitcher and stir to combine. Serve over ice and garnish with the lavender buds and lemon slices.

INGREDIENTS:

- 4 CUPS COCONUT WATER
- 2 CUPS FRESH LEMON JUICE
- LAVENDER SYRUP (SEE PAGE 174), TO TASTE

GUNSHOP FIZZ

GARNISH: 1 CUCUMBER SLICE

Place the bitters, lemon juice, syrup, strawberries, cucumber slices, and strips of citrus peel in a cocktail shaker and muddle. Let sit for 2 minutes. Add ice, shake vigorously, and strain into a Collins glass filled with ice. Top with the Sanbitter and garnish the additional slice of cucumber.

INGREDIENTS:

- 2 OZ. PEYCHAUD'S BITTERS
- 1 OZ. LEMON JUICE
- 1 OZ. SIMPLE SYRUP
- 2 STRAWBERRIES, HULLED
- 3 CUCUMBER SLICES
- 3 STRIPS OF GRAPEFRUIT PEEL
- 3 STRIPS OF ORANGE PEEL
- SPLASH OF SAN PELLEGRINO SANBITTER

LEMON-RASPBERRY SPRITZER

YIELD: MAKES 8 SERVINGS

Place the raspberries and lemon slices in a half-gallon pitcher or jar, cover with the seltzer water, and steep in the refrigerator for 2 to 4 hours.

INGREDIENTS:

- 1 PINT RASPBERRIES
- 1 LEMON, SLICED THIN
- 8 CUPS SELTZER WATER

INDUSTRY INSIDERS

I am not a cocktail professional. I don't own a bar and can't claim to even have worked in one. I've made cocktails for friends at home, but most of my expertise is gleaned from my time on various barstools. I've learned much while working on this book, but reading and drinking only gets you so far. I felt that this book would be incomplete without input from the "other side of the bar." Those people who know about jiggers, shrubs, esoteric syrups, and the like, and greet you when you sit down to ask for a menu. I needed real-world input from people who live and breathe cocktails on a daily basis, and I searched far and wide to get it. While some of the insights absorbed from this globe-trotting sojourn appear earlier in the book, I accumulated far too much valuable material to be restricted to particular spirits. I hope you find the various tips and numerous recipes from these industry insiders as enlightening as I did.

A note on some of the recipes in this chapter: I have elected not to convert the recipe measurements for those provided using metric measurements. Precision is a big part of why the cocktails these folks produce are delicious. So, if you want to try to make them, you may have to go old school and brush up on the metric system by consulting the conversion table on page 807.

MIZUNARA: THE LIBRARY Q&A WITH CHANDRAKANT MOHANTY, DIRECTOR, AND MASAHIKO ENDO, BARTENDER-IN-CHIEF

Tucked away on the fourth floor of an office building in the Wan Chai district of Hong Kong, this whisk(e)y paradise is as sophisticated as its bookish name implies. It boasts Japanese style and service, along with over 700 whiskies, many of them extremely rare Japanese varieties.

What can you tell us about how the bar started?

The Library opened in February 2015, after over two years of planning and preparations. From the concept stage until launching, the vision was always to bring through the simplicity and elegance of Japanese culture and hospitality via a whisk(e)y and cocktail bar. Whether the choice of the location to facilitate a Japanese garden on the terrace, the single-piece natural wood counter imported from Japan, the detailed design of the barstools, the soft leather sofa sets, the glassware, the design of the leather menu, or the wide selection of the whiskies and cocktails, the single focus was that of "detail without compromise." Every part of Mizunara has a story behind it!

However, the most important aspect of the vision was to bring in the right quality of team to manage and operate the bar, which would be the key to delivering the overall vision of Mizunara. Consequently, it felt like the stars were somewhat aligned when Masahiko Endo, an award-winning bartender from Fukuoka, Japan, was brought in as the bartender-in-chief at an early stage of the planning. Subsequently, the focus has been to continuously bring in top-shelf bartenders with a great sense of hospitality, passion, and pride in what they do. After all, isn't it always about the people?

Can you tell us about the theme of the bar and what is the focus of, and influences upon, your cocktails?

The core of our bar is based on the theme of Japanese hospitality and is primarily based on the philosophy of the traditional Japanese tea ceremony. One of the main philosophies that we adhere to is *Ichigo ichie*, which means "treasure every encounter, for it will never recur."

With this in our mind, we always strive to host every guest that comes through the door to the best of our ability, not only in the context of the cocktails or whiskies that we serve, but also the overall experience we want them to have at Mizunara.

Since we are following the philosophy of Japanese tea ceremony, our signature cocktails usually include Japanese ingredients like matcha green tea, yuzu, and shiso.

What does your team look for when creating a new cocktail for your menu?

The Mizunara team is always seeking a variety of new ingredients, whether they are local or of Japanese origin, or from some other region. However, the key is that the final outcome of any cocktail should be enjoyable and have the right flavors for our guests.

As you are based in Hong Kong, does the food and culture of Hong Kong influence the cocktails as well?

Yes, we also use some Chinese local ingredients like jasmine tea, baijiu, dried tangerine peel.

I've read that Endo-san feels that water is an important element in a cocktail? Can you elaborate further?

Almost every cocktail, excluding the hot ones of course, uses ice. And water from ice increases the amount of the cocktail. For example, when we shake 60 ml of liquid for a cocktail, the final amount will be 80 to 90 ml, which means one-third to one-quarter is water from ice. In our opinion, the key to making cocktails is how to mix that water into the cocktails thoroughly. In another way, you could say that it is important to think how to emulsify them. If you can't mix water well inside the cocktail,

you can feel the thin/watery taste, since it is separate. To be emulsified properly, we have to know the humidity and temperature on that day, also check how sweet, bitter, sour, or fresh the ingredients are and then think about how to shake, stir, or throw. We have to incorporate many of these elements because of the dilution, then adjust them appropriately from time to time.

What are the best parts of running a cocktail bar in Hong Kong? Are there any downsides or things that make it difficult?

Hong Kong is a very vibrant city and the dining and bar industry has evolved over the past few years. While we are always focused on being true to our philosophy of Japanese-styled hospitality, it is great to see and learn from all that is around us and continuously explore new ingredients and flavors.

One of the best parts of operating a bar in Hong Kong is that we get to meet a variety of guests from different parts of the world, all of them with different interests, different stories and perspectives. We learn every day.

The downsides of working in the food and beverage industry are the odd, long working hours, fewer holidays, and the opposite time schedule compared to people with day jobs. Every job has some downside. But if you are passionate and have a great sense of pride in what you do the challenges make it equally exciting.

Blue Hawaiian, Brandy Alexander, Pink Squirrel, Rusty Nail, Tom Collins, White Russian, Grasshopper, Rob Roy, Pink Lady: If you had to pick one of these classic cocktails to add to your menu how would you reimagine your choice to make it fit in with your style?

For Pink Squirrel, we would add some matcha tea to give it subtle bitterness, and bring in the complex flavors from the tea itself. At the same time, it enhances the visual appearance by changing the color of the cocktail to an attractive green.

For Rob Roy, we would use some smoky whisky and English black tea to give it a smoky and an aromatic flavor.

Do you have a favorite cocktail?

Manhattan, Gimlet.

Do you have a favorite alcohol to work with when making cocktails?

Whisk(e)y and sherry.

Q&A WITH GERMAN LACANNA, CO-OWNER OF VERNE COCKTAIL CLUB

With a cocktail menu inspired by the work of Jules Verne, this popular Buenos Aires watering hole looks and feels like you have stepped into one of the author's classic fictions.

What can you tell us about how Verne Cocktail Club came to be?

It was created from the idea of mixing French literature, classic cocktails, and a steampunk aesthetic. I am an Argentinian who lived in France for 10 years. I have studied literature and taught it at a French university for 4 years. Also, I have always enjoyed drinking good quality cocktails. With three French partners we decided to open a bar that brought together all of our powerful ideas in a single theme: Jules Verne. Once in Argentina I met Fede Cuco, whom I first met on Twitter. Fede is a passionate cocktail lover, a great bartender, and also an expert in the history of cocktails in Argentina. Together we built Verne Cocktail Club.

Can you tell us about the theme of the bar and how it influences your cocktails?

Verne Cocktail Club is a cocktail bar with retro-futuristic aesthetics. That means a lot! It's a place inspired by Jules Verne's books on the sensorial suggestion of inviting you to travel toward the origins of cocktail making. We embrace steampunk aesthetics—Chesterfield leather armchairs, tables and chairs with Victorian touches, Persian rugs, walls covered with rusty iron—and a cocktail list nostalgic for the beginning of the 20th century. Verne intends to become a timeless place in the midst of the Buenos Aires night. It is possible to taste craft cocktails with ingredients that are not typical in Argentina, such as eucalyptus smoke, Szechuan peppercorns, or Chartreuse elixir, besides the classic drinks from the early 1900s, and a wide variety of absinthe.

Our menu is divided into two parts, and each one takes as a starting point a novel by Jules Verne. The first one is called: "Around the World in Eight Cocktails," where we craft eight cocktails inspired by eight places that Phileas Fogg visited: London, Paris, Bombay, Suez, Hong Kong, Yokohama, San Francisco, and New York. Each of the cocktails in this section is inspired by those places. For example, our signature cocktail, Opium Fashioned, is a bourbon Old Fashioned with black tea syrup and eucalyptus smoke that represents the opium dens Phileas Fogg went to in Hong Kong.

The second part of the menu is called: "The Lighthouse at the End of the World." As this novel is located in Argentina, we pay tribute to Argentine ingredients and products, especially those that have been forgotten.

What does Fede Cuco look for when creating a new cocktail for your menu?

We have four menus per year, one for each season. So at first he looks for fresh ingredients to work sustainably. As a classic bartender he prefers cocktails with no more than three or four ingredients. He usually starts "playing" with one new ingredient or a new bottle, making different drinks for the guests. Then he tries to improve his ideas. He works in that way for one month to finish a new cocktail. For him, it is important to make a tasty cocktail, as he always begins from the point of view of the guest. He doesn't like vodka and doesn't create vodka cocktails.

How does being a cocktail bar in a country with such a rich wine culture affect the cocktails you offer?

Nowadays, there is a big cocktail trend in our country so now it is not really difficult. But the big issue is about the price, as people still prefer to pay for one bottle of wine rather than four cocktails. In our bar we have only 10 bottles of wine, as we are a cocktail bar and we want to accentuate this aspect. We have only a few selected bottles, none of them very popular, as we don't want to sell wine.

What are the benefits of running a cocktail bar in Buenos Aires? Are there any downsides or things that make it difficult?

The benefit is that bartenders here are creating a big community. They are all very motivated and very creative. They love their job! In fact, the downside is also the benefit here: we do not have a huge variety of bottles to work with in Argentina. We don't have rye whiskey for example, only one variety of Cognac, and very few liquors. During the last five years, it was almost impossible to have single malts. We had to adapt and learn to work with what's available. Making our own syrups, being more and more creative. That was difficult but we learned a lot.

Blue Hawaiian, Brandy Alexander, Pink Squirrel, Rusty Nail, Tom Collins, White Russian, Grasshopper, Rob Roy, Pink Lady: If you had to pick one of these cocktails to add to your cocktail menu how would you reimagine your choice to make it fit in with your style?

We had a version of the Rusty Nail on our first menu! It was in our section "The Lighthouse at the End of the World." We created an Argentine version of it using Caña Legui instead of Drambuie. Legui is a fine Argentine liqueur extracted from sugarcane, made with an infusion of aromatic herbs, produced in the Province of San Juan. Using this kind of "forgotten" sugarcane liquor, something that our grandpas used to drink, fit perfectly well with our idea of making classic cocktails with few ingredients but always with our personal touch.

Verne Cocktail Club Signature Cocktails:

Opium Fashioned: Bourbon (Bulleit) - Black tea syrup - Angostura - Eucalyptus smoke

Jazmin Blanco: Gin (Beefeater) - Honey - Lemon - Cardamom - Jasmine tea

Jean Picaporte: Whisky (Johnnie Walker Black Label) - Malbec wine reduction - Absinthe - Angostura

Q&A WITH JULIA RITZ TOFFOLI, FOUNDER AND PRINCIPAL OF WOMEN WHO WHISKEY

Women Who Whiskey is an educational whisk(e)y club for women. Both for amateurs and connoisseurs, Women Who Whiskey gives its members the opportunity to learn about different whiskies and cocktail culture, and to join a network of like-minded women with a taste for knowledge and strong drinks. But don't let the name of her company fool you, for as much as Toffoli knows about whiskies, she knows just as much about gin, and the rest of the cocktail universe.

Can you tell us a bit about yourself?

My first taste of cocktail culture was in France, as a little girl, seeing my older relatives prepare their daily aperitif. I marveled at how a syrupy, clear liqueur—Pastis—would instantly turn cloudy when ice water was added, its pungent licorice taste so surprising (I was occasionally allowed a small sip). And I remember being entranced by the ritual of preparation: matching highball glasses lined up on a tray, elegant, long-handled spoons, tiny bowls of mixed nuts and bridge crackers, a crystal ice bucket so clear I was convinced it must have also been made of ice.

Though my parents didn't make cocktails at home—we were more of a wine-with-dinner family—my fascination with the alchemy of mixology never left me. As a child, I would create elaborate concoctions of flavored syrups and sparkling waters. And then, as an adult, I rekindled my interest in cocktails, first with easy-to-make (but also easy-to-ruin) mixed drinks, like Rye & Gingers and Gin & Tonics, and eventually with more complex classics, like Manhattans and Old Fashioneds.

When I founded Women Who Whiskey, in 2011, my primary ambition was to create a space for women in the traditionally male-dominated world of whisk(e)y. But I was also new to New York at the height of the cocktail revival, and I knew a whisk(e)y club was the perfect way to explore my new, exciting city through its plethora of cocktail and whisk(e)y bars.

While I know you from the whisk(e)y world, I also know you as an excellent hostess. Other than whisk(e)y, is there a spirit that you like to work with when you craft a cocktail?

Whisk(e)y, to me, is the sine qua non of the cocktail—essential in all the best classics, though I'm sure many bartenders would challenge that assertion.

And while I admire and respect the breadth and flourish that rum tiki cocktails offer, gin, to me, is second in line, a spirit even more versatile than whisk(e)y, dare I say. It works in the laciest, frothiest, most ethereal cocktails, like a Bee's Knees or a Gin Fizz, but sturdily holds its own in bolder drinks, like my favorite non-whisk(e)y classic, the Negroni. Even a simple Gin & Tonic, made with a decent tonic (hard pass on the Schwepps) and a fragrant garnish, holds up against complex, multi-ingredient cocktails.

And for gin skeptics who "don't like drinking Christmas trees," don't worry—it's not all juniper-y London Dry gin out there. There's a gin renaissance happening now, with countless craft varietals across a spectrum of botanical notes and *terroirs*. From Scotland there's The Botanist Gin, from Spain there's Nordés and Gin Mare, and even craft whiskey distilleries in the U. S. are producing some amazing new genevers, like Finn's Gin, from Chicago Distilling Company, or Dorothy Parker Gin, from New York Distilling Company.

What do you like about cocktails versus a straight spirit?

While a straight spirit is like a warm hug, a good cocktail is like a riveting conversation. With multiple flavor notes, textures, fragrances, and even changing temperatures, a cocktail is an experience in itself, but also a way to use complementary ingredients to highlight hidden elements of your favorite spirits that may not shine when enjoying the spirit neat. A lemony, foamy Whisk(e)y Sour is across the spectrum from a bitter, boozy Boulevardier. Both are whisk(e)y cocktails, but each sings a completely different tune.

Can you tell us how you go about making a cocktail?

To be perfectly candid, compared to the industry experts who make most of my drinks, my cocktails skills leave a lot to be desired. I've never gotten into the habit of mixing drinks at home, so my technique needs a little work, plus there are a number of obvious-yet-elusive cocktail staples that I haven't stocked my home bar with yet, like Bénédictine, [Luxardo], or even triple sec! But practice makes perfect, so every once in a while, mostly when we're entertaining, I try my hand, and have learned a few tricks along the way.

Like any good French chef will advise, mise en place—the art of preparing everything you need in advance—is essential. The last thing you want is for ice to be melting in the mixing glass and over-diluting your cocktail while you're rummaging around for those bitters you swear you had. Having everything at arm's length before you start avoids this problem, and will alert you to any missing ingredients.

If possible, make multiple drinks—of the same drink!—at the same time. It's easier to "mini-batch" ingredients in a single mixing glass, and then pour it out into multiple glasses, than it is to make the same drink three times in a row. Just remember to double-check your measurements, and make sure you're scaling properly! I've ruined one too many Manhattans by tripling the vermouth but only doubling the whisk(e)y.

A fancy, fragrant garnish goes a long, long way to making an amateur drink look professional—and possibly Instagram-worthy! Garnishes are more than just for looks, too. They say that 80 percent of taste is smell, so adding a garnish with a strong scent—a citrus peel, a sprig of fresh herbs, or even a burnt cinnamon stick—is essentially like adding an extra ingredient without having to add it to the drink. A mix of notes on the nose and the palate increases a cocktail's complexity. And let's face it, they also just look good. For the more ambitious, you can pre-prep some garnishes in advance—wheels of citrus peel wrapped around a Luxardo cherry and secured with a toothpick—and have them on hand when you're mixing drinks, so that you don't need to fuss with preparing garnishes while your guests are waiting.

Keep it simple—you can make a great drink without eight micro-ingredients—and, if necessary, substitute. At the end of the day,

bitters are bitters, and one orange liqueur is like another.

Make a test cocktail to try before you labor over a batch and realize the vermouth has gone off. If you are substituting something, you want to make sure it works. And most importantly: not all recipes are created equal.

Can you share a few of the cocktails you've created?

In my short-lived career as a cocktail columnist for The Whiskey Reviewer, I've tried my hand at mixology, not just making cocktails according to someone else's recipe, but actually crafting my own—to mixed results (no pun intended). So here I'll stick to what I'm good at—creative variations on time-tested classics, from my home bar to yours.

BOURBON BERRY BRAMBLE

GARNISH: 1 STRIP OF MEYER LEMON ZEST & 3 BERRIES

In a mixing glass, muddle berries, jam, and 1 or 2 slices of lemon. Add simple syrup and bourbon and stir. Pour everything into a tumbler over ice. Top with sparkling water, and garnish with the strip of lemon zest and the additional berries skewered on a swizzle stick.

INGREDIENTS:

- 4–6 FRESH BERRIES (BLACKBERRIES AND RASPBERRIES WORK BEST)
- 1 TEASPOON RASPBERRY JAM
- 1 MEYER LEMON, SLICED
- 1 TEASPOON SIMPLE SYRUP
- 2 OZ. BOURBON
- SPARKLING WATER, TO TOP

MIDNIGHT MANHATTAN

GARNISH: 1 TO 2 LUXARDO CHERRIES

Combine ingredients in a mixing glass filled with ice and stir gently for a minute or so. Strain into a chilled coupe. Garnish with a Luxardo cherry or two skewered on a toothpick.

INGREDIENTS:

- 2 OZ. RYE WHISKEY
- ¾ OZ DOLIN VERMOUTH DE CHAMBERY ROUGE
- 5–7 DASHES OF FEE BROTHERS CARDAMOM BITTERS

CAMPFIRE OLD FASHIONED

GARNISH: 1 STRIP OF LEMON PEEL & 1 STRIP OF ORANGE PEEL

Place the ingredients in a chilled mixing glass, add ice, and stir gently for 20 to 25 seconds. Strain into a chilled rocks glass containing a large ice cube, express the lemon peel and orange peel over the cocktail, and then use them as garnishes.

KAMPOT PEPPER SIMPLE SYRUP

In a medium saucepan, combine sugar, water, and peppercorns. Bring to a boil, stirring regularly, until the sugar has dissolved. Reduce heat to a simmer and cook for 20 minutes. Remove from heat and let cool to room temperature. Strain and store in the refrigerator for up to 1 month.

**Kampot pepper is an especially fragrant varietal of black pepper from Cambodia. If you can't find it, any black pepper will work.*

INGREDIENTS:

- 2 OZ. HIGH WEST CAMPFIRE WHISKEY
- ½ TEASPOON KAMPOT PEPPER SIMPLE SYRUP (SEE RECIPE BELOW)
- 2 DASHES OF ANGOSTURA BITTERS
- DASH OF REGAN'S ORANGE BITTERS

KAMPOT PEPPER SIMPLE SYRUP:

- 1 CUP WATER
- 1 CUP GRANULATED SUGAR
- 1 TABLESPOON WHOLE FRESH BLACK KAMPOT PEPPERCORNS*
- 1 TABLESPOON BLACK PEPPERCORNS, CRACKED

Q&A WITH THOMAS MEROLLA, BAR MANAGER AT BLACKBIRD ORDINARY

Dan Binkiewicz has launched several of Miami's hottest innovative cocktail bars, including Purdy Lounge and Sweet Liberty. With Blackbird Ordinary, which is in Miami's Brickell neighborhood, he has aimed to keep prices reasonable and the drinks interesting in the name of being a "gateway to craft cocktails."

What can you tell us about how the bar started?

I actually did not open the place. Blackbird Ordinary was opened by Dan Binkiewicz and his partners seven years ago. They recruited a legend and inspiration to all of us, John Lermayer. They put together an amazing program in the perfect location at the perfect time.

Can you tell us about the theme of the bar and what is the focus of, and influences upon, your cocktails?

Being called Blackbird Ordinary, the theme is all things birds. From antique bird paintings to the names of the cocktails: bird is the word. The focus of, and influence for our cocktails, are the freshest ingredients and a high appreciation for the classics while understanding the modern palate.

What does your team look for when creating a new cocktail for your menu?

Fresh, balanced, creative, and time-efficient due to the volume we execute!

How do the food and culture of Miami influence the cocktails that you offer?

The Miami culture certainly dictates certain flavors and flavor pairings that we work into our program. As it should.

What are the best parts of running a cocktail bar in Miami? Are there any downsides or things that make it difficult?

I love Miami! I would have to say one of the best parts of running a cocktail program in Miami is the diversity of employees and customers from around the world. So there are many variables to consider when working on a new menu to please all in Miami.

Miami is a drinking town with lots of options for cocktails. What do you think Blackbird Ordinary offers that makes it stand out?

Unquestionably our atmosphere! Our service is second to none, that is what we strive for nightly.

We have an indoor/outdoor bar, thanks to a retractable roof. A large stage outside for live music.

Excellent selection of both music and programming that appeals to everyone. Our training program, both hiring and ongoing, is an integral part of our product and services. And a staff that is friendly, knowledgeable, and ready to create a handcrafted memory for our guests.

Blue Hawaiian, Brandy Alexander, Pink Squirrel, Rusty Nail, Tom Collins, White Russian, Grasshopper, Rob Roy, Pink Lady: If you had to pick one of these classic cocktails to add to your cocktail menu how would you reimagine your choice to make it fit in with your menu?

South Florida? Tom Collins all day! An amazingly simple blueprint with endless variations. I would probably just make an Earl Grey tea simple syrup and add a touch of Dolin Blanc, to add another layer of flavor.

Do you have a favorite cocktail?

There are too many to list. I do not have a particular favorite.

Do you have a favorite alcohol to work with when making cocktails?

I would say gin and whisk(e)y are probably my two favorite spirits to work with at this moment. But that changes one month to the next.

BLACKBIRD

GARNISH: 1 BLACKBERRY & 1 SPRIG OF MINT

Place the ingredients in a cocktail shaker filled with ice and shake vigorously. Strain into a pint glass, add pebble ice,* and garnish with the blackberry and sprig of mint.

**If pebble ice isn't available, use crushed ice.*

INGREDIENTS:

- 2 OZ. SWEET TEA VODKA
- ½ OZ. BLACKBERRY PUREE
- ¾ OZ. FRESH LEMON JUICE
- ¾ OZ. SIMPLE SYRUP

THE WOODPECKER

GARNISH: CANDIED GINGER

Place all of the ingredients, except for the soda water, in a mason jar filled with ice and stir until chilled. Top with the soda water and garnish with the candied ginger.

INGREDIENTS:

- 2 OZ. WOODFORD RESERVE
- 1 OZ. GINGER SYRUP (SEE PAGE 255, SUBSTITUTE SUGAR FOR THE HONEY)
- ¼ OZ. FRESH LIME JUICE
- 3 DASHES OF AROMATIC BITTERS
- SODA WATER, TO TOP

Q&A WITH NICOLAS TORRES, OWNER OF TRUE LAUREL

Even with the success David Barzelay and Nicolas Torres had after opening the acclaimed restaurant Lazy Bear in San Francisco's Mission District, they decided Torres's gifts as a mixologist needed room to grow. Enter True Laurel, a cocktail bar imbued with mid-century whimsy—there is a reason the room's design centerpiece is a wall sculpture inspired by Isamu Noguchi's playscapes—that is reflected in a rotating list of cocktails that celebrates the never-ending abundance of local ingredients.

What can you tell us about how the bar was started?

Chef David and I had been working together for about 3 years at Lazy Bear, and we were always looking for ways to improve the bar program. One day we realized that our ideas may have outgrown what we could do within the confines of Lazy Bear, so we searched for a new space that could focus a little more on drinks, but carry a similar ethos.

What is the theme of the bar and its focus?

I don't think we were going for a theme. Our focus is working with seasons and the farmers that supply our stuff. We want to use the most of the bounty California has to offer, and we want to use what we can get to the extent that we hopefully waste as little as possible. There are definitely bars we looked at for flow and back-of-house operations, but as for look and feel we really took our own path, and found it very important to do so.

What do you look for when creating new cocktails?

I usually start with the produce and work backward. I'm typically looking for ways to use good produce, rare wines, and common spirits. This formula has been good to me. I strive for balance and a certain lightness.

How do the food and culture of San Francisco influence the cocktails that you offer?

I eat and drink out all the time. It's really killing my wallet, but I believe if you want to be part of a culture you really have to partake.

What are the best parts of running a cocktail bar in San Francisco? Are there any downsides or things that make it difficult?

This city is saturated with food and cocktails, it is very gluttonous at times. The hard part is staying competitive. The city is always looking for what's next. It also constantly pushes you as an artist to perform. At the same time, there is so much support in the industry, and we all try to learn from each other.

Blue Hawaiian, Brandy Alexander, Pink Squirrel, Rusty Nail, Tom Collins, White Russian, Grasshopper, Rob Roy, Pink Lady: If you had to pick one of these classic cocktails to add to your cocktail menu how would you make it fit in with your style?

Tom Collins for sure, I still order them all the time. It's a beautiful cocktail. Like a lot of simple sours, or fizz in this case, the details really matter. Simple yet complex, you can learn so much from that drink. It is the base of so many fizzes, coolers, daisies that came after it.

Do you have a personal favorite cocktail?

I'm a huge Highball fan, brandy and soda please.

Do you have a favorite spirit to work with when making cocktails?

I think about wines and fortified wines more than I think about spirits, or at least when I'm trying to use a certain spirit I often think what wine would go well with it.

TOP DAWG

INGREDIENTS:

- SUDACHI SALT, FOR THE RIM
- 3¾ OZ. FERMENTED SHINKO PEAR-AND-TONIC SYRUP
- 1½ OZ. RANCIO

Sudachi Salt: Combine the zest of 1 sudachi with 1 tablespoon of Black Lava salt.

Fermented Syrup: In a large container with a lid, combine 2 quarts of shinko pear juice, 1 cup of rich tonic syrup, and 1 teaspoon wine yeast. Keep the mixture at room temperature for 2 days and then strain.

Wet the rim of a highball glass and dip it into the salt. Combine the syrup and rancio in a container and force carbonate the mixture. Add ice to the glass and pour the cocktail into it.

Q&A WITH JASON LONIGRO OF EMERIL'S CHOP HOUSE AT THE SANDS CASINO RESORT

Emeril Lagasse is one of the original celebrity chefs. Born in Massachusetts, the young chef came into his own running the kitchen at the legendary Commander's Palace in New Orleans. From there, Lagasse opened his first restaurant in 1992, and since then he has been a constant fixture of the culinary landscape. In 2009, Lagasse grew his business into the Northeast United States with Emeril's Chop House at the Sands Casino Resort in Bethlehem, Pennsylvania. And, as General Manager Jason Lonigro will tell you, it isn't a quality chop house without an inventive bar program.

What can you tell us about how you got into the world of cocktails and a bit about what you do at present?

Right out of high school I became a server at the W Hotel in New Orleans. After a few months one of the bartenders quit, and I kind of lied my way into picking up those shifts. I was lucky enough to be trained by Marvin Allen, who is currently the head bartender of The Carousel Bar at Hotel Monteleone in New Orleans. From there I started working for Emeril's restaurants and the rest is history. I'm currently the general manager of Emeril's Chop House at the Sands Casino Resort in Bethlehem, Pennsylvania.

What do you look for when creating a new cocktail for one of your menus?

When creating a seasonal cocktail list I really start with three things. First, I look at the variety of base spirits to feature, based on seasonality, so that the menu has a little to offer everyone. I then look at the diversity of builds from stirred and boozy to light and lower ABV. For example, I love stirred bourbon cocktails, but that shouldn't be the only style featured on the menu. And last, I look at flavor profiles to fit the season from bold, spice-driven flavors in the fall and winter to fresh, vegetal tones in the spring and summer.

How does managing a bar in the Lehigh Valley differ from other locations where you've worked?

Since we are located in a casino that is very close to other cities we entertain a lot of guests from Philadelphia, New Jersey, and New York, along with those from the Lehigh Valley. No matter what market you are working in, the end goal of giving the guest what they want is always the same. The only challenging aspect can be from guests from out of state who question how wines and spirits are priced, not realizing that Pennsylvania has some of the highest wine and spirit taxes in the country.

What are the benefits of being part of a big restaurant group when it comes to getting spirits that you want to work with? Are there any downsides or factors that make it difficult?

No matter who you work for Pennsylvania makes it very difficult to source certain alcoholic beverages due to it being totally under the state's control. When trying to source out limited release bourbons and whiskies we are limited to using the state-run lottery system. Whereas in a non-control state we would normally be allocated Van Winkle bourbons, for example, in Pennsylvania we are limited to the one bottle we have the opportunity to win, which last year was a bottle of Old Rip Van Winkle 10 Year. There are other advantages and disadvantages with the state system we have to work in, but I'm very lucky to be in a casino with an amazing purchasing department that helps source things for us.

Blue Hawaiian, Brandy Alexander, Pink Squirrel, Rusty Nail, Tom Collins, White Russian, Grasshopper, Rob Roy, Pink Lady: If you had to pick one of these cocktails to add to your cocktail menu how would you reimagine your choice to make it fit in with your menu?

I love playing with drinks that you wouldn't think to find in a fine dining steak house. We actually featured a Pink Squirrel on our Spring/Summer menu because it's the perfect, opulent steak house dessert drink. We kicked it up with homemade vanilla ice cream, and used crème de noyaux and crème de cacao from Tempus Fugit. I also did a fun riff on the Alabama Slammer, replacing Southern Comfort with our house made "Northern Comfort," which we created by altering an old recipe from The Picayune's Creole Cook Book: Cuffs & Buttons, the recipe the Southern Comfort is allegedly modeled after. We've also been playing around with a Rusty Nail variation by approaching it as more of an Old Fashioned, using four types of scotch (Dewar's 12 Year, Macallan Double Cask, Glenfiddich Fire & Cane, and Monkey Shoulder) and adding a few dashes of orange bitters.

What spirits do you like to work with when making cocktails?

I love Amaro, bourbon, and mezcal. The layers of complexity an Amaro can lend is where the fun is, and incorporating multiple ones into one cocktail build can really enhance things from there.

Do you have a favorite cocktail?

I can't say that I have a favorite, but my go-to is a Boulevardier with high-proof bourbon. In warmer months I love mezcal, Campari, and fresh lime juice shaken over ice.

Q&A WITH FRANKIE COSGROVE, BAR MANAGER AT BABEL AT BULLITT HOTEL

Located in Belfast, Ireland, Babel's carefully curated shrub cocktail menu is inspired by its unique "living walls." Featuring over 300 fresh plants, including edible herbs and flowers such as basil, mint, thyme, and sage, these living walls stand behind both the indoor and outdoor bars, and the harvested items become elements of the drinks, from shrubs to infusions and garnishes.

What can you tell us about how your bar came to be?

Babel opened in November 2017, coming into the run-up of Christmas. However, its intended development was being planned for much longer, spanning back to 2016 when the hotel itself was initially opened. We always knew there was going to be a rooftop bar—but when that rooftop bar would come to be and what identity it would take was anyone's guess. Needless to say, we were elated with the final result once the time came.

The grounds of the hotel were initially derelict. I remember walking down Church Lane here in Belfast and looking into the entrance, thinking, *There is no way this is going to be the grounds of such a big investment.* It was a narrow lane that looked unfit for any purpose, so the fact that it has now come to be one of Belfast's most popular hospitality hot spots really is a credit to how serious we, as a city, take our hospitality sector.

Opening a rooftop bar in Belfast was always something that people thought was madness. The sun doesn't exactly shine 365 days of the year here, but we were well prepared. We have our large outdoor terrace with its beautiful, panoramic views, and which receives a majority of the sunshine during those rare moments. We also have an ornate indoor cocktail area that many customers thoroughly enjoy. It has been compared to other cocktail lounges throughout the world, including ones in New York and London, which is always pleasant to hear! Essentially, there is always a space regardless of that day's weather.

Can you tell us about the theme of your bar and how that theme influences your cocktails?

I think that Babel's main theme is "innovation," and I feel this one word encompasses all that we have to offer. Last year alone has been a complete roller coaster and there has never been a moment where we sit idly by waiting for ideas to arrive at our doorstep by some miracle. We like to be proactive!

Our main menu has a strong focus on the use of shrubs as ingredients, which is quite unusual. The flavor they impart is phenomenal, and it is helping us be more sustainable through prolonging the shelf life of the fruit that we order in. Considering that fruit is one of the biggest waste products for bars worldwide, this is something we are extremely proud of. As a team, we are extremely enthusiastic about keeping up-to-date with current affairs throughout the world of drinks. Whether it's visiting drinks festivals, chatting to fellow bartenders, or checking out the latest, or oldest, drinks literature available, we always feel there is something to learn that we can then adapt around our own personalities to deliver bespoke products.

What do you and your team look for when creating new cocktails for your menu?

We never look for a single criterion. Babel's menu has been created in a way whereby all drinks will not appeal to all people, but there will be a drink in there which will ultimately appeal to everyone! We have simple and sweet, we have smoky and bitter, and, of course, we have that one drink that is perceived to be a bartender's drink. Ultimately, we take great pride in the profession we have chosen and there is great satisfaction in knowing that customers are choosing to come to our venue to enjoy our creations. And it is because of this we will always endeavor to make drinks that will leave a lasting impression.

We also try to keep it fresh and, as mentioned before, innovative. One example was for Halloween when we came up with a concept to base a seasonal menu around different fears as opposed to what other people were doing: dry ice, black coloring, cocktails named after some type of monster, etc. As Halloween is a time when people like to be scared, we wanted to put a psychological spin on our offering, which I thought was cool. One drink was based on the fear of sharp objects and was garnished with "glass shards," another was based on the fear of pumpkins and incorporated pumpkin shrub. As a huge fan of crème de violette, an Aviation naturally went on there also.

What can you tell us about the cocktail scene in Belfast? Are there any downsides or things that make it difficult?

The cocktail scene is amazing. For such a small city there is so much to offer. We have gin bars, rum bars, jazz bars, 5-star hotel cocktail bars . . . the list goes on. The people who work in the industry are brilliant, also. When you have a bad day at work, you can always call in to unwind—there's always an ear to bend and offer emotional support. It really is a great network to be part of. The cocktail scene itself is still in its development stages, which is really exciting, but with bars such as ours, Bert's, and The Merchant (all of which are within walking distance from each other!) I won't be surprised when Belfast starts to get more recognition on an international level. As for the negatives, there are always going to be factors that make any job difficult, but I feel the positives outweigh these 10 to 1.

Blue Hawaiian, Brandy Alexander, Pink Squirrel, Rusty Nail, Tom Collins, White Russian, Grasshopper, Rob Roy, Pink Lady: If you had to pick one of these cocktails to add to your cocktail menu how would you reimagine your choice to make it fit in with your style?

There are quite a few of our cocktails that have been influenced by the classics. It's only natural: in order to create new libations you should have a sound knowledge of how cocktails came to be. We have a drink in our menu that is a cross between a Last Word and a Rob Roy. I know that seems counterintuitive, but it works! It's called the Final Curtain and consists of rye, Cognac, Yellow Chartreuse, maraschino liqueur, Boker's Bitters. It's stirred down and has lime oils expressed over the top of it and is garnished with a pickled cherry. The base spirit is obviously different, but anyone who opts for a Last Word is looking for something that packs a punch so the rye and Cognac work well. The sour cherry is still evident and although yellow Chartreuse has been substituted for its green brethren, it still has that herbaceous hit. The only thing missing was the sourness from lime, but we realized that a simple expression of oils was the perfect way to round it off. The cherry is soaked in a pickling agent for up to two weeks. Many people comment these would be amazing on a cheese board, but we reserve them for this particular cocktail. I feel this drink is amazing at showcasing what we are about. Many places are now trying to get their fix through obscurity and get carried away. It is great to see and is something we will also look at to push our limits, but the Final Curtain showcases something that we are proud of: simple elegance.

Do you have a spirit you prefer to work with when making cocktails?

I think everyone has a personal favorite when it comes to spirits, at least, I know I do, at least for a month or two, then I find something else that catches my attention! I personally prefer working with things that most people don't enjoy. It's more of a challenge and more rewarding when someone comments that they didn't think they would have liked a particular drink when they heard it was made with "insert base spirit here," but it has surprised them. Tequila is a fun spirit to play with at the moment. It was such a shooter, but more and more recently it's becoming mainstream and the public is more inclined to try premium, 100 percent agave-based tequilas. I've also become a lot more interested in experimenting with vermouths after having had one of the most refreshing cocktails I have had the pleasure of tasting, which used Belsazar Rosé and water—the exact ingredients have completely escaped me—created by Barney O' Kane of Little Red Door, Paris.

When you get the chance to sit down and have a cocktail, what is your cocktail of choice?

At the moment I am actually trying out classic Daiquiris, but with different base rums, a horizontal tasting as it were. I always go to a beautiful jazz bar called Bert's. The guys there are fantastic. The chat is always great, the reception from the moment you walk through the doors to the moment you leave is faultless, and perhaps most importantly, they do a banging Daiquiri! If it has been a particularly stressful week, I will perhaps try a Champs-Elysees or Last Word to get a Chartreuse hit. Classics aside, if a bartender ever recommends something they are working on I can never say no!

Babel's shrub-forward drink program has set the Belfast cocktail scene abuzz. Give any of these special ingredients a go and you'll quickly see why.

BLACKBERRY & LIME SHRUB

INGREDIENTS:

- 215 G BLACKBERRIES
- ZEST OF 5 LIMES
- 200 G SUGAR
- 235 ML APPLE CIDER VINEGAR

Place blackberries, lime zest, and sugar in a medium bowl. Crush the berries and stir to combine.

Cover bowl with plastic wrap and place in refrigerator. Allow to macerate for a day.

Position a fine-mesh strainer over a small bowl and strain the mixture to remove the solids.

Combine strained syrup with the vinegar. Whisk well to incorporate any undissolved sugar.

You may have some sugar clinging to the berry solids in the strainer; if so, set the strainer with the solids over another small bowl. Pour the syrup-and-vinegar mixture over the solids to wash the sugar into the bowl. Repeat as needed.

Pour syrup-and-vinegar mixture into a clean mason jar. Cap it, shake it well to incorporate any undissolved sugar, and place in the refrigerator for a week before using.

Discard the solids or save them for another preparation.

CHAMOMILE TEA SYRUP

Place the water and sugar in a saucepan and bring to a boil while stirring the mixture.

When the sugar is dissolved, remove the saucepan from heat, add the chamomile tea, and let cool completely.

When the mixture is cool, strain into a glass bottle and store in the refrigerator.

INGREDIENTS:

- 500 ML WATER
- 500 G SUGAR
- 3 TABLESPOONS CHAMOMILE TEA

CHILLI & MANGO SHRUB

Place the mango, vinegar, and chilies in a jar with a tight-fitting lid and stir to combine. Cover and steep at room temperature for 3 days, while gently shaking the jar each day.

After 3 days, strain the mixture while squeezing to remove as much liquid as possible.

Place the strained liquid and sugar in a saucepan and bring to a boil over medium heat. Reduce heat to low and simmer for 10 minutes. Remove from heat and let cool completely. Makes approximately 1 cup.

INGREDIENTS:

- 165 G MANGO, DICED
- 175 ML APPLE CIDER VINEGAR
- 3 RED CHILIES, CHOPPED
- 170 G SUGAR

DRAGON FRUIT & CANTALOUPE SHRUB

Place the flesh of the dragon fruit and cantaloupe in a food processor with the sugar and puree until combined. Place the mixture in a nonreactive container and let steep for 2 days, while shaking regularly.

After 2 days, strain the liquid into a bowl, while squeezing to remove as much liquid as possible.

Gradually pour the vinegar over the strainer to wash as much of the undissolved sugar into the strained liquid. Transfer the shrub to a container and store in the refrigerator.

INGREDIENTS:

- 2 DRAGON FRUITS
- 1 CANTALOUPE
- 200 G SUGAR
- 250 G WHITE WINE VINEGAR

PASSION FRUIT SHRUB

Place the water, sugar, and passion fruit pulp in a saucepan and cook, while stirring, over medium heat. When the sugar is dissolved, remove pan from heat and let cool completely. Pour the mixture over the vinegar, bottle, and store in the refrigerator.

INGREDIENTS:

1 L WATER

1.3 KG SUGAR

PULP FROM 1 CASE OF PASSION FRUITS

500 ML WHITE WINE VINEGAR

RASPBERRY & THYME SHRUB

Place the raspberries and sugar in a bowl, mash the berries so that they release their juice, and stir to combine. Cover and store in the refrigerator for 2 days.

Place the thyme and vinegar in a nonreactive container and let stand for 2 days.

Strain the macerated raspberries through a fine sieve. Working in increments, pour the infused vinegar over the strainer to dissolve as much of the remaining mixture as possible.

Transfer the shrub to a mason jar and refrigerate for 1 week before using.

INGREDIENTS:

250 G RASPBERRIES

225 G SUGAR

8 SPRIGS OF THYME

200 ML APPLE CIDER VINEGAR

RHUBARB & PLUM SHRUB

Crush the plums with your hands and place them in a bowl. Cover with the sugar, stir to combine, and refrigerate for 2 days, while stirring occasionally.

After 2 days, place the mixture in a saucepan with the water and rhubarb. Bring to a boil over medium heat, reduce the heat so that the mixture simmers, and cook until the rhubarb starts to break down.

Remove from heat, let cool, strain, add the vinegar, and stir to combine.

INGREDIENTS:

200 G PLUMS, CHOPPED

255 G SUGAR

200 ML WATER

300 G RHUBARB, DICED

200 ML WHITE WINE VINEGAR

NAMASTEA-INFUSED PIMM'S

Place the tea leaves in the bottle of Pimm's and steep overnight. Strain before using.

INGREDIENTS:

- 3 TEASPOONS FREEBIRD NAMASTEA
- 1 (750 ML) BOTTLE OF PIMM'S NO. 1

STRAWBERRY-PEPPERCORN SHRUB

Place the strawberries, sugar, and pepper in a large jar, cover, and shake to combine. Store in the refrigerator for at least 2 hours and up to 1 day.

Add vinegar, cover, shake to combine, and store in the refrigerator for 2 days.

After 2 days, strain the mixture through a fine sieve, transfer the liquid to a mason jar, and shake to incorporate any undissolved sugar. Transfer to the refrigerator and let stand for 1 week before using.

INGREDIENTS:

- 250 G STRAWBERRIES, SLICED
- 115 G SUGAR
- 2 TEASPOONS COARSELY GROUND BLACK PEPPER
- 235 ML APPLE CIDER VINEGAR

TEA SYRUP

Place the water and sugar in a saucepan and bring to a boil over medium heat. Remove from heat, add the tea bags, and steep for 20 to 25 minutes.

Remove tea bags, let cool completely, and store in the refrigerator.

INGREDIENTS:

- 100 ML WATER
- 100 G SUGAR
- 2 BAGS OF BLACK TEA

PICKLED CHERRIES

Rinse the cherries. Dry them and transfer to a large container.

Place the remaining ingredients in a saucepan and bring to a boil over medium heat. Reduce heat to low and simmer for 5 minutes.

Pour the syrup over the cherries and let stand for 3 minutes. Transfer the mixture to a sterilized jar and let stand until cool. Transfer to the refrigerator and let stand for 2 weeks before using.

INGREDIENTS:

- 600 G CHERRIES
- 500 ML WHITE WINE VINEGAR
- 250 ML WATER
- 200 G LIGHT MUSCOVADO SUGAR
- 1 CINNAMON STICK
- 1 BAY LEAF

BASIL-INFUSED HONEY SYRUP

INGREDIENTS:

500 ML HONEY

250 ML BOILING WATER

4 SPRIGS OF BASIL

Place the honey and boiling water in a large jar and stir to combine. Add the basil, cover, and let cool completely. Strain before using.

GUINNESS & SAGE SYRUP

INGREDIENTS:

500 ML GUINNESS

500 ML BROWN SUGAR

PINCH OF SAGE LEAVES

Place the Guinness and brown sugar in a saucepan and simmer over medium-low heat, while stirring, until the sugar is dissolved. Remove from heat, transfer to a sterilized jar, and add the sage leaves. Steep overnight and strain before using.

PICKLED POMEGRANATE SEEDS

INGREDIENTS:

4 LARGE POMEGRANATES

400 ML RED WINE

400 ML RED WINE VINEGAR

400 G DEMERARA SUGAR

5 CLOVES

5 PINK PEPPERCORNS

3 CARDAMOM PODS

1 STAR ANISE POD

1 CINNAMON STICK

1 TABLESPOON CORIANDER SEEDS, TOASTED

ZEST OF ½ ORANGE

Cut the pomegranates into quarters and remove the seeds. Place the seeds in a bowl and set aside.

Place the remaining ingredients in a saucepan and bring to a boil. Remove from heat and let stand overnight. Strain the mixture through a sieve, and then add the pomegranate seeds. Transfer to 4 sterilized 500 ml jars and store in the refrigerator for 2 to 3 days before using.

PINEAPPLE SHRUB

Remove the skins and cores of the pineapples and place them in a container with the vinegar. Chop the flesh into chunks, transfer to a container, and cover with the sugars. Use your hands to crush the pineapple chunks and release their juices.

Let stand for 2 days. After 2 days, strain the contents of both containers and combine the infused vinegar with the pineapple syrup. Whisk to incorporate any undissolved sugar.

If there is undissolved sugar in the strainer, pour the shrub over the sugar, repeating until it has been incorporated.

Transfer the shrub to a mason jar, cover, and shake to combine. Store in the refrigerator for 1 week before using.

INGREDIENTS:

- 4 PINEAPPLES
- 1 L APPLE CIDER VINEGAR
- 500 G CASTER SUGAR
- 500 G BROWN SUGAR

DELICIOUS BERRY SYRUP

Place the sugar and water in a saucepan and cook, while stirring, over medium heat until the sugar has dissolved. Remove from heat, add the tea leaves, and let steep for 1 day. Strain before using.

INGREDIENTS:

- 500 G CASTER SUGAR
- 500 G WATER
- 4 TEASPOONS FREEBIRD DELICIOUS BERRY TEA

HIBISCUS GRENADINE

Place the pomegranate juice and tea in a saucepan and cook over medium heat until the liquid has reduced by half. Add the sugar, stir until it is dissolved, and then strain the liquid into a container. Let cool completely, add the vodka and citric acid, and refrigerate.

INGREDIENTS:

- 2 L FRESH POMEGRANATE JUICE
- 20 G HIBISCUS & POMEGRANATE TEA
- 1.3 KG CASTER SUGAR
- 35 ML VODKA
- 1 TEASPOON CITRIC ACID

BABEL SIGNATURE RECIPES

THE BABEL

GARNISH: 1 SPRIG OF MINT, 1 BLACKBERRY, & 1 SPRIG OF ROSEMARY

Place all of the ingredients, except for the soda water, in a cocktail shaker filled with ice and shake vigorously. Strain into a wine glass filled with crushed ice and top with the soda water. Spear the blackberry with the rosemary and use it and the sprig of mint as a garnish.

INGREDIENTS:

- 50 ML HAVANA CLUB 3-YEAR RUM
- 25 ML FRESH LIME JUICE
- 15 ML SIMPLE SYRUP
- 20 ML BLACKBERRY & LIME SHRUB (SEE PAGE 784)
- PINCH OF MINT LEAVES
- SODA WATER, TO TOP

FINAL CURTAIN

GARNISH: 1 STRIP OF LIME PEEL & PICKLED CHERRIES (SEE PAGE 787)

Place the ingredients in a mixing glass filled with ice and stir until chilled. Strain into a coupe, express the lime peel over the cocktail, and then discard it. Garnish with the Pickled Cherries.

INGREDIENTS:

- 25 ML RITTENHOUSE RYE
- 25 ML HENNESSY VS
- 5 ML YELLOW CHARTREUSE
- 10 ML LUXARDO
- 5 ML SIMPLE SYRUP
- 2 DASHES OF DR. ADAM ELMEGIRAB'S BOKER'S BITTERS

ANKLE-BITER

GARNISH: SAGE LEAVES

Combine all of the ingredients, except for the soda water, in a cocktail shaker filled with ice and shake vigorously. Strain into a rocks glass filled with ice and garnish with the sage leaves.

INGREDIENTS:

- 50 ML BELVEDERE CITRUS
- 50 ML GRAPEFRUIT JUICE
- 15 ML SIMPLE SYRUP
- 2 DASHES OF LEMON BITTERS
- PINCH OF SAGE
- SODA WATER, TO TOP

MAI-P-A

GARNISH: 1 SPRIG OF MINT & 1 ORANGE WHEEL

Place all of the ingredients, except for the beer, in a cocktail shaker filled with ice and shake vigorously. Strain into a rocks glass filled with ice, top with the beer, and garnish with the mint and orange wheel.

INGREDIENTS:

- 20 ML APPELTON VX RUM
- 20 ML HAVANA CLUB 7-YEAR RUM
- 20 ML FRESH LIME JUICE
- 10 ML COINTREAU
- 10 ML ORGEAT
- 10 ML PASSION FRUIT SHRUB (SEE PAGE 786)
- DASH OF ANGOSTURA BITTERS
- HIGH WIRE GRAPEFRUIT IPA, TO TOP

HIGH WIRE
GRAPEFRUIT PALE ALE

Q&A WITH RICHARD POPE, OWNER OF MULBERRY BAR

Verdant flora isn't restricted to the lovely patio at Mulberry Bar in Toronto, Ontario. Owner Richard Pope's fascination with glassed-in Parisian spaces makes for a lush, fern-filled interior where customers quaff cocktails like the Coco Chanel (rhum, coconut liqueur, lime, almond orgeat, Fernet-Branca) and the Umbrella Over Cherbourg (rhubarb and chocolate liquers, rose water, saffron, lemon).

How was this bar started?

I've owned and run Northwood, down the street from Mulberry Bar, for nearly 6 years, and Mulberry is our newer sister location with a different feel, look, and menu.

Can you tell us about the theme of the bar and the focus of the cocktails?

No specific bars have inspired the look here, but French design in general has. Particularly Parisian—in Paris there are glass arcades everywhere, hence the atrium we created inside. We've also since developed a section of the menu dedicated to our favorite (memories of) cocktails at Parisian cocktail bars, changed up after each time we visit the bars there. We've called this section the Arcades Project after Walter Benjamin's famous cataloguing of Parisian culture.

What do you look for when creating new cocktails for your menu?

I typically begin with flavor combinations, like grape and walnut, and build up from there—from grape: Cognac, wine, verjus; bitters from the walnut. Then I add whatever else goes well with these base flavors.

How do the food and culture of Toronto influence the cocktails that you offer?

Not sure. We've found our niche and happily exist within it.

What are the best parts of running a cocktail bar in Toronto? Are there any downsides or things that make it difficult?

The best parts: creating unique and fun experiences for patrons, from the interior design to the playlists to the lighting to, of course, the cocktail menu. What matters is how everything comes together. There aren't really downsides, besides the high costs of Toronto rent and alcohol prices.

Blue Hawaiian, Brandy Alexander, Pink Squirrel, Rusty Nail, Tom Collins, White Russian, Grasshopper, Rob Roy, Pink Lady: If you had to pick one of these classic cocktails to add to your cocktail menu how would you reimagine your choice to make it fit in with your style?

Pink Squirrel. I'd probably add rose water to play on the flavor combo of almond and rose. Rose would work well with the pink color of the drink, too. Maybe a touch of Cherry Heering as well.

Do you have a favorite cocktail?

Only of the moment. My current favorite is our recently developed Paris Plages: Cortel Napoleon brandy, Briottet banana liqueur, verjus, pineapple syrup. It's glug glug, the sort of drink you'd want all day, all night at one of Paris' pop-up summer beaches.

Do you have a favorite alcohol to work with when making cocktails?

Calvados. My uncle makes his own in Normandy, France, and we grew up drinking it after dinner every night.

Q&A WITH RAFAEL BARBOSA OF PORT MORRIS DISTILLERY

Tucked away in the Bronx is a craft distillery that produces *pitorro,* which is a Puerto Rican version of moonshine.

What can you tell us about how the Port Morris Distillery came to be?

In 2010, after selling a previous business, my partner William Valentin and I were discussing *pitorro*, which is from Puerto Rico and known as "moonshine rum."

We came up with the idea to start distilling pitorro here on the mainland. And what better place than the Bronx? We contacted my uncle, a long-time moonshiner, and the rest is history.

What makes your spirit unique or different from current offerings?

My opinion is that most craft distillers are doing the same thing: whisk(e)y, gin, vodka, and it all tastes the same. Even when a brand calls its product moonshine it's usually 80 proof white whiskey. Moonshine to me is something that's made from the heart, an old family recipe. That's how we approach our pitorro shine, which is what we use as the basis to make all our products. We use techniques that have been passed down to me from Puerto Rico, while using New York apples and honey, along with brown sugar, to make our mash.

What are the benefits of having a small distillery in the Bronx? Are there any downsides or things that make it difficult?

We are the only distillery in the borough so we get lots of support from the local community. The downside is that there isn't a craft cocktail culture in the Bronx, and being the only one here people forget. The craft movement is making its way here but is taking time. We are the forefront of this wave.

Q&A WITH DARYL PRYOR, HEAD BARTENDER AT B&GC DENVER

"When you have a choice, choose happy": these words, uttered by aviation pioneer Florence Lowe "Pancho" Barnes, also serve as the motto for B&GC in Denver, a speakeasy-styled basement bar. Nostalgia meets hip behind the street level's golden doorbell, and once you've descended the stairs, you won't want to keep the drinks a secret.

What can you tell us about how B&GC came to be?

B&GC is really the brainchild of Brandon Wise, the vice president of beverage for Sage Restaurant Group. Brandon has spent years developing fantastic cocktail programs for Sage's hotel restaurants. As the Halcyon was being put together in Denver, the team realized they had a great space tucked away in the basement. When asked what he would like to see there, he knew immediately. With B&GC, we really wanted to create a unique environment to create really intimate cocktail experiences for our guests.

Can you tell us about the theme of the bar and how it influences your cocktails?

B&GC is a vintage American cocktail bar. Our idea is not to limit ourselves to a particular period, but rather to celebrate the timeless spirit of the American cocktail. We want our drinks to feel like classics, even if we're exploring new or unfamiliar flavors. Even with the seeming exclusivity, it's supremely important to the team that we connect with our guests, whether it's through conversation or the beverages we're making for them. In that sense, we don't look to challenge our guests with flavors. More so, we want to showcase or highlight new spirits or ingredients or flavor combinations in a way that excites them.

What you do and your team look for when creating a new cocktail for the menu?

One of our guiding principles is that we want our drinks to evoke the sense that these cocktails could be something you'd find on a classic cocktail menu, had the products or ingredients in them been readily available at the time. There are drinks that we make that step far outside the box, but we still believe in their core structure and balance echoing the sentiments of the simple, enduring classics. We don't want to use eccentric techniques and flavors just for the sake of being new and different. When we turn toward these things, our idea is that they should, first and foremost, make sense within the cocktail. They should highlight the soul of the drink, rather than be the soul of the drink themselves.

How does being a "speakeasy" with such a distinct and beautiful style affect how you create cocktails and update your menu? Even the bathroom wallpaper is memorable.

Working in such a beautiful space can be a little intimidating. People post more pictures of that wallpaper to social media than they do pictures of the drinks! We joke a lot that, from the minute someone steps through the door of B&GC, we've already won, just a little. There's a certain expectation, though, once someone walks down the alley and into a dimly lit, concrete hallway, only to end up in this gorgeous, moody, austere room. If the drinks didn't land, we'd have a real façade on our hands. It's important that our cocktails showcase the heart and soul that create the space. That people can see we're not tricking them. Too many times, people expect a "speakeasy" to be pretentious, overwrought, and unwelcoming. When guests look at our menu and seem intimidated or confused, we tell them, "You've been to a bar before. It's just like that, but darker."

What can you tell us about the cocktail scene in Denver? Are there any downsides or things that make it difficult?

I dig this city in a big, big way. The cocktail scene is growing so quickly, and there are so many young, hungry bartenders who want to grow with it rather than out of it. The public at large is growing with us, too. If anything, the biggest challenge can be keeping up with the people on the other side of the bar. We'll hear things like "Oh yeah, I have a bottle of that on my backbar, what else do you have?" or "I was just making those for my friends last week." When just a few years ago, this was all fairly new to them. It pushes us to grow more knowledgeable as a community, and this community of bartenders is damn supportive of each other.

Blue Hawaiian, Brandy Alexander, Pink Squirrel, Rusty Nail, Tom Collins, White Russian, Grasshopper, Rob Roy, Pink Lady: If you had to pick one of these cocktails to add to your cocktail menu how would you reimagine your choice to make it fit in with your style?

We actually have a Rusty Nail on our classics menu. Our classics section tends to reach for B-side cocktails, things that don't always get printed or called for anymore, but that we think are worth drinking. I call it our Hipster Classics section. We try to stick to traditional builds as much as possible, with some modern tweaks to speak more to the modern palate. With the Rusty Nail, we dialed back the Drambuie to dry out the cocktail a little and added a dash of Fee Brothers Peach Bitters to brighten things up. Our base is Auchentoshan's American Oak, which is light and toasty. It's a few simple updates that help to lift the cocktail above its reputation while still staying true to what it is.

A QUIET DIVORCE

GARNISH: 1 STRIP OF ORANGE PEEL

Combine all ingredients in a mixing glass filled with ice and stir until chilled and slightly diluted. Strain into a Nick & Nora glass, express the orange peel over the cocktail, and then use it as a garnish.

INGREDIENTS:

- 2 OZ. RITTENHOUSE RYE
- ¾ OZ. DUBONNET ROUGE
- ¼ OZ. AMARO NONINO QUINTESSENTIA
- 2 DASHES OF BITTERCUBE TRINITY BITTERS

DISTANT LOVER

GARNISH: MINT LEAVES

Place all of the ingredients in a cocktail shaker filled with ice and shake vigorously. Double-strain into a rocks glass containing a large piece of ice and garnish with a slightly ridiculous amount of mint.

INGREDIENTS:

- 1½ OZ. HENRY MCKENNA BONDED BOURBON
- ½ OZ. BRANCA MENTA
- ½ OZ. GRADE B MAPLE SYRUP
- ¾ OZ. FRESH LEMON JUICE
- 3 DASHES OF STRONGWATER RIZA BITTERS

BARCELONA WILDWOOD

GARNISH: 1 CUCUMBER SLICE & 3 DROPS OF ROSE WATER

Place all of the ingredients in a cocktail shaker filled with ice and shake until chilled. Double-strain into a coupe, float the cucumber slice on top, and top with the rose water.

INGREDIENTS:

- 1½ OZ. AVUA PRATA CACHAÇA
- ½ OZ. MIDORI
- ¼ OZ. NARDINI MANDORLA
- ½ OZ. FRESH LIME JUICE
- 2 SPOONFULS OF POWDERED SUGAR
- 1 EGG WHITE

A NOTE FROM PORTLAND, OREGON

Emily Ross-Johnson is a spirits specialist and brand ambassador based in Portland, OR. She and I go back a bit as she founded and ran the Astoria Whiskey Society in Queens. When I started the Manhattan Whiskey Club, Emily was the person who provided the most guidance. Currently, she represents Oxley Gin as their Portland ambassador, enjoys creating, styling, and photographing cocktails for her popular blog, fern + shaker, and also serves as the vice president for the Oregon chapter of the United States Bartenders' Guild.

I've always known Emily to craft a mean cocktail, and I've asked her to share a few of her favorites.

POMEGRANATE PISCO SOUR

Place all of the ingredients, except for the bitters, in a cocktail shaker with no ice and dry shake for 1 minute. Add ice and shake for 10 seconds. Double-strain into a coupe, add the bitters, and use a toothpick to swirl them.

INGREDIENTS:

- 2 OZ. CAMPO DE ENCANTO GRAND & NOBLE PISCO
- 1 OZ. FRESH LIME JUICE
- 1 OZ. BG REYNOLDS LUSH GRENADINE TROPICAL SYRUP
- 1 EGG WHITE
- 4–5 DROPS OF BOY DRINKS WORLD PASSION FRUIT BITTERS

ROSY CHEEKS

GARNISH: ROSE PETALS

Rose Syrup: Combine 4 tablespoons culinary-grade rose petals, 1 cup sugar, and 1 cup water in a saucepan and bring to a boil. Reduce heat and simmer for 5 minutes. Remove from heat and let cool. Strain into an airtight container and store for up to a month in the fridge.

Place all of the ingredients, except for the sparkling wine, in a cocktail shaker filled with ice. Shake for 10 seconds and strain into a champagne flute or coupe. Top with sparkling wine and garnish with the rose petals.

INGREDIENTS:

- ½ OZ. ROSE SYRUP
- 1½ OZ. THE BOTANIST GIN
- ½ OZ. MEYER LEMON JUICE
- DRY SPARKLING WINE, TO TOP

¿QUE ONDA, BLANCA?

GARNISH: GRATED NUTMEG & 1 ORCHID BLOSSOM

Place all of the ingredients in a cocktail shaker filled with ice and shake vigorously. Strain into a highball glass filled with ice and garnish with the grated nutmeg and the orchid.

INGREDIENTS:

- 1 OZ. PIERRE FERRAND 1840 COGNAC
- 1 OZ. FLOR DE CANA 7 YEAR GRAN RESERVA RUM
- ½ OZ. BERGAMOT-ORANGE JUICE
- ½ OZ. OLOROSO SHERRY
- ½ OZ. COINTREAU
- ½ OZ. GRENADINE

ONE NIGHT IN DUBLIN . . .

. . . a friend and I were walking near St. Stephen's Green. When we ducked into the Urchin Bar for a pit stop as we made our way to The Palace Bar, we had the pleasure of meeting Milan Ormanović. He made a bespoke cocktail that I loved and I have asked him to share a few of his cocktails with you. He's been working as a bartender for more than 16 years, and when I asked him what drove him to cocktails in particular, he felt it was the creativity—the flavors and flavor combinations drive his interest. These days, if you make your way to Dublin you might find him hard at work at the Americana in the Devlin Hotel, where it's all about local: local products, local spirits.

MILAN'S MANHATTAN

GARNISH: 1 WIDE STRIP OF ORANGE PEEL & 1 BRANDY-SOAKED CHERRY

Place all of the ingredients in a mixing glass filled with ice and stir until chilled. Strain into a Nick & Nora glass and garnish with the orange peel and the brandy-soaked cherry.

INGREDIENTS:

- 2 OZ. RYE WHISKEY
- ¾ OZ. SWEET VERMOUTH
- 1 TABLESPOON SOUR CHERRY SYRUP
- 2 DASHES OF ANGOSTURA BITTERS
- DASH OF ORANGE BITTERS

IRISH COFFEE NO. 3

GARNISH: 1 STRIP OF ORANGE PEEL & DEHYDRATED YOGURT

Add the ingredients to a sherry glass in the order they are listed in. Express the orange peel over the cocktail, discard, and garnish with the dehydrated yogurt.

INGREDIENTS:

- 30 ML POWERS JOHN'S LANE IRISH WHISKEY
- 5 ML BERMET
- 70 ML COCONUT COLD BREW COFFE
- 10 ML SUGARCANE JUICE

Q&A WITH GREG BOEHM, OWNER OF COCKTAIL KINGDOM, MACE, BOILERMAKER, AND KATANA KITTEN

Greg Boehm, Mud Puddle Books publisher, and the owner of Cocktail Kingdom and several New York City bars, has his finger on the pulse of contemporary cocktail culture. His deep appreciation for the history of cocktails, and his collection of over 3,000 vintage books related to drinks and drinking (which was recently digitized, and upon request, can be accessed by the public) is a big part of the reason why.

Can you tell us a bit about yourself and how you got into the industry?

Sterling, my family's publishing company, published *Classic Cocktails* by Salvatore Calabrese in 1997. At that time I would be in London fairly often and I spent many of those nights at the Library Bar where Salvatore's team would make amazing cocktails. I was hooked, and I started collecting antique cocktail books as my interest in cocktails grew. A couple years later I started importing high-quality barware, and finally started designing and manufacturing barware.

What can you tell us about the creation of Cocktail Kingdom?

Cocktail Kingdom started when I published very accurate facsimile reproductions of some of the most important cocktail books from the 1800s and early 1900s. As I came to know many great bartenders, I was asked to import barware from Japan and Germany, which I did. After talking with many of the top cocktail bartenders, I realized there was an opportunity to design and sell barware both based on antiques and more modern styles. Today, Cocktail Kingdom sells barware and glassware to more than 60 countries. We have special barware lines with many of the industry greats, such as David Wondrich, Jeff "Beachbum" Berry, Jeffrey Morganthaler, Gaz Regan, and Dale DeGroff.

What are the themes of your bars?

Boilermaker is my oldest bar. I wanted to create a place that was more of a "local" that could also make great cocktails. It is the kind of bar that gets better with age. I was actually happy when the banquettes started to get beat up a little. Mace was the next bar that I opened. Nico de Soto was one of my absolute favorite bartenders. The cocktails he made were so good. So he and I decided to open a small bar with spice-focused cocktails. Since Nico and I travel so extensively, and spices are truly international, it was a good fit. The walls are decorated with jars of spices that I carried back from places like Madagascar and India. Next up was Existing Conditions. Don Lee and I had worked together at Cocktail Kingdom for a few years, and we had often discussed opening a bar together. When Don asked if I would want to include Dave Arnold in the mix, I jumped at the chance. We now have a relaxed bar that uses technology and a bit of science to offer a unique cocktail program.

What do you and your team look for when starting a new bar?

I just go with gut instinct when deciding to open a new bar. I do not even put together a business plan. It is all about team building for me. Of course, finding the right space for the right price is important too.

As a longtime member of the cocktail industry, what are your thoughts on the cocktail scene in New York? Are there any downsides or things that make it difficult?

New York has an amazing cocktail scene. However, recently I have been seeing things that make me nervous. Every restaurant and bar seem to feel pressure to have a cocktail program. This means that places offer cocktails even if there is no talented bartender to execute them well. This worries me because I am meeting drinkers who stay away from cocktails after a few bad experiences. It is important to me that cocktail bartenders learn the classic cocktails and a bit of history so they can be well rounded and create good drinks.

Q&A WITH ZACH SHARAGA, CO-FOUNDER OF MACE AND OWNER OF DEAR MAMA COFFEE

Not only did Zach Sharaga expose yours truly to the wide world of cocktails, but he is a friend. Since the days of Louis 649, Zach has kept busy with Dear Mama Coffee and Mace, which he helped to open with Greg Boehm.

What were you doing before opening Louis 649?

I opened Louis 649 at the ripe young age of 20. Before that, I was working in retail for Gap and Club Monaco, for a total of three years. Those experiences gave me a solid foundation and the courage to embark on entrepreneurship.

What was the theme of Louis 649 and how did that theme influence your cocktails?

Louis 649 was a neighborhood bar with an approachable menu of spirits and cocktails. We made sure everyone working there knew about the drinks on our menu and could talk shop if the guest was inquisitive or interested. Cocktails were a way for us to always keep our bar dynamic and offered us a common language with guests from all walks of life. Everyone has a cocktail story—whether it's the memory of a parent who always mixed an Old Fashioned after dinner or someone trying a Martini for the first time—so we took to understanding the history of drinks and had a passion to share the knowledge over the bar.

You're expanding Dear Mama Coffee and involved with Mace. What has changed about opening a bar today compared to when you started Louis 649?

The cocktail scene in the early aughts was just starting to pick up steam. Sasha Petraske's Milk & Honey had been open for a few years. A lot of industry professionals and budding cocktail enthusiasts were strongly influenced by how Sasha's bars were dedicated to classics. Creating a bar now versus then is different because cocktail programs nowadays are ubiquitous, which isn't necessarily a good thing. All bars and restaurants are attempting to offer a cocktail program. But very few hit the mark. There is a lot of responsibility that comes with understanding the craft and being able to execute at a very high level for guests who spend their hard-earned money.

What do you look for when creating new cocktails?

We aim to incorporate new artisanal liqueurs and spirits and include a broad scope of flavors as a way to introduce new beverages to drinkers.

Blue Hawaiian, Brandy Alexander, Pink Squirrel, Rusty Nail, Tom Collins, White Russian, Grasshopper, Rob Roy, Pink Lady: If you had to pick one of these cocktails to add to a menu how would you reimagine your choice to make it fit in with your style?

White Russian. I would use different coffee roast profiles to create variations of house-made coffee liqueur and experiment with alternative milks. The combinations are endless.

Do you have a spirit you prefer to work with when making cocktails?

It's difficult to pick a single category but if I had to, it would likely be whisk(e)y. It's my favorite category and one that offers a wide range of flavor notes to accompany.

When you get the chance to sit down and have a cocktail, what is your cocktail of choice?

A properly made Manhattan with rye whiskey.

I've included my notes from your Cocktail 101 class in 2011 (see pages 18-19). What advice would you give today's budding cocktail makers?

Taste, taste, taste—above all else! Following a written recipe when too many other variables are not factored in is a recipe for disaster. People don't consider the specific spirit and how it affects a cocktail, for example 80-proof rye versus 100-proof rye, or the quality and taste of their ice, or the lemon juice they may be using.

METRIC EQUIVALENTS

VOLUME MEASURES

⅛ teaspoon = 0.6 ml
¼ teaspoon = 1.23 ml
½ teaspoon = 2.5 ml
1 teaspoon = 5 ml
1 tablespoon (3 teaspoons) = ½ fluid ounce = 15 ml
2 tablespoons = 1 fluid ounce = 29.5 ml
¼ cup (4 tablespoons) = 2 fluid ounces = 59 ml
⅓ cup (5⅓ tablespoons) = 2.7 fluid ounces = 80 ml
½ cup (8 tablespoons) = 4 fluid ounces = 120 ml
⅔ cup (10⅔ tablespoons) = 5.4 fluid ounces = 160 ml
¾ cup (12 tablespoons) = 6 fluid ounces = 180 ml
1 cup (16 tablespoons) = 8 fluid ounces = 240 ml

WEIGHTS

1 ounce = 28 grams
2 ounces = 57 grams
4 ounces (¼ pound) = 113 grams
8 ounces (½ pound) = 227 grams
16 ounces (1 pound) = 454 grams

APPENDIX

As you have no doubt noticed, there is a dizzying array of drinks in this book, and many of them feature unusual and exotic garnishes. As I mention in the Introduction, one of the greatest assets of having so many recipes in one place is that you can use them to come up with your own take on a cocktail. In the name of such experimentation, the following garnishes are not used in any specific recipes, but could come in handy if you set out to create your own bespoke drinks.

Citrus Basket: using key or kaffir limes or dwarf lemons to create handled citrus "baskets" that hold edible seeds such as pomegranate, watermelon, persimmon, akebia, melon, cherimoya, or other edible fruit seeds, is a stunning yet whimsical layered look. Cut the citrus while either holding it in one hand or placing it on a cutting board. Using a channel knife or serrated knife, cut a wide strip in the vertical midsection of the fruit, working from the top to the horizontal middle. Cut around the strip and remove the two sections of fruit. Cut the fruit away from the lower portion of the wide strip to make a "basket" handle. Carefully remove the pulp from the bottom half of the fruit. Mold back into shape and fill the basket with a few of the edible seeds.

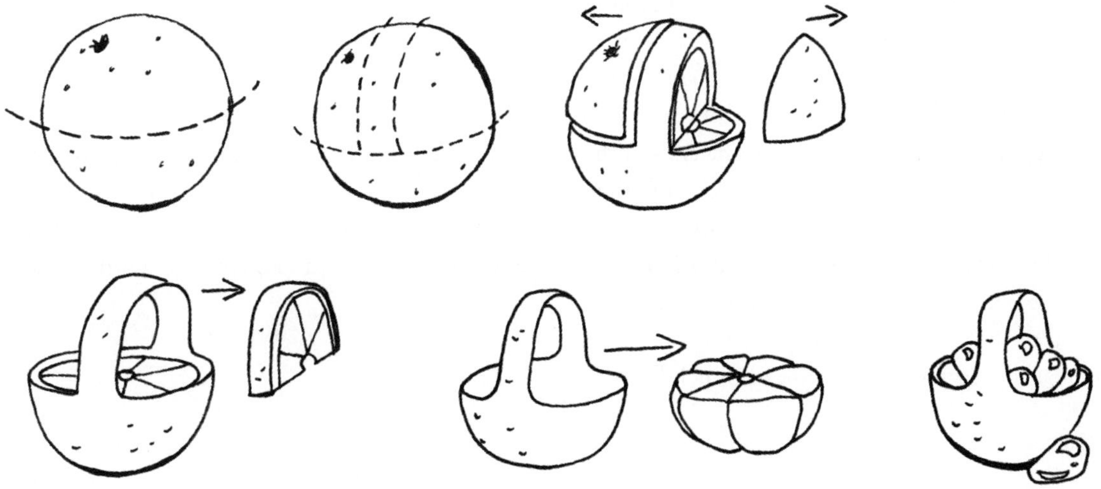

Flower: this "gateway garnish" is relatively simple to make. Using a vegetable peeler or a Y-shaped garnish peeler, hold the fruit in one hand or place it on a cutting board. Start at one end and cut a thin, long, uninterrupted strip of peel. Take the strip of peel and wrap as tightly as possible to form a floret. You can secure with a small toothpick or allow the florets to "blossom" and open accordingly.

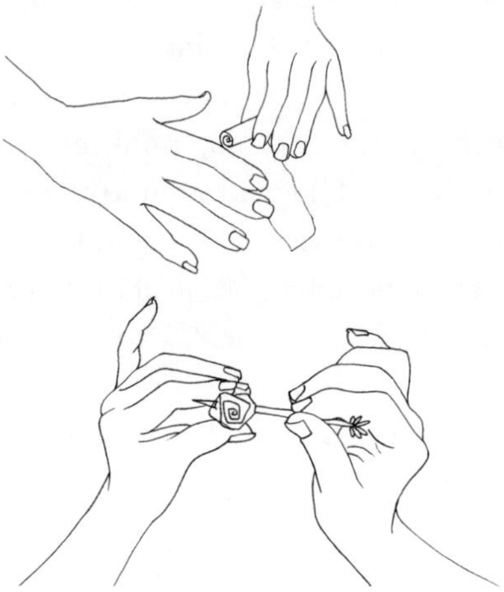

Butterfly: cut a thin strip of citrus peel around one side of the fruit with a vegetable peeler or channel knife. Repeat on the other side of the fruit. On a cutting board, cut the strips into 1-inch-long pieces. Next, cut off the ends of the citrus. Cut the citrus into thin wheels, and then cut the wheels into thirds. To assemble the Butterfly, place two of the wheel thirds on a clean citrus leaf with the pointed ends touching. Use two of the 1-inch-long strips as the antennae. Float the Butterfly in a drink or punch bowl.

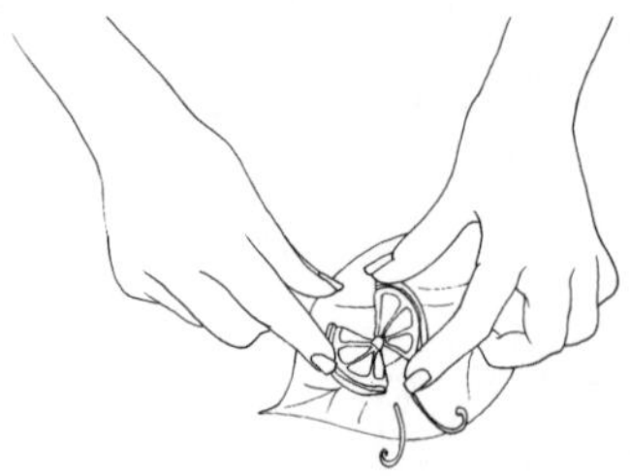

Ship Ahoy!: using a serrated knife, cut a lemon or lime into eight wedges. Take a lemon or lime wedge, cut straight across the top, and remove the center section. Cut a thin strip from a different citrus peel (orange, tangerine, or pummelo, for example) to create the ship's sail. Stand a toothpick in the center of the fruit wedge. Skewer the strip of peel to create the sail. Cut a cherry into quarters and add one of the cherry pieces to the tip of the toothpick to make a flag! You can also use a cranberry or a blueberry as your flag.

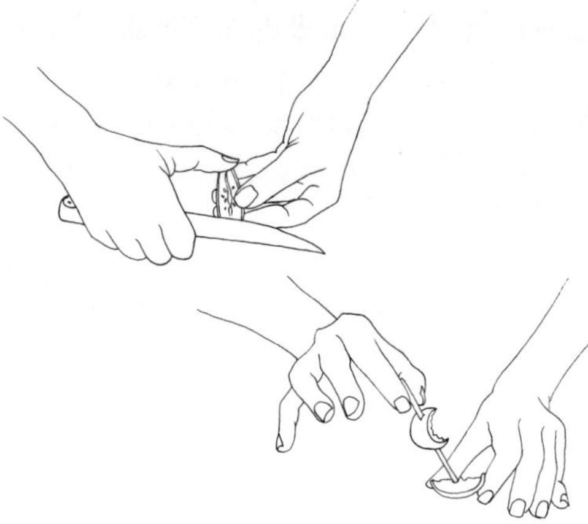

Pineapple Firebird: an exotic garnish for tiki cocktails. The outside skin or "pine" is the tail of the bird. To create, you'll need a knife, a maraschino cherry with its stem, and a toothpick.

Remove the pineapple top about an inch from the base of the leaves. Vertically section the pineapple top. Each section should have a bit of pineapple flesh and a plume of leaves. Cut a slit at a 45-degree angle from the inner flesh toward the outer shell of the pineapple. Insert the toothpick vertically through the smaller segment of flesh. Put the cherry on the toothpick; the stem should hang over the drink, giving the illusion that the bird is drinking from the glass.

Cucumber Rose: using a vegetable peeler or paring knife, slice the cucumber lengthwise to create thin ribbons. Roll one end of a ribbon to a tight center. Keep turning the ribbon around the center by holding in one hand and turning with the other until you reach the end of the ribbon. Hold in place with a clothespin or toothpick. Garnish with a cherry tomato or olive for added dimension and color.

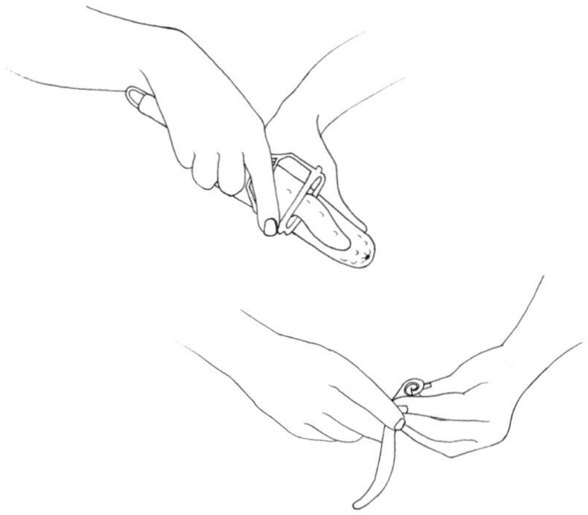

Cucumber Ship: Use three to four cucumber ribbons and cut into triangles. Insert a toothpick into the tiered or layered cucumbers and top with a sail!

Cucumber Tree: using the same method as in the Cucumber Rose, cut a cucumber into ribbons, then loop over and back on a toothpick, spreading the "tree branches" from larger/wider to shorter as you approach the "top" of the tree. Add a tiny olive, ear of pickled baby corn, carrot ribbons, or beet strings to form a kind of maypole. You can perch on the glass rim while using the olive or corn on the bottom as the "trunk" of the tree, or simply place the garnish in the glass.

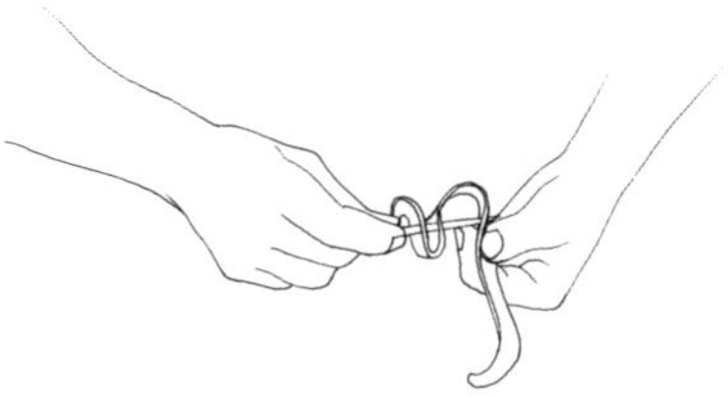

Cucumber Waffle Cut: score a peeled cucumber, and then, using a crinkle knife, cut the cucumber into wheels. The waffle cut slices can be topped with an edible flower and floated in a drink, or cut to perch on the side of the glass. You can also skewer two or three on a toothpick with an olive on each end and place in the glass.

Banana Dolphin: Brian Miller details his method for this dramatic tour de force:

"Shape three 'fins' for the tiki dolphin out of pineapple leaves. Remove any brown areas from the leaves and make sure your leaf selections are green and firm. Two of the leaves should be the same size (these will be the flippers), and the third leaf should be bigger and will become the fin.

"Cut off the bottom fifth of a banana. Slice off a quarter inch of the stem tip of the banana. Slice through the stem to make the dolphin's mouth. Make a slit at the top part of the banana (the dolphin's back), and insert the larger of the pineapple leaves.

"Make two slits at the sides of the peel about halfway down the banana. Insert the smaller pineapple leaves to create the flippers. Next make a slit at a 45-degree angle about an inch from the bottom of the banana. This is how you will make the dolphin stand on the lip of the glass."

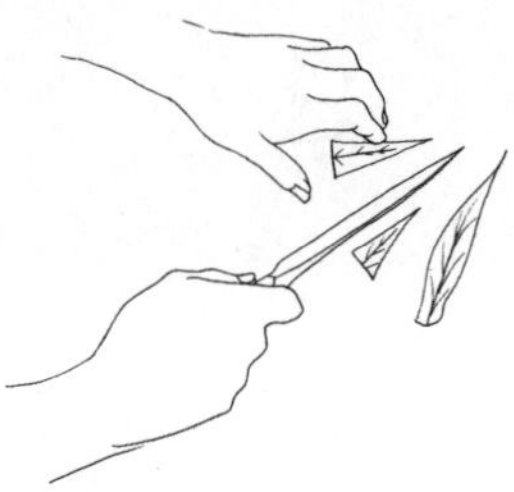

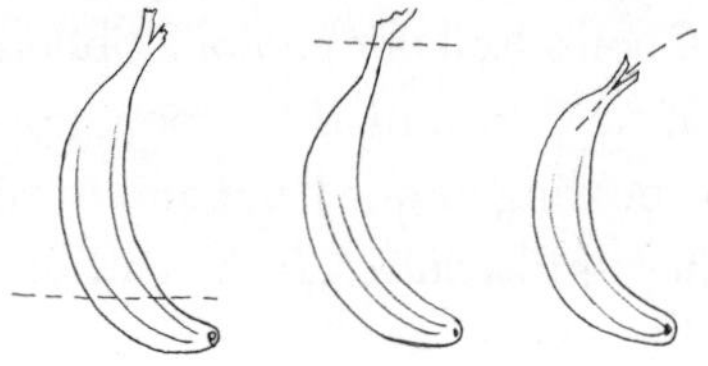

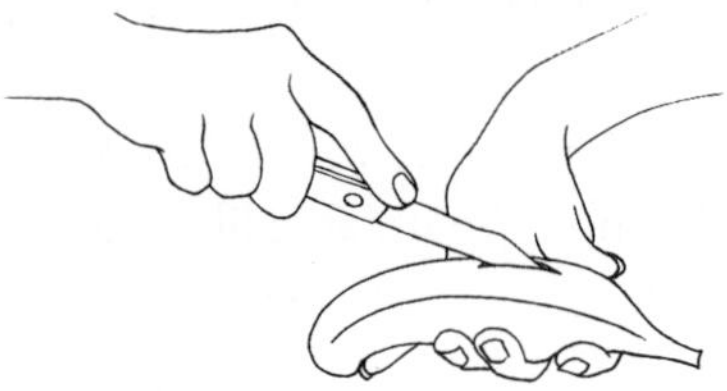

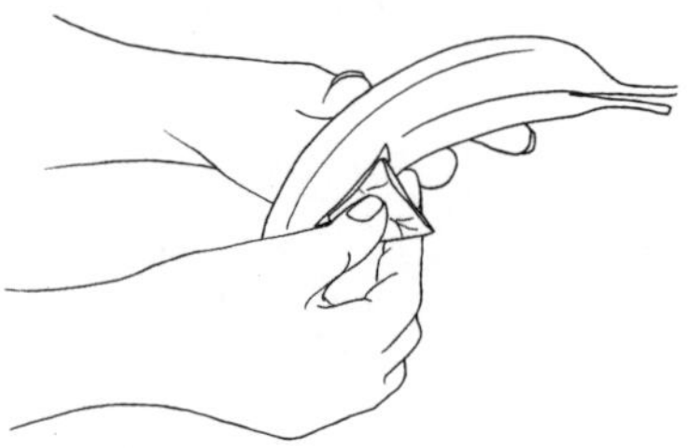

GLOSSARY

Absinthe mist: fill a small, travel-sized spray bottle with absinthe. Coat the inside of the glass with 1 to 2 sprays.

Advocaat: a traditional Dutch alcoholic beverage typically made from egg yolks, sugar, and brandy. A popular drink throughout Europe around the holidays, it has a smooth, custard-like consistency.

Amaro: an Italian herbal liqueur that is usually consumed as an after-dinner digestif. It comes in a number of varieties, among which Cynar, Fernet-Branca, and Amaro Averna are the best known. It typically carries a bittersweet flavor.

Aperitif/Digestif: a drink that stimulates your appetite or a drink that helps you digest your meal. Examples of aperitifs are Suze and soda, any champagne-based cocktail, Lillet, or a kir. Digestifs are drinks made with brandy, Chartreuse, Bénédictine, or Calvados.

Aperol: a popular aperitif consisting primarily of gentian, rhubarb, and cinchona. It is similar in taste to Campari, but Aperol is less bitter and contains less than half of the alcohol.

Appellation of Origin: a legally defined and protected geographical indication that identifies where a particular product comes from. Champagne and Cognac are two of the most famous examples of alcohol to receive the designation.

Applejack: a strong, apple-flavored alcoholic beverage that is similar to apple brandy and is traditionally produced by freeze distillation rather than the more commonplace evaporative method. Applejack was so popular in Colonial America that for a time it was used as currency in New Jersey.

Aquavit: a liquor distilled from grain and potatoes which receives its distinct flavor from caraway, the primary member of a mixture of spices and herbs. Largely produced in Scandinavian countries, where it is a traditional feature of holiday celebrations.

Bar spoon: a long spoon with a threaded shaft that enables it to navigate around ice cubes and distribute the liquid in a manner that ensures evenly mixed cocktails.

Bénédictine: a popular French liqueur that contains 27 herbs and spices and is typically paired with brandy. The recipe for this sweet beverage is highly classified and rumored to be known to only three people at a given time.

Bitters: there are two different categories of bitters. There are bitter-flavored liqueurs, which are used as additions or as the base for a variety of cocktails. Examples include Campari, Suze, Aperol, Amaro, and Cocchi Rosa. The other category is simply called bitters, which come in small bottles, the most well known being Angostura Bitters. These are infused and very flavorful alcohol-based liquids that are typically used in extremely small quantities to add flavor to a cocktail. They are made by a variety of companies (Fee Brothers, Scrappy's, and Bittermens are a few reliable outfits) and come in a myriad of flavors such as orange, chocolate, celery, and lavender, to name just a few. A key component in a number of today's craft cocktails, it is wise to have a variety of flavors on hand if you are going to get serious about mixology.

Bourbon whiskey: a type of whisk(e)y popular in the American South, distilled from a mash of at least 51 percent corn and aged in new, charred oak barrels. Due to the high levels of corn, bourbon tends to be sweeter than most whiskies and commonly features notes of vanilla, oak, and caramel.

Brut: an appellation given to the driest sparkling wine. It is occasionally broken down further into "extra brut" and "brut natural," with the latter indicating that no sugar has been added.

Calvados: an apple or pear brandy that hails from the Normandy region of France. It is distilled from cider and aged in oak casks for at least two years.

Cava: a sparkling wine from Spain that can be white or Rosé and is known for its crisp, tart taste.

Cocktail shaker: a sealed container used to mix cocktails by shaking. It is usually filled with ice before use to quickly cool beverages.

Cognac: named for the French town it is produced in, this is a variety of brandy produced by double distilling very dry, acidic white wine and aging it in oak casks for at least two years, though many offerings will rest for longer than that.

Cordials: a sweet substance made from fruit or flowers that is added to a cocktail or consumed alone. While cordials are thought of as alcoholic in the United States, they are typically nonalcoholic in other countries.

Crémant: initially used to describe less fizzy varieties of sparkling wine, it is now a designation applied to French sparkling wine that is produced outside of the Champagne region.

Crème: refers not to the presence of cream, but to a liqueur with a large amount of sugar added, to the point where it acquires a nearly syrup-like consistency.

Curaçao: a liqueur flavored by the dried peel of the laraha citrus fruit (a descendant of the Seville orange) that is grown on the island of the same name. Blue or orange food coloring is typically added to curaçao to provide the exotic look it can lend to a cocktail.

Dash: a quick addition, usually of a liquid ingredient. It is roughly equivalent to 1 teaspoon, but not an exact measurement.

Dollop: a large spoonful, usually in reference to whipped cream.

Domaine de Canton: a popular ginger liqueur that is made from a mixture of baby Vietnamese ginger, varieties of Cognacs, vanilla, honey, and ginseng, and renowned for its light, yet strong flavor.

Double-strain: single straining is done using the traditional Hawthorne strainer and will be what's required for most drinks. Some cocktails, though, require two filters to produce a more appealing mouthfeel. To double-strain, place a fine-mesh strainer over the glass and pour your drink through the Hawthorne strainer and the mesh strainer.

Drambuie: this famously smooth liqueur is made from scotch whisky, honey, herbs, and spices.

Dry shake: shaking ingredients in a cocktail shaker without ice. This technique is typically utilized in drinks involving egg white, in order to emulsify it.

Dusting: a small amount of a spice or powder, usually in reference to cinnamon or nutmeg.

Eau de vie: a clear, fruit brandy that is the result of double distillation and fermentation. In France, it is the generic term used to describe distilled spirits.

Express: twisting a strip of citrus peel over a cocktail in order to impart the oils into the drink and enhance its flavor and aroma.

Falernum: a sweet syrup containing almond, ginger, and lime flavors that is available in alcoholic and nonalcoholic options and frequently used in tropical and Caribbean-inspired cocktails.

Float: a technique where a small amount of alcohol is layered on top of a cocktail. Alcohol that is floated should be poured very slowly, an effect a number of bartenders achieve by pouring the liquid over the back of a bar spoon.

Fortified wine: a wine to which a distilled spirit, usually brandy, has been added in order to preserve and flavor it.

Frangelico: a popular hazelnut-and-herb flavored liqueur that is produced in Italy and colored with caramel.

Galliano: a sweet Italian liqueur that contains a blend of 30 herbs and features flavors of vanilla, anise, and subtle notes of citrus.

Garnish: an element, typically a slice of fruit or vegetable or a strip of peel, to be added to a drink after the cocktail has been mixed and added to the glass. Usually employed to provide an accent flavor and/or an aesthetic element to a drink.

Grenadine: red, nonalcoholic syrup that is used to provide sweetness and/or color to cocktails. Initially composed of pomegranate juice, sugar, and water, it is now commonly produced using artificial ingredients.

Griottines: morello cherries that possess a considerable depth of flavor thanks to the kirsch or, less commonly, eau de vie that they have been soaked in.

Hawthorne strainer: a common strainer featuring a handle, a disc, and a spring that fits inside of a mixing container in order to filter out the ice.

Herbsaint: an anise-flavored liqueur that was originally created in New Orleans to be a substitute for absinthe, which was banned in the United States.

Kümmel: a Dutch liqueur flavored with caraway seed, cumin, and fennel, lending it a smooth, savory quality that works well in cocktails.

Lactart: a solution made from lactic acid, which lends buttermilk its pleasant, sour taste. Can be used to add a tart and refreshing element to cocktails in place of citrus juice.

Lillet: an aperitif wine that is a blend of wines from the Bordeaux region in France and citrus liqueurs. Typically served chilled, it is also part of the Vesper Martini, which Ian Fleming had James Bond order in *Casino Royale*, the first 007 novel.

Liqueur: a combination of a distilled spirit and a flavorful element that is typically sweet. Usually very strong in flavor, a liqueur is primarily used to provide an accent in cocktails, rather than consumed on its own. Popular examples are crème de menthe, Kahlua, Grand Marnier, and Midori.

Liquor: an alcoholic substance made from grains, plants, or sugarcane that are fermented in order to be consumed straight or used as the base of a cocktail. Examples are rum, vodka, gin, brandy, tequila, and whisk(e)y.

London Dry gin: a gin made from a completely neutral base spirit that has been distilled to 96 percent alcohol by volume. In order to be classified London Dry, all flavors must be added through natural materials during distillation, with nothing other than sugar or water able to be added after it has been distilled.

Luxardo: a relatively dry liqueur that is produced through distillation, this sour cherry beverage is made from the pits and sour fruit of the marasca cherry.

Luxardo maraschino cherries: candied in marasca cherry juice and sugar, the deep, dark red of these cherries is a far cry away from what most think of when they hear maraschino cherry.

Mixing glass: a glass other than the intended drinking vessel in which to mix ingredients together. A pint glass is commonly used, though some professionals prefer a mixing glass with a lip that makes it easy to pour from.

Muddle: lightly mashing ingredients in the bottom of a glass or cocktail shaker to better release their flavor. Can be done with any blunt instrument, but a specific tool known as a muddler also exists.

Orange Blossom Water: the product of distilling fresh bitter orange blossoms, it is employed in cooking and cocktail making due to the considerable taste and aroma a small amount can provide.

Orgeat: a sweet syrup made from almonds, sugar, and either rose or orange blossom water. Nutty and slightly floral, it is a component of the Mai Tai and a number of other tropical cocktails. To make at home: in a saucepan, combine ½ quart white sugar and 1 quart almond milk and cook over medium heat, while stirring constantly, until the sugar dissolves. When the mixture is about to boil, remove from heat and cover. Let cool for a minimum of 2 hours, then add orange blossom water and almond extract. Label and store.

Overproof: refers to a spirit that is more than 50 percent ethanol when it is bottled.

Part: the suggested ratio of a particular component in a cocktail recipe. Allows the recipe to be easily adapted to different kinds of glassware.

Pastis: an anise-flavored spirit that emerged in France following the ban on absinthe. It is traditionally consumed on hot days in the South of France, where it is typically diluted with water and served on ice.

Pimm's: a series of liqueurs that utilize different base alcohols. The most popular, Pimm's No. 1, is a gin-based digestif that has a hints of spice and citrus and a reddish-brown tint. It is frequently mixed with lemonade and garnished with slices of various fruits.

Pinch: a small amount of material that can be picked up and held between two fingers. Roughly equivalent to 1⁄16 of a teaspoon, though not an exact measure.

Pisco: a brandy produced in wine-making regions in Peru and Chile. Due to its heightened aromatic profile, it is frequently substituted for gin to put a twist on traditionally gin-based cocktails.

Port: a frequently sweet fortified wine that is often served as an after-dinner drink. Most commonly used to describe wines that are produced in the Douro region of Portugal.

Rim: dipping the wet rim of a glass into a salt, sugar, or mixture before pouring the cocktail into it. Used to accent cocktails without affecting the balance of flavors in what is being mixed.

Rinse: adding a small amount (approximately ⅛ oz.) of a strongly flavored ingredient to a glass and quickly swirling so that it coats the inside of the glass and does not overpower the cocktail. The Sazerac is the most popular cocktail that utilizes the rinse method.

Rosé: a wine produced in the manner of a white wine but which has been colored with the skin of red grapes.

Rye whiskey: distilled from a mash of at least 51 percent rye and aged in charred oak barrels, rye is typically spicier than bourbon, its close cousin. Also refers to Canadian Whisky, which generally only contains a small amount of rye in its mash bill.

Sake: an alcoholic beverage made by fermenting rice that has been polished to remove the bran. The national drink of Japan, sake comes in a number of varieties, and is typically chilled before being consumed.

Scotch whisky: malt or grain whisky from Scotland that has been aged in oak casks for at least three years. The common use of peat as a fuel source for drying the malted barley used to make Scotch provides the smoky element that this whisky is famous for.

Short shake: a little less vigorous and time-consuming than a traditional shake. Essentially, you just want to combine and chill the ingredients.

Sherry: a fortified wine that is made from white grapes that are grown in Andalusia, Spain. After the wine has been fortified, it is stored in casks of North American oak.

Shochu: a Japanese beverage that is usually distilled from rice, barley, sweet potatoes, buckwheat, or brown sugar, and frequently features a nutty or earthy taste.

Shrub: a syrup that is commonly a 1:1:1 ratio of fruit, sugar, and vinegar. The ingredients are heated and strained, with the result either added to cocktails or enjoyed on its own once cool.

Slice of fruit: a common garnish. Refers to a slice taken from a fruit wheel.

Sloe gin: a sweet, red liqueur that is the result of steeping sloe drupes, a relative of the plum, in gin.

Spent: refers to a piece of citrus, fruit, or vegetable that the juice has been removed from.

Splash: a quick addition, usually of a liquid ingredient. Larger than a dash, it is roughly equivalent to 1 tablespoon, but not an exact measurement.

Strip: a thin slice of peel taken from a citrus fruit.

Squeeze: a rough measurement that refers to the amount of juice contained in a wedge of citrus.

St-Germain: a sweet elderflower liqueur that is commonly paired with light alcohols such as vodka, gin, and tequila in order to provide complexity.

Swizzle method: a practice that utilizes a swizzle stick to combine and aerate cocktails made with crushed ice. If a cocktail recipe calls for you to employ the swizzle method, place a swizzle stick in the cocktail, hold it between the palms of your hands, and rotate the stick quickly by sliding your hands back and forth.

Syrup: there is simple syrup, which is basically just sugar heated in water until it dissolves, and flavored syrups, which are made in a similar fashion but add a flavoring element such as ginger, lemongrass, lime, or passion fruit. Used to sweeten and add flavor to a cocktail, a number of syrups can be picked up at the store (such as grenadine, which is actually a pomegranate syrup), but making them yourself typically produces better results. A few basic recipes for syrups follow:

Simple syrup (1:1): in a small saucepan, combine 1 cup granulated sugar and 1 cup water. Cook over medium heat, while stirring, until the sugar is completely dissolved. Let cool to room temperature, and then store in an airtight container for up to 1 week in the refrigerator. For demerara or honey syrup, replace the granulated sugar with demerara sugar or honey, respectively.

Rich simple syrup (2:1): in a small saucepan, combine 2 cups granulated sugar with 1 cup water. Cook over medium heat, while stirring, until the sugar is completely dissolved. Let cool to room temperature, and then store in an airtight container for up to 1 week in the refrigerator. For demerara or honey syrup, replace the granulated sugar with demerara sugar or honey, respectively.

Tincture: a typically alcoholic extract of plant or animal material. Produced by steeping an element in a solvent such as alcohol or vinegar for 2 to 3 weeks.

Top: to fill the remainder of a glass with a particular ingredient, most commonly utilized when adding something that is carbonated, like sparkling wine or seltzer water.

Torch: running a match or lighter over the surface of a garnish in order to add a smoky element to a cocktail. Most commonly employed with citrus peels and herbs such as rosemary.

Twist: a strip of citrus peel sliced around the diameter of the fruit to give it a corkscrew shape.

Umeshu: a sweet and sour Japanese liqueur that is made by steeping unripe Chinese plums in sugar and alcohol.

Verjus: the pressed juice of unripe red or white grapes. It is acidic, though less than vinegar, for which it is often substituted.

Vermouth: dry vermouth is white; sweet vermouth is red. As in most things, the brand and quality matter. The French producers Dolin and Noilly Prat are trustworthy for dry vermouth, while Italian giants Cocchi and Carpano offer the most reliable sweet vermouth.

Virgin: refers to a nonalcoholic version of a drink that is commonly alcoholic.

Wedge: a triangular slice of fruit (most commonly citrus) used as a garnish. Its juice is often squeezed into the drink for added flavor.

Wheel: a thin, circular slice of a fruit or vegetable that commonly refers to citrus fruits. Also known as "rounds."

Whip shake: this method utilizes two hands and a very small amount of ice (1 or 2 cubes) to shake a cocktail as hard as possible in a short period of time, resulting in a cocktail with a creamy consistency.

RESOURCES

These books were of immense help when putting together *Drink*—they are all outstanding resources.

Dale DeGroff
The Craft of the Cocktail: Everything You Need to Know to Be a Master Bartender (Clarkson Potter, 2002)

This is the book that got me started, my first real cocktail book.

Stefan Van Eycken
Whisky Rising: The Definitive Guide to the Finest Whiskies and Distillers of Japan (Cider Mill Press, 2017)

My go-to book on Japan. If I had to choose just one of these books to hold onto, this is it.

Amanda Schuster
New York Cocktails: An Elegant Collection of Over 100 Recipes Inspired by the Big Apple (Cider Mill Press, 2017)

I love Amanda's writing, and this book taught me things I didn't know about the bars in the city I live in.

Nico Martini
Texas Cocktails: An Elegant Collection of Over 100 Recipes Inspired by the Lone Star State (Cider Mill Press, 2018)

The magic word here is "shrubs," a piece of the spirits world that I was not familiar with until I dug into this book.

Doni Belau
Paris Cocktails: An Elegant Collection of Over 100 Recipes Inspired by the City of Light (Cider Mill Press, 2015)

Somehow, this made me love Paris even more, exposing me to a number of amazing bars that I have yet to visit.

Shane Carley
The Home Bartender, 2nd Edition (Cider Mill Press, 2018)

This is the modern version of the scrawled bartender's notes, only it's too good to hide behind the register.

Amy Hunter
Infused Water and Ice (Cider Mill Press, 2018)

Without this book, the chapter on nonalcoholic drinks would have been nothing but mocktails. For that alone, you should be grateful.

Madeline Teachett
The Little Pink Book of Cocktails (Cider Mill Press, 2008)

This book may be little, but it packs a wallop.

IMAGE CREDITS

Endpapers, Rare bottles from True Laurel image courtesy of RRPR CREATIVE: photography by Wes Rowe; Page 86, courtesy of Strelka; Pages 160-161, courtesy of Tasting Groups Limited; pages 164-165, courtesy of Gin Palace; pages 168-169, courtesy of The Ritz Hotel, Paris; pages 204-206, courtesy of Quinary; pages 324-325, courtesy of LeBLANC+SMITH; pages 425-426 and page 429, courtesy of Kailley Lindman; page 505, courtesy of Maison Noilly Prat; pages 510-511, courtesy of 878 Bar; pages 766-769, courtesy of Mizunara: The Library; pages 770-771, courtesy of @verneclub; page 774, courtesy of Julia Ritz Toffoli; pages 778-779, courtesy of RRPR CREATIVE: photography by Wes Rowe; page 791, courtesy of Babel at Bullitt Hotel; page 796, courtesy of Emily Ross-Johnson; page 798, (bottom right) courtesy of Kurt Maitland, (top and bottom left) courtesy of Milan Ormanović; pages 800-803, courtesy of Cocktail Kingdom: page 800 photography by Alex Kikis, page 801 (top) photography by Eric Medsker, page 801 (bottom) photography by Michael Marquand, pages 802-803 photography by Scott Gordon Bleicher.

The following images are used under official license from Shutterstock.com: pages 4-8; pages 11-14; pages 20-24; pages 26-30; pages 34-35; pages 43-45; page 47; page 55 (bottom left); page 63; page 65 (top); page 73 (top left, top right); page 81 (top left); page 85; page 88 (top left, bottom right); page 91 (top right); pages 92-93; page 98 (bottom right); page 102; pages 106-107; page 112; pages 114-115; page 119 (top left, top right); pages 120-121; page 123; page 131 (top); page 134 (top left, bottom right); page 138 (bottom); pages 144-145; pages 150-151; page 157 (top); page 177 (top left, bottom right); pages 208-209; page 217 (top left, top right, bottom left); page 242 (top right); page 253 (top right); page 258 (bottom right); pages 270-271; page 281 (bottom left); page 285 (top left); page 286 (bottom); page 293 (bottom right); page 294 (bottom left); page 297 (bottom left); page 306 (top left); pages 326-327; page 335 (bottom right); pages 338-339; pages 350-351; page 353 (top left, bottom right); page 356 (top right); page 359 (bottom); pages 360-361; page 362 (top left); page 375 (bottom left); page 379 (top left, top right); pages 380-381; page 389 (bottom right); page 394 (top); page 403 (top right, bottom); page 414 (top right); pages 430-431; page 437; page 438 (bottom); pages 444-445; page 466 (top right); page 469 (bottom); pages 470-471; page 475; pages 480-481; page 483; page 487 (top); page 488 (bottom); pages 498-499; page 501 (top); page 502 (top); pages 506-507; pages 520-521; page 524; page 535; page 536 (top); pages 544-545; pages 550-551; pages 556-557; page 567; pages 574-575; pages 592-593; page 595; pages 597-598; page 608 (top left); page 614; page 619; pages 630-634; page 638; pages 642-643; pages 645-646; page 655; page 658; pages 662-663; page 669; pages 670-671; pages 700-701; page 704; page 707 (top left, top right); page 708 (top right); page 711 (bottom); page 712; page 722 (top); page 725 (top); page 726; pages 728-730; pages 740-741; pages 750-751; page 761 (top); pages 762-763; page 765; pages 804-807; page 808.

All other images courtesy of Cider Mill Press Book Publishers.

ACKNOWLEDGMENTS

First and foremost, this goes out to my family—my mom, Hilma; my father, Garvis; my sister, Renee; my nephew, Reece—for their love and support in all of my endeavors.

My godmother, Angela Noriega—whose kindness and generosity helped me through the early days of my return to New York City.

Richard Thomas—for being a great friend and for pulling me into the crazy world of spirits.

Amanda Schuster—for taking time when she didn't have to and for writing a great book like *New York Cocktails*, which was a godsend to me when working on this book.

Cider Mill Press for giving me the opportunity to write my first book. Special thanks to Carlo DeVito, who thought I could step out of my lane and write a book on cocktails of all things. Hopefully, I've repaid his faith. Extra special thanks to my editor, Buzz Poole, who kept me on target and without whom I'd still be out trying to get additional Q&As to add to the book.

My whisk(e)y/spirit friends in New York—your knowledge and friendship have been priceless.

All of the bartenders and industry insiders who took the time to talk to me, to teach me, and to demonstrate their skills and talents. This goes out to both those included in the book as well the ones I've met in my travels. I'd also like to thank the Brandy Library in general, and Flavien Desoblin in particular. The knowledge and wisdom you have shared continues to prove invaluable.

My friends—who have all had to put up with me babbling on about writing some book and me drifting off to talk to the bartender when we were hanging out. This practice might continue, but at least, in this instance, I had an excuse.

Last, but not least, I'd like to thank Anthony Bourdain—whose TV shows, books, and mere presence in this world have been an inspiration to me. He passed away while I was working on this book and it would be impossible to deny his influence on my writing. As I was working on these acknowledgements his book, *Appetites: A Cookbook*, fell on one of my feet. Perhaps he was trying to tell me something, or maybe I just need better bookshelves. Regardless, he shall be missed.

INDEX

ABOUT THE AUTHOR

Kurt Maitland started his spirits journey with drams of Jameson in college, and has been exploring the world of spirits in general, and whisk(e)y in particular, ever since. He lives in New York City and is the deputy editor of the popular The Whiskey Reviewer website, the curator of the Manhattan Whiskey Club, and the owner of Whiskey Selections.

ABOUT CIDER MILL PRESS BOOK PUBLISHERS

Good ideas ripen with time. From seed to harvest, Cider Mill Press brings fine reading, information, and entertainment together between the covers of its creatively crafted books. Our Cider Mill bears fruit twice a year, publishing a new crop of titles each spring and fall.

CIDER MILL PRESS
BOOK PUBLISHERS

"Where Good Books Are Ready for Press"

501 Nelson Place
Nashville, Tennessee 37214

cidermillpress.com

BOURBON 8 YEAR
Walker'
DeLuxe
DECANTE
FIFTH
This Whiskey is 8 Years Old
FITZGERALD
OLD FITZGERALD
FITZGERALD
BOURBON WHISKEY
led in Bond
BOTTLED
YEARS OLD
OLD
OVERHOLT
THIS WHISKEY IS 6 YEARS OLD
THE WHISKEY IS 5 YEARS OLD
The Pacific-Union Club
KENTUCKY STRAIGHT BOURBON WHISKEY
Sour Mash
DISTILLED AND BOTTLED BY
James B. Beam Distilling Co.
ESPECIALLY FOR
The Pacific-Union Club
SAN FRANCISCO
CLUB BOURBON
KENTUCKY STRAIGHT BOURBON WHISKEY
Stitzel-Weller Distillery
LOUISVILLE, JEFFERSON COUNTY, KENTUCKY
THE PACIFIC-UNION CLUB
KENTUC
WHISKE
BOTTLED IN BOND
Established
1810
1 QUART
100 PROOF
OLD OVERHOLT
STRAIGHT RYE WHISKEY
DISTILLED BY
A. Overholt & Co. Inc.
BROAD FORD, PA., U.S.A.